MCA
Microsoft® Certified Associate
Azure® Network Engineer
Study Guide

MCA
Microsoft® Certified Associate Azure® Network Engineer
Study Guide
Exam AZ-700

Puthiyavan Udayakumar

Kathiravan Udayakumar

SYBEX®
A Wiley Brand

To the Wiley team for all their support.
—Kathiravan Udayakumar

To my mother and father, who taught me everything.
To my beloved better half—thanks for everything you do for me in thriving in our life journey.
To my dearest brother and mentor of my lifetime.
—Puthiyavan Udayakumar

Acknowledgments

We want to express our sincere thanks to Sybex for continuing to support this project.

Although this book bears our name as authors, numerous people contributed to its design and development of the content. They helped make this book possible, or at best, it would be in a lesser form without them. Kenyon Brown was the acquisitions editor and so helped get the book started. Christine O'Connor, the managing editor, oversaw the book as it progressed through all its stages. Jon Buhagiar was the technical editor who checked the text for technical errors and omissions—but any remaining mistakes are our own. Tom Dinse, the development editor, helped keep the text understandable. Liz Welch, the copyeditor, helped keep the text grammatical. Barath Kumar Rajasekaran, content refinement specialist, and others from his team helped check the text for typos and shaped the content.

About the Authors

Puthiyavan Udayakumar is an infrastructure architect with over 14 years of experience in modernizing and securing IT infrastructure, including the cloud. He has been writing technical books for more than 10 years on various infrastructure and security domains. He has designed, deployed, and secured IT infrastructure out of on-premises and the cloud, including servers, networks, storage, and desktops for various industries, such as pharmaceutical, banking, healthcare, aviation, and federal entities. He is an Open Group Master Certified Architect (Open CA).

Kathiravan Udayakumar is Head of Delivery & Chief Architect for Oracle Digital Technologies (Europe Practice) at Cognizant, covering various elements of the technology stack in on-premises and the cloud. He has over 18 years of experience in architecture, design, implementation, administration, and integration with greenfield IT systems, ERP, cloud platforms, and solutions across various business domains and industries. He has a passion for networking from his undergraduate studies and has a Cisco Certified Network Associate (CCNA). He also proposed protocols for optimal routings in complex networks, DRIP (Differential Routing Information Protocol) to avoid pinhole congestion in his undergraduate thesis.

About the Technical Editor

Jon Buhagiar (Network+, A+, CCNA, MCSA, MCSE, BS/ITM) is an information technology professional with two decades of experience in higher education. During the past 22 years he has been responsible for network operations at Pittsburgh Technical College and has led several projects, such as virtualization (server and desktop), VoIP, Microsoft 365, and many other projects supporting the quality of education at the college. He has achieved several certifications from Cisco, CompTIA, and Microsoft and has taught many of the certification paths. He is the author of several books, including Sybex's *CompTIA A+ Complete Study Guide: Exam 220-1101 and Exam 220-1102* (2022), *CompTIA Network+ Review Guide: Exam N10-008* (2021), and *CCNA Certification Practice Tests: Exam 200-301* (2020).

Contents at a Glance

Introduction   *xxv*

Assessment Test   *xxxvii*

Chapter 1   Getting Started with AZ-700 Certification for
                Azure Networking   1

Chapter 2   Design, Deploy, and Manage a Site-to-Site VPN Connection
                and Point-to-Site VPN Connection   75

Chapter 3   Design, Deploy, and Manage Azure ExpressRoute   145

Chapter 4   Design and Deploy Core Networking
                Infrastructure: Private IP and DNS   203

Chapter 5   Design and Deploy Core Networking
                Infrastructure and Virtual WANs   255

Chapter 6   Design and Deploy VNet Routing and Azure
                Load Balancer   317

Chapter 7   Design and Deploy Azure application gateway,
                Azure front door, and Virtual NAT   381

Chapter 8   Design, Deploy, and Manage Azure Firewall and
                Network Security Groups   459

Chapter 9   Design and Deploy Azure Web Application
                Firewall and Monitor Networks   543

Chapter 10   Design and Deploy Private Access to Azure
                Services   615

Appendix   Answers to Review Questions   679

Index   *697*

Contents

Introduction   *xxv*

Assessment Test   *xxxvii*

**Chapter   1   Getting Started with AZ-700 Certification for
                  Azure Networking   1**

Basics of Cloud Computing and Networking   2
    The Need for Networking Infrastructure   3
    The Need for the Cloud   3
    Basics of Networking   6
    Enterprise Cloud Networking   10
Microsoft Azure Overview   11
    Azure Cloud Foundation   12
    Azure Global Infrastructure   14
    Azure Networking Terminology   20
    Azure Networking Overview   21
    Azure Networking Services   23
Azure Virtual Network   26
    VNet Concepts and Best Practices   28
    Deploying a Virtual Network with Azure PowerShell   35
Configure Public IP Services   37
    Basic SKUs   38
    Standard SKUs   39
    Configure a Basic SKU Public IP   40
    Configure a Standard SKU Public IP with Zones   40
Configuring Domain Name Services   40
    Configure an Azure DNS Zone and Record Using
      Azure PowerShell   42
Configuring Cross-Virtual Network Connectivity with
  Peering   43
    Configuring Peering between Two Virtual Networks
      in the Same Region   45
Configuring Virtual Network Traffic Routing   46
    Using Forced Tunneling to Secure the VNet Route   52
Configuring Internet Access with Azure Virtual NAT   53
    Deploy the NAT Gateway Using Azure PowerShell   54
Summary   56
Exam Essentials   56
Hands-On Lab: Design and Deploy a Virtual Network
  via the Azure Portal   57
    Activity 1: Prepare the Network Schema   58
    Activity 2: Build the Aviation Resource Group   60

Activity 3a: Build the CoreInfraVnet Virtual Network
and Subnets   60
Activity 3b: Build the EngineeringVnet Virtual Network
and Subnets   64
Activity 3c: Build the BranchofficeVnet Virtual Network
and Subnets   66
Activity 4: Validate the Build of VNets and Subnets   68
Review Questions   70

**Chapter   2   Design, Deploy, and Manage a Site-to-Site VPN
Connection and Point-to-Site VPN Connection   75**

Overview of Azure VPN Gateway   76
Designing an Azure VPN Connection   79
Design Pattern 1   86
Design Pattern 2   87
Design Pattern 3   88
Choosing a Virtual Network Gateway SKU for Site-to-Site VPN   89
Using Policy-Based VPNs vs. Route-Based VPNs   92
Building and Configuring a Virtual Network Gateway   94
Building and Configuring a Local Network Gateway   97
Building and Configuring an IPsec/IKE Policy   101
Configuration Workflow   104
Diagnosing and Resolving VPN Gateway Connectivity Issues   109
Choosing a VNet Gateway SKU for Point-to-Site VPNs   112
Configuring RADIUS, Certificate-Based, and Azure AD
Authentication   116
Configuration Workflow for Native Azure Certification
Authentication   117
Configuration Workflow for Native Azure Active Directory   124
Configuration Workflow for Windows Active Directory   127
Diagnosing and Resolving Client-Side and Authentication Issues 133
Summary   136
Exam Essentials   136
Review Questions   140

Chapter   3   Design, Deploy, and Manage Azure ExpressRoute   145

Getting Started with Azure ExpressRoute   146
Key Use Case for ExpressRoute   151
ExpressRoute Deployment Model   151
Choosing Between the Network Service Provider and
ExpressRoute Direct   153
Designing and Deploying Azure Cross-Region Connectivity
between Multiple ExpressRoute Locations   156
Selecting ExpressRoute Circuit SKUs   156
Estimating Price Based on ExpressRoute SKU   156

Select a Peering Location   157
Select the Proper ExpressRoute Circuit   157
Select a Billing Model   159
Select a High Availability Design   159
Pick a Business Continuity and Disaster Recovery
   Design Pattern   162
Choosing an Appropriate ExpressRoute SKU and Tier   169
Designing and Deploying ExpressRoute Global Reach   171
Deploying ExpressRoute Global Reach   173
   Use Case 1: Enabling Circuits in the Same Region 173
   Use Case 2: Enabling Circuits in Different Regions 174
Designing and Deploying ExpressRoute FastPath   175
Evaluate Private Peering Only, Microsoft Peering Only,
   or Both   176
Setting Up Private Peering   178
Setting Up Microsoft Peering   181
Building and Configuring an ExpressRoute Gateway   182
Connect a Virtual Network to an ExpressRoute Circuit   186
Recommend a Route Advertisement Configuration   190
Configure Encryption over ExpressRoute   191
Deploy Bidirectional Forwarding
   Detection   192
Diagnose and Resolve ExpressRoute Connection Issues   193
Summary   196
Exam Essentials   196
Review Questions   199

**Chapter   4   Design and Deploy Core Networking
Infrastructure: Private IP and DNS   203**

Designing Private IP Addressing for VNets   204
Deploying a VNet   210
Preparing Subnetting for Services   213
   Subnetting Design Considerations   214
   Example Case Study: Preparing Subnetting for Services 218
Configuring Subnetting for Services   220
Preparing and Configuring a Subnet Delegation   223
   Configure Subnet Delegation   225
Planning and Configuring Subnetting for Azure Route Server   226
Designing and Configuring Public DNS Zones   231
Creating an Azure DNS Zone and Record Using PowerShell   233
Designing and Configuring Private DNS Zones   235
   Creating a Private DNS Zone and Record Using
   PowerShell   238
Designing Name Resolution Inside a VNet   240
   VMs and Role Instances   243
   Web Apps   243

	Linking a Private DNS Zone to a VNet	245
	Summary	248
	Exam Essentials	249
	Review Questions	251

Chapter 5   Design and Deploy Core Networking Infrastructure and Virtual WANs   255

Overview of Virtual Network Peering, Service Chaining, and Gateway Transit	256
Configure VPN Gateway Transit for Virtual Network Peering	258
Design VPN Connectivity between VNets	263
Deploy VNet Peering	266
Deployment Model 1: Running in the Same Azure Subscription and Deployed Using Azure Resource Manager	267
Deployment Model 2: Running in Different Subscriptions and Deploying Using Resource Manager	270
Deployment Model 3: Running in the Same Subscription and Deploying One VNet Using Resource Manager and Another Using the Classic Model	273
Deployment Model 4: Running in Different Subscriptions and Deploying One VNet Using Resource Manager and Another Using the Classic Model	275
Design an Azure Virtual WAN Architecture	277
Choosing SKUs and Services for Virtual WANs	289
Connect a VNet Gateway to an Azure Virtual WAN and Build a Hub in a Virtual WAN	291
Build a Virtual Network Appliance (NVA) in a Virtual Hub	299
Set Up Virtual Hub Routing	304
Build a Connection Unit	306
Summary	309
Exam Essentials	310
Review Questions	312

Chapter 6   Design and Deploy VNet Routing and Azure Load Balancer   317

Design and Deploy User-Defined Routes	318
Basic Routing Concepts	318
Azure Routes	321
Associate a Route Table with a Subnet	328
Set Up Forced Tunneling	329

Diagnose and Resolve Routing Issues	334
Design and Deploy Azure Route Server	336
Route Server Design Pattern 1	338
Route Server Design Pattern 2	339
Choosing an Azure Load Balancer SKU	344
Choosing Between Public and Internal Load Balancers	349
Build and Configure an Azure Load Balancer (Including Cross-Region)	353
Build and Configure Cross-Region Load Balancer Resources	361
Deploy a Load Balancing Rule	366
Build and Configure Inbound NAT Rules	370
Build Explicit Outbound Rules for a Load Balancer	371
Summary	374
Exam Essentials	375
Review Questions	377

Chapter 7   Design and Deploy Azure application gateway, Azure front door, and Virtual NAT   381

Azure Application Gateway Overview	383
How Application Gateway Works	385
Scaling Options for Application Gateway and WAF	389
Overview of Application Gateway Deployment	390
Front-End Setup	390
Back-End Setup	390
Health Probes Setup	391
Configuring Listeners	393
Redirection Overview	394
Application Gateway Request Routing Rules	395
Redirection Setting	397
Application Gateway Rewrite Policies	397
Features and Capabilities of Azure Front Door SKUs	409
Health Probe Characteristics and Operation	411
Secure Front Door with SSL	412
Front Door for Web Applications with a High-Availability Design Pattern	413
SSL Termination and End-to-End SSL Encryption	421
Multisite Listeners	423
Back-Ends, Back-End Pools, Back-End Host Headers, and Back-End Health Probes	424
Routing and Routing Rules	426
URL Redirection and URL Rewriting in Front Door Standard and Premium	427
Design and Deploy Traffic Manager Profiles	429

How Traffic Manager Works 430
Traffic Manager Routing Methods 432
Priority-Based Traffic Routing 433
Weighted-Based Traffic Routing 433
Performance-Based Traffic Routing 435
Geographic-Based Traffic Routing 436
Multivalue-Based Traffic Routing 437
Subnet-Based Traffic Routing 437
Building a Traffic Manager Profile 438
Virtual Network NAT 442
Using a Virtual Network NAT 443
Allocate Public IP or Public IP Prefixes for a NAT Gateway 445
Associate a Virtual Network NAT with a Subnet 447
Summary 451
Exam Essentials 451
Review Questions 455

Chapter 8   **Design, Deploy, and Manage Azure Firewall and
Network Security Groups** **459**

Azure Firewall and Firewall Manager Features 460
How Azure Firewall Manager Works 467
How Azure Firewall and Firewall Manager Protect
VNets 468
Build and Configure an Azure Firewall Deployment 476
Azure Firewall Policy 495
Build and Configure a Secure Hub within an Azure Virtual
WAN Hub 501
Build and Configure a Secure Hub within an Azure
Virtual WAN Hub Using Azure PowerShell 503
Integrate an Azure Virtual WAN Hub with a Third-Party
Network Virtual Appliance 507
High-Level Use Case for Network Virtual Appliances 508
Create and Attach a Network Security Group to a Resource 509
Create an Application Security Group and Attach It to a NIC 519
Create and Configure NSG Rules and Read Network
Security Group Flow Logs 524
Validate NSG Flow Rules 531
Verify IP Flow 534
Summary 536
Exam Essentials 536
Review Questions 539

Chapter 9   **Design and Deploy Azure Web Application
Firewall and Monitor Networks** **543**

Azure Web Application Firewall Functions and Features 544
WAF on Application Gateway 547
WAF on Front Door 549

WAF on Azure CDN from Microsoft 550
Set Up Detection or Prevention Mode 551
Azure Front Door WAF Policy Rule Sets 553
Managed Rule Sets 555
Custom Rule Sets 558
WAF Policies 560
Application Gateway WAF Policy Rule Sets 566
Per-Site WAF Policy 568
Per-URI Policy 568
Managed Rules 568
WAF Policies 572
Custom Rules 573
Deploy and Attach WAF Policies 580
Set Up Network Health Alerts and Logging Using
Azure Monitor 582
Build and Configure Azure Network Watcher 591
Build and Configure a Connection Monitor Instance 595
Build, Configure, and Use Traffic Analytics 600
Build and Configure NSG Flow Logs 604
Enable and Set Up Diagnostic Logging 607
Enabling Diagnostic Logging 608
Summary 609
Exam Essentials 609
Review Questions 611

Chapter 10 Design and Deploy Private Access to Azure Services 615

Overview of Private Link Services and Private Endpoints 616
Key Benefits of Private Link 618
How Private Link Integrates into an Azure Virtual
Network 619
How Azure Private Endpoint Works 619
Plan Private Endpoints 628
Configure Access to Private Endpoints 632
Azure Private Link RBAC Permissions 634
Integrate Private Link with DNS and Private Link Services
with On-Premises Clients 634
Use Case 1: Workloads on Virtual Networks without a
Custom DNS Server 635
Use Case 2: Workloads That Use a DNS Forwarder
On-Premises 637
Use Case 3: Using a DNS Forwarder for Virtual Network
Workloads and On-Premises Workloads 640
Set Up Service Endpoints and Configure Service Endpoint
Policies 642

Overview of Service Tags and Access to Service Endpoints	646
Configure Access to Service Endpoints	651
Integrating App Services into Regional VNets	657
Azure Regional VNet Integration	658
How Azure Regional VNet Integration Works	659
Subnet Requirements	660
Access Management	661
Route Management	661
Application Route Management	662
Configure Azure Kubernetes Service (AKS) for Regional VNet Integration	665
Configure Clients to Access the App Service Environment	670
Summary	673
Exam Essentials	673
Review Questions	675

Appendix   Answers to Review Questions   679

Chapter 1: Getting Started with AZ-700 Certification for Azure Networking	680
Chapter 2: Design, Deploy, and Manage a Site-to-Site VPN Connection and Point-to-Site VPN Connection	681
Chapter 3: Design, Deploy, and Manage Azure ExpressRoute	683
Chapter 4: Design and Deploy Core Networking Infrastructure: Private IP and DNS	685
Chapter 5: Design and Deploy Core Networking Infrastructure and Virtual WANs	686
Chapter 6: Design and Deploy VNet Routing and Azure Load Balancer	688
Chapter 7: Design and Deploy Azure application gateway, Azure front door, and Virtual NAT	690
Chapter 8: Design, Deploy, and Manage Azure Firewall and Network Security Groups	691
Chapter 9: Design and Deploy Azure Web Application Firewall and Monitor Networks	693
Chapter 10: Design and Deploy Private Access to Azure Services	694

Index	697

Table of Exercises

Exercise	1.1	Deploying a Virtual Network with the Azure Portal	31
Exercise	1.2	Setting Up Azure Az PowerShell	36
Exercise	1.3	Deploying a Route Table with the Azure Portal	49
Exercise	1.4	Deploying a Route Using the Azure Portal	52
Exercise	2.1	Creating a Virtual Network Gateway in the Azure Portal	94
Exercise	2.2	Creating a Local Network Gateway in the Azure Portal	98
Exercise	2.3	Creating and Configuring an IPsec/IKE Policy for a VPN Gateway Connection	105
Exercise	2.4	Resetting the Azure VPN via the Azure Portal	109
Exercise	2.5	Building a Point-to-Site VPN Using Azure Active Directory	125
Exercise	2.6	Building a Point-to-Site VPN Using Active Directory Domain Server(AD DS)	130
Exercise	3.1	Creating a Network Gateway Subnet in the Azure Portal	183
Exercise	3.2	Creating a Virtual Network Gateway in the Azure Portal	184
Exercise	3.3	Troubleshoot Azure ExpressRoute Connectivity	194
Exercise	4.1	Deploying a Virtual Network in Azure via Azure Cloud Shell	211
Exercise	4.2	Adding a Subnet via the Azure Portal	220
Exercise	4.3	Changing a Subnet via the Azure Portal	222
Exercise	4.4	Deleting a Subnet via the Azure Portal	223
Exercise	4.5	Delegating a Subnet	225
Exercise	4.6	Removing a Subnet Delegation	225
Exercise	4.7	Creating an Azure DNS Zone and Record Using PowerShell	234
Exercise	4.8	Creating a DNS Zone and Record with PowerShell in Azure	239
Exercise	4.9	Configuring a Virtual Network Link	247
Exercise	5.1	Configuring User-Defined Routing via the Azure Portal	261
Exercise	5.2	Create a Virtual WAN Using the Azure Portal	292
Exercise	5.3	Create a Virtual HUB in a Virtual WAN Using the Azure Portal	293
Exercise	5.4	Connect a Virtual Network to a Virtual WAN Hub Using the Azure Portal	294
Exercise	5.5	Connect a VNet Gateway to Azure Virtual WAN	295
Exercise	5.6	Create an NVA via the Azure Portal	301
Exercise	5.7	Create a Route Table via the Azure Portal	305
Exercise	6.1	Configure User-Defined Routing Using the Azure Portal	325

Exercise 6.2   Change User-Defined Routing Settings Using the Azure Portal. 327

Exercise 6.3   Associate a Route Table with a Subnet Using the Azure Portal 328

Exercise 6.4   Use User-Defined Routes to Create a Route Table That Adds a
Default Route and Associates the Route Table with a
Subnet to Enable Forced Tunneling 331

Exercise 6.5   Configure Azure Load Balancing Rules via the Azure Portal 367

Exercise 6.6   Configure Azure Load Balancing Inbound NAT Rules via the Azure
Portal. 370

Exercise 6.7   Configure Azure Load Balancing Outbound Rules via the Azure
Portal. 373

Exercise 7.1   Design and Deploy an Azure Application Gateway via the Azure
Portal. 401

Exercise 7.2   Deploy Front Door for Web Applications with a High-Availability
Design Pattern 414

Exercise 7.3   Build a Traffic Manager Profile 439

Exercise 7.4   Create a NAT Gateway 446

Exercise 7.5   Associate a VNet NAT with a Subnet. 448

Exercise 8.1   Deploy Network Prerequisites: Develop a Resource Group. 481

Exercise 8.2   Deploy Network Prerequisites: Deploy a Virtual Network via the Azure
Portal. 482

Exercise 8.3   Deploy Network Prerequisites: Create a Virtual Machine. 485

Exercise 8.4   Deploy an Azure Firewall 490

Exercise 8.5   Configure the Outbound Default Route Through the Azure Firewall. 493

Exercise 8.6   Configure an Application Rule 497

Exercise 8.7   Create DNAT Rule 499

Exercise 8.8   Create a Network Security Group 514

Exercise 8.9   Attach a Network Security Group to a Resource. 517

Exercise 8.10 Create a New Application Security Group. 521

Exercise 8.11 Create a New Application Group 522

Exercise 8.12 Create Network Security Group Rules. 524

Exercise 8.13 IP Flow Verify Using the Azure Portal. 535

Exercise 9.1   Set Up Detection or Prevention Mode Using the Azure Portal 551

Exercise 9.2   Set Up Rule Sets for Front Door Using the Azure Portal 561

Exercise 9.3   Set Up Rule Sets for Azure Application Gateway Using the Azure
Portal. 575

Exercise 9.4   Set Up Rule Sets for a WAF Policy Using the Azure Portal. 580

Exercise 9.5   Set Up Network Health Alerts Using the Azure Portal 587

Exercise **9.6** Build and Configure an Azure Network Watcher 594
Exercise **9.7** Build and Configure a Connection Monitor Instance 598
Exercise **9.8** Build and Configure an NSG Flow Log Using the Azure PowerShell 602
Exercise **9.9** Build and Configure NSG Flow Logs Using the Azure Portal 605
Exercise **10.1** Set Up a Private Link Service and Private Endpoints 623
Exercise **10.2** Create a Private Endpoint Using the Azure Portal 630
Exercise **10.3** Create a Subnet 644
Exercise **10.4** Enable a Service Endpoint 645
Exercise **10.5** Bind Network Access to Azure PaaS Resources 651

Introduction

Welcome to *MCA Microsoft® Certified Associate Azure® Network Engineer Study Guide*. This book offers a firm grounding for Microsoft's Exam AZ-700: Designing and Implementing Microsoft Azure Networking Solutions. This introduction provides a basic overview of this book and the Microsoft Certified Associate AZ-700 exam.

What Is Azure?

Organizations worldwide can become more digitally connected with Microsoft Azure, and networking can transform their processes. In a cloud environment, networking as a service provides scale, speed, elasticity, and managed oversight to customers. The network engineer's role continues to evolve in the cloud landscape as professionals migrate workloads to the cloud, manage hybrid connectivity, empower remote workers, and support strategic scenario-led digital transformations.

About the AZ-700 Certification Exam

The AZ-700 certification exam tests your knowledge and understanding of Microsoft Azure networking solutions. Specifically, the certification aims to validate your expertise in designing, deploying, and maintaining Azure networking solutions, including hybrid networking, routing, security, connectivity, and private access to Azure services.

You will be tested on your capabilities to translate requirements into secure, scalable, and reliable cloud network design and deployment of networking solutions.

Why Become a Certified Microsoft Azure Network Engineer Associate?

Would you like to demonstrate your Microsoft Azure networking skills and experience to your company or clients by planning, designing, deploying, and managing their Azure networking solutions?

Because Microsoft certification is a globally recognized and industry-endorsed proof of mastering real-world skills, those with such a certification are known to be more productive and efficient. Microsoft certifications differentiate you by proving your broad set of skills and experience with current Microsoft network solutions.

A Microsoft certification exam is a great way to demonstrate your level of expertise and build your résumé. You can validate your product knowledge and experience by taking the Microsoft certification AZ-700 exam.

> During and following the COVID-19 pandemic that began in 2020, many testing organizations changed their on-site testing procedures, some even offering remote exam proctoring. In light of this, be sure you check with Microsoft's website and the provider where you plan to take the exam prior to registration and again prior to exam day for the latest, up-to-the-minute changes in exam site procedures.

Preparing to Become a Certified Microsoft Azure Network Engineer Associate

Exam takers should have expertise in planning, implementing, and maintaining Azure networking solutions because the exam benchmarks your ability in these areas: hybrid networking; core networking infrastructure; routing; networking; and VPN access to Azure services.

The best preparation for the exam is by studying and hands-on practice. By studying this book, you will learn the necessary information and skills to prepare for the Azure Network Engineer Associate Certification AZ-700.

We recommend planning to devote 10 weeks or so of intensive study for the AZ-700 exam. Here are some recommendations to maximize your learning time; you can modify this list as necessary based on your own learning experiences:

- Get hands on with the Azure portal daily, read articles about Azure, and learn Azure networking terminology.

- Take one or two evenings to read each chapter in this book and work through its review materials.

- Answer all the review questions and take the practice exam provided on the book's website.

- Complete the exercises for each chapter.

  - Review the Microsoft Azure AZ-700 skills measured on Microsoft's page for this exam at:

    `https://query.prod.cms.rt.microsoft.com/cms/api/am/binary/RE4PaHw`

- You'll find a "skills measured" section on every exam and Microsoft certification page. Listed below are the primary skills that will be assessed for the AZ-700 exam. A detailed outline can be downloaded from the Microsoft site for this exam.
  - Design, implement and manage hybrid networking.
  - Design and implement core networking infrastructure.
  - Design and implement routing.
  - Secure and monitor networks.
  - Design and implement private access to Azure services.
- Use the flashcards included with the online study tools for this book to reinforce your understanding of concepts.
- Take free hands-on learning courses on Microsoft Learn at:

  `https://docs.microsoft.com/en-us/learn/paths/design-implement-microsoft-azure-networking-solutions-az-700`
- Read the Microsoft Azure documentation at:

  `https://docs.microsoft.com/en-us/azure/?product=popular`

How to Become a Microsoft Certified Azure Network Engineer

You can register for your exam from the Microsoft Certification AZ-700 exam details page once you are prepared:

`https://docs.microsoft.com/en-us/learn/certifications/exams/az-700`

On the certification details page, you'll find the choice to register in the "Schedule Exam" section.

You can take the exam online or at a local testing center, so you need to choose a test center or use online proctoring. There are advantages to each. Local test centers provide a secure environment. By taking your exam online, you can take it almost anywhere at any time. However, a reliable connection and a secure browser are required. When you take your test online, your system will first be checked to be sure it meets the requirements.

Who Should Buy This Book

Anybody who wants to pass the Microsoft AZ-700 exams will benefit from reading this book. If you're new to Azure networking, this book covers the material you will need to learn starting from the basics. It continues by providing the knowledge you need up to a proficiency level sufficient to pass the AZ-700 exams. You can pick up this book and learn from it even if you've never used Azure networking before, although you'll find it an easier read if you've at least casually used networking or virtual networking for a few days. If you're already familiar with networking, this book can serve as a review and a refresher course for the information you might not be entirely aware of. Reading this book will help you pass the Microsoft AZ-700 exams in either case.

This book is written with the assumption that you know at least a little bit about Azure and basic networking: what it is, and specifically what virtual machines, TCP/IP, the Domain Name System (DNS), virtual private networks (VPNs), firewalls, software-defined networking (SDN), wide area networks (WANs), and encryption technologies are. We also assume that you know some basics about creating Azure login accounts or setting up your Azure subscription. You can still use this book to fill in gaps in your knowledge.

How This Book Is Organized

This book consists of 10 chapters plus supplementary information. The chapters are organized as follows:

Chapter 1, "Getting Started with AZ-700 Certification for Azure Virtual Networking," covers the basics of cloud networking, introduction to Azure virtual networks, configuring public IP address services, designing name resolution for your virtual network, enabling cross-virtual network connectivity with peering, deploying virtual network traffic routing, and configuring Internet access with Azure virtual NAT.

Chapter 2, "Design, Deploy, and Manage a Site-to-Site VPN Connection and Point-to-Site VPN Connection," covers designing a site-to-site VPN connection, building and configuring a virtual network gateway, how to choose a virtual network (VNet) gateway SKU that is appropriate for your network, how to use policy-based VPN versus route-based VPN, building and configuring a local network gateway and IPsec/IKE policy, preparing and configuring RADIUS authentication, certificate-based authentication, OpenVPN authentication, and Azure Active Directory authentication, deploying a VPN client configuration file, diagnosing and resolving VPN gateway connectivity issues, and diagnosing and resolving client-side and authentication issues.

Chapter 3, "Design, Deploy, and Manage Azure ExpressRoute," covers how to choose between the network service provider and direct model (ExpressRoute Direct), designing and deploying Azure cross-region connectivity between multiple ExpressRoute locations, how to choose an appropriate ExpressRoute SKU and tier, designing and deploying ExpressRoute Global Reach, designing and deploying ExpressRoute FastPath, evaluating between private peering only, Microsoft peering only, or both, how to set up private peering, how to set up Microsoft peering, building and configuring an ExpressRoute gateway, connecting a virtual network to an ExpressRoute circuit, recommending a route advertisement configuration, configuring encryption over ExpressRoute, deploying bidirectional forwarding detection, and diagnosing and resolving ExpressRoute connection issues.

Chapter 4, "Design and Deploy Core Networking Infrastructure: Private IP and DNS," covers designing private IP addressing to VNets, deploying a VNet, preparing and configuring subnetting for services, including VNet gateways, Private Endpoints, firewalls, application gateways, and VNet-integrated platform services, preparing and configuring subnet delegation, designing public and private DNS zones, designing name resolution inside a VNet, and joining a private DNS zone to a VNet.

Chapter 5, "Design and Deploy Core Networking Infrastructure and Virtual WANs," covers designing service chaining inclusive of gateway transit, designing VPN connectivity between VNets, deploying VNet peering, design an Azure virtual WAN architecture, how to choose SKUs and services, connecting a VNet gateway to Azure virtual WANs, building a hub in a virtual WAN, building a virtual network appliance (NVA) in a virtual hub, setting up virtual hub routing, building a connection unit.

Chapter 6, "Design and Deploy VNet Routing and Azure Load Balancer," covers designing and deploying user-defined routes (UDRs), attaching a route table with a subnet, setting up forced tunneling, diagnosing and resolving routing issues, how to choose an Azure Load Balancer SKU, how to choose public and internal Azure Load Balancer-building and configuring an Azure Load Balancer (including cross-region), deploying a load balancing rule, building and configuring inbound NAT rules, and building explicit outbound rules for a load balancer.

Chapter 7, "Design and Deploy Azure application gateway, Azure front door, and Virtual NAT," covers defining Azure Application Gateway deployment options, how to choose between manual and autoscale, building a back-end pool, building and configuring health probes, listeners, and routing rules, building and configuring HTTP settings and Transport Layer Security (TLS), how to choose an Azure Front Door SKU, setting up health probes, including customization of HTTP response codes, setting up SSL termination and end-to-end SSL encryption, setting up multisite listeners, back-end targets, and routing rules, including redirection rules, building a routing method (mode), endpoints and HTTP settings, how to use a virtual network NAT, allocate public IP or public IP address prefixes for a NAT gateway, and associating a virtual network NAT with a subnet.

Chapter 8, "Design, Deploy, and Manage Azure Firewall and Network Security Groups," covers designing, building, and configuring an Azure firewall deployment, building and configuring Azure firewall rules and policies, building and configuring a secure hub within an Azure virtual WAN hub, integrating an Azure virtual WAN hub with a third-party NVA, creating an NSG and attaching it to a resource, creating an application security group (ASG) and attaching it to a NIC, creating and configuring NSG rules, reading NSG flow logs, validating NSG flow rules, and verifying IP address flow.

Chapter 9, "Design and Deploy Azure Web Application Firewall and Monitor Networks," covers setting up Detection or Prevention mode, setting up rule sets for Azure Front Door, including Microsoft-managed and user-defined, setting up rule sets for Application Gateway, including Microsoft-managed and user-defined, deploying and attaching WAF policies, setting up network health alerts and logging by using Azure Monitor, building and configuring a Connection Monitor instance, building, configuring, and using traffic analytics, building and configuring NSG flow logs, enabling diagnostic logging, and Azure Network Watcher.

Chapter 10, "Design and Deploy Private Access to Azure Services," covers setting up a Private Link service and Private Endpoints, preparing Private Endpoints, building and configuring access to remote endpoints, integrating Private Link with DNS and with on-premises clients, setting up service endpoints and configuring service endpoint policies, building service tags and access to service endpoints, building app service for regional VNet integration, building Azure Kubernetes Service (AKS) for regional VNet integration, and building clients to access App Service Environment.

Chapter Features

Each chapter begins with a list of the Azure Network Engineer Associate AZ-700 exam objectives covered in that chapter. Note that the book doesn't cover the goals in order. Thus, you shouldn't be alarmed at some of the odd ordering of the objectives within the book.

The exercises within each chapter are intended to reinforce the content just learned. We have listed a few elements you can use to prepare for the exam for each chapter:

Exam Essentials   This section aims to provide an overview of the critical information presented in the chapter. It should be possible for you to complete each task or convey the information requested.

Review Questions   There are 20 review questions at the end of each chapter. The answers to these questions are provided in the Appendix at the back of the book; you can check your answers there. You should review the chapter or the sections you are having trouble understanding if you can't answer at least 80 percent of these questions correctly.

The review questions, assessment test, and other testing elements included in this book are *not* derived from the AZ-700 exam questions, so don't memorize the answers to these questions and assume that doing so will enable you to pass the exam. You should learn the underlying topic, as described in the text of the book. This will let you answer the questions provided with this book *and* pass the exam. Learning the underlying topic is also the approach that will serve you best in the workplace—the goal of a certification like AZ-700.

To get the most out of this book, you should read each chapter from start to finish and then check your memory and understanding with the chapter-end elements. Even if you're already familiar with a topic, you should skim the chapter; Azure networking is complex enough that there are often multiple ways to accomplish a task, so you may learn something even if you're already competent in an area.

Interactive Online Learning Environment and Test Bank

We've put together some great online tools to help you pass the AZ-700 exam. The interactive online learning environment that accompanies *MCA Microsoft® Certified Associate Azure® Network Engineer Study Guide* provides a test bank and study tools to help you prepare for the exam.

Items available among these companion files include the following:

Practice Tests   All of the questions in this book appear in our proprietary digital test engine—including the 30-question assessment test at the end of this introduction, a 65-question practice exam, and the 200 questions that make up the review question sections at the end of each chapter. In addition, there is a 30-question bonus exam.

Electronic "Flashcards"   The digital companion files include 100 questions in flashcard format (a question followed by a single correct answer). You can use these to review your knowledge of the AZ-700 exam objectives.

Glossary   The key terms from this book, and their definitions, are available as a fully searchable PDF.

Interactive Online Learning Environment and Test Bank

You can access all these resources at www.wiley.com/go/sybextestprep. Once there, select your book from the list, complete the registration, including the question to show you own the book, and you will be emailed your personal PIN code. When you receive the PIN code, follow the directions in the email or go to www.wiley.com/go/sybextestprep where you will activate the PIN code and sign up for an account or add your new book to an existing account.

Conventions Used in This Book

This book uses certain typographic styles in order to help you quickly identify important information and to avoid confusion over the meaning of words such as on-screen prompts. In particular, look for the following styles:

- *Italicized text* indicates key terms that are described at length for the first time in a chapter. (Italics are also used for emphasis.)

- A `monospaced font` indicates the contents of configuration files, messages displayed at a text-mode Linux shell prompt, filenames, text-mode command names, and Internet URLs.

- *`Italicized monospaced text`* indicates a variable—information that differs from one system or command run to another, such as the name of a client computer or a process ID number.

- **`Bold monospaced text`** is information that you're to type into the computer, for example at a shell prompt. This text can also be italicized to indicate that you should substitute an appropriate value for your system.

In addition to these text conventions, which can apply to individual words or entire paragraphs, a few conventions highlight segments of text:

A tip provides information that can save you time or frustration and that may not be entirely obvious. A tip might describe how to get around a limitation or how to use a feature to perform an unusual task.

A note indicates information that's useful or interesting or provides additional relevant information that's somewhat peripheral to the main text.

Sidebars

A sidebar is like a note but longer. The information in a sidebar is useful, but it doesn't fit into the main flow of the text.

EXERCISES

An exercise is a procedure you should try out on your own Azure environment to help you learn about the material in the chapter. Don't limit yourself to the procedures described in the exercises, though! Try other PowerShell commands and procedures to really learn about Azure networking.

Using This Book

To get the most out of this book, all you need is an Azure subscription (paid), and a connection to the Internet, which is required to use and practice the online exercises for this book.

In addition to its web-based console, the Azure portal is available for desktop, tablet, and mobile devices. JavaScript must be enabled on your browser to use the portal. Make sure you use the latest browser for your operating system.

There are detailed explanations of real-world examples and scenarios included in this book covering all AZ-700 networking exam objectives. With this exam reference, IT network professionals will learn the critical thinking and decision-making skills they need to succeed.

While we have made every effort to ensure this book is as accurate as possible, Azure is constantly changing. In this book, some screenshots referring to the Azure portal may look different from what you see on your monitor because the Azure portal is different now than it was when the book was published. Additionally, minor interface changes, a name change, and so forth might have taken place as well.

As a network engineer, your responsibilities include designing and deploying Azure networking solutions. You're expected to maintain performance, resiliency, scale, and security of networking solutions. This book will help you design, deploy, and manage networking solutions using the Azure portal, PowerShell, Azure command-line interface, and Azure Resource Manager (ARM) templates.

For those preparing for the examination, this book will provide prescriptive guidance.

While this book covers all the topics found on the exam, you won't find every question that might appear in the real exam. We cannot cover specific questions because only Microsoft examination team members have access to exam questions, and Microsoft continuously adds new exam questions. So view this book as a complement to your related real-world experience and other study materials.

Technology Requirements

In addition to a paid Azure subscription and a connection to the Internet, the following are good to have for going through the book easily:

- **An Azure Subscription (must have):** You can sign up by visiting `https://azure.microsoft.com`.
- **PowerShell:** Run `$PSVersionTable.PSVersion` to check which version of PowerShell you have installed. You must have PowerShell 7.0.6 LTS or PowerShell 7.1.3 or higher.
- **Azure PowerShell Module:** Download the latest PowerShell module for Azure networking modules. You will not have it all by default.
- **Azure PowerShell:** To run PowerShell, a Windows 10 or 11 machine with 4 GB of RAM is sufficient.

AZ-700 EXAM OBJECTIVES

The structure of this book follows Microsoft's published "Exam AZ-700: Designing and Implementing Microsoft Azure Networking Solutions – Skills Measured" document (available at `https://query.prod.cms.rt.microsoft.com/cms/api/am/binary/RE4OV0k`). AZ-700 covers the following five major topic areas:

Subject Area	% of Exam
Design, Implement, and Manage Hybrid and Private Networking	10%–15%
Design and Implement Core Networking Infrastructure	20%–25%
Design and Implement Routing	25%–30%
Secure and Monitor Networks	15%–20%
Design and Implement Private Access to Azure Services	10%–15%

The book's 10 chapters are mapped to the Azure skills measured. The following tables show which chapter covers which objective.

Skill Measured: Design, Implement, and Manage Hybrid Networking

Exam Objective	Chapter
Introduction and Azure Networking Overview	1
Design, implement, and manage a site-to-site VPN connection	2
Design, implement, and manage a point-to-site VPN connection	2
Design, implement, and manage Azure ExpressRoute	3

Skill Measured: Design and Implement Core Networking Infrastructure

Exam Objective	Chapter
Design and implement private IP addressing for VNetx	4
Design and implement name resolution	4

Exam Objective	Chapter
Design and implement cross-VNet connectivity	5
Design and implement an Azure Virtual WAN architecture	5

Skill Measured: Design and Implement Routing

Exam Objective	Chapter
Design, implement, and manage VNet routing	6
Design and implement an Azure Load Balancer	6
Design and implement Azure Application Gateway	7
Implement Azure Front Door	7
Implement an Azure Traffic Manager profile	7
Design and implement an Azure Virtual Network NAT	7

Skill Measured: Secure and Monitor Networks

Exam Objective	Chapter
Design, implement, and manage an Azure Firewall deployment	8
Implement and manage network security groups (NSGs)	8
Implement a Web Application Firewall (WAF) deployment	9
Monitor networks	9

Skill Measured: Design and Implement Private Access to Azure Services

Exam Objective	Chapter
Design and implement Azure Private Link service and Azure Private Endpoint	10
Design and implement service endpoints	10
Configure VNet integration for dedicated platform as a service (PaaS) services	10

Microsoft reserves the right to change exam domains and objectives without prior notice. The most up-to-date information can be found on the Microsoft website at:

`https://docs.microsoft.com/en-us/learn/certifications/azure-network-engineer-associate`

Like all exams, the MCA Azure Network Engineer certification from Microsoft is updated periodically and may eventually be retired or replaced. At some point after Microsoft is no longer offering this exam, the old editions of our books and online tools will be retired. If you have purchased this book after the exam was retired, or are attempting to register in the Sybex online learning environment after the exam was retired, please know that we make no guarantees that this exam's online Sybex tools will be available once the exam is no longer available.

How to Contact the Publisher

If you believe you've found a mistake in this book, please bring it to our attention. At John Wiley & Sons, we understand how important it is to provide our customers with accurate content, but even with our best efforts an error may occur.

In order to submit your possible errata, please email it to our Customer Service Team at wileysupport@wiley.com with the subject line "Possible Book Errata Submission."

Assessment Test

1. Sybex wants to configure record types in Azure DNS. Which of the following are supported record types?

   A. A

   B. AAAA

   C. CNAME

   D. All the above

2. Sybex wants to create a VNet. Which of the following protocol(s) are supported in an Azure virtual network?

   A. TCP

   B. UDP

   C. ICMP TCP/IP

   D. All of the above

3. True or False: Sybex wants to use HTTP/2. Azure Front Door provides the support for this requirement.

   A. True

   B. False

4. Azure ExpressRoute will allow Sybex to connect its on-premises network to Microsoft's cloud. Which of the following options is not an ExpressRoute standard that Sybex can use?

   A. Any to any connection

   B. Site-to-site VPN

   C. Point-to-site VPN

   D. CloudExchange co-location

5. True or False: Customers want to move from standard to WAF SKU without downtime.

   A. True

   B. False

6. True or False: It is possible for Sybex to reserve a private IP address for a VM that they will create at a later time.

   A. True

   B. False

7. True or False: You can use global VNet peering with Azure Basic Load Balancer.

   A. True

   B. False

8. True or False: You can have ExpressRoute circuits from different service providers.

    A. True

    B. False

9. True or False: You want to create an always-on VPN. Active VPN profiles can connect automatically and remain connected based on triggers, such as user sign-in, network state change, or device screen activity. You can deploy this solution for Windows 10 users.

    A. True

    B. False

10. True or False: You want to use your own favorite network virtual appliance (in an NVA VNet) with Azure Virtual WAN. Azure virtual WAN can support this requirement.

    A. True

    B. False

11. You want to deploy peering in Azure ExpressRoute; which of the following is supported?

    A. Microsoft peering

    B. Private peering

    C. Public peering

    D. All of the above

12. You want to create an ExpressRoute and site-to-site VPN connections side by side. Can they coexist?

    A. Yes

    B. No

13. Application Gateway is a dedicated deployment in your virtual network. Is it possible to share?

    A. Yes

    B. No

14. You want to build a virtual network; what management tools should you use?

    A. Azure portal

    B. PowerShell

    C. Azure CLI

    D. All of the above

15. You want to use Azure DNS private zone. Does Azure store your customers' personal content?

    A. Yes, it does store customers' content.

    B. No, it does not store customers' content.

    C. Metadata only is stored.

    D. None of the above is stored.

16. You want to use Virtual WAN for transit connectivity between VPN and ExpressRoute. Does the Azure Virtual WAN support this?

    A. Yes

    B. No

17. You want to use the virtual network gateway management solution feature to provide an easy way to view and disconnect current point-to-site VPN sessions; is it possible to deploy this solution to network engineers?

    A. Yes

    B. No

18. True or False: It is possible to set custom routing policies on VNets and subnets.

    A. True

    B. False

19. Which of the following prerequisites must you meet in order to make calls to Private Endpoints?

    A. Make sure that your DNS lookups resolve to the Private Endpoint.

    B. Make sure clients can access the intranet.

    C. Make sure clients can access the Internet.

    D. None of the above.

20. You wants to create a site-to-site VPN. What management tools should you use?

    A. Azure portal

    B. PowerShell

    C. Azure CLI

    D. All of the above

21. Azure Firewall supports which of the following rule collections?

    A. Application

    B. NAT

    C. Network

    D. All the above

22. True or False: You want to configure DNSSEC, and Azure DNS supports that.

    A. True

    B. False

23. True or False: You want to use Application Gateway to redirect HTTP-to-HTTPS. It is a supported feature by Azure Application Gateway.

    A. True

    B. False

24. Your company wishes to establish a secure communication tunnel between your remote offices. Which of the following technologies cannot be used?

    A. Site-to-site VPN

    B. Point-to-site VPN

    C. ExpressRoute

    D. Implicit FTP over SSL

25. True or False: You want to use Application Gateway to redirect HTTP-to-HTTPS. It is a supported feature by Azure Front Door.

    A. True

    B. False

26. True or False: You can add a virtual machine from the same availability set to other back-end pools of a load balancer with different availability sets.

    A. True

    B. False

27. True or False: It is possible for you to have public IP addresses in your VNets.

    A. True

    B. False

28. True or False: The Network Watcher service is zone-resilient by default.

    A. True

    B. False

29. You want to create Private Endpoints in the same virtual network. How many are supported?

    A. A maximum of one

    B. A maximum of two

    C. More than one

    D. None of the above

30. An Azure VNet does not support which of the following? (Choose all that apply.)

    A. Multicast

    B. Broadcast

    C. Unicast

    D. None of above

Answers to Assessment Test

1. D. An Azure DNS zone can use Alias records for the following types of records: A, AAAA, and CNAME. See Chapter 4 for more information.

2. D. VNets allow the use of TCP, UDP, and ICMP TCP/IP protocols. Within VNets, Unicast is supported, except for Dynamic Host Configuration Protocol (DHCP) via Unicast (source port UDP/68 / destination port UDP/67) and UDP source port 65330, which is reserved for hosts. See Chapter 1 for more information.

3. A. True. Only Azure Front Door clients can access HTTP/2 support. HTTP/1.1 is the communication protocol used to contact back-ends in the back-end pool, and the back-end pool supports HTTP/2 by default. See Chapter 7 for more information.

4. B. A site-to-site virtual private network is not an ExpressRoute model. See Chapter 2 for more information.

5. A. True. Microsoft supports customers changing from Standard to WAF SKU without disruption. See Chapter 9 for more information.

6. B. False. Private IP addresses cannot be reserved. A DHCP server's VM or role instance receives a private IP address if it is available. If you want a private IP address assigned to a VM, it may or may not be that one. See Chapter 1 for more information.

7. B. Azure Basic Load Balancer does not support global VNet peering. You need to use Standard Load Balancer instead. See Chapter 6 for more information.

8. A. True. ExpressRoute circuits are available from various service providers, and one service provider is responsible for each ExpressRoute circuit. See Chapter 3 for more information.

9. A. True. The Windows 10 VPN client has a new feature, Always-On, which allows a VPN connection to be maintained. The active VPN profile can automatically connect and remain connected using Always-On based on triggers such as user authentication, network state changes, or device screen activation. See Chapter 2 for more information.

10. A. True. It is possible to connect your favorite network virtual appliance (NVA) VNet to the Azure Virtual WAN. See Chapter 5 for more information.

11. D. There are three types of routing domains supported by ExpressRoute: private peering, Microsoft peering, and public peering. (At some point in the future, public peering will be deprecated.) See Chapter 3 for more information.

12. A. Site-to-site VPN connections and ExpressRoute work together. There are several advantages to configuring site-to-site VPN and ExpressRoute. You can set up a site-to-site VPN as a secure failover path for ExpressRoute or set up site-to-site VPNs to connect to sites that aren't connected through ExpressRoute. See Chapter 2 for more information.

13. B. If Application Gateway is a dedicated deployment in your virtual network, it cannot be shared with any other customers. See Chapter 7 for more information.

14. D. You can use the Azure portal, PowerShell, and Azure CLI to build or set up a VNet. See Chapter 1 for more information.

15. B. The Azure DNS private zones do not store any customer content. See Chapter 4 for more information.

16. A. Virtual WAN allows transit connectivity between VPNs and ExpressRoute. This implies that VPN-connected sites or remote users can communicate with ExpressRoute-connected sites. See Chapter 5 for more information.

17. A. With the Azure virtual network gateways, current point-to-site VPN sessions can be viewed and disconnected easily. See Chapter 2 for more information.

18. A. True. An organization can create a route table and associate it to a subnet. See Chapter 6 for more information.

19. A. Make sure your DNS lookups resolve to the Private Endpoint if you want to make calls to Private Endpoints. See Chapter 10 for more information.

20. D. Azure VPN gateways provide connectivity between Azure and customer premises. You can use the Azure portal, PowerShell, and Azure CLI. See Chapter 2 for more information.

21. D. Azure Firewall supports rules and rule collections of three types: application, network, and NAT rules. See Chapter 8 for more information.

22. B. False. As of today, Azure DNS does not support the Domain Name System Security Extensions (DNSSEC). See Chapter 4 for more information.

23. A. True. Application Gateway supports redirects. See Chapter 7 for more information.

24. D. FTP over SSL can't be used to deploy a secure communication tunnel. See Chapter 2 for more information.

25. A. True. In addition to the host, path, and query string redirection, Azure Front Door supports URL redirection. See Chapter 7 for more information.

26. B. False. You cannot add a virtual machine from the same availability set to different back-end pools of a load balancer. See Chapter 6 for more information.

27. A. True. You can have public IP addresses in your own VNets. See Chapter 1 for more information.

28. A. True. Microsoft Azure Network Watcher service is zone-resilient by default. See Chapter 9 for more information.

29. C. It is possible to have more than one Private Endpoint in the same VNet or subnet, and different ones can connect to different services. See Chapter 10 for more information.

30. A, B. An Azure VNet does not support multicast and broadcast. See Chapter 6 for more information.

Chapter 1

Getting Started with AZ-700 Certification for Azure Networking

THE MICROSOFT AZ-700 EXAM OBJECTIVES COVERED IN THIS CHAPTER INCLUDE:

- ✓ Basics of Cloud Networking
- ✓ Introduction to Azure Virtual Networks
- ✓ Configuring Public IP Services
- ✓ Configuring Domain Name Services
- ✓ Configuring Cross-Virtual Network Connectivity with Peering
- ✓ Configuring Virtual Network Traffic Routing
- ✓ Configuring Internet Access with Azure Virtual Network NAT

In this chapter, we focus on prerequisites for AZ-700 preparation. This chapter shows you how to design and deploy essential Microsoft Azure networking resources such as virtual networks, public and private IPs, DNS, virtual network peering, routing, and Azure Virtual Network NAT.

Azure provides infrastructure as a service (IaaS), platform as a service (PaaS), and software as a service (SaaS) through its cloud computing service. It includes network, storage, compute, database, analytics, security, and many more cloud computing services. In this chapter, you learn the basics of cloud computing, and we provide an overview of Azure networking services.

Basics of Cloud Computing and Networking

Let's get started with the basics of cloud computing and networking.

Information technology (IT) resources are delivered via the Internet on demand on a pay-per-use basis through cloud computing. Organizations can rent (rather than own) and maintain physical datacenters and servers from a cloud service provider, like Microsoft Azure, and access technology services in real time as needed.

Despite cloud computing's profound impact on IT, real transformation opportunities are still to come. Cloud-first cultures have emerged in companies of all sizes in recent years, as more resources are dedicated to following a cloud-first strategy.

When comparing cloud computing to traditional on-premises IT, and depending on the cloud services organization chosen, cloud computing helps lower IT costs and increase agility and time-to-value. In addition, IT can scale up or down more efficiently and cheaply.

Let's start by defining the term *cloud computing*. The definition provided by the National Institute of Standards and Technology (NIST) is as follows:

> Cloud computing is a model for enabling ubiquitous, convenient, on-demand network access to a shared pool of configurable computing resources (e.g., networks, servers, storage, applications, and services) that can be rapidly provisioned and released with minimal management effort or service provider interaction. (http://nvlpubs.nist.gov/nistpubs/Legacy/SP/nistspecialpublication800-145.pdf).

With cloud computing, you can instantly access computing services, including servers, storage, databases, networking, software, analytics, and intelligence, via the Internet to innovate more rapidly, adapt resources more efficiently, and achieve economies of scale. Typically, you only pay for the cloud services you use, allowing you to reduce your operating costs, run your infrastructure more efficiently, and scale up or down as your business needs change.

The Need for Networking Infrastructure

Networking is defined by NIST as follows:

> Information system(s) implemented with a collection of interconnected components. Such components may include routers, hubs, cabling, telecommunications controllers, key distribution centers, and technical control devices. (`http://csrc.nist.gov/glossary/term/network#`).

Computer networking relates to two or more connected computers sharing resources such as files, data, printers, applications, an intranet, or an Internet connection, or a combination of these resources.

Computer network infrastructure is needed by enterprises to meet end users' needs for hardware and software. Connecting servers, desktops, and mobile devices through a network is crucial. It is expensive and complex to manage IT infrastructure in an enterprise. It requires specialized IT staff members and costly hardware and software to run correctly. It is possible for organizations to build private cloud networks on their premises or to build hybrid cloud networks using the public cloud and on-premises cloud resources. Virtual routers, firewalls, and bandwidth and network management software can be included as part of these network resources.

Organizations used to set up their own IT departments to acquire, deploy, and maintain networking applications. A new application or evolving use case often required additional hardware, such as a server. In turn, this meant more capital expenditures and more support time required of IT personnel. Typically, the IT department was already stretched by managing one location. As a result, the costs and support time associated with deploying and maintaining network equipment and applications were compounded even further.

The Need for the Cloud

Organizations today turn to the cloud to drive agility, deliver differentiation, accelerate time-to-market, and increase scale. The cloud model has become the standard approach to building and delivering applications for the modern digital era.

IT infrastructures are experiencing abnormal wear and tear to meet clients' expectations for speedy, secure, and stable services. Organizations often find that improving and managing a hardy, scalable, and secure IT foundation is prohibitively expensive as they strive to develop their IT systems' processing and storage capabilities.

DevOps (development and operations), DevSecOps (development, security, and operations), and site reliability engineering (SRE) can converge on what matters most with cloud computing and withdraw undifferentiated trades, such as procurement, support, and retention planning. The adoption of cloud computing has led to numerous distinct models and deployment strategies tailored to fit the specific needs of users. Cloud service and deployment organizations offer consumers varying degrees of control, flexibility, and management.

Cloud deployment models are defined by where the infrastructure resides and who controls it. One of the most critical decisions IT organizations should make is their deployment model. NIST defines four types of cloud deployment:

Public Cloud   The cloud infrastructure is provisioned for open use by the general public. It may be owned, managed, and operated by a business, academic, or government organization, or some combination of them. It exists on the premises of the cloud provider.

Private Cloud   The cloud infrastructure is provisioned for exclusive use by a single organization comprising multiple consumers (e.g., business units). It may be owned, managed, and operated by the organization, a third party, or some combination of them, and it may exist on- or off-premises.

Community Cloud   The cloud infrastructure is provisioned for exclusive use by a specific community of consumers from organizations that have shared concerns (e.g., mission, security requirements, policy, and compliance considerations). It may be owned, managed, and operated by one or more of the organizations in the community, a third party, or some combination of them, and it may exist on- or off premises.

Hybrid Cloud   The cloud infrastructure is a composition of two or more distinct cloud infrastructures (private, community, or public) that remain unique entities but that are bound together by standardized or proprietary technology that enables data and application portability (e.g., cloud bursting for load balancing between clouds).

```
(http://nvlpubs.nist.gov/nistpubs/Legacy/SP/
nistspecialpublication800-145.pdf)
```

Cloud networks also play a critical role in the way organizations approach their expanding infrastructure needs, regional expansions, and redundancy plans. Many organizations choose a multidatacenter strategy and leverage multiple clouds from several cloud service providers.

Enterprise networks can be designed, deployed, operated, and managed by a single platform in cloud networking. A cloud infrastructure offers enterprise-class network capabilities without requiring additional hardware appliances or IT resources.

A cloud-defined network can be either public or private, and a company can host it. In comparison to conventional networks, cloud networking services are unique. Data is stored in various front- and back-end storage servers accessible through the Internet and is retrieved through an application-based software infrastructure.

A cloud provider provides public cloud networking to end users who connect via the Internet without deploying anything on their own organization's infrastructure. A pay-per-use model is also available for public cloud networking services. A private cloud network refers to a set of computing services hosted on a proprietary network behind a firewall and is offered to a limited number of users. For example, a company's internal IT department using a private cloud infrastructure essentially hosts applications within their private cloud network and provides those applications to their own IT users.

Cloud-native networking features allow enterprises to deploy locations within minutes and to operate distributed networks using cloud-based services. They also provide unparalleled levels of centralized control and network visibility. The cloud is usually a subscription service as well, so no capital costs are required up front.

In a nutshell, a cloud network is essentially a method of connecting to your network using the Internet or cloud technologies in conjunction with wide area networks (WANs). The network resources include virtual routers, bandwidth, firewalls, and network management software.

Like cloud computing, cloud networking focuses on centralized computing resources that different clients or customers share. Through the network, users are connected and are able to communicate with one another. The cloud can manage more network functions, making it less necessary for customers to maintain their networks.

Cloud networking fits into the following three categories: cloud-enabled networks, cloud-based networks, and cloud-native network functions (CNFs; see Figure 1.1):

FIGURE 1.1   Cloud networks

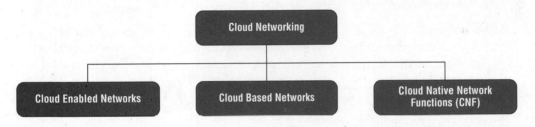

Cloud-Enabled Networks   The network remains on-premises while one or more resources are in the cloud. The core network infrastructure, such as packet forwarding, routing, and data, stays in-house. Still, network management, monitoring, maintenance, and security services are done through the cloud or the Internet.

Cloud-Based Networks   In cloud-based networking, all networking resources are in the cloud. This includes network management resources and physical hardware. Cloud-based networking connects the applications and resources deployed on the web.

Cloud-Native Network Functions (CNFs)   Functions that are traditionally performed on physical hardware devices (e.g., IPv4 router, L2 switch, firewall, virtual private networking [VPN]) can be accessed through cloud-native devices.

The organization is rapidly adopting cloud networking within enterprises. However, there are always concerns that need to be resolved, such as security, privacy, high availability, poor application performance, compliance, business continuity, and localization. Despite those concerns, the fact is that many organizations are moving to the cloud. And they are beginning to appreciate their actual benefits, such as lower costs, fast deployment, productivity, mobility, instant scalability, minimal downtime, and enhanced security.

Basics of Networking

Let's start our journey with the basics of networking. An understanding of the foundations of networking, such as the various devices you can use to build a network, is essential for a career as an Azure network engineer, administrator, or architect.

Computer networks facilitate communication across all types of businesses, entertainment, and research organizations. Because of computer networks, there is the Internet, online search, email, audio and video sharing, online commerce, live streaming, and social networks.

In parallel with cloud networking needs are the types of computer networks developed to meet those needs. There are a variety of sizes, shapes, and kinds of networks.

Types of Networks

Different types of networks are classified into the categories shown in Figure 1.2 to make identifying them easier.

FIGURE 1.2   Network classification

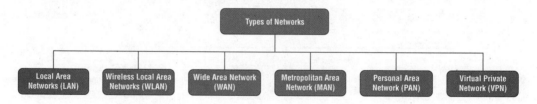

Local Area Network (LAN)   Connects computers over relatively short distances, enabling them to share data, files, and resources. In an office building, school, or hospital, a LAN may connect all the computers. Networks are typically managed and owned privately.

Wireless Local Area Network (WLAN)   Has the same capabilities as local area networks. However, it connects using wireless technology.

Wide Area Network (WAN)   Connects computers over long distances, such as from region to region or even continent to continent. WANs connect billions of computers worldwide via the Internet. You will typically see collective or distributed ownership models for WAN management.

Metropolitan Area Network (MAN)   MANs are typically larger than LANs and smaller than WANs. Governmental entities and cities usually own and operate MANs.

Personal Area Network (PAN)   A network provider for individuals. PANs allow a smartphone, smartwatch, tablet, and laptop to connect and share data without the need for an access point or other third-party network services.

Virtual Private Network (VPN)   As a point-to-point connection between two network endpoints, a virtual private network (VPN) provides security. A VPN builds an encrypted tunnel that keeps a user's identity and access credentials, as well as the data they are sending, safe from hackers.

Several characteristics set a LAN apart from a WAN. Knowing the difference between them helps you to prepare the services to deploy across these networks.

- A LAN is a privately operated network typically covered in a single location. In contrast, a WAN is used to connect geographically separate offices. Multiple organizations utilize WANs.

- LANs operate at speeds of 10 Gbps or more. A WAN usually works at a rate of less than one gigabit per second.

- A LAN is less populated compared to other network types. In contrast, a WAN is more populated compared to other network types.

- In-house management and administration of a LAN are possible. However, WANs typically require a third party to configure and set up, which increases the cost.

A network can't exist unless the devices can communicate with each other. It doesn't matter if your system is part of an on-premises network or a larger one like the Azure cloud. It is the same principle for all networks.

A network protocol provides a unified method of communication, but network standards govern the hardware and software that use them.

With today's technology, you can seamlessly add your computer or network to the thousands of hardware suppliers that are out there. A network standard enables devices to communicate with each other.

The network standard allows for backward compatibility and connectivity among network-enabled devices. Standards are published by the International Telecommunication Union (ITU), the American National Standards Institute (ANSI), and the Institute of Electrical and Electronics Engineers (IEEE). Without network standards, it is unlikely that networks could be built or networked devices could connect reliably.

Networking Terminology

Before taking the AZ-700 certification exam, you must familiarize yourself with the terms used in networking.

Let's get started with protocol suites. Protocol suites are used to communicate between computers on a network. Protocol stacks are collections of communication protocols, such as the Internet Protocol (IP) suite.

The IP suite is well known and consists of two types: Open Systems Interconnection (OSI) and Transmission Control Protocol/Internet Protocol (TCP/IP). The IP suite is a network model that varies between four and seven layers.

The OSI model describes a logical network and computer packet transfer. Today's Internet operates using the TCP/IP protocol rather than OSI. As a model of network communication,

OSI defines systems that can communicate or interconnect with other systems. It serves to visualize and communicate how networks function and isolate and troubleshoot problems in networks using the OSI 7-layer model. Seven layers of the OSI model are the Physical Layer, Data Link Layer, Network Layer, Transport Layer, Session Layer, Presentation Layer, and Application Layer.

The TCP/IP protocol suite is the most used and the most widely available protocol suite since both TCP and IP are primary protocols. TCP/IP is made up of several layers. Each layer represents a different possible use of the protocol. It is common for each layer to have more than one protocol option for carrying out its duties. The four layers are Application, Transport, Network, and Data Link.

Figure 1.3 compares the OSI and the TCP/IP models.

FIGURE 1.3   OSI model compared to TCP/IP model

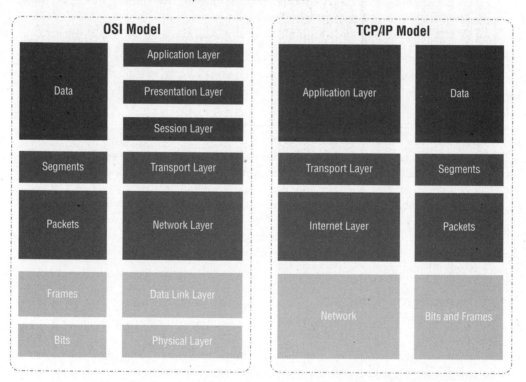

In computer networking, there are a few more standard terms you need to know:

IP Address   The *IP address* is a unique number associated with every device attached to a network communicating over the Internet Protocol. An IP address identifies the host network of a device and its location within the host network. When sending data, the protocol header usually contains the IP address of the sending device and the destination device.

Media Access Control (MAC)   Network protocols are used to communicate, but network standards govern hardware and software that use network protocols. There are six pairs of hexadecimal numbers in the *Media Access Control (MAC)* address, typically separated by a colon. The first six hexadecimal numbers are the manufacturer's organizationally unique identifier (OUI), and the last six are used to identify the device.

Routers   *Routers* are devices that transmit information contained in data packets between networks. The router analyzes packet data to determine how to send the information to its destination. Routers forward packets of data until they are received at the destination node.

Switches   Ethernet *switches* allow packets to be transferred between network nodes and help ensure the packets arrive at their destination. Switches rather than routers are used in networks to transfer data between network nodes.

Switching is the method of transferring data between devices on a computer network. Generally, there are three types: circuit switching, packet switching, and message switching.

Ports   Network devices are connected by *ports*, which identify a specific connection. Each port has a unique number. In the same way that an IP address is equivalent to an address for a hotel, ports are the suites or rooms. Computers use port numbers to determine which applications, services, or processes should receive messages.

Repeaters   A *repeater* is a two-port device that echoes network signals. Repeaters are used when network devices are a great distance from each other. The repeater doesn't interpret or modify data packets before it resends them, nor does it augment the signal. The repeater re-creates the data packet at the original strength, bit by bit.

Bridge   A *bridge* divides a network into network segments and can isolate, segregate, and transmit data packets between these segments. Bridges use the network device's MAC address to determine the data package's destination. Typically, a bridge is used to improve network performance by reducing redundant network traffic on network portions.

Network Cable Types   Ethernet, coaxial, and fiber optic are the most used *cable* types. You choose a cable type depending on the size, arrangement, and physical distance between the network elements.

Firewall   A *firewall* is a security device that can aid in defending your network by scrubbing traffic and blocking hackers from gaining access to the private data on your system.

Ethernet   *Ethernet* is a network standard used on wired LANs as well as MANs and WANs. Ethernet has replaced other wired LAN technologies like ARCNet and Token Ring and is an industry standard. Despite Ethernet's association with wired networks, fiber optics is also used with Ethernet today.

Packets   *Packets* are the smallest units of data being transferred across a network. Data packets (in pieces) are the envelopes through which data is transported over a network.

Network Address Translation (NAT)   It is a process that enables multiple IP addresses to be mapped into a single unique IP address. An organization that wants various devices to share a single IP address uses a NAT configuration. In NAT, a single device, such as a router, acts as an intermediary between the Internet (or public network) and a local network (or private network), which indicates that only a single unique IP address is needed to illustrate a whole group of devices to anything outside their network.

Virtual Private Network (VPN)   A *virtual private network (VPN)* establishes a protected connection over a public network. It encrypts your data and conceals your identity online, which means your online activities are less likely to be tracked and your information is less likely to be stolen by third parties. Data is encrypted in real time.

Virtualization   Virtualization makes it possible for network architects to design, implement, and manage networks more efficiently than ever before. Network functions virtualization (NFV) and software-defined networking (SDN) are two key capabilities that enable cloud capability transformation.

Software-Defined Network (SDN)   A *software-defined network (SDN)* separates a router's control plane from the forwarding plane. Network administrators and architects use a central control point for configuration and management. As a result, dynamic, agile, and scalable networks are created that can be quickly adapted to changing business needs by using the virtualized infrastructure of modern datacenters.

Network Functions Virtualization (NFV)   *Network functions virtualization (NFV)* allows network functions to be virtualized without requiring specialized hardware (routers, firewalls, VPN terminators, software-defined wide area networking [SD-WAN], and so forth). With VNF, you can deploy your network functions on demand using high-performance x86 hardware.

Enterprise Cloud Networking

Cloud networks are IT infrastructure that enables users, devices, and applications to communicate to cloud-hosted services. Cloud network design and deployment goals are to continuously provide reliable and secure connected digital services to employees, partners, customers, and, increasingly, physical objects.

A cloud network can be divided into three domains:

Private Cloud and Hybrid Clouds   These types are responsible for network connections to and among applications, workloads, and data, within on-premises datacenters and private and public cloud services. The network design should support low latency, security, and mission-critical reliability.

Campus, Branch, and Internet of Things (IoT)   These types are responsible for providing fixed and remote access to users and things. They are present in all areas of an organization, both in offices and in functional spaces such as manufacturing and warehouse facilities. The network design should support transparent, secure access and high density.

Wide Area Networks (WANs)   WANs are responsible for network connections to facilities, buildings, or campuses to other branches, datacenters, or the public cloud. The network design should support user experience and bandwidth efficiency.

Typically, each part is designed, deployed, and optimized for its purpose and business objectives.

The following are critical characteristics of cloud networking:

Connectivity   The cloud network should be designed to provide proper connectivity for all users, devices, and applications in a company, based on their roles, purposes, and locations.

Scalability and Flexibility   IT networks must support digital initiatives to quickly adapt to rapidly changing services and products, including growth, scaling, and expansion.

Security and Defense   Cloud networks are primary detectors of threats, enforcers of security, and enforcers of compliance in addition to security applications and devices, such as firewalls and secure Internet gateways. These services will identify, profile, verify, monitor, authenticate, control access to, segment, and manage devices and accounts.

Optimization   The goal of proactive network optimization is to resolve issues quickly, prioritize essential traffic, and ensure privacy and security. Cloud networks can improve the user experience.

Zero-Trust Standards   *Zero trust* is a security framework that requires all users, whether inside or outside the organization's network, to be authenticated, authorized, and constantly validated for security configuration before gaining access to applications and data.

Users, applications, and data must be protected across mobility and cloud adoption. If the security framework facilitates zero-trust access, attackers are less likely to move laterally through a network.

Microsoft Azure Overview

The Microsoft Azure cloud computing platform is Microsoft's public cloud platform. Offerings include infrastructure as a service (IaaS), platform as a service (PaaS), and software as a service (SaaS) solutions, with some offering pay-as-you-go options. With its global reach and 90+ compliance features, Azure is an essential choice for enterprises.

Large businesses approach Azure by moving their existing lower environments to Azure. Migrating workloads to the cloud is a great start; however, the cloud is more than moving the workloads to the cloud because Azure offers constant improvement and new updates on a wider variety of services for enterprise digital needs.

Organizations consume Azure services via a web-based unified console, the Azure portal, as an alternative to command-line tools. With the Azure portal, a consumer can manage Azure tenant subscriptions by using a graphical user interface. The Azure portal also allows consumers to:

- Deploy, manage, and monitor all subscribed Azure services
- Create custom dashboards for a structured view of services consumed by organizations at various levels
- Configure accessibility choices for a better experience

In this section, you will learn about two key concepts:

- The foundation of the Azure cloud
- Azure's global infrastructure

Figure 1.4 provides an overview of the Azure cloud.

FIGURE 1.4   The building blocks of Azure

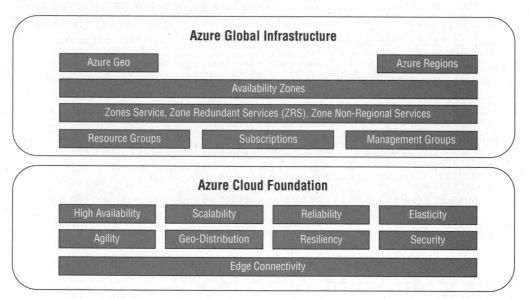

Azure Cloud Foundation

First, you need to understand the foundation of the Azure cloud. The cloud offers the following advantages:

High Availability   Azure has a wide variety of service-level agreements (SLAs) that provide various degrees of high availability options based on the application requirements for the services available to end users. Azure leverages services that are distributed across various regions.

Reliability   Reliability refers to an Azure cloud service's ability to function under certain circumstances for a specified period. Reliability is a subprocess of cloud services that maintain IT functionality. It is closely associated with availability and is typically defined as the ability to run at a specified moment or time interval as agreed between Microsoft and cloud consumers.

Scalability   Applications in the cloud can scale both vertically and horizontally:

> **Scaling Vertically**   Azure allows you to increase compute capacity by adding vCPU or vRAM to a virtual machine (VM).

> **Scaling Horizontally**   Azure allows you to increase compute capacity by adding instances of resources such as VMs.

Elasticity   An elastic infrastructure can expand or contract as needed to adapt to workload changes in an autonomous way. With elasticity, the number of resources allotted will match the number of resources needed at any point in time. Scalability ensures adaptability to changing demand by statically adding and removing resources to meet an application's needs within the limits of the infrastructure.

Agility   A significant advantage of the cloud is its ability to scale rapidly. For example, suppose you have web applications running in Azure, and the developer decides to add two more VMs for the application. In that case, the developer can scale out to three VMs in seconds. Azure takes care of allocating the resources for the developer. All a developer has to do is tell Azure how many VMs are needed. This kind of speed and versatility in Azure is called *cloud agility*.

Geo-Distribution   Organizations can deploy applications and data to regional datacenters around the globe. They can efficiently deploy applications in multiple regions.

Resiliency   By taking advantage of cloud-based backup services, data replication, and geo-distribution, organizations have a fallback solution in the event of a disaster.

Security   Azure security is the highest priority for customers, and Azure users benefit from a cloud architecture developed to meet the obligations of security-sensitive businesses.

Edge   Your organization can focus on business insights instead of managing data by leveraging Azure IoT Edge's cloud analytics and custom business logic. You can scale out your IoT solution by packaging your business logic into standard containers. Once deployed, those containers can be monitored via the cloud from any device.

Azure Global Infrastructure

The second key concept to understand about Azure cloud is its global infrastructure, developed with two essential elements: one is physical infrastructure, and the other is connective network components. The physical infrastructure consists of over 200 physical datacenters, organized into regions and connected by extensive interconnected networks.

Azure's global infrastructure is classified into Azure geography, Azure regions pairs, Azure regions, Azure availability zones, and availability sets, as shown in Figure 1.5.

FIGURE 1.5 Azure global infrastructure logical view

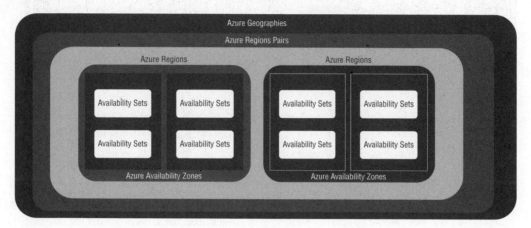

Azure Geography

Azure geography is defined with one or more regions to fulfill the data residency and compliance requirements that are often demanded by businesses.

Azure geography is fault-tolerant to withstand region failure through its dedicated high-capacity networking elements. Azure cloud geography holds at least two regions segregated by a considerable physical distance. As a result of this pattern, Azure achieves disaster recovery in the region.

Azure users are encouraged to replicate data in multiple regions. Microsoft guarantees round-trip network performance of 2 milliseconds or less between regions.

Azure's existing and upcoming geography, as of this writing, are listed in Table 1.1.

TABLE 1.1   Azure geography

Existing geography	Upcoming geography
Africa	Belgium
Asia Pacific	Austria
Australia	Chile
Brazil	Denmark
Canada	Finland
China	Greece
Europe	Indonesia
France	Israel
Germany	Italy
India	Malaysia
Japan	Mexico
Korea	New Zealand
Norway	Poland
Sweden	Qatar
Switzerland	Spain
United Arab Emirates	Taiwan
United Kingdom	
United States	

Azure Region

An *Azure region* is a set of physical datacenters installed within a security and latency-defined network perimeter and connected through a dedicated and secured low-latency network.

Azure gives organizations the freedom of choice to install and configure applications on demand. An Azure region is equipped with discrete pricing and IT service availability.

Azure developed regions with logical boundaries called regional pairs. Each regional team contains two regions within the geographically defined boundaries.

An Azure region is a specific geographical boundary, and each region is typically hundreds of miles apart.

Azure's existing and upcoming regions, as of this writing, are listed in Table 1.2.

TABLE 1.2   Azure region

Existing region	Upcoming region
Africa	Belgium
South Africa North	Belgium Central
Asia Pacific	Austria
East Asia	Austria East
Southeast Asia	
Australia	Chile
Australia East	Chile Central
Australia Central	
Australia Southeast	
Brazil	Denmark
Brazil South	Denmark East
Canada	Finland
Canada East	Finland Central
Canada Central	
China	Greece
China East	Greece Central
China East 2	
China North	
China North 2	
China North 3	
Europe	Indonesia
North Europe	Indonesia Central
West Europe	

Existing region	Upcoming region

France
   France Central
	Israel
	   Israel Central

Germany
   Germany Central
   Germany Northeast
   Germany West Central
	Italy
	   Italy North

India
   South India
   Central India
	Malaysia
	   Malaysia West

Japan
   Japan East
   Japan West
	Mexico
	   Mexico Central

Korea
   Japan Central
	New Zealand
	   New Zealand North

Norway
   Norway East
	Poland
	   Poland Central

Sweden
   Sweden Central
	Qatar
	   Qatar Central

Switzerland
   Switzerland North
	Spain
	   Spain Central

United Arab Emirates
   UAE North
	Taiwan
	   Taiwan North

United Kingdom
   UK South
   UK West
	India
	   Southcentral India

United States
   Central US
   East US
   East US 2
   East US 3
   South Central US
   West US 2
   West US 3
	United Sates
	   East US 3
	   North Central US
	   West Central US
	   West US

Azure Availability Zones

Azure developed a cloud pattern known as *availability zones* to achieve maximum availability for IT services that demand maximum uptime. Azure is enabled with a minimum of three availability zones within each region where they exist.

Availability zones enable the cloud to be consumed with high availability and fault tolerance. Azure availability zones provide a software and networking solution to help business achieve high availability (HA).

An Azure region is divided into availability zones, which are physical locations. A region includes a datacenter and several other datacenters that are individually powered, cooled, and networked. Within a region, physical separation of availability zones limits the impact of incidents such as flooding, major storms, or superstorms that could disrupt site access, safe passage, utility uptime, and resources if a zone fails.

By deploying IT services to two or more availability zones, the business achieves maximum availability. Azure offers a service level agreement of 99.99 percent uptime for virtual machines provided two or more VMs are deployed into two or more zones.

Azure offers three types of availability zones:

Microsoft Azure Zonal Services   These include IT services such as VMs, managed disks used in VMs, and public IP addresses used in VM. To achieve the HA design pattern, the IT function must explicitly install zonal services in two or more zones.

Microsoft Azure Zone-Redundant Services (ZRS)   These include services such as zone-redundant storage and SQL databases. To use the availability zones with ZRS and SQL database services, you need to specify the option to make them zone redundant during the deployment.

Microsoft Azure Nonregional Services   Azure services are constantly ready from Azure geographies and are resilient to zone-wide blackouts and region-wide blackouts.

Azure Resources Groups

Azure resources groups consist of virtual machines, storage accounts, networks, web apps, databases, and more. It is typical for azure administrators to organize resources related to an application into groups such as production and nonproduction.

It is critical for enterprises to secure, manage, and accurately track their cloud resources. Resource hierarchy in Azure allows administrators to organize and manage cloud resources for organizations.

In the hierarchy, the topmost account is the root account. There may be multiple management groups in larger enterprises, such as IT, human resources (HR), and finance. Subscriptions are available within each management group to manage the administration and costs of various groups of functions—for example, a production environment may be separated from a nonproduction environment.

An Azure resource only exists in a single resource group and cannot be attached to two different resource groups. However, you can move resources from one resource group to another as your design requirements change. Deleting the resource group deletes all the resources associated with that group.

Azure Availability Sets

The *availability sets* in Azure datacenters protect applications from hardware failures; the availability zones in Azure datacenters protect applications against a complete loss of the Azure datacenter.

Availability sets take the virtual machine and configure multiple copies of it. Each copy is isolated within a separate physical server, compute rack, storage units, and network switches within a single datacenter within an Azure region.

When Azure administrators create a virtual machine, they can specify the availability set but they can't change it or move it in or out of an availability set after deployment. If the Azure administrator wants to make changes, they need to re-create the virtual machine. Virtual machines are the only type of resource that can use availability sets; no other resource can use them.

Availability sets allow Azure administrators to create two or more virtual machines in different physical server racks in an Azure datacenter. Azure offers a service level agreement of 99.95 percent within an availability set and provides a service level agreement of 99.99 percent with availability zones.

Azure Subscriptions

An *Azure subscription* is automatically initiated as soon as you sign up for Azure cloud and all the resources created within the subscription. However, an enterprise or business can create additional subscriptions that are tied to an Azure account. Other subscriptions' use cases apply whenever companies want to have logical groupings for Azure resources, especially for reports on resources consumed by departments.

Azure subscriptions are offered in the following three categories:

Free Trial   Completely free access for a limited time per account for limited resources; expired accounts cannot be reused.

Pay-As-You-Go   Pay only for resources consumed in Azure. No capital expenditure is involved and cancellation is possible at any time.

Pay-As-You-Go Dev/Test   A subscription for Visual Studio that can be used for development and testing. No production usage.

Each Azure subscription has a unique identifier called the *subscription ID*. Microsoft recommends using the subscription ID to identify the subscription.

As with the tenant to which a subscription belongs, each subscription has its own unique ID. You need the ID for a subscription or tenant as you execute different activities, and you can find the ID in the Azure portal.

Management Groups

Management groups are an efficient method of enforcing policies and privilege control to Azure cloud resources. A similar approach to a resource group, a management group is a logical container for structuring Azure resources. However, management groups can hold a single Azure subscription or a nested management group. Azure management group hierarchy supports up to six levels, and it is impossible to have multiple parents in a single management group or a single subscription.

Azure Networking Terminology

Understanding Azure-specific terms is vital to using Azure networking components. This understanding will enable you to discuss and take the exam more effectively. The key terms that appear most frequently throughout this book are listed here:

Azure Application Gateway   A web traffic load balancer that allows you (as an Azure network engineer) to manage your web applications' traffic.

Azure Content Delivery Network (CDN)   Describes a global solution for caching content at geographically dispersed nodes to ensure high-bandwidth delivery.

Azure DNS   A naming database in which Internet domain names are found and turned into IP addresses.

Azure Firewall   Describes a cloud-based network security service that protects your Azure virtual network resources managed by Microsoft.

Azure Front Door Service   Enables an enterprise to define, manage, and monitor the global routing and failover of all web traffic to their websites, including high availability and performance optimization.

Azure Load Balancer   Drives traffic in a balanced method across multiple targets in multiple Azure availability zones, and it offers load balancing at layer 4 for all UDP and TCP protocols with high performance and low latency. It manages inbound and outbound connections.

Azure Monitor for Networks   Provides a complete look at health and metrics for all installed network resources without any configuration. Azure Monitor maximizes the availability and performance of your apps by giving you a complete solution for gathering, analyzing, and executing on telemetry from Azure virtual networks and on-premises environments.

Azure NAT Gateways   Enables outbound Internet traffic from Azure instances in a private subnet.

Azure Network Watcher   Helps you monitor, diagnose, and view Microsoft or user defined metrics; logs are enabled or disabled for Azure resources in an Azure virtual network.

Azure Subnet   Describes a logical subdivision of an IP network. It can be private or public.

Azure Traffic Manager   A DNS-based traffic load balancer. It lets you spread traffic to your public-facing applications over the global Azure regions.

Azure Virtual Network (VNet)   Describes a logically isolated section of the cloud where you can launch Azure services and resources.

Azure Virtual Network Peering   Enables you to seamlessly connect two or more virtual networks in Azure. These virtual networks are perceived as one for connectivity purposes, and the traffic between virtual machines in peered virtual networks uses the Microsoft backbone infrastructure.

Azure Virtual Network Routing   Describes how traffic from subnetwork gateways and subnets is directed.

Azure Virtual Network Service Endpoint   Privately connects a virtual private cloud to other cloud and endpoint services.

Azure Virtual Network Terminal Access Point   A tool that continuously collects network data from virtual machines and streams it to network packet collectors.

Azure VPN Gateway   A type of virtual network gateway that facilitates encrypted communication between an Azure virtual network and an on-premises location over the public Internet.

Azure Web Application Firewall (WAF)   Protects your web applications from exploits and vulnerabilities such as SQL injection, XSS, and other common web attacks.

Network Security Group   Describes a list of security rules that allow or deny network traffic to Azure resources.

Azure Networking Overview

Azure networking delivers hybrid network, cloud-native apps with zero-trust and low-latency networking services. Critical functions of Azure networking are connecting compute resources and providing access to applications. As part of Azure's networking capabilities, you can connect to the Azure global datacenters' features and services.

Azure's vast network of highly available, scalable, performant, and secure public and private fiber infrastructure, spanning over 60 regions and over 170 points of presence throughout the world, lets you meet even the most extreme workload demands. With services that seamlessly work across on-premises, multiple clouds, and edge locations, you can offer your business a consistent, low-latency experience. Using Azure networking, you can concentrate on delivering your application logic.

With Azure's optimal routing for best performance, you can deliver predictable, low-latency performance for your business applications since the traffic is routed through the

Microsoft global network by default (known as *cold potato routing*). You can use a vast network across regions with a 1 ms latency for resilient cloud deployments spanning multiple regions and availability zones. With Azure ExpressRoute, network engineers can achieve performance up to 100 Gbps reliably, enable optimized SaaS and SD-WAN connectivity through the Azure Peering Service, and deliver robust security. A comprehensive range of choices enables Azure network engineers to set up organization traffic routes between Azure and the Internet with routing preference. Applications gain their highest performance with ultra-low latency via Azure Load Balancer.

Using Azure routing preferences, you can control how traffic is routed between Azure and the Internet. The Microsoft network and ISP networks (public Internet) can route traffic. These options can also be referred to as *cold potato* routing and *hot-potato* routing.

The Microsoft network routes Internet traffic closest to the user. Azure provides an optimized network experience (cold potato routing) by accepting and delivering traffic where it is most relevant (cold potato routing).

In this competitive egress tier, Microsoft uses the transit ISP network to minimize travel on its global network. Hot potato routing allows Internet traffic to enter and exit Microsoft's network closest to the hosted service region.

Azure uses and allocates two different types of IP addresses—public IP addresses and private IP addresses:

- Communication of resources within an Azure resource group is made possible via the private IP address. Resources cannot access an external IP address through the network. In addition to the VM network interface and internal load balancer, an application gateway can also be connected using a private address.

- Azure resources can communicate over the Internet with Azure services that are available for public viewing. Thus, resources can be accessed from outside the network through public IP addresses. In addition to the VM network interface and the public-facing, Internet-facing load balancer, an application gateway, VPN gateway, and Azure firewall tools can use public addresses.

Here are two types of IP allocation in Azure networking:

Dynamic IP Address   As a default, dynamic allocation is used. Once assigned, dynamic IP addresses can only be released if a network interface is deleted or moved to a different subnet within the same virtual network, or if the allocation method is changed from dynamic to static and another IP address is specified.

Static IP Address   The static IP address allocation method uses a custom allocation method to assign the unreserved open addresses in a subnet range. A static IP address is fixed in time and does not change.

Azure subnets are a small network of IP addresses that covers a range of addresses. VNets can be split into subnets for organizations in Azure. An Azure VNet must have a subnet range and topology specified. Subnets are subparts of big blocks of IP addresses that are used in VNets. Each virtual machine and resource in a network will receive an IP address based on the subnets assigned.

Azure virtual WANs enable on-premises, multicloud, and branch deployments. They enhance edge and 5G scenarios by enabling Azure Edge Zones, Azure Edge Zones with the carrier, and Azure Private Edge Zones.

Cloud services are available from Azure Edge facilities, which are 5G-connected.

A private Edge Zone is a small Azure extension installed on a customer's premises. Cloud computing and storage can be performed locally using this distributed public cloud offering. Azure managed services enable enterprises to deploy industrial IoT applications with 5G network functions and other networking components.

In Azure Edge Zones with the carrier, the same Azure hardware is deployed in a carrier's datacenter. It is the same hardware used in Microsoft's standard cloud availability regions in both cases.

Azure network engineers and architects can utilize services that support the zero-trust approach to security to safeguard workloads and virtual networks running on Azure. You can use microsegmentation to secure virtual network infrastructure, an Azure web application firewall (WAF) and Azure Bastion to protect applications, and Azure DDoS Protection to detect threats intelligently.

Azure Networking as a service enables the connectivity and scale you need without requiring Azure network engineers to build or manage down to the fiber. The Azure engineer can manage traffic for applications using Azure App Gateway, and protect that traffic using the Azure WAF; establish and monitor global routing with Azure Front Door; and get turnkey firewall abilities with Azure Firewall and VNet NAT to guarantee reliable outbound connectivity from predictable IP address space.

Azure Networking Services

During every phase of IT transformation, networks used to be an essential part of every IT ecosystem to have a well-functioning infrastructure. It is no wonder that networking is a necessary part of the cloud.

Azure virtual networks facilitate Azure resources, such as virtual machines, web applications, and databases, to interact with each other, with business users on the Internet, and with your on-premises computers. Azure networks are web-based connections that link resources in Azure.

The following key networking capabilities are available through Azure virtual networks:

- Isolation and micro-segmentation
- Internet communications
- Communicate among Azure resources
- Communicate with on-premises resources
- Route and filter network traffic
- Attach virtual networks

In addition to Virtual Network Services and the Azure Content Delivery Network, Azure Network Services provides tools to connect network engineers and cloud and on-premises resources.

With Azure, engineers and architects can access a range of networking services that can be used individually or in combination. Four vital groups of services are offered in Azure (see Figure 1.6):

FIGURE 1.6   Overview of Azure Network Services

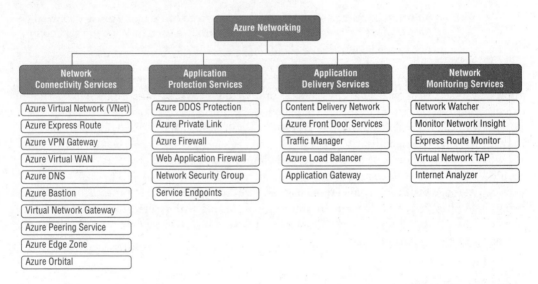

Network Connectivity Services   Provide connectivity between Azure resources and on-premises resources by using the following networking services:

- Virtual Network (VNet)
- ExpressRoute
- VPN Gateway

- Virtual WAN
- Virtual Network NAT Gateway
- Azure DNS
- Azure Bastion
- Virtual Network Gateway
- Peering service
- Edge zone
- Orbital

Application Protection Services   Azure provides several networking services that can be used to protect applications:

- DDoS protection
- Private Link
- Firewall
- Web Application Firewall
- Network Security Groups
- Service Endpoints

Application Delivery Services   Azure allows users to deliver applications using any combination of networking services:

- Content Delivery Network (CDN)
- Azure Front Door Service
- Traffic Manager
- Application Load Balancer
- Application Gateway

Network Monitoring   Azure enables you to monitor your network resources using the following services:

- Network Watcher
- ExpressRoute Monitor
- Azure Monitor
- Internet Analyzer
- Terminal Access Point (TAP)

Azure Virtual Network

Azure Virtual Network (VNet) is the fundamental building block for a private network. VNets provide a secure communication channel between Azure resources, such as virtual machines (VMs) and other network components. VNets are like traditional datacenters but have the advantage of Azure's infrastructure, including scalability, availability, reliability, broad network access, hybrid connectivity, segmentation, isolation, and security.

VNet is the representation of your own networks in the cloud. The Azure cloud is logically isolated and dedicated to your subscription. VNets can be used to provision and manage virtual private networks (VPNs) in Azure. Alternatively, they can be linked to other VNets in Azure or your on-premises infrastructure to create hybrid or hybrid cross-premises solutions. You can link each VNet you make with another VNet and an on-premises network if the Classless Inter-Domain Routing (CIDR) blocks don't overlap. The administrator can also control VNet settings; subnets can also be segmented.

> CIDR (Classless Inter-Domain Routing) is also called *supernetting*. It improves the efficiency of Internet Protocol (IP) addresses, replacing the previous system of classes A, B, and C networks. CIDR was originally aimed at reducing the rapid exhaustion of IPv4 addresses by slowing the increase of router routing tables. As a result, Internet addresses have become more plentiful.

Azure Network Communication with the Internet   A VNet's outbound communications are enabled by default for all resources. You can share an inbound connection to a resource by assigning a public IP address or using a public load balancer. Manage your outbound connections using a public IP or public load balancer.

Azure Communication between Azure Resources   Azure resources are used in three main ways: by the virtual network, VNet peering, and virtual network service endpoint.

Azure Virtual Networks and Azure Kubernetes Service are also available for connections between VMs and Azure resources, including the App Service Environment.

> What is Kubernetes? Containerized, legacy, cloud-native, and apps being refactored into microservices can be deployed and managed with Kubernetes across environments, including private cloud and major public cloud providers like Amazon Web Services (AWS), Google Cloud, IBM Cloud, and Microsoft Azure.

Azure resources like Azure SQL databases and storage accounts can be accessed via service endpoints. As soon as you create a VNet, your services and virtual machines will be able to work together directly in the cloud.

The following methods are used by Azure resources to communicate securely with each other:

By a Virtual Network   Azure public virtual networks are used to deploy virtual machines, as well as Azure App Service Environments, Azure Kubernetes Services (AKS), and Azure Virtual Machine Scale Sets.

By VNet Peering   Virtual networks can be connected, allowing resources to communicate with another using virtual network peering. Connecting virtual networks in different Azure regions is possible.

By a Virtual Network Service Endpoint   Directly connect your virtual network server with Azure services, such as Azure Storage and Azure SQL Database, so your virtual network can access their private address space and identity. You can secure Azure service resources to just a virtual network using service endpoints.

Azure Network Communication with the Private Cloud   Protect your datacenter by extending it securely. With Azure ExpressRoute, your on-premises computers and networks can be connected to a virtual network via a point-to-site VPN, site-to-site VPN, or Microsoft VPN. Connecting your on-premises computers and network to a virtual network may be accomplished through any of the following options:

Azure ExpressRoute   Establishes a connection between your network and Azure via an ExpressRoute partner. It is a private connection. Traffic does not go over the Internet.

Point-to-Site VPN   An Internet-based virtual private network (VPN) between a virtual network and a single computer in your network is known as a point-to-site VPN. Those who wish to establish connections to virtual networks must configure their computers to do so. You can use this connection type if you are a first-time Azure user, work on a proof of concept (PoC), or are a developer. A virtual network's communication with your computer is done over the Internet using an encrypted tunnel.

Site-to-Site VPN   A site-to-site VPN creates a virtual network connection between your corporate VPN device and the Azure VPN gateway. Access to a virtual network is enabled through this connection type for any resource on-premises you authorize. An encrypted tunnel connects your VPN device on-premises with the Azure VPN gateway.

Filter Network Traffic   Using firewalls, gateways, proxies, and network address translation (NAT) services, you can filter network traffic between subnets while maintaining network security. There are two options for filtering network traffic between subnets:

Network Virtual Appliances   Virtual network appliances perform network functions such as firewalls, WAN optimization, or other functions using virtual machines.

Network Security Sets   Network security sets and application security sets allow you to filter network traffic entering and leaving resources by IP and protocol addresses, ports, and sources.

Route Network Traffic   Azure routes traffic between subnets, connected virtual networks, on-premises networks, and the Internet. To override Azure's default routes, implement one of the following two options:

Route Tables   It is possible to create custom route tables with routes that control where traffic is routed for each subnet.

Border Gateway Protocol (BGP) Routes   By connecting your virtual network to your on-premises network using an Azure VPN Gateway or ExpressRoute connection, you can propagate your on-premises BGP routes to your virtual network.

Integrate Azure Services   Virtual machines or compute resources in an Azure virtual network can access Azure services privately when Azure services are integrated into the virtual network. Your virtual network can be integrated in the following ways:

- Virtualizing the service by creating dedicated instances. The services can then be accessed privately within the virtual network and from the on-premises network.

- From your virtual network and on-premises networks, you can access a specific service instance using Private Link.

- Similarly, it is possible to connect to the service through service endpoints by building a virtual network. The virtual network can be protected with service endpoints.

VNet Concepts and Best Practices

You can deploy virtual networks and connect your cloud resources easily once you understand core concepts and best practices, which we'll discuss in this section.

Address Space

VNets require a unique private IP address space, either public or private (RFC 1918). Virtual networks in Azure are assigned a private IP address from the address space that you specify. A virtual network can be created in more than one region per subscription. Virtual networks can contain multiple subnets.

The following is a list of nonroutable address spaces:

- `10.0.0.0 - 10.255.255.255` (10/8 prefix)

- `172.16.0.0 - 172.31.255.255` (172.16/12 prefix)

- `192.168.0.0 - 192.168.255.255` (192.168/16 prefix)

Setting the address space for a virtual network is one of the most critical configurations. In this case, the entire network will be divided into subnets using the whole IP range. There are five address spaces that you cannot add to your virtual network:

- `224.0.0.0/4`, which is used for Azure multicast
- `255.255.255.255/32`, which is used for Azure broadcast
- `127.0.0.0/8`, which is used for Azure loopback
- `169.254.0.0/16`, which is used for Azure link-local
- `168.63.129.16/32`, which is used for Azure internal DNS

You must not use an overlapping address space, since doing so will prevent you from connecting virtual networks.

Subnets

Using subnets, you can segment the virtual network into one or more subnetworks, each of which receives a portion of the virtual network's address space. After that, Azure resources can be deployed within a specific subnet. With subnets, you can segment your VNet address space for your organization's internal network, much like in a traditional network. Address allocation is also made more efficient this way.

The Azure cloud services reserve five IP addresses for each subnet:

- `x.x.x.0`, which is the network address used by Azure.
- `x.x.x.1`, which Azure reserves for the default gateway.
- `x.x.x.2` and `x.x.x.3`, which map the Azure DNS IPs to the VNet space.
- `x.x.x.255`, which is a network broadcast address for subnets of size `/25` and higher. This will be a different address in smaller subnets.

CIDR is the format used to define the internal address space of a virtual network. Any network you connect to must have a unique address space within your subscription. The smallest IPv4 subnet supported is `/29` and the largest is `/2` (CIDR IPv4 subnet definitions). `/64` is the minimum size for IPv6 subnets.

Let's imagine choosing an address space of `10.0.0.0/24` for your first virtual network. The addresses defined in this address space range from `10.0.0.1` to `10.0.0.254`.

Now suppose you want to create a second virtual network and choose an address space of `10.0.0.0/8`. The IP addresses in this address space range from `10.0.0.1` to `10.255.255.254`.

The IP addresses for your first and second virtual networks overlap, and as a result, you cannot connect the two virtual networks. Technically it is possible, however, to use `10.0.0.0/16`, which ranges from `10.0.0.1` to `10.0.255.254`, and `10.1.0.0/16`, which ranges from `10.1.0.1` to `10.1.255.254`. None of these address spaces overlap with any of your virtual networks.

The virtual network address space can be partitioned into one or more subnets within each address range. Or you can define custom routes to route traffic between subnets. Alternatively, all virtual networks' address ranges can be combined into one subnet.

When considering your design and deployment, keep the following in mind:

- You must use CIDR to specify each subnet's address range.
- You can build several subnets and allow a service endpoint for some subnets.
- You can use subnets for traffic management.
- Virtual network service endpoints allow you to regulate access to Azure resources by subnet.
- You can use network security groups (NSGs) to further segment your network based on IP address classification.
- The default limit per virtual network is 3,000 subnets, but that can be scaled up to 10,000 with Microsoft support.
- You can use tags to organize Azure resources, resource groups, and subscriptions logically. As you apply the same tag to multiple resources and groups, you can categorize them and view consolidated billing.

Regions

An Azure region is required for all Azure resources. A resource can only be created in the same region and subscription as the resource in a virtual network. Virtual networks can, however, be connected between regions and subscriptions. Consider the geographic location of the people (consumers) of resources when determining where to deploy them. VNets are limited to a single Azure region; however, you can pair them with different virtual networks from different regions.

Subscriptions

VNets are only accessible from the current subscription. Azure subscriptions and Azure regions support multiple virtual networks.

When designing your Azure network, your naming conventions are crucial. An effective naming convention uses essential information about each resource to compose resource names. The correct name makes it easy to identify the type of resource, associated workload, deployment environment, and Azure region hosting the resource. There is no need to include the entire VNet address space in your subnets. If you need address space in the future, plan it and reserve it. In comparison to having multiple small VNets, VNets should be centralized to reduce management overhead, according to Microsoft. Microsoft recommends securing your virtual network by applying Network Security Groups to the subnets.

You can create, configure, and manage your VNet using the Azure portal, PowerShell, or the Azure CLI.

Exercise 1.1 shows you how to create a new virtual network using the Azure portal.

EXERCISE 1.1

Deploying a Virtual Network with the Azure Portal

1. Log in to a personal or business account in the Azure portal at `portal.azure.com`. You will see a page like this:

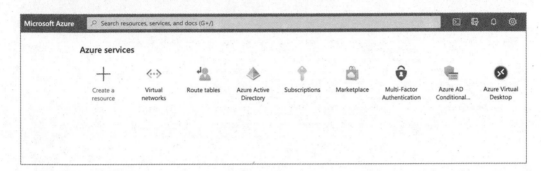

2. Click Create A Resource, type **virtual network** in the search box, and click Create.

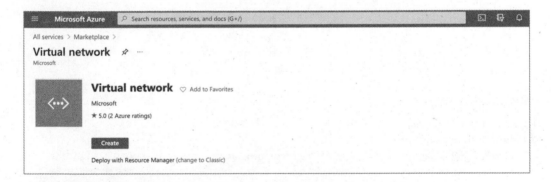

3. Select the Basics tab and enter the following settings:

Project Details

Subscription   Choose your subscription.

Resource Group   Choose a resource group or create a new resource group.

Instance Details

Name   Type a name for your new VNet using your organization's naming standards.

Region   Choose the region you want to deploy to or a region close to your resource needs.

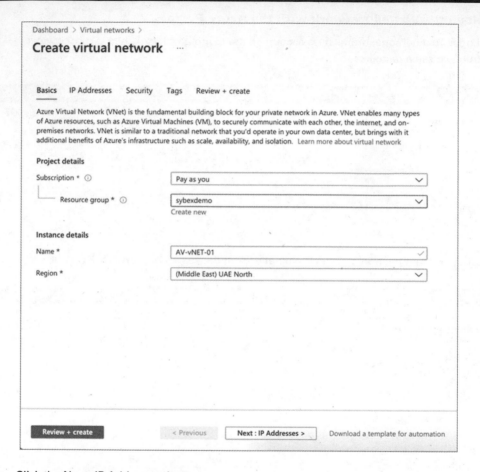

4. Click the Next: IP Addresses button.

5. On the IP Addresses page, enter the following settings. Before you get started, determine the first IPv4 address space range of the subnet.

    IP Address Space   In CIDR notation, enter one or more address prefixes to define the virtual network's address space. After creating the virtual network, you can add address spaces.

The subnet's address range in CIDR notation must be contained by the address space of the virtual network. Do not use special characters in subnet names, only letters, numbers, underscores, periods, or hyphens.

6. In the Add Subnet pane, enter the subnet name and address range. You can include the services you want to connect to the virtual network. Azure service endpoints provide a means of securely connecting to Azure services, thus eliminating the need for a public IP address.

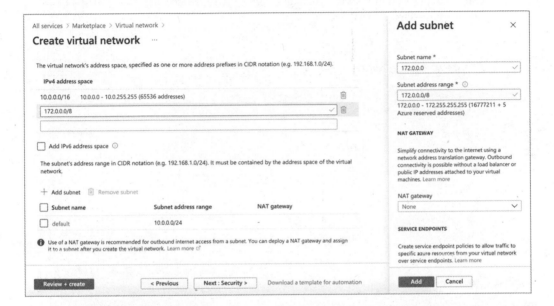

7. Click the Next: Security button.

8. On the Security page, specify whether you want to enable or disable BastionHost, DDoS Protection Standard, and Firewall. You need to provide additional information for these services:

    BastionHost   A new PaaS service in your virtual network, Azure Bastion, is fully platform-managed. RDP/SSH connections are made secure and seamless over SSL directly from the Azure console. You do not need a public IP address for your virtual machines when you connect through Azure Bastion.

DDoS Protection Standard   Standard DDoS protection is available. Your virtual network will be protected against the impacts of a distributed denial-of-service (DDoS) attack with adaptive tuning, attack notifications, and telemetry. Azure provides essential DDoS protection by default at no additional cost.

Firewall   The Azure Firewall is a managed service from Microsoft that offers network security for your virtual networks.

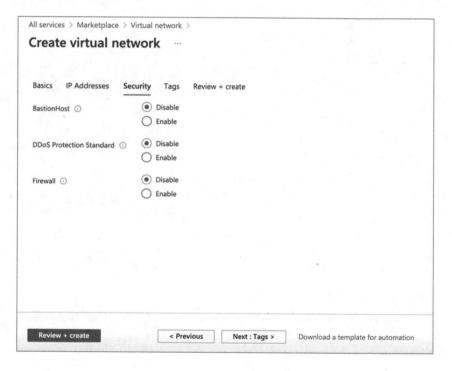

For this exercise, keep all three choices disabled.

9. When you click Next: Tags, you'll see the Tags page. For this exercise, skip this page and click Next: Review + Create.

10. On the Review + Create page, wait for the validation pass status before you click Create.

All services > Marketplace > Virtual network >

Create virtual network ...

✓ Validation passed

Basics   IP Addresses   Security   Tags   **Review + create**

Basics

Subscription	Pay as you
Resource group	(new) sybexdemo
Name	SY-vNET1-TEST-DEMO
Region	UAE North

IP addresses

Address space	10.0.0.0/16,172.0.0.0/8
Subnet	default (10.0.0.0/24)

Tags

None

Security

BastionHost	Disabled
DDoS protection plan	Basic
Firewall	Disabled

[Create]   [< Previous]   [Next >]   Download a template for automation

11. Finish by clicking Create.

Deploying a Virtual Network with Azure PowerShell

Using PowerShell, you can manage Azure resources directly from PowerShell's Az PowerShell module. PowerShell's power comes from its ability to automate Azure resources, such as continuous integration/continuous delivery (CI/CD) pipelines to better manage your Azure infrastructure.

The *Azure Az PowerShell* module is a set of cmdlets for managing Azure resources directly from PowerShell. PowerShell provides powerful features for automation that can be leveraged for managing your Azure resources.

Microsoft recommends using PowerShell to interact with Azure instead of Azure Resource Manager. Azure Az PowerShell allows you to automate and manage Azure resources from

PowerShell. Deploying the Azure virtual network using Az can also automate deployment tasks.

You must first install the latest versions of the Az modules before you can continue.

All versions of PowerShell 7.*x* and later work with Azure Az PowerShell. When PowerShell 7.*x* or later is used, Azure PowerShell needs no additional requirements.

Exercise 1.2 shows you how to set up Azure Az PowerShell.

EXERCISE 1.2

Setting Up Azure Az PowerShell

1. If you are running a Windows machine:

    a. Select Start ≻ All Programs ≻ Accessories, and select the Windows PowerShell folder. Then launch Windows PowerShell.

    b. In the Run box, enter **PowerShell_ISE**.

    Here is the command used to verify the PowerShell version:

    ```
    $PSVersionTable.PSVersion
    ```

    The PowerShell script execution policy needs to be set to RemoteSigned or Unrestricted:

    ```
    Set-ExecutionPolicy -ExecutionPolicy RemoteSigned -Scope CurrentUser
    ```

    The Az PowerShell module is installed for the current user only:

    ```
    Install-Module -Name Az -Scope CurrentUser -Repository PSGallery -Force
    ```

2. Connect to the Azure subscription through a PowerShell console. Use the following command to connect to an Azure account:

    ```
    Connect-AzAccount
    ```

3. Create the resource group for the virtual network before you create the virtual network. New-AZResourceGroup is used to create resource groups. In this exercise, the SY-TEST-DEMO resource group will be created in the WestUS location:

    ```
    $rg = @{
        Name = 'SY-TEST-DEMO'
        Location = 'WestUS'
    }
    New-AzResourceGroup @rg
    ```

4. New-AzVirtualNetwork allows you to build a virtual network. An example of how to create a virtual network named SY-VNET1-TEST-DEMO in the location WestUS is shown here:

    ```
    $vnet = @{
        Name = 'SY-VNET1-TEST-DEMO'
    ```

```
        ResourceGroupName = 'SY-TEST-DEMO'
        Location = 'WestUS'
        AddressPrefix = '10.0.0.0/16'
    }
    $virtualNetwork = New-AzVirtualNetwork @
```

PowerShell deploys virtual networks without requiring subnet definitions, which is different when deploying them from the portal. Creating subnets can be done independently of deploying virtual networks by executing the following command:

```
    $subnet = @{
        Name = 'default'
        VirtualNetwork = $SY-DMZ
        AddressPrefix = '172.0.0.0/24'
    }
    $subnetConfig = Add-AzVirtualNetworkSubnetConfig @subnet
```

Configure Public IP Services

An Azure resource that communicates with the external world outside of the secure zone demands public IP addresses, and vice versa.

An Internet resource can communicate inbound with Azure resources using a public IP address. Internet-facing Azure services and Azure resources can communicate via *public IP addresses*. When you assign the address to a resource and then unassign it, it is dedicated to that resource.

Azure addresses are assigned to specific resources until they are unassigned by an Azure administrator. Azure's network address translation service allows resources without a public IP address to communicate outbound by using an available IP address that isn't assigned to them.

You can associate a public IP address resource with VM network interfaces, Internet-facing load balancers, VPN gateways, NAT gateways, application gateways, Azure Firewall, and Bastion Host.

Public IP addresses are deployed with an IPv4 or Ipv6 address, either dynamic or static.

A public IP address is listed as a resource's property and the allocation method. Table 1.3 and Table 1.4 illustrate the public IP services for various Azure network services.

TABLE 1.3   Public IP address for key Azure Network Services (Part 1)

Top-level resource	Virtual machine	Internet-facing load balancer	Virtual network gateway (VPN)	Virtual network gateway (ER)
IP address association	Network interface	Front-end configuration	Gateway IP configuration	Gateway IP configuration
Dynamic IPv4	Yes	Yes	Yes (non-AZ only)	Yes

TABLE 1.3   Public IP address for key Azure Network Services (Part 1) *(continued)*

Top-level resource	Virtual machine	Internet-facing load balancer	Virtual network gateway (VPN)	Virtual network gateway (ER)
Static IPv4	Yes	Yes	Yes (AZ only)	No
Dynamic IPv6	Yes	Yes	No	Yes (preview)
Static IPv6	Yes	Yes	No	No

Support for public IPv6 is not available for all resource types as of this writing. Check Microsoft Azure Online Resources at `http://docs.microsoft.com/en-us/azure/virtual-network/public-ip-addresses` for the most up-to-date information.

TABLE 1.4   Public IP address for Key Azure Network Services (Part 2)

Top-level resource	NAT gateway	Application gateway	Azure Firewall	Bastion Host
IP Address association	Gateway IP configuration	Front-end configuration	Front-end configuration	Public IP configuration
Dynamic IPv4	No	Yes (V1 only)	No	No
Static Ipv4	Yes	Yes (V2 only)	Yes	Yes
Dynamic Ipv6	No	No	No	No
Static Ipv6	No	No	No	No

Public IP addresses are available in two SKU types: Basic and Standard. Basic SKU public IP addresses were created before SKUs were introduced. You can now specify the SKU you would like a public IP address to use.

Basic SKUs

You can assign basic IP addresses for Basic SKUs using static or dynamic allocation methods:

- **For IPv4:** A static or dynamic allocation method can be used.
- **For IPv6:** Only available through dynamic allocation.

You can have an adjustable inbound originated idle flow timeout of 4–30 minutes, with a default of 4 minutes, and a fixed outbound originated idle flow timeout of 4 minutes.

Microsoft recommends having network security groups restrict inbound or outbound traffic, but doing so is not mandatory.

The Basic SKU does not support routing preference or cross-region load balancers functionality or availability zone scenarios.

You can assign basic public IP addresses to any Azure resource with a public IP address, including network interfaces, VPN gateways, application gateways, and load balancers exposed to the Internet.

Standard SKUs

Standard SKUs have static IP addresses. Their idle timeout for inbound initiated flows can be adjusted from 4 to 30 minutes; their idle timeout for outbound originated flows is fixed at 4 minutes.

Standard IP addresses are secure by default and closed to inbound traffic. Using a network security group allows inbound traffic explicitly.

You can assign a standard IP address to a network interface, a public load balancer, an application gateway, or a VPN gateway. It is possible to create standard IPs zonally (zone-redundant but guaranteed in a specific availability zone) or zone-redundant by default.

Azure does not support bringing your own public IP from on-premises networks into Azure. Regardless of location, a public IP address is assigned from a pool of available addresses. The public IP address resource cannot be specified by setting the allocation method to static.

Each Azure cloud has its own unique range of public IP addresses. An IP address cannot be transferred between regions. Each IP address has a specific region. In the case of a company with datacenters in multiple locations, the public IP address range will be different in each location. To balance traffic between regionally specific instances, you can use technology such as Azure Traffic Manager.

It is possible to create a prefix for public IP addresses that ensures a static range. The addresses will not be specified when creating the prefix but will be fixed afterward. It will be a range of contiguous IP addresses. An advantage to public IP addresses is that you can set firewall rules for them knowing they won't change. Almost any resource in Azure that supports public IP addresses can be assigned an address from a public IP address prefix.

For the AZ-700 exam, keep in mind that, for communicating with Azure resources, you need to update your firewall rules. Whenever a scenario arises in your day job, changing the IP address requires updating the A records for DNS name resolution.

With IP address-based security, Azure resources communicate with other apps and services. Certificates associated with IP addresses are used for TLS/SSL.

A DNS record for a custom domain can be configured using Azure DNS or an external DNS provider for services that use a public IP address.

The DNS label for a public IP resource can be specified by choosing this option. It works for IPv4 (A record of 32 bits) and IPv6 (128 bits). Azure-managed DNS maps `domainnamelabel.location.cloudapp.azure.com` to the public IP.

An example is deploying a public IP with sybexapp as a domain name label and East US as the Azure location. In this case, the fully qualified domain name `sybexapp.eastus .cloudapp.azure.com` resolves to the public IP address of the resource.

Configure a Basic SKU Public IP

The following code deploys the Azure resource group `SY-TEST-DEMO` to a Basic static public IPv4 address named mysybexpip using `New-AzPublicIpAddress`.

```
$ip = @{
    Name = 'mysybexpip'
    ResourceGroupName = 'SY-TEST-DEMO'
    Location = 'westus2'
    Sku = 'Basic'
    AllocationMethod = 'Static'
    IpAddressVersion = 'IPv4'
}
New-AzPublicIpAddress @ip
```

Configure a Standard SKU Public IP with Zones

The following code deploys the Azure resource group `SY-TEST-DEMO` to a zone-redundant public IPv4 address named mysybexpip using `New-AzPublicIpAddress`.

```
$ip = @{
    Name = 'mysybexpip'
    ResourceGroupName = 'SY-TEST-DEMO'
    Location = 'westus2'
    Sku = 'Standard'
    AllocationMethod = 'Static'
    IpAddressVersion = 'IPv4'
    Zone = 1,2,3
}
New-AzPublicIpAddress @ip
```

Configuring Domain Name Services

On the Internet, the *Domain Name System (DNS)* works like a telephone directory. Domain names, such as `www.microsoft.com` or `www.wiley.com`, enable users to access information online. IP addresses are how browsers communicate with each other. Domain names are converted to IP addresses so that browsers can access Internet resources.

An IP address (such as `172.168.1.1`) is converted into a computer-friendly hostname (such as `www.microsoft.com`) following DNS resolution. IP addresses identify every Internet-connected device, and they are used to find the appropriate Internet device, like a street addresses used to locate a specific home. Whenever a user tries to load a web page, the address they type into their web browser (`www.microsoft.com`) must be translated into a machine-friendly address necessary to locate the `Microsoft.com` page.

Using Azure infrastructure, Azure DNS hosts DNS domains and provides name resolution. Azure allows you to manage DNS records using the same credentials, APIs, tools, and billing facilities that you use to manage other Azure services.

The Azure DNS name servers host DNS domains hosted by Azure DNS. DNS in Azure uses anycast networking. Your domain is routed to the closest available DNS server during each DNS query to provide high performance and high availability.

As a network engineer you could create a virtual network that allows VMs and other resources deployed in Azure to communicate with one another depending on how you use Azure to host IaaS, PaaS, and hybrid solutions. Even though IP addresses can be used for communication, it is much simpler to use a permanent name that is easy to remember.

The Azure DNS offering is classified into three types: public, private DNS for resources available from your resources, and Azure-provided DNS (Internal DNS).

Domain Name System translates human-readable domain names (for example, `www.microsoft.com`) to machine-readable IP addresses. DNS domains in Azure DNS are hosted on Azure's global DNS nameserver network. Azure public DNS uses anycast networking. The closest DNS server answers each DNS query for your domain, ensuring fast performance and high availability.

With Azure DNS, you can manually create address records within relevant zones. As a network engineer, you will most often use the following:

- **Host:** A/AAAA (IPv4/IPv6)

- **Aliases:** CNAME

With Azure DNS, domain names can be managed and resolved on a virtual network without adding custom DNS services.

A DNS zone hosts DNS records. In order for your domain name to be hosted in Azure DNS, you must create a DNS zone first. This domain zone is then used to develop every DNS entry for your domain.

When a VNet is deployed, it automatically creates an internal DNS zone, supports automatic registration, does not require manual record creation, and is created when the VNet is created. This is a free service.

As of this writing, Azure does not provide any capabilities for authoritative name resolution. In this case, DNS zone names and records would be managed by Azure automatically in a way that you could not control.

The internal DNS defines a namespace as follows: `.internal.cloudapp.net`. The DNS domain name of any VM created in a VNet is `myVM.internal.cloudapp.net`. There are several things to keep in mind. First, recognize that it's the Azure resource name, not the guest OS name on the VM.

In Azure, private DNS zones can only be accessed by internal resources. They are global in scope so that you can access them from any region, subscription, VNet, and tenant. When the zone can be read, you can use it for resolving names. Global replication makes private DNS zones highly resilient. They cannot be accessed through Internet resources.

Your virtual network can benefit from Azure Private DNS, which provides a reliable and secure DNS service. Azure Private DNS manages and resolves domain names without the need to configure custom DNS for the virtual network using Azure Private DNS.

With private DNS zones, the Azure-provided names during deployment can be replaced with your own custom names. Your virtual network architecture can be tailored to suit your organization's needs if you use a custom domain name. In a virtual network and connected virtual networks, Private DNS is used to resolve VM name resolution. As an added feature, the split-horizon configuration enables private and public DNS zones to share a zone name.

Virtual networks must be linked to private DNS zones to resolve their records. Virtual networks linked to a private zone have access to a full set of DNS records. Once a new DNS zone has been deployed, resource records based on Azure resource names can be manually created or generated automatically as part of auto-registration.

Additionally, virtual networks can be auto-registered. Virtual network links with auto-registration enable the private zone to be used to store the DNS records for virtual machines within the virtual network. Azure DNS updates the zone record as soon as a virtual machine is created, its IP address is changed, or it is deleted when auto-registration is enabled.

A forward DNS lookup is allowed across virtual networks connected to the private zone, and a reverse DNS lookup is allowed for virtual networks linked to the private zone.

You can set up private DNS zones with pointers, MX records, Start of Authority (SOA) records, service records, and texts.

Configure an Azure DNS Zone and Record Using Azure PowerShell

Use the `New-AzDnsZone` cmdlet to create a DNS zone. The following example creates a DNS zone called sybex.com in the resource group named SY-TEST-DEMO. You can create your own DNS zone by substituting the values in the sample:

```
New-AzDnsZone -Name sybex.com -ResourceGroupName SY-TEST-DEMO
```

Using the `New-AzDnsRecordSet` cmdlet, you can create recordsets. Here is an example that creates a record with the relative name www in the resource group SY-TEST-DEMO within the DNS zone. sybex.com. sybex.com is the fully qualified name of the recordset. The record type is A, the IP address is 10.20.20.20, and the time to live (TTL) is 1,800 seconds.

```
New-AzDnsRecordSet -Name www -RecordType A -ZoneName sybex.com -
ResourceGroupName
SY-TEST-DEMO -Ttl 1800 -DnsRecords
(New-AzDnsRecordConfig -IPv4Address "10.20.20.20")
```

Use the following command to list the DNS records in your zone:

```
Get-AzDnsRecordSet -ZoneName sybex.com -ResourceGroupName SY-TEST-DEMO
```

Configuring Cross-Virtual Network Connectivity with Peering

Virtual network peering in Azure enables seamless communication with virtual networks. In Azure, virtual networks can peer with one another. A VPN gateway will provide an encrypted connection in the region, but VNet peering will share connections in the various azure regions. This is mostly used for disaster recovery or cross-region data replications. Figure 1.7 depicts Hub Cross virtual network connectivity with peering.

FIGURE 1.7   Cross-virtual network connectivity with peering

With VNet peering, you can route traffic privately between virtual networks via IPv4 addresses. Peer VNets can communicate with each other as if they are in a single network.

Virtual networks peering with each other are private. For connectivity purposes, these networks seem to be one. Peer virtual networks communicate between VMs using Microsoft's backbone infrastructure, not the Internet, gateways, or encryption required by public virtual networks.

In large-scale operations, connections between various parts of infrastructure will often be needed for the following demands:

- A VNet peering network is like an inter-VLAN routing network in an on-premises network, so it is identical to a VLAN-to-VLAN communication network.

- Azure infrastructure must connect to virtual networks to share traffic for applications, backup, replication, and recovery.

- Connection of virtual machines of different virtual networks can be done through VNet peering within or across geographical regions.

A global peering can be created between two public clouds in Azure, China, or government cloud regions. Only virtual networks from the same Azure government cloud region can be peer-to-peer.

The advantages of using virtual network peering, regional or global, network infrastructure includes a low-latency, high-bandwidth connection between resources in different virtual networks. You can apply network security groups in either virtual network to block access to other virtual networks or subnets. VNet peering allows data transfer between virtual networks across Azure subscriptions, Azure Active Directory tenants, deployment models, and Azure regions. VNet peering allows virtual peer networks deployed through the Azure Resource Manager.

It is possible to translate traffic from one virtual network to another or a gateway in a peer network by using user-defined routes. Configure user-defined routes as the next-hop IP address of virtual machines in virtual peer networks to enable service chaining. Using user-defined routes, service chaining could also be enabled via virtual network gateways.

Hub-and-spoke networks provide the capability to host infrastructure components such as virtual networking appliances and VPN gateways. When all spoke, networks were connected to the hub network, they could all peer with it. Traffic flows through virtual network appliances or VPN gateways in the virtual hub network. Figure 1.8 shows a hub-and-spoke deployment model.

FIGURE 1.8 Hub-spoke deployment model

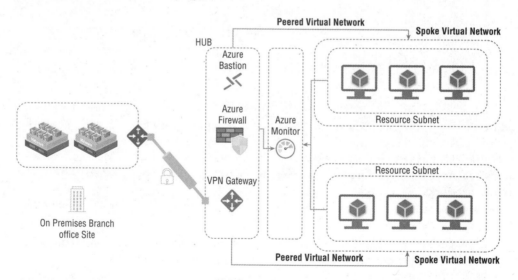

Peering virtual networks lets an entity in a virtual peer network or a VPN gateway be the next hop in a route. The next hop type of an Azure ExpressRoute gateway cannot be specified for user-defined routes between virtual networks.

Peer-to-peer networks can also have their gateways. Virtual networks can connect to on-premises networks through their gateways. Even peer-to-peer virtual networks can be connected using gateways.

Both options of virtual network interconnection require peering configurations for traffic to flow. The Azure backbone is used to transport traffic.

Virtual networks created with different deployment models can be connected via a gateway. When Resource Manager is configured as a virtual network, the gateway must be part of it.

Peering virtual networks that share a single ExpressRoute connection led to traffic flowing through the peering relationship. Traffic on Azure uses the backbone network. You can still connect to each virtual network using a local gateway. If you opt for a shared gateway, you can use transit to connect on-premises.

The following are constraints for peered virtual networks:

- In a global peer-to-peer virtual network, resources in one virtual network can't communicate with an internal load balancer (ILB).

- Basic load balancing is not supported over global virtual networks peering.

Configuring Peering between Two Virtual Networks in the Same Region

Peering between virtual networks can be created using `Add-AzVirtualNetworkPeering`.

The following is the sample configuration for a peer network in the same Azure region:

```
$rgName='SY-TEST-DEMO'
$location='westus'
# Configure virtual network 1.
$vnet1 = New-AzVirtualNetwork -ResourceGroupName $rgName -Name 'sybexvnet1' -
AddressPrefix '10.1.0.0/16'
-Location $location
# Configure virtual network 2.
$vnet2 = New-AzVirtualNetwork -ResourceGroupName $rgName -Name 'sybexvnet2' -
AddressPrefix '10.2.0.0/16'
-Location $location
# Configure Peer between VNet1 to Vnet2.
Add-AzVirtualNetworkPeering -Name 'sybexvnet1Tosybexvnet2'
-VirtualNetwork $vnet1
-RemoteVirtualNetworkId $vnet2.Id
# Configure Peer between VNet2 to VNet1
Add-AzVirtualNetworkPeering -Name 'sybexvnet2Tosybexvnet1' -VirtualNetwork
$vnet2
-RemoteVirtualNetworkId $vnet1.Id
```

Cloud customers need fast, secure, and private connections across regions and VNets. Different types of workloads require different customer needs. For example, for global data replication, you need high bandwidth and low-latency connections. With Azure, you can connect VNets through peering or VPN gateways to cater to changing customer needs. So alternate VNet peering and VPN gateways also can be used. A VPN gateway sends data between an Azure virtual network and an on-premises location over the Internet.

Additionally, you can use a VPN gateway to transfer traffic between VNets. Each VNet can only have one VPN gateway. Detailed analysis is required before you decide whether a VPN gateway or VNet peering is needed. Moreover, VPN gateways and VNet peering can coexist through gateway transit.

VPN gateways are configured as transit points in peered virtual networks when virtual networks have peered. As a result, the virtual peer network can access other resources via the remote gateway. One gateway can be part of a virtual network. It is possible to use Gateway Transit both for network peering and for global network peering.

If the virtual network is permitted to use Gateway Transit, resources outside of the peering can be accessed. Upon configuring global peering, each VNet will have a peering entry added to its routing table, which will give you changes in the peered VNets.

Configuring Virtual Network Traffic Routing

Routing is the process of selecting a path across one or more networks. A routing principle can be applied to any network, from telephone networks to public transportation. Routes are the paths by which Internet Protocol packets (IP) travel from their origin to their destination in packet-switching networks like the Internet. The routers make these Internet routing decisions.

Routers use internal routing tables to determine how to route packets across networks. Each router maintains a routing table that records how packets should be routed to each destination. Just as timetables are helpful to passengers as they decide which train they should take, routing tables work like that for networks.

However, with many cloud computing service provides, routers are fully managed, and the same principle applies to Azure. Every subnet within an Azure virtual network is automatically assigned a routing table, and its system default routes are added to the table. Custom routes can override Azure's system routes, and you can add additional routes to the route tables. In Azure, outbound traffic is routed based on routes in the subnet's route table.

A virtual network's subnets are automatically assigned system routes by Azure. Creating system routes or removing them is not possible, but you can override custom routes. The Azure cloud platform makes default system routes for each subnet. When a specific custom route is used, it can add additional routes to subnets or all subnets.

Essentially, data can be routed between source and destination in different ways depending on where it originates. The ubiquitous TCP/IP-based networking protocol is used everywhere to establish connectivity and send data.

By default, Azure routes, address prefixes, and next-hop types are available for each route. Azure uses the route that carries the prefix whenever a virtual network is created if traffic leaving a subnet is sent to an IP address within the route's address prefix. Within each subnet of the virtual network, Azure automatically creates the routes shown in Table 1.5.

TABLE 1.5   Azure default system routes

Source	Default			
Address prefixes	**Unique to the virtual network**	0.0.0.0/ 0	10.0.0.0/ 8	192.168.0.0/ 16	100.64.0.0/ 10
Next hop type	Virtual network	Internet	None	

Every time a packet of data is transmitted between two computers connected by a network, there is a hop. A node is a virtual machine that serves as a gateway for the data packets to reach their destination. From that definition, it makes sense that the fewer hops, the more quickly the packet will reach its destination.

Traffic directed to the address prefix listed in Table 1.5 is routed by Azure using the next-hop types listed there. The following list defines the next-hop types.

Hop Type Virtual Network   In a virtual network, traffic is routed between addresses within its address space. Azure provides a route with an address prefix that corresponds to each address range defined in the address space of a virtual network. Azure creates a unique route for each range of addresses within a virtual network address space. As traffic flows between subnets, Azure uses an address range-specific routing engine. Traffic between subnets does not need to go through gateways in Azure. Although each subnet in a virtual network has its own address space, Azure does not create default routes for address ranges that fall within the address space of a virtual network.

Hop Type Internet   Traffic is routed to the Internet based on the address prefix. By default, the system uses the address prefix 0.0.0.0/0. Any addresses that don't match a range within a virtual network are automatically routed to the Internet if Azure's default routes are not overridden. A destination address for an Azure service will be routed directly to the service over Azure's backbone network rather than via the Internet. No traffic between Azure services crosses the Internet, regardless of where the virtual network resides or where an Azure service instance is deployed. Custom routes can be added to Azure's default system route for 0.0.0.0/0.

Hop Type None   No traffic is routed outside of the subnet if it is routed to the None next hop type. The following address prefixes are automatically routed by Azure:

- `10.0.0.0/8` and `192.168.0.0/16`: Reserved in RFC 1918 for private use.
- `100.64.0.0/10`: Reserved as per RFC 6598.

Consider assigning one of the previous address ranges to the virtual network's address space. If assigned, Azure automatically changes the next hop type for the route to the virtual network. Address ranges outside of the four reserved address prefixes can be assigned to the address space of a virtual network, and Azure will remove the route for the prefix and add a route for the address range you added, with the virtual category network as the next hop type.

If you enable additional networking capabilities, Azure will add default system routes, as shown in Table 1.6. Azure can add default routes to either specific subnets or the entire virtual network.

TABLE 1.6   Azure optional default routes

Source	Default	Virtual network gateway	Default
Address prefixes	Unique to the virtual network, for example: `10.1.0.0/16`	Prefixes advertised from on-premises via BGP, or configured in the local network gateway	Multiple
Next hop type	VNet peering	Virtual network gateway	VirtualNetwork-ServiceEndpoint
Subnet within virtual network that route is added to	All	All	Only the subnet a service endpoint is enabled for

The following are three optional default routes that exist as part of virtual network traffic routing.

VNet Peering   Each virtual network created when peering with another has a route for each address set in its address area.

Virtual Network Gateway   Azure adds *virtual network gateways* to virtual networks, which are counted as the next hops in routes. Virtual network gateways are listed as sources because they add routes to the subnet. Assume your on-premises network gateway exchanges routing information with an Azure virtual network gateway via the Border Gateway Protocol (BGP). In that case, each route propagated from the on-premises network gateway will be added as a route. When writing this book, there is a limit (i.e., Aggregate BGP routes 4,000 per VPN gateway is the maximum supported configuration limitation) to the number of routes you can propagate in Azure virtual network gateways. As per Microsoft recommendations, you must summarize on-premises routes to the largest address ranges possible.

Virtual Network Service Endpoint   As soon as you enable a *service endpoint* to a service, the Azure route table is updated with the public IP addresses for the service. Each subnet in a virtual network has a service endpoint enabled; therefore, only the route for that subnet is added to the route table. Azure services periodically change their public IP addresses. When the route table addresses change, Azure automatically manages them.

You can create custom routes by creating user-defined routes or exchanging BGP routes between your on-premises network gateway and an Azure virtual network gateway. Azure virtual appliances can manage traffic between subnets and the Internet through network routes. IP forwarding must be enabled on the network interfaces before traffic can be received and forwarded. If more than one route type is present in a UDR route table, user-defined routes will be preferred over the default system route. A specific route is consumed when multiple routes match the destination.

Next-hop types for user-defined routes include virtual appliances, virtual network gateways, VNets, None, and Internet. The virtual network service endpoint cannot be defined as the next hop type in user-defined routes. The Azure virtual network peering and service endpoint configurations only allow VNet peering or virtual network service endpoint next hops.

Exercise 1.3 shows you how to create a new route table using the Azure portal.

EXERCISE 1.3

Deploying a Route Table with the Azure Portal

1. Log in to a personal or business account in the Azure portal at `portal.azure.com`. You will see a page like this:

2. In the Azure portal search box, type **Route table**. When *route table* appears in the search results, select it to launch the Route Table wizard. On the first page, choose Create Route Table, as shown here:

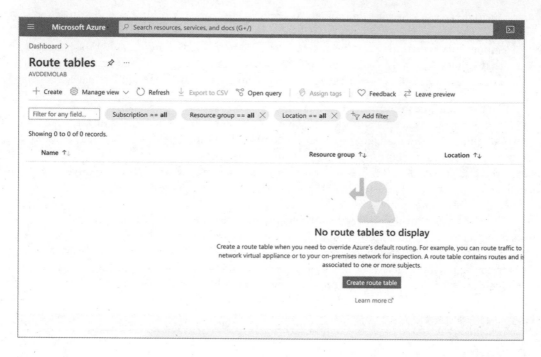

3. On the Basics page, enter the following settings:

Project Details

Subscription   Choose your subscription.

Resource Group   Choose a resource group or create a new resource group; in our case, it is Sybex.

Instance Details

Region   Choose the region you want to deploy to or that is close to your resource needs.

Name   Assign a name to your new route table according to your naming standards; in our case, it is SybexRoutePublic.

Propagate Gateway Routes Choose Yes.

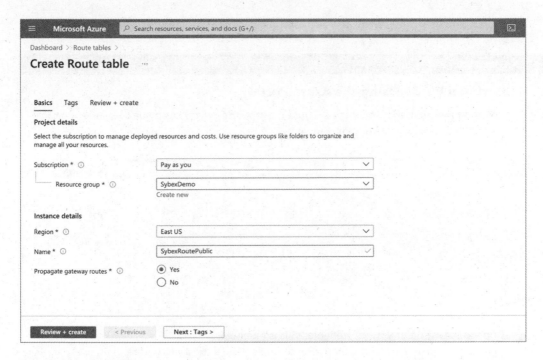

4. Select the Review + Create tab, or click the Review + Create button at the bottom of the page to go to the screen shown here:

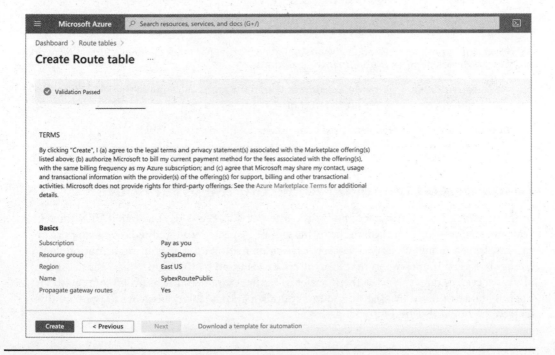

To create a new route using the Azure portal, take the steps shown in Exercise 1.4.

EXERCISE 1.4

Deploying a Route Using the Azure Portal

1. Log in to a personal or business account in the Azure portal at `portal.azure.com`. You will see a page like the one shown here:

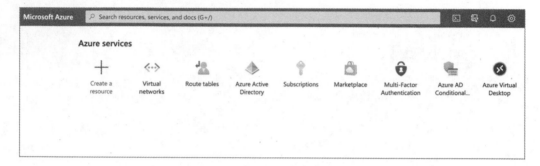

2. Choose the name of your route table; in this example, we're using SybexRoutePublic. In the Settings section of the SybexRoutePublic wizard, choose Routes.

3. In the route's wizard, click the + Add button and make the following settings:

Route Name	Type **ToPrivateSubnet**.
Address Prefix	Use the address of the private subnet you used.
Next Hop Type	Choose Virtual Appliance, Virtual Network Gateway, Virtual Network, Internet, or None.
Next Hop Address	Provide an address within the address range of the DMZ subnet or your preferred choice.

4. Complete the wizard and associate your network with the route table.

Using Forced Tunneling to Secure the VNet Route

In *forced tunneling*, all traffic bound for the Internet is forced to go through a VPN tunnel to your on-premises location, where the traffic will be inspected and audited. For many organizations, forced tunneling is a critical security requirement. Suppose your organization doesn't configure forced tunneling. In that case, all Internet-bound traffic from your VMs in Azure always traverses directly out to the Internet from the Azure network infrastructure without the possibility of monitoring it or auditing it. Information security breaches are potentially triggered by unauthorized Internet access.

Forced tunneling can be deployed by using Azure PowerShell or the Azure portal. To configure forced tunneling, you must deploy a routing table, attach a user-defined default route to the VPN gateway, and connect the routing table to the relevant VNet subnets. Tunneling allows you to restrict and inspect Internet access from your Azure VMs and cloud services.

VNets that have route-based VPN gateways can be forced to tunnel. On-premises VPN devices must be configured with `0.0.0.0/0` as traffic selectors, and you must set a default connection among the cross-premises sites connected to the virtual network.

Configuring Internet Access with Azure Virtual NAT

A gateway resource is part of a virtual network's NAT and provides outbound Internet connectivity. The NAT gateway used on the virtual network is specified in its subnet. In a subnet, NAT provides source network address translation. VMs are given static IP addresses when creating outbound flows via NAT gateway resources. Public IP addresses, public IP prefixes, or both can be used to deploy static IP addresses. When a public IP prefix resource is used, all IP addresses of the entire public IP prefix resource are consumed by the NAT gateway resource. Up to 16 static IP addresses can be assigned to a NAT gateway.

There is a severe shortage of IPv4 address ranges worldwide, which makes accessing Internet resources very expensive. The problem of internal resources on a private network sharing routable IPv4 addresses with external resources on a public network led to NAT.

If you want to allow communication between internal resources and an external IP address, you can use a NAT service rather than purchasing an IPv4 address for each resource.

Azure NAT services map IP prefixes and ports associated with IP addresses. The public IP address or IP prefix resource can be used for NAT. Public IP prefixes can be used directly or distributed across multiple NAT gateways. Traffic will be routed to all IP addresses within the prefix range. A VNet can be connected via NAT to the Internet. Return traffic from the Internet is only permitted when there is an active flow.

You configure each subnet's NAT in a VNet to allow outbound connectivity by defining which NAT gateway resource to use. All outbound UDP and TCP traffic from a VM instance will be connected to the Internet through NAT after the configuration is complete. Additional configuration is not required, and you don't need to define routes. Subnets replace the default Internet destination with NAT, which takes precedence over other outbound scenarios.

Azure NAT scales to support dynamic workloads, so there is no need to preplan or preallocate addresses. A NAT system can provide up to 64,000 concurrent flows for UDP and TCP, respectively, for each attached public IP address, by using port network address translation (PNAT or PAT). NAT can support up to 16 public IP addresses.

With Azure NAT, you can use Standard SKU resources such as load balancing, public IP addresses, and public IP prefixes.

It is possible for NAT and compatible Standard SKU features to know how a flow was initiated. A coexisting inbound and outbound scenario is likely. Due to this feature's understanding of flow direction, these scenarios will receive the correct network address translation. The following resources are used with NAT to connect your subnet(s) to the Internet. NAT provides all Internet access from a subnet(s).

The following are crucial limitations:

- Basic resources such as a load balancer must be located on a non-NAT subnet.

- NAT supports the IPv4 address family, and the IPv6 prefix cannot be used for NAT.

- NAT can't traverse multiple virtual networks, and IP fragmentation is not supported.

Deploy the NAT Gateway Using Azure PowerShell

You can use Azure PowerShell to create a NAT gateway to provide outbound connectivity for a VM. Keep the following in mind:

- A NAT gateway requires one or more public IP addresses to access the Internet. In our next example, you use the `New-AzPublicIpAddress` cmdlet to create a resource called `sybexpublicip` under your `sybexrgnat`.

- You can build a worldwide Azure NAT gateway using the `New-AzNatGateway` cmdlet. The following code creates a gateway resource named `sybexrgnat` that uses the public IP address `sybexpublicip`. Ten minutes is the idle timeout.

- You can build a virtual network called `sybexvnet` with a subnet named `sybexsubnet` using the `New-AzVirtualNetworkSubnetConfig` cmdlet in the `sybexrggroup` that uses `New-AzVirtualNetwork`. Virtual network IP addresses are `10.1.0.0/16`. In the virtual network, the subnet address is `10.1.0.0/24`.

- You can deploy an Azure Bastion host named `my bastion host` to access the VM. You create a bastion host by using the `New-AzBastion` cmdlet. With `New-AzPublicIpAddress`, you assign a public IP address to the bastion host.

```
## Deploy public IP address for NAT gateway ##
$ip = @{
    Name = 'sybexpublicip'
    ResourceGroupName = 'sybexrgnat'
    Location = 'westus2'
    Sku = 'Standard'
    AllocationMethod = 'Static'
}
```

```
$publicIP = New-AzPublicIpAddress @ip

## Create NAT gateway resource ##
$nat = @{
    ResourceGroupName = 'sybexrgnat'
    Name = 'sybexnatgateway'
    IdleTimeoutInMinutes = '10'
    Sku = 'Standard'
    Location = 'westus2'
    PublicIpAddress = $publicIP
}
$natGateway = New-AzNatGateway @nat
## Deploy subnet config and associate NAT gateway to subnet##
$subnet = @{
    Name = 'sybexsubnet'
    AddressPrefix = '10.1.0.0/24'
    NatGateway = $natGateway
}
$subnetConfig = New-AzVirtualNetworkSubnetConfig @subnet
## Deploy Azure Bastion subnet. ##
$bastsubnet = @{
    Name = 'AZBastionSubnet'
    AddressPrefix = '10.1.1.0/24'
}
$bastsubnetConfig = New-AzVirtualNetworkSubnetConfig @bastsubnet
## Deploy the virtual network ##
$net = @{
    Name = 'myVNet'
    ResourceGroupName = 'sybexrgnat'
    Location = 'eastus2'
    AddressPrefix = '10.1.0.0/16'
    Subnet = $subnetConfig,$bastsubnetConfig
}
$vnet = New-AzVirtualNetwork @net
## Deploy public IP address for bastion host. ##
$ip = @{
    Name = 'sybexbastionip'
    ResourceGroupName = 'sybexrgnat'
    Location = 'eastus2'
    Sku = 'Standard'
    AllocationMethod = 'Static'
}
```

```
$publicip = New-AzPublicIpAddress @ip

## Deploy bastion host ##
$bastion = @{
    ResourceGroupName = 'sybexrgnat'
    Name = 'sybexbastionip'
    PublicIpAddress = $publicip
    VirtualNetwork = $vnet
}
New-AzBastion @bastion -AsJob
```

Summary

This chapter explored several topics related to the basics of cloud networking and presented a brief overview of cloud computing.

As your organization moves to Microsoft Azure, you must design and deploy a secure cloud networking environment that provides a secure platform for cloud and on-premises resources. End users must obtain the infrastructure resources they need seamlessly and securely.

In this chapter, you learned how to deploy virtual networks and configure public IP services, name resolution, cross-VNet connectivity, Azure Virtual Network NAT, and virtual network routing.

Exam Essentials

Be sure you are following the right certification path.   There are several Azure certification paths. Make sure your career path aligns with your goals. This book covers Exam AZ700: Microsoft Azure, Designing and Implementing Networking Solutions. For this exam, candidates must know how to plan, implement, and maintain Azure networking solutions, including hybrid networking, connectivity, routing, security, and private access to Azure services.

Be able to define cloud computing.   Users can access infrastructure over the Internet and use computing resources without installing and maintaining them on-premises. A cloud service provider (CSP) offers on-demand access to computing resources, including applications, servers (physical and virtual), data storage, development tools, networking capabilities, and more, all hosted in a remote datacenter. The CSP charges a monthly fee for these resources or charges based on usage.

Understand networking in the cloud.   Cloud networking can be classified as cloud-enabled networking, cloud-based networking, or cloud-native network functions (CNFs). CNFs perform functions traditionally performed on physical hardware devices (e.g., IPv4 router, L2 Switch, firewall, VPN), but they can be accessed through cloud-native devices. Cloud networking critical characteristics include connectivity, scalability and flexibility, security and defense, optimization, and zero-trust standards.

Know the key concepts of Azure.   Azure offers high availability, scalability, reliability, elasticity, agility, geo-distribution, resiliency, security, and an edge to give end users maximum uptime. Key concepts include Azure geography, regions, availability zones, zone-redundant services, resource groups, subscriptions, and management groups.

Understand Azure networking services.   In Azure, networking services provide a variety of capabilities that can be combined or used separately. Networking services encompass four broad areas: connectivity services, application protection services, application delivery services, and network monitoring services.

Be familiar with Azure network connectivity services.   You can integrate Azure resources with on-premises resources by using any or a combination of Azure networking services: virtual networks (VNets), virtual WANs, ExpressRoute, VPN gateways, Virtual Network NAT Gateways, Azure DNS, Peering service, and Azure Bastion.

Know Azure network application protection services.   The following networking services in Azure can help you protect your applications: load balancers, private links, DDoS protection, firewalls, network security groups, web application firewalls, and virtual network endpoints.

List Azure network application delivery services.   These networking services are used to deliver applications in the Azure network: content delivery networks (CDNs), Azure Front Door Service, Traffic Manager, Application Gateway, Internet Analyzer, and load balancer.

Be able to describe Azure network monitoring.   Using the following networking services in Azure, you can monitor your network resources: Network Watcher, ExpressRoute Monitor, Azure Monitor, or VNet Terminal Access Point (TAP).

Be able to describe Azure virtual networking.   The following key networking capabilities are available through Azure virtual networks: isolation and microsegmentation, Internet communications, communications among Azure resources and with on-premises resources, routing and filtering of network traffic, and attaching virtual networks. Azure subscriptions and regions support multiple virtual networks.

Hands-On Lab: Design and Deploy a Virtual Network via the Azure Portal

This exercise helps you to get started with AZ- 700 exam's prerequisites.

Imagine an aviation company migrating infrastructure and applications to Azure. You are responsible for planning, preparing, designing, and deploying three virtual networks and subnets to support Azure resources.

The CoreInfraVnet virtual network is deployed in the UAE North region. The CoreInfraVnet virtual network will have the most significant number of resources, and it will have connectivity to on-premises networks through a VPN connection. The network will provide mission-critical web services, databases, and other critical systems to the aviation business's operations. Additionally, management payloads such as domain controllers and DNS will be located here. The company is anticipating growth; acquisition is in the pipeline and therefore needs ample address space.

The EngineeringVnet virtual network is deployed in the North Europe region, near the location of your organization's engineering facilities. In this virtual network, engineering facilities operations will be managed. Your organization anticipates retrieving data from many internally connected devices, including engineering materials. To expand its IP address space in the future, it needs ample address space.

The BranchofficeVnet virtual network is deployed in the East India region, near the organization's support services team. The support services team uses this virtual network. Organizational resources are limited and are not expected to grow any time soon. The business requires a few virtual machines and a few IP addresses.

To complete the exercise, you need to perform the four-step process shown in Figure 1.9.

FIGURE 1.9   Step-by-step workflow

Activity 1: Prepare the network schema.

Activity 2: Build the Aviation resource group.

Activity 3: Build the CoreInfraVnet, EngineeringVnet, and BranchofficeVnet virtual network and subnets.

Activity 4: Validate the build of VNets and subnets.

Azure portal access is required for this exercise. A free trial is available at `http://azure.com/free` if you do not already have one.

Let's get started with Activity 1.

Activity 1: Prepare the Network Schema

Gathering your network infrastructure requirements is the first step in planning your IP address scheme. By reserving an additional IP address and subnet, you will prepare for future growth.

Azure networks are similar in features and functions compared to on-premises networks, but they differ in structure. Azure's network is not based on the hierarchical network design found on-premises. It is possible to scale up and scale down Azure's infrastructure based on demand. The Azure network provisioning process takes only a few seconds to complete. Hardware devices like routers and switches do not exist. You slice your infrastructure into pieces that fit your needs.

Virtual networks in Azure use private IP addresses. There is no difference in the private IP address ranges compared to on-premises addresses. Administrators have full control over IP address assignment, name resolution, security settings, and security rules in Azure virtual networks. Subnets can be added or removed based on the IP address block CIDR.

You can divide your virtual network into multiple subnets. There is a portion of your virtual network's IP address space assigned to each subnet. Subnets can be added, removed, expanded, or shrunk if they do not contain virtual machines or services.

In the context of the AZ-700 exam, keep in mind that Azure virtual networks can communicate across all subnets by default. It is possible, however, to deny communication between subnets using a network security group. A /29 subnet mask is used to support the smallest subnet. It uses a subnet mask of /8 for its largest subnet.

Based on the following table, virtual networks are designed to accommodate existing resources while allowing for growth. Our networking infrastructure for this exercise will be built on these virtual networks and subnets.

Virtual network	Azure region	Virtual network address space	Subnet purpose	Subnet range
CoreInfraVnet	UAE North	10.40.0.0/16	Gateway Subnet	10.40.0.0/27
			Management Subnet	10.40.20.0/24
			Apps Subnet	10.40.30.0/24
			Database Subnet	10.40.40.0/24
			PublicWebApps Subnet	10.40.50.0/24
EngineeringVnet	North Europe	10.60.0.0/16	Engineering System Subnet	10.60.20.0/24
			Device 1 Unit Subnet	10.60.30.0/24
			Device 1 Unit Subnet	10.60.40.0/24
BranchofficeVnet	East India	10.80.0.0/16	Branchoffice Subnet	10.80.20.0/24

Activity 2: Build the Aviation Resource Group

To create an Aviation resource group using the Azure portal, take the following steps:

1. Log in to a personal or business account in Azure portal at `http://portal.azure.com`.

2. Select the resource group under the Azure services.

3. In the resource group, choose to create and provide the following inputs:

Setting	Inputs
	Basics details
Name	Choose your name for your resource group.
Region	Choose the region you want to deploy to or that is close to your resource needs.

4. Once the resource group has been created, click Review + Create.

Activity 3a: Build the CoreInfraVnet Virtual Network and Subnets

To create CoreInfraVnet using the Azure portal, take the following steps:

1. Log in to a personal or business account in the Azure portal at `http://portal.azure.com`. (See Figure 1.10.)

FIGURE 1.10   Azure portal

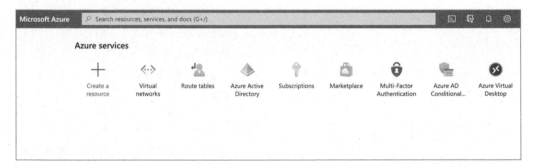

2. Click the Create A Resource button in the Azure portal, enter **virtual network** in the search box, and click Create Virtual Network to bring up the Virtual Network page shown in Figure 1.11.

FIGURE 1.11   Azure portal: Virtual Network

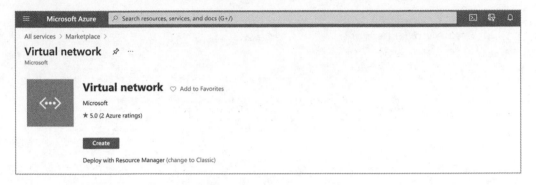

3. On the Basics tab shown in Figure 1.12, enter the following inputs.

Setting	Inputs
	Project details
Subscription	Choose your subscription.
Resource group	Choose a resource group or create a new resource group. In this example we use UAE North.
	Instance details
Name	Provide your new VNet name using your defined naming standards.
Region	Choose the region you want to deploy to or that is close to your resource needs.

4. On the IP Addresses tab shown in Figure 1.13, use the following information to deploy the subnet:

Virtual network	Azure region	Virtual network address space	Subnet purpose	Subnet range
CoreInfraVnet	UAE North	10.40.0.0/16	Gateway Subnet	10.40.0.0/27
			Management Subnet	10.40.20.0/24
			Apps Subnet	10.40.30.0/24
			Database Subnet	10.40.40.0/24
			PublicWebApps Subnet	10.40.50.0/24

FIGURE 1.12   Create Virtual Network: Basics

To begin deploying each subnet, select + Add Subnet. To complete building each subnet, click Add.

5. Once the CoreInfraVnet and its subnets have been created, select Review + Create. You can now click Create after your configuration has passed validation (see Figure 1.14).

FIGURE 1.13   Create Virtual Network: IP Addresses

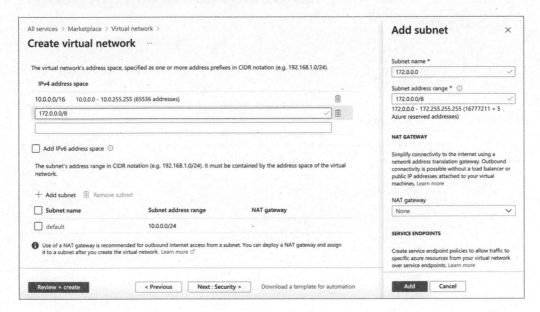

FIGURE 1.14   Create Virtual Network: Review + Create

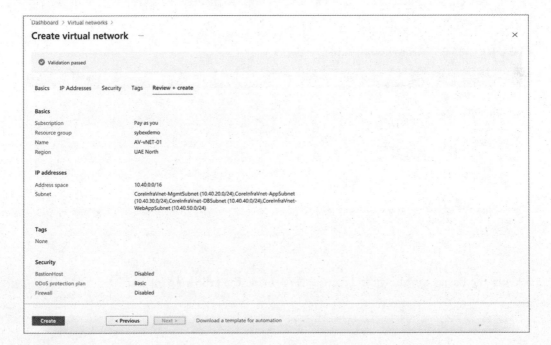

Activity 3b: Build the EngineeringVnet Virtual Network and Subnets

To create EngineeringVnet using the Azure portal, take the following steps:

1. Log in to a personal or business account in Azure portal at `http://portal.azure.com` (see Figure 1.15).

FIGURE 1.15   Azure portal

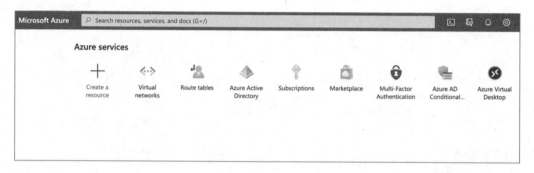

2. Click the Create A Resource button in the Azure portal, enter **virtual network** in the search box, and click Create Virtual Network to display the screen shown in Figure 1.16.

FIGURE 1.16   Azure portal: Virtual Network

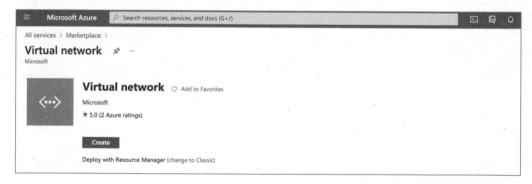

3. On the Basics tab shown in Figure 1.17, provide the following inputs:

Setting	Inputs
	Project details
Subscription	Choose your subscription.
Resource Group	Choose a resource group or create a new resource group. We are using North Europe.
	Instance details
Name	Provide your new VNet name using your defined naming standards.
Region	Choose the region you want to deploy to or that is close to your resource needs.

FIGURE 1.17   Create Virtual Network: Basics

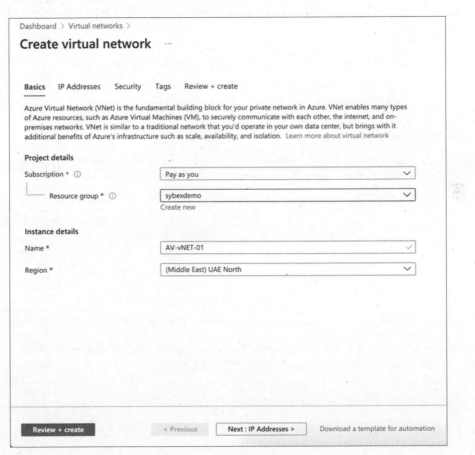

4. On the IP Addresses tab, enter the following information:

Virtual network	Azure region	Virtual network address space	Subnet purpose	Subnet range
EngineeringVnet	North Europe	`10.60.0.0/16`	Engineering System Subnet	`10.60.20.0/24`
			Device 1 Unit Subnet	`10.60.30.0/24`
			Device 1 Unit Subnet	`10.60.40.0/24`

5. Once the EngineeringVnet and its subnets have been created, select Review + Create. You can now click Create after your configuration has passed validation.

Activity 3c: Build the BranchofficeVnet Virtual Network and Subnets

To create BranchofficeVnet using the Azure portal, take the following steps:

1. Log in to a personal or business account in the Azure portal at `http://portal.azure.com` (see Figure 1.18).

FIGURE 1.18   Azure portal

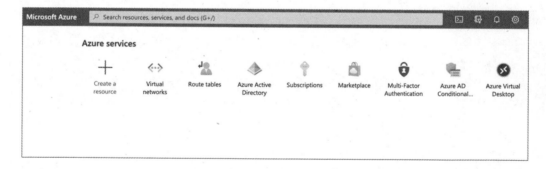

2. Click the Create A Resource button in the Azure portal, enter **virtual network** in the search box, and click Create Virtual Network to display the screen shown in Figure 1.19.

3. On the Basics tab shown in Figure 1.20, provide the following inputs:

FIGURE 1.19   Azure portal: Virtual Network

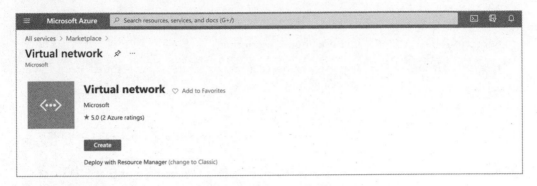

FIGURE 1.20   Create Virtual Network: Basics

Setting	Inputs
	Project details
Subscription	Choose your subscription.
Resource Group	Choose a resource group or create a new resource group. We are using East India.
	Instance details
Name	Provide your new VNet name using your defined naming standards.
Region	Choose the region you want to deploy to or that is close to your resource needs.

4. On the IP Addresses tab, enter the following information.

Virtual network	Azure region	Virtual network address space	Subnet purpose	Subnet range
BranchofficeVnet	East India	10.80.0.0/16	Branchoffice Subnet	10.80.20.0/24

To begin deploying each subnet, select + Add Subnet. To complete building each subnet, click Add.

5. Once the BranchofficeVnet and its subnets have been created, select Review + Create. You can now click Create after your configuration has passed validation.

Activity 4: Validate the Build of VNets and Subnets

To validate a VNet creation using the Azure portal, take the following steps (see Figure 1.21):

FIGURE 1.21   Virtual Network: Validate

1. Log in to a personal or business account in the Azure portal at `http://portal.azure.com`.

2. Choose All Resources and verify that all your VNets and subnets appear.

3. Verify that each VNets that build shows planned and configured IP ranges against each subnet.

Review Questions

1. Which of the following are types of cloud computing models provided by Azure? (Choose all that apply.)

   A. Infrastructure as a service

   B. Platform as a service

   C. Software as a service

   D. Report as a service

2. Which of the following cloud deployment models is provisioned for exclusive use by a single organization comprising multiple consumers?

   A. Private cloud

   B. Public cloud

   C. Community cloud

   D. Hybrid cloud

3. Which of the following cloud deployment models is provisioned for exclusive use by a specific community of consumers from organizations that have shared concerns (e.g., mission, security, and compliance considerations)?

   A. Private cloud

   B. Public cloud

   C. Community cloud

   D. Hybrid cloud

4. Which of the following is provisioned for open use by the general public and may be owned, managed, and operated by a business, an academic organization, a government organization, or a combination?

   A. Private cloud

   B. Public cloud

   C. Community cloud

   D. Hybrid cloud

5. Which of the following protects your Azure virtual network resources by providing managed cloud-based network security?

   A. Azure Firewall

   B. Azure Virtual WAN

   C. Azure Virtual WAF

   D. None of above

6. Which of the following Azure network modules is responsible for providing fixed and remote access to users and Internet devices?

A. WANs (wide area networks)

B. Campus, branch, and Internet of Things (IoT)

C. Private cloud

D. Hybrid cloud

7. Which of the following Azure networking services allows customers to connect to Microsoft cloud services such as Microsoft 365, Dynamics 365, SaaS services, Azure, and any other Microsoft service accessible on the Internet?

A. Azure Firewall

B. Azure Peering Service

C. Azure Virtual WAF

D. None of above

8. VMs and managed disks are IT services that are provided by which of the following?

A. Azure Zonal Services

B. Azure Zonal Redundant Services

C. Azure Non-Regional Services

D. Azure Resource Groups

9. For Azure subscriptions, which of the following statements is true?

A. Azure subscriptions require Microsoft approval to allocate resources.

B. Azure subscriptions do not require Microsoft approval to allocate resources.

C. Azure subscriptions do not require customer data owner approval to allocate resources.

D. Azure subscriptions do not require customer application owner approval to allocate resources.

10. Azure management groups can support up to how many levels of hierarchy?

A. 5

B. 8

C. 6

D. 4

11. What is an Azure subnet?

A. The physical subdivision of an IP network that private Azure management groups can support up to

B. The physical subdivision of an IP network that can be either private or public

C. The logical subdivision of an IP network that can be either private or public

D. The logical subdivision of an IP network that can be only public

12. You can protect your website against SQL injection by using which of the following?

    A. Azure web application firewall

    B. Azure Firewall

    C. Azure NAT gateway

    D. Azure Vault

13. Which of the following are true? (Choose four.)

    A. VNets can be split into subnets.

    B. AWS WAF and Azure Bastion are used to protect applications.

    C. Network customization services is one of Azure's networking services.

    D. CDN and application load balancer are application delivery services.

    E. Internet Analyzer and Terminal Access Points are network monitoring services.

14. Azure communicates securely with other resources through various methods, mainly Virtual Network, _____, and Virtual Network Service Endpoint.

    A. WAN (Wide Area Networks)

    B. VNet Peering

    C. Subnetting

    D. Hybrid networks

15. Identify all correct statements.

    A. VNet Peering allows you to connect virtual networks in different Azure regions.

    B. ExpressRoute enables a public traffic between on-premises and cloud.

    C. Network Security allows you to filter both incoming and outgoing network traffic.

    D. WAN optimization is performed by routing tables.

16. For Azure subscriptions and regions, which of the following statements is valid?

    A. Azure subscriptions and regions support multiple virtual networks.

    B. Azure subscriptions and regions do not support multiple virtual networks.

    C. Azure subscriptions and regions do not support more than two virtual networks.

    D. None of the above.

17. Identify all correct statements.

    A. x.x.x.1 is the network address used by Azure.

    B. x.x.x.0 is reserved by Azure for the default gateway.

    C. x.x.x.0 is the network address used by Azure.

    D. x.x.x.1 is the default gateway reserved by Azure.

18. Identify all correct statements.

    A. Resource Group is an optional field when creating subnets.

    B. Tags cannot be added to Azure subnets.

    C. Firewall is enabled by default for all Azure VNets.

    D. Firewall is disabled by default for all Azure VNets.

19. How many concurrent flows can a NAT system provide for UDP and TCP?

    A. 64,000

    B. 32,000

    C. 128,000

    D. 256,000

20. How many public IP addresses can NAT support?

    A. 24

    B. 16

    C. 32

    D. 64

Chapter

2

Design, Deploy, and Manage a Site-to-Site VPN Connection and Point-to-Site VPN Connection

THE MICROSOFT AZ-700 EXAM OBJECTIVES COVERED IN THIS CHAPTER INCLUDE:

✓ **Design, Implement, and Manage a Site-to-Site VPN Connection**

- Design a site-to-site VPN connection for high availability
- Select an appropriate virtual network (VNet) gateway SKU.
- Identify when to use policy-based VPN versus route-based VPN
- Create and configure a local network gateway
- Create and configure Ipsec/IKE policy
- Create and configure a virtual network gateway
- Diagnose and resolve virtual network gateway connectivity issues

✓ **Design, Implement, and Manage a Point-to-Site VPN Connection**

- Select an appropriate virtual network (Vnet) gateway SKU
- Plan and configure RADIUS authentication
- Plan and configure certificate-based authentication
- Plan and configure OpenVPN authentication
- Plan and configure Azure Active Directory (Azure AD) authentication.
- Implement a VPN client configuration file
- Diagnose and resolve client-side and authentication issues

As organizations move to Azure, they should design their networks with security as a top priority. Design and deployment should ensure that communication between the on-premises environment and Azure workloads is secure and reliable.

You need to know how to design and implement a hybrid connectivity solution that addresses the short- and long-term goals of an organization's global enterprise IT footprint.

The following are key prerequisites for reading this chapter: you must have experience with networking concepts, including IP addressing, DNS, and routing, as well as methods of connecting to networks such as VPNs or WANs. You should also be familiar with the Azure portal and Azure PowerShell.

This chapter has two parts. In the first part, you learn about designing, implementing, and managing site-to-site VPN connections; choosing an appropriate virtual network (VNet) gateway SKU; and identifying when to use policy-based VPN versus route-based VPN. You also create and configure a local network gateway, IPsec/IKE policy, and a virtual network gateway, and you diagnose and resolve virtual network gateway connectivity issues.

In the second part of this chapter, you learn about designing, implementing, and managing a point-to-site VPN connection, and choosing an appropriate virtual network (VNet) gateway SKU. You also learn to plan and configure RADIUS authentication, certificate-based authentication, OpenVPN authentication, and Azure Active Directory (Azure AD) authentication, and how to diagnose and resolve client-side and authentication issues.

Overview of Azure VPN Gateway

A *virtual private network (VPN)* connects your organization to the Azure resource in a protected manner and allows you to use public networks securely. VPNs encrypt and hide your end-user data exchange over the Internet. Third parties will have difficulty tracking your activities on the web and stealing your data when you use a VPN.

By creating a tunnel between an on-premises network and an Azure network, VPNs allow end users on the public network to access private networks as if they were directly connected. In recent years, the use of VPNs has increased in the business sector, thanks to consumers seeking more privacy as they browse the web.

VPNs mask an individual's IP address by redirecting the network through a VPN server, which is run remotely by the VPN host. A VPN encrypts the data you send to the VPN server, so user data is protected from unauthorized access by their Internet service provider (ISP) and other third parties.

You must create a secure connection between on-premises networks and the Microsoft Azure Platform. With an Internet connection or a dedicated link, you can create such a connection.

Hybrid networks are networks that connect on-premises resources and virtual resources. An Azure VNet can be connected via a virtual private network (VPN), a private, interconnected network. Using an encrypted tunnel, a VPN connects to another network. Typically, they connect two or more trusted private networks over an untrusted network, such as the Internet. Traffic traveling over the untrusted network is encrypted to prevent eavesdropping or other attacks.

An encrypted connection is required to integrate your on-premises environment with Azure, and a dedicated link or an Internet connection can be used.

There must be a bridge between your on-premises network and Azure when you want to integrate the two. This can be achieved through a VPN gateway. *VPN gateways* enable the transmission of encrypted traffic between networks. VPN gateways can route VPN tunnels that utilize any available bandwidth since they support multiple connections. A VPN gateway is needed for every virtual network, and its connections use the same amount of bandwidth. Azure provides virtual network connectivity through VPN gateways as well.

Azure architects must plan adequately for the construction of virtual network gateways. The provisioning process creates gateway virtual machines and deploys them on the gateway subnet when you create a virtual network gateway. You can configure the gateway settings on these VMs.

It's essential to understand the different Azure configurations available for VPN gateway connections. As of this writing, three varieties exist: point-to-site, site-to-site, and ExpressRoute. Each of them requires different designs and structures. If you can determine which meets your needs, that will be the best option.

Gateway types determine how virtual network gateways are used and what the gateway does. A VPN gateway is created when you specify the gateway type VPN. It's a different type of gateway from an ExpressRoute gateway. VPN and ExpressRoute can be the two network gateways in a virtual network.

VPN gateways are deployed to the gateway subnet and configured with the settings you specify when they are created. Depending on the gateway SKU selected, this process could take 45 minutes. Create an IPsec/IKE VPN tunnel connection between the VPN gateway and another VPN gateway (VNet-to-VNet) or create a site-to-site IPsec/IKE VPN tunnel between the VPN gateway and an on-premises VPN device (site-to-site). Additionally, you can set up a point-to-site VPN connection (OpenVPN, IKEv2, or SSTP) to access your virtual network remotely, such as from a conference or your home.

Multiple resources must be configured in a recommended order to work as expected for a VPN gateway connection. You must configure some networking resources in a specific order, but most resources can be configured independently.

You can use a configuration tool like the Azure portal to create and configure resources. It is possible to switch to another tool, such as PowerShell, to configure additional resources or to modify existing resources. The Azure portal does not currently allow you to configure every resource and resource setting.

In Azure availability zones (AZs), VPN gateways can be deployed. Using virtual network gateways deployed in AZs can improve scalability, reliability, and availability. You can separate your gateways logically and physically within a region while protecting your on-premises network from failures at the zone level.

These design elements determine the Azure VPN gateway connections:

- Network throughput (Mbps or Gbps)
- Network backbone (Internet or private)
- VPN device compatibility and VPN gateway type
- Azure VPN Gateway SKU
- Method of routing (route-based or Border Gateway Protocol [BGP]).
- Network connection resiliency pattern (active/passive or active/active)
- Network protocols supported (Secure Socket Tunneling Protocol [SSTP], Internet Protocol Security [IPsec], OpenVPN, Multiprotocol Label Switching [MPLS], virtual private LAN service [VPLS])
- Organizationwide multiple client connections or a site-to-site link
- Availability of a public (static) IP address
- Service-level agreement (SLA) and pricing

You can choose the most appropriate connectivity method based on Table 2.1 and the best choice for various use cases.

Use Case 1 When you want to access Azure virtual networks securely from a remote location, choose a point-to-site VPN.

Use Case 2 When you are using Azure cloud services for development, preproduction, proof-of-concept, and small-to-medium-scale production workloads, choose a site-to-site VPN.

Use Case 3 When you want full access to all Azure services, enterprise-class workloads requiring backup, big data, Azure as a disaster recovery site, and many more cloud-native use cases, choose an ExpressRoute.

TABLE 2.1 Planning table

Type	Point-to-site	Site-to-site	ExpressRoute
Azure supported services	Azure native services and VMs	Azure native services and VMs	Private peering, Azure Peering (no support for CDN, Azure Front Door, Azure Virtual Desktop, MFA, Logica apps, Traffic Manager), public peering
Typical bandwidths	Condition to the gateway SKU	Typically < 1 Gbps aggregate	50 Mbps, 100 Mbps, 200 Mbps, 500 Mbps, 1 Gbps, 2 Gbps, 5 Gbps, 10 Gbps
Protocols supported	SSTP, OpenVPN, and IPsec	IPsec	Direct connection over VLANs, network service provider's VPN technologies (MPLS and VPLS)

Type	Point-to-site	Site-to-site	ExpressRoute
Network routing	Route-based	Static routing and route-based (dynamic routing VPN)	BGP
DR pattern	Active/passive	Active/passive or active/active	Active/passive

Designing an Azure VPN Connection

In this section you learn about the Azure VPN gateway connection design patterns and deployment topology. We'll begin with a site-to-site VPN.

A *site-to-site* VPN is established by connecting two gateways at different sites using the Internet, a private network, or an outsourced IPsec network. Any organization can access its IT resources quickly and safely, regardless of whether they are hosted on-premises or in the cloud.

A site-to-site VPN's primary function is providing secure access to sensitive information and network resources, such as internal customer and sales systems, cloud applications, and local file storage used by end users across many devices.

Cross-premises and hybrid configurations can be supported by site-to-site connectivity. A site-to-site VPN gateway is a network connection over an IPsec/IKE (IKEv1 or IKEv2) VPN tunnel. The traffic is encrypted at one end and sent over the public Internet to the other end, which decrypts it and routes it to its destination. A VPN device on-premises that comes with public IP addresses is required for site-to-site VPN connections. The technology enables the connection of geographically displaced sites or networks using a public Internet connection or a WAN connection. VPN connections require an on-premises VPN device with a public IP address assigned to it.

The typical deployment topology in Figure 2.1 shows a single-site, site-to-site VPN to establish a VPN tunnel (IPSec VPN tunnel) between Azure and an on-premises site.

FIGURE 2.1   Single-site VPN connection

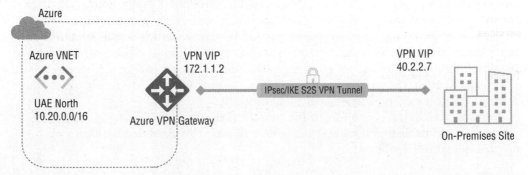

The VPN gateway can be configured in active/standby mode with a single public IP address or active/active mode with two public IP addresses. IPsec tunnels are active in active/standby mode, and tunnels are on standby. This setup allows traffic to flow through the active tunnel, but traffic switches over to the standby tunnel in case of an issue with that tunnel. Microsoft recommends that you configure the VPN gateway in an active/active mode. Both IPsec tunnels are active simultaneously, and data flows through both tunnels simultaneously. A further advantage of the active/active mode is that customers can experience higher throughput.

You can create multiple VPN connections from your virtual network gateway, typically connecting to multiple on-premises sites. Multiconnection VPNs require route-based VPNs (or a dynamic gateway if you use a classic VNet).

Figure 2.2 shows a typical deployment topology: a multisite, site-to-site VPN to establish a VPN tunnel (IPSec VPN tunnel) between Azure and on-premises sites.

FIGURE 2.2 Multiple-site VPN connection

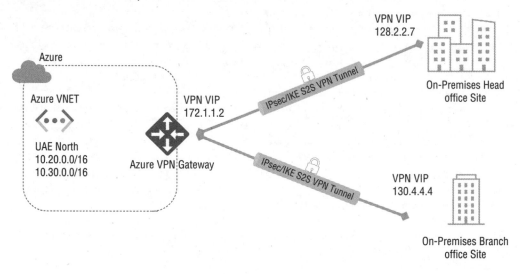

You can set up a VPN gateway in active/standby mode using one public IP or active/active method using two public IPs. With a VPN gateway in active/active mode, both of the IPsec tunnels are simultaneously active, with data flowing through both tunnels at the same time.

Furthermore, your organization benefits from an increase in throughput in an active/active configuration mode. Active standby refers to having one IPsec tunnel active and another on standby. If the active tunnel experiences any issues, traffic switches over to the standby tunnel.

One of the crucial prerequisites is to ensure your organization's environment has a compatible VPN device on-premises to build and manage it.

The second technical prerequisite is that your VPN device needs to have an external IPv4 address. The virtual network subnets you wish to connect to cannot overlap with your on-premises network subnets.

To configure a site-to-site (S2S) cross-premises VPN connection using a VPN gateway, you need a VPN device. Connecting on-premises networks with virtual networks or any time you desire secure connections between them is possible using S2S connections.

In Azure environments, static routing is called policy-based routing and dynamic routing is called route-based.

Applying a multisite design model offers numerous advantages, including the following:

- Settings and management are simplified. There is no room for configuration drifts.

- The VPN gateway ensures that all data and traffic between the client in-house and the Azure cloud are encrypted.

- Azure consumers' networking needs can be served by scaling and extending the design model.

Microsoft has validated a variety of standard VPN devices in partnership with network device manufacturers. The VPN gateways in the following table should be compatible with all the devices in each family. These devices were compatible as of this writing, but refer to the Microsoft site for the most updated information.

TABLE 2.2   Microsoft-validated VPN devices and device configuration

Vendor	Device family	Minimum OS version
A10 Networks	Thunder CFW	ACOS 4.1.1
Allied Telesis	AR Series VPN Routers	AR-Series 5.4.7+
Arista	CloudEOS Router	vEOS 4.24.0FX
Barracuda Networks	Barracuda CloudGen Firewall	Policy-based: 5.4.3
		Route-based: 6.2.0
Check Point	Security gateway	R80.10
Cisco	ASA	8.3
		8.4+ (IKEv2*)
Cisco	ASR	Policy-based: IOS 15.1
		Route-based: IOS 15.2
Cisco	CSR	Route-based: IOS-XE 16.10
Cisco	ISR	Policy-based: IOS 15.0
		Route-based*: IOS 15.1

TABLE 2.2   Microsoft-validated VPN devices and device configuration *(continued)*

Vendor	Device family	Minimum OS version
Cisco	Meraki (MX)	MX v15.12
Cisco	vEdge (Viptela OS)	18.4.0 (active/passive mode)
		19.2 (active/active mode)
Citrix	NetScaler MPX, SDX, VPX	10.1 and above
F5	BIG-IP series	12
Fortinet	FortiGate	FortiOS 5.6
Hillstone Networks	Next-Gen Firewalls (NGFW)	5.5R7
Internet Initiative Japan (IIJ)	SEIL Series	SEIL/X 4.60
		SEIL/B1 4.60
		SEIL/x86 3.20
Juniper	SRX	Policy-based: JunOS 10.2
		Route-based: JunOS 11.4
Juniper	J-Series	Policy-based: JunOS 10.4r9
		Route-based: JunOS 11.4
Juniper	ISG	ScreenOS 6.3
Juniper	SSG	ScreenOS 6.2
Juniper	MX	JunOS 12.x
Microsoft	Routing and Remote Access Service	Windows Server 2012
Open Systems AG	Mission Control Security gateway	N/A
Palo Alto Networks	All devices running PAN-OS	PAN-OS
		Policy-based: 6.1.5 or later
		Route-based: 7.1.4

Vendor	Device family	Minimum OS version
Sentrium (Developer)	VyOS	VyOS 1.2.2
ShareTech	Next Generation UTM (NU series)	9.0.1.3
SonicWall	TZ Series, NSA Series	SonicOS 5.8.x
	SuperMassive Series	SonicOS 5.9.x
	E-Class NSA Series	SonicOS 6.x
Sophos	XG Next Gen Firewall	XG v17
Synology	MR2200ac	SRM1.1.5/ VpnPlusServer-1.2.0
	RT2600ac	
	RT1900ac	
Ubiquiti	EdgeRouter	EdgeOS v1.10
Ultra	3E-636L3	5.2.0.T3 Build-13
WatchGuard	All	Fireware XTM
		Policy-based: v11.11.x
		Route-based: v11.12.x
Zyxel	ZyWALL USG series ZyWALL ATP series ZyWALL VPN series	ZLD v4.32+

* IKEv2 support has been added to Cisco ASA versions 8.4+, allowing custom IPsec/IKE policy to be used with the `UsePolicyBasedTrafficSelectors` option to connect to the Azure VPN gateway.

 A network gateway that lets you connect to your virtual network from another network or physically is called a site-to-site VPN gateway connection.

A *point-to-site* VPN gateway connection lets you build a secure connection to the Azure virtual network from an individual end-user computer. You connect to a point-to-site network using the end user's computer. Connecting to Azure VNets from a remote location, such as from home or during a conference, is an excellent solution for telecommuters. If you have only a few clients connecting to a VNet, a point-to-site VPN is also appropriate for site-to-site VPN. A point-to-site connection requires no public IP address or VPN device on-premises, in contrast to site-to-site connections. If both links' requirements are compatible, using a point-to-site link and a site-to-site link through a single VPN gateway is possible.

Figure 2.3 shows the deployment model of a point-to-site (P2S) VPN.

FIGURE 2.3   Point-to-site VPN connection

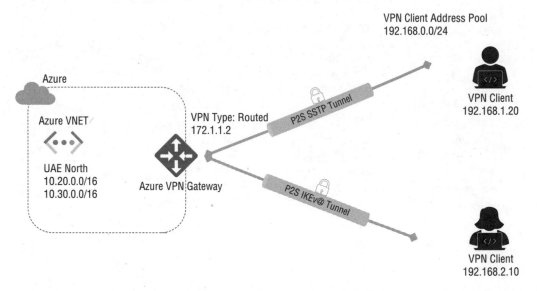

Virtual networks can be joined to each other (VNet-to-VNet) similar to on-site locations of virtual networks. Both connectivity types provide an IPsec/IKE tunnel via a VPN gateway. You can combine communications between VNets with multisite configurations. Network topologies can be established that combine premise-to-premise and premise-to-virtual connectivity.

A network gateway that lets you connect to your virtual network from client endpoints is called a point-to-site VPN gateway connection.

Point-to-site provides you with secure access to Azure VNets. Your local network limits your access to a site-to-site connection, whereas point-to-site enables you to connect anywhere. Using certificate-based authentication, the VPN server and client use the same certificate to verify the connection and access. Consequently, you can access Azure VNets at any time and from anywhere. An on-demand connection of this type is typically used for maintenance and management tasks. Consider a site-to-site connection if you require a constant connection.

The typical deployment topology in Figure 2.4 shows a VNet-to-VNet VPN to establish a VPN tunnel (IPsec VPN tunnel) within the same or a different region, within the same or different subscriptions, or within the same or different deployment models.

FIGURE 2.4   VNet-to-VNet VPN connection

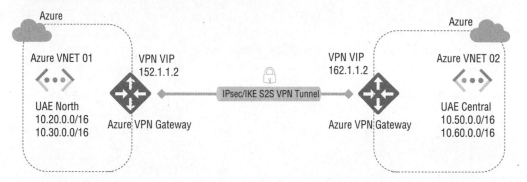

Microsoft 365 and other Microsoft cloud services can be connected to Azure using ExpressRoute. A network connectivity provider facilitates the connection between an organization network on-premises and the Azure cloud using ExpressRoute. Network connectivity can be provided by any-to-any (IP VPN) networks, point-to-point Ethernet networks, or virtual cross-connection through providers located at colocation facilities. Site-to-site VPN and ExpressRoute can coexist.

Next, let's explore highly available configuration options for cross-premises and VNet-to-VNet connectivity using Azure VPN gateways.

As part of every Azure VPN gateway, two instances are configured in active/standby mode. The standby instance will automatically take over (failover) when the active instance is down for planned maintenance or an unplanned outage. An interruption will occur during the switchover (failback). If this is scheduled maintenance, the connection should be restored in a matter of minutes. If unexpected issues arise, the connection recovery time will be longer, about one to three minutes in the worst-case scenario. End users connecting to point-to-point VPN from the client machines will need to reconnect from the clients' devices after the gateway disconnects the clients' point-to-site connections.

Figure 2.5 shows the high availability deployment model of active/standby mode.

The ultimate objective of reliability is to avoid a single-point failure in your network design and deployment. Every network function or element can fail, but you should strive to build a robust system that can tolerate any individual component's failure.

As cloud network operations become more pervasive, network functions become further dependent on them; failure such as hardware failure, natural disasters, and data corruption should not disrupt or stop networks from functioning. The network function should allow the business to operate with highly reliable and secure network systems. Network architects must consider such networks' reliability throughout their design and use.

FIGURE 2.5 VPN gateway redundancy

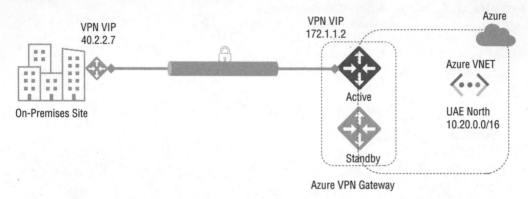

The following three sections describe design patterns that support availability for your cross-premises connections:

Design Pattern 1 Avoids failures or interruptions on your on-premises network and VPN devices

Design Pattern 2 Avoids failures or interruptions on Azure network failover automatically

Design Pattern 3 Avoids failures or interruptions on the Azure network and on-premises network

Design Pattern 1

You can use multiple VPN devices from the on-premises network to connect to your Azure VPN gateway, as shown in Figure 2.6.

FIGURE 2.6 Multiple on-premises VPN devices

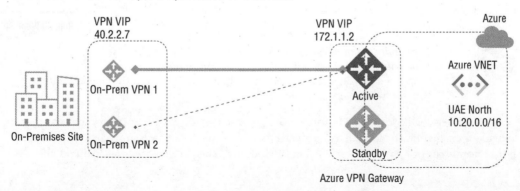

A single Azure VPN gateway provides multiple active tunnels to your on-premises devices at the exact location.

You need to build multiple site-to-site VPN connections from on-premises VPN devices to Azure. When you want to connect more than one VPN device from the same on-premises network to Azure, you must meet the following requirements:

- You need to build one local network gateway for every VPN device.

- You need a connection from the Azure VPN gateway to each local network gateway.

- In your VPN device's `GatewayIpAddress` property, you must give each gateway a unique public IP address.

- You must use BGP for this configuration and specify a unique BGP peer IP address in the `BgpPeerIpAddress` property of each local network gateway representing a VPN device.

- To maximize the performance of your Azure VPN gateway, you should use BGP to advertise the same prefixes of the same on-premises networks simultaneously. Traffic will be forwarded through these tunnels simultaneously.

- Equal-cost multipath routing (ECMP) is the best approach. There is a limit of 10 tunnels per Azure VPN gateway and 30 tunnels per high performance gateway.

Despite this design pattern, the Azure VPN gateway is still operating in active/standby mode, so the interruptions and failover behaviors previously mentioned will still occur.

Design Pattern 2

The Azure VPN gateway is set up for active/active deployment so that both VM instances establish site-to-site VPN tunnels with your on-premises VPN device, as illustrated in Figure 2.7.

FIGURE 2.7 Active/active VPN gateway

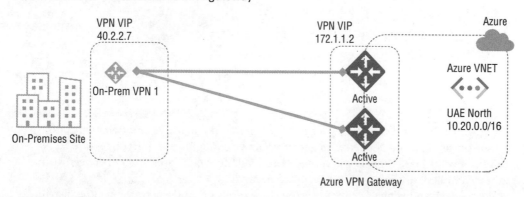

Azure gateway instances will each have their own IP address in this deployment model. Your on-premises VPN device specified in your local network gateway and connection will establish an IPsec/IKE site-to-site VPN tunnel. There is one connection for both VPN tunnels. On-premises VPN devices will still need to be configured to accept or establish two site-to-site VPN tunnels to the Azure VPN gateways' two public IP addresses.

Because the Azure gateway instances are in an active/active deployment model, the traffic from your Azure virtual network to on-premises network will be routed via both tunnels concurrently.

Whenever you send packets to your on-premises network from Azure, Azure uses the same tunnel. A different tunnel could be used to transmit packets to Azure from your on-premises network.

In case of planned maintenance or an unplanned event on one gateway instance, your VPN device on-premises will be disconnected from that instance using IPsec. Consequently, your VPN devices will automatically remove or withdraw routes, ensuring that data travels through an IPsec tunnel that is active. As for Azure, the affected instance will be switched over to the active model automatically.

Design Pattern 3

The most reliable design pattern is integrating the active/active gateways on your network and Azure, as shown in Figure 2.8.

FIGURE 2.8   Dual-redundancy: active/active VPN gateway

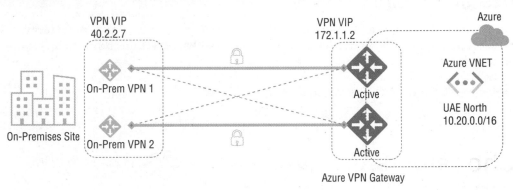

Here you create and configure your two local network gateways and two connections for your on-premises VPN devices in an active/active configuration for your Azure VPN gateway. Several IPsec tunnels will provide full-mesh network connectivity between your Azure virtual network and your on-premises network.

All gateways and tunnels are active from the Azure side, and the traffic will be distributed among all four tunnels simultaneously, but each TCP or UDP flow will proceed through the same tunnel or path. Rather than directly increasing performance, high availability is the primary objective. The use of IPsec tunnels may result in a slight improvement in throughput. Since spreading is statistical, measuring how different application traffic conditions may affect aggregate throughput is difficult.

There are two local network gateways and two connections needed to support two on-premises VPN devices. BGP is required for two connections to be able to connect to the same network.

Connecting Azure VNets can be configured in the same way as active/active connections. Figure 2.9 shows an active/active configuration applied to VNet-to-VNet connections.

FIGURE 2.9   Highly available VNet-to-VNet

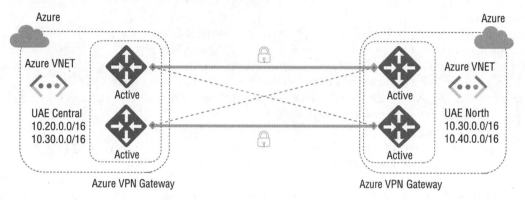

Both virtual networks will have active/active VPN gateways, which can be connected to form the same full-mesh connectivity of four tunnels between them. By doing so, you ensure that your virtual networks will always have tunnels between them during any planned maintenance, providing even better availability. Even though the same topology requires two connections for cross-premises connectivity, each gateway would require only one connection for VNet-to-VNet connectivity. Additionally, BGP is optional if transit routing over VNet-to-VNet connections is not required.

Choosing a Virtual Network Gateway SKU for Site-to-Site VPN

You must specify the gateway stock-keeping-unit (SKU) you want to use to create a virtual network gateway. Considering types of workloads, throughputs, features, and SLAs, determine the appropriate SKU.

VpnGw SKUs can be resized within a generation, except the Basic SKU. The Basic SKU has feature limitations, and resizing it is not possible. The Basic SKU VPN gateway must be deleted and replaced with an alternate SKU VPN gateway.

The following is a high-level design and deployment consideration:

- The size can be changed between VpnGw1, VpnGw2, or VpnGw3.

- There is no resizing from Basic, Standard, or High-Performance SKUs to new VpnGw1, VpnGw2, or VpnGw3 SKUs.

- VPN gateway generation, generation change, or generation switching are not allowed. Generation 1 supports only Basic and VpnGw1, whereas Generation 2 supports only VpnGw4 and VpnGw5.

The critical KPI is VPN gateway throughput. You need to measure how much data passes through a VPN gateway each second. Gateway types and SKUs have different throughput thresholds.

On a VPN gateway, site-to-site and point-to-site connections share the same bandwidth, so increasing the bandwidth on one can slow down the other. When your VPN gateway has reached its maximum throughput, you might consider decreasing your throughput requirements or increasing the gateway's capacity. The average metrics and point-to-site bandwidth need to identify when your throughput thresholds are approaching so that you can take remedial steps before performance degrades.

Specifying the gateway SKU when creating a virtual network gateway is essential. Choose the SKU that best meets your needs depending on the types of workloads, throughputs, features, and SLA. Table 2.3 contains the available SKUs as of this writing.

TABLE 2.3   Gateway SKUs by tunnel, connection, and throughput

VPN gateway generation	SKU	S2S/ VNet-to-VNet	P2S SSTP connections	P2S IKEv2/ OpenVPN connections	Aggregate throughput benchmark	BGP support	Zone-redundant
Gen1	Basic	10 Max	128 Max	Not supported	100 Mbps	No	No
Gen1	VpnGw1	30 Max	128 Max.	250 Max	650 Mbps	Yes	No
Gen1	VpnGw2	30 Max	128 Max	500 Max	1 Gbps	Yes	No
Gen1	VpnGw3	30 Max	128 Max	1000 Max	1.25 Gbps	Yes	No
Gen1	VpnGw1AZ	30 Max	128 Max.	250 Max	650 Mbps	Yes	Yes
Gen1	VpnGw2AZ	30 Max	128 Max	500 Max	1 Gbps	Yes	Yes
Gen1	VpnGw3AZ	30 Max	128 Max	1000 Max	1.25 Gbps	Yes	Yes
Gen2	VpnGw2	30 Max	128 Max	500 Max	1.25 Gbps	Yes	No

VPN gateway generation	SKU	S2S/ VNet-to-VNet	P2S SSTP connections	P2S IKEv2/ OpenVPN connections	Aggregate throughput benchmark	BGP support	Zone-redundant
Gen2	VpnGw3	30 Max	128 Max.	1000 Max	2.5 Gbps	Yes	No
Gen2	VpnGw4	30 Max	128 Max	5000 Max	5 Gbps	Yes	No
Gen2	VpnGw5	30 Max	128 Max	10000 Max	10 Gbps	Yes	No
Gen2	VpnGw2AZ	30 Max	128 Max	500 Max	1.25 Gbps	Yes	Yes
Gen2	VpnGw3AZ	30 Max	128 Max	1000 Max	2.5 Gbps	Yes	Yes
Gen2	VpnGw4AZ	30 Max	128 Max	5000 Max	5 Gbps	Yes	Yes
Gen2	VpnGw5AZ	30 Max	128 Max	10000 Max	10 Gbps	Yes	Yes

Every connection has a separate limit. For example, you can connect 128 SSTP protocols and 250 IKEv2 protocols over a VpnGw1 SKU.

The maximum throughput is 1 GB per tunnel. Table 2.3 shows that Microsoft aggregates tunnel measurements to compute the throughput benchmarks and calculations. As per Microsoft VPN, gateways are measured based on the point-to-site and site-to-site combined throughput. Throughput constraints may negatively influence site-to-site connections if you have many point-to-site connections. Because of Internet traffic conditions and your application's behavior, Microsoft cannot guarantee aggregate throughput.

Pricing plays a significant role. Organizations consuming Azure VPN gateways pay for two items: one is the hourly compute costs for the virtual network gateway, and another is the egress data transfer from the virtual network gateway. An hourly compute cost is associated with each virtual network gateway. Your virtual network gateway price is based on the gateway SKU that you specify. Besides the cost of the gateway, there is the cost of data transfer. It is the same cost for active/active as for active/passive.

Data transfer prices are determined based on egress traffic from the origin virtual network gateway and vary according to the following:

- If you send traffic to your on-premises VPN device, the data transfer rate to the Internet will be calculated.

- If you send traffic among virtual networks in different regions, the price will depend on the region you're in.

- Only traffic sent between virtual networks in the same region incurs data fees. Traffic between VNets in the same region has no cost.

Using Policy-Based VPNs vs. Route-Based VPNs

Two types of VPN gateways are currently supported by Azure:

Policy-Based   VPN devices based on policy define the encryption/decryption process through IPsec tunnels based on the sequence of network prefixes. Typically, packet filtering is performed by firewall devices. To the packet processing engine, IPsec tunnel encryption and decryption are added.

Route-Based   In route-based VPN devices, traffic is selected from any-to-any (wildcard) and routed to a specific IPsec tunnel depending on the routing table. Virtual tunnel interfaces (VTIs) are used to model IPsec tunnels on router platforms as network interfaces.

SKUs for VPN gateways offer streamlined feature sets, as shown in Table 2.4.

TABLE 2.4   Gateway SKU by feature set

Category	Policy-based VPN gateway	Route-based VPN gateway	Route-based VPN gateway
Azure gateway SKU	Basic(*)	Basic(**)	VpnGw1, VpnGw2, VpnGw3, VpnGw4, VpnGw5
IKE version	IKEv1	IKEv2	IKEv1 and IKEv2
Max site-to-site connections	1	10	30
Max point-to-site connections	0	0	100*

* Basic SKUs are considered legacy SKUs, and the Basic SKUs have some limitations. There is no way to resize a gateway that uses a Basic SKU to another SKU; instead, you must change to a new SKU, requiring you to delete and re-create your VPN gateway.

** Route-based VPN gateways can be connected to multiple policy-based firewall devices on-premises by configuring `PolicyBasedTrafficSelectors`.

When you configure a custom IPsec/IKE policy, Azure route-based VPN gateways can connect to policy-based VPN devices that use prefix-based traffic selectors. With this feature, you can connect to multiple on-premises policy-based VPN/firewall devices from an Azure virtual network and VPN gateway, removing the one-connection limitation of the current Azure policy-based VPN gateways.

One key factor in determining whether to enable a policy-based connection with Azure route-based VPN gateways is to ensure that devices supporting IKEv2 are on your premises.

IKEv1 connections were traditionally only supported by Azure's Basic SKUs, whereas IKEv2 connections were supported by all VPN gateway SKUs other than Basic SKUs. Since the Basic SKU allows only one connection, along with other limitations such as performance, customers with legacy devices that only support IKEv1 protocols have been limited in their experience. Except for the Azure VPN gateway Basics SKU, VPN gateway SKUs that support IKEv1 protocols are now available to provide a better user experience.

Transit for IKEv1 and IKEv2 connections on the same VPN gateway is enabled automatically when both are applied.

IPsec and IKE protocol standards support a wide range of cryptographic algorithms in various combinations. By default, Azure VPN gateways use a set of default cryptographic algorithms and parameters if you don't request specific parameters and algorithms. A variety of third-party VPN devices in default configurations are compatible with the default policy sets. This means that the proposed policies and proposals can't account for all combinations of available cryptographic algorithms and key strengths.

You can now configure the Azure VPN gateways to use specific cryptographic algorithms and key strengths, rather than the Azure default policy sets, for communications that require specific cryptographic algorithms or parameters, typically due to compliance or security requirements.

The custom IPsec/IKE connection policy can only link Azure virtual networks with policy-based VPN devices on-premises. You must specify the full policy when enabling policy-based traffic selection (IPsec/IKE encryption algorithms, key strengths, and SA lifetimes).

Depending on your VPN device and the kind of VPN connection you intend to establish, you can accept different types of VPN connections when you are connecting over a point-to-site or virtual network, or when you are creating a VPN type gateway in conjunction with an ExpressRoute gateway.

Your choice will depend on the device that your organization has on-premises. The decision is easier if your hardware device supports either policy-based or route-based in your corporate network.

The term *static routing* is now commonly used to describe policy-based routing. An access control list (ACL)will be created in the VPN configuration so that traffic can travel from your network to Azure. To implement policies, you will make an access control list (ACL).

Policy-based routing (aka dynamic routing) occurs when the devices themselves update the routing. Devices 1 and 2 report what they support, and you can have wildcards compatible with either. Route-based is more flexible. Microsoft supports both options equally, the legacy approach and the more modern approach, but it depends on the device.

A route-based VPN gateway comes in three types: Basic, Standard, and High Performance. When coexisting with an ExpressRoute gateway, the gateway must be set up for Standard or High performance. If the active/active mode is to be enabled, high-performance SKUs must be selected. The policy-based VPN gateway is only available as a Basic SKU.

In Azure availability zones, VPN gateways can be deployed. In this way, virtual network gateways provide resiliency, scalability, and higher availability. As a result of using Azure availability zones, gateways are physically, logically, and geographically separated. This provides security and prevents network failures at the zone level.

Building and Configuring a Virtual Network Gateway

Using Azure, you can integrate on-premises servers and network equipment with the cloud and work in a hybrid environment.

A virtual network gateway is the second component required for setting up a connection to an Azure VNet. A point-to-site or site-to-site connection must be created with this device, which is directly connected to the virtual network. Whenever a site-to-site connection is created, the VPN type needs to match the VPN device style on the local network.

Active/active mode ensures high availability by utilizing two IP addresses with separate gateway configurations. The *Border Gateway Protocol (BGP)* is used to exchange routing and reachability information among the various autonomous systems. Each design is assigned an autonomous system number (ASN).

On-premises and Azure are connected through Azure VPN gateways. Azure also lets you create gateways.

In Exercise 2.1 you create a virtual network gateway in the Azure portal.

EXERCISE 2.1

Creating a Virtual Network Gateway in the Azure Portal

1. Log in to a personal or business account in the Azure portal at `portal.azure.com` to open the page shown here.

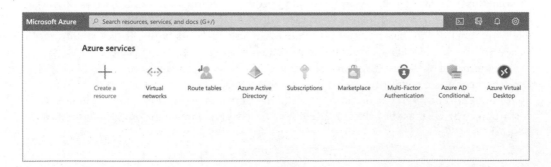

2. Click the Create A Resource button in the Azure portal, enter the virtual network gateway name in the search box, and click Create Virtual Network Gateway to open the screen shown here.

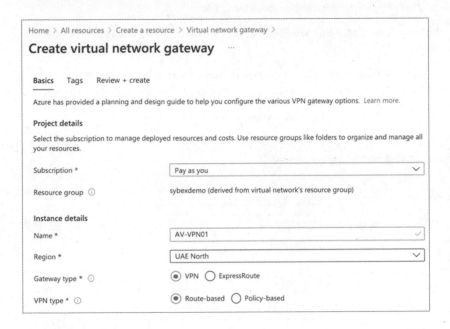

Enter the following information:

Name: **AV-VPN01**

Region: **UAE North**

Gateway Type: VPN

VPN Type: Route-based

SKU: Basic

Generation: Generation1

Virtual Network: **AV-vNET-01** (which you created in Chapter 1)

Gateway Subnet Address Range: **10.40.0.0/24**

Public IP Address: Create New

Public IP address name: **AV-VNet-PUBLICIP**

Among the crucial parameters that you need to provide are the following:

IP address (i.e., the public IP address of the local firewall)

Address space (i.e., the local address space that you want to connect to)

Optionally, Border Gateway Protocol (BGP) settings

Assignment: VPN gateway establishes only Dynamic.

Enable Active/Active Mode: Choose Enabled only if you build an active/active gateway configuration.

BGP should be set to disable unless a setting is explicitly required. By setting a different ASN when creating the VPN gateway or by changing it afterward, you can override this default ASN 65515.

3. Choose Review + Create; once validation passes, click Create to build the VPN gateway as shown here:

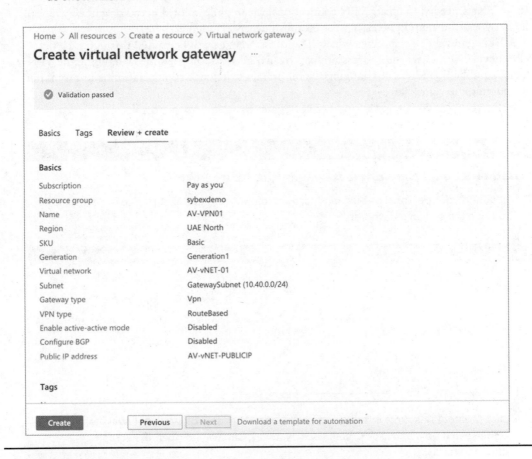

Home > All resources > Create a resource > Virtual network gateway >

Create virtual network gateway ...

✓ Validation passed

Basics   Tags   **Review + create**

Basics

Subscription	Pay as you'
Resource group	sybexdemo
Name	AV-VPN01
Region	UAE North
SKU	Basic
Generation	Generation1
Virtual network	AV-vNET-01
Subnet	GatewaySubnet (10.40.0.0/24)
Gateway type	Vpn
VPN type	RouteBased
Enable active-active mode	Disabled
Configure BGP	Disabled
Public IP address	AV-vNET-PUBLICIP

Tags

Create   Previous   Next   Download a template for automation

Building and Configuring a Local Network Gateway

When a site-to-site connection is created, configurations must be provided for both sides of the connection—Microsoft Azure and on-premises. Even though a local network gateway is created in Azure, it is part of your local network (on-premises) and specifies its configuration. Site-to-site connections between virtual networks and the local network depend on creating the VPN connection. In this section, you'll learn how to use the Azure portal to create and configure a local network gateway.

Local network gateways connect virtual network gateways to on-premises networks. Virtual network gateways are directly connected to virtual networks and contain all the Azure VNets needed to create VPN connections. Meanwhile, a local network gateway has all the network information necessary for establishing a VPN connection.

A VPN gateway also specifies which IP address prefixes will be routed through it to the VPN device. You select the address prefixes from a network on-premises. Changing the VPN device's public IP address or changing the on-premises network configuration is just a matter of updating the values later.

In Exercise 2.2 you create a local network gateway in the Azure portal.

EXERCISE 2.2

Creating a Local Network Gateway in the Azure Portal

1. Log in to your personal or business account in the Azure portal at `portal.azure.com` to open the screen shown here:

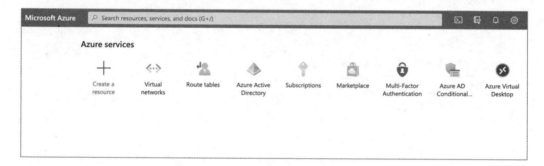

2. Click Create A Resource in the Azure portal, enter the local network gateway name in the search box, and click Create Local Network Gateway to open the screen shown here:

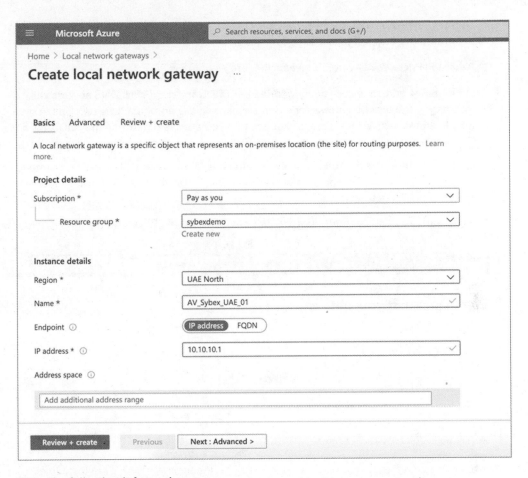

Enter the following information:

Region: UAE North

Name: AV_Sybex_UAE_01

Endpoint: IP Address or FQDN (in our example, IP Address)

IP Address: 10.10.10.1

In this scenario, choose the IP Address option. Enter the IP address allocated by your Internet service provider for on-premises VPN devices. A public IP address is needed to connect the Azure VPN gateway to the on-premises VPN device. As for where the public IP address of the on-premises VPN device can be found, you can use the values listed in the example, but you will have to locate the public IP address afterward. Azure cannot connect otherwise.

If your organization has a dynamic public IP address, that could change after a certain period, usually determined by your ISP. In that case, you can use a constant DNS name with a dynamic DNS service to point to the on-premises VPN device's current public IP address. The Azure VPN gateway will resolve the fully qualified domain name (FQDN) to determine the public IP address to connect to.

Azure VPN gateway key points to consider are as follows:

- Limited IPv4 addresses are not supported per FQDN in Azure VPN. DNS servers will return only the first IP address for a domain name if the domain name resolves to multiple IP addresses. Microsoft recommends that you always determine the FQDN for one IPv4 address to eliminate the uncertainty. IPv6 is not supported.

- Every 5 minutes, the Azure VPN gateway refreshes its DNS cache. For each separate tunnel, the gateway attempts to resolve the FQDN. FQDN resolution is also triggered by resetting the gateway.

3. Optionally, you can configure Border Gateway Protocol (BGP) settings as shown here:

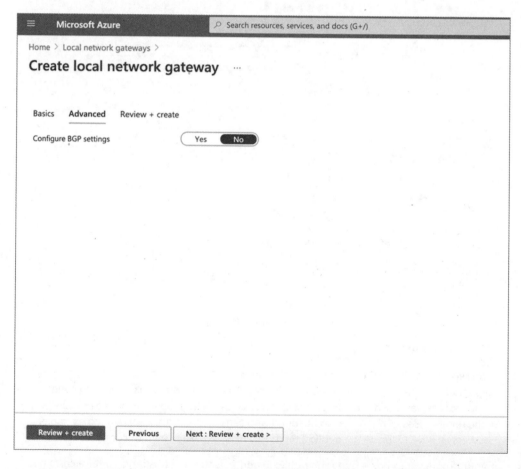

4. Click Review + Create; once validation passes, click Create Local Network Gateway to open the screen shown here:

Building and Configuring an IPsec/IKE Policy

An Internet Protocol Security (IPsec) packet runs on an IP address and provides the basis for sending IP packets securely across the Internet. With IPv6, IPsec must be implemented; with IPv4, doing so is optional. IP packets that have been encrypted are accompanied by security headers, which provide information on the cryptographic protection applied and instructions for decoding. The Encapsulating Security Payload (ESP) header ensures privacy and protects against malicious modification by performing authentication and optional encryption. Network address translation (NAT) routers can be used to transmit traffic through them.

An Authentication Header (AH) is used to protect against malicious modification by performing authentication. This technique cannot protect traffic that traverses NAT routers.

Internet Key Exchange (IKE) exchanges secret keys without user intervention as part of the IPsec protocol set. To set up a secure connection, IKE is used, which gives access to secure keys without requiring any user interaction.

The IKE and IPsec protocols support various combinations of cryptographic algorithms. Security and compliance requirements are met with Azure VPN gateways and encrypted conditions.

The IPsec and IKE protocol standards support various combinations of cryptographic algorithms. Only those gateway SKUs (route-based) configured with IPsec/IKE policy will be protected against IPsec attacks. Azure engineers and architects are only able to specify one combination of policies per connection. You can select all IKE (Main Mode) and IPsec (Quick Mode) algorithms. Policies cannot be specified in part. Consult the vendor specifications of on-premises VPN devices to ensure the policy is supported. Site-to-site connections cannot be established if the guidelines are incompatible.

IPsec policies determine what IP traffic needs to be secured using IPsec and how that traffic should be protected. A computer can only have one IPsec policy active at a time. IP filtering rules are shaped by a variety of selection criteria referred to as *policy conditions*. You can filter traffic by IP address, port, protocol, destination, routing information, and security class. Policy conditions may describe dynamic critical exchange filters or dynamic VPN tunnels for other types of IPsec policies.

Table 2.5 is a list of the cryptographic algorithms supported by Azure key strengths; you can use it in your design based on your organization's requirements.

TABLE 2.5 Supported list of cryptographic algorithms

IPsec/IKE	Options
IKE Encryption	AES256
	AES192
	AES128
	DES3
	DES
IKE Integrity	SHA384
	SHA256
	SHA1
	MD5
DH Group	DHGroup24
	ECP384
	ECP256
	DHGroup14
	DHGroup2048
	DHGroup2
	DHGroup1
	None

IPsec/IKE	Options
IPsec Encryption	GCMAES256
	GCMAES192
	GCMAES128
	AES256
	AES192
	AES128
	DES3
	DES
	None
IPsec Integrity	GCMASE256
	GCMAES192
	GCMAES128
	SHA256
	SHA1
	MD5
PFS Group	PFS24
	ECP384
	ECP256
	PFS2048
	PFS2
	PFS1
	None
QM SA Lifetime	(Optional; default values are used if not specified)Seconds (integer; minimum 300/default 27,000 seconds) KBytes (integer; minimum 1024/default 102,400,000 KBytes)
Traffic Selector	UsePolicyBasedTrafficSelectors ($True/$False; Optional; default is $False if not specified)
DPD timeout	Seconds (integer: minimum 9/maximum 3600; default is 45 seconds)

> Please refer to the following Microsoft site to learn more about crypto-graphic algorithm support:
>
> https://docs.microsoft.com/en-us/azure/vpn-gateway/ipsec-ike-policy-howto#supported-cryptographic-algorithms--key-strengths

For SSL VPN or VNet-to-VNet connections, you must keep certain factors in mind when configuring IPsec/IKE policies. Your organization's on-premises VPN device configuration must match or contain the following algorithms and parameters that you configure in the Azure IPsec/IKE policy.

IKE corresponds to Main Mode or Phase 1 with the following:

- IKE encryption algorithm
- IKE integrity algorithm
- DH Group

IPsec corresponds to Quick Mode or Phase 2 with the following:

- IPsec encryption algorithm
- IPsec integrity algorithm
- PFS Group > * Traffic Selector (if `UsePolicyBasedTrafficSelectors` is used)

If the `UsePolicyBasedTrafficSelectors` option is set to $True in the Azure VPN gateway, it will configure the gateway to connect to a policy-based VPN firewall on-premises. In addition, if you enable `PolicyBasedTrafficSelectors`, ensure your VPN device has the traffic selectors configured with all combinations of your on-premises network (local network gateway) prefixes to/from Azure virtual networks, and not any-to-any.

The security association (SA) lifetimes are local specifications only and do not need to match. The IKE Main Mode SA lifetime is fixed at 28,800 seconds on Azure VPN gateways.

If AES with Galois/Counter Mode (GCM) is used for the IPsec Encryption algorithm, you must choose the same GCM AES algorithm and critical length for IPsec Integrity, such as GCM AES 128 for both.

When an Azure VPN gateway is used, the Dead Peer Detection (DPD) timeout value defaults to 45 seconds. Shorter time delays will cause IKE to rekey more aggressively, resulting in the connection appearing disconnected. This might not be an option in some cases, such as when on-premises locations are far from Azure regions or when the connection could experience packet loss. Microsoft recommends setting a timeout of 30 to 45 seconds.

Configuration Workflow

Exercise 2.3 details how to create and configure an IPsec/IKE policy for a VPN gateway connection. Figure 2.10 shows the high-level design for this exercise.

FIGURE 2.10   VPN gateway connection

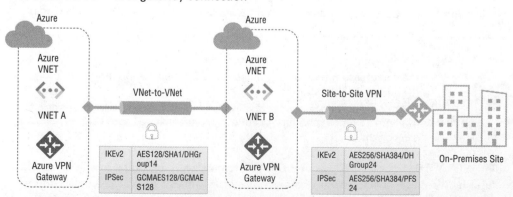

EXERCISE 2.3

Creating and Configuring an IPsec/IKE Policy for a VPN Gateway Connection

This exercise focuses on the following workflow to achieve the design shown in Figure 2.10.

Build the virtual network, VPN gateway, and local network gateway.

Build a new site-to-site VPN connection with an IPSec/IKE policy.

Build a new VNet-to-VNet connection with an IPSec/IKE policy.

You previously performed the first task via the Azure portal in Chapter 1; now you'll explore a way to do this using Azure PowerShell.

1. Begin by declaring your variables. For production (and exam) purposes, change the values as needed. Here you are going to connect VNet B to on-premises site 1.

```
$Sub1          = "pay as you"
$RG1           = "sybexdemo"
$Location1     = "UAE North"
$VNetName1     = "VNETB"
$APPSubName1   = "AppPool"
$DBSubName1    = "DBPool
$GWSubName1    = "GTSubnet"
$VNetPrefix11  = "10.11.0.0/16"
$VNetPrefix12  = "10.12.0.0/16"
$APPSubPrefix1 = "10.11.0.0/24"
$DBSubPrefix1  = "10.12.0.0/24"
$GWSubPrefix1  = "10.12.255.0/27"
$DNS1          = "8.8.8.8"
$GWName1       = "UAEVNETBGW"
$GW1IPName1    = "UAEVNETBGWIP1"
$GW1IPconf1    = "uaegw1ipconf1"
$Connection16  = "UAEVNETBtoOnPrem1"
$LNGName6      = "OnPrem1"
$LNGPrefix61   = "10.61.0.0/16"
$LNGPrefix62   = "10.62.0.0/16"
$LNGIP6        = "131.107.72.22"
```

2. Once the variables are prepared, set up a new resource group based on your subscription:

```
Connect-AzAccount
Select-AzSubscription -SubscriptionName $Sub1
New-AzResourceGroup -Name $RG1 -Location $Location1
```

A virtual network, VNETB, is created with three subnets and a VPN gateway in the following sample. It is best to always use GatewaySubnet as the name of your gateway subnet when substituting values:

```
$Appsub1 = New-AzVirtualNetworkSubnetConfig
-Name $APPSubName1   -AddressPrefix $APPSubPrefix1
$DBsub1 = New-AzVirtualNetworkSubnetConfig
-Name $DBSubName1      -AddressPrefix $DBSubPrefix1
$GWsub1 = New-AzVirtualNetworkSubnetConfig
-Name $GWSubName1   -AddressPrefix $GWSubPrefix1
New-AzVirtualNetwork -Name $VNetName1 -ResourceGroupName $RG1
-Location $Location1 -AddressPrefix $VNetPrefix11,$VNetPrefix12
-Subnet $Appsub1,$DBsub1,$GWsub1
$gw1pip1    = New-AzPublicIpAddress
-Name $GW1IPName1 -ResourceGroupName $RG1 -Location $Location1
-AllocationMethod Dynamic
$vnetb       = Get-AzVirtualNetwork -Name $VNetName1
-ResourceGroupName $RG1
$subnet1     = Get-AzVirtualNetworkSubnetConfig -Name "GatewaySubnet"
-VirtualNetwork $vnetb
$gw1ipconf1 = New-AzVirtualNetworkGatewayIpConfig -Name $GW1IPconf1
-Subnet $subnet1 -PublicIpAddress $gw1pip1
New-AzVirtualNetworkGateway -Name $GWName1 -ResourceGroupName $RG1
-Location $Location1 -IpConfigurations $gw1ipconf1
-GatewayType Vpn -VpnType RouteBased -GatewaySku VpnGw1
New-AzLocalNetworkGateway -Name $LNGName6
-ResourceGroupName $RG1 -Location $Location1
-GatewayIpAddress $LNGIP6
-AddressPrefix $LNGPrefix61,$LNGPrefix62
```

3. Build a site-to-site VPN connection with an IPsec/IKE policy. It is a two-stage process:

   ▪ Build an IPsec/IKE policy.

   ▪ Build the site-to-site VPN connection with the IPsec/IKE policy.

The Azure VPN gateway will only send or accept IPsec/IKE proposals that are encrypted using selected cryptographic algorithms and key strengths when an IPsec/IKE policy is specified on a connection. You must ensure that the VPN device using the link uses the exact policy combination. Site-to-site VPN tunnels cannot be established otherwise.

a. The following example script builds an IPsec/IKE policy with the following algorithms and parameters:

IKEv2: AES256, SHA384, DHGroup24

IPsec: AES256, SHA256, PFS None, SA Lifetime 14400 seconds and 102,400,000 KB

```
$ipsecpolicy6 = New-AzIpsecPolicy -IkeEncryption AES256
-IkeIntegrity SHA384 -DhGroup
DHGroup24 -IpsecEncryption AES256 -IpsecIntegrity SHA256
-PfsGroup None
-SALifeTimeSeconds 14400
-SADataSizeKilobytes 102400000
```

Because you use GCM AES for IPsec (whether for the AZ-700 exam or in production), you must use the same GCM AES algorithm and key length you did for IPsec encryption.

b. The following code builds the site-to-site VPN connection with the IPsec/IKE policy. (You previously created the site-to-site connection.)

```
$vnetbgw = Get-AzVirtualNetworkGateway -Name $GWName1
-ResourceGroupName $RG1
$lng6 = Get-AzLocalNetworkGateway  -Name $LNGName6
-ResourceGroupName $RG1
New-AzVirtualNetworkGatewayConnection -Name $Connection16
-ResourceGroupName $RG1 -VirtualNetworkGateway1 $vnetbgw
-LocalNetworkGateway2 $lng6 -Location $Location1
-ConnectionType IPsec -IpsecPolicies $ipsecpolicy6
-SharedKey 'AzureA12bC3'
```

In addition to adding -UsePolicyBasedTrafficSelectors $True to the create connection cmdlet, you can set up a connection with an on-premises policy-based VPN device.

4. Build a new VNet-to-VNet connection with the IPsec/IKE policy. It is a two-stage process:

- Build a second virtual network, VPN.

- Create a VNet-to-VNet connection with the IPsec/IKE policy.

A VPN gateway configured with the specified cryptographic algorithms and key strengths will only send or accept IPsec/IKE proposals. The IPsec policies must be identical for both connections. Otherwise, the VNet-to-VNet connection will not be established.

a. Begin by declaring your variables. For production (and exam) purposes, change the values as needed. Here we are going to connect VNET A to VNET B:

```
$RG2          = "sybexdrdemo"
$Location2    = "East US 2"
$VNetName2    = "VNETA"
$AppSubName2   = "APP"
```

```
$DBSubName2    = "DB"
$GWSubName2    = "GWSubnet"
$VNetPrefix21  = "10.21.0.0/16"
$VNetPrefix22  = "10.22.0.0/16"
$FESubPrefix2  = "10.21.0.0/24"
$BESubPrefix2  = "10.22.0.0/24"
$GWSubPrefix2  = "10.22.255.0/27"
$DNS2          = "8.8.8.8"
$GWName2       = "VNetAGW"
$GW2IPName1    = "VNetAGWIP1"
$GW2IPconf1    = "gw2ipconf1"
$ConnectionBA  = "VNetBtoVNetA"
$ConnectionAB  = "VNetAtoVNetB"
```

b. Implement your IPsec/IKE policy on the VNet-to-VNet connection. The two gateways in this example belong to the same subscription. As a result, it is possible to build and configure both connections using the same IPsec/IKE policy in the same PowerShell session, as shown in the following code.

```
$vnetagw = Get-AzVirtualNetworkGateway
-Name $GWName1  -ResourceGroupName $RG1
$vnetbgw = Get-AzVirtualNetworkGateway
-Name $GWName2  -ResourceGroupName $RG2
New-AzVirtualNetworkGatewayConnection
-Name $Connection12 -ResourceGroupName $RG1
-VirtualNetworkGateway1 $vnetagw -VirtualNetworkGateway2 $vnetbgw
-Location $Location1 -ConnectionType Vnet2Vnet
-IpsecPolicies $ipsecpolicy2 -SharedKey 'AzureA1b2C3'
New-AzVirtualNetworkGatewayConnection
-Name $Connection21 -ResourceGroupName $RG2
-VirtualNetworkGateway1 $vnetbgw -VirtualNetworkGateway2 $vnetagw
-Location $Location2 -ConnectionType Vnet2Vnet
-IpsecPolicies $ipsecpolicy2 -SharedKey 'AzureA1b2C3'
```

Once steps 1 to 4 are complete, the connection will be established in just a few minutes, and the network design will be complete.

Diagnosing and Resolving VPN Gateway Connectivity Issues

An Azure virtual network cannot connect to an on-premises network after deploying a site-to-site VPN connection between the on-premises and Azure VNet. This section provides troubleshooting steps to help you resolve this problem. When you lose cross-premises VPN connectivity within one or more site-to-site VPN tunnels, you may need to reset an Azure VPN gateway or gateway connection. Your organization's on-premises VPN device will appear to be functioning correctly but cannot establish a VPN tunnel with Azure.

There are two VM instances, one active and the other on standby. The gateway keeps its current public IP address. When you reset the gateway, the designs are applied again at the gateway after it has rebooted. Thus, you will not need to change the routing configuration of your VPN router with the new public IP address of the Azure VPN gateway.

Resetting the gateway reboots the currently active instance of the Azure VPN gateway immediately. The standby instance will not be available during the failover (a reboot of the active instance). One minute should be the maximum gap. After the first reboot, if the connection is not restored, reissue the same command to reboot the second VM instance (now the active gateway). There will be a slight delay when both instances (active and standby) are rebooted if two reboots are ordered back-to-back. Because of this, the VPN connection will remain down for up to 45 minutes while the VMs are rebooted. If your cross-premises connectivity problem persists after two reboots, you should submit a Microsoft support request via the Azure portal.

Check each IPsec site-to-site (S2S) VPN tunnel's key items listed next before resetting your gateway. Mismatches between the items will result in site-to-site VPN tunnels being disconnected. By verifying and correcting the configurations for your on-premises and Azure VPN gateways, you can avoid unnecessary reboots and disruptions for the other working connections on the gateways.

The Azure VPN reset can be performed via the Azure portal or the PowerShell cmdlet. Exercise 2.4 shows the steps for performing the reset via the Azure portal.

EXERCISE 2.4

Resetting the Azure VPN via the Azure Portal

1. Log in to your personal or business account in the Azure portal at `portal.azure.com` to open the screen shown here:

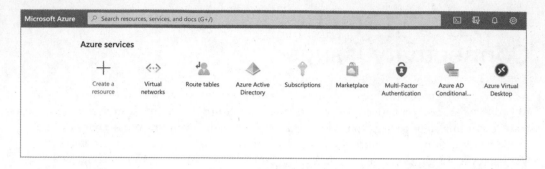

2. Go to the virtual network gateway and click Reset.

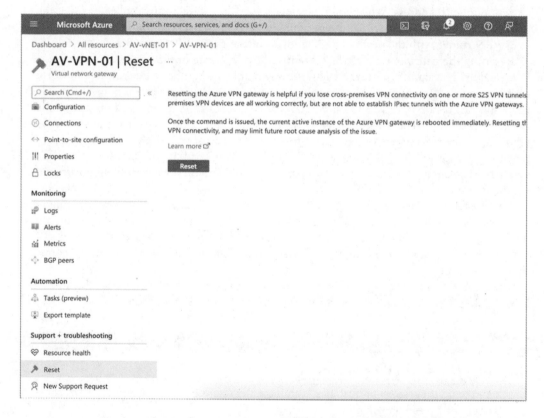

Via Azure PowerShell, the `Reset-AzVirtualNetworkGateway` cmdlet can be used to reset a gateway. Make sure you use the latest version of the PowerShell Az cmdlets before you perform the reset. The following syntax resets a virtual network gateway named VNETAGWV in the SybexDemo resource group:

```
$gw = Get-AzVirtualNetworkGateway -Name VNETAGW
-ResourceGroupName SybexDemo Reset-AzVirtualNetworkGateway
-VirtualNetworkGateway $gw
```

If the problem persists after a reset, follow these steps:

- Build a VNet.
- Build the VPN gateway.
- Make certificates.
- Plan your VPN client address pool.
- Define tunnel model and authentication model.
- Upload root certificate public key information.
- Install an exported client certificate.
- Set up configuration for VPN clients.
- Validate the client connection and connect to Azure.
- Verify that the organization's on-premises VPN device is a Microsoft-validated VPN device and is using a valid operating system version. On-premises devices may need to be validated as a VPN device by the manufacturer to determine compatibility. Verify that the on-premises VPN devices are configured according to recommendations.
  The site to validate the compatibility is:

  https://docs.microsoft.com/en-us/azure/vpn-gateway/
  vpn-gateway-about-vpn-devices#devicetable

3. Verify the security shared key by checking that the on-premises VPN key matches the Azure Virtual Network VPN key. You can view the Azure VPN shared key by using one of the following methods:

   a. Log in to a personal or business account on the Azure portal at `portal.azure.com`.
      Go to the VPN gateway site-to-site connection you deployed, and in the Settings section, click Shared Key.

   b. You can use the Azure PowerShell `Get-AzVirtualNetworkGatewayConnection SharedKey` cmdlet to query and display the shared key used for the connection:

   ```
   Get-AzVirtualNetworkGatewayConnectionSharedKey -Name <Connection name>
   -ResourceGroupName <Resource group name>
   ```

4. Verify the virtual private network peer IP addresses.

   Local network gateway objects in Azure should represent on-premises IP addresses identically. In on-premises devices, you should review the Azure gateway IP definition.

5. Verify user-defined routing (UDR) and network security groups (NSGs) on the gateway subnet.

    Search for and remove UDR and NSGs on the gateway subnet, and then test the results. If the issue is fixed, verify the configuration that the UDR or NSG applied.

6. Verify the on-premises VPN device's external interface address.

    If the VPN device's Internet-facing IP address is contained in the Azure Local Network definition, users might experience sporadic disconnections.

7. Verify that the subnets match Azure policy-based gateways.

    The Azure virtual network address space(s) and on-premises definitions must match precisely, and the gateway and local subnets must match exactly in the on-premises network definitions.

8. Verify the Azure gateway health probe.

    When you navigate to the following URL and open Health Probe, you receive a response from an active VPN gateway:

    `<YourVirtualNetworkGatewayIP>:8081/healthprobe`

    If you don't receive a response, the gateway might not be functioning correctly, or there may be an NSG in the gateway subnet.

9. Verify that the on-premises VPN device has the Perfect Forward Secrecy (PFS) feature enabled.

Perfect Forward Secrecy (PFS) and Forward Secrecy (FS) refers to an encryption system that constantly and automatically changes the keys that are used to encrypt and decrypt information. Using this approach, even if the most recent key is hacked, very little sensitive information will be exposed.

Perfect Forward Secrecy can cause problems with disconnection. Perfect forward secrecy should be disabled if it's enabled in the VPN device. Updating the IPsec policy on the VPN gateway is next.

Choosing a VNet Gateway SKU for Point-to-Site VPNs

A point-to-site VPN is also a helpful alternative to a site-to-site VPN when you have only client machines that need to connect to an Azure VNet. A point-to-site VPN gateway connection permits you to build a secure Azure virtual network from an individual client computer.

A point-to-site link is set by starting it from the client machine. This solution is helpful for telecommuters who want to connect to Azure VNets from a remote location.

A point-to-site VPN can adopt one of the following protocols: OpenVPN Protocol, an SSL/TLS-based VPN protocol, Secure Socket Tunneling Protocol (SSTP), and IKEv2 VPN.

Azure accepts a point-to-site VPN connection with the following authentication methods:

- Native Azure certificate authentication
- Native Azure Active Directory authentication
- Active Directory (AD) domain server

Windows and Mac users use native VPN clients for point-to-site (P2S). Azure provides native clients with a VPN configuration zip file containing settings needed for connections:

- Users install an installer package to configure their VPN client on Windows devices.
- The mobile config file is installed on Mac devices by users.

As part of the zip file, you can also find the values of some basic Azure settings used to create profiles. The key performance indicators (KPIs) include:

- Routes
- The VPN gateway address
- Configured tunnel types
- The root certificate for gateway validation

You must specify the gateway SKU to use to create a virtual network gateway by considering types of workloads, throughputs, features, and SLAs, and determine the appropriate SKU.

You can resize VpnGw SKUs in the same generation (except for resizing the Basic SKU because it is a legacy SKU and has feature limitations). Creating a new gateway based on the generation and SKU size combo will allow you to switch from Basic to another VpnGw SKU.

There is a separate limit for point-to-site connections. One VpnGw1 has 128 SSTP and 250 IKEv2 connections, for example.

Specifying the gateway SKU when creating a virtual network gateway is essential. Choose the SKU that best meets your needs depending on the types of workloads, throughputs, features, and SLAs. Table 2.6 shows the available SKUs as of this writing.

A single gateway collectively aggregates multiple tunnels to measure the aggregate throughput benchmark shown in Table 2.6. Maximum throughput of 1 Gbps is possible on a single tunnel. Site-to-site and point-to-site are the benchmarks for an aggregate VPN throughput. The limitation of throughput can adversely affect a site-to-site connection if you have many point-to-site connections. As a result of Internet traffic conditions and the behavior of business applications, aggregate throughput benchmark performance cannot be assured by Microsoft.

TABLE 2.6   VNet gateway SKU for point-to-site VPNs

VPN gateway generation	SKU	S2S/ VNet-to-VNet	P2S SSTP connections	P2S IKEv2/ OpenVPN connections	Aggregate throughput benchmark	BGP support	Zone-redundant
Gen1	Basic	Max 10	Max 128	Not supported	100 Mbps	No	No
Gen1	VpnGw1	Max 30	Max 128	Max 250	650 Mbps	Yes	No
Gen1	VpnGw2	Max 30	Max 128	Max 500	1 Gbps	Yes	No
Gen1	VpnGw3	Max 30	Max 128	Max 1000	1.25 Gbps	Yes	No
Gen1	VpnG-w1AZ	Max 30	Max 128	Max 250	650 Mbps	Yes	Yes
Gen1	VpnG-w2AZ	Max 30	Max 128	Max 500	1 Gbps	Yes	Yes
Gen1	VpnG-w3AZ	Max 30	Max 128	Max 1000	1.25 Gbps	Yes	Yes
Gen2	VpnGw2	Max 30	Max 128	Max 500	1.25 Gbps	Yes	No
Gen2	VpnGw3	Max 30	Max 128	Max 1000	2.5 Gbps	Yes	No
Gen2	VpnGw4	Max 30	Max 128	Max 5000	5 Gbps	Yes	No
Gen2	VpnGw5	Max 30	Max 128	Max 10000	10 Gbps	Yes	No
Gen2	VpnG-w2AZ	Max 30	Max 128	Max 500	1.25 Gbps	Yes	Yes
Gen2	VpnG-w3AZ	Max 30	Max 128	Max 1000	2.5 Gbps	Yes	Yes
Gen2	VpnG-w4AZ	Max 30	Max 128	Max 5000	5 Gbps	Yes	Yes
Gen2	VpnG-w5AZ	Max 30	Max 128	Max 10000	10 Gbps	Yes	Yes

Table 2.7 shows the IKEv2 policies that are allowed to be configured on VPN gateways for point-to-site VPNs.

TABLE 2.7 Point-to-site VPN IKEv2 policies

Cipher	Integrity	Pseudo-random function (PRF)	Diffie-Hellman Group (DH-Group)
GCM_AES256	GCM_AES256	SHA384	GROUP_24
GCM_AES256	GCM_AES256	SHA384	GROUP_14
GCM_AES256	GCM_AES256	SHA384	GROUP_ECP384
GCM_AES256	GCM_AES256	SHA384	GROUP_ECP256
GCM_AES256	GCM_AES256	SHA256	GROUP_24
GCM_AES256	GCM_AES256	SHA256	GROUP_14
GCM_AES256	GCM_AES256	SHA256	GROUP_ECP384
GCM_AES256	GCM_AES256	SHA256	GROUP_ECP256
AES256	SHA384	SHA384	GROUP_24
AES256	SHA384	SHA384	GROUP_14
AES256	SHA384	SHA384	GROUP_ECP384
AES256	SHA384	SHA384	GROUP_ECP256
AES256	SHA256	SHA256	GROUP_24
AES256	SHA256	SHA256	GROUP_14
AES256	SHA256	SHA256	GROUP_ECP384
AES256	SHA256	SHA256	GROUP_ECP256
AES256	SHA256	SHA256	GROUP_2

Table 2.8 shows the IPsec policies that are allowed to be configured on VPN gateways for point-to-site VPNs.

> **TIP** Using a point-to-site VPN, you can connect from your office or your home workstation to the Azure network so that you can use those resources as if they were local and extend the Azure VM network to them.

TABLE 2.8 Point-to-site VPN IPsec policies

Cipher	Integrity	PRF
GCM_AES256	GCM_AES256	GROUP_NONE
GCM_AES256	GCM_AES256	GROUP_24
GCM_AES256	GCM_AES256	GROUP_14
GCM_AES256	GCM_AES256	GROUP_ECP384
GCM_AES256	GCM_AES256	GROUP_ECP256
AES256	SHA256	GROUP_NONE
AES256	SHA256	GROUP_24
AES256	SHA256	GROUP_14
AES256	SHA256	GROUP_ECP384
AES256	SHA256	GROUP_ECP256
AES256	SHA1	GROUP_NONE

Configuring RADIUS, Certificate-Based, and Azure AD Authentication

Your organization's devices can be safely connected to Azure's private, secure virtual network over the public Internet. Converge the on-premises office network with the Azure network. Provide rules that limit the access a particular device has to portions of your on-premises network, or to all of it at once. You can also access the virtual network in Azure by redirecting all Internet traffic from devices to the access server. You can access even local networks if they choose to allow VPN connections.

Azure's point-to-site solution is cloud-based and can be set up quickly to meet the growing demand for remote working. The capacity can efficiently and promptly be increased and then turned off when no longer needed. OpenVPN Protocol, SSL/TLS-based VPN protocols, Secure Socket Tunneling Protocol (SSTP), and IKEv2 VPN protocols can be used for point-to-site VPNs.

Figure 2.11 shows the high-level design pattern we will use in the upcoming two sections.

FIGURE 2.11   Point-to-site VPN connection with Azure

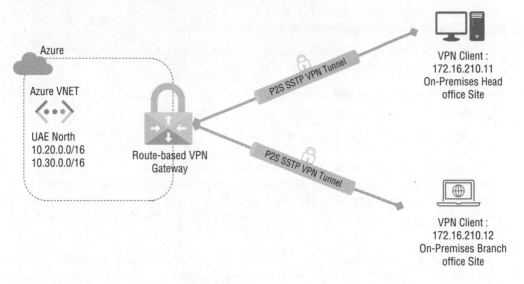

To establish a point-to-site VPN connection with Azure, the user must first authenticate. A user can do so in three ways:

- Native Azure certificate authentication
- Native Azure Active Directory authentication
- Active Directory (AD) domain server

Configuration Workflow for Native Azure Certification Authentication

In this section, we will explore the configuration for native Azure certification authentication—the end user authenticates using their client certificate. Client certificates are generated from the root certificates and are then installed on client computers. You can generate a self-signed certificate or use a root certificate generated by an enterprise solution.

When the VPN gateway establishes a point-to-site connection, the VPN gateway validates the client certificate. A root certificate needs to be uploaded to Azure for validation.

Following is an overview of the step-by-step workflow used to build a point-to-site VPN using Azure certificate authentication:

Step 1: Build a VNet.

Step 2: Build the VPN gateway.

Step 3: Make certificates.

Step 4: Plan your VPN client address pool.

Step 5: Define the tunnel and authentication models.

Step 6: Upload the root certificate public key information.

Step 7: Install an exported client certificate.

Step 8: Set up configuration for VPN clients.

Step 9: Validate the client connection and connect to Azure.

The rest of this section provides a detailed discussion of how a point-to-site VPN can be built using Azure certificate authentication.

Step 1: Build a virtual network.   Please refer to Chapter 1, Exercise 1.1, "Deploying a Virtual Network with the Azure Portal," for step-by-step instructions.

You should coordinate with your on-premises network administrator when establishing a virtual network as part of a cross-premises architecture to carve out an IP address range that can be used specifically for this virtual network. Traffic will be routed unexpectedly if there are duplicate address ranges on both sides of the VPN connection. Moreover, if this virtual network is connected to another virtual network, the address space cannot overlap with that virtual network. Make sure the network configuration is appropriate.

Step 2: Build a VPN gateway.   Please refer to Exercise 2.1: "Creating a Virtual Network Gateway in the Azure Portal" for step-by-step instructions.

RADIUS or IKEv2 authentication is not supported by the Basic gateway SKU. You should not use the Basic SKU if you plan on having Mac clients connect to your virtual network.

Don't add network security groups (NSGs) to the subnet when working with gateway subnets. If you add a network security group to this subnet, you might experience problems with your virtual network gateway (VPN and ExpressRoute gateways).

Step 3: Make certificates.   Route-based VPN users can use certificates issued by certificate authorities (CAs) if authentication is required. The VPN tunnel's gateways are configured to trust the CA that signed the other gateway's certificate. If the primary identity information is correct, all certificates issued by a trusted CA are accepted as valid and can be added, renewed, or changed without affecting VPN traffic. A certificate must always be provided for gateways connected to Stonesoft IPsec VPN clients. VPN clients can be identified with certificates, but the use of certificates isn't required.

In VNets over point-to-site VPN connections, certificates are used to authenticate clients. The public key information is uploaded to Azure once a root certificate is obtained. Azure then considers the root certificate as "trusted" to connect point-to-site (P2S) to the virtual network. In addition, each client computer is issued a certificate derived from the trusted root certificate. Client certificates are used to authenticate clients when they attempt to connect to a VNet.

For the root certificate, the certificate administrator needs to obtain the CER file. Alternatively, you can use self-signed certificates generated with an enterprise solution. The root certificate file should be exported as a Base64 encoded X.509 CER file. The file can be uploaded later to Azure.

Step 4: Plan your VPN client address pool.   Next, plan the VPN client address pool. The address pool is private and specified by you. A dynamic IP address is assigned dynamically to VPN clients connecting over point-to-site VPNs. When connecting from on-premises, use a private IP range that does not overlap with the VNet you want to access. A configured address pool is equally divided among all the configured protocols if SSTP is one of them.

Once the virtual network gateway is built (step 2), go to the Settings section of the Virtual Network Gateway Wizard. In Settings, choose Point-To-Site Configuration. Click Configure Now to open the configuration page.

In the Point-To-Site Configuration Wizard, add the private IP address range that you want to use in the Address Pool field. Once the range is specified, the client receives a dynamic IP address. The minimum subnet mask is /29 for active/passive and /28 for active/active configuration.

Figure 2.12 shows the point-to-site configuration.

FIGURE 2.12   Point-to-site configuration

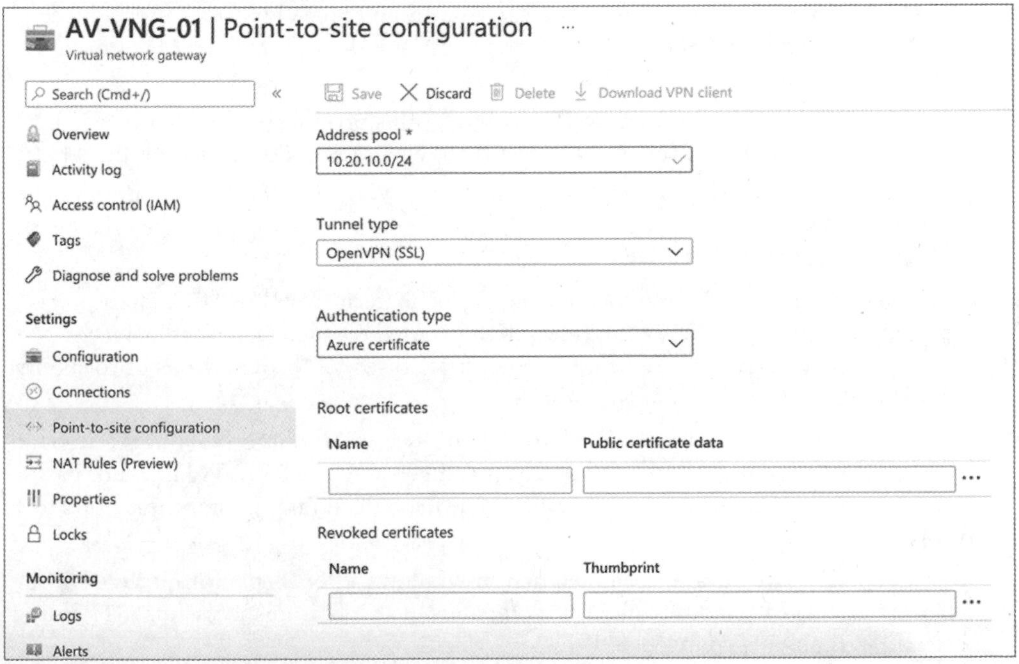

Step 5: Define the tunnel and authentication models. In this step you configure tunnel types and the authentication model.

Your gateway uses the Basic SKU when no tunnel type or authentication type is displayed on the point-to-site configuration page. The Basic SKU does not support IKEv2 or RADIUS authentication. If you want to define the tunnel and authentication types, then it can be achieved by deleting the existing basics gateway SKU and creating it with a different one if these settings are required.

You can use the five tunnel types shown in Figure 2.13 to configure the point-to-site VPN:

FIGURE 2.13 Tunnel types

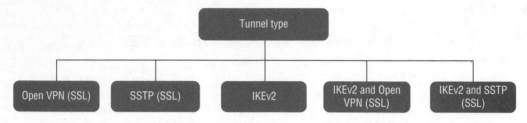

- OpenVPN is a virtual private network system that allows you to create secure point-to-point or site-to-site connections in routed or bridged configurations and remote access. It is an SSL-based solution that can penetrate firewalls since most firewalls open the outbound TCP port that 443 SSL uses. You can connect to OpenVPN from Android (versions 11.0 and later), iOS (versions 11.0 and later), Windows, Linux, or Mac (macOS versions 10.13 and later).

- Secure Socket Tunneling Protocol (SSTP) is Microsoft's proprietary SSTP over SSL. It can penetrate firewalls because most firewalls allow outgoing TCP traffic on the 443 SSL port.

- Internet Key Exchange version 2 (IKEv2) is an encrypted tunneling protocol used by VPNs to encrypt Internet traffic.

- IKEv2 is a protocol used for authenticating keying material for IPsec. IKE Phase 1 was replaced by IKEv2 (RFC 2409). In IPsec, IKEv2 is used to implement secure packet exchange at the IP layer. It can be used to negotiate IPsec VPN connections or to specify encryption and authentication algorithms.

- IKEv2 and Open VPN(SSL) is a standards-based IPsec VPN solution that uses outbound UDP ports 500 and 4500 and an IP protocol number of 50. IKEv2 VPN may not pass through proxy servers or firewalls because some firewalls do not permit these ports to be opened.

- IKEv2 and SSTP are always attempted first in Windows VPN clients for mixed environments consisting of Windows and Mac computers. If IKEv2 is unsuccessful, SSTP is used instead. You can only connect via IKEv2 on Mac OS X.

Let's do deep dive with OpenVPN from the AZ-700 exam perspective. VPNs are accessed through software called OpenVPN. The OpenVPN client is built into a lot of devices since it is widely used in the industry. Setting up a new VPN connection to a virtual network in Azure should be easier with OpenVPN support for Azure VPN gateways.

Today's digital-first world demands a high level of security and privacy. By setting up a VPN with OpenVPN in Azure, you can offer online privacy and security as well as an additional layer of protection. This applies to both personal and enterprise usage. No matter what Wi-Fi network or hotspot end users connect to, they will remain secure when they are connected to the Internet via a VPN.

The following figure 2.14 depicts the Point-to-site VPN.

FIGURE 2.14   Point-to-site VPN

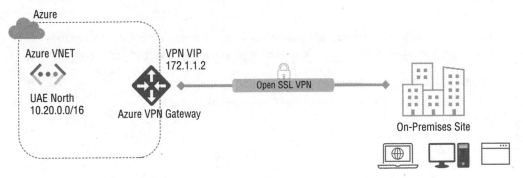

You can use either the Azure portal or the Azure PowerShell method to deploy the OpenVPN solution.

In the Azure portal, navigate to your preferred virtual network gateway and select Point-To-Site Configuration. For Tunnel Type, choose OpenVPN (SSL) from the drop-down menu, as shown in Figure 2.15.

FIGURE 2.15   Point-to-site configuration: Tunnel Type

AV-VNG-01 | Point-to-site configuration ···
Virtual network gateway

Search (Cmd+/) «   💾 Save ✕ Discard 🗑 Delete ⬇ Download VPN client

- 🛡 Overview
- 📓 Activity log
- 👥 Access control (IAM)
- 🏷 Tags
- 🔧 Diagnose and solve problems

Settings

- 🖥 Configuration
- ⊘ Connections
- ‹–› Point-to-site configuration
- ⊞ NAT Rules (Preview)
- ⫴ Properties

Address pool *

| 10.20.10.0/24 | ⌄ |

Tunnel type

| OpenVPN (SSL) | ⌄ |

- OpenVPN (SSL)
- SSTP (SSL)
- IKEv2
- IKEv2 and OpenVPN (SSL)
- IKEv2 and SSTP (SSL)

Name   Public certificate data

To configure this using PowerShell, use the `Get-AzVirtualNetworkGateway` and `Set-AzVirtualNetworkGateway` cmdlets to configure OpenVPN.

```
$gw = Get-AzVirtualNetworkGateway -ResourceGroupName SybexDemo -name AV-VNG-01
Set-AzVirtualNetworkGateway -VirtualNetworkGateway $gw -VpnClientProtocol OpenVPN
```

Clients running strongSwan on Android and Linux and native clients for iOS and macOS must use only IKEv2 tunnels for connectivity. Clients on Windows will first try IKEv2, and if that fails, they will use SSTP. For OpenVPN tunnel connections, you can use the OpenVPN client.

Step 6: Upload the root certificate public key information.   Next, select the Authentication type; you must choose Azure Certificate, as shown in Figure 2.16.

FIGURE 2.16   Point-to-site configuration: Authentication Type

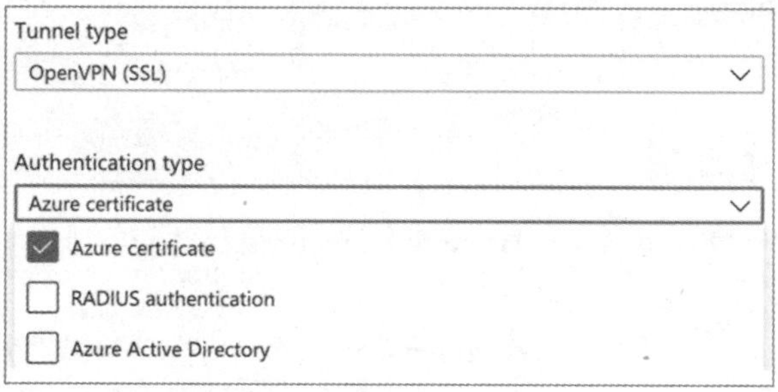

Authentication of a client using a client certificate generated from the trusted root certificate can be carried out once the public certificate data has been uploaded to Azure.

As a next step, you have to export the root certificate as a Base-64 encoded X.509 (CER) as shown in Figure 2.17. A text editor can open the certificate when the certificate is exported in CER format. Private keys do not have to be exported to the Azure portal.

FIGURE 2.17   Point-to-site configuration: Root Certificate

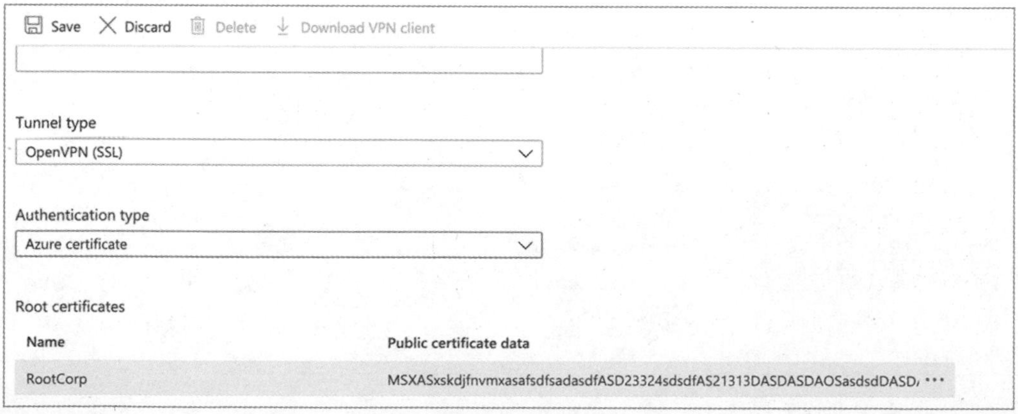

Notepad is an excellent text editor for opening the certificate. If you need to copy the certificate data, make sure you copy it in one continuous line without carriage returns. It may be necessary to change the view in the text editor to Show Symbol/Show All Characters to see carriage returns and line feeds. Copy as one continuous line and paste it in the Public Certificate Data field. The number of trusted root certificates you can attach is 20.

Commit your configuration by clicking the Save button in the Point-to-Site Configuration Wizard.

Step 7: Install an exported client certificate.   You need to install a client certificate to establish point-to-site (P2S) from a computer other than the one on which you generated the client certificates. If you export a client certificate, you need to use the password created when you exported it.

You should ensure that the client certificate and the entire certificate chain are exported as PFX files. Otherwise, the client's computer will not authenticate correctly since the root certificate information is not present.

Step 8: Set up configuration for VPN clients.   Using P2S, each computer connects to the virtual network gateway using a VPN client natively installed in the operating system. Client configuration packages are used to configure each VPN client. Client configuration packages contain VPN gateway–specific settings. Adding VPN connections to Windows computers can be done without a VPN client by modifying the VPN settings.

Following is the list of supported operating systems to use point-to-site VPN:

- Windows Server OS 2008 R2 (64-bit only)
- Windows Server OS 2012 (64-bit only)
- Windows Server OS 2012 R2 (64-bit only)
- Windows Server OS 2016 (64-bit only)
- Windows Server OS 2019 (64-bit only)
- Windows Client OS 8.1 (32-bit and 64-bit)
- Windows Client OS 10
- macOS version 10.11 or later
- Linux (strongSwan)
- iOS

Select Download VPN Client at the top of the point-to-site configuration page. In addition to generating the configuration package, client configuration packages are created within a few minutes. You may not see any indications during this process until the packet has been generated.

Configure the VPN client according to the architecture of the Windows operating system. Use the VpnClientSetupAmd64 installer package for 64-bit processors. Choose the VpnClientSetupX86 installer package for 32-bit processor architectures.

Step 9: Validate the Client Connection and Connect to Azure.   On the client computer, make sure the client certificate is installed. If you are using native Azure certificate authentication, a client certificate must be provided. Navigate to the Manage User Certificates section to find the client certificate. Current User/Personal/Certificates contains the client certificate.

Verify that the root certificate has been installed by selecting Trusted Root Certification Authorities/Certificates under Manage User Certificates. To complete authentication, you must see the root certificate listed.

To connect, select In-Network Settings and click VPN. There is a name for the virtual network connected to the VPN connection.

Use an elevated command prompt to confirm that your VPN connection is active. Look at the results. In your configuration, you specified Point-to-Site VPN Client Address Pool as the address pool for receiving IP addresses.

From the Microsoft AZ-700 exam, keep in mind that client computers do not automatically reestablish their VPN connections by default. In point-to-site VPNs, autoreconnect and Dynamic DNS are not supported.

Configuration Workflow for Native Azure Active Directory

In this section, we explore the native *Azure Active Directory*. Native Azure Active Directory authentication allows users to connect to Azure using their Azure Active Directory (AD) credentials. As of this writing, only Windows 10 and the OpenVPN protocol are supported by native Azure AD authentication. VPN using Azure AD requires native authentication, which supports conditional access and multifactor authentication.

The following is an overview of the step-by-step workflow for building a point-to-site VPN using Azure AD:

Step 1: Validate the Azure AD tenant.

Step 2: Create Azure AD tenant users.

Step 3: Set up Azure AD authentication on the VPN gateway.

Step 4: Install and configure a VPN client.

The first step in the workflow is to validate whether the Azure AD tenant exists or not. If it exists, proceed with step 2. Otherwise, request your identity and platform administrator of Azure to provision Azure AD tenant for your enterprise organization.

> **NOTE** More information about Azure AD tenant setup is available here: `https://docs.microsoft.com/en-us/azure/active/directory/fundamentals/active/directory-access-create-new-tenant`

The second step in the workflow, Azure AD user creation, is also performed by the identity and platform administrator at the enterprise organization.

> **NOTE** More information about Azure AD user creation is available here: `https://docs.microsoft.com/en-us/azure/active/directory/fundamentals/add-users-azure-active/directory`

Exercise 2.5 begins with workflow step 3.

EXERCISE 2.5

Building a Point-to-Site VPN Using Azure Active Directory

1. Log in to a personal or business account in the Azure portal at `portal.azure.com` to open the page shown here:

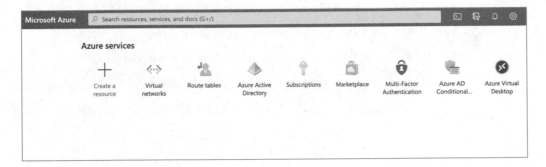

2. Go to your virtual network gateway and choose Point-To-Site Configuration.

3. Select OpenVPN (SSL) as the Tunnel type to enable Azure AD authentication at the VPN gateway.

4. Choose Azure Active Directory under Authentication, then fill in the following information (step 3 in the workflow overview).

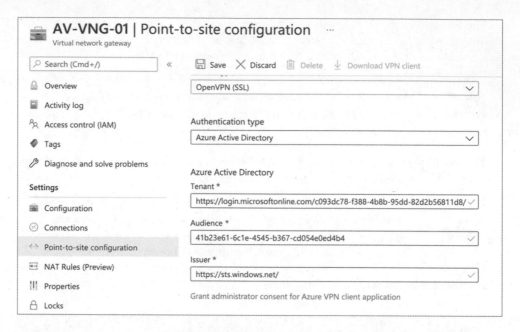

Tenant: Tenant ID for the Organization Azure AD tenant:

    login.microsoftonline.com/{AzureAD TenantID}

Audience: Application ID of the Azure VPN Azure AD Enterprise App

>   Type 41b23e61-6c1e-4545-b367-cd054e0ed4b4 for Azure Public

>   Type 51bb15d4-3a4f-4ebf-9dca-40096fe32426 for Azure Government

>   Type 538ee9e6-310a-468d-afef-ea97365856a9 for Azure Germany

>   Type 49f817b6-84ae-4cc0-928c-73f27289b3aa for Azure China 21Vianet

Issuer: URL of the Secure Token Service along with an Organization Azure AD Tenant ID

    sts.windows.net/{AzureAD TenantID}

5.   Set up a virtual network connection via a point-to-site VPN using Azure AD from the client machine (step 4 in the workflow overview).

You can download the Azure VPN client from the following site. This VPN client also supports certificate-based client profiles and RADIUS client profiles, as shown here:

    https://go.microsoft.com/fwlink/?linkid=2117554

Azure VPN Client

Microsoft Corporation • Productivity

The Azure VPN Client lets you connect to Azure securely from anywhere in the world. It supports Azure Active Directory, certificate-based and RADIUS authentication.

E ESRB   EVERYONE

Free

Get

⚠ See System Requirements

6. Build and download the client profile by choosing Download VPN Client in the Point-To-Site Configuration Wizard; extract the downloaded zip file and browse to the unzipped `AzureVPN` folder.

   The Azure VPN client must be downloaded and configured for every endpoint to access the VNet via the VPN client. A client profile can be created, exported, and imported to multiple endpoints so that you can configure various endpoints together.

7. Note where the `azurevpnconfig.xml` file is located. The Azure VPN Client imports the `azurevpnconfig.xml` file directly into the Azure VPN application. Also, every user who needs to connect can be emailed this file. To join Azure VPN successfully, you must have Azure AD credentials.

Configuration Workflow for Windows Active Directory

In this section, we explore the configuration for the *Active Directory (AD) domain server*. AD Domain authentication allows users to authenticate with the organization's domain credentials. In addition, RADIUS servers need to be integrated with AD servers. Existing RADIUS deployments can also be incorporated.

In Azure VNet or on-premises, RADIUS servers can be deployed. Through the Azure VPN gateway, the RADIUS server and connecting devices pass authentication messages back and forth. Access to the RADIUS server through the gateway is essential. Azure must be connected to those sites via a VPN site-to-site connection for on-premises sites with RADIUS servers.

Additionally, RADIUS servers support AD certificates. Point-to-site certificate authentication can be done using organization's certificates and RADIUS server instead of Azure certificates. Certificates that have been revoked or that are root certificates are not required on Azure. That is an advantage.

Additionally, RADIUS servers can integrate with external identity management systems. Point-to-site VPNs now offer multiple authentication options, including multifactor authentication.

Use a RADIUS server to handle user authentication in a point-to-site configuration. In Azure VNet or on-premises, the RADIUS server can be deployed. For high availability, you can configure two RADIUS servers.

By logging in with their organization's domain credentials, users can access Azure. The AD server must be integrated with a RADIUS server. Organizations can also leverage RADIUS deployments.

Your Azure VNet or on-premises RADIUS server can be located anywhere. Azure requires a site-to-site VPN connection from the Azure site to the RADIUS server located on-premises. The VPN gateway connects to the RADIUS server and forwards authentication messages to and from the connected device during authentication. It must be possible for the VPN gateway to reach the RADIUS server.

As well as Active Directory, RADIUS servers integrate with other external identity systems. Point-to-site VPNs now have a variety of authentication options, including multifactor authentication. The vendor documentation for your RADIUS server should include a list of the identity systems it integrates with. When connecting to RADIUS servers on-premises, you can only use a site-to-site connection VPN. No ExpressRoute connections are allowed.

The following are the key design and deployment considerations:

- Public IP addresses are required for VPN gateways in this mode of authentication.
- VPN Type should be route-based.
- The RADIUS server should be deployed before deployment.

Creating your virtual network gateway requires first requesting the IP address resource. The IP address of the resource is dynamically assigned during the creation of the VPN gateway. Currently, only dynamic IP addresses can be allocated for public resources. There is no option to request a static public IP address.

The IP address, however, does not change once it has been assigned to your VPN gateway. Only when a gateway is deleted and re-created will the public IP address change. This setting doesn't change if you resize, reset, or upgrade your VPN gateway internally.

Figure 2.18 shows the high-level design pattern we will use in this section.

FIGURE 2.18   Authenticating using Active Directory domain server(AD DS)

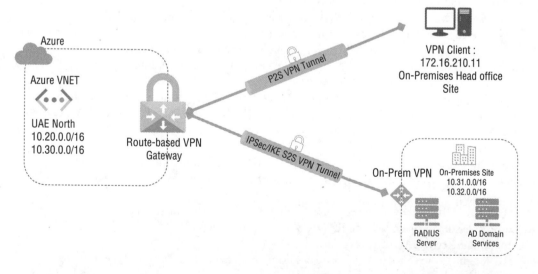

Here is an overview of the step-by-step workflow for building a point-to-site VPN using domain authentication:

Step 1: Create a VNet and public IP.

Step 2: Set up an on-premises RADIUS server.

Step 3: Deploy a VPN gateway.

Step 4: Add the RADIUS server and client address pool.

Step 5: Install and configure a VPN client.

The rest of this section provides a detailed discussion of how a point-to-site VPN can be built using domain authentication.

Step 1: Create a VNet and public IP.   Please refer to Chapter 1, Exercise 1.1, "Deploying a Virtual Network with the Azure Portal" for step-by-step instructions.

Step 2: Set up an on-premises RADIUS server.   The deployment and configuration guides provided by your RADIUS vendor contain detailed instructions for this step.

In this book, we are not focusing on setting up the RADIUS server. However, we will cover what is required from the RADIUS server. RADIUS clients must be configured on the on-premises VPN gateway as a RADIUS client. The virtual network gateway subnet you created earlier in this chapter must be specified when adding this RADIUS client.

RADIUS clients must use the IP address and the shared secret of the RADIUS server once the installation and configuration are complete. The CA IP address of a RADIUS server VM should be used if the RADIUS server is in the Azure VNet.

Step 3: Deploy a VPN gateway. Please refer to Exercise 2.1, "Creating a Virtual Network Gateway in the Azure Portal," for step-by-step instructions.

RADIUS or IKEv2 authentication is not supported by the Basic gateway SKU. You should not use the Basic SKU if you plan on having Mac clients connect to your virtual network.

`VpnType` and `RouteBasedType` are the required `-GatewayType` and `-VpnType` parameters.

Step 4: Add the RADIUS server and client address pool. Select the RADIUS authentication method via the Azure portal Point-to-Site Configuration Wizard, as shown in the following Exercise 2.6.

Exercise 2.6 begins with workflow step 4.

Key Considerations for Setting Your Environment

Clients connected to VPNs receive their IP addresses from the address pool. Choose an IP address range that does not overlap the on-premises location or the VNet from which you will connect. Make sure you have configured a large enough address pool.

It is possible to specify the RADIUS server by name or by IP address. The VPN gateway may not recognize on-premises servers if the name is selected, and the server resides on-premises. The IP address of the server should be specified in that case. An on-premises RADIUS server's secret should match what you have entered for the RADIUS secret.

Point-to-site (P2S) connections require that the client device from which you connect be configured. Windows, macOS, and Linux clients can establish P2S VPN connections.

RADIUS authentication offers several methods of authentication: username/password and certificates, among others. Each authentication method requires a different VPN client configuration. VPN clients can be configured using client configuration files that contain the required settings.

Authentication can be configured to use, or not use, Active Directory. Be sure to authenticate all users connecting through RADIUS, regardless of the scenario.

You can only configure username/password authentication for the EAP-MSCHAPv2 when configuring username/password authentication.

EXERCISE 2.6

Building a Point-to-Site VPN Using Active Directory Domain Server(AD DS)

1. Log in to a personal or business account in the Azure portal at `portal.azure.com` to open the page shown here:

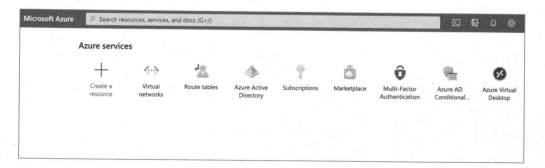

2. Go to your virtual network gateway and choose Point-To-Site Configuration.

3. Select OpenVPN (SSL) as the Tunnel type to enable RADIUS authentication at the VPN gateway.

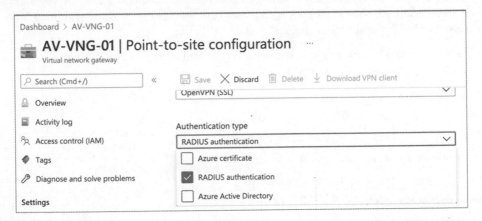

The following graphic shows the Azure portal choices. Primary Server IP Address and Primary Server Secret are mandatory; Secondary Server IP Address and Secondary Server Secret are optional.

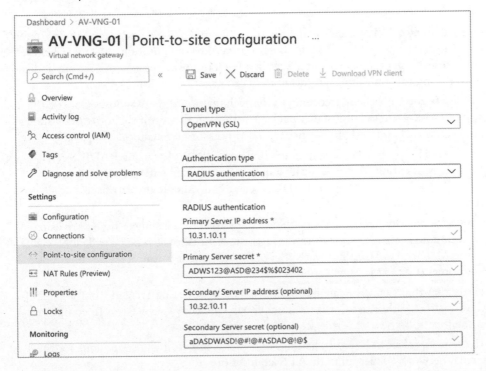

This completes, the configuration of Point-to-Site VPN Using Active Directory Domain Server(AD DS).

Step 5: Install and configure a VPN client.   Set up configuration for the VPN client. Using P2S, each computer connects to the virtual network gateway using a VPN client natively installed in the operating system. Client configuration packages are used to configure each VPN client. Client configuration packages contain VPN gateway-specific settings. Adding VPN connections to Windows computers can be done without a VPN client by modifying the VPN settings.

The following is the list of client-supported operating systems for P2S VPNs. Azure supports Windows, Mac, and Linux:

- Windows Server OS 2008 R2 (64-bit only)
- Windows Server OS 2012 (64-bit only)
- Windows Server OS 2012 R2 (64-bit only)
- Windows Server OS 2016 (64-bit only)
- Windows Server OS 2019 (64-bit only)
- Windows Client OS 8.1 (32-bit and 64-bit)
- Windows Client OS 10
- macOS version 10.11 or later
- Linux (strongSwan)
- iOS

Select Download VPN Client at the top of the Point-To-Site Configuration page (refer to the previous image). In addition to generating the configuration package. Client configuration packages are created within a few minutes. You may not see any indications during this time until the packet has been generated.

Configure the VPN client according to the architecture of the Windows OS. Use the `VpnClientSetupAmd64` installer package for 64-bit processors. Choose the installer package `VpnClientSetupX86` for a 32-bit processor architecture.

The EAP-TLS protocol can be used to configure VPN clients using RADIUS certificate authentication. To authenticate a user for a VPN, an enterprise certificate is typically used. Check that your RADIUS server can validate the certificates of all connected users.

On the client computer, make sure the client certificate is installed. If you are using native Azure certificate authentication, a client certificate must be provided. Navigate to the Manage User Certificates section to find the client certificate. `Current User/Personal/Certificates` contains the client certificate.

Verify that the root certificate has been installed by selecting Trusted Root Certification Authorities/Certificates under Manage User Certificates. To complete authentication, the root certificate must be listed.

To connect, select In-Network Settings and click VPN. You will see a name for the virtual network connected to the VPN connection.

Use an elevated command prompt to confirm that your VPN connection is active. Look at the results. In your configuration, you specified the Point-To-Site VPN Client Address Pool as the address pool for receiving IP addresses.

A virtual network gateway in Azure lets you view and terminate current point-to-site VPN sessions. A session update occurs every five minutes. Updates may take several minutes.

List active sessions with this PowerShell command:

```
Get-AzVirtualNetworkGatewayVpnClientConnectionHealth -VirtualNetworkGatewayName
<name of the azure virtual network gateway>  -ResourceGroupName <name of the azure
 resource group>
```

To disconnect a session, you need to copy the VpnConnectionId and use the following PowerShell command:

```
Disconnect-AzVirtualNetworkGatewayVpnConnection -VirtualNetworkGatewayName <name of
the azure virtual network gateway> -ResourceGroupName <name of the azure resource
group> -VpnConnectionId <VpnConnectionId of the session you want to disconnect>
```

Diagnosing and Resolving Client-Side and Authentication Issues

This section lists the top five common point-to-site connection problems that you might experience with respect to point-to-site VPN client-side issues.

1. A certificate could not be found.
2. The message received was unexpected or badly formatted.
3. A certificate chain processed but terminated.
4. The target URI is not specified.
5. The Azure VPN custom script failed.

Problem Statement 1   A certificate could not be found.

Possible Symptom   The following error message appears when you attempt to connect to an Azure virtual network using the VPN client:

```
A certificate could not be found that can be used with this Extensible
Authentication Protocol. (Error 798)
```

Cause   The client certificate is not present in the respective location.

Solution The following certificates should be in their respective location.

Certificate name	Certificate location
AzureClient.pfx	Current User\Personal\Certificates
AzureRoot.cer	Local Computer\Trusted Root Certification Authorities

Problem Statement 2   The message received was unexpected or badly formatted.

Possible Symptom   The following error message appears when you attempt to connect to an Azure virtual network gateway using IKEv2:

```
The network connection between your computer and the VPN server could not be
established because the remote server is not responding
```

Cause   Windows without support for IKE fragmentation results in the problem.

Solution   IKEv2 is supported on Windows 10 and Windows Server 2016. IKEv2 must be installed, and the following registry key value must be set on a local computer to use it. SSTP is only available for operating systems before Windows 10.

Registry key name	Path	Value
DisableCertReqPayload REG_DWORD key	HKEY_LOCAL_MACHINE\SYSTEM\ CurrentControlSet\Services\ RasMan\ IKEv2\	1

Problem Statement 3   A certificate chain processed but terminated.

Possible Symptom   The following error message appears when you attempt to connect to an Azure virtual network by using the VPN client:

```
The message received was unexpected or badly formatted. (Error 0x80090326)
```

Cause   The following conditions must be valid for this problem to occur:

- In the gateway subnet, the user-defined routes (UDRs) are set incorrectly with the default route.
- An Azure VPN gateway does not upload the root certificate public key.
- A corrupted or expired key is being used.

Solution Here are the steps you can take to fix this issue:

1. Remove the UDR from the gateway subnet. Verify that the UDR is properly forwarding all traffic.
2. The Azure portal can be used to check whether the root certificate has been revoked. Remove the root certificate and re-upload it if it is not revoked.

Problem Statement 4 The target URI is not specified.

Possible Symptom The following error message appears:

`File download error. Target URI is not specified.`

Cause The gateway type is incorrect.

Solution There must be only one type of VPN gateway, VPN, and it must be route-based.

Problem Statement 5 The Azure VPN custom script failed.

Possible Symptom The following error message appears when you attempt to connect to an Azure virtual network by using the VPN client:

`Using a shortcut might cause this problem when you connect to the site-to-point VPN.`

Solution Rather than opening the VPN package through a shortcut, open it directly.

Refer to the following Microsoft site for the latest common recurring problems, causes, and solutions:

`https://docs.microsoft.com/en-us/azure/vpn-gateway/vpn-gateway-troubleshoot-vpn-point-to-site-connection-problems`

VPN Client Configuration Location in Windows

VPN client configuration files are in the following location: `C:\Users\%UserName%\AppData\Roaming\Microsoft\Network\Connections<VirtualNetworkId>`.

VPN Certificate Location in Windows

The `AzureClient.pfx` certificate is in `Current User\Personal\Certificates`.

The `Azuregateway-GUID.cloudapp.net` certificate is in `Current User\Trusted Root Certification Authorities`.

The `AzureGateway-GUID.cloudapp.net` and `AzureRoot.cer` certificates are in `Local Computer\Trusted Root Certification Authorities`.

VPN Client Log Location in Windows

VPN log files are in the following location: `C:\Users\%UserName%\AppData\Local\Package\Microsoft.AzureVPN_GUID\LocalState\Logfiles`.

Use Wireshark for Mac OS X

IKE_SA packets should be filtered on isakmp. Under Payload: Security Association, you can find the SA proposal details. If you do not see a server response, verify that you have enabled the IKEv2 protocol on the Azure Gateway Configuration page in the Azure portal.

Summary

You should now be able to deploy, configure, and manage VPNs for your organization to connect on-premises devices and Azure. You should also be able to design and implement a hybrid connectivity solution that will address the short- and long-term goals of your organization's global enterprise IT footprint.

When an organization migrates resources and services to Azure, as network architects and engineers, we must set up communication between the on-premises and Azure workloads securely and reliably.

This chapter covered two topics for the AZ-700 exam: Design, implement, and manage a site-to-site VPN connection, and Design, implement, and manage a point-to-site VPN connection.

In the next chapter, you will learn to design, implement, and manage Azure ExpressRoute.

Exam Essentials

Understand the design pattern for a site-to-site VPN connection for high availability. There are two Azure VPN gateway instances in active/standby configuration for every Azure VPN gateway. If the active instance is interrupted for maintenance or unplanned, the standby instance automatically takes over (failover) and resumes the S2S VPN or VNet-to-VNet connections. You have many options for configuring Azure VPN gateways for cross-premises and VNet-to-VNet connectivity, including multiple on-premises VPN devices, an active/active Azure VPN gateway, and a combination of both.

Know the appropriate VNET gateway SKU. Virtual network gateways send encrypted traffic between your virtual network and your on-premises location over a public network. There can only be one gateway per type of virtual network. It is imperative to make sure the gateway type you choose is appropriate for your configuration when creating a virtual network gateway. You can specify either VPN or ExpressRoute. You must specify the gateway SKU you want to use when creating a virtual network gateway. Select the SKU that meets your requirements based on your workloads, throughput, features, and service level agreements.

Know when to use policy-based VPN vs. route-based VPN. Policy-based: to encrypt/decrypt traffic through IPsec tunnels, VPN devices use a combination of prefixes from both networks. Firewalls typically filter packets, and packet filtering and processing engines encrypt and decrypt IPsec tunnels.

It is vital to understand if you want to set up a VPN-based mesh topology in Azure or between multiple on-premises sites. There is an active/active VPN, and redundancy is available.

Route-based: any-to-any (wildcard) traffic selectors are used by VPN devices, with routing/forwarding tables directing traffic to different IPsec tunnels. IPsec tunnels are typically built on router platforms, which model each IPsec tunnel as a network interface or VTI (virtual tunnel interface).

A single S2S VPN connection is allowed, either with an on-premise firewall or another VNet in Azure. Mesh topologies cannot be used. Although peering is available within Azure, the VNet gateway can still only connect to a single on-premises endpoint.

There is no active/active VPN. Redundancy is not available.

Understand how to build and configure a local network gateway. Local network gateways are objects that represent your on-premises location for routing purposes (the site). The site gets a name by which Azure can refer to it, and the IP address of your on-premises VPN device is specified. The VPN gateway also specifies the IP address prefixes that will be routed to the VPN device through the VPN gateway. Prefixes selected by you are those on your on-premises network. If the on-premises network changes or you need to change the public IP address for the VPN device, you can easily update the values.

Each FQDN can have only one IPv4 address. The Azure VPN gateway will use the first IP address that the DNS servers return if the domain name resolves to multiple IP addresses. To eliminate uncertainty, Microsoft recommends that your FQDN resolve to a single IPv4 address. IPv6 is not supported.

A DNS cache for the Azure VPN gateway is updated every five minutes. For disconnected tunnels, the gateway only attempts to resolve FQDNs, and resetting the gateway will also trigger FQDN resolution.

Understand how to build and configure a IPsec/IKE policy. Different cryptographic algorithms can be combined with the IPsec and IKE protocols. IKE/IPsec policy is only available for the following gateway SKUs: VpnGw1*5 and VpnGw1AZ*5AZ (route-based) and Standard and High Performance (route-based).

These are the five steps for configuring an IPsec/IKE policy for S2S VPN or VNet-to-VNet connections: start with the creation of a virtual network and a VPN gateway. Then create a local network gateway for a cross-premises connection or another virtual network and gateway for a VNet-to-VNet connection. Next, create an IPsec/IKE policy with selected algorithms and parameters, and then create a connection (IPsec or VNet2VNet) with the IPsec/IKE policy. Finally, add, update, or remove an IPsec/IKE policy for an existing connection.

Understand how to build and configure a virtual network gateway.   Requirements to create a VPN gateway are the VPN device, a static public IP address, and a valid Azure subscription.

The virtual network gateway uses gateway subnets. When configuring your virtual network, you specify an IP address range for the gateway subnet, and these addresses will be used to access virtual network gateway resources.

The process consists of these steps: create and manage a VPN gateway using the Azure portal, create a virtual network, and create a VPN gateway.

Know the method for diagnosing and resolving virtual network gateway connectivity issues.   Through a VPN gateway connection, you can establish secure, cross-premises connectivity between your Azure virtual network and your IT infrastructure on-premises.

VPN gateway connections can fail for a variety of reasons. For example, if you attempt to connect an on-premises network to an Azure virtual network with a site-to-site VPN connection, the connection will stop working and you cannot reconnect.

You can troubleshoot multiple VPN gateway-related events using diagnostic logs, including configuration activity, VPN tunnel connectivity, IPsec logging, BGP route exchanges, and point-to-site advanced logging.

Know how to choose an appropriate virtual network gateway SKU.   The gateway SKU you want to use is required when you're creating a virtual network gateway. Identify the SKU that satisfies your needs based on the workload, throughput, features, and service level agreements.

Basic and different types of VpnGw SKUs exist for a point-to-site VPN.

VpnGw SKUs may be resized within the same generation, except for the Basic SKU, a legacy SKU with limited features. The Basic SKU VPN gateway must be deleted and a new gateway with the desired generation and size created.

Know the prerequisites for authenticating point-to-site using RADIUS.   When deploying RADIUS authentication on a point-to-site connection, you will need the following prerequisites: a route-based VPN gateway and a RADIUS server for user authentication. You can deploy the RADIUS server on-premises or within the Azure virtual network. Connecting Windows devices to the VNet will require the installation of a VPN configuration package. A VPN client configuration package contains the settings that enable a VPN client to connect via point-to-site.

Know the prerequisites for authenticating point-to-site using certificate-based authentication.   When deploying certificate authentication on a point-to-site connection, you will need the following: a route-based VPN gateway, the public key (CER file) for a root certificate, a client certificate that is generated from the root certificate, and a VPN client configuration.

You must have a subscription to Azure. You can activate your MSDN subscriber benefits or sign up for a free Azure account if you don't already have one.

Know the prerequisites for authenticating point-to-site using Azure AD.   It would be best if you verified that you have a tenant in Azure AD, a Global Admin account, and a user account.

You must have a subscription to Azure. You can activate your MSDN subscriber benefits or sign up for a free Azure account if you don't already have one.

Know how to generate the VPN client configuration file.   You can generate the VPN client configuration files using the Azure portal or Azure PowerShell.

To connect to a virtual network using point-to-site (P2S), you must configure the client device that will connect to the virtual network. Using Windows, macOS, or Linux client devices, you can establish P2S VPN connections.

There are many authentication options available with RADIUS: username/password, certificate, and other authentication types. Depending on the authentication type, the VPN client configuration may differ.

Review Questions

1. Application service managers need dynamic IP addresses for specific resources on their VNets. Which SKU should be chosen?

   A. Basic SKU

   B. Standard SKU

   C. Advanced SKU

   D. Enterprise SKU

2. What are the two types of virtual private networks?

   A. Policy-based

   B. Dynamic

   C. Route-based

   D. Static

3. Which of the following should you consider when creating Azure VPN gateway connections?

   A. Network throughput

   B. Network backbone

   C. Azure VPN gateway SKU

   D. All of the above

   E. All of the above and a few more

4. For a point-to-site VPN type connection, which of the following statements is valid? (Choose two.)

   A. Site-to-site supports both the active/active and the active/passive pattern.

   B. Site-to-site supports only the active/active pattern.

   C. Point-to-site and ExpressRoute support the active/passive pattern and the active/active pattern.

   D. Point-to-site and ExpressRoute supports only the active/passive pattern.

5. Dynamic routing is supported by which of the following?

   A. Site-to-site

   B. Point-to-site

   C. Both (site-to-site and point-to-point)

   D. Point-to-point only

6. Site-to-site VPN supports which of the following?

   A. OpenVPN

   B. IPsec

   C. Both (OpenVPN and IPsec)

   D. None of the above

7. Azure peering is supported by which of the following?

   A. Point-to-site

   B. Site-to-site

   C. Point-to-point

   D. ExpressRoute

8. ExpressRoute supports which of the following?

   A. BGP (Border Gateway Protocol)

   B. Static routing

   C. Active/passive DR

   D. Both A and C

9. Which of the following can VPN gateways support?

   A. Point-to-point and site-to-site

   B. Policy-based and route-based

   C. Point-to-point, site-to-site, and ExpressRoute

   D. None of the above

10. Policy-based VPN gateway devices can support a maximum of how many site-to-site connections?

    A. 30

    B. 10

    C. 1

    D. Unlimited

11. For policy-based VPN devices, which of the following statements is valid?

    A. Policy-based VPN devices do not support the IKE v1 protocol.

    B. Policy-based VPN devices support the IKE v1 and IKE v2 protocols.

    C. Policy-based VPN devices do not support the IKE v1 and IKE v2 protocols.

    D. Policy-based VPN devices support only the IKE v1 protocol.

12. What is the maximum throughput in a site-to-site VPN connection?

    A. 1 GB per tunnel

    B. 1 GB per VM

    C. 10 GB per tunnel

    D. 10 GB per VM

13. Azure VPN gateway cost is based on which of the following? (Choose all that apply.)

    A. Compute cost for the VPN gateway

    B. Number of application transactions through the tunnel

    C. Data transfer speed

    D. Egress of data transfer

14. Which are types of route-based VPN gateways? (Choose all that apply.)

    A. Basic

    B. Standard

    C. High performance

    D. Super fast

15. Which of the following are the steps for building a point-to-site VPN using Azure certificate authentication?

    A. Build the VNet, build the VPN gateway, create certificates, plan for the VPN client address pool, define the tunnel and authentication models, and upload the root certificate.

    B. Build the VPN gateway, build the VNet, create certificates, plan for the VPN client address pool, define the tunnel and authentication models, and upload the root certificate.

    C. Either A or B is correct.

    D. Follow all steps in A and then set up VPN clients to complete.

16. What are the default settings when a VPN gateway is configured for high availability?

    A. Active/standby

    B. Active/active

    C. Dual redundancy

    D. None of the above

17. What type of server is required to authenticate a user connecting through a point-to-site connection using Active Directory Domain Server(AD DS)?

    A. Active Directory from on-premises

    B. Active Directory from Azure

    C. Azure AD

    D. RADIUS

18. Which authentication types are supported by a point-to-site VPN connection?

    A. RADIUS authentication

    B. Certificate-based authentication

    C. OpenVPN authentication

    D. Azure Active Directory authentication

    E. All of the above

19. To resolve point-to-site VPN client-side issues, you have checked the client OS compatibility, certificate deployed, and configuration files deployed in client OS. What are the other potential items to be checked for any issue?

    A. Verify that NIC drivers exist in the client OS.

    B. Check local firewall policies and make sure the execution of apps is not blocked.

C. Check if client-specific hibernate or sleep time is configured after a specified or sufficient time.

D. Check Internet access, valid client credentials, DNS server resolvable, VPN server reachable, and responding.

E. None of the above; you have checked all required items already.

F. All of the above.

20. Which of the following Tunnel type configuration is supported by point-to-site configuration? (Choose all that apply.)

A. OpenVPN (SSL)

B. SSTP (SSL)

C. IKEv2 and OpenVPN (SSL)

D. IKEv2 and SSTP (SSL)

E. OpenVPN (SSL) and SSTP (SSL)

Chapter
3

Design, Deploy, and Manage Azure ExpressRoute

THE MICROSOFT AZ-700 EXAM OBJECTIVES COVERED IN THIS CHAPTER INCLUDE:

✓ **Design, implement, and manage Azure ExpressRoute**

- Choose between provider and direct model (ExpressRoute Direct)
- Design and implement Azure cross-region connectivity between multiple ExpressRoute locations
- Select an appropriate ExpressRoute SKU and tier
- Design and implement ExpressRoute Global Reach
- Design and implement ExpressRoute FastPath
- Choose between private peering only, Microsoft peering only, or both
- Configure private peering
- Configure Microsoft peering
- Create and configure an ExpressRoute gateway
- Connect a virtual network to an ExpressRoute circuit
- Recommend a route advertisement configuration
- Configure encryption over ExpressRoute
- Implement Bidirectional Forwarding Detection
- Diagnose and resolve ExpressRoute connection issues

When an organization migrates resources and services to Azure, as a network architect or engineer, you must set up communication between the on-premises and Azure workloads securely and reliably. Azure ExpressRoute lets you connect your enterprise networks on-premises with Microsoft cloud services, such as Azure and Microsoft 365. Using ExpressRoute, you can connect your on-premises network to the Microsoft cloud without experiencing the delays, disruptions, and fluctuating bandwidth that can plague a VPN connection between a corporate network and the Microsoft cloud. At a very high level, this chapter focuses on how Azure ExpressRoute works, what it does, and when you should use it.

To get the most out of this chapter, you must have experience with networking concepts, including IP addressing, DNS, and routing. You must also know how to connect to networks such as VPNs or WANs, and you should be familiar with the Azure portal and Azure PowerShell.

By the end of this chapter, you will be able to design, deploy, and manage Azure ExpressRoute for your organization to connect between on-premises and Azure networks. You should also be able to design and implement a hybrid connectivity solution that will address the short- and long-term goals of your organization's global enterprise IT footprint.

Getting Started with Azure ExpressRoute

In addition to the Azure VPN gateway (covered in Chapter 2, "Design, Deploy, and Manage a Site-to-Site VPN Connection and Point-to-Site VPN Connection"), many organizations use the Azure ExpressRoute method to connect Azure virtual networks (VNets) to on-premises resources. This is because a VPN may not meet every business requirement. A VPN, for example, is limited to a maximum network speed of 1.25 Gbps. Business users who need higher speeds shouldn't opt for VPNs. In other words, all traffic is also sent over the public Internet, which can be prohibitively expensive for some end users.

Microsoft *Azure ExpressRoute*, which uses private connectivity, serves as an alternative method of connecting your on-premises networks to Microsoft Azure cloud services. It meets most enterprise organizations' needs, including security and resiliency.

An ExpressRoute circuit represents a logical connection between your on-premises infrastructure and Microsoft cloud services through a connectivity provider, as shown in Figure 3.1.

FIGURE 3.1   ExpressRoute circuits

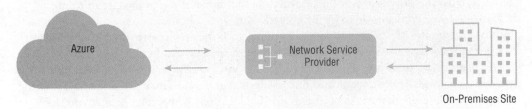

Your organization can choose from a variety of ExpressRoute circuit types. You can connect each circuit to the on-premises infrastructure through different connectivity providers, either within the same region or in different regions.

Service providers help organizations connect their on-premises infrastructure to the Azure cloud using ExpressRoute. Network service providers offer a wide variety of services.

> Visit the following URL for the latest list of all ExpressRoute connectivity service providers:
>
> https://docs.microsoft.com/en-us/azure/expressroute/
> expressroute-locations#partners

Organizations worldwide can gain performance advantages through an ExpressRoute connection since the connection is directly made through the ExpressRoute connectivity provider's infrastructure to the edge of Microsoft's network. However, even with ExpressRoute, you may experience suboptimal connectivity since the Internet is typically provided through partnerships and relationships among telecommunications providers.

The provider takes direct responsibility for setting up an optimized connection with the Microsoft network when the organization chooses a dedicated and private connection with a connectivity provider.

To provide fiber-optic connectivity at speeds of up to 10 Gbps, Azure offers a service via ExpressRoute. As shown in Figure 3.2, the ExpressRoute feature allows you to connect to Azure from your on-premises network through a Microsoft Enterprise Edge (MSEE) router. The MSEE router sits on the edge of its network, and in most cases, the connection will also be through a router in your on-premises network.

FIGURE 3.2   ExpressRoute with MSEE

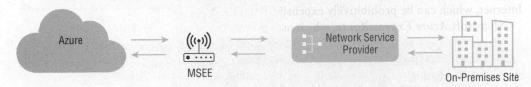

Since ExpressRoute does not traverse the public Internet, bandwidth is more reliable. You must trust the provider with the information that flows through the circuit to use the ExpressRoute configuration. With ExpressRoute Direct, you can connect directly to a physical port on the MSEE router without dealing with the service provider. You can also choose ExpressRoute Direct if the organization needs greater bandwidth.

Microsoft refers to ExpressRoute connections as *circuits*. The ExpressRoute service depends on ExpressRoute circuits and ExpressRoute gateways. There are different zones for ExpressRoute circuits that are deployed at peering locations or peering, or *meet-me*, locations. ExpressRoute gateways are deployed in Azure. You can choose from several plans that have different bandwidth limitations. Each circuit has a fixed bandwidth.

There is a mapping between a circuit and a connectivity provider and peering site. Each peering shares the bandwidth for the circuit. Circuits may peer with up to two peers. Different routings are used depending on the kind of service requested through these peerings, such as Microsoft peering and private peering:

- Through Microsoft peering, you can access Microsoft public services such as Microsoft 365, Dynamics 365, and Power Platform.

- Through private peering, you can access private Azure resources such as Azure VMs.

Border Gateway Protocol (BGP) is primarily used by autonomous systems to exchange network routing and reachability across autonomous systems. The internal BGP is known as iBGP (internal), and the external BGP is eBGP (external). Border Gateway Protocol 4 (BGP-4) is defined by RFC 4271.

Peerings consist of two independent BGP sessions, each configured redundantly for high availability. Resiliency requires that these sessions transit over different physical connections.

What is BGP?

BGP (Border Gateway Protocol) is the Internet's postal service. When someone drops a letter in a mailbox, the postal service processes this piece of mail and selects the quickest, most efficient route to deliver it. Furthermore, when data is sent across the Internet, BGP is responsible for checking all possible routes that data can travel and choosing the best path, which usually involves switching between autonomous systems.

The Internet works because of BGP. It makes it possible for data to be routed over the Internet. BGP ensures that fast and efficient communication can occur.

The public Internet is advertised with the IP addresses of Microsoft's cloud services. Microsoft also advertises the relevant IP prefixes for the services specified by the peerings for those circuits through the ExpressRoute BGP connection.

It is the responsibility of your network team to set up internal routing to send data to Microsoft. They must:

- Prioritize the route of Microsoft online services traffic through the subnet connected to ExpressRoute.
- Configure routing for Microsoft online services traffic via a BGP session for the subnet connected to ExpressRoute.

The traffic that flows to Microsoft datacenters will be routed to the appropriate service within the datacenter, and Microsoft manages that process.

Azure ExpressRoute has no up-front cost, no termination fees, and charges for only what the organization uses.

Azure ExpressRoute lets you establish a private connection between Azure datacenters and the on-premises or co-location environments. They are faster, more reliable, and have lower latency than typical Internet connections since ExpressRoute links don't go over the public Internet.

High availability is a crucial feature of ExpressRoute. A circuit of 5 Gbps has redundant connections, so the actual bandwidth allocated to the circuit is 10 Gbps. For short bursts, Microsoft will let an organization use the extra bandwidth.

The following list details the critical features offered by Azure ExpressRoute:

Layer 3 Connectivity   The Azure cloud network uses BGP (described earlier in this section), an industry-standard dynamic routing protocol to exchange routes between your organization's on-premises network, your instances in Azure, and Microsoft's public addresses. As part of Microsoft's cloud service, ExpressRoute establishes multiple BGP sessions with the on-premises networks for different traffic profiles.

Redundancy   A Microsoft Enterprise Edge (MSEE) router is located at each ExpressRoute location and connects two ExpressRoute circuits. Microsoft wants a double BGP connection from the connectivity provider/network edge to each MSEE. Network connectivity service providers use redundant devices to ensure that your connections are properly handed over to Microsoft. Redundant devices/Ethernet services may not be deployed depending on your decision at the organization's end.

Connectivity to Microsoft Cloud Services   Connecting to Azure and Microsoft 365 via ExpressRoute enables access to your services securely and reliably.

Connectivity to All Regions within a Geopolitical Region   Connecting to Microsoft via a peering location will allow organizations to access regions within the geopolitical region. For example, if you connect to Microsoft in Amsterdam through ExpressRoute, you have access to all Microsoft cloud services hosted in Northern and Western Europe.

Global Connectivity with ExpressRoute Premium   *ExpressRoute Premium* allows your organization to extend connectivity across geopolitical boundaries. If connecting to Microsoft via ExpressRoute from Amsterdam, for example, your organization can use all Microsoft cloud services regardless of where the cloud is hosted. The cloud services can also be accessed in South America or Australia and North and West Europe. However, national clouds are excluded from consideration.

On a standard ExpressRoute circuit, an organization can have 10 virtual network connections, whereas Premium consumers can have 100 virtual network connections.

When ExpressRoute is deployed within the same geographic region as Dynamics 365, ExpressRoute Premium is not required.

Local Connectivity with ExpressRoute Local   When you enable Local SKU, you can transfer data to an ExpressRoute location close to the Azure region. Local includes data transfer in its port charge.

On-Premises Connectivity between Locations with ExpressRoute Global Reach   Connecting ExpressRoute circuits from on-premises networks to ExpressRoute Global Reach allows data exchange between on-premises sites.

For example, imagine an oil and gas company with a private datacenter in Abu Dhabi connected to an ExpressRoute circuit in the UAE North region. Another private datacenter in Dubai is connected to an ExpressRoute circuit in UAE Central. These two ExpressRoute circuits allow the organization to connect its private datacenters with ExpressRoute Global Reach.

Microsoft's network will carry the cross-datacenter traffic from the on-premises networks in this configuration.

Rich Connectivity Partner Ecosystem   Across ExpressRoute's ecosphere, connectivity providers, and system integrators are continuously growing.

ExpressRoute Direct   *ExpressRoute Direct* offers customers a direct connection to the Microsoft global network through peering locations worldwide. Dual 100 Gbps connectivity is provided by ExpressRoute Direct, which supports active/active connections. Organizations can take advantage of the ExpressRoute Direct service through a service provider.

Connectivity to National Clouds   For specific segments and geopolitical regions, Microsoft operates fully isolated cloud environments.

Bandwidth Choices and Dynamic Scaling   Azure customers can choose between a variety of ExpressRoute bandwidth options. There are various bandwidths to choose from, such as 50 Mbps, 100 Mbps, 200 Mbps, 500 Mbps, 1 GB, 2 GB, 5 GB, and 10 GB. Without hindering an organization's connections, ExpressRoute circuit bandwidth can be increased (under the best conditions).

Key Use Case for ExpressRoute

Azure and Microsoft 365 are two cloud services that organizations can link to using ExpressRoute. The ExpressRoute service lets organizations extend their on-premises networks into the Microsoft cloud through a private connection with the help of a connectivity provider. Connectivity is provided by an IPVPN (any-to-any) or Ethernet network or virtual cross-connection through a connectivity provider at a co-location facility. In addition to better reliability, faster speeds, consistent latencies, and more security, ExpressRoute connections do not use the public Internet.

With ExpressRoute, you can connect to Azure quickly and reliably with bandwidths up to 100 Gbps, making it ideal for use cases such as data migration, replication for business continuity, disaster recovery, and high availability scenarios. For instance, shifting large amounts of data with a high-performance computing application or moving large virtual machines between user acceptance testing environments to development environments from Azure to your on-premises production environments is a cost-effective solution.

With ExpressRoute, it is possible to extend an on-premises datacenter, adding compute and storage capacity to existing datacenters in the cloud. Organizations can benefit from the public cloud's scale, economies, and performance without sacrificing network performance, thanks to Azure's high throughput and fast latencies.

Using ExpressRoute's predictable, reliable, and high-throughput connections, you can deploy hybrid applications and develop on-premises and Azure applications without compromising security or performance. For instance, an intranet application in Azure authenticates and manages corporate end users without leaking the data to the public Internet.

For the Microsoft AZ-700 exam, keep the following in mind:

- A private connection created through Azure ExpressRoute allows you to connect Azure datacenters, Azure services, and infrastructure on-premises or a co-location facility.

- The time taken for failure deduction to be computed over an ExpressRoute circuit can be reduced from a few 10ths of a second to less than a second by enabling Bidirectional Forwarding Detection (BFD).

- Connectivity can be extended across geopolitical boundaries with ExpressRoute Premium. For example, if you connect to Microsoft in the UAE North region through ExpressRoute, you will have access to all Microsoft cloud services hosted in all regions worldwide.

- Site-to-site VPN connections can be configured as a backup for ExpressRoute in the cloud. Virtual networks linked through Azure's private peering path are eligible for this connection.

ExpressRoute Deployment Model

In four different deployment models, you can build and configure connectivity between consumers' on-premises networks and the Microsoft cloud. Network connectivity service providers may offer one or more connectivity deployment models, such as cloud exchange co-location, point-to-point Ethernet connection, any-to-any (IPVPN) connection, and ExpressRoute Direct.

Let's start with the co-located at a cloud exchange deployment model, shown in Figure 3.3. In this case, you can order virtual cross-connections to the Microsoft cloud through the co-location provider's Ethernet exchange. Through cross-connections on Layer 2 or 3, Microsoft cloud infrastructure and your on-premises infrastructure in co-location facilities can be integrated.

FIGURE 3.3   ExpressRoute with cloud exchange co-location

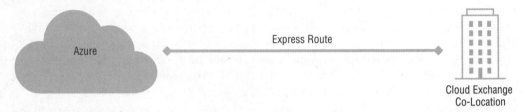

The second model is point-to-point Ethernet connection, through which you can connect Microsoft cloud customers' on-premises datacenters or remote offices. Microsoft cloud customers' on-premises datacenters can connect to Microsoft cloud via managed Layer 3 or Layer 2 connections through point-to-point Ethernet. Figure 3.4 shows the deployment model for a point-to-point Ethernet connection.

FIGURE 3.4   ExpressRoute with a point-to-point Ethernet connection

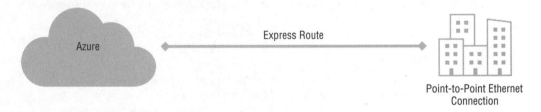

In the third network model, any-to-any (IPVPN), you can integrate Microsoft's cloud WAN with your organization's WANs. A VPN provider (likely an MPLS VPN) provides connectivity between cloud client datacenters and branch offices. Connecting a Microsoft cloud to your WAN makes it appear like any other branch office. Your WAN provider typically manages Layer 3 connectivity.

Figure 3.5 shows the any-to-any (IPVPN) deployment model.

The fourth deployment model is direct from ExpressRoute sites; you can connect directly into Microsoft's global network from a peering location strategically placed around the globe. The ExpressRoute Direct router provides dual 100 Mbps or 10-Gbps connectivity. Active/active connectivity is supported at scale. Figure 3.6 shows the deployment model direct from ExpressRoute sites.

FIGURE 3.5 ExpressRoute with any-to-any (IPVPN) connection

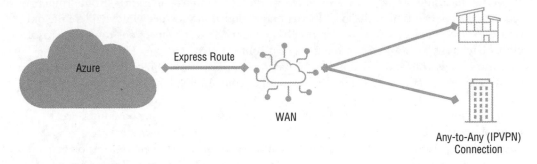

WAN

Any-to-Any (IPVPN)
Connection

FIGURE 3.6 ExpressRoute Direct connection

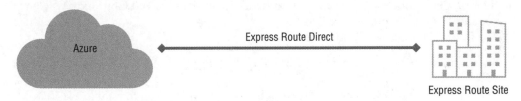

Express Route Site

Choosing Between the Network Service Provider and ExpressRoute Direct

Azure ExpressRoute enables you to build a secure connection among their on-premises datacenter/branch offices and the Azure cloud. It is necessary to have an existing Azure account to access ExpressRoute. If the desired connectivity provider is not supported, ExpressRoute customers must establish a relationship with a supported connectivity provider or connect to Microsoft cloud services through an exchange.

The following are essential network requirements when you're planning an ExpressRoute deployment:

- You need redundancy at each peering location.
- You need redundancy for disaster recovery.
- Routing with BGP management is required.
- Microsoft only accepts public IP addresses through Microsoft peering.
- Consider network security when connecting to the Microsoft cloud via ExpressRoute.

ExpressRoute Direct enables you to connect directly into Microsoft's global network at peering locations strategically distributed worldwide. Connecting ExpressRoute routers requires the cooperation of the local carrier and co-location provider, which will be the only means for cloud customers to use ExpressRoute Direct. Direct connections to the Microsoft global backbone are available through ExpressRoute Direct.

Port pairings will be billed at a fixed amount in ExpressRoute Direct. There is no additional charge for standard circuits and premium circuits. Billing for egress is based on the zone where the peering location is located.

When you create the ExpressRoute Direct resource or after either or both links are enabled, ExpressRoute Direct's port pairs are billed 45 days later. Customers are given a 45-day grace period to complete the cross-connection process with their co-location provider.

Azure storage and other big data services can be accessed via ExpressRoute Direct for massive data ingestion. Circuits on ExpressRoute Direct 100 Gbps are available with a 40 Gbps or 100 Gbps circuit SKU. Port pairs are only 100 Gbps or 10 Gbps, and there is no limit on the number of virtual circuits created. Circuit sizes are 100 Gbps ExpressRoute Direct and 10 Gbps ExpressRoute Direct.

The following are benefits of ExpressRoute:

- ExpressRoute extends your on-premises networks over a private connection to Azure and Microsoft 365 clouds using a connectivity provider.

- Using Ethernet networks, the ExpressRoute platform allows you to establish IPVPNs between any location and any IP address. A co-location facility can provide your organization with virtual cross-connections.

- Connections over ExpressRoute are typically faster and more secure since they never cross the public Internet.

The following are benefits of ExpressRoute Direct:

- Ingestion of massive amounts of data into services like Azure Storage and Cosmos DB is possible.

- Banking, government, and retail are some industries that require physical isolation because of regulations.

- Distribution of circuits is based on business units.

For the Microsoft AZ-700 exam, keep in mind the significant differences between ExpressRoute via a network service provider and via ExpressRoute Direct, shown in Table 3.1.

TABLE 3.1   Difference between ExpressRoute and ExpressRoute Direct

ExpressRoute via a network service provider	ExpressRoute Direct
Utilizes network service providers to facilitate fast onboarding and connectivity to existing infrastructure	Needs 100 Gigabit/10 Gigabit infrastructure, as well as full management at all layers.
Integrates with a number of providers, including Ethernet and Multiprotocol Label Switching (MPLS)	Data ingestion and direct/dedicated capacity for regulated industries.

ExpressRoute via a network service provider	ExpressRoute Direct
Offerings of circuits at speeds between 50 Mbps and 10 Gbps	Using 100 Gbps ExpressRoute Direct, you can mix and match circuit SKUs: 5, 10, 40, 100 Gbps. You may choose from a variety of circuit SKUs such as 1, 2, 5, 10 GBps on ExpressRoute Direct with 10Gbps. ExpressRoute Direct supports tagging of QinQ and Dot1Q VLANs.*
Designed for a single tenant	Designed for single tenants with multiple business units and multiple work environments.

* By using QinQ VLAN Tagging, ExpressRoute circuits can be divided into separate routing domains. A circuit's S-Tag is dynamically assigned by Azure at circuit creation and cannot be changed. A unique C-Tag will be used for each peering on the circuit (Private and Microsoft). On ExpressRoute Direct ports, the C-Tag does not have to be unique across circuits. With Dot1Q VLAN Tagging, a single VLAN can be tagged for each ExpressRoute Direct port pair. All peerings and circuits using the ExpressRoute Direct port pair must use the same C-Tag.

You have many decisions to make when planning an ExpressRoute deployment. Here are some essential points to think about:

- Pick among provider and direct models.
- Focus on route advertisement.
- Enable Bidirectional Forwarding Detection (BFD).
- Build and set up encryption over ExpressRoute.
- Network traffic from Azure to on-premises networks.
- Network traffic from on-premises networks to Azure.
- Design redundancy for an ExpressRoute.
  - Build and configure ExpressRoute and site-to-site coexisting connections.
  - Deploy a zone-redundant VNet gateway in Azure availability zones.
- Build and configure a site-to-site VPN as a failover path for ExpressRoute.
- Apply cross-region connectivity to link various ExpressRoute locations.
- Research service level agreements (SLAs) and pricing.

Designing and Deploying Azure Cross-Region Connectivity between Multiple ExpressRoute Locations

Through ExpressRoute, on-premises infrastructure can be seamlessly connected to Azure services. Let's review some design decisions you need to make before deploying an ExpressRoute circuit.

ExpressRoute must be configured according to several prerequisites. The inevitable result of these can be unexpected costs and activities that hurt the project and other services.

ExpressRoute does not provide a physical connection; instead, it offers private connectivity over an established physical connection. A connectivity provider must first set up the physical connectivity. Connecting ExpressRoute to existing ExpressRoute partners can be done via various Microsoft network service providers.

The following are the seven important design areas to focus on for ExpressRoute. These are each discussed in the sections that follow.

- Select an ExpressRoute circuit SKU.
- Select a peering location.
- Estimate price based on the chosen SKU.
- Select the appropriate ExpressRoute circuit.
- Select a billing model.
- Design for high availability.
- Select a business continuity and disaster recovery design pattern.

Selecting ExpressRoute Circuit SKUs

There are three different circuit solutions offered by Microsoft Azure ExpressRoute: local, standard, and premium. These three SKU types each offer a different price structure.

The local SKU comes with an unlimited data plan automatically.

With the standard and premium SKUs, you can choose from a metered or an unlimited data plan. There is no charge for ingress data unless you want the Global Reach add-on.

Estimating Price Based on ExpressRoute SKU

Connectivity providers charge a fee to establish a private connection. These costs can range widely, depending on the number and type of connections required.

Before using ExpressRoute, use the Azure pricing calculator to estimate costs since the cost could affect the network design. In addition to gathering requirements, determine how much network bandwidth cloud users consume with their hosted services.

Bandwidth is used when data is transferred between as well as among Azure datacenters; other transfers are expressly covered by ExpressRoute pricing.

1. To access the Azure price calculator, visit
   https://azure.microsoft.com/en-us/pricing/calculator
2. Choose Networking, then choose Azure ExpressRoute to begin.
3. Choose the proper zone depending on peering location.
4. Pick the SKU, circuit speed, and the data plan you would like to assess.
5. Enter an estimate of the amount of outbound data you might use over a month in the Additional Outbound Data Transfer field.
6. Include the Global Reach add-on within the estimate if you desire.

Select a Peering Location

Regions in Azure are entirely different from ExpressRoute locations, so for the Microsoft AZ-700 exam, knowing about their differences is critical when exploring hybrid networking in Azure.

Azure Regions   Microsoft Azure regions are global datacenters where Azure's compute, networking, and storage resources can be found. You must choose the location of an Azure resource when deploying it. Setting the location of the resource ensures that the Azure datacenter (or availability zone) in which the resource will be deployed can be determined.

ExpressRoute Locations (Peering Locations)   MSEE devices are located in co-location facilities called ExpressRoute locations (sometimes referred to as peering places or meet-me locations). You can connect to Microsoft's global network through ExpressRoute facilities that are globally distributed. ExpressRoute partners and ExpressRoute Direct customers make cross-connections to Microsoft's network at these locations. You can access Azure services across all regions if connected to an ExpressRoute location within the geopolitical region.

Select the Proper ExpressRoute Circuit

Table 3.2 lists the Azure regions to ExpressRoute locations within each geopolitical region.

TABLE 3.2 Azure ExpressRoute regions and location availability

Geography region	Azure regions	ExpressRoute locations
Australia Government	Australia Central, Australia Central 2	Canberra, Canberra2
Europe	France Central, France South, Germany North, Germany West Central, North Europe, Norway East, Norway West, Switzerland North, Switzerland West, UK West, UK South, West Europe	Amsterdam, Amsterdam2, Berlin, Copenhagen, Dublin, Dublin2, Frankfurt, Frankfurt2, Geneva, London, London2, Madrid, Marseille, Milan, Munich, Newport (Wales), Oslo, Paris, Stavanger, Stockholm, Zurich
North America	East US, West US, East US 2, West US 2, West US 3, Central US, South Central US, North Central US, West Central US, Canada Central, Canada East	Atlanta, Chicago, Chicago2, Dallas, Denver, Las Vegas, Los Angeles, Los Angeles2, Miami, Minneapolis, Montreal, New York, Phoenix, Quebec City, Queretaro (Mexico), Quincy, San Antonio, Seattle, Silicon Valley, Silicon Valley2, Toronto, Toronto2, Vancouver, Washington DC, Washington DC2
Asia	East Asia, Southeast Asia	Bangkok, Hong Kong, Hong Kong2, Jakarta, Kuala Lumpur, Singapore, Singapore2, Taipei
India	India West, India Central, India South	Chennai, Chennai2, Mumbai, Mumbai2, Pune
Japan	Japan West, Japan East	Osaka, Tokyo, Tokyo2
Oceania	Australia Southeast, Australia East	Auckland, Melbourne, Perth, Sydney, Sydney2
South Korea	Korea Central, Korea South	Busan, Seoul, Seoul2
UAE	UAE Central, UAE North	Dubai, Dubai2
South Africa	South Africa West, South Africa North	Cape Town, Johannesburg
South America	Brazil South	Bogota, Campinas, Rio de Janeiro, Sao Paulo, Sao Paulo2

To connect Azure regions to ExpressRoute locations within geopolitical regions, and to identify the service provider and satellite operators, visit

https://docs.microsoft.com/en-us/azure/expressroute/
expressroute-locations#locations

Select a Billing Model

Microsoft offers a variety of ExpressRoute options based on the desired bandwidth of the private connection between the on-premises network and the selected Azure region. In most cases, you need to determine the amount of data you will use every month by evaluating your current usage. Then you can decide the type of ExpressRoute SKU that meets your needs. You select between the Local, Standard, and Premium SKUs when deploying ExpressRoute. There are metered versions of all these options, where you pay by the giga-bytes used or for an unlimited version.

You can also connect your network directly to a Microsoft edge node, which connects to Microsoft's global network to connect any Azure region. In addition to ExpressRoute Direct, Microsoft global network fees are charged.

Cloud customers have the option to choose a billing model that fits their needs. Here are the billing models available:

Unlimited Data   Data transfer inbound and outbound is not billed separately but will appear together on your monthly bill.

Metered Data   The service is billed monthly; inbound data transmission is free. Transfers outbound are charged per gigabyte. There are regional variations in data transfer rates.

ExpressRoute Premium Add-On   There is an ExpressRoute Premium add-on for the ExpressRoute circuit:

- ExpressRoute Premium provides connectivity across geographical boundaries.
- The maximum number of VNets per ExpressRoute circuit can be increased from 10 to a more significant number with a Premium add-on, depending on the bandwidth of the circuit.
- Azure public and Azure private peering limits are raised from 4,000 to 10,000 routes with Premium.

Select a High Availability Design

To ensure high availability, you must maintain the redundancy of ExpressRoute circuits throughout your entire end-to-end network.

In a nutshell:

- Redundancy is required for the on-premises network.
- Cloud service providers should maintain redundancy.

Having redundancy implies at a minimum preventing single-point failures. Network devices can also be powered and cooled redundantly, which will further improve availability.

The rest of this section discusses the factors you should consider when designing for high availability. Let's start with a physical layer:

- If both the primary and secondary connections of ExpressRoute circuits are terminated on the same customer premises equipment (CPE), availability of the consumer's on-premises networks is compromised.

- If you configure the primary and secondary connections through the same CPE port, your partner is forced to compromise high availability on their network segment.

You can terminate the two connections over different subinterfaces, or you can merge them within your partner's network. (A "partner" offers a wide variety of network connectivity and datacenters. Partners may be able to provide fast, reliable, and private connections between your organization's on-premises infrastructure and Azure.) If ExpressRoute circuits are terminated in different locations, however, you can compromise the performance of the connection. A substantial difference in network latency between primary and secondary connections that terminate at different locations will result in suboptimal network performance if traffic is actively load-balanced. Figure 3.7 illustrates this situation.

FIGURE 3.7 An ExpressRoute circuit optimized to maximize its availability

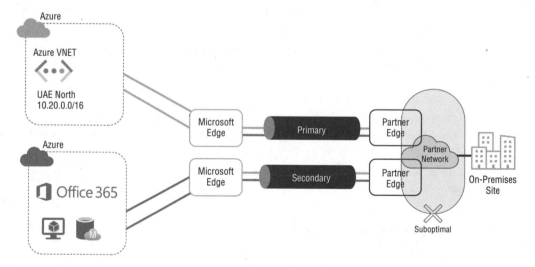

Active/active connections are configured for ExpressRoute circuits on the Microsoft network. However, the redundant connections on an ExpressRoute circuit can be forced to operate in passive/active mode by a route advertisement. The standard techniques used to make one path preferred over another include more specific route advertising and prepending BGP autonomous system (AS) paths.

To improve high availability, Microsoft recommends operating both the connections of an ExpressRoute circuit in active/active mode. If the connections work in an active/active design pattern, the Microsoft network will load-balance the traffic across the links on a per-flow basis. If the active path fails for one of the connections of an ExpressRoute circuit, the active/passive mode may fail for the other connection as well. Most failures when switching over are due to a passive connection that is not managed correctly and is advertising stale routes. In addition, whenever an ExpressRoute circuit fails, running both primary and secondary connections in active/active mode results in about half of the flows being rerouted. The mean time to recovery will improve significantly by implementing a proactive approach.

> Mean time to repair (MTTR), a metric for incident management, measures how long it takes to diagnose and fix IT problems on average. The MTTR measures the time it takes to restore the service to the end user after an incident. In the end, it's all about how quickly a network can return to business as usual.

Microsoft prefers using AS path prepending during a maintenance period (or in an unplanned event affecting a connection) to move traffic to the healthy connection. You will need to ensure that the traffic can route over the healthy path when path prepend is configured from Microsoft. The required route advertisements must be configured appropriately to avoid any service disruption.

A Microsoft peering service is designed to facilitate communication between public servers. The common practice, shown in Figure 3.8, is for on-premises Private Endpoints to be network address translated (NATed) with a public IP on the partner or customer network before being handed off for peering. How you use NAT influences how quickly you recover following the failure of one ExpressRoute connection, assuming that they are both used in active/active mode.

FIGURE 3.8   NAT choices for Microsoft peering

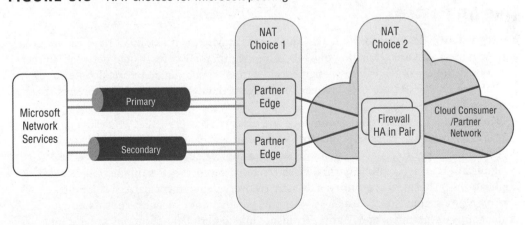

A common NAT pool should be your first choice for traffic distribution to split traffic between the primary and secondary connections. There is no requirement for common NAT pools to introduce a single point of failure to compromise high availability before breaking the traffic. After primary or secondary connections fail, the NAT pool is still accessible. Consequently, networks can reroute packets to recover faster from failures.

A NAT pool with independent NATs should be your second choice for traffic distribution between primary and secondary connections. In an ExpressRoute circuit, NAT is applied after traffic is divided between the primary and secondary connections. Traffic will return to the same edge device from which it exited. To meet the stateful requirements of NAT, each primary and secondary device is assigned an independent NAT pool.

ExpressRoute is unable to reach the appropriate NAT pool if the connection fails. All broken network flows need to be reestablished by either TCP or the application layer after the corresponding timeout. When Azure fails, it cannot reach on-premises servers until the ExpressRoute circuit's primary or secondary connections have been restored.

A key design consideration is that an ExpressRoute circuit cannot reach the on-premises server if a port for the IP address from the NAT pool is mapped to it via NAT choice 2. This will occur if a connection is lost during NAT choice 2 (a NAT pool with independent NATs).

Both the private and Microsoft peering connections under ExpressRoute support Bidirectional Forwarding Detection (BFD). You can activate BFD on ExpressRoute to speed the detection of link failures between MSEE devices and ExpressRoute routers—that is, between customer edge routers (CEs) and provider edge routers/switches (PEs). In this book, we refer to this as CE/PE. Your edge routing devices or partner edge routing devices can be configured using ExpressRoute.

BFD is supported over private peering in ExpressRoute. Microsoft Enterprise Edge and their BGP neighbors on the on-premises side experience reduced failure detection times due to BFD. BFD accelerates failure recovery by allowing for more time to recover from failures.

Pick a Business Continuity and Disaster Recovery Design Pattern

ExpressRoute is designed for high availability so that Microsoft resources have carrier-grade connectivity. There are no single points of failure within the ExpressRoute network. In the previous section, you read about design considerations to maximize ExpressRoute circuit availability. In this section, you will read about geo-redundant ExpressRoute circuits that can provide disaster recovery.

The use case for the business continuity and disaster recovery (BC/DR) design pattern is that cloud customers, Microsoft, network service providers, or any other cloud service provider can face opportunities or situations where a complete regional service degrades. A significant reason for this is natural disasters. So, if business relies on mission-critical applications or business continuity, a disaster recovery deployment pattern is a must.

Any Azure region can serve as a failover site, whether your business runs its mission-critical apps on-premises or in Azure. To ensure mission-critical operations are not interrupted during ExpressRoute connectivity, Microsoft recommends that disaster recovery plans include geo-redundant network connectivity.

Difficulties in managing various ExpressRoute circuits start with asymmetrical routing. You create parallel paths when they interconnect two or more networks simultaneously, using more than one connection. Without best architectural design practices, similar methods could lead to asymmetrical routing. In the case of stateful entities (NAT, firewalls), asymmetric routing could obstruct traffic flow. ExpressRoute peering does not involve stateful entities like NAT or firewalls, so you will not commonly encounter them. Therefore, asymmetrical routing with private peering over ExpressRoute won't obstruct traffic flow.

Although you may or may not have stateful entities, the network's performance may not be harmonious if they load balance traffic across geo-redundant parallel paths. These geo-redundant parallel paths can pass through the same metros or different metros.

To access global commercial locations within the same location with dual connections, and for a detailed list of metros that have two ExpressRoute locations, visit:

```
https://docs.microsoft.com/en-us/azure/expressroute/
expressroute-locations-providers#global-commercial-azure
```

For example, the Azure region Tokyo has Tokyo and Tokyo2. Architects could design redundant connections by connecting two Azure locations with two parallel paths in the identical metro area. In this design, when the on-premises applications fail, Microsoft's end-to-end latency remains roughly constant. It may, however, no longer be possible to connect both paths during a natural disaster such as a tsunami or earthquake.

With parallel paths, you need to use the Premium SKU for both circuits to choose a location outside the geopolitical region. Choose a second location in the same geopolitical region when you need redundancy from multiple metro areas. This configuration has an advantage because there is a lower chance of a natural disaster causing an outage of both links, resulting in increased end-to-end latency.

Use Case 1

The small business unit network connectivity with the BC/DR pattern is shown in Figure 3.9. This figure shows established geo-redundant ExpressRoute connectivity between an on-premises network and an Azure VNet within an Azure region. An active preferred path is indicated by the solid gray line, and the dotted line shows a standby path.

When designing ExpressRoute connectivity for disaster recovery, follow these best practices:

- Apply geo-redundant ExpressRoute circuits.
- Apply diverse service provider network(s) for different ExpressRoute circuits.
- Develop each of the ExpressRoute circuits with a high availability pattern.
- Terminate the different ExpressRoute circuits in different locations on the on-premises network.

FIGURE 3.9   Geo-redundant ExpressRoute connectivity

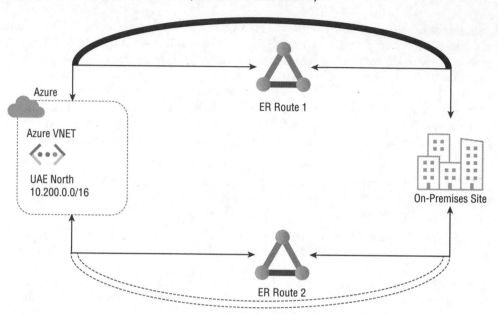

Azure uses equal-cost multipath (ECMP) routing to load-balance all ExpressRoute routes if you advertise identical routes over all ExpressRoute paths. In contrast, for geo-redundant ExpressRoute circuit paths (especially latency), you must consider different network performance aspects. You may prefer the ExpressRoute circuit with minimal latency because it will perform more consistently during regular operation.

Azure can support multiple ExpressRoute circuits by using any of the following techniques:

- Perform more specific route advertising over a preferred ExpressRoute circuit(s) than over other ExpressRoute circuits.

- Set up a higher connection weight for the connection between the virtual network and the ExpressRoute circuit preferred by the virtual network.

- Advertise routes via the AS path prepended to ExpressRoute circuits that have a lower preference.

Figure 3.10 illustrates the influence of route advertisements on ExpressRoute path selection. This example of SMB network connectivity with the BC/DR pattern illustrates IP addresses advertised by the active preferred path through ExpressRoute 1 and as /24 through ExpressRoute 2 over a /24 address range via the standby path.

In Azure's normal state, /25 is more specific than /24, so traffic destined to 10.1.10.0/24 is sent over ExpressRoute 1. It is only through ExpressRoute 2 that the VNet might receive the route advertisement 10.1.11.0/24 in this failed state; therefore, the standby is utilized.

FIGURE 3.10   ExpressRoute path selection using more specific route advertisement

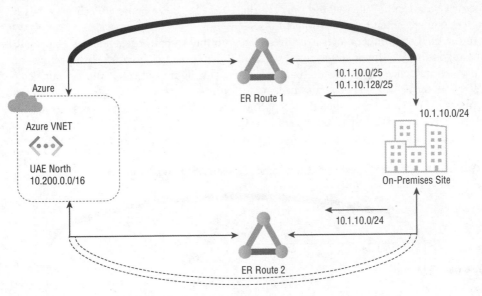

The next technique is setting up a higher connection weight for the connection between the virtual network and the ExpressRoute circuit preferred by the virtual network. Figure 3.11 shows ExpressRoute path selection using connection weight. Connectivity weight is set to 0 by default. This example shows ExpressRoute 1 with a weight of 100. VNets will prefer the connection with the highest weight among route prefixes advertised over more than one ExpressRoute circuit.

FIGURE 3.11   ExpressRoute path selection using connection weight

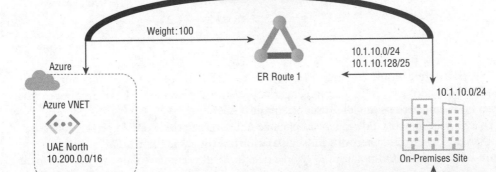

The standby circuit is used in this scenario when both connections of ExpressRoute 1 go down because the VNet would only see the `10.1.10.0/24` route advertisements via ExpressRoute 2 when ExpressRoute 1 fails.

In the final technique, routes are advertised with the AS path prepended to ExpressRoute circuits that have a lower preference. Figure 3.12 demonstrates how AS path prefixes can be used to influence ExpressRoute path selection. This figure illustrates the default behavior of eBGP in terms of route advertisements over ExpressRoute 1. Also, autonomous system numbers (ASNs) are prefixed to the AS path of routes advertised over ExpressRoute 2 by the on-premises network. As part of the eBGP route selection process, if VNet receives the same route over multiple ExpressRoute circuits, it prefers the route with the shortest AS path.

FIGURE 3.12   ExpressRoute path selection with AS path prepended

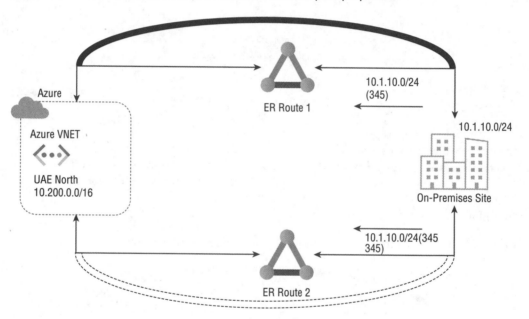

ExpressRoute 1 would continue to advertise `10.1.10.0/24` only if both connections failed. If both connections failed, the longer AS path would no longer be of any importance. When both connections fail, the standby circuit is used.

To avoid asymmetric flows, if you influence Azure to prioritize one ExpressRoute over another, the on-premises network must also prioritize the same ExpressRoute path for Azure-bound traffic. On-premises networks use the local preference value to decide which ExpressRoute circuit to prioritize over another. A local preference value is part of the iBGP protocol, and the BGP route with the highest local preference value is preferred.

Microsoft recommends that you actively manage your ExpressRoute circuits and periodically conduct disaster recovery drills and failover operations when using ExpressRoute circuits as standby.

Use Case 2

This use case is an example of enterprise distributed network connectivity with the BC/DR pattern. Let's consider the example shown in Figure 3.13. Using ExpressRoute circuits in two other peering locations, an organization has two on-premises locations connected to two different infrastructures as service deployments in two separate Azure regions.

FIGURE 3.13 Two different Azure regions via ExpressRoute circuits in two different peering locations

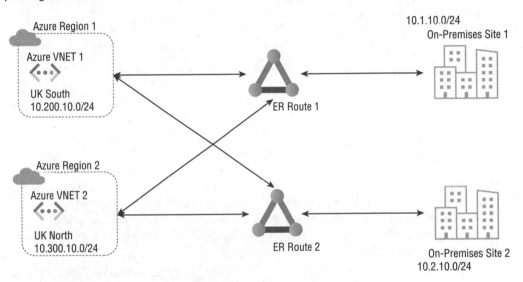

In disaster recovery, all traffic flows through a local ExpressRoute circuit between Azure and on-premises networks in a constant state. All traffic flows between Azure and the remote ExpressRoute circuit handle the on-premises network if the local ExpressRoute circuit fails.

Choice 1 The bolded lines in Figure 3.14 show traffic between on-premises site 1 networks and Azure VNet1. The light lines at the bottom of the figure indicate the paths for traffic flow between Azure VNet2 and on-premises site 2 networks. Solid straight lines represent the desired direction in a steady state. They show the related ExpressRoute circuit that carries steady-state traffic flow when the corresponding dashed lines are broken.

FIGURE 3.14   Disaster recovery—choice 1

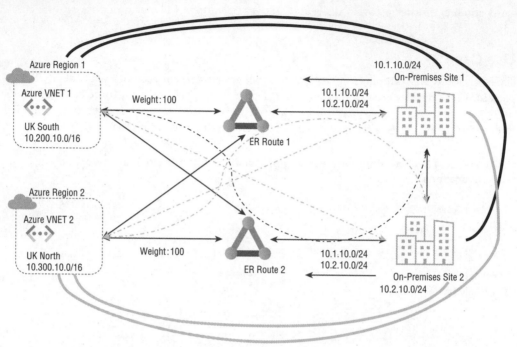

Connectivity weight influences VNets to choose on-premises network-bound traffic to be routed through local peering locations instead of ExpressRoute. You must ensure symmetrical reverse traffic flow to complete the design. The ExpressRoute circuit is preferred when iBGP is used between on-premises BGP routers (when ExpressRoute circuits go out on-premises).

Choice 2   This choice is depicted in Figure 3.15. In this diagram, bolded lines represent routes between Azure region 1 VNet1 and the on-premises networks. On-premises cloud networks and Azure region 2 VNet2 are shown with light lines to show the traffic flow paths. All traffic between the VNets and the on-premises locations passes primarily over Microsoft's backbone when doing business, represented by solid lines. The data will go through the interconnection between on-premises locations only in the failover state.

Changing the interconnection configuration between the on-premises and Azure locations is necessary to influence the choice of network route for traffic bound for Azure. However, it would help if you determined which interconnection link is preferable within their on-premises network based on their routing protocol. You can choose the wireless networks' local or metric preferences for iBGP (Open Shortest Path First [OSPF] or Intermediate System to Intermediate System [IS-IS]), and a more specific route because the AS path prefix will influence the VNet path selection more precisely.

FIGURE 3.15   Disaster recovery—choice 2

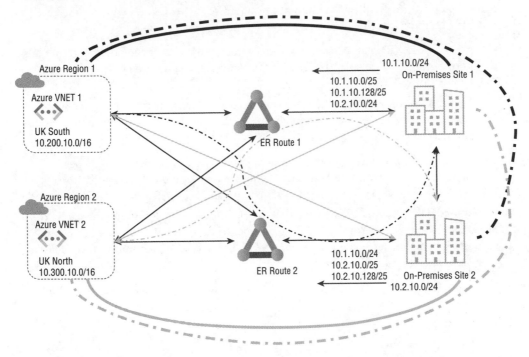

For the Microsoft AZ700 exam, keep in mind that:

- Microsoft peering allows organizations to consume a subset of supported services with route filters.
- Online services provided by Microsoft (Microsoft 365 and Azure PaaS) are connected through Microsoft peering.

Choosing an Appropriate ExpressRoute SKU and Tier

Creating a *virtual network gateway* is the first step toward connecting Azure virtual networking and on-premises networks via ExpressRoute. Virtual network gateways serve two primary purposes:

- Used when a network exchanges IP routes with another network
- For network traffic routing

This section will explore methods for choosing gateway types, gateway SKUs, and predicted performance based on SKU.

Gateway Type   You need to specify several settings when creating a virtual network gateway. One of the required configurations, GatewayType, defines whether the gateway is a VPN or ExpressRoute. The two gateway types are as follows:

- You can use VPN gateways to send encrypted traffic across the public Internet, also known as the Microsoft VPN gateway. VNet-to-VNet, site-to-site, and point-to-site connections all use a VPN gateway.

- You can use the ExpressRoute gateway to send network traffic on a private connection. In the ExpressRoute configuration, this is referred to as the ExpressRoute gateway.

The number of virtual network gateways per gateway type is limited to one per virtual network. For Example You can use one virtual network gateway that uses -GatewayType VPN and one that uses -GatewayType ExpressRoute.

Gateway SKUs   You can create virtual network gateways by specifying the gateway SKUs they want to use. You can allocate more CPUs and network bandwidth to the gateway when choosing a higher gateway SKU. Therefore, throughput to a virtual network can be higher thanks to the gateway.

Gateways for virtual networks powered by ExpressRoute are available in the following SKUs:

- Standard
- HighPerformance
- UltraPerformance

You can generally resize `AzVirtualNetworkGateway` PowerShell cmdlets to upgrade gateways to more powerful models using the `Resize-AzVirtualNetworkGateway` PowerShell cmdlet. You can upgrade from Standard and HighPerformance SKUs. It would be best to re-create a non-availability-zone gateway to upgrade it to the UltraPerformance SKU. The gateway does not have to be deleted and rebuilt to upgrade an AZ-enabled SKU. Keep in mind that replacing a gateway may result in downtime.

Table 3.3 lists the characteristics and tiers of ExpressRoute SKUs.

TABLE 3.3   Comparison of gateway SKUs

Gateway SKU	VPN gateway and ExpressRoute coexistence	Max. number of circuit connections
ERGw1Az/Standard SKU	Yes	4
ERGw2Az/HighPerformance SKU	Yes	8
ErGw3Az/UltraPerformance SKU/	Yes	16

Gateway Subnet   It is helpful to create gateway subnets before creating ExpressRoute gateways. Subnets for virtual network gateway hosts and services are in the gateway subnet. You can deploy virtual network gateways to gateway subnets that have been configured to use ExpressRoute gateway settings. Never add anything (such as more virtual machines) to the gateway subnet. `GatewaySubnet` must be the name of the gateway subnet where you want the virtual network gateway VMs and services to be deployed.

For gateway VMs and gateway services, a gateway subnet is populated with IP addresses. You must specify how many IP addresses the gateway subnet contains when you create the subnet. Depending on the configuration, you may need more IP addresses.

A configuration combining ExpressRoute with a VPN gateway, for example, requires a larger gateway subnet than most others. You should expect subnets to have enough IP addresses to accommodate any additional configurations. You can create a gateway subnet as small as /29; however, Microsoft recommends making at least a /27 gateway subnet (/27, /26, etc.) if enough address space is available. If 16 ExpressRoute circuits are interconnected, the gateway subnet should be /26. Microsoft recommends an a /64 IPv6 range. This range can accommodate almost any configuration, including, for example, a dual-stack gateway subnet.

Azure availability zones (AZs) can also be used for ExpressRoute gateway deployments. Separating them in this manner protects on-premises network connectivity to Azure against zone-level failures on both a physical and a logical level.

As of this writing, the following SKU types exist for ExpressRoute with zone-redundant gateways:

- ErGw1AZ
- ErGw2AZ
- ErGw3AZ

Other deployment options are available to fit your needs. You can deploy a virtual network gateway to a specific zone with the SKUs listed here. For ExpressRoute IPv6-based private peering, choose an AZ SKU that you can deploy in a dual-stack gateway subnet.

Designing and Deploying ExpressRoute Global Reach

You can access many Microsoft cloud services such as Azure and Microsoft 365 from private datacenters or corporate networks. ExpressRoute offers private and reliable connections to the Microsoft cloud for on-premises network users.

For example, consider the scenario as shown in Figure 3.16; you have a branch office at an on-premises site 1 and site 2. Both sites have high-speed connectivity to Azure services; however, the branches cannot communicate directly.

FIGURE 3.16   ExpressRoute without Global Reach

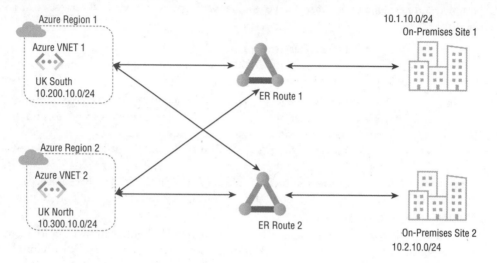

The *ExpressRoute Global Reach* service allows you to link ExpressRoute circuits to form private networks between on-premises cloud networks. As shown in Figure 3.17, adopting ExpressRoute Global Reach allows the on-premises network at site 2 (`10.2.10.0/24`) to directly exchange data with site 1 through ExpressRoute circuits in Microsoft's global network.

FIGURE 3.17   ExpressRoute Circuits in Microsoft Global network Without global reach

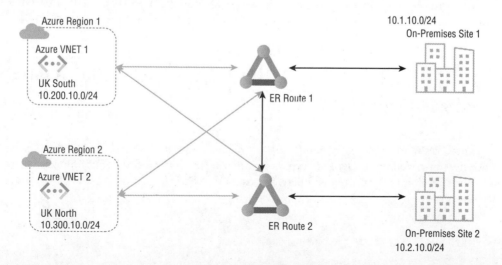

One of the principal use cases for ExpressRoute Global Reach is to connect an organization's branch offices worldwide. By leveraging ExpressRoute Global Reach, you can use existing service providers to connect their branches in their primary country. This is useful for remote offices located outside the region, where the current service provider does not provide services. You can use the ExpressRoute Global Reach link and connect their branch location office to the primary office.

To take advantage of this benefit, you must have the Premium SKU with the ExpressRoute Global Reach add-on.

At of this writing, ExpressRoute Global Reach is supported in the following countries: Australia, Canada, Denmark, France, Germany, Hong Kong SAR, India, Ireland, Japan, South Korea, Netherlands, New Zealand, Norway, Singapore, South Africa (Johannesburg only), Sweden, Switzerland, Taiwan, the United Kingdom, and the United States.

Let's now look at the steps for deploying ExpressRoute Global Reach.

Deploying ExpressRoute Global Reach

First, you should identify the ExpressRoute circuits that you wish to use. When two ExpressRoute circuits are located in supported countries/regions and created at different peering locations, you can enable ExpressRoute Global Reach between them.

Use Case 1: Enabling Circuits in the Same Region

First we'll look at example syntax used to enable ExpressRoute circuits in the same region. Circuits 1 and 2 can be obtained by using the following commands. This subscription contains both circuits.

```
$ckt_1 = Get-AzExpressRouteCircuit -Name "CloudConsumer_ER1_name"
-ResourceGroupName "CloudConsumer_resource_group"
$ckt_2 = Get-AzExpressRouteCircuit -Name "CloudConsumer_ER2_name"
-ResourceGroupName ""CloudConsumer_resource_group""
```

Now, pass the peering ID of circuit 2 into the following command:

```
Add-AzExpressRouteCircuitConnectionConfig
-Name 'CloudConsumer_connection_name' -ExpressRouteCircuit $ckt_1 -
PeerExpressRouteCircuitPeering $ckt_2.Peerings[0].Id
-AddressPrefix '10.0.0.0/29'
```

-AddressPrefix must be a /29 IPv4 subnet, for instance, 10.0.0.0/29. For this example, we'll use the IP addresses in this subnet to build connectivity between two ExpressRoute circuits:

```
"/subscriptions/{CloudConsumer_subscription_id}/resourceGroups
/{CloudConsumer_resource_group}/providers/Microsoft.Network
```

```
/expressRouteCircuits/{CloudConsumer_circuit_name}/peerings
/AzurePrivatePeering".
```

Whatever subnet you use here should not be used in the Azure virtual network or your on-premises network.

To commit the change, use the following command:

```
Set-AzExpressRouteCircuit -ExpressRouteCircuit $ckt_1
```

When the early process finishes, you will connect on-premises networks on both sides by two ExpressRoute circuits in the same region.

Use Case 2: Enabling Circuits in Different Regions

Next is an example of enabling ExpressRoute circuits in different regions. First, you generate an authorization key, as shown in the following code:

```
$ckt_2 = Get-AzExpressRouteCircuit -Name "CloudConsumer_circuit_2_name" -
ResourceGroupName "CloudConsumer_resource_group"
Add-AzExpressRouteCircuitAuthorization -ExpressRouteCircuit $ckt_2 -Name
"Name_for_auth_key"
```

Next, execute the following command on circuit 1. Enter the private peering ID and authorization key for circuit 2.

```
Add-AzExpressRouteCircuitConnectionConfig -Name
'CloudConsumer_connection_name' -
ExpressRouteCircuit $ckt_1 -PeerExpressRouteCircuitPeering
"circuit_2_private_peering_id" -AddressPrefix '__.__.__.__/29'
-AuthorizationKey
'########-####-####-####-############'
```

To commit the change, use the following:

```
Set-AzExpressRouteCircuit -ExpressRouteCircuit $ckt_1
```

Now connect your on-premises networks on both sides by two ExpressRoute circuits in different regions.

To disable connectivity among your on-premises networks, run the following commands against the circuit where the configuration was made:

```
$ckt_1 = Get-AzExpressRouteCircuit -Name "CloudConsumer_circuit_1_name" -
ResourceGroupName "CloudConsumer_resource_group"
Remove-AzExpressRouteCircuitConnectionConfig -Name "Cloud_connection_name" -
ExpressRouteCircuit $ckt_1
Set-AzExpressRouteCircuit -ExpressRouteCircuit $ckt_1
```

Finally, disconnect your on-premises networks via ExpressRoute circuits.

Designing and Deploying ExpressRoute FastPath

A virtual network's *FastPath* protocol improves communications between your on-premises and Azure virtual networks by accelerating the data path. Network routes and traffic are routed through ExpressRoute's virtual network gateway. Through FastPath, network traffic is sent directly to VMs within the virtual network, bypassing the gateway.

FastPath is available on all ExpressRoute circuits. It still requires a virtual network gateway to be built to exchange routes between virtual and on-premises networks. When you build the virtual network gateway, you need to specify the gateway SKU. As a result of selecting a higher gateway SKU, the gateway is allocated more CPUs and network bandwidth, increasing the virtual network's bandwidth.

Microsoft offers ExpressRoute virtual network gateway SKUs such as Standard, High-Performance, UltraPerformance, ErGw1Az, ErGw2Az, and ErGw3Az. However, to use ExpressRoute FastPath, the virtual network gateway must be either UltraPerformance or ErGw3AZ.

When designing FastPath, keep in mind that it comes with these limitations and doesn't support the following subsystem integration:

- UDRs (user-defined routes) on the gateway subnet
- Basic load balancer
- Private Link

Typically, ExpressRoute FastPath is controlled and enabled by engineers if their virtual network gateways are UltraPerformance or ErGw3AZ. FastPath enhances on-premises cloud connectivity with Azure virtual networks and improves packet-per-second rates.

You can enable ExpressRoute networking directly to VMs connected to a local or peering virtual network through FastPath and virtual network peering, bypassing the ExpressRoute virtual network gateway in the data path.

The following is a deployment example that configures FastPath on a new connection:

```
$circuit = Get-AzExpressRouteCircuit -Name "SybexCircuit"
-ResourceGroupName "SybexRG"
$gw = Get-AzVirtualNetworkGateway -Name "SybexGateway"
-ResourceGroupName "SybexRG"
$connection = New-AzVirtualNetworkGatewayConnection
-Name "SybexConnection" -ResourceGroupName "SybexRG"
-ExpressRouteGatewayBypass -VirtualNetworkGateway1 $gw -PeerId $circuit.Id -
ConnectionType ExpressRoute
-Location "SybexLocation"
```

The following is a deployment example that updates an existing connection to enable FastPath:

```
$connection = Get-AzVirtualNetworkGatewayConnection -Name "SybexConnection"
-ResourceGroupName "SybexRG"
$connection.ExpressRouteGatewayBypass = $True
Set-AzVirtualNetworkGatewayConnection
-VirtualNetworkGatewayConnection $connection
```

The following is a deployment example that removes an ExpressRoute link from the subscription to the gateway. You use the `Remove-AzVirtualNetworkGatewayConnection` command to eliminate the link between the gateway and the circuit:

```
Remove-AzVirtualNetworkGatewayConnection "MyConnection"
-ResourceGroupName "MyRG"
```

> FastPath sends network traffic straight to virtual machines in the virtual network, detouring the gateway and avoiding traffic being routed into the VNet gateways, directly connecting all the VNets to the ExpressRoute FastPath circuit.

Evaluate Private Peering Only, Microsoft Peering Only, or Both

ExpressRoute circuits can be set up by peering in three Azure domains: Azure public, Azure private, and Microsoft. Each peering is configured identically on a pair of routers in an active/active or load-sharing configuration for high availability. Two Azure services are based on the IP address schemes: Azure public and Azure private. Figure 3.18 depicts two types of peering.

Cloud services, such as virtual machines and cloud services deployed within a virtual network, can be connected to Azure through the private peering domain. Azure recognizes the private peering domain as an extension of the core network. Azure VNets can be configured to be bidirectionally connected to the on-premises core network. Connecting to VMs and cloud services directly via their private IP addresses is enabled by Azure private peering. You can connect more than one virtual network to the private peering domain.

Microsoft 365 was created to be accessed securely and reliably via the Internet. Because of this, Microsoft recommends ExpressRoute for specific scenarios.

FIGURE 3.18 Peering types

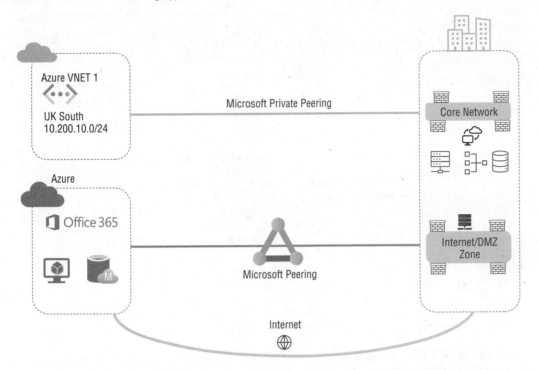

FIGURE 3.18 Peering types

Connectivity to Microsoft online services (Microsoft 365 and Azure PaaS services) occurs through Microsoft peering. Microsoft enables bidirectional connectivity between the consumer's WAN and Microsoft's cloud services through the peering routing domain. You must connect to Microsoft cloud services only over public IP addresses owned by your organization or your network connectivity providers.

Table 3.4 shows the baseline for evaluating Azure public, Azure private, and Microsoft peerings.

TABLE 3.4 Comparison of Peering

KPIs to compare	Azure private peering	Microsoft peering	Azure public peering*
Max. # prefixes supported per peering	4,000 by default; 10,000 with ExpressRoute Premium	200	200
IP address ranges supported	Any valid IP address within your WAN	Public IP addresses owned by your organization or your connectivity provider	Public IP addresses owned by your organization or your connectivity provider

TABLE 3.4   Comparison of Peering *(continued)*

KPIs to compare	Azure private peering	Microsoft peering	Azure public peering*
Routing interface IP addresses	RFC1918 and public IP addresses	Public IP addresses registered to organization in routing registries	Public IP addresses registered to organization in routing registries
AS number requirements	Private and public AS numbers—you must own the public AS number if you choose to use one	Private and public AS numbers; however, you must prove ownership of public IP addresses	Private and public AS numbers; however, you must prove ownership of public IP addresses
IP protocols support	IPv4, IPv6 (as of this writing it was preview)	IPv4, IPv6	IPv4
MD5 hash support	Yes	Yes	Yes

* Key point to consider: Azure public peering (As per Microsoft it is deprecated for new circuits)

ExpressRoute circuits can support one or more enabled routing domains. Support for more than one can be achieved by dividing them into multiple routing domains. You can combine all routing domains onto a single VPN to form a single domain.

Microsoft recommends that public and Microsoft peering links be configured to connect to the DMZ, whereas private peering is linked directly to the core network.

There are different peering types, and each requires its own BGP session. Pairs of BGP sessions ensure high availability. You must configure and manage the routes if they connect via layer 2 connectivity providers.

Network Performance Monitor (NPM) can be used to monitor ExpressRoute circuits' availability, connectivity, and bandwidth utilization. Monitoring the health of Azure private peering and Microsoft peering is performed by NPM.

Setting Up Private Peering

By using *Azure's private peering* domain, Azure compute services, such as IaaS and PaaS, can be connected within a virtual network. Azure will peer with the organization's network over the private peering domain. Azure VNets and core networks can be connected bidirectionally. Connecting directly to VMs and cloud services is possible with peering.

ExpressRoute circuits can be configured with private peering. You can set up peerings in any order you wish. The peering setup for each network must be performed individually, however.

To connect to Microsoft cloud services through ExpressRoute, you must meet a few prerequisites:

- Azure must be valid and active.

- You must connect to the Microsoft cloud via an ExpressRoute connection or through a cloud exchange service provider.

- There must be redundancy of peering locations, disaster recovery, routing, NAT, quality of service (QoS), and network security requirements of each peering location.

- An active ExpressRoute circuit is needed.

- Ensure that both sides of the tunnel use the key if the security requirements call for a shared key/MD5 hash. The maximum number of characters is 25.

ExpressRoute workflows are configured to make provisioning and routing of circuits easy. This rest of this section outlines the steps to provision an ExpressRoute circuit from end to end, accomplishing the following tasks:

- Validate all prerequisites.

- Order connectivity or configure ExpressRoute Direct.
    - ExpressRoute partner model
    - ExpressRoute Direct model

- Create an ExpressRoute circuit.
    - ExpressRoute partner model
    - ExpressRoute Direct model

- Start consuming the ExpressRoute circuit.

- Set up routing domains.
    - Azure private peering
    - Microsoft peering

- Network service provider provisions connectivity.

Configure the ExpressRoute circuit. Check the provider's status to ensure that the connectivity provider fully provisions the circuit before continuing.

If your network connectivity provider offers managed Layer 3 services, you can request that their network connectivity provider enable Microsoft peering. However, if the network connectivity provider doesn't manage routing for you, you can take the following steps.

To configure private peering for the circuit, ensure that you have the following information before getting started:

- You need an IP address space not reserved for virtual networks, which comprises two subnets. The primary link will use one subnet, and the secondary link will use the other.

You will assign the first usable IP address to your organization's router from each subnet since Microsoft uses the second functional IP address for its router. Here are the options:

- IPv4: Two /30 subnets
- IPv6: Two /126 subnets
- Both: Two /30 subnets and two /126 subnets

- The VLAN ID on which the peering is to be established. You should use the same VLAN ID on both primary and secondary links.

- The AS number for peering can be a 2-byte or 4-byte AS number. You can do peering using your own AS numbers, except for AS numbers 65515 to 65520.

- The route from the on-premises edge router must be advertised through BGP to Azure.

- The MD5 hash may be used depending on security needs, but it is optional.

The following is a deployment example of configuring Azure private peering for the circuit:

```
Add-AzExpressRouteCircuitPeeringConfig -Name "AzurePvtPeering"
-ExpressRouteCircuit $ckt -PeeringType AzurePrivatePeering
-PeerASN 100 -PrimaryPeerAddressPrefix "10.0.0.0/30"
-SecondaryPeerAddressPrefix "10.0.0.10/30" -VlanId 200
Set-AzExpressRouteCircuit -ExpressRouteCircuit $ckt
```

Next is a deployment example of configuring Azure private peering for the circuit with an MD5 hash:

```
Add-AzExpressRouteCircuitPeeringConfig -Name "AzurePvtPeering"
-ExpressRouteCircuit $ckt -PeeringType AzurePrivatePeering
-PeerASN 100 -PrimaryPeerAddressPrefix "10.0.0.0/30"
-SecondaryPeerAddressPrefix "10.0.0.10/30" -VlanId 200
-SharedKey "AX1YBZ2EC3D4"
```

And here is a deployment example for getting Azure private peering details:

```
$ckt = Get-AzExpressRouteCircuit -Name "ExpressRouteARMCircuit"
-ResourceGroupName "SybexExpressRouteResourceGroup"
Get-AzExpressRouteCircuitPeeringConfig -Name "AzurePvtPeering"
-ExpressRouteCircuit $ckt
```

Next, we'll explore a method for creating and getting the Azure private peering configuration for an ExpressRoute circuit through PowerShell.

Setting Up Microsoft Peering

The Internet is a secure and reliable way to access Microsoft 365. Consequently, ExpressRoute is recommended for this.

Azure PaaS services and Microsoft 365 services are connected by *Microsoft peering*. The Microsoft peering routing domain allows bidirectional connectivity between WANs and Microsoft cloud services. To access Microsoft cloud services, you must use public IP addresses owned or controlled by your organization or your connectivity providers. They should also adhere to all cloud service regulations.

ExpressRoute circuits can be configured with Microsoft peering. You can set up peerings in any order you wish. The peering setup for each network must be performed individually, however.

For your organization to connect to Microsoft cloud services through ExpressRoute, the following prerequisites must be met:

- Microsoft Azure must be valid and active.

- You must connect to the Microsoft cloud via an ExpressRoute connection or through a cloud exchange service provider.

- There must be redundancy of peering locations, disaster recovery, routing, NAT, QoS, and network security requirements of each peering location.

- An active ExpressRoute circuit is needed.

- Ensure that both sides of the tunnel use the key if the security requirements call for a shared key/MD5 hash. The maximum number of characters is 25.

Configure the ExpressRoute circuit. Check the provider's status to ensure that the connectivity provider fully provisions the circuit before continuing.

If the network connectivity provider offers managed Layer 3 services, you can request that your network connectivity provider enable Microsoft peering. However, follow the process described next if the network connectivity provider doesn't manage the route. Then you to have configure Microsoft peering for the circuit.

Ensure that you have the following prerequisites in place before getting started:

- You need a pair of subnets owned by your organization and registered within a cloud registry. There will be a primary link and a secondary link, and one subnet will be used for each connection. A router will be assigned the first usable IP address from each subnet and Microsoft's router will be assigned the second usable IP address. Here are three options for this pair of subnets:

  - IPv4: Two /30 subnets. All are public IPv4 addresses.

  - IPv6: Two /126 subnets. These are required publicly available IPv6 addresses.

  - IPv4 and IPv6: Two /30 subnets and two /126 subnets.

- You need the VLAN ID on which the peering is to be established. You should use the same VLAN ID on both primary and secondary links.

- The AS number for peering can be a 2-byte or 4-byte AS number.

- List all prefixes you plan to advertise over BGP. You can send a comma-separated list if you plan to send a set of prefixes. Those prefixes must be registered in an RIR (Regional Internet Registry) or IRR (Internet Routing Registry).

- Your advertising prefixes registered to peer AS numbers can be specified if they are not registered to peering AS numbers.

- For the Routing Registry Name, you may specify an RIR/IRR rather than an AS number or prefix.

- The MD5 hash may be used depending on your security needs, and it is optional.

Let's use Azure PowerShell to create and obtain the Microsoft peering configuration for an ExpressRoute circuit.

The following is a deployment example of configuring Microsoft peering for the circuit:

```
Add-AzExpressRouteCircuitPeeringConfig -Name "MSPeering" -ExpressRouteCircuit
$ckt -PeeringType MicrosoftPeering -PeerASN 100
-PeerAddressType IPv4 -PrimaryPeerAddressPrefix "124.0.0.0/30"
-SecondaryPeerAddressPrefix "124.0.0.4/30" -VlanId 300
-MicrosoftConfigAdvertisedPublicPrefixes "124.1.0.0/24"
-MicrosoftConfigCustomerAsn 23
-MicrosoftConfigRoutingRegistryName "ARIN"
Set-AzExpressRouteCircuit
-ExpressRouteCircuit $ckt
```

Next is a deployment example for getting Microsoft peering for the circuit:

```
$ckt = Get-AzExpressRouteCircuit -Name "ExpressRouteARMCircuit"
-ResourceGroupName ""ExpressRouteResourceGroup""
Get-AzExpressRouteCircuitPeeringConfig -Name ""MSPeering""
-ExpressRouteCircuit $ckt
```

Building and Configuring an ExpressRoute Gateway

In this section, you build and configure a gateway for a preexisting VNet. The steps in Exercise 3.1 walk you through the process.

EXERCISE 3.1

Creating a Network Gateway Subnet in the Azure Portal

1. Log into a personal or business account in the Azure portal at `https://portal
   .azure.com` and choose Virtual Networks (FrontEnd in this example).

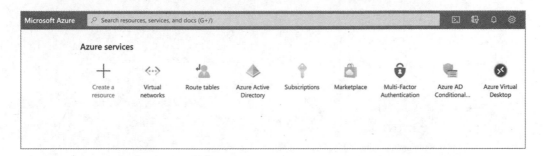

2. On the Settings tab of the VNet, choose Subnets to expand Subnet settings and add
   Gateway Subnet, as shown here:

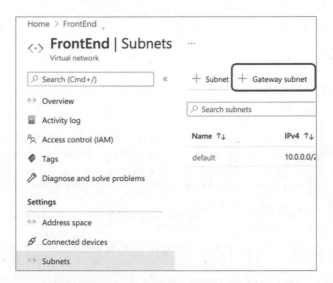

3. In the Name field for the subnet, the value GatewaySubnet is automatically filled in
   (see the following graphic). Azure needs this value to recognize the subnet as the
   gateway subnet. Change the autofilled IP address range values to match the configuration. Microsoft recommends that you create a gateway subnet of /27 or larger (/26,
   /25, etc.). You must create a /26 or larger IP address subnet if you plan to connect 16
   ExpressRoute circuits to your gateway.

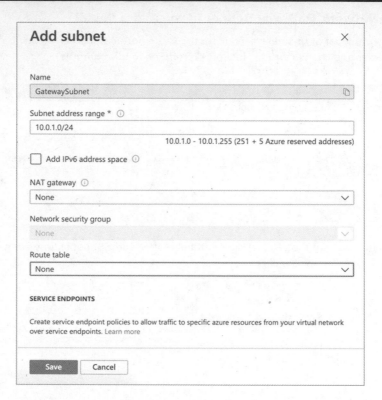

4. Click Add IPv6 Address Space and enter the IPv6 address range values for dual-stack virtual networks using private peering over ExpressRoute. Save the values and create the gateway subnet by clicking OK to finish creating the gateway subnet.

Next, in Exercise 3.2, you create a virtual network gateway in the Azure portal.

EXERCISE 3.2

Creating a Virtual Network Gateway in the Azure Portal

1. Log into a personal or business account in the Azure portal at `https://portal`
    `.azure.com`.

2. Choose Create A Resource and type **Virtual Network Gateway** in the search box. Choose Virtual Network Gateway from the results. In the Virtual Network Gateway Wizard, click Create.

3. On the Create Virtual Network Gateway page (shown next), enter or choose these settings:
   - Name: **AV-ER01.**
   - Region: UAE North.
   - Gateway Type: ExpressRoute.
   - SKU: There are three types of ExpressRoute gateways: Standard, HighPerformance, and UltraPerformance.

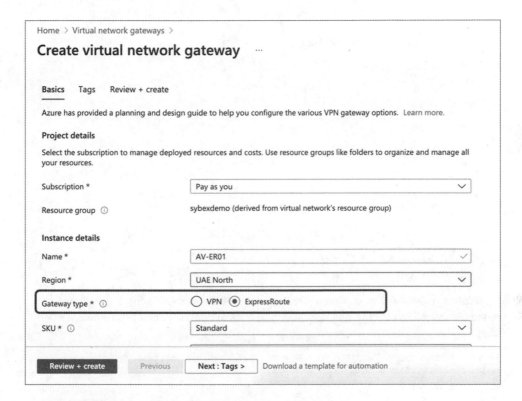

4. On the Basics tab, enter these settings (see the next graphic):
   - Virtual Network: **FrontEnd** (created in Chapter 1)
   - Gateway Subnet Address Range: **10.0.1.0/24**
   - Public IP Address: Create New
   - Public IP Address Name: **VNet1GWpip**

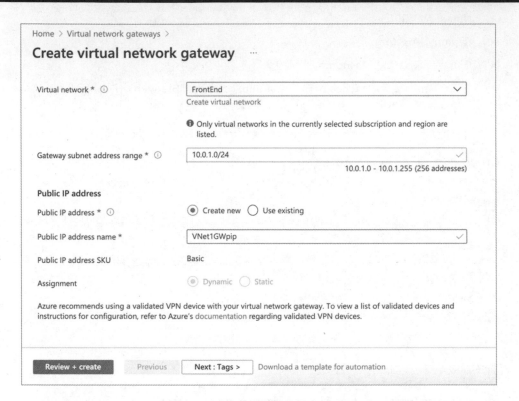

5. To create a gateway, click Review + Create, then click Create. Once the settings are validated, Azure will create the gateway. A virtual network gateway can be created in up to 45 minutes.

   This completes the virtual network gateway creation for the ExpressRoute.

Connect a Virtual Network to an ExpressRoute Circuit

This section covers connecting VNets to ExpressRoute circuits using PowerShell. A virtual network may belong to the same subscription or a different subscription as the ExpressRoute circuit it's connecting to.

Here are important deployment considerations:

- An ExpressRoute circuit can link up to 10 virtual networks. A standard ExpressRoute circuit allows only virtual networks in the same geographic region.

- VNets can be linked to an unlimited number of ExpressRoute circuits. Subscriptions for ExpressRoute circuits can be the same, different, or a mix of both.

- You can link virtual networks outside the ExpressRoute circuit's geopolitical region by enabling the ExpressRoute Premium add-on. Using the Premium add-on, you can also connect up to 10 virtual networks to the ExpressRoute circuit.

- To establish a connection from the ExpressRoute circuit to the ExpressRoute virtual network gateway, the number of IP address spaces advertised by the local or peer virtual networks must be equal to or less than 200 (as of this writing). Following the successful creation of a connection, you can add up to 1,000 IP address spaces to local or peer virtual networks.

- The previous sections discussed the prerequisites, routing requirements, and workflows that should be considered when constructing ExpressRoutes.

- Make sure you have your Azure private peering configured for circuits.

- Set up Azure private peering and establish BGP peering between the on-premises network and Microsoft for end-to-end connectivity.

- Create and provision virtual networks and virtual network gateways for every organization.

The following cmdlet connect a virtual network gateway to an ExpressRoute circuit running in the same subscription. You must be run this code after the virtual network gateway has been created and can be linked:

```
$circuit = Get-AzExpressRouteCircuit -Name "SybexCircuit"
-ResourceGroupName "SybexRG"
$gw = Get-AzVirtualNetworkGateway
-Name "SybexExpressRouteGw"
-ResourceGroupName "SybexRG"
$connection = New-AzVirtualNetworkGatewayConnection
-Name "ERConnection" -ResourceGroupName "SybexRG"
-Location "UAE North"
-VirtualNetworkGateway1 $gw -PeerId $circuit.Id
-ConnectionType ExpressRoute
```

Consumers of Azure services can share an ExpressRoute circuit among multiple subscriptions. Figure 3.19 is a simple diagram showing how ExpressRoute circuits are shared across multiple subscriptions.

FIGURE 3.19   ExpressRoute shared deployment mode

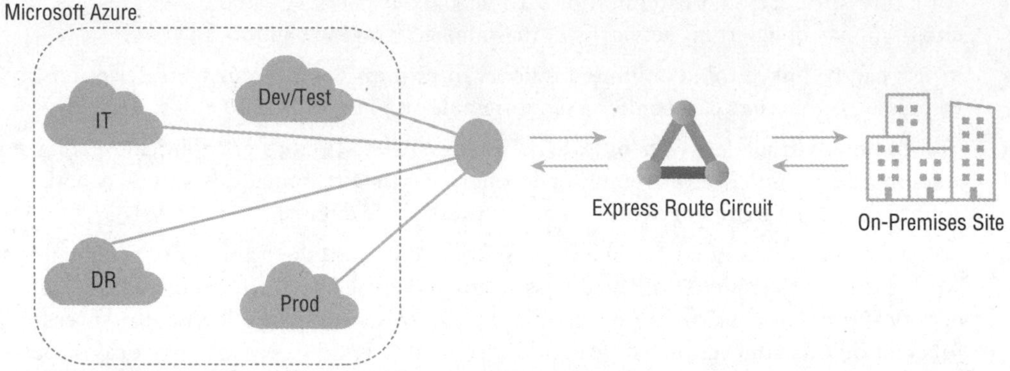

Each of the multitenant subscriptions within the large cloud represents different departments within the enterprise. Each department can own an ExpressRoute circuit. Tenants use their subscriptions to deploy their services but can connect back through an ExpressRoute circuit to the on-premises network. Another subscription within the company may use the ExpressRoute circuit.

The subscription owner will be charged for bandwidth and connectivity for ExpressRoute circuits. All virtual networks share the bandwidth.

At a high level, there are two roles within the Azure environment. The circuit owner is a power user who can access the ExpressRoute circuit resource and has full authority to create, review, add, and delete authorization. They can create authorization for circuit users to redeem.

The circuit user has the lowest authority to redeem and release connections. Circuit users own virtual network gateways that are not included in the same subscription as an ExpressRoute circuit. The circuit users may redeem authorizations (per virtual network).

Modifying and revoking authorizations are at the discretion of the circuit owner. Revoking an authorization results in all link connections being deleted from the subscription whose access was revoked.

For circuit users to connect their virtual network gateways to the ExpressRoute circuit, the circuit owner creates an authorization, which establishes an authorization key. Authorizations can be used only once. The following code shows how this is done:

```
$circuit = Get-AzExpressRouteCircuit -Name "SybexCircuit"
-ResourceGroupName "SybexRG"
Add-AzExpressRouteCircuitAuthorization
-ExpressRouteCircuit $circuit -Name "SybexAuthorization1"
Set-AzExpressRouteCircuit
-ExpressRouteCircuit $circuit
$circuit = Get-AzExpressRouteCircuit -Name "SybexCircuit"
-ResourceGroupName "SybexRG"
```

```
$auth1 = Get-AzExpressRouteCircuitAuthorization
-ExpressRouteCircuit $circuit -Name "SybexAuthorization1"
```

The next example shows how a circuit owner reviews an authorization key:

```
$circuit = Get-AzExpressRouteCircuit -Name "SybexCircuit"
-ResourceGroupName "SybexRG".
$authorizations = Get-AzExpressRouteCircuitAuthorization
-ExpressRouteCircuit $circuit
```

Here is how you add an authorization key (the required role is circuit owner):

```
$circuit = Get-AzExpressRouteCircuit -Name "SybexCircuit"
-ResourceGroupName "SybexRG"
Add-AzExpressRouteCircuitAuthorization
-ExpressRouteCircuit $circuit -Name "SybexAuthorization2"
Set-AzExpressRouteCircuit -ExpressRouteCircuit $circuit
$circuit = Get-AzExpressRouteCircuit -Name "SybexCircuit"
-ResourceGroupName "SybexRG"
$authorizations = Get-AzExpressRouteCircuitAuthorization
-ExpressRouteCircuit $circuit
```

The following code shows deleting an authorization key (required role is circuit owner):

```
Remove-AzExpressRouteCircuitAuthorization
-Name "SybexAuthorization2"
-ExpressRouteCircuit $circuit
Set-AzExpressRouteCircuit -ExpressRouteCircuit $circuit
```

The circuit user must obtain the peer ID and the circuit owner's authorization key. Globally unique identifiers (GUIDs) are used for authorization keys.

You can use this command to check the peer ID:

```
Get-AzExpressRouteCircuit -Name ""SybexCircuit"" -ResourceGroupName
""SybexRG""
```

Circuit users can redeem link authorizations by running the following cmdlets; the minimum required role is circuit user.

```
$id = ""/subscriptions/********************************/resourceGroups/
ERCrossSubTestRG/providers/
Microsoft.Network/expressRouteCircuits/SybexCircuit"
$gw = Get-AzVirtualNetworkGateway -Name "ExpressRouteGw"
-ResourceGroupName "SybexRG"
$connection = New-AzVirtualNetworkGatewayConnection
-Name "SybexER_01" -ResourceGroupName "RemoteResourceGroup"
-Location "UAE North" -VirtualNetworkGateway1 $gw
-PeerId $id -ConnectionType ExpressRoute -AuthorizationKey
"^^^^^^^^^^^^^^^^^^^^^^^^^^^^^^^^^^^^^^^^^^^^^"
```

Consumer virtual networks can be connected to multiple ExpressRoute circuits. Several ExpressRoute circuits can provide the same prefix. As shown in the following code, you can modify a connection's RoutingWeight to specify which connection to use for traffic destined for this prefix. That connection receives traffic.

```
$connection = Get-AzVirtualNetworkGatewayConnection -Name
"SybexVirtualNetworkConnection"
-ResourceGroupName "SybexRG"
$connection.RoutingWeight = 100
Set-AzVirtualNetworkGatewayConnection
-VirtualNetworkGatewayConnection $connection
```

On the on-premises side, Microsoft peering is typically terminated on the perimeter network (also known as DMZ, demilitarized zone, and screened subnet), whereas private peering is terminated on the core network zone. Firewalls generally are used to separate the zones. You should filter through only the public IP addresses that are advertised over Microsoft peering when configuring Microsoft peering exclusively for enabling tunneling over ExpressRoute.

Recommend a Route Advertisement Configuration

Organizations must set up and manage the ExpressRoute to connect to Microsoft cloud services. Some connectivity providers offer managed services for setting up and managing the routing. Find out if your organization's network connectivity providers supply this service. Otherwise, follow these guidelines:

- You must reserve a few blocks of IP addresses to configure routing between your networks and MSEE routers.

- High availability configurations using Microsoft do not support router redundancy protocols—for example, Hot Standby Router Protocol (HSRP) and Virtual Router Redundancy Protocol (VRRP). Microsoft's solution uses a pair of redundant BGP sessions for high availability.

- Public or private IPv4 addresses can be used for private peering by cloud service consumers. These addresses aren't advertised online. Private peering allows Microsoft to isolate traffic end to end, so overlapping addresses with other customers is impossible.

- Customers of Microsoft's cloud services can connect to the Microsoft peering path. Services on the list include Microsoft 365 services, such as Exchange Online, SharePoint Online, Skype for Business, and Microsoft Teams. Connectivity between Microsoft peering sites is bidirectional. For traffic to reach Microsoft cloud services, valid public IPv4 addresses must be used.

- A session between the MSEEs and your routers is established via eBGP. Routing exchanges are done using BGP. There is no requirement for BGP authentication. MD5 hashes can be configured if necessary.

- Microsoft uses AS 12076 for Azure public, Azure private, and Azure peering. From 65515 to 65520, Microsoft reserves ASNs for internal use. AS numbers in both 16- and 32-bit formats are supported.

- The Azure private peering allows for advertising up to 4,000 IPv4 addresses and 100 IPv6 addresses. The ExpressRoute Premium add-on allows you to increase this number to 10,000 IPv4 prefixes. During a BGP session for Azure public and Microsoft peering, Microsoft will accept up to 200 prefixes.

- Transit routers cannot be configured with ExpressRoute. For transit routing services, you must rely on the providers of their network connectivity.

- Azure private peering sessions can only use default routes. All traffic from the associated virtual networks will be routed to your network in such a case. Default routes into private peering will result in the Internet path from Azure being blocked. Services hosted in Azure must rely on corporate edges to route traffic to and from the Internet.

- The following items must be in place before you can connect to Azure services and infrastructure services:

  - Peering between Azure public endpoints is enabled.

  - Each subnet requiring Internet connectivity can be connected to the cloud by using user-defined routing.

  - Peering paths with Microsoft with routes tagged with appropriate community values will be advertised publicly by Microsoft. Microsoft, however, will not honor any community values tagged to routes advertised to Microsoft.

Configure Encryption over ExpressRoute

ExpressRoute ensures the privacy and integrity of data traversing between Microsoft's network and the cloud as part of its encryption capabilities.

Data is encrypted at the media access control (MAC) level or Network Layer 2 by MACsec, an IEEE standard. The MACsec protocol can encrypt the physical links between your networks and Microsoft's network devices when connecting to Microsoft via ExpressRoute Direct. By default, MACsec is not enabled on ExpressRoute Direct ports. Azure Key Vault lets cloud users store their MACsec keys for encryption in the cloud.

The MACsec protocol encrypts all traffic on a physical link with a key that belongs to one entity (i.e., the customer). This protocol is only available with ExpressRoute Direct. MACsec encrypts all network control traffic, BGP data, and customer data traffic once enabled.

As an alternative to preshared keys, Microsoft supports MACsec configuration. This means you need to update your keys on your devices and Microsoft's via an API. You will lose connectivity when a critical mismatch between the two sides occurs. Microsoft strongly recommends scheduling a maintenance window for the configuration change. After you switch your network traffic to another link, you can update the ExpressRoute Direct configuration on one link to reduce downtime. When MACsec is configured and there is a key mismatch, your end user loses connectivity to Microsoft. Microsoft won't fall back to unencrypted connections, because that would expose your data.

MACsec encryption and decryption happen in hardware on the routers Microsoft uses, which has no impact on performance. Nonetheless, you should check with your network device vendor to see whether MACsec has any performance implications.

As of this writing, Microsoft supports the following encryption ciphers:

- GCM-AES-128
- GCM-AES-256
- GCM-AES-XPN-128
- GCM-AES-XPN-256

The IPsec standard is an Internet Engineering Task Force (IETF) standard. At the IP level, IPsec encrypts data at Network Layer 3. You can use the IPsec protocol to encrypt connections between your on-premises and VNets on Azure.

MACsec secures your physical connections to Microsoft. Your physical network and your virtual network on Azure are connected and secured using IPsec. You can enable IPsec independently.

Deploy Bidirectional Forwarding Detection

Bidirectional Forwarding Detection (BFD) is supported both by ExpressRoute over private peering and by Microsoft peering. By configuring BFD over ExpressRoute, you can speed up the link failure detection between MSEE devices and routers that connect to your ExpressRoute circuits (CE/PE). If you have chosen a managed Layer 3 connection service, you can configure ExpressRoute over your edge routing devices or your partner's edge routing devices.

You can enable ExpressRoute circuits through Layer 2 connections or managed Layer 3 connections. If there is more than one Layer 2 device in the ExpressRoute path, the overlying BGP session is responsible for detecting link failures.

MSEE devices are configured to keep alive for 60 seconds and to hold for 180 seconds in BGP. When a link fails, it may take up to 3 minutes for traffic to be switched to an alternative link.

You can configure a lower BGP hold-and-keep-alive time on your edge peering device. BGP sessions will be established based on the lower value when the BGP timers don't match the peer devices. As little as 3 seconds can be specified as the BGP keep-alive period and as little as 10 seconds as the hold time. BGP is a process-intensive protocol, so Microsoft does not recommend setting a very aggressive timer.

BFD is configured by default on all newly created ExpressRoute private peering interfaces on MSMEs. So, you only need to configure BFD on your primary and secondary devices to enable BFD. Two steps are involved in configuring BFD: configuring the BFD on the interface and linking it to the BGP session.

BFD peers determine their transmission rate based on which of them is slower. A 300-millisecond transmission/receive interval is set for MSEE's BFDs. Depending on the scenario, the interval may be set as high as 750 milliseconds. These intervals can be made longer by configuring a higher value, but they cannot be made shorter.

Diagnose and Resolve ExpressRoute Connection Issues

In this section you learn how to check and troubleshoot Microsoft Azure ExpressRoute connectivity. A connection provider typically facilitates a private connection that extends an on-premises network into the Microsoft cloud with ExpressRoute. ExpressRoute connections usually consist of three different network zones:

- An organization's network
- Network service provider
- Microsoft Azure datacenter

The following list shows various checkpoints you need to verify and validate:

- Verify CircuitProvisioningState is enabled and not disabled.
- Verify ServiceProviderProvisioningState is provisioned.
- Validate Peering Configuration.
- Validate ARP.
- Validate BGP and routes on the MSEE.
- Confirm the traffic flow.

Follow the steps in Exercise 3.3 to troubleshoot Azure ExpressRoute connectivity.

EXERCISE 3.3

Troubleshoot Azure ExpressRoute Connectivity

1. Verify `CircuitProvisioningState` is enabled.

   Use the following cmdlet to select an ExpressRoute circuit within a resource group:

   ```
   Get-AzExpressRouteCircuit -ResourceGroupName "Sybex-ER-RG" -Name "Sybex-ER-Ckt"
   ```
   Determine whether an ExpressRoute `CircuitProvisioningState` is enabled:

   ```
   CircuitProvisioningState        : Enabled
   ```

2. Verify `ServiceProviderProvisioningState` is provisioned.

   Use the following cmdlet to verify service provider provisioning state:

   ```
   Get-AzExpressRouteCircuit -ResourceGroupName "Sybex-ER-RG" -Name "Sybex-ER-Ckt"
   ```
   In the output, use the following fields to determine whether an ExpressRoute `ServiceProviderProvisioningState` is provisioned, and the following status example shows it is provisioned.

   ```
   ServiceProviderProvisioningState : Provisioned
   ```

3. Validate the peering configuration: Microsoft peering (traffic to public endpoints of PaaS and SaaS) or Azure private peering (traffic to private virtual networks in Azure). Use the following cmdlet to get Azure private peering configuration details:

   ```
   $ckt = Get-AzExpressRouteCircuit -ResourceGroupName "Sybex-ER-RG"
   -Name "Sybex-ER-Ckt"
   Get-AzExpressRouteCircuitPeeringConfig -Name "SybexPrivatePeering"
   -ExpressRouteCircuit $ckt
   ```

   Use this command to get Azure public peering configuration details:

   ```
   $ckt = Get-AzExpressRouteCircuit -ResourceGroupName "Sybex-ER-RG"
   -Name "Sybex-ER-Ckt"
   Get-AzExpressRouteCircuitPeeringConfig -Name "SybexPublicPeering"
   -ExpressRouteCircuit $ckt
   ```

   Use this command to get Microsoft public peering configuration details:

   ```
   $ckt = Get-AzExpressRouteCircuit -ResourceGroupName "Sybex-ER-RG"
   -Name ""Sybex-ER-Ckt""
   Get-AzExpressRouteCircuitPeeringConfig -Name ""MSSybexPeering""
   -ExpressRouteCircuit $ckt
   ```

4. Validate Address Resolution Protocol (ARP). A peering's IP address and MAC address can be found in the ARP table. For each interface (primary and secondary), the ARP table includes the following items:

   - Aligning the IP address of your on-premises routers to the MAC address.

   - Aligning the IP address on an Azure ExpressRoute router with the MAC address.

   - Validating Layer 2 configurations and troubleshooting Layer 2 connectivity issues can be helped by knowing the age of the mapping ARP tables.

5. Validate BGP and routes on the MSEE.

   Use the following command to get the routing table from MSEE for the primary path of the private routing context:

   ```
   Get-AzExpressRouteCircuitRouteTable -DevicePath Primary
   -ExpressRouteCircuitName "Sybex-ER-Ckt" -PeeringType AzurePrivatePeering
   -ResourceGroupName "Sybex-ER-RG"
   ```

   Check if the primary and secondary peer subnets assigned to an MSEE and a CE/PE-MSEE match the configuration on the linked CE/PE-MSEE and if the state of an eBGP peering between them is active or idle. You should also check if the MSEEs are using the correct `VlanId`, `AzureAsn`, and `PeerAsn` and if these values map to those used on the PE-MSEE/CE linked to it. If MD5 hashing is chosen, the shared key should be the same on the CE/PE-MSEE pair and MSEE.

6. Confirm the traffic flow. Use the following command to get traffic statistics for both the primary and secondary paths within a peering context:

   ```
   Get-AzExpressRouteCircuitStats -ResourceGroupName "Sybex-ER-RG"
   -ExpressRouteCircuitName $CircuitName
   -PeeringType 'SybexPrivatePeering'
   ```

Address Resolution Protocol (ARP) is the protocol that bridges Layer 2 and Layer 3 of the OSI (Open Systems Interconnection) model and acts as an adhesive between Ethernet and IP in typical TCP/IP stacks. By determining a device's IP address, we can discover its MAC address.

ExpressRoute circuits are uniquely identified by their service keys. Microsoft or an ExpressRoute partner can assist you if you provide the service key to identify the circuit. Azure resources record information about changes—in this case, who last modified the resource.

Summary

In this chapter, you learned about ExpressRoute and how to design an Azure consumer network with ExpressRoute and perform required ExpressRoute configuration. You also learned how to decide on the appropriate SKU based on business requirements. We discussed ExpressRoute Global Reach and ExpressRoute FastPath, and you gained a detailed understanding about ExpressRoute peering, private peering, and Microsoft peering.

You should now be able to design, deploy, and manage Azure ExpressRoute for your organization to connect between on-premises and Azure networks. You should also be able to design and implement a hybrid connectivity solution that will address the short- and long-term goals of your organization's global enterprise IT footprint.

Exam Essentials

Understand the difference between a provider and a direct model (ExpressRoute Direct).   Using ExpressRoute Direct, you can connect directly to Microsoft's global network at peering locations strategically distributed worldwide. With ExpressRoute Direct, you can have dual 10 Gbps or 100 Gbps connections and active/active connectivity at scale. ExpressRoute uses a service provider to provide fast connectivity to existing infrastructure and enable onboarding. Ethernet and MPLS providers are supported. ExpressRoute uses service provider–supported SKUs of 50 Mbps up to 10 Gbps.

Be able to design and implement Azure cross-region connectivity between multiple ExpressRoute locations.   Based on specific organizational requirements, ExpressRoute can be designed and implemented in various ways.

The following services can be accessed via ExpressRoute connections:

- Microsoft Azure services
- Microsoft 365 services

These provide support for all regions within a geographic region, with access to all regions within that region from any of the peering locations.

Know the appropriate ExpressRoute SKU and tier.   Three different circuit solutions are offered by ExpressRoute: Local, Standard, and Premium. These SKU types have different pricing structures from which you can choose: metered (pay by the gigabyte used) or an unlimited version.

Understand how to design and deploy ExpressRoute.   ExpressRoute enables you to seamlessly connect on-premises networks to Azure services. Before deploying an ExpressRoute circuit, you must choose ExpressRoute circuit SKUs, select a peering location, choose the right ExpressRoute circuit, and decide on a billing model.

Be able to design and deploy ExpressRoute FastPath. ExpressRoute virtual network gateways are used to route network traffic and exchange network routes. FastPath is designed to improve the performance of the data path between your on-premises network and your virtual network. With FastPath enabled, network traffic is sent directly to VMs within the virtual network, bypassing the gateway.

Understand the peering associated with an ExpressRoute circuit. Two peering options are associated with an ExpressRoute circuit: Azure private and Microsoft. For high availability, every peering is configured identically on two routers (active/active or load-sharing configurations). Azure services are divided into Azure public and Azure private, based on the IP address scheme used.

Know how to create and configure an ExpressRoute gateway. You must first create a virtual network gateway in order to connect your Azure virtual network with your on-premises network through ExpressRoute. A virtual network gateway exchanges IP routes between networks and routes traffic. FastPath requires an UltraPerformance or ErGw3AZ virtual network gateway. If you plan to use FastPath with ExpressRoute-based IPv6-based private peering, ensure that the SKU is ErGw3AZ. Remember that FastPath is only available on circuits using ExpressRoute Direct.

Understand how to connect a virtual network to an ExpressRoute circuit. Using the Azure portal, you can create a connection to link a virtual network to an Azure ExpressRoute circuit. The virtual networks you connect to your Azure ExpressRoute circuit can either be in the same subscription or part of another subscription. A standard ExpressRoute circuit can connect up to 10 virtual networks. Standard ExpressRoute circuits require all virtual networks to be in the same geopolitical region. The maximum number of ExpressRoute circuits in a single VNet is 16. ExpressRoute circuits can be in the same subscription, different subscriptions, or both.

Know how to configure a route advertisement. To configure routing between your network and the MSEE's routers, you need to reserve a few blocks of IP addresses. To configure peerings, you can use private IP addresses or public IP addresses. Azure must not use overlapping address ranges for configuring routes and creating virtual networks. You must use public IP addresses to set up the BGP sessions. Through Routing Internet Registries and Internet Routing Registries, Microsoft must be able to verify ownership of IP addresses.

Know how to configure encryption over ExpressRoute. Through an Azure ExpressRoute circuit, you can establish an IPsec/IKE VPN connection from your on-premises network to Azure using Azure Virtual WAN. Using this technique, on-premises and Azure virtual networks can be connected securely over ExpressRoute without going over the public Internet or using public IP addresses. Setting up the connection is straightforward:

- Connect ExpressRoute to a private peering and ExpressRoute circuit.
- Set up a VPN connection.

This configuration includes ExpressRoute and VPN paths for routing between on-premises and Azure networks.

Know how to implement Bidirectional Forwarding Detection.   Bidirectional Forwarding Detection (BFD) is supported over private and Microsoft peering in ExpressRoute. You can use BFD over ExpressRoute to increase the speed of link failure detection between MSEE and routers that are configured for your ExpressRoute circuit (CE/PE). ExpressRoute can be configured on your edge routing devices or your Partner Edge routing devices (if you choose managed Layer 3 connection service).

Understand how to diagnose and resolve ExpressRoute connection issues.   ExpressRoute extends an on-premises network into the Microsoft cloud over a private connection that a connectivity provider commonly facilitates. ExpressRoute connectivity traditionally involves three distinct network zones: customer network, provider network, and Microsoft data-center. Logical steps in troubleshooting an ExpressRoute circuit start with verifying circuit provisioning and state and moving on to validating peering configuration, validating ARP, validating BGP and routes on the MSEE, confirming the traffic flow, performing a private peering connectivity test, and verifying availability of the virtual network gateway.

Review Questions

1. What is the best use of ExpressRoute?
   A. To connect securely and reliably to Azure services
   B. To connect on-premises services from a remote office
   C. To interconnect on-premises services within an organization
   D. None of the above

2. What is the best use case to connect ExpressRoute Premium?
   A. Only available within a metro area
   B. Local resources available within a region
   C. Resources in different geography regions
   D. None of the above

3. Which bandwidth options are available with ExpressRoute?
   A. 50 Mbps
   B. 100 Mbps
   C. 500 Mbps
   D. 1 GB
   E. All the above and a few more

4. From Microsoft Azure VPN, which of the following is valid?
   A. Azure VPN is the right choice to connect Azure and Microsoft 365.
   B. Azure S2S VPN is not the right choice to connect Azure and Microsoft 365 services.
   C. Azure P2S VPN is the only way to connect Azure and Microsoft 365 services.
   D. None of the above.

5. ExpressRoute Direct is Azure's offering for which of the following? (Choose all that apply.)
   A. Data ingestion
   B. Dedicated capacity for regulated industry
   C. A connection that requires more bandwidth than usual
   D. None the above

6. What is the maximum number of prefixes supported through Azure private peering?
   A. 4,000 by default
   B. 10,000 with ExpressRoute
   C. 200
   D. None of the above

7. How would you select a peering service to connect Microsoft 365 and PaaS services?

   A. Azure PaaS and Microsoft 365 can be accessed via private peering.

   B. Azure PaaS and Microsoft 365 can be accessed via Microsoft peering.

   C. Azure PaaS and Microsoft 365 can be accessed via public peering.

   D. None of the above.

8. ExpressRoute supports which of the following?

   A. BGP (Border Gateway Protocol)

   B. Static routing

   C. Active/passive disaster recovery

   D. Both A and C

9. Identify the billing models available with Azure ExpressRoute.

   A. Unlimited data

   B. Metered data

   C. ExpressRoute Premium add-on

   D. All of the above

10. Which of these is the most important consideration for Azure ExpressRoute configuration?

   A. Peering IP address

   B. Peering region

   C. High availability and disaster recovery

   D. VPN type

11. Through Microsoft peering, you want to consume certain services. What should you configure?

   A. Network firewall

   B. Network switch

   C. Route filter

   D. None of the above

12. IPv4 is supported in which of the following?

   A. Azure private peering

   B. Azure public peering

   C. Microsoft peering

   D. All the above

13. Azure private peering by default supports which of these?

   A. 4,000 prefixes

   B. 400 connections

   C. 4,000 by default and cannot be extended further

   D. None of the above

14. Any valid IP address within an organization's WAN is supported by which of the following?

    A. Azure private peering

    B. Azure public peering

    C. Microsoft peering

    D. All the above

15. What is the maximum number of circuit connections supported by the UltraPerformance gateway SKU?

    A. Unlimited

    B. 64

    C. 8

    D. 32

    E. None of the above

16. An ExpressRoute connection established via a third-party network provider can provide a maximum speed of _____.

    A. 100 Gbps

    B. 10 Gbps

    C. 50 Gbps

    D. 1 Gbps

17. FastPath is supported in which type of ExpressRoute SKU?

    A. Standard

    B. HighPerformance

    C. UltraPerformance

    D. All the above

18. From a FastPath perspective, which of the following is valid?

    A. FastPath enables sending traffic directly to a VM within a virtual network.

    B. FastPath enables sending traffic proxy to a VM within a virtual network.

    C. FastPath is not able to send traffic directly to a VM within a virtual network.

    D. None of the above.

19. Identify the best practices recommended by Microsoft when designing ExpressRoute DR. (Choose all that apply.)

    A. Apply geo-redundancy.

    B. Avoid diverse network suppliers.

    C. Use high availability.

    D. Terminate at the same location.

20. Which of the following is a valid statement about Azure ExpressRoute?

   A. It is necessary to have an existing Azure account to access Azure ExpressRoute.

   B. It is not necessary to have an existing Azure account to access Azure ExpressRoute.

   C. It is necessary to have an existing Azure minimum credit to access Azure ExpressRoute.

   D. None of the above.

Chapter

4

Design and Deploy Core Networking Infrastructure: Private IP and DNS

THE MICROSOFT AZ-700 EXAM OBJECTIVES COVERED IN THIS CHAPTER INCLUDE:

✓ **Design and implement private IP addressing for VNets**

- Create a VNet
- Plan and configure subnetting for services, including VNet gateways, private endpoints, firewalls, application gateways, and VNet-integrated platform services
- Plan and configure subnet delegation
- Plan and configure subnetting for Azure Route Server

✓ **Design and implement name resolution**

- Design public DNS zones
- Design private DNS zones
- Design name resolution inside a VNet
- Configure a public or private DNS zone
- Link a private DNS zone to a VNet

The following are critical prerequisites for reading this chapter: you must have experience with networking concepts, including knowledge of IP addresses, DNS, routing, and networks like VPNs or WANs. You should also be familiar with the Azure portal and Azure PowerShell.

This chapter has two parts. First, you will read about designing private IP addresses for virtual networks (VNets), deploying VNets using Azure command-line tools and the Azure portal, and steps for preparing and configuring services for subnetting that include VNet gateways, Private Endpoint, firewalls, application gateways, and VNet-integrated platform services. Security aspects such as network security groups (NSGs) and access control lists (ACLs) for subnets are also discussed in detail, along with deployment and configuration steps. You will also learn about subnet delegation, planning, and subnetting for Azure route services.

In the second part, you will learn to design and deploy a domain name system (DNS) in private and public zones. Setting up DNS for name resolution inside VNets is explored in detail along with linking a private DNS zone to a VNet.

By the end of this chapter, you will understand some of the most crucial aspects of designing and deploying private IP addressing for VNets. Additionally, you will have detailed insight into designing and deploying name resolution.

Designing Private IP Addressing for VNets

In Chapter 1, "Getting Started with AZ-700 Certification for Azure Networking," you read about Azure virtual networks (VNets). Let's do a quick recap to get you prepared for what you'll learn about in this chapter.

The *Azure VNet* is the fundamental building block for a private network. VNets provide a secure communication channel between Azure resources, such as virtual machines (VMs). VNets are like traditional datacenters but have the advantage of Azure's infrastructure, such as scalability, availability, reliability, broad network access, hybrid connectivity, segmentation, isolation, and security.

Azure VNets are the representation of your own networks in the cloud. The Azure cloud is logically isolated and dedicated to your subscription. VNets can be used to provision and manage virtual private networks (VPNs) in Azure. Alternatively, they can be linked to other VNets in Azure or your on-premises IT infrastructure to create hybrid or hybrid cross-premises solutions. You can link each VNet you make with another VNet and an on-premises network if the Classless Inter-Domain Routing (CIDR) blocks don't overlap. You can also control VNet settings, and subnets can be segmented.

The Azure VNet enables Azure resources to communicate with the Internet and on-premises networks securely. Critical scenarios include the following:

- Communication between Azure resources
- Contact with on-premises resources
- Filtering and routing of network traffic
- Integration with Azure services

Organizations can use VNets to do the following:

Build a dedicated private cloud-native VNet.   Organizations do not always need cross-premises configurations. By creating a VNet, you allow your organization's services and VMs within cloud consumer VNets to communicate directly and securely within the cloud. You can still configure endpoint connections for VMs and services that need Internet connectivity as part of Azure's virtual network solution.

Securely connect an on-premises datacenter.   Organizations can use VNets to securely connect their on-premise datacenters to the cloud via traditional site-to-site (S2S) VPNs. Azure provides secure connections between cloud-based enterprise VPN gateways and S2S VPNs using IPsec.

Provide organizations with the ability to support a range of hybrid cloud scenarios.   The cloud can be securely connected to on-premises systems such as mainframes and Unix servers.

Azure VNets use private IP addresses. Private IP addresses fall within the same range as on-premises addresses. You have complete control over IP address assignment, name resolution, security settings, and security rules in an Azure VNet just as you do with on-premises networks. According to the CIDR for the IP address block, you can add or remove subnets.

Azure networks usually consist of essential components such as the following:

- Virtual networks
- Network security groups
- Subnets
- load balancers
- Firewalls

Azure's network structure is like an on-premises network, but its features and functions are different. Unlike on-premises networks, the Azure network does not follow a typical hierarchical structure. Azure allows you to scale infrastructure up and down on demand following cloud computing principles. It takes seconds for an organization's Azure resources to be provisioned, and routers and switches aren't required. You can logically segment a network according to your organization's demand since the entire infrastructure is virtual.

Network segmentation is an architectural practice that separates a network into numerous segments or subnets, each operating as its small network. This allows you to control traffic flow between subnets based on acceptable policies. Your organization can use segmentation to enhance monitoring, increase performance, localize technical problems, and significantly enhance security.

You can typically implement an NSG and a firewall. Subnets enable you to separate front- and back-end services, such as web servers and DNS, from each other. The Network layer filters traffic between internal and external servers. Firewalls can perform Network layer filtering as well as Application layer filtering. Your business can improve isolation of your resources for secure network architecture by using NSGs and a firewall.

A virtual network is a network in the cloud that is intended to serve cloud consumers. Virtual networks can be divided into multiple subnetworks. The cloud consumer virtual network is assigned a portion of each subnet. If there are no VMs or services deployed in a subnet, you can add, delete, expand, and shrink virtual networks.

In Azure VNets, all subnets can communicate by default. However, you can block communication between subnets by setting up an NSG. Subnet mask /29 is the smallest supported subnet; the largest supported subnet is /8.

You must know how to connect Azure virtual network resources with your organization's on-premises networks and configure IP addresses in the VNet. There are three types of resources that can have IP addresses assigned to them in Azure virtual networks:

- Virtual machine network interfaces
- load balancers
- Application gateways

You can establish them as dynamic (DHCP lease) or static (DHCP reservation). Organization on-premises and Azure virtual networks use private IP addresses:

- Dynamic private IP addresses are assigned using DHCP leases and are subject to change throughout their life span. Azure assigns the IP addresses in a subnet's address range that are currently unassigned or unreserved. If addresses 10.0.0.4–10.0.0.9 are already assigned to other resources, Azure gives 10.0.0.10 to a new resource.
- As a default, dynamic allocation is used. When an IP address has been assigned, it is released if it is:
  - Deleted
  - Reassigned
  - Modified to static

When you change the allocation method from dynamic to static, Azure assigns the previous dynamically assigned address as the static address. A static private IP address is assigned by DHCP reservation and does not change throughout the Azure resource. When a resource is stopped or deallocated, static IP addresses persist.

A subnet's address range, for instance, is `10.0.0.0/16`, and the addresses `10.0.0.4-10.0.0.9` are used by other resources. You can assign any address between `10.0.0.10` and `10.0.255.254`. Statically assigned addresses can only be released when you remove network interfaces.

When the allocation method is changed, Azure assigns a static IP address as a dynamic IP address. If the available address in the subnet is not set, the reassignment will occur. A network interface's address changes when it is assigned to a different subnet.

To assign the network interface to a different subnet, you must change the allocation method from static to dynamic. Then you set the allocation method back to static after assigning the interface to a different subnet. Affix the interface to an IP address in the new subnet's range.

For virtual machines in Linux or Windows, network interface cards or network interface cards are assigned one or more private IP addresses. The allocation method for private IP addresses can be dynamic or static, depending on the business requirement. For Azure internal load balancers and Azure application gateways, you can assign the private IP address to the front-end configuration.

Next let's turn to the fundamentals of IP addressing for Azure virtual networks.

The Azure VNet is fundamental to your organization's network. The scope of IP addresses is defined when you create a VNet. You are responsible for assigning IP addresses, setting security policies, and controlling security rules in the virtual network. Azure private IP addressing works the same way it does in on-premises networks. The Internet Assigned Numbers Authority (IANA) reserves private IP addresses for an organization's network based on the requirements of the cloud consumer's network:

- `10.0.0.0/8`
- `172.16.0.0/12`
- `192.168.0.0/16`

In a virtual network, a subnet is a set of IP addresses. You can divide the virtual network into multiple subnets. CIDR specifies the address range for each subnet. The CIDR format is used to represent a block of IP addresses in a network. CIDRs, established as part of IP addresses, indicate the length of the network prefix.

Take, for example, the CIDR `192.168.10.0/24`. The network address is `192.168.10.0`. `192.168.10.0` is part of the network address, whereas the last 8 bits are assigned to specific hosts. Address ranges for virtual networks and on-premise networks cannot overlap.

All Azure subnets are assigned three IP addresses by default. To comply with protocols, the first and last IP addresses of all subnets are also dedicated. An internal DHCP service manages the lease of IP addresses within Azure. Azure cloud consumers are not able to configure the `.1`, `.2`, and `.3` IP addresses—Azure reserves these IP addresses for internal use.

You must compile requirements for your infrastructure before planning a network IP address scheme. These requirements will also help you prepare for future growth by reserving extra IP addresses and subnets. Here are questions you might ask to determine your requirements:

- What is the number of devices on your network?
- When do you plan on adding more devices to your network?

- What devices do you need to separate based on the services running on the infrastructure?
- Do you need multiple subnets?
- How many devices is your organization planning on adding to subnets in the future?
- In the future, how many subnets are you planning to add?

Keep in mind while designing IP schema that CIDR allows a more flexible allocation of IP addresses than was possible with the original system of IP address classes. You need to determine your business's requirements to slice the IP block into subnets and hosts. You should be familiar with the criteria for determining the number of devices on the network per subnet and how many subnets cloud users require.

Azure uses the first three IP addresses on each subnet. Protocol conformance is also reserved for the first and last IP addresses of a subnet. As a result, there are two *n-5 addresses on an Azure subnet, where n is the number of host bits.

Virtual networks can be deployed, and your cloud resources connected easily, when you understand the core concepts and best practices for implementing VNets (refer to Chapter 1 for a refresher). The rest of this section discusses the core concepts and best practices to follow while designing IP addresses for VNets.

Address Space VNets require a unique private IP address space, either public or private (RFC 1918). Virtual networks in Azure are assigned a private IP address from the address space that you specify. A virtual network can be created in more than one region per subscription. Virtual networks can contain multiple subnets.

In your design and deployment, take into consideration this list of non-routable address spaces:

- `10.0.0.0 - 10.255.255.255 (10/8 prefix)`
- `172.16.0.0 - 172.31.255.255 (172.16/12 prefix)`
- `192.168.0.0 - 192.168.255.255 (192.168/16 prefix)`

Setting the address space for a virtual network is one of the most critical configurations. The entire network will be divided into subnets using the whole IP range. There are five address spaces that you cannot add to your virtual network:

- `224.0.0.0/4` is used for Azure multicast.
- `255.255.255.255/32` is used for Azure broadcast.
- `127.0.0.0/8` is used for Azure loopback.
- `169.254.0.0/16` is used for Azure link-local.
- `168.63.129.16/32` is used for Azure internal DNS.

Also, having overlapping address spaces will prevent you from connecting virtual networks.

Subnets   Using subnets, you can segment the virtual network into one or more subnetworks, each of which receives a portion of the virtual network's address space. After that, Azure resources can be deployed within a specific subnet. Using subnets, you may segment your VNet address space for the organization's internal network, much like in a traditional network. Address allocation is also made more efficient in this way.

The Azure cloud services reserve five IP addresses for each subnet, starting from x.x.x.0 to x.x.x.3, and the last address in the subnets.

- x.x.x.0 is the network address used by Azure.
- x.x.x.1 is reserved by Azure for the default gateway.
- x.x.x.2 and x.x.x.3 map the Azure DNS IPs to the VNet space.
- x.x.x.255 is a network broadcast address for subnets of size /25 and greater. This will be a different address in smaller subnets.

According to Azure CIDR, the largest CIDR subnet supported in Azure is /29, and the smallest is /2 (CIDR IPv4 subnet definitions). /64 is the minimum size for IPv6 subnets.

Consider the following in the design and deployment process:

- VNets are Layer 3 overlays. The Azure platform does not support Layer 2 semantics.
- A routing table can be deployed and associated with a subnet.
- CIDR must be used to specify each subnet's address range.
- You can build several subnets and allow a service endpoint for some subnets.
- Azure VNet does not support multicast or broadcast.
- Subnets can be used for traffic management.
- Virtual network service endpoints permit you to regulate access to Azure resources by subnet.
- You can use network security groups to segment your network further based on IP address classification.
- You will not be able to ping default routers within a VNet.
- You will not be able to use tracert to diagnose connectivity.
- The default limit per virtual network is 3,000 subnets, but that can be scaled up to 10,000 with Microsoft support.
- VNets can be extended by adding subnets whenever available space in the network's address range remains, and the subnet address range is not already assigned to another subnet.

- Availability sets tell Azure that several cloud consumer VMs perform the same workload, so they shouldn't be vulnerable to the same fault or update domain. If your organization selects an availability set while creating a VM in the portal, you can only deploy your VM to the VNet where the other VMs are deployed, and the option to create a new VNet is removed.

- It is impossible to move VMs from one VNet to another without deleting and then re-creating them, but you can move the subnet in which a VM is located within the same VNet. A new IP address is assigned to the NIC by changing its configuration. The static IP address is outside of the address range of the new subnet. Static IP addresses must be replaced with dynamic ones before moving the VM.

Deploying a VNet

In Chapter 1, you worked through the step-by-step deployment of Azure VNets using the Azure portal and Azure PowerShell. In this chapter you'll create a VNet using the Azure cloud shell.

VMs can communicate privately and with the Internet through a virtual network. In this section, you'll deploy a virtual network and then deploy two VMs into it.

Subnetworks are ranges of IP addresses within the virtual network. To organize and secure a virtual network, you can divide it into multiple subnets. Each NIC in a VM belongs to one virtual network subnet. NICs connected to different subnets within a virtual network can communicate without any additional configuration.

When setting up the virtual network, you specify their topology, including the available address spaces and subnets. Select address ranges that do not overlap when connecting the virtual network to other virtual networks or on-premises networks. Any address range in Azure is treated as a private virtual network IP address space. An IP address is a private address that only the computer can access. Only the address range of the virtual network, interconnected virtual networks, and the on-premises location can be accessed.

By default, security boundaries do not exist between subnets. This allows virtual machines within each subnet to communicate. Use NSGs to control traffic flows between subnets and VMs if your deployment needs security boundaries.

An *access control list (ACL)* defines whether network traffic is allowed or denied for subnets or NICs in an NSG. NSGs can be associated with subnets or individual NICs. ACLs are applied to all VMs in a subnet if an NSG is associated with that subnet. By associating an NSG directly to a NIC, you can restrict NIC traffic.

To create a new virtual network using the Azure cloud shell, follow the steps in Exercise 4.1.

EXERCISE 4.1

Deploying a Virtual Network in Azure via Azure Cloud Shell

Before creating a virtual network, you must create a resource group to host the virtual network if it does not exist already. Using `az group create`, create a resource group. This example deploys a resource group named SybexvNet-rg in the Westus location:

```
az group create \
        --name SybexVNet-rg \
        --location westus
```

1. Log into a personal or business account in the Azure cloud shell at `https://shell .azure.com`.

2. Use the following code to deploy a default virtual network named SybexVNet with one subnet named `default`:

```
az network vnet create \
        --name SybexVNet \
        --resource-group SybexVNet-rg \
        --subnet-name default
```

3. Using `az vm create create`, deploy a default virtual machine named SybexVM1. If there are no SSH keys in the default key location, the following command creates them. You can specify a specific set of keys by using the `--ssh-key-value` option.

```
az vm create \
        --resource-group SybexVNet-rg \
        --name SybexVM1 \
        --image UbuntuLTS \
        --generate-ssh-keys \
        --no-wait
```

IP addresses are assigned to resources in either a dynamic or a static manner. IP addresses are dynamically assigned to Azure resources by default. IP addresses are not provisioned when a resource is deployed. When creating a VM or restarting a stopped VM, you provide the IP address. When you stop or delete a VM, the IP address is released.

Set the allocation method explicitly to `static` to ensure the VM's IP address remains the same. An IP address will be assigned immediately in this case. You can release it only when the VM is deleted or changes its allocation method to dynamic.

4. The static IP address for Sybex virtual machine 1 can be set with the following command:

```
az network nic ip-config update \
        --name SybexVM1 \
        --resource-group SybexVNet-rg  \
```

```
    --nic-name SybexVM1Nic \
    --private-ip-address 10.10.0.11
```

5. You can create VM2 using the same method, `no-wait`, since you used `no-delay` in the previous VM deployment.

```
az vm create \
    --resource-group SybexVNet-rg \
    --name SybexVM2 \
    --image UbuntuLTS \
    --private-ip-address 10.10.0.12 \
    --generate-ssh-keys \
    --no-wait
--no-delay
```

6. A static IP address for Sybex virtual machine 2 can be set with the following command:

```
az network nic ip-config update \
--name SybexVM2 \
--resource-group SybexVNet-rg  \
--nic-name SybexVM2Nic \
--private-ip-address 10.10.0.12
```

If an Azure VM doesn't have a public IP address or is in a back-end pool of an Azure load balancer, it will have a default outbound access IP. Outbound access IP addresses aren't configurable by default.

When the VM is assigned a public IP address or placed in a standard load balancer with or without outbound rules, the default outbound access IP is disabled. When an Azure VNet NAT gateway resource is assigned to the subnet of a VM, the default outbound access IP is disabled. In Flexible Orchestration mode, VMs created by virtual machine scale sets do not have default outbound access.

For the Microsoft AZ-700 exam, keep in mind that the Azure route table is associated with zero or more virtual network subnets after it is created, and a subnet can be associated with one or more route tables. You can create route tables and associate them with subnets so that their routes are combined with, or overridden by, the default routes Azure adds to a subnet by default.

All resources connected to a subnet will be governed by the rules associated with an NSG. You can further restrict traffic by associating an NSG with a virtual machine or NIC. An NSG is associated with a "north/south" traffic subnet filter, which means packets flow into and out of the subnet. NSGs associated with network interfaces filter "east/west" traffic, which is how VMs connect within a subnet.

Preparing Subnetting for Services

This section covers preparing subnetting for services, including VNet gateways, Private Endpoint, firewalls, application gateways, and VNet-integrated platform services.

Subnetworks are networks within networks. They are efficient because they are connected. By using subnetting, you ensure that network traffic can travel a shorter distance without traversing unnecessary routers to reach its destination. In this section you'll prepare the subnet for each service listed here:

- VNet gateway
- Private Endpoints
- Azure firewall
- Application gateway
- VNet-integrated platform services

Here is an overview of each service in this list:

Virtual Network Gateway   Recall from Chapter 3, "Design, Deploy, and Manage Azure ExpressRoute," that VM gateways are composed of two or more VMs deployed to a subnet that you create called the gateway subnet. VM gateways run routing tables and specific gateway services. You can create these VMs when you create the virtual network gateway. You cannot directly configure the VMs that are part of the virtual network gateway.

A *virtual network gateway* in Azure is configured with a setting that specifies the type of gateway. A virtual network gateway's type determines how it will be used and what actions it will take. A VPN gateway that uses the gateway type VPN is distinct from an ExpressRoute gateway, which uses a different gateway type. Two virtual network gateways can be present in a virtual network: one VPN gateway and one ExpressRoute gateway.

Private Endpoints   A Private Endpoint is an interface using a private IP address in a virtual network. The Azure Private Link provides you with a secure and private connection to the service. You can add the service to the cloud consumer virtual network by enabling a Private Endpoint.

The service could be provided by Azure, such as Azure Storage, Azure Cosmos DB, Azure SQL Database, and the cloud consumer's own service using a Private Link service.

Azure Firewall   Azure Firewall is a cloud-native security service that uses a well-designed intelligent firewall to protect business workloads from threats. It's a stateful firewall with high availability and unrestricted scalability built into it. The firewall can inspect both east-west traffic and north-south traffic.

Standard and Premium versions of Azure Firewall are available.

Azure Firewalls are managed across multiple subscriptions using Azure Firewall Manager. A firewall policy enables Firewall Manager to apply a standard set of network/application rules and configurations to firewalls within cloud tenants.

Both VNets and virtual wide area networks (secure virtual hubs) can be protected with Firewall Manager. Secure virtual hubs simplify routing traffic to the firewall using the virtual WAN route automation solution in a few clicks.

Azure Application Gateway   Cloud consumers can manage cloud consumer web applications using a web traffic load balancer. Traditionally, load balancers operate at the Transport layer (Open Systems Interconnection (OSI) Layer 4—TCP and UDP) and route traffic based on source IP address and port to a destination IP address and port.

Application gateways can route a request based on additional attributes, such as the URI path or the host headers.

VNet-Integrated Platform Services   App Service VNet integration allows your business applications to access resources via virtual networks. You can place several Azure resources in a non-Internet routable network. A virtual network integration does not allow cloud consumer apps to be accessed privately.

App Service has two variations:

- In one variation, there are four dedicated compute pricing tiers: Basic, Standard, Premium, and Premium v2.
- In the other variation, the App Service Environment deploys directly into your organization's Azure VNet with dedicated infrastructure and uses the Isolated and Isolated v2 pricing tiers.

Subnetting Design Considerations

Now let's prepare and configure subnetting. An IP address prefix is assigned to a subnet, which helps define address space segments within a CIDR block. You can provide connectivity for various workloads by adding NICs to subnets and connecting them to virtual machines.

Consider creating multiple subnets in a VNet in the following scenarios:

A subnet does not have enough private IP addresses for all NICs.   When the number of NICs in the subnet exceeds the subnet address space, you must create multiple subnets. Azure reserves five private IP addresses on each subnet that cannot be used: the first and last addresses of the address space (for subnet addresses and multicast) and three addresses for internal use (for DHCP and DNS).

Security is the top priority.   For workloads with multilayered structures, subnets can be used to separate groups of VMs, which can then be applied with different NSGs.

You want to provide hybrid connectivity. On-premises datacenter(s) can be connected to a cloud consumer's VNets using VPN gateways and ExpressRoute circuits. ExpressRoute circuits and VPN gateways require their own subnets.

You want to use virtual appliances. Azure VNets can be configured with virtual appliances such as firewalls, WAN accelerators, and VPN gateways. Routing traffic to those appliances and isolating them on their own subnet is a necessity.

The following are the high-level best practices that can be used to design and deploy subnets:

- To provide isolation, you can divide a virtual network into one or more subnets. Subnets are allotted a portion of the virtual network's address space.

- You can create multiple subnets within a virtual network.

- A virtual network's traffic is routed between all of its subnets by default.

- Subnet decisions are made based on your organization's requirements.

- CIDR is used to create subnets.

Your address space in Azure is used to assign private IP addresses to resources in a virtual network. For example, if you deploy a virtual machine into a VNet with an address space of $10.0.0.0/16$, the VM will be assigned a private IP address of $10.0.0.4$. Keeping in mind that Azure reserves five IP addresses per subnet is essential. The addresses are $x.x.x.0$-$x.x.x.3$ and the subnet's last address. Each subnet has $x.x.x.1$-$x.x.x.3$ reserved for Azure services.

- **Network address:** $x.x.x.0$
- **Default gateway reserved:** $x.x.x.1$
- **Reserved for mapping Azure DNS IPs to the VNet:** $x.x.x.2$ and $x.x.x.3$
- **Network broadcast address:** $x.x.x.255$

Subnets can be segmented within a virtual network up to the limits. When planning whether one subnet or multiple virtual networks will be created in a subscription, consider the following factors:

- CIDR addresses must be assigned to each subnet within the address space of the virtual network. The address range cannot overlap with another subnet.

- Azure service resources can require, or create, their own subnet, so there needs to be enough unallocated space for them to do so if they are deployed in a virtual network. For example, a virtual network must have a dedicated subnet for the Azure VPN Gateway when it is connected to an on-premises network.

Table 4.1 illustrates various Azure services that can be hosted with a dedicated subnet or shared.

TABLE 4.1   Azure services hosted on a dedicated subnet or shared

Setting	Azure services	Inputs
Compute	Virtual machines: Linux or Windows	No
	Virtual machine scale sets	No
	Cloud service: Virtual network (classic) only	No
	Azure Batch	No
Networks	Application Gateway – WAF	Yes
	VPN Gateway	Yes
	Azure Firewall	Yes
	Azure Bastion	Yes
	Network Virtual Appliances	No
Data	RedisCache	Yes
	Azure SQL Managed Instance	Yes
Analytics	Azure HDInsight	No
	Azure Databricks	No
Identity	Azure Active Directory Domain Services	No
Containers	Azure Kubernetes Service (AKS)	No
	Azure Container Instance (ACI)	Yes
	Azure Container Service Engine with Azure Virtual Network CNI plug-in	No
	Azure Functions	Yes
Web	API Management	Yes
	Web Apps	Yes
	App Service Environment	Yes
	Azure Logic Apps	Yes

Setting	Azure services	Inputs
Hosted	Azure Dedicated HSM	Yes
	Azure NetApp Files	Yes
Azure Spring Cloud	Deploy in Azure virtual network (VNet injection)	Yes

- Traffic in an Azure virtual network is routed between all subnets by default. You can override Azure's default routing to prevent Azure from routing traffic between subnets or from using a virtual network appliance to route traffic between subnets. For example, if you require traffic flowing between resources in the same virtual network to be routed through a virtual network appliance (NVA), they deploy the resources to different subnets.

- You can configure a virtual network service endpoint to restrict Azure resources such as Azure storage accounts or Azure SQL databases to specific subnets. You might create several subnets and enable service endpoints on some but not all of them. In addition, you can deny access to Internet resources.

  An organization's Azure service resources can be secured to only virtual networks using endpoints. VNet service endpoints connect to Azure services with a safe and direct route over the Azure backbone network. By using service endpoints, you ensure that a private IP address in the VNet can access an Azure service's endpoint without needing a public IP address on the VNet. The following Azure services and regions offer service endpoints:

  - Azure Storage (Microsoft.Storage)
  - Azure SQL Database (Microsoft.Sql)
  - Azure Synapse Analytics (Microsoft.Sql)
  - Azure Database for PostgreSQL server (Microsoft.Sql)
  - Azure Database for MySQL server (Microsoft.Sql)
  - Azure Database for MariaDB (Microsoft.Sql)
  - Azure Cosmos DB (Microsoft.AzureCosmosDB)
  - Azure Key Vault (Microsoft.KeyVault)
  - Azure Service Bus (Microsoft.ServiceBus)
  - Azure Event Hubs (Microsoft.EventHub)
  - Azure Data Lake Store Gen 1 (Microsoft.AzureActiveDirectory)
  - Azure App Service (Microsoft.Web)
  - Azure Cognitive Services (Microsoft.CognitiveServices)

- One or more network security groups can be assigned to each subnet in a virtual network. Each Azure subnet can be associated with a different NSG. Several rules control traffic to and from the sources and destinations of each NSG.

Example Case Study: Preparing Subnetting for Services

For this example, imagine that you are an Azure network architect, and you work for XYZ Company with two datacenters in the United States and two datacenters in Europe. Two other business units maintain six applications that you want to migrate to Azure as a pilot project. Figure 4.1 depicts the logical building blocks.

FIGURE 4.1   Subnetting: example building blocks

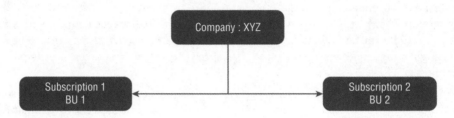

The applications' basic architecture is as follows:

- Apps are currently hosted in one of XYZ Company's U.S. datacenters.

- On Linux servers running Ubuntu, OpCoApp1, OpCoApp2, OpCoApp3, and OpCoApp4 are web applications. A separate application server hosts RESTful services on Linux servers for each application. RESTful services connect to a MySQL database back-end.

- Both OpCoApp5 and OpCoApp6 run on Windows servers running Windows Server 2016. The applications connect to SQL Server databases.

- Address space `10.0.0.0/8` is used by on-premises datacenters.

Your customer has already engaged the consulting company, and they concluded that the following are the requirements with respect to the number of subscriptions and VNets:

- Resource consumption by other business units should not affect each business unit.

- All applications should be tested and developed on the same test/development VNet within each business unit.

- Two Azure datacenters are located on each continent (America and Europe).

- For easier management, you should minimize VNets and subnets.

To fulfill these requirements, the following is one of the ways forward.

You need to have a subscription for every business unit based on those requirements. You should also consider the "one subscription per business unit, two VNets per group of apps" pattern since you may want to minimize the number of VNets. This method prevents resource consumption by one business unit from counting against other business units' limits.

Each Azure virtual network must also have an address space specified. As cloud consumers need connectivity between the on-premises datacenters and the Azure regions, the address space used by Azure VNets cannot clash with the on-premises network, and each VNet's address space should not conflict with any already existing VNets. You could satisfy these requirements by using address spaces other than the existing subnet's.

The following are the requirements with respect to the number of subnets and NSGs:

- For easier management, minimize VNets and subnets.

- The applications are separate from each other.

- Customers can access the applications over the Internet using HTTP/S.

- An encrypted tunnel allows users connected to the on-premises datacenters to access each application.

- Datacenters on-premises should be connected via existing VPN devices.

- A daily replication of Azure databases should be done to other Azure locations.

To fulfill these requirements, the following is one of the ways forward.

You could use one subnet per Application layer and NSGs to filter traffic per application based on those requirements. This method limits you to three subnets per VNet (front-end, Application layer, and Data layer) and one NSG per application per subnet. In this case, you should consider using NSGs for each app and one subnet per Application layer, as shown in Figure 4.2.

FIGURE 4.2   NSG planning

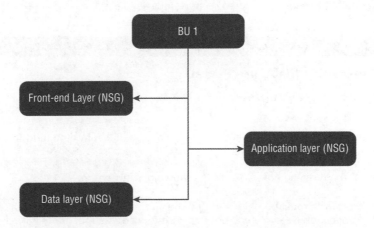

In addition, it would be helpful if you were able to deploy an extra subnet for the VPN connectivity between the VNets and the on-premises datacenters. You need to specify the address space for each subnet.

The following are the requirements with respect to the number of access controls:

- The company's network group should be in complete control of the VNet configuration.

- In each business unit, developers should be able to deploy VMs only to existing subnets.

To fulfill these requirements, the following is one of the ways forward.

Using these requirements, you would be able to include networking team members in the built-in Network Contributor role in each subscription, and create a custom role for application developers to be able to add VMs to existing subnets.

Several Azure roles in addition to Network Contributor are built into Azure role-based access control (RBAC). You can assign these roles to users, groups, service principals, and managed identities. The assignments are what permit users to access Azure resources.

For the Microsoft AZ-700 exam, keep in mind that a virtual network is a communication boundary that isolates VNets from one another. VNets allow virtual machines and services to communicate. In other words, if you want to open a communication channel between VNets, you should configure VNet peering.

Configuring Subnetting for Services

In this section, you will add, change, and delete a virtual network subnet. To create and add a subnet using the Azure portal, follow the steps in Exercise 4.2.

EXERCISE 4.2

Adding a Subnet via the Azure Portal

1. Log into a personal or business account in the Azure portal at `https://portal .azure.com`.

2. Choose the name of the virtual network you want to add a subnet to, and from Settings, choose Subnets, then Subnet.

3. In the Add Subnet dialog box, fill out the following information:

    Name   The name must be unique within the virtual network. For example, Azure Application Gateway will not deploy into a subnet that starts with a number. Microsoft recommends naming the service with a letter as the first character for maximum compatibility with other Azure services.

Address Range	Virtual networks must have unique ranges within their address spaces.
	Within the virtual network, the range cannot overlap with other subnet address ranges.
	Classless Inter-Domain Routing (CIDR) must be used to specify the address space.
	Create a gateway subnet if you intend to connect a virtual network to a VPN gateway.
	Each subnet's first and last addresses are reserved for protocol conformance by Azure. Azure services will use the remaining three addresses.
Network Security Group	You can associate an existing network security group with the subnet to filter traffic in and out of a subnet. The NSG must belong to the same subscription and be in the same location as the virtual network.
Route Table	You may associate an existing route table with a subnet to control traffic routing to other networks. Routing tables must exist in the same subscription and location as virtual networks.
Subnet	Depending on the configuration of the subnet, it may have one or more service endpoints. From the list of services, select the service or services you wish to enable service endpoints for. Azure will configure the location automatically. Azure configures the service endpoints according to the region of the virtual network by default. It automatically configures Azure Storage endpoints to pair with Azure paired regions to support regional failover scenarios.
	If you want to remove a service endpoint, deselect the box next to the service you want to remove.
	Once you enable a service endpoint, you must also allow network access for the subnet for a resource created with the service.
	For instance, if you enable the service endpoint for Microsoft. Storage, you must also allow network access to all Azure storage accounts to which you want to grant network access.
	Check the route for any network interface in a subnet to determine whether a service endpoint is enabled for the subnet. When configuring an endpoint, you see a default route with the address prefixes of the service, and a next-hop type of VirtualNetworkServiceEndpoint.
Subnet Delegation	Depending on the subnet, it may be possible to enable one or more delegations. When deploying a service, subnet delegation grants explicit permission to the service to create service-specific resources within a subnet. In the Services section, choose the service you want to delegate.

4. The subnet will be added to the virtual network when it is selected and you click OK.

To change a subnet using the Azure portal, follow the steps in Exercise 4.3.

EXERCISE 4.3

Changing a Subnet via the Azure Portal

1. Log into a personal or business account in the Azure portal at `https://portal.azure.com`.

2. Choose the name of the virtual network you want to add a subnet to, and from Settings, choose Subnets, then Subnet.

3. In the list of subnets, choose the subnet you want to modify. In the Add Subnet dialog box, fill out the following information:

Address Range	If no resources are deployed on the subnet, you can change the address range. You must either remove any resources from the subnet or move them to another subnet if there are any resources in the subnet.
User	You can control access to the subnet by using built-in roles or cloud consumer custom roles.
Network Security Group	You can associate an existing network security group with the subnet to filter traffic in and out of a subnet. The network security group must belong to the same subscription and be in the same location as the virtual network.
Route Table	You may associate an existing route table with a subnet to control traffic routing to other networks. Routing tables must exist in the same subscription and location as virtual networks.
Subnet	Depending on the configuration of the subnet, it may have one or more service endpoints. From the list of services, select the service or services you wish to enable service endpoints for. Azure will configure the location automatically. Azure configures the service endpoints according to the region of the virtual network by default. It automatically configures Azure Storage endpoints to pair with Azure paired regions to support regional failover scenarios.
	If you want to remove a service endpoint, deselect the box next to the service you want to remove.
	Once you enable a service endpoint, you must also allow network access for the subnet for a resource created with the service.
	For instance, if you enable the service endpoint for Microsoft.Storage, you must also allow network access to all Azure storage accounts to which you want to grant network access.
	Check the route for any network interface in a subnet to determine whether a service endpoint is enabled for the subnet. When configuring an endpoint, you see a default route with the address prefixes of the service, and a next-hop type of VirtualNetworkServiceEndpoint.

Subnet Delegation	Depending on the subnet, it may be possible to enable one or more delegations. When deploying a service, subnet delegation grants explicit permission to the service to create service-specific resources within a subnet. In the Services section, select the service you want to delegate.

4.   This is the final step; here, you should commit the change.

To delete a subnet using the Azure portal, follow the steps in Exercise 4.4.

EXERCISE 4.4

Deleting a Subnet via the Azure Portal

You can delete a subnet only if it does not have any resources. Resources in the subnet must be deleted before you can delete the subnet. You follow a different process to delete a resource.

1.   Log into a personal or business account in the Azure portal at `https://portal.azure.com`.

2.   Choose the name of the virtual network you want to add a subnet to, and from Settings, choose Subnets, then Subnet.

3.   From the list of subnets, choose the subnet you want to delete.

4.   Click Delete, and then choose Yes in the authorization dialog box.

Preparing and Configuring a Subnet Delegation

You can use *subnet delegation* for Azure PaaS services that need to be injected into a cloud consumer's virtual network. Subnet delegation offers customers complete control over how Azure services are integrated into their virtual networks.

You can delegate subnets to Azure services so that those services can set up some basic network configuration rules that will allow them to operate their instances stably. Because of this, you should take the following key deployment issues into consideration:

- Consider deploying the service in a shared subnet instead of a dedicated one.
- Postdeployment, add the network intent policies that are required for the service to function.

You can gain the following advantages by delegating subnets to specific services:

- The ability to establish a subnet for one or more Azure services and manage the instances in that subnet. To better manage resources and access, the virtual network owner may define the following for delegated subnets:
  - Security groups for network filtering traffic
  - Routing policies with user-definable routes
  - Service endpoint configurations integrated with routing policies
- Assign preconditions to injected services in network intent policies to better integrate them with the virtual network.

The virtual network's owners need to delegate one of the subnets for a specific Azure service by performing subnet delegation. The Azure service then deploys the instances into this subnet for consumption by cloud consumer workloads.

Delegated subnet Azure services still have the same basic properties as nondelegated subnet Azure services; for example:

- Instances can be injected into customer subnets, but existing workloads cannot be affected.
- These services apply flexible policies that the customer overrides.

According to the deployment model, the impact of subnet delegation on the subnet varies. Each Azure service can decide what properties it supports or does not support in a delegated subnet, such as:

- It supports a shared subnet with other Azure services or VMs that are in the same subnet, or it supports a dedicated subnet with instances of this service only.
- It associates an NSG with the delegated subnet.
- An NSG that supports the delegated subnet can also be associated with any other subnet.
- It enables routing tables to be associated with the delegated subnet.
- It allows a subnet to be associated with a routing table associated with a delegated subnet.
- The delegated subnet must contain at least one IP address.
- A delegated subnet must be assigned IP addresses from the Private IP Address space (10.0.0.0/8, 192.168.0.0/16, 172.16.0.0/12).
- Custom DNS configurations have a DNS entry in Azure.
- Prior to deleting a virtual network or subnet, the delegation must be removed.
- Delegated subnets cannot be used with Private Endpoints.

The following policies can also be added to injected services:

- Security policies, which are a set of rules defining how a given service should operate
- A route policy, which is the collection of routes necessary for a service to function

Configure Subnet Delegation

When deploying a service, subnet delegation gives explicit permission for the service to create subnet-specific resources. Exercise 4.5 and Exercise 4.6 present methods to add and remove a delegated subnet for an Azure service.

EXERCISE 4.5

Delegating a Subnet

Using the Azure portal:

1. Log into a personal or business account in the Azure portal at `https://portal`
   `.azure.com`.

2. In the portal's search bar, type the virtual network's name. When the virtual network's name appears in the search results, choose it.

3. In Settings, choose Subnets, then your subnet.

4. On the Subnet page, from the Subnet Delegation list, choose the services listed beneath Delegate Subnet To A Service (for instance, `Microsoft.DBforPostgreSQL/ serversv2`).

Using Azure PowerShell:

You can use `Add-AzDelegation` to add a delegation (in this example, `SybexDelegation`) to the subnet (in this example, `sybexSubnet`). This example delegation uses `Microsoft.DBforPostgreSQL/serversv2`:

```
$vnet = Get-AzVirtualNetwork -Name "SybexVNet" -ResourceGroupName "SybexRG"
  $subnet = Get-AzVirtualNetworkSubnetConfig -Name "SybexSubnet" -VirtualNetwork
 $vnet
  $subnet = Add-AzDelegation -Name "SybexDelegation" -ServiceName
"Microsoft.DBforPostgreSQL/serversv2" -Subnet $subnet
  Set-AzVirtualNetwork -VirtualNetwork $vnet
```

EXERCISE 4.6

Removing a Subnet Delegation

Using the Azure portal:

1. Log into a personal or business account in the Azure portal at `https://portal.azure`
   `.com`.

2. In the portal's search bar, type the virtual network's name. When the virtual network's name appears in the search results, choose it.

EXERCISE 4.6 *(continued)*

3. In Settings, choose Subnets, then your subnet.

4. On the Subnet page, from the Subnet Delegation list, choose None from the services listed under Delegate Subnet To A Service.

Using Azure PowerShell:

You can use Remove-AzDelegation to remove a delegation (in this example, SybexDelegation) to the subnet (in this example, sybexSubnet):

```
$vnet = Get-AzVirtualNetwork -Name "SybexVnet" -ResourceGroupName "SybexRG"
  $subnet = Get-AzVirtualNetworkSubnetConfig -Name "SybexSubnet" -VirtualNetwork
$vnet
  $subnet = Remove-AzDelegation -Name "SybexDelegation" -Subnet $subnet
  Set-AzVirtualNetwork -VirtualNetwork $vnet
```

You can connect to your intranet system via PaaS services that have a public endpoint. For example, consider a scenario where you would like to connect Azure NetApp Files or Azure Databricks. You may grant the DataBricks service or the NetappFiles service control over certain aspects of a subnet within an existing VNet. This is called *subnet delegation*. PaaS services allow specific configuration changes, such as adding network security group rules (if a subnet is attached to an NSG) or configuring custom routes.

There is no way to delegate a subnet to more than one resource type in Azure, and that's why you frequently build dedicated subnets for Azure PaaS services.

Planning and Configuring Subnetting for Azure Route Server

Azure Route Server allows the dynamic routing of cloud consumer virtual networks and consumer network virtual appliances (NVAs). Using Azure Route Server, you can exchange routing information directly with any networking device that supports the Border Gateway Protocol (BGP) routing protocol and the Azure software-defined network (SDN) in the Azure VNet without manually setting up routing tables or configuring them. High availability is built into Azure Route Server, a managed service.

Figure 4.3 shows how Azure Route Server works with a software-defined wide area network (SD-WAN) NVA and a security NVA in a virtual network.

FIGURE 4.3   Azure Route Server with an SD-WAN NVA

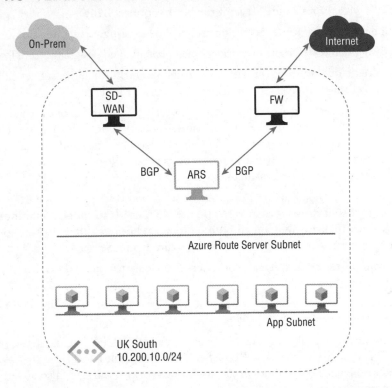

Upon establishing the BGP peering, Azure Route Server will receive a route from the SD-WAN appliance (10.250.0.0/16) and a default route (0.0.0.0/0) from the firewall. Once configured, the virtual network's routes are automatically applied to each VM. Therefore, the SD-WAN appliance will receive all traffic destined for the on-premises network. The firewall will also forward Internet traffic. Both NVAs will receive the virtual network address (10.1.0.0/16) from Azure Route Server. This information can be propagated to the on-premises network by the SD-WAN appliance.

You can configure, manage, and deploy your organization's virtual networks more easily with Azure Route Server. The following are the key benefits:

- Whenever an organization's virtual network addresses are updated, you no longer need to update the routing table on your NVA manually.

- Users of Azure networking no longer need to manually update user-defined routes whenever an NVA announces new routes or withdraws old ones.

- Using Azure Route Server, your NVA can peer with multiple instances, and the NVA can be configured with BGP attributes. Azure Route Server should know which NVA instance is active or passive based on your organization's Azure network design (e.g., active-active for performance or active-passive for resiliency).

- There is a common standard protocol between NVA and Azure Route Server. You can peer NVAs with Azure Route Server if the NVA supports BGP.

- You can deploy Azure Route Server on any new or existing virtual network.

The following are the key points to consider when planning and designing Azure Route Server:

- You can create one route server within a virtual network. An entire subnet called Route Server Subnet must be reserved for the deployment of the service.

- Azure Route Server supports virtual network peering; if you peer one virtual network with another and enable the Use Remote Gateway setting on the other, Azure Route Server will learn the address space of that virtual network and send it to all the virtual peering networks. An NVA will also program its routes into the routing table of the VMs connected to a peering virtual network.

- BGP is the only protocol Azure Route Server supports. To deploy Azure Route Server in a dedicated subnet in a virtual network, the NVA needs to support multihop external BGP. When configuring BGP on an NVA, you must choose a different Autonomous System Number (ASN) that the one used by Azure Route Server.

- During routing exchanges, Azure Route Server propagates the BGP routes to your organization's virtual network.

- A public IP address is required for Azure Route Server to communicate with the back-end service that manages routing configurations.

You can configure Azure Route Server to peer with an NVA in a virtual network using Azure PowerShell. Using Azure Route Server, routes are learned from the NVA and programmed in the virtual machines in the virtual network. Routes are also advertised to the NVA using Azure Route Server.

Use the `New-AzResourceGroup` command to create a resource group. You must make a resource group to host Azure Route Server before starting it. The following example creates a resource group named `SybexRouteServerRG` in the `UAENorth` location:

```
$rg = @{
    Name = 'SybexRouteServerRG '
    Location = 'UAENorth'
}
New-AzResourceGroup @rg
```

`New-AzVirtualNetwork` allows you to create a virtual network. A default virtual network named `SybexVNet` is created in the `UAENorth` location:

```
$vnet = @{
    Name = 'SybexVNet'
    ResourceGroupName = 'SybexRouteServerRG '
    Location = 'UAENorth'
    AddressPrefix = '10.0.0.0/16'
}
$virtualNetwork = New-AzVirtualNetwork @vnet
```

There is a dedicated subnet called `ARSSubnet` that Azure Route Server requires. When deploying Route Server, you can receive an error message if the subnet size is less than /27 or a short prefix (such as /26 or /25). `Add-AzVirtualNetworkSubnetConfig` creates the `ARSSubnet` configuration:

```
$subnet = @{
    Name = 'ARSSubnet'
    VirtualNetwork = $virtualNetwork
    AddressPrefix = '10.0.0.0/24'
}
$subnetConfig = Add-AzVirtualNetworkSubnetConfig @subnet
$virtualnetwork | Set-AzVirtualNetwork
```

An assigned public IP address is required so that the back-end service can manage Route Server configuration. Create an IP address named `SybexARSIP` with `New-AzPublicIpAddress`:

```
$ip = @{
    Name = 'sybexARSIP'
    ResourceGroupName = 'SybexRG'
    Location = 'UAENorth'
    AllocationMethod = 'Static'
    IpAddressVersion = 'Ipv4'
    Sku = 'Standard'
}
$publicIp = New-AzPublicIpAddress @ip
```

Azure Route Server can be created with `New-AzRouteServer`. ARS is the name of the Azure Route Server created in the `UAENorth` location in this example. In the previous section, we created `ARSSubnet` with `HostedSubnet`.

```
$rs = @{
    RouteServerName = 'SybexARS'
    ResourceGroupName = 'SybexRG'
    Location = 'UAENorth'
    HostedSubnet = $subnetConfig.Id
    PublicIP = $publicIp
}
New-AzRouteServer @rs
```

BGP peering can be established between Route Server and the NVA with `Add-AzRouteServerPeer`.

The `CC_nva_ip` represents the virtual network address of the NVA. In the NVA, this is the ASN. ASNs other than those from 65515 to 65520 can be any 16-bit number. Microsoft reserves the range of ASNs in this range.

```
$peer = @{
    PeerName = 'SybexNVA"
    PeerIp = '192.168.0.1'
    PeerAsn = '65501'
    RouteServerName = 'SybexARS'
    ResourceGroupName = 'SybexRG'
}
Add-AzRouteServerPeer @peer
```

Use the same command with a different `PeerName`, `PeerIp`, and `PeerAsn` if you want to set up peering with a different NVA or another instance of a different NVA.

The IP and ASN of Azure Route Server are required to complete the configuration on the NVA. You can get this information by using `Get-AzRouteServer`:

```
$routeserver = @{
    RouteServerName = 'SybexARS'
    ResourceGroupName = 'SybexRG'
}
Get-AzRouteServer @routeserver
```

If you have an ExpressRoute and an Azure VPN gateway in the same virtual network, and you want those two to exchange routes, you can enable route exchange on Azure Route Server. With the `-AllowBranchToBranchTraffic` flag, Azure Route Server can exchange routes with gateway(s):

```
$routeserver = @{
    RouteServerName = 'SybexARS'
    ResourceGroupName = 'SybexRG'
    AllowBranchToBranchTraffic
}
Update-AzRouteServer @routeserver
```

Use `Update-AzRouteServer` without the `-AllowBranchToBranchTraffic` flag to disable route exchange between Azure Route Server and the gateway(s):

```
$routeserver = @{
    RouteServerName = 'SybexARS'
    ResourceGroupName = 'SybexRG'
}
Update-AzRouteServer @routeserver
```

For the Microsoft AZ-700 exam, keep in mind that limitations of Azure Route Server include:

- Currently, BGP supports eight peers.
- Every BGP peer can advertise 100 routes toward Azure Route Server.

- The maximum number of routes Azure Route Server can advertise for ExpressRoute or the VPN gateway is 200.
- Azure Route Server can support a maximum of 2,000 virtual machines in a virtual network (including peered virtual networks).

Designing and Configuring Public DNS Zones

A *domain name system (DNS)* converts a hostname (`www.xyz.com`) into an IP address (`192.168.2.2`). Each Internet device has an IP address, which is used to identify it, much like a street address helps to locate a house. There must be a translation between the address typed into a web browser (`xyz.com`) and what the machine can use to access the `xyz.com` website.

Domains are grouped into hierarchies in the DNS. The top-level domains include `.com`, `.net`, `.org`, `.uk`, or `.jp` below the root domain. `org.uk` and `co.jp` are second-level domains beneath the top-level domains. DNS name servers around the world host domains in the DNS hierarchy that are distributed globally.

Your public domain's host names can be resolved by Azure DNS. You could configure Azure DNS to host `www.mycompany.xyz` to your web server's IP address if you purchased the `mycompany.xyz` domain name from a domain name registrar.

With *Azure DNS*, your organization can use a globally distributed and high-availability name server infrastructure to host your organization domain. You can manage DNS records with credentials, APIs, tools, and billing, and you can support other Azure services by hosting domains in Azure DNS.

You can't use Azure DNS to purchase a domain name for your organization. Customers of the App Service can buy a domain name through a third-party registrar or use App Service domains, and organizations can host their domains in Azure DNS for record management.

Azure DNS's nonfunctional features include these built-in features (see Figure 4.4):

FIGURE 4.4   Design principles of Azure public DNS zones

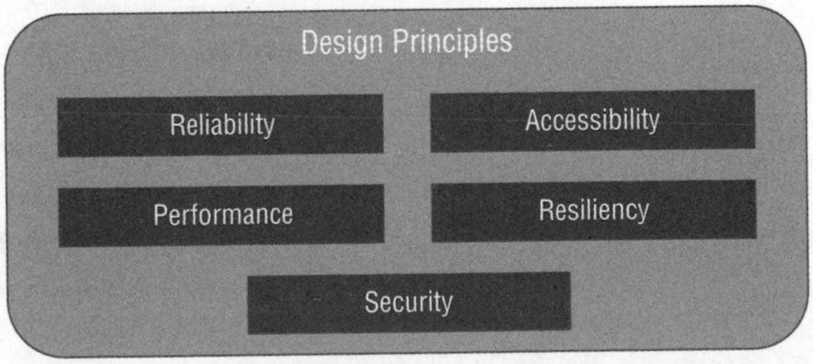

Design Principles

Reliability   Accessibility

Performance   Resiliency

Security

Reliability and Performance   Azure DNS hosts DNS domains on its global DNS name servers, and it uses anycast networking. The closest DNS server answers the domain's DNS query to ensure high performance and availability.

Security   Azure DNS is built on Azure Resource Manager, which offers these features:

- By using Azure RBAC, you have control over who has access to specific actions.
- Logs can be used to determine if a problem occurred when troubleshooting the activity.
- Resources, resource groups, and subscriptions can be locked so that other users will not delete or modify critical resources.

Accessibility   Azure DNS can manage DNS for Azure services and provide DNS for external resources. Azure DNS can be accessed through the Azure portal with the same credentials, support contract, and billing information. DNS billing is based on the number of DNS zones and queries hosted in Azure.

Currently, Azure DNS does not support DNSSEC. Most businesses can minimize the need for DNSSEC by using HTTPS/TLS consistently in their applications. Organizations can host DNS zones with third-party DNS hosting providers if DNSSEC is a critical requirement.

Azure DNS supports alias record sets. Your organization can use an alias record set to reference an Azure resource, such as an Azure public IP address, an Azure Traffic Manager profile, or an Azure Content Delivery Network (CDN) endpoint. The alias record set points to the IP address of the service instance. Whenever the IP address of the underlying resource changes, the alias record set seamlessly updates itself.

Azure DNS also supports private DNS domains. This feature lets you use custom domain names in private virtual networks rather than using Azure-provided names.

The DNS records for domains are stored in DNS zones. You will need to create a DNS zone for your domain name to host it in Azure DNS, and DNS records will then be added to this zone.

When you design a DNS zone in Azure DNS, consider the following:

- The zone's name must be unique within the resource group, and it cannot already exist. Otherwise, it fails.
- Different Azure subscriptions or resource groups can use the same zone name.
- Whenever multiple zones have the same name, each instance is assigned a different name server address. With the domain name registrar, only one set of addresses can be configured.
- You do not need to own a domain name to create a DNS zone in Azure DNS. However, you need to hold the domain name for Azure DNS to be configured as a name server for the domain name with the domain name registrar.
- As of this writing, the following maximum configurations are possible:
  - **Public DNS zones per subscription:** 250
  - **Record sets per public DNS zone:** 10,000

- **Records per record set in public DNS zones:** 20
- **Alias records for a single Azure resource:** 20

    During your requirements gathering, it's essential that you understand the following concepts in DNS:

    DNS Record   A record that points an IPv4 address to a domain.

    CNAME Records   CNAME doesn't respond with an IP address but rather with a pointer to the DNS record that contains it.

    Weighted Routing   You can assign weights to service endpoints and distribute traffic according to those weights using weighted routing. This is one of four routing mechanisms available in Traffic Manager.

    Priority Routing   Based on the health of the endpoints, priority routing is determined. All traffic is sent to the highest priority endpoint by default, but traffic is sent to the secondary endpoint when a failure or disaster occurs.

Resiliency   Recovery from a disaster involves recovering from severe application functionality loss. To select the best disaster recovery solution, business and technology owners must consider which level of functionality they need during a disaster, such as being unavailable, partially available via reduced functionality, or fully functional. Enterprise customers choose multiregion architectures to reduce the risk of application failures and infrastructure failures. To achieve high availability and failover through redundant architecture, you have several options. Examples include:

- Active/passive with cold standby
- Active/passive with pilot light
- Active/passive with warm standby

When Azure architects set up disaster recovery architecture, there are two design aspects to consider:

- Replicating instances, data, and configurations between a primary and a standby environment. Azure Site Recovery with partner appliances/services like Veritas or NetApp can provide disaster recovery natively.
- Diverting network traffic to the standby site from the primary site. Using Azure DNS, Azure Traffic Manager (DNS), or third-party global load balancers is one option for disaster recovery.

Creating an Azure DNS Zone and Record Using PowerShell

In this section you create a DNS zone and record it with PowerShell in Azure. You can also perform these steps through the Azure portal or Azure CLI.

First, you need to create a DNS zone before you can use Azure DNS. DNS zones contain DNS records for a particular domain, and each zone can hold DNS records for a single domain.

In a DNS zone, DNS records are maintained for this domain and its subdomains. The DNS name servers are configured to answer queries on a domain and point to a destination.

In Exercise 4.7, you'll create a DNS zone for the domain organization that wants to host in Azure DNS. DNS records for a particular domain are stored in a DNS zone. Each DNS record for your domain is then created inside this DNS zone. Finally, you must configure the name servers for the domain to publish the cloud consumer DNS zone to the Internet (see Figure 4.5).

FIGURE 4.5   Azure DNS zone example

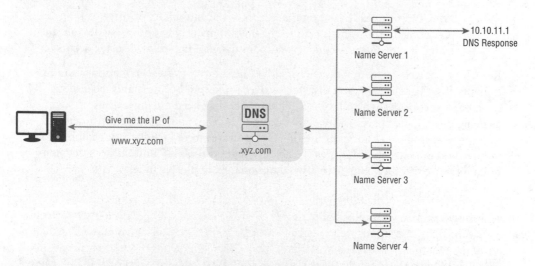

EXERCISE 4.7

Creating an Azure DNS Zone and Record Using PowerShell

1. Before creating a DNS zone, use the New-AzResourceGroup cmdlet to create a resource group. You must create a resource group to host the DNS.

   ```
   New-AzResourceGroup -name SybexRG -location "UAENorth"
   ```

2. The New-AzDnsZone cmdlet allows you to create a DNS zone. Use the following example to create a DNS zone called xyz.com under the sybexRG resource group. Create a DNS zone by substituting cloud consumer values for those in the example.

   ```
   New-AzDnsZone -Name xyz.com -ResourceGroupName sybexRG
   ```

3. The New-AzDnsRecordSet cmdlet lets you create record sets. In the following example, you create a record with the relative name www in the DNS zone xyz.com

in the resource group sybexRG. The fully qualified name is XYZ.COM. The address is "10.10.11.1", and the TTL is 3600 seconds.

```
New-AzDnsRecordSet -Name www -RecordType A -ZoneName xyz.COM -ResourceGroupName
sybexRG -Ttl 3600 -DnsRecords (New-AzDnsRecordConfig -IPv4Address "10.10.11.1")
```

For the Microsoft AZ-700 exam, keep in mind that Azure DNS billing is determined by the number of DNS zones hosted in Azure DNS and the number of DNS queries they receive. Organizations receive discounts based on their usage.

Azure guarantees that valid DNS requests will be answered 100 percent of the time by at least one Azure DNS name server.

Designing and Configuring Private DNS Zones

The DNS is responsible for translating (or resolving) service names to IP addresses. Using Azure infrastructure, Azure DNS provides naming resolution for domains. Not only does Azure DNS support Internet-facing DNS domains, but it also supports private DNS zones.

Azure *Private DNS* offers a secure and reliable DNS service for virtual networks. A virtual network and connected virtual networks provide naming resolution for VMs. With Azure Private DNS, you don't have to configure a custom DNS solution to manage and resolve domain names in the virtual network. Private DNS zones allow your organization's own custom domain name instead of those provided by Azure during deployment. You can customize your organization's virtual network architecture to meet its needs with a custom domain name. You can also configure zone names with a split-horizon view, allowing private and public DNS zones to share the same name. Figure 4.6 illustrates the private domain name services.

It is helpful to link the virtual network with a private DNS zone to resolve the records of a private DNS zone from a virtual network. The linked virtual networks have full access to the private zone's DNS records and can resolve them. You can also enable autoregistration on a virtual network link. The DNS records for the VMs in the virtual network are registered in the private zone when you enable autoregistration on the virtual network link. If autoregistration is enabled, Azure DNS will update the zone record whenever a VM is created, its IP address changes, or it is deleted.

According to Microsoft's best practice, the private DNS zone shouldn't be a local domain. Some of the operating systems don't support this.

The following are some of the advantages of Azure Private DNS:

FIGURE 4.6   Private DNS resolution

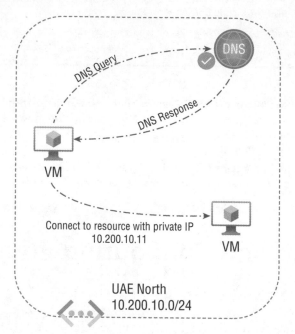

Excludes the Demand for Custom DNS Solutions   For managing DNS zones in their virtual networks, many customers used custom DNS solutions. The native Azure infrastructure now allows you to work with DNS zones, which means you don't have to create and manage custom DNS solutions.

Extensive DNS Record Types   Azure DNS supports A, AAAA, CNAME, MX, PTR, SOA, SRV, and TXT records.

Automatic Hostname Record Management   Azure automatically maintains VMs in the specified virtual networks and custom DNS records. You can optimize cloud consumer domain names using this method without creating custom DNS solutions or modifying applications.

Resolution of Hostnames among Virtual Networks   A private DNS zone can be shared between multiple virtual networks, unlike Azure-provided hostnames. In scenarios such as virtual network peering, this capability simplifies the discovery of cross-network services.

Easy-to-Use Tools   The service relies on well-established Azure DNS tools (the Azure portal, Azure PowerShell, Azure CLI, Azure Resource Manager templates, and the REST API).

Integrated Split-Horizon DNS Support   Azure DNS lets you create zones with the same name that resolve different responses within a virtual network and on the public

Internet. Split-horizon DNS is typically used to provide a dedicated service version in the cloud consumer virtual network.

Support for All Azure Regions   In the Azure public cloud, Azure DNS private zones can be established across all Azure regions.

The following are some of the Azure private DNS capabilities:

- Virtual machines automatically register from a private zone linked to a virtual network with autoregistration enabled.

  A record pointing to the private IP address of a virtual machine gets added to the private zone. Azure DNS also automatically removes the corresponding DNS record from the linked private zone when a VM in a virtual network link with autoregistration is deleted.

- The private zone supports forward DNS resolution across virtual networks that are linked to it.

  The virtual networks are not peering with each other for cross-virtual network DNS resolution. You might want to peer virtual networks in different scenarios (for example HTTP traffic).

- Virtual-network peering supports reverse DNS.

  For a private IP associated with a private zone, reverse DNS will return an FQDN that includes the host/record name and the zone name as the suffix.

The Azure private DNS service provides reliable and secure DNS management and resolution of domain names in a virtual network without adding a custom DNS service.

Before you enable Azure private DNS, there are a few concepts you should know. It is possible to associate a virtual network with a private DNS zone in two ways:

- A *registration network* is a virtual network configured against a specific DNS zone. A virtual machine within that virtual network will automatically register its hostname with the private DNS zone once it is registered.

- The behavior of a virtual network configured as a *resolution network* varies slightly. The DNS won't automatically register virtual machines, but they will still resolve hostnames in the private DNS zone.

Resolving networks have the advantage of allowing multiple DNS zones to be registered against a single DNS zone. VNets can share a standard DNS zone this way. Ideally, this is used when applications are spread across multiple VNets.

Consider the following Azure private DNS limitations when designing:

- If automatic registration of VM DNS records is enabled, only one private zone can be associated with a particular virtual network. Nevertheless, you can connect multiple virtual networks to a single DNS zone.

- The reverse DNS service is only available for private IP addresses in a linked virtual network.

- When reverse DNS for a private IP address is set to `internal.cloudapp.net`, the default suffix for the virtual machine will be `internal.cloudapp.net`. In the case of virtual networks connected to a private zone with autoregistration enabled, reverse DNS for a private IP address returns two FQDNs: one with the default suffix `internal.cloudapp.net` and another with the private zone suffix.

- Currently, conditional forwarding isn't supported natively. (Using a conditional forwarder, you can specify a domain to be forwarded to, such as `contoso.com`, in a DNS server. A DNS query for that domain is forwarded to the configured DNS server instead of the local DNS server trying to resolve the query.)

- Azure DNS private zones provide domain name resolution within a virtual network and between virtual networks. The virtual networks do not have to be peering explicitly. A private DNS zone must be linked to every virtual network.

- The CanNotDelete lock prevents accidental zone deletion, and a custom role should not have permission to delete zones.

- DNS-related security issues can be mitigated using a DNS firewall.

- Virtual networks belonging to different subscriptions can be linked to a private zone. You must have written permission to operate the virtual networks and the private DNS zone. Different Azure roles can grant permissions for writing. Classic Network Contributor Azure roles, for example, have written consent for virtual networks. The private DNS zones Contributor role has written permissions for the private DNS zones.

- As of this writing, the following maximum configuration was possible:

  - 1,000 private DNS zones per subscription
  - 25,000 record sets per private DNS zone
  - 20 records per record set for private DNS zones
  - 200 DNS queries queued (pending response) per virtual machine
  - 1,000 DNS queries a virtual machine can send to Azure DNS resolver, per the second set
  - A total of 1,000 private DNS zones a virtual network can get linked

Creating a Private DNS Zone and Record Using PowerShell

Azure private DNS operates similar to an Azure DNS zone, except that it operates within a virtual network rather than on public records. This feature is used to resolve custom domain names and names within the Azure virtual network.

You need to create a DNS zone for your domain before you can host it in Azure DNS. DNS zones are used for hosting DNS records for a specific domain, and your organization's domain DNS records are then created within this DNS zone. You specify the list of virtual networks allowed to resolve records in a private DNS zone to your organization's virtual network. These networks are called *linked virtual networks*. Azure DNS updates the zone records whenever a VM is created, changes its IP address, or is deleted when autoregistration is enabled.

In Exercise 4.8, you create a DNS zone and record it with PowerShell in Azure. You can perform these steps through the Azure portal or Azure CLI.

EXERCISE 4.8

Creating a DNS Zone and Record with PowerShell in Azure

1. Before creating a DNS zone, use the New-AzResourceGroup cmdlet to create a resource group. You must create a resource group to host the DNS:

   ```
   New-AzResourceGroup -name SybexRG -location "UAENorth"
   ```

2. The New-AzPrivateDnsZone cmdlet allows you to create a private DNS zone. The following example builds a virtual network named sybexVNet. The SybexRG resource group creates a DNS zone named sybex.xyz.com, links it to the SybexVNet virtual network, and provides automatic registration:

   ```
   Install-Module -Name Az.PrivateDns -force
   $DownStreamSubnet = New-AzVirtualNetworkSubnetConfig -Name DownStreamSubnet
   -AddressPrefix "10.2.0.0/24"
   $vnet = New-AzVirtualNetwork `
     -ResourceGroupName MyAzureResourceGroup `
     -Location uaenorth `
     -Name sybexVNet `
     -AddressPrefix 10.4.1.0/16 `
     -Subnet $DownStreamSubnet
   $zone = New-AzPrivateDnsZone -Name sybex.xyz.com -ResourceGroupName sybexRG
   $link = New-AzPrivateDnsVirtualNetworkLink -ZoneName sybex.xyz.com`
     -ResourceGroupName sybexRG -Name "sybexlink" `
     -VirtualNetworkId $vnet.id -EnableRegistration
   ```

3. Deploy two virtual machines so that you can test the private DNS zone:

   ```
   New-AzVm `
       -ResourceGroupName "sybexRG" `
       -Name "SybexVM01" `
       -Location "UAE North" `
       -subnetname DownStreamSubnet `
       -VirtualNetworkName "sybexVnet" `
       -addressprefix 10.4.1.0/24 `
       -OpenPorts 3389
   New-AzVm `
       -ResourceGroupName "sybexRG" `
       -Name "SybexVM02" `
       -Location "UAE North" `
       -subnetname DownStreamSubnet `
   ```

```
-VirtualNetworkName "sybexVnet" `
-addressprefix 10.4.1.0/24 `
-OpenPorts 3389
```

4. Build an additional DNS record. The `New-AzPrivateDnsRecordSet` cmdlet allows you to build record sets. In this example, a record will be created with the relative name app in the DNS zone `sybex.xyz.com`, in resource group SybexRG. App `.private.contoso.com` is the fully qualified name of this record set. A record of type "A" was found with an IP address of "10.4.1.6" and a TTL of 3600 seconds.

```
New-AzPrivateDnsRecordSet -Name app -RecordType A -ZoneName app.xyz.com `
    -ResourceGroupName sybexRG -Ttl 3600 `
    -PrivateDnsRecords (New-AzPrivateDnsRecordConfig -IPv4Address
"10.4.1.6")
```

The following cmdlet lets you list the DNS records in your organization's zone:

```
Get-AzPrivateDnsRecordSet -ZoneName sybex.xyz.com -ResourceGroupName
MyAzureResourceGroup.
```

You can test using the `ping` command and validate by setting the VM's guest OS to allow inbound ICMP.

> You can use a private DNS zone when you want to use your own custom domain name for your Azure resources rather than the Azure-provided domain name. Such a DNS zone satisfies organizational needs.

Designing Name Resolution Inside a VNet

You may be required to enable communication between VMs and other resources deployed in a virtual network using Azure IaaS, PaaS, and hybrid solutions. Even though you can use IP addresses to enable communication, it is much easier to use easily recognizable names that do not change.

The following methods can be used by resources deployed in virtual networks to resolve domain names to internal IP addresses:

- Private DNS zones in Azure
- Azure-provided name resolution
- Your organization's managed DNS server

Which of these you use depends on how resources need to communicate and what type of name resolution is used.

In the previous section, you read about private DNS zones in Azure. In this section, you learn about Azure-provided name resolution.

Name resolution provided by Azure offers only basic authoritative DNS capabilities. If your organization needs a fully featured DNS solution for virtual networks, you must use Azure DNS private zones or cloud consumer-managed DNS servers. Let's assume your organization uses the Azure-provided name resolution option. When this happens, DNS zone names and records will be managed by Azure, and your organization will not be able to control DNS zone names or the life cycle of DNS records.

VMs and role instances within the same virtual network or cloud service can also use Azure to resolve internal names, in addition to public DNS resolution. Cloud services share the same DNS suffix, so the hostname alone suffices. However, different cloud services have different DNS suffixes in virtual networks deployed using the classic deployment model. FQDNs are required to resolve the other cloud service names in this case. Virtual networks deployed with Azure Resource Manager maintain a consistent DNS suffix, so the FQDN is not required. Network interfaces and VMs can both be given DNS names. Azure provides name resolution without any configuration needed, but it may not be appropriate for all deployment scenarios.

Azure-provided name resolution includes the following advantages and implementation considerations:

- It's easy to use because no configuration is required.

- It's extremely reliable. It's not necessary to manage and create clusters of your DNS servers.

- Both on-premises and Azure hostnames can be resolved using the service in conjunction with cloud consumer DNS servers.

- It is possible to resolve names between VMs and role instances within the same cloud service without an FQDN.

- Name resolution can be used in Azure Resource Manager deployed virtual networks without requiring FQDNs. For names to be resolved in different cloud services, virtual networks in the classic deployment model need an FQDN.

- Rather than using autogenerated names, choose hostnames that describe your deployments best.

The following are some key points to consider while adopting Azure-provided name resolution:

- It is not possible to modify the DNS suffix created by Azure-provided name resolution because it is fully managed by Microsoft.

- All DNS lookups are scoped to a single virtual network. It is impossible to resolve DNS names created for one virtual network from another virtual network.

- Organizations cannot register their records manually.

- There's no WINS or NetBIOS support. VMs cannot be accessed through Windows Explorer.

- DNS-compatible hostnames are required. 0–9, a–z, and "-" are the only valid characters for names.

- DNS query traffic for each VM is throttled. Most applications should not be affected. Organizations must enable client-side caching if they observe request throttling.

- Client-side caching: it is not necessary to send every DNS query across the network. Client-side caching reduces latency by resolving recurring DNS queries from a local cache and improves network resilience to blips. A DNS record contains a time-to-live (TTL) mechanism, which allows the cache to keep the record, if possible, without affecting its freshness. As a result, most situations can be handled by client-side caching. DNS caching packages (such as dnsmasq) are available in several different flavors (such as Ubuntu [uses resolvconf], SUSE [uses Netconf], and CentOS [uses NetworkManager]).

- Client-side retries: UDP is the primary protocol for DNS. The DNS protocol handles retry logic since the UDP protocol does not guarantee message delivery. DNS clients (operating systems) may exhibit different retry logic, depending on the creator's preference:

  - Windows operating systems retry after one second, then again after 2 seconds, 4 seconds, and 4 more seconds.

  - Linux defaults to trying after 5 seconds. Microsoft recommends changing the retry specifications to five times, with one-second intervals.

- A DNS cache is built into the default Windows DNS client. Caching is not included by default in some Linux distributions. Cloud consumers may want to add a DNS cache to each Linux VM if there isn't one already.

- A maximum of 180 VMs can be registered in a classic deployment model for each virtual network. Azure Resource Manager does not have this restriction.

- 168.63.129.16 is the Azure DNS IP address. This is a fixed IP address that will not change.

- Virtual networks based on Azure Resource Manager support reverse DNS. Cloud consumers can issue reverse DNS queries (PTR queries) to map virtual machine IP addresses to their FQDNs.

- All PTR queries for virtual machine IP addresses return FQDNs of the form vmname .internal.cloudapp.net, and a forward lookup on FQDNs of the form vmname .internal.cloudapp.net will resolve to the virtual machine's IP address.

- The reverse DNS queries will return two records if the virtual network is linked to an Azure DNS private zone. The first record will be in the format *vmname .privatednszonename*, and the second will be in the form *vmname*.internal. cloudapp.net.

- Even if a virtual network peers with other virtual networks, a reverse DNS lookup is still limited to that virtual network. NXDOMAIN returns in reverse DNS queries (PTR queries) for IP addresses of virtual machines located in peered virtual networks.

- By creating a reverse lookup zone and linking it to your organization's virtual network, you can disable the reverse DNS function in a virtual network.

Now let's move on to organization-managed DNS servers. The next two sections cover VMs, role instances, and web apps.

VMs and Role Instances

Azure might not be able to satisfy all the needs of organizations when it comes to naming resolution. For example, your organization might need to use Microsoft Windows Server Active Directory domains or resolve DNS names between virtual networks. Azure offers cloud users the option of using their DNS servers to address these scenarios.

A virtual network's DNS servers can forward queries to the recursive resolvers in Azure. The virtual network can use these resolvers to resolve hostnames. Domain controllers (DCs) running in Azure, for example, can respond to DNS queries for their domains and forward all other requests to Azure. By forwarding queries, your organization's VMs can see both Azure-provided hostnames and on-premises resources (via the DC). Virtual IP `168.63.129.16` provides access to the recursive resolvers in Azure.

Additionally, DNS forwarding enables DNS resolution between virtual networks and allows on-premises machines to resolve Azure hostnames. It is required that the DNS server VM reside in the same virtual network and be configured to forward hostname queries to Azure to resolve the hostname. Each virtual network has a different DNS suffix, so organizations can use conditional forwarding rules to direct DNS queries to the correct virtual network. By using this method, two virtual networks and an on-premises network can resolve DNS between themselves.

Each VM that uses Azure-provided name resolution receives an internal DNS suffix (`.internal.cloudapp.net`) from Azure Dynamic Host Configuration Protocol (DHCP). Because the hostname records are in the `internal.cloudapp.net` zone, this suffix enables hostname resolution. When organizations use their name resolution solution, this suffix will not be supplied to VMs because it interferes with other DNS architectures (like domain-joined scenarios). Azure provides a nonfunctional placeholder instead (`reddog.microsoft.com`).

Your organization should provide its DNS solution if forwarding queries to Azure does not meet your requirements. It should include the following:

- By using dynamic domain name services (DDNS), for example, you can resolve host-names appropriately. Customers using DDNS might need to disable DNS record scavenging. Scavenging might remove DNS records prematurely on Azure DHCP leases.

- Use recursive resolution if external domains need to be resolved.

- It should be accessible (TCP and UDP on port 53) from the clients it serves and have Internet access.

- Ensure there is no access from the Internet so that threats posed by external agents can be mitigated.

Web Apps

Organizations need name resolution from cloud consumer web apps linked to a virtual network to VMs in the virtual network. Setting up a custom DNS server that has a DNS forwarder that forwards queries to Azure (virtual IP `168.63.129.16`) is just the beginning.

To perform name resolution from a web application built using an app service linked to a virtual network to VMs in a different virtual network, you need to configure custom DNS servers on each virtual network, as follows:

- Configure a VM to serve as a DNS server in your target network, directing queries to the recursive resolver in Azure (virtual IP `168.63.129.16`). Azure Resource Manager Quickstart Templates and GitHub offer examples of DNS forwarders.

- Install a DNS forwarder on the virtual network of the source. By configuring this DNS forwarder, queries will be forwarded to the DNS server in the virtual network the organization is targeting.

- In your organization source's virtual network settings, configure the DNS server.

- Enable virtual network integration for your web app to link to the original virtual network.

If your organization is using its own DNS servers, Azure can specify multiple DNS servers for each virtual network. The classic deployment model allows you to select various DNS servers per network interface. DNS servers specified for network interfaces or cloud services are prioritized over DNS servers set for virtual networks in the virtual network.

Table 4.2 shows various scenarios and their associated name resolution solutions that can be adopted in your design.

TABLE 4.2 Name resolution solutions

Deployment scenarios	Solution	DNS suffix
Resolving names for resources that are in the same Azure Cloud Service role or virtual network.	Private DNS zones in Azure or Azure-provided name resolution.	Hostname or fully qualified domain name
Resolving names between VMs in different virtual networks or roles in different cloud services.	Private DNS zones in Azure or organization-managed DNS server.	Fully qualified domain name
By using virtual network integration, resolve names from an Azure App Service (Web App, Function, or Bot) to VMs or role instances in the same virtual network.	DNS servers are managed by the organization for forwarding queries between virtual networks for resolution by Azure (DNS proxy).	Fully qualified domain name
App Service Web Apps in one virtual network are resolved to VMs in another virtual network.	DNS servers are managed by the organization for forwarding queries between virtual networks for resolution by Azure (DNS proxy).	Fully qualified domain name
Resolving names of on-premises computers and services from VMs or role instances in Azure.	Managed DNS servers (on-premises domain controllers, local read-only domain controllers, or DNS secondary servers synced using zone transfers, for instance).	Fully qualified domain name

Deployment scenarios	Solution	DNS suffix
Hostnames in Azure need to be resolved from on-premises computers.	The DNS proxy server in the corresponding virtual network forwards queries to Azure for resolution.	Fully qualified domain name
Reverse DNS for organization internal IPs.	Private DNS zones in Azure or organization-managed DNS server or cloud consumer–managed DNS server.	N/A
Instances of VMs or roles located on different cloud services, not in a virtual network, resolve their names.	Virtual machines and role instances in different cloud services cannot communicate outside of a virtual network. Not applicable.	N/A

Linking a Private DNS Zone to a VNet

You need to link a virtual network to a private DNS zone created in Azure. The private DNS zone is accessible once the VMs are connected to that virtual network. It has a collection of virtual network link child resources. These resources represent connections to virtual networks. Registration or resolution virtual networks can be linked to a private DNS zone.

Registration Virtual Network An interface between a private DNS zone and a virtual network is created. The autoregistration option is available to cloud consumers. If this setting is enabled, the virtual network becomes a private DNS zone registration network. Each time a VM is deployed to the virtual network, a DNS record is automatically created. DNS records will also be created for already deployed VMs.

Consequently, the private DNS zone becomes the registration zone for that virtual network. There can be multiple registration virtual networks in the private DNS zone. For each virtual network, however, there can be only one registration zone.

Resolution Virtual Network Organizations may link virtual networks to their private DNS zone without autoregistration. Virtual networks are treated as resolution networks only, and there will be no automatic creation of DNS records in the private zone for VMs deployed in this virtual network. Nonetheless, VMs deployed in the virtual network can successfully query DNS records within the private zone. Manually created records can be stored in a private DNS zone and automatic records from other virtual networks.

There can be multiple resolution zones within a private DNS zone, and it is possible to have numerous resolution zones within a virtual network.

The following are some key points to consider when using a virtual network link:

- The classic deployment model does not support virtual networks deployed by Microsoft.

- There can only be one connection between a private DNS zone and a virtual network in the cloud.

- In a private DNS zone, each virtual network link must have its own unique name. Several private DNS zones may have the same name.

- Check the Link Status field once the organization has created a virtual network link. The link status can change to complete after a few minutes, depending on the size of the virtual network.

- Organizations can delete virtual networks, all linked virtual networks, and the associated DNS records by deleting the virtual networks.

- The associated virtual network link can be removed by updating the DNS zone associated with the linked virtual network. During this process, automatically registered virtual machine records are removed from the zone.

- Without first unlinking the virtual network from a private zone, the deletion operation succeeds, and all links to the DNS zone are automatically cleared.

Configuring a Virtual Network Link   The organization creates a virtual network link to link a cloud at the consumer's private DNS zone to the organization's virtual network.

Manage DNS records for VMs deployed in a virtual network using the Azure DNS private zone's autoregistration feature. This setting is enabled when an organization links a virtual network with a private DNS zone. Every VM in the virtual network will have its DNS record created.

The A and PTR records are created for each VM. Additionally, DNS records are automatically created in the linked private DNS zone for newly deployed VMs. Any associated DNS records are also removed from the private DNS zone whenever a VM is deleted.

When creating a virtual network link, select the Enable Auto Registration check box. The following are some key restrictions to consider:

- Only VMs can be registered automatically. All other resources, such as internal load balancers, can be created manually in the private DNS zone linked to the virtual network by cloud consumers.

- A DNS record is created automatically for the VM's primary NIC only. You can create DNS records manually for other network interfaces if cloud consumers' VMs have more than one NIC.

- DHCP-based virtual machine NICs automatically create DNS records. Autoregistration doesn't create records for the VM if you use static IPs, such as configuring multiple IP addresses in Azure.

- The automatic registration of IPv6 (AAAA records) is not supported.

- One private DNS zone can be associated with a specific virtual network when automatic VM DNS registration is enabled. Consumers of cloud services can link multiple virtual networks to a single DNS zone; however, they link many virtual networks to one DNS zone.

- As of this writing, the following maximums are possible:

  - For private DNS zones with autoregistration enabled, the maximum number of virtual network links per zone is 1,000 and the maximum number of virtual network links per zone is 100.

  - With autoregistration enabled, a virtual network can link to only one private DNS zone.

  - The maximum number of private DNS zones a virtual network can link to is 1,000.

Exercise 4.9 walks you through the high-level workflow for configuring a virtual network link.

EXERCISE 4.9

Configuring a Virtual Network Link

1. Log into a personal or business account in the Azure portal at `https://portal.azure.com`.

2. Open the Cloud consumer private DNS zone and select Virtual Network Links (for example, `Sybex.xyz.com`) private zone.

3. In the left pane, choose Virtual Network Links and click Add, as shown here:

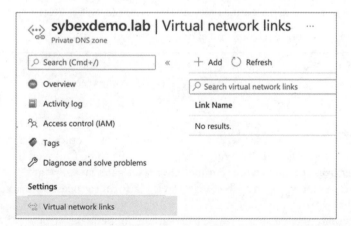

4. For a new virtual network, fill in the Link Name field (see the following image), then select values for the Subscription and Virtual Network fields (only virtual networks within the selected subscription will be available). You can also provide the resource ID of your virtual network, rather than selecting options from the drop-down menu.

Add virtual network link

sybexdemo.lab

Link name *

Sybexdemo

Virtual network details

> ℹ Only virtual networks with Resource Manager deployment model are supported for linking with Private DNS zones. Virtual networks with Classic deployment model are not supported.

☐ I know the resource ID of virtual network ℹ

Subscription * ℹ

Pay as you

Virtual network *

Configuration

☑ Enable auto registration ℹ

OK

5. For an existing virtual network, choose a virtual network (for example, SybexVNet.)

6. Select the Enable Auto Registration check box and click OK.

Summary

In this chapter you learned about designing private IP addresses for VNets, deploying the VNets using Azure command-line tools and the Azure portal, and steps to be followed in preparing and configuring services for subnetting that includes VNet gateways, Private Endpoint, firewalls, application gateways, and VNet-integrated platform services. Security aspects such as network security groups (NSGs) and ACLs were also discussed in detail, along with deployment and configuration steps. You learned about subnet delegation, planning, and configuring subnetting for Azure route services as well.

Along with designing subnets, you learned how to design and deploy DNS in private and public zones. We also explored setting up DNS for name resolution for VNets as well as linking a private DNS zone to a VNet.

Exam Essentials

Know how to deploy virtual networks. In Azure, a virtual network is a fundamental component of your private network. The service enables Azure resources, such as virtual machines, to communicate securely and access the Internet. The Azure virtual network enables Azure resources to communicate with the Internet and on-premises networks securely. You can create virtual networks using the Azure portal, Azure PowerShell, Azure CLI, and the ARM template.

Be able to prepare and configure subnetting for services, including VNet gateways, Private Endpoints, firewalls, application gateways, and VNet-integrated platform services. Subnet addresses are the IP addresses within a virtual network. Subnets help organize and secure virtual networks. Each NIC in a VM is connected to one virtual network subnet. If NICs in a virtual network are connected to different (or the same) subnets, they can communicate with each other without any additional configuration. A Layer 3 overlay network-based solution lets you extend on-premises subnets to Azure. You can use ARM templates, Azure PowerShell, and Azure CLI to create subnets.

Be able to prepare and configure subnet delegation. You can inject a specified Azure PaaS service into your virtual network by delegating a subnet. Subnet delegation gives customers complete control over integrating Azure services into their virtual networks. The virtual network owners must perform a subnet delegation exercise to designate one of the subnets for a particular Azure service. The Azure service then uses this subnet to deploy instances for consumption by customers.

Be able to prepare and configure subnetting for Azure Route Server. A dedicated subnet is required for Azure Route Server. At least /27 or a short prefix (such as /26 or /25) is required for the subnet. UDRs can't be configured on Azure Route Server subnets. Azure Route Server does not route data traffic between NVAs and VMs. Azure Route Server does not support RouteServerSubnet.

Know how to design Public DNS zones. Azure DNS hosts DNS domains and provides name resolution by using Azure infrastructure. Your Azure-hosted domains enable you to manage DNS records using credentials, APIs, tools, and billing as well as other Azure services. Azure DNS cannot be used to purchase domain names. Instead, App Service domains or third-party domain registrars can be used. When using Azure DNS, domain records are hosted there. Private domains can also be hosted in Azure DNS. This feature lets you use your own custom domain names in your private virtual networks rather than the Azure-provided names available today. There are alias records available through Azure DNS. Among the Azure resources that an alias record set can refer to are Azure public IP addresses, Azure Traffic Manager profiles, and Azure Content Delivery Network (CDN) endpoints. Azure DNS does not currently support DNSSEC.

Know how to design private DNS zones. Azure Private DNS offers reliable and secure DNS services for virtual networks. With Azure Private DNS, domain names are managed and resolved on the virtual network without the need to configure a custom DNS solution. You can deploy Azure services without using the Azure-provided names by using private DNS zones. When automatic VM DNS record registration of VMs is enabled, a specific virtual network can be linked to only one private zone if you wish to link more than one virtual network to one DNS zone. Reverse DNS works only for private IP space in the linked virtual network. Conditional forwarding is not natively supported.

Be able to link a private DNS zone to a VNet. Azure Private DNS provides a reliable, secure DNS service to manage and resolve domain names in a virtual network without adding a custom DNS solution. You can use your custom domain names by using private DNS zones rather than the Azure-provided names available today. The records in a private DNS zone aren't resolvable from the Internet, and DNS resolution against a private DNS zone works only from virtual networks linked to it. Microsoft doesn't support single-labeled private DNS zones. A private DNS zone can have a maximum of 34 labels.

Review Questions

1. Each VNet can be divided into _____ subnets.

    A. Fixed max of 3,000

    B. Fixed max of 10,000

    C. Max of 10,000 by default and unlimited with extension request to Microsoft

    D. Max of 3,000 by default and up to 10,000 with extension request to Microsoft

2. Which of the following is valid for Azure VNets?

    A. You will not be able to ping default routers within a VNet.

    B. You will be able to ping default routers within a VNet.

    C. You will be able to ping a default gateway within a VNet.

    D. None of the above.

3. Which of the following is valid for Azure VNets?

    A. Azure VNet can support multicast and broadcast using UDP.

    B. Azure VNet can support broadcast only using UDP.

    C. Azure VNet cannot support multicast and broadcast using UDP.

    D. Azure VNet can support multicast only using UDP.

4. Azure virtual network can connect which of the following Azure resources?

    A. Virtual machines and scale sets

    B. App Service Environment

    C. Azure Kubernetes Services

    D. All of the above

5. Regarding Azure public IP addresses, which of the following is valid?

    A. Public IP addresses allow Internet resources to communicate with Azure resources inbound.

    B. Public IP addresses do not allow Internet resources to communicate with Azure resources inbound.

    C. Public IP addresses do not allow Internet resources to communicate with Azure resources outbound and inbound.

    D. None of the above.

6. For specific resources within their VNet, application owners should use dynamic IP addresses. How do they select the right SKU?

    A. Basic SKU

    B. Standard SKU

    C. Basic or Standard

    D. None of the above

7. One of the following needs the resources in one VNet to communicate with resources in a subnet in a different VNet. How should the Azure networking be configured?

   A. Azure DNS

   B. Internal DNS

   C. VNet peering

   D. Azure availability zones

8. _____ is a cloud-native security service that protects cloud consumer workloads from threats.

   A. Azure Firewall

   B. Azure Application Gateway

   C. Private Endpoint

   D. All the above

9. Identify the resource types to which IP addresses are assigned in a subnet. (Choose all that apply.)

   A. Virtual machine network interface

   B. load balancer

   C. Application gateways

   D. Azure switches

10. What is the maximum number of private DNS zones available per subscription?

   A. 1,000

   B. 10,000

   C. Capped by subscription type

   D. Unlimited

11. You are required to set up DNS that resolves names for resources in the same Azure Cloud Service role or virtual network. Which one of the following should you use?

   A. Use private DNS zones in Azure or Azure-provided name resolution.

   B. Use private DNS zones in Azure or a cloud consumer managed DNS server.

   C. Use public DNS zones in Azure or a cloud consumer managed DNS server.

   D. Virtual machines and role instances in different cloud services cannot communicate outside of a virtual network.

12. What should you use to resolve names between VMs in different virtual networks or roles in different cloud services?

   A. Private DNS zones in Azure or Azure-provided name resolution.

   B. Private DNS zones in Azure or a cloud consumer managed DNS server.

   C. Public DNS zones in Azure or a cloud consumer managed DNS server.

   D. Virtual machines and role instances in different cloud services cannot communicate outside of a virtual network.

13. Which of these deployment scenarios are applicable for DNS resolution? (Choose all that apply.)

 A. Resolution across virtual networks

 B. Resolution scoped to a single virtual network

 C. Split-horizon functionality

 D. None of the above

14. How many requests can a virtual machine send to a DNS server?

 A. 1,000 per minute

 B. 1,000 per second

 C. No limit

 D. Configured by cloud customer administrator

15. How many private DNS zones can link to a virtual network?

 A. 1,000

 B. 2,000

 C. No limit

 D. Configured by cloud customer administrator

16. Which of the following provides a secure and reliable DNS service for your virtual network?

 A. Azure Private DNS

 B. Azure Hybrid DNS

 C. A third-party DNS service

 D. None of the above

17. Which of the following is the fixed Azure DNS IP address?

 A. 168.63.129.16

 B. 168.63.129.01

 C. 168.63.129.00

 D. 168.63.127.16

18. Which of the following is valid for an Azure DNS zone configuration?

 A. You can override the resolution with the private IP address of your Private Endpoints.

 B. You cannot override the resolution with the private IP address of your Private Endpoints.

 C. You cannot override the resolution with your Private Endpoints' private IP address until SKU is upgraded.

 D. None of the above.

19. Which of the following is valid regarding a DNS suffix?

 A. You can change the DNS suffix when you are using Azure-provided DNS services.

 B. You cannot change the DNS suffix when you are using Azure-provided DNS services.

 C. You can remove the DNS suffix when you are using Azure-provided DNS services.

 D. None of the above.

20. Which of the following methods can be used by resources deployed in virtual networks to resolve domain names to internal IP addresses?

   A. Private DNS zones in Azure

   B. Azure-provided name resolution

   C. The organization's managed DNS server

   D. All of the above

Chapter

5

Design and Deploy Core Networking Infrastructure and Virtual WANs

---

THE MICROSOFT AZ-700 EXAM OBJECTIVES COVERED IN THIS CHAPTER INCLUDE:

✓ **Design and implement cross-VNet connectivity**

- Design service chaining, including Gateway Transit
- Design VPN connectivity between VNets
- Implement VNet peering

✓ **Design and implement an Azure Virtual WAN architecture**

- Design an Azure Virtual WAN architecture, including selecting types and services
- Connect a VNet gateway to Azure Virtual WAN
- Create a hub in Virtual WAN
- Create a network virtual appliance (NVA) in a virtual hub
- Configure virtual hub routing
- Create a connection unit

In this chapter, you will learn how to design and implement hybrid networking solutions such as cross-VNet connectivity and Azure Virtual WAN and Virtual WAN hubs.

A VNet represents your own network in the Azure cloud, which is logical isolation dedicated to your subscription. You can use VNets in Azure to create and manage virtual private networks (VPNs). VNets can be linked with other VNets in Azure or your on-premises IT infrastructure to create hybrid or cross-premises solutions.

With Azure Virtual WAN, many networking, security, and routing capabilities are combined into a single operational interface, and you will gain a lot of insight into these capabilities by reading this chapter.

As a network engineer, you have to ensure that users access resources such as file compute, storage, databases, and applications on-premises and in Azure. You must design and implement a core networking solution to achieve your organization's global enterprise IT footprint's short-term and long-term goals.

After reading this chapter, you will have a broad overview of some of the most crucial aspects of designing and deploying core networking infrastructure, cross-VNet IP, and Virtual WAN.

Overview of Virtual Network Peering, Service Chaining, and Gateway Transit

The virtual network peering capability in Azure connects two or more virtual networks seamlessly so that they appear as one network. In peer-to-peer virtual networks, traffic is carried over a *Microsoft backbone* infrastructure. Microsoft's private network is the only way for traffic to reach other virtual machines (VMs) on the same network.

Peering with an Azure virtual network is supported in the following ways:

- Peering between virtual networks in the same Azure region
- Azure global virtual network peering that connects virtual networks across regions

Azure VNet local or global peering offers the following benefits:

- The connection of resources in different virtual networks is low-latency and high-bandwidth.
- The virtual network can communicate with another virtual network.
- Data can be transferred between Azure subscriptions, Azure Active Directory tenants, deployment models, and Azure regions.

- Azure Resource Manager allows virtual networks to peer.

- Resource Manager also allows peering between virtual networks created through the classic deployment model and those created through Resource Manager.

- Neither virtual network will experience downtime at the time that peering is created or after peering is created.

The following constraints apply only when virtual networks globally peer:

- Resources in one virtual network cannot communicate with an internal load balancer (ILB).

- Global virtual network peering does not work for all services that use a basic load balancer.

Peer-to-peer networks share a private network. They communicate over the Microsoft backbone. A public Internet connection, gateways, or encryption are not needed for communication between virtual networks.

In a peering network, resources can directly connect to other resources. All VMs in a virtual network peering in the same region experience the same latency. A VM's bandwidth is proportionate to its size and determines its network throughput. Peering doesn't restrict bandwidth in any way.

Using Azure network security groups (NSGs), you can block access to other virtual networks and subnets in a virtual network and open or close the NSG rules between virtual networks when configuring peering.

You can apply NSGs to block or deny specific access between virtual peer networks. The default setting is full connectivity.

Your organization can use *Azure service chaining* to deliver traffic from a VNet to a virtual appliance in a peering virtual network through user defined routes (UDRs). An example of a network in which service chaining is designed and deployed is shown in Figure 5.1.

FIGURE 5.1   Service chaining

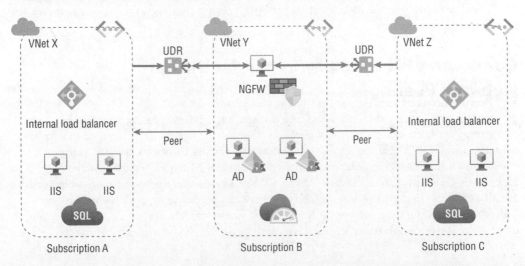

Azure's service chaining enables the design of UDRs between virtual networks and virtual appliances and gateways within peer networks. You can configure UDRs as the next-hop IP address for virtual machines in virtual peer networks. In addition to UDRs, *virtual network gateways* can be used to enable service chaining.

You can deploy hub-and-spoke networks, where a virtual hub network hosts infrastructure components such as virtual network appliances (VNAs) or VPN gateways. Each spoke virtual network would then connect to the virtual hub network. The virtual hub network consists of VNAs or VPN gateways.

Virtual network peering enables a UDR to have as its next hop an IP address of a virtual machine in the peering virtual network or a VPN gateway. With Azure ExpressRoute gateways specified as next hops, you cannot route between virtual networks.

Virtual networks, including peer networks, can each have a gateway. An on-premises network can be connected to a virtual network through its gateway. Even peer-to-peer virtual networks can connect to gateways in Azure.

Traffic between virtual networks flows through the peering configuration when you configure both options for interconnectivity. This traffic is routed through the Azure backbone.

The gateway can also act as a transit point to an on-premises network as part of the virtual network peering. In this case, the virtual network can't have a gateway since it is using a remote gateway. Virtual networks have only one gateway.

On-premises virtual network peering as well as global virtual network peering support Gateway Transit. Virtual network peering supports the creation of virtual networks by using different deployment models as gateways. In the Resource Manager model, the gateway must be included in the virtual network.

By peering virtual networks that share an ExpressRoute connection, you send their traffic through the peering relationship, and Azure backbone networks handle that traffic. You can still use local gateways in each virtual network to connect to an on-premises circuit. Alternatively, you can configure transit to connect to on-premises systems via a shared gateway.

In a peering environment, Gateway Transit enables a virtual network to use a VPN/ExpressRoute gateway. The Gateway Transit technology supports both network-to-network connectivity as well as cross-premises connectivity. Traffic to the gateway (entry or exit) in the virtual network peering incurs virtual network peering charges on the spoke network (or non-gateway network).

Configure VPN Gateway Transit for Virtual Network Peering

By merging two Azure virtual networks into one, virtual network peering seamlessly connects two virtual networks for connectivity purposes. One virtual network can connect to another network using a VPN gateway in the virtual network peering through Gateway Transit.

As shown in Figure 5.2, peer virtual networks can use Azure VPN gateways through Hub-RM's Gateway Transit feature. VNet-to-VNet, site-to-site, and point-to-site connections are all available on the VPN gateway. Peering between deployment models can be done via transit. When configuring between different deployment models, transit needs to be configured in the Resource Manager deployment model, not the classic deployment model.

FIGURE 5.2   Virtual network peering using Gateway Transit

A *hub-and-spoke network* architecture enables spoke virtual networks to share the hub's VPN gateway instead of deploying VPN gateways for each spoke virtual network. Routes to the gateway-connected virtual networks or on-premises networks will propagate to the virtual network peering through Gateway Transit. Alternatively, you can disable automatic route propagation. Assign the routing table to the subnets to prevent the route distribution by building a table with the Disable BGP Route Propagation option.

One of the critical limitations for service chaining is nontransparency. Service chaining is shown in the example in Figure 5.3. If VNet X and VNet Y, and VNet Y and VNet Z are peering, VNet peering does not apply to VNet X and VNet Z.

FIGURE 5.3   Azure peering nontransparency

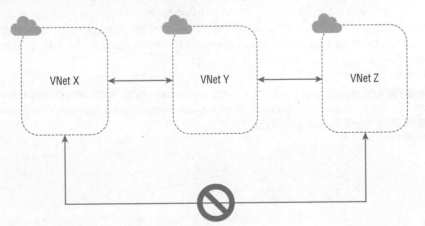

You can design and deploy hub-and-spoke networks to overcome the limitations of VNet peering, where the virtual hub network can host infrastructure components such as a VNA or VPN gateway, as shown in Figure 5.4. A virtual hub network would then be able to peer with all the spoke networks. The virtual hub network can be connected to VNAs or VPN gateways. In this way, all the networks can communicate with each other without any restrictions.

FIGURE 5.4   Hub-and-spoke model

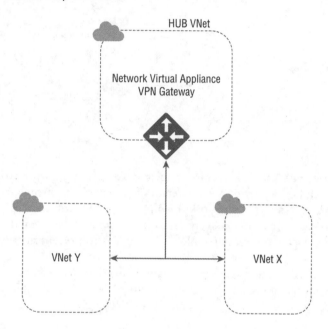

Also, traffic flows through the peering configuration when a virtual network is connected to a gateway and to a virtual network peering. To complete the design and deployment of service chaining, it is essential to implement the custom routing and validate the service chaining. To implement the custom routing, enable IP forwarding for the NIC of the VM, configure UDR, and configure routing in the VM.

Virtual network peering enables a route to be redirected to a virtual machine within a virtual network peering, or to a VPN gateway, as the next hop. With service chaining, you can create UDRs between one virtual network and a virtual appliance, or virtual network gateway, in a virtual network peering.

Using the example shown in Figure 5.4, you can create or update peering using Power-Shell as shown in the following code:

```
$SpokedemoRG = "SpokesybexRG1"
$SpokedemoRM = "SpokesybexRM"
$HubdempRG   = "HubsybexRG1"
$HubdemoRM   = "HubsybexRM"
$spokermdemovnet = Get-AzVirtualNetwork -Name $SpokedemoRM
-ResourceGroup $SpokedemoRG
$hubrmdemovnet   = Get-AzVirtualNetwork -Name $HubdemoRM
-ResourceGroup $HubdemoRG
Add-AzVirtualNetworkPeering `
  -Name SpokeRMtoHubRM `
  -VirtualNetwork $spokermdemovnet `
  -RemoteVirtualNetworkId $hubrmdemovnet.Id `
  -UseRemoteGateways
Add-AzVirtualNetworkPeering `
  -Name HubRMToSpokeRM `
  -VirtualNetwork $hubrmdemovnet `
  -RemoteVirtualNetworkId $spokermdemovnet.Id `
  -AllowGatewayTransit
```

The following method demonstrates how to enable IP forwarding on a network interface via PowerShell:

```
$nic = Get-AzNetworkInterface -ResourceGroupName "SybeRG" -Name "NIC1"
$nic.EnableIPForwarding = 1
$nic | Set-AzNetworkInterface
```

In the first command, the network interface NIC1 is stored in the $nic variable. The second command changes IP forwarding to true, and the third command applies the changes. If you want to disable IP forwarding on a network interface, follow the example, but be sure to modify the second command to $nic.EnableIPForwarding = 0.

Exercise 5.1 demonstrates how to configure user-defined routing via the Azure portal.

EXERCISE 5.1

Configuring User-Defined Routing via the Azure Portal

1. Log into a personal or business account in the Azure portal at portal.azure.com as shown here.

EXERCISE 5.1 *(continued)*

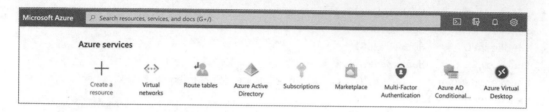

2. Click Create A Resource, enter **route table** in the search box, to open the window shown here and click Create.

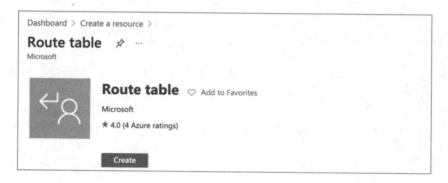

3. Once the Create Route Table Wizard opens, configure the following settings in the Route Table column (see the following image):

Subscription	Choose your Azure subscription.
Resource Group	Choose an existing resource group or create a new one.
Region	Pick the Azure datacenter where you want to deploy the VM. Virtual networks and virtual machines must share the same route table.
Name	Provide a name for the route table.

It is safe to choose No for Propagate Gateway Routes, since this prevents on-premises routes from propagating to the network interfaces in the associated subnets.

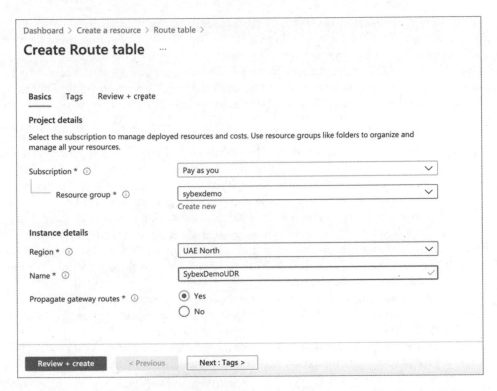

Dashboard > Create a resource > Route table >

Create Route table   ...

Basics   Tags   Review + create

Project details

Select the subscription to manage deployed resources and costs. Use resource groups like folders to organize and manage all your resources.

Subscription * ⓘ | Pay as you   ∨ |

    Resource group * ⓘ | sybexdemo   ∨ |
                                Create new

Instance details

Region * ⓘ | UAE North   ∨ |

Name * ⓘ | SybexDemoUDR   ∨ |

Propagate gateway routes * ⓘ   ◉ Yes
                                  ○ No

[**Review + create**]   [< Previous]   [Next : Tags >]

4. To finish creating the route table, select Review + Create, then click Create. Once the settings are validated, the route table will be deployed.

Microsoft recommends using an organization firewall VM as a gateway when creating user-defined routes. You must also configure routes to each subnet using the firewall VM for traffic between the two subnets to pass through the firewall VM. Subnets should be assigned route tables. As per Microsoft, giving more than one route table to a subnet is impossible.

Finally, to perform the validation of the service chaining, ensure that you have configured Windows Firewall with Advanced Security on the target Azure VM and use `Test-NetConnection -ComputerName` to check if service chaining is supported between peering virtual networks in a Windows VM.

Design VPN Connectivity between VNets

A VPN is useful for several reasons, such as protecting cloud customers' privacy when using an open network, but there are cases where it shouldn't be used, such as to circumvent regional data regulation.

The definition of virtual private networking is sending private data securely across an unsecured network to a third network. In general, we are referring to an unsecured network like the Internet, which has several potential security risks due to its design.

VNet-to-VNet (VPN gateway) connections are the oldest means of internal connectivity. You must set up a separate subnet with a VPN gateway in each VNet you want to connect to. A secure tunnel such as IPsec/ Internet Key Exchange (IKE) can then be provided between these VPN gateways.

Connecting VNets is as simple as configuring a VNet-to-VNet connection. A virtual network connection to another network using the VNet-to-VNet connection type creates a link similar to a site-to-site IPsec connection to an on-premises location. In both cases, a VPN gateway is used to provide a secure tunnel using IPsec/IKE, and they function alike when communicating. They differ, however, in how local network gateways are configured.

You will automatically create and populate the local network gateway address space when you make a VNet-to-VNet connection. The other VNet automatically routes to the updated address space when you update the address space for one VNet. Establishing a VNet-to-VNet connection is faster and easier than setting a site-to-site connection. But the local network gateway isn't visible.

You can specify additional address spaces for the local network gateway or if you plan to add additional connections later and need to adjust the local network gateway. In this case, you should create the configuration by following the site-to-site steps.

A point-to-site client pool address space is not included in the VNet-to-VNet connection. You may create a site-to-site connection between the virtual network gateways if transitive routing is needed for point-to-site clients or you can use VNet peering.

Assume you are working with a complicated network configuration. You may connect your organization's VNets using the site-to-site steps rather than the VNet-to-VNet steps. You need to create and configure the local network gateways manually when the organization uses site-to-site steps. A local network gateway for each VNet treats the other VNet as a local site. You can use this to specify an additional address space for the local network gateway. You must update the corresponding local network gateway if a VNet's address space changes, which doesn't happen automatically.

Consumers of cloud services may want to connect virtual networks with a VNet-to-VNet connection for the following reasons:

- Geo-redundancy across regions and geo-presence

  - You can set up an organization network with geo-replication or synchronization and secure connectivity without accessing the Internet.

  - Using Azure Traffic Manager and load balancer, you can set up highly available workloads across multiple Azure regions with geo-redundancy. SQL Always-On can be set up across multiple Azure regions via availability groups.

- Regional multi-tier applications with isolation or an administrative boundary

  - For reasons of isolation or administration, you can connect multiple virtual networks within the same region.

Communications between VNets can be combined with multisite configurations. A mixed network topology combines cross-premises and inter-virtual connectivity. Figure 5.5 shows this configuration.

FIGURE 5.5   VPN connectivity deployment model

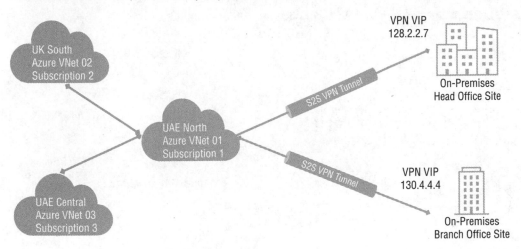

Azure VNet peering is an Azure feature. You can use Azure global VNet peering to connect regions. Virtual networks can be in the same region or different regions. The Azure global VNet peering service is the same in all other respects. Figure 5.6 shows VPN connectivity between VNets in the same region.

FIGURE 5.6   VNet-to-VNet VPN connection in the same region

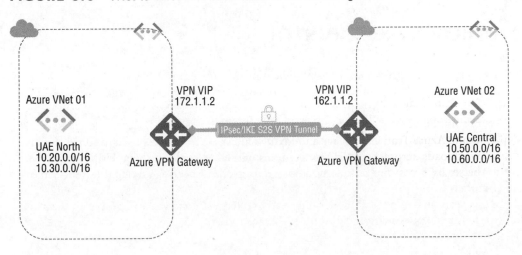

You can connect virtual networks in different regions and from different subscriptions, and the subscriptions don't need to be associated with the same Active Directory tenant. The configuration establishes a connection between two virtual network gateways. Figure 5.7 shows VPN connectivity between VNets in different regions.

FIGURE 5.7   VNet-to-VNet VPN connection in different regions

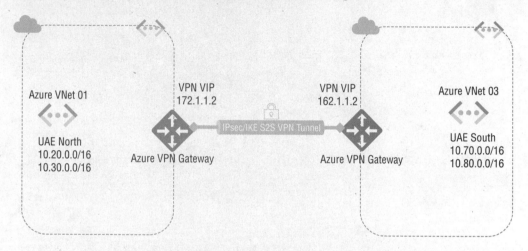

A VPN gateway's data traffic is limited based on the service level selected. Depending on the subscription, the virtual networks may be in the same region or in different regions. You can build a configuration using various tools, such as the Azure portal, PowerShell, and Azure Cloud Shell, depending on the deployment pattern of your VNet.

Deploy VNet Peering

In this section, you learn about the deployment models for Azure VNet peering.

Two virtual networks can peer with each other. Different deployment models can be used in the same subscription, or different subscriptions can be used in the same subscription.

Azure solutions can be deployed and managed using Resource Manager and classic deployment models. You interact with them through two different API sets, and the deployed resources can differ significantly. There is no compatibility between them. However, in this section we present a mitigation methodology to implement peering among different deployment models.

In this section, deployment models one and two have subscriptions *deployed* in the same or different regions using Azure Resource Manager.

Deployment models 3 and 4 have subscriptions *created* in the same or different region. One is deployed using Resource Manager and another using Azure Classic.

Deployment Model 1: Running in the Same Azure Subscription and Deployed Using Azure Resource Manager

Azure's command-line interface (CLI), Azure PowerShell, or an Azure Resource Manager template can be used to create a virtual network peering.

 Throughout this chapter, we will be using only Azure PowerShell as the preferred method of deployment.

You can peer virtual networks with one another using virtual network connections. The resources in both virtual networks will communicate with each other with the same latency and bandwidth as if they were in the same virtual network. In this section, you explore how to set up the virtual network peering running in the same Azure subscription.

1. Set up two VNets.

2. Connect two VNets with virtual network peering.

3. Build a VM into each virtual network.

4. Communicate among VMs.

You must first create a resource group for the virtual network.

Use the New-AzResourceGroup command to create a resource group. You have to create a resource group to host the Azure Route Server before starting it. The following example creates a resource group named SybexRG in the UAENorth location:

```
$rg = @{
    Name = 'SybexRG'
    Location = 'UAENorth'
}
New-AzResourceGroup @rg
```

New-AzVirtualNetwork allows you to create a virtual network. A default virtual network named VNET1 is created in the UAENorth location:

```
$virtualNetwork1 = New-AzVirtualNetwork `
  -ResourceGroupName 'SybexRG
  -Location UAE North `
  -Name VNET1 `
  -AddressPrefix 10.0.0.0/16
```

With `Add-AzVirtualNetworkSubnetConfig`, configure a virtual network subnet. This is a dedicated subnet called `VNET1Subnet`.

```
$subnetConfig = Add-AzVirtualNetworkSubnetConfig `
  -Name VNET1Subnet `
  -AddressPrefix 10.0.0.0/24 `
  -VirtualNetwork $ virtualNetwork1
```

`Set-AzVirtualNetwork` creates the subnet by writing the subnet configuration to the virtual network:

```
$virtualNetwork1 | Set-AzVirtualNetwork
```

With one subnet and an address range of `10.1.0.0/16`, create a virtual network:

```
# Create the virtual network.
$virtualNetwork2 = New-AzVirtualNetwork `
  -ResourceGroupName SybexRG `
  -Location UAE Central `
  -Name VNet2`
  -AddressPrefix 10.1.0.0/16
# Create the subnet configuration.
$subnetConfig = Add-AzVirtualNetworkSubnetConfig `
  -Name VNET1Subnet `
  -AddressPrefix 10.1.0.0/24 `
  -VirtualNetwork $virtualNetwork2
# Create the subnet configuration to the virtual network.
$virtualNetwork2 | Set-AzVirtualNetwork
```

Add virtual network peering with `Add-AzVirtualNetworkPeering`. Here is an example of `myVirtualNetwork1` peering with `myVirtualNetwork2`:

```
Add-AzVirtualNetworkPeering `
  -Name myVirtualNetwork1-myVirtualNetwork2 `
  -VirtualNetwork $virtualNetwork1 `
  -RemoteVirtualNetworkId $virtualNetwork2.Id
```

`PeeringState` is initiated in the output returned by the previous command. The initiated peering remains in the initiated state until the peering from `myVirtualNetwork2` to `myVirtualNetwork1` is created. Create a peering from `vNet2` to `vNet1`:

```
Add-AzVirtualNetworkPeering `
  -Name VNet2- VNet1 `
  -VirtualNetwork $virtualNetwork2 `
  -RemoteVirtualNetworkId $virtualNetwork1.Id
```

With the output from the previous command, the peering state is connected. `MyVirtualNetwork1 – myVirtualNetwork2` peering was also changed to

Connected by Azure. You can verify that the peering state for the `myVirtualNetwork1`–`myVirtualNetwork2` peering has changed to `Connected` by issuing `Get-AzVirtualNetworkPeering`:

```
Get-AzVirtualNetworkPeering `
  -ResourceGroupName 'SybexRG '
  -VirtualNetworkName VNet1 `
  | Select PeeringState
```

`PeeringState` for the peerings in both virtual networks must be `Connected` before resources from one virtual network can communicate with resources from the other virtual network.

The `New-AzVM` command creates a virtual machine. The following example creates a VM named `SybexVm1` in the `vNET1` network. Using the `-AsJob` option, you can make the VM in the background and proceed to the next step. Enter the username and password to log into the VM when prompted.

```
New-AzVm `
  -ResourceGroupName "SybexRG" `
  -Location "UAE North" `
  -VirtualNetworkName "vNET1" `
  -SubnetName " VNET1Subnet " `
  -ImageName "Win2019Datacenter" `
  -Name "SybexVm1" `
  -AsJob
```

Deploy VM2 named SybexVm2 in virtual network 2:

```
New-AzVm `
  -ResourceGroupName "SybexRG" `
  -Location "UAE North" `
  -VirtualNetworkName "vNET2" `
  -SubnetName " VNET1Subnet " `
  -ImageName "Win2019Datacenter" `
  -Name "SybexVm2" `
  -AsJob
```

It takes a few minutes for the VM to be created. After Azure creates the VM and returns results to PowerShell, you can continue.

In Azure, VMs that do not have a public IP address or that are part of an internal Basic Azure Load Balancer pool receive an outbound access IP address. An outbound IP address is provided by default and cannot be customized.

When a public IP address is assigned to the virtual machine or the virtual machine is placed in the back-end pool of a Standard load balancer with or without outbound rules, the default outbound access IP is disabled. If an Azure virtual network NAT gateway resource is assigned to the subnet of the virtual machine, the default outbound access IP is disabled.

By default, outbound access is not enabled for virtual machines created by virtual machine scale sets in Flexible Orchestration mode.

 Flexible Orchestration mode in Azure offers a unified Azure VM provisioning experience through flexible orchestration. VMs can be spread across fault domains within availability zones and regions to provide high availability guarantees (up to 1,000 VMs).

You can connect to a VM's public IP address from the Internet. Use `Get-AzPublicIpAddress` to return the public IP address of a VM. Here is an example of how to retrieve the public IP address of the SybexVM1 VM:

```
Get-AzPublicIpAddress `
  -Name SybexVM1 `
  -ResourceGroupName SybexRG | Select IpAddress
```

To access SybexVM1 from a desktop/laptop computer, run the following command. (Replace `<publicIpAddress>` with the IP address returned by the previous command.)

```
mstsc /v:<publicIpAddress>
```

Remote Desktop Protocol (RDP) files are created, downloaded, and opened on the admin workstation. Enter the appropriate username and password on the RDP screen. (Admins may need to select More Choices, then select a different account to specify the credentials the admin used when they created the VM.) During the sign-in process, a certificate warning may appear. If the warning appears, click Continue.

By enabling ICMP on the SybexVm1 VM, the admin can use PowerShell to ping it later from SybexVm2.

Deployment Model 2: Running in Different Subscriptions and Deploying Using Resource Manager

Resource Manager can be used to peer virtual networks between each other. Each virtual network has its own subscription to a different Azure Active Directory (Azure AD) tenant. It is possible to peer two virtual networks so that the resources in the two networks can communicate with each other with the same bandwidth and latency as if they were on the same virtual network. In this section, you explore how to set up virtual network peering running in different Azure subscriptions.

Let's look at the essential prerequisites for this deployment model scenario. When you are working with virtual network peering, you must have the following roles assigned to their accounts:

- **Network Contributor:** Deployed by Resource Manager for a virtual network
- **Classic Network Contributor:** Used for classic deployment models of virtual networks

You must assign their account to a custom role if it is not assigned to one of the roles in the previous list. This custom role must be assigned the actions shown in Table 5.1.

TABLE 5.1   Custom roles

Setting	Azure services description
`Microsoft.Network/virtualNetworks/ virtualNetworkPeerings/write`	Permission required to build a peering from virtual network X to virtual network Y. Virtual network X must be a virtual network (Azure Resource Manager).
`Microsoft.Network/virtualNetworks/ peer/action`	Permission required to build a peering from virtual network Y (ARM) to virtual network X.
`Microsoft.Network/virtualNetworks/ virtualNetworkPeerings/read`	Permission to read a virtual network peering.
`Microsoft.Network/virtualNetworks/ virtualNetworkPeerings/delete`	Permission to delete a virtual network peering.
`Microsoft.ClassicNetwork/ virtualNetworks/peer/action`	Permission required to build a peering from virtual network Y (classic) to virtual network X.

For this setup, imagine you have two users' IDs enabled with different privileges for different subscriptions.

Enter the `Connect-AzAccount` command in PowerShell to log in as User1. Creating a virtual network peering requires permissions on the Azure engineer's account.

You must first create a resource group for the virtual network using the `New-AzResourceGroup` command. This resource group will host the Azure Route Server before starting it. The following example creates a resource group named `SybexRGA` in the `UAENorth` location:

```
$rg = @{
    Name = 'SybexRGA '
    Location = 'UAENorth'
}
New-AzResourceGroup @rg
```

`New-AzVirtualNetwork` allows you to create a virtual network. The following code creates a default virtual network named `VNetX` in the `UAENorth` location:

```
$virtualNetwork1 = New-AzVirtualNetwork `
  -ResourceGroupName 'SybexRGA
  -Name VNetX `
```

```
 -AddressPrefix 10.0.0.0/16
 - Location = 'UAENorth'
```

Use the `New-AzRoleAssignment` cmdlet to provide access. Access is provided by assigning the right RBAC role to them at the right scope.

```
New-AzRoleAssignment `  -SignInName User2@azure.com `
-RoleDefinitionName "Network Contributor" `
-Scope /subscriptions/<SubscriptionA-Id>/resourceGroups/myResourceGroupA/
providers/Microsoft.Network/VirtualNetworks/VNETX
```

Log User1 out from Azure and log User2 in. To create a virtual network peering, the logged-in account must have the necessary permissions.

```
$virtualNetwork1 = New-AzVirtualNetwork `
 -ResourceGroupName 'SybexRGB
 -Name VNetY `
 -AddressPrefix 10.1.0.0/16
 - Location = 'UAECentral'
New-AzRoleAssignment `  -SignInName User1@azure.com `
-RoleDefinitionName "Network Contributor" `  -Scope /subscriptions/
<SubscriptionA-Id>/resourceGroups/myResourceGroupA/providers/
Microsoft.Network/VirtualNetworks/VNETY
```

Once deployed, log User2 out from Azure via PowerShell and log User1 in and build the peering from VNetX to VNetY. The following is the sample configuration to build peering from VnetX to VnetY.

```
$vNetX=Get-AzVirtualNetwork -Name VNetX -ResourceGroupName SybexRGA
Add-AzVirtualNetworkPeering `
 -Name 'VNetXToVNetY' `
 -VirtualNetwork $VNetX `
 -RemoteVirtualNetworkId "/subscriptions/<SubscriptionB-Id>/resourceGroups/
myResourceGroupB/providers/Microsoft.Network/virtualNetworks/myVnetY"
```

Verify and validate the peering of VNetX, using the following sample configuration:

```
Get-AzVirtualNetworkPeering `
 -ResourceGroupName SybexRGA `
 -VirtualNetworkName VNetX `
 | Format-Table VirtualNetworkName, PeeringState
```

The state `Initiated` will change to `Connected` once you set up the peering to VNetX from VNetY.

Once deployed, log User1 out from Azure via PowerShell and log User2 in and build the peering from VNetY to VNetX. The following is the sample configuration to build peering from vNetY to vNetX:

```
# Peer myVnetY to myVNetX.
$vNetY=Get-AzVirtualNetwork -Name VNetY -ResourceGroupName SybexB
Add-AzVirtualNetworkPeering `
  -Name 'VNetYToVNetX' `
  -VirtualNetwork $VNetX `
  -RemoteVirtualNetworkId "/subscriptions/<SubscriptionB-Id>/resourceGroups/
myResourceGroupB/providers/Microsoft.Network/virtualNetworks/VNetY"
```

Verify and validate the peering of vNetY, using the following sample configuration:

```
Get-AzVirtualNetworkPeering `
  -ResourceGroupName SybexRGB`
  -VirtualNetworkName VNetX `
  | Format-Table VirtualNetworkName, PeeringState
```

The state `Initiated` will change to `Connected` once you set up the peering to VNetY from VNetX. Both virtual networks must be in the `Connected` state before peering can be established. You can now connect any Azure resources they create within either virtual network using IP addresses. The resources in the virtual networks cannot resolve names across the virtual networks if you use default Azure name resolution. You must create a DNS server for your organization to resolve names across virtual networks in a peering.

Deployment Model 3: Running in the Same Subscription and Deploying One VNet Using Resource Manager and Another Using the Classic Model

This section discusses how to create virtual network peering in the same Azure subscription but with different deployments, one using Azure Resource Manager and the other using the classic model.

By peering, two separate virtual networks can communicate with each other with the same bandwidth and latency as if they were in the same virtual network. Virtual networks deployed using the classic deployment model can't be peered with each other. You can, however, use the Azure VPN Gateway to connect virtual networks created by the classic deployment model.

For the setup in this section, imagine you have two users' IDs enabled with the same privileges for the same subscription.

You must first create a resource group for the virtual network using the New-AzResourceGroup command. You must create a resource group to host the Azure Route Server before starting it. The following example creates a resource group named SybexRouteServerRG in the UAENorth location:

```
$rg = @{
    Name = 'SybexRGA '
    Location = 'UAENorth'
}
New-AzResourceGroup @rg
```

The New-AzVirtualNetwork command allows you to create a virtual network. The following code creates a default virtual network named VNetX in the UAENorth location:

```
$virtualNetwork1 = New-AzVirtualNetwork `
  -ResourceGroupName 'SybexRGA
  -Name VNetX `
  -AddressPrefix 10.0.0.0/16
 - Location = 'UAENorth'
```

Imagine that VNetY is created using the classic method of deployment. In that case, you must create an existing network configuration in an XML file as follows.

```
<VirtualNetworkSite name="VNetY" Location="UAE North">
  <AddressSpace>
    <AddressPrefix>10.1.0.0/16</AddressPrefix>
  </AddressSpace>
  <Subnets>
    <Subnet name="default">
      <AddressPrefix>10.1.0.0/24</AddressPrefix>
    </Subnet>
  </Subnets>
</VirtualNetworkSite>
```

Once deployed, build the peering from VNetX to VNetY. The following is the sample configuration to build peering from VNetX to VNetY:

```
# Peer VNetX to VNetY.
Add-AzVirtualNetworkPeering `
  -Name VNetXToVNetY `
  -VirtualNetwork $VNet1 `
  -RemoteVirtualNetworkId /subscriptions/<subscription Id>/resourceGroups/
Default-Networking/providers/Microsoft.ClassicNetwork/virtualNetworks/VNetY
```

Verify and validate the peering of vNetX using the following configuration:

```
Get-AzVirtualNetworkPeering `
  -ResourceGroupName Sybex`
  -VirtualNetworkName VNetX `
  | Format-Table VirtualNetworkName, PeeringState
```

The state `Initiated` will change to `Connected` once you set up the peering to VNetX from VNetY. Both virtual networks must be in the `Connected` state before peering can be established. You can now connect any Azure resources you create within either virtual network using IP addresses. The resources in the virtual networks cannot resolve names across the virtual networks if your organization uses default Azure name resolution. It would help if you created a DNS server for your organization to resolve names across virtual networks in a peering.

Deployment Model 4: Running in Different Subscriptions and Deploying One VNet Using Resource Manager and Another Using the Classic Model

This section discusses how to create virtual network peering in different Azure subscriptions and with different deployment models, one using Resource Manager and another using the classic model.

By peering two virtual networks together, you ensure that resources within them can communicate at the same bandwidth and latency as though they were in the same virtual network.

It is not possible to peer virtual networks that each use the classic deployment model. While Azure networks can peer with virtual networks from different supported regions, in this section we use virtual networks that exist in the same region.

For the setup in this section, imagine you have two users' IDs enabled with different privileges for different subscriptions.

You must first create a resource group for the virtual network using the `New-AzResourceGroup` command. You must create a resource group to host the Azure Route Server before starting it. The following example creates a resource group named `SybexRGA` in the `UAENorth` location:

```
$rg = @{
    Name = 'SybexRGA '
    Location = 'UAENorth'
}
New-AzResourceGroup @rg
```

The `New-AzVirtualNetwork` command allows you to create a virtual network. A default virtual network named `VNetX` is created in the `UAENorth` location:

```
$virtualNetwork1 = New-AzVirtualNetwork `
  -ResourceGroupName 'SybexRGA
  -Name VNetX `
  -AddressPrefix 10.0.0.0/16
 - Location = 'UAENorth'
```

Assign the RBAC role to the principal at the scope using `New-AzRoleAssignment`:

```
New-AzRoleAssignment `  -SignInName User2@azure.com `  -RoleDefinitionName
"Network Contributor" `  -Scope /subscriptions/<SubscriptionA-Id>/
resourceGroups/myResourceGroupA/providers/Microsoft.Network/
VirtualNetworks/VNetX
```

Imagine that VNETY is created using the classic method of deployment. In that case, you must create a network configuration in an XML file as follows:

```
<VirtualNetworkSite name="VNetY" Location="UAE North">
  <AddressSpace>
    <AddressPrefix>10.1.0.0/16</AddressPrefix>
  </AddressSpace>
  <Subnets>
    <Subnet name="default">
      <AddressPrefix>10.1.0.0/24</AddressPrefix>
    </Subnet>
  </Subnets>
</VirtualNetworkSite>
```

Access Resource Manager by typing the **Connect-AzAccount** command and assigning User1 permissions to VNetY. Following is the sample deployment:

```
New-AzRoleAssignment `
  -SignInName User1@azure.com `
  -RoleDefinitionName "Classic Network Contributor" `
  -Scope /subscriptions/<SubscriptionB-id>/resourceGroups/Default-Networking/
providers/Microsoft.ClassicNetwork/virtualNetworks/VNetY
```

Once deployed, build the peering from VNetX to VNetY using the following code:

```
# Peer VNetX to VNetY.
Add-AzVirtualNetworkPeering `
  -Name VNetXToVNetY `
  -VirtualNetwork $vnet1 `
  -RemoteVirtualNetworkId /subscriptions/<subscription Id>/resourceGroups/
Default-Networking/providers/Microsoft.ClassicNetwork/virtualNetworks/VNetY
```

Verify and validate the peering of vNetX using this code:

```
Get-AzVirtualNetworkPeering `
  -ResourceGroupName Sybex`
  -VirtualNetworkName VNetX `
  | Format-Table VirtualNetworkName, PeeringState
```

The state `Initiated` will change to `Connected` once you set up the peering to VNetX from VNetY. Both virtual networks must be in the `Connected` state before peering can be established. You can now connect any Azure resources you create within either virtual network using IP addresses. The resources in the virtual networks cannot resolve names across the virtual networks if your organization uses default Azure name resolution. You must create a DNS server for your organization to resolve names across virtual networks in a peering.

> For the AZ-700 exam, keep in mind that peer-to-peer virtual networks now have private network traffic. Data can be transferred between Azure subscriptions, deployment models, and regions using virtual network peering. Virtual network peering does not cause downtime.
>
> Azure virtual networking does not support peer-to-peer transitive routing by default. However, a virtual network appliance and custom routing rules can implement peer-to-peer transitive routing.

Design an Azure Virtual WAN Architecture

Azure Virtual WAN is an Azure Network Service from Microsoft that offers high-speed global transit and secure connectivity between branches, datacenters, hubs, and users. It supports branch-to-Azure VPN, user-to-user VPN, and ExpressRoute connectivity. The Hub-to-VNet connection (between the VNet and the virtual workload network) is automated. Azure Virtual WAN can also be used to connect branches across regions by using the Azure private backbone.

Virtual WAN combines networking, security, and routing functionality into a single operational interface. Benefits include:

- Virtual WAN Partner devices such as SD-WAN or VPN CPE that can automate branch connectivity
- Site-to-site VPN connectivity
- Remote user VPN (point-to-site) connectivity
- ExpressRoute (Private) connectivity

- Intra-cloud connectivity
- VPN ExpressRoute inter-connectivity
- Routing
- Azure Firewall
- Encryption for private connectivity

An Azure VPN Gateway and a Virtual WAN VPN Gateway differ in the following ways:

- Virtual WANs provide site-to-site connectivity, designed for speed, scalability, and ease of use. In contrast to a regular virtual network gateway that uses the VPN gateway type, a Virtual WAN VPN gateway uses a Virtual WAN VPN. When you connect an ExpressRoute circuit to a Virtual WAN hub, it uses a different resource for the ExpressRoute gateway than the regular virtual network gateway that uses the ExpressRoute gateway type.

- VPN and ExpressRoute support Virtual WANs with an aggregate throughput of 20 Gbps maximum. A Virtual WAN also offers automation for connectivity with an ecosystem of CPE branch devices. These devices are available from a growing ecosystem of SD-WAN and VPN partners and are equipped with built-in automation that automatically provisions and connects to Azure Virtual WAN.

VPN gateways are limited to 30 tunnels. For large-scale VPN connections, you should use Virtual WAN. The number of branch connections per virtual hub can reach 1,000, with a combined bandwidth of up to 20 Gbps. A connection is an active-active tunnel from the on-premises VPN device to the virtual hub. You can also have multiple virtual hubs per region, so cloud users can connect over 1,000 branches to a single Azure region by deploying multiple Virtual WAN hubs in that region, each with their own site-to-site VPN gateway.

The following benefits are offered by Virtual WANs:

Integrated Connectivity Solutions in the Hub and Spoke   Configure on-premises to Azure and create connectivity between the two.

Automated Spoke Setup and Configuration   Integrate organization workloads and virtual networks seamlessly into the Azure hub.

Intuitive Troubleshooting   Azure engineers can see the entire flow within Azure and take appropriate action based on this information.

Virtual WAN-based hub-and-spoke architecture includes the following benefits:

- More limited operational burden by substituting existing hubs with a fully managed Azure Virtual WAN service.
- By removing the need for network virtual appliances, a managed service can save you money.
- Added secure hubs with Azure Firewall and Virtual WAN minimize misconfiguration-related security risks.
- There is a separation of responsibilities between central IT (SecOps, InfraOps) and workloads (DevOps).

The Virtual WAN architecture is a hub-and-spoke architecture that provides scale and performance for branches (VPN/SD-WAN devices), users (Azure VPN/OpenVPN/IKEv2 clients), ExpressRoute circuits, and virtual networks.

Using Virtual WAN, you can build a global transit network architecture that provides transitive connectivity between endpoints distributed across various types of "spokes" using a cloud-hosted network "hub."

The following is a high-level description of how availability zones and resiliency are handled in Virtual WANs. In a Virtual WAN, hubs and services are centralized within a hub. Users may set up as many virtual networks as they need. A Virtual WAN hub provides VPN, ExpressRoute, and other services. Azure Firewall is automatically deployed across availability zones (except for regions that don't support availability zones). A region can become an availability zone after the initial deployment in the hub of the user re-creates the gateways, triggering an availability zone deployment. All gateways in a hub are set up as active-active, which provides built-in redundancy for the hub. Multi-hub connectivity is available if users wish to maintain resiliency across regions.

Azure Firewall can currently be deployed to support availability zones via Azure Firewall Manager, PowerShell, or CLI. There was no way to deploy a firewall across availability zones as of this writing. This means organizations need to delete and re-deploy their Azure Firewall.

Virtual WAN is a global concept, but it is a regional resource deployed through Resource Manager. All hubs within a Virtual WAN will continue to function in the event of an issue with the Virtual WAN region, but new hubs cannot be created until the Virtual WAN region is available.

Figure 5.8 shows the high-level building blocks of Virtual WAN resources.

FIGURE 5.8   Virtual WAN building blocks

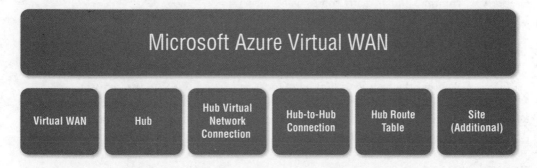

To set up an end-to-end Virtual WAN, you should design the following resources on demand:

VirtualWAN   The *virtualWAN* resource is an overlay of the Azure network for the organization. It includes multiple resources. The Virtual WAN provides links to all your organization's virtual hubs that you wish to have. In a Virtual WAN, resources are isolated and cannot be connected to a standard hub, and there is no communication between virtual hubs.

Hub   A *virtual hub* is a network managed by Microsoft. Service endpoints are located on the hub to enable connectivity. From the on-premises network of the organization (VPN site), you can connect to a VPN gateway inside the virtual hub, connect ExpressRoute circuits to a virtual hub, or connect mobile users to a point-to-site gateway inside the virtual hub. Your organization's networks in regions are centered around the hub, and a region may have more than one virtual hub.

There is a difference between a hub gateway and a virtual network gateway that organizations use for ExpressRoute and VPN Gateway. For example, in the case of a Virtual WAN, an organization does not establish a site-to-site connection between their on-premises site and their VNet. Instead, it uses a site-to-site connection. All traffic passes through the hub gateway. The organization's VNets do not require a virtual network gateway. Through its virtual hub and virtual hub gateway, the Virtual WAN enables the organization's VNets to scale efficiently.

Hub Virtual Network Connection   The *hub virtual network connection* allows seamless communication between the hub and the organization's virtual network. There can be only one virtual network per virtual hub.

Hub-to-Hub Connection   A Virtual WAN links all hubs together. As a result, a branch, user, or VNet connected to a local hub can use the complete mesh architecture to communicate with another branch, user, or VNet. Through the hub-to-hub connected framework, organizations can connect VNets within a hub transiting through the virtual hub and VNets across the hub.

Hub Route Table   You can create virtual hub routes and add them to virtual hub route tables. You may add as many routes as necessary.

Site (Additional Virtual WAN resources)   Currently, a VPN site is only used to connect sites. It represents your organization's on-premises VPN device. You can automatically export configurations to Azure by collaborating with a Virtual WAN partner.

Figure 5.9 shows the high-level building blocks of Virtual WAN connectivity.

In Azure, the hub serves as a central point of connectivity with your on-premises networks. These virtual networks peer with the hub and can be used to isolate workloads. A VPN gateway or ExpressRoute connection connects the on-premises datacenter(s) with the hub. One of the main features of this approach is that Azure Virtual WAN replaces hubs as a managed service.

Virtual WAN provides cloud networking. As part of this service, Microsoft hosts and manages the networking components. Through Virtual WAN, you can create global transit networks, enabling a ubiquitous, any-to-any kind of connectivity between globally distributed cloud workloads in VNets, branch sites, SaaS and PaaS applications, and users. Figure 5.10 shows an overview of Virtual WAN capabilities.

FIGURE 5.9   Virtual WAN connectivity

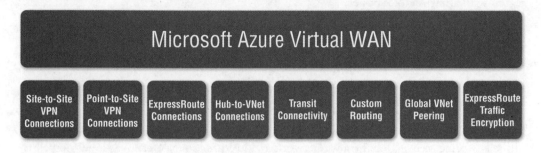

FIGURE 5.10   Global transit network with Virtual WAN

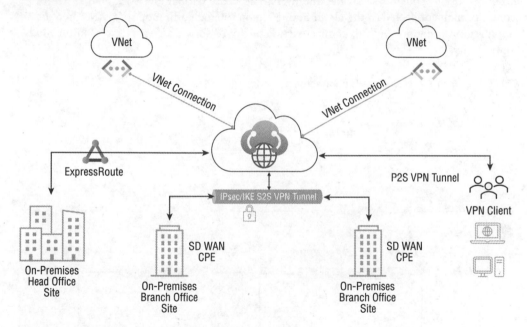

In the Virtual WAN architecture, Virtual WAN hubs are provisioned in Azure regions to which you can choose to connect your branches, VNets, and remote users. The physical branch sites are connected to the hub by Premium or Standard ExpressRoute or site-to-site-VPNs. VNets are connected to the hub by VNet connections. Remote users can directly connect to the hub using the user's VPN (point-to-site VPNs). Virtual WAN also supports cross-region VNet connections, where a VNet in one region can be connected to a Virtual WAN hub in a different region.

You can establish a Virtual WAN by creating a single Virtual WAN hub in the region with the largest number of spokes (branches, VNets, users) and connecting the spokes in other regions to the hub. This is a good option when your enterprise footprint is mostly in one region with a few remote spokes.

Azure regions can serve as hubs to which you can connect. Using the Microsoft backbone for any-to-any (any spoke) connectivity, all hubs are fully connected in a standard Virtual WAN. A Virtual WAN CPE solution (SD-WAN/VPN) using SD-WAN/VPN devices can provide connectivity to Azure manually or through a Virtual WAN CPE (SD-WAN/VPN) partner solution. Connectivity automation (exporting device information into Azure, downloading the Azure configuration, and establishing connectivity) is supported by Microsoft with Virtual WAN.

Cross-regional connectivity between cloud and on-premises network endpoints is one of the key principles of global transit network architecture. Your enterprise cloud footprint can span multiple cloud regions, and it is optimal (latency-wise) to access the cloud from a region close to your physical sites and users. The Azure Global Network enables traffic from a branch connected to the cloud in one region to reach a branch or a VNet in a different region using hub-to-hub connectivity. Figure 5.11 shows an overview of hub-to-hub connectivity.

FIGURE 5.11 Hub-to-hub connectivity

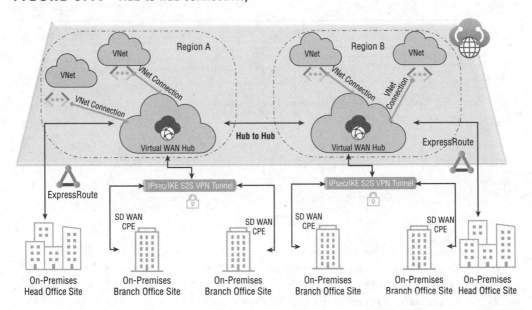

A single Virtual WAN can support multiple hubs automatically connected via hub-to-hub links, enabling the global connection between branches and VNets distributed across various regions. Moreover, hubs in the same Virtual WAN can be associated with different regional security and access policies.

Virtual WANs are typically used for the following design situations:

- Access to shared services and central control are necessary for connecting workloads.
- For enterprise security, a firewall and separate management of each spoke's workload are necessary.

Many Azure customers adopt the Azure hub-and-spoke connectivity model to use the default transitive routing behavior for simple and scalable cloud networks. Azure Virtual WAN builds on these concepts. It provides new capabilities that enable global connectivity topologies between on-premises and Azure applications, allowing you to leverage the scale of the Microsoft network to augment your existing global networks.

Virtual WAN hubs enable any-to-any connectivity over the global transit network. Architecture described in the rest of this section, full or partial mesh connectivity between spokes, is eliminated or reduced, which is a more time-consuming and challenging process. Furthermore, hub-and-spoke networks are easier to set up and maintain than mesh networks.

Through any-to-any connectivity (in the context of a global architecture), an enterprise with globally distributed users, branches, datacenters, virtual networks, and applications can connect via the transit hub(s). Azure Virtual WAN serves as the global transit system.

Figure 5.12 depicts the any-to-any connection types branch-to-VNet (1), branch-to-branch (2), and remote user-to-VNet (3):

FIGURE 5.12   Virtual WAN traffic paths 1, 2, and 3

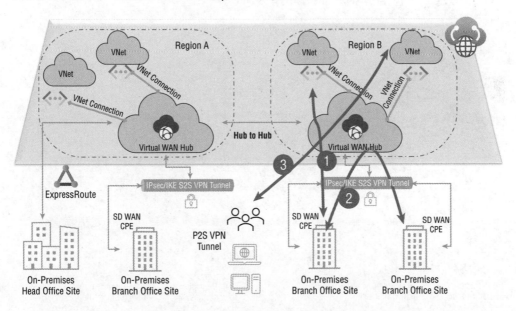

Network Connectivity from Branch-to-VNet (1)   Branches can be connected via Azure Virtual WAN to Azure IaaS enterprise workloads that are deployed in Azure VNets. You can connect branches to the Virtual WAN via ExpressRoute or site-to-site VPN. Through VNet connections, traffic transits to VNets that are connected to the Virtual WAN hubs. Virtual WAN does not require explicit Gateway Transit since it automatically enables Gateway Transit to branch offices.

Network Connectivity from Branch-to-Branch (2)   Branches can be connected to an Azure Virtual WAN hub using ExpressRoute circuits and site-to-site VPN connections. You can connect the branches to the Virtual WAN hub in the region closest to the branch.

By leveraging the Azure backbone, you can connect branches. Even so, be sure to weigh the benefits of using Azure Virtual WAN versus a private WAN when connecting branches.

Remote User to a Virtual Network (3)   By connecting a remote user client to a Virtual WAN, you can enable secure, direct remote access to Azure. Employees in remote offices no longer need to use a corporate VPN to access the cloud.

Figure 5.13 shows the any-to-any connection types remote user-to-branch (4), VNet-to-VNet (5), and branch-to-hub-hub-to-branch (6).

FIGURE 5.13   Virtual WAN traffic paths 4, 5, and 6

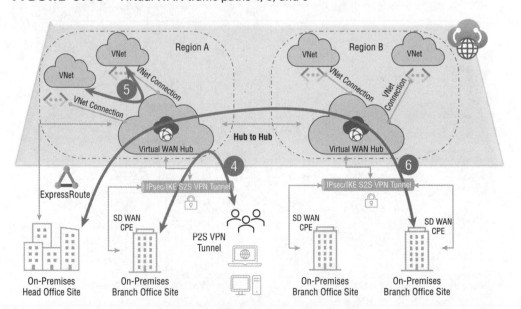

Remote User to an On-Premises Branch Office (4)   In Azure Virtual WAN, you can enable centrally managed secure remote access. Remote users can transit through the cloud to access on-premises workloads and applications using the remote user-to-branch path. Remote users have access to both Azure and on-premises workloads through this path.

Organization VNet-to-VNet Transit (5)   Multi-tier applications implemented across multiple VNets can be interconnected with the VNet-to-VNet transit. You have the option of connecting VNets through VNet peering. This is useful for scenarios in which transit through the VWAN hub is not necessary.

Organization Branch-to-Branch Cross-Region (6)   Similar to branch-to-branch (2), ExpressRoute circuits or site-to-site VPN connections can be used to connect branches to an Azure Virtual WAN hub. The branches can be connected to the Virtual WAN hub that is located closest to the branch.

You can use this option to connect branches to the Azure backbone. However, carefully weigh the benefits of connecting branches over Azure Virtual WAN versus using a private WAN, even though this feature is available.

The branch-to-branch connection can be disabled through the Virtual WAN. VPN sites and ExpressRoute sites connected by VPN (site-to-site and point-to-site) will not propagate routes. Branches-to-VNet or VNet-to-VNet connections will not be affected by this configuration. Using the Azure portal you can disable this setting by selecting Setting ➤ Branch-to-Branch ➤ Disabled from the Virtual WAN Configuration menu.

Figure 5.14 shows the any-to-any connection types branch-to-hub-hub-to-VNet (7) and VNet-to-hub-hub-to-VNet (8).

FIGURE 5.14   Virtual WAN traffic paths 7 and 8

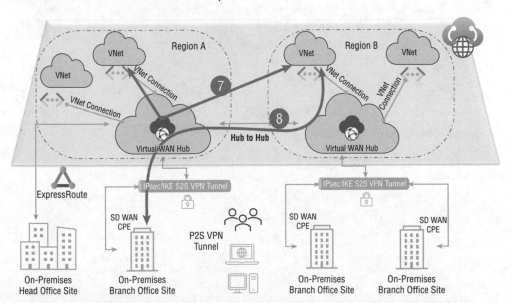

Organization Branch-to-VNet Cross-Region (7)   Similar to branch-to-VNet, Virtual WAN provides a branch-to-VNet cross-region path that allows you to connect your branches to Azure IaaS enterprise workloads hosted in Azure VNets. Through ExpressRoute or a site-to-site VPN, branches can be connected to the Virtual WAN, and traffic flows from the Virtual WAN hubs to the VNets connected to them via VNet connections. A VPN does not require explicit Gateway Transit since the VPN automatically enables Gateway Transit to the branch site.

Organization VNet-to-VNet Cross-Region (8)   Like the VNet-to-VNet cross-region, multi-tier applications implemented across multiple VNets can be interconnected with the VNet-to-VNet transit. You can connect VNets through VNet peering, which is useful for scenarios in which transit through the Virtual WAN hub is not necessary.

A virtual hub reproduces a learned default route to a VNet, site-to-site VPN, point-to-site VPN, or ExpressRoute connection. When the Enable Default flag is set to Enabled on a VPN/ExpressRoute connection, the virtual hub propagates the learned default route. This flag becomes visible when a user edits a virtual network connection, a VPN connection, or an ExpressRoute connection. When adding a virtual network connection to a virtual hub, it is enabled by default. Sites and ExpressRoute circuits that are connected to a hub have this flag disabled by default. The default route does not originate in the Virtual WAN hub; it is propagated if the hub already knows it because it deployed a firewall or if another site connected to the hub has forced tunneling enabled.

Figure 5.15 shows the any-to-any connection types VNet-to-VNet secured transit (9) and Security Service for third parties (10).

FIGURE 5.15   Virtual WAN traffic paths 9 and 10

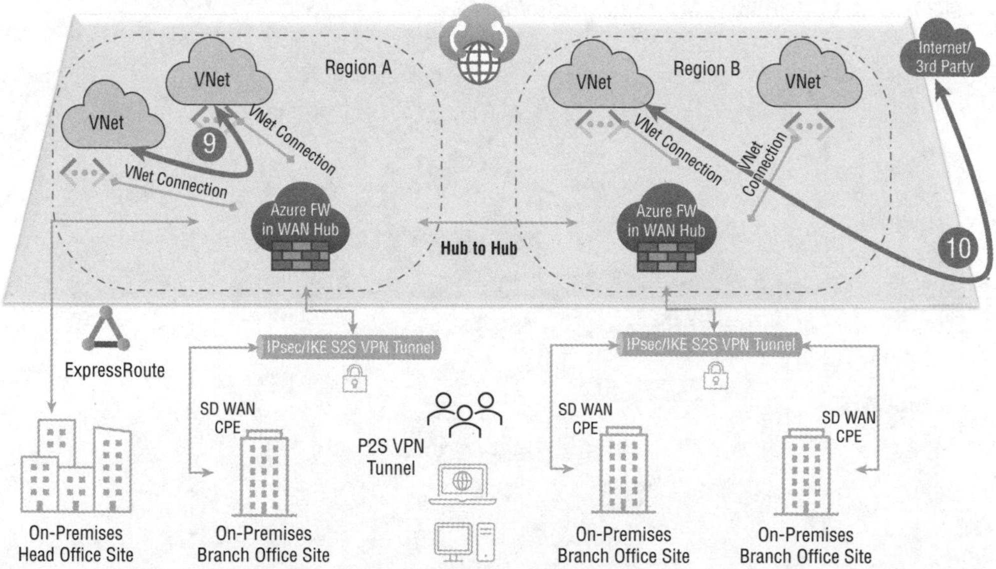

Azure Virtual WAN hubs connect all the networking endpoints across the hybrid network and view all transit traffic. Secured virtual hubs can be created by deploying the Azure Firewall inside Virtual WAN hubs to enable cloud-based security, access, and policy control. Azure Firewall Manager can orchestrate Azure firewalls in Virtual WAN hubs.

Security for global transit networks can be managed and scaled using Azure Firewall Manager. With Azure Firewall Manager, you can work traffic routing, global policy management, and advanced Internet security services via a third party along with the Azure Firewall.

VNet-to-VNet Secured Transit (9)   In the Virtual WAN hub, the VNet-to-VNet secured transit enables VNets to connect via the Azure Firewall.

Security Service for Third Parties (10)   VNet-to-Internet enables VNets to connect to Azure Firewalls via the Virtual WAN hub. The Azure Firewall does not block traffic to the Internet from third-party security services that are supported. A supported third-party security service can be used to configure the VNet-to-Internet path using Azure Firewall Manager.

Figure 5.16 shows the any-to-any connection types branch-to-Internet or third-party security service (11) and cross-region secured branch-to-branch transit (12).

FIGURE 5.16   Virtual WAN traffic paths 11 and 12

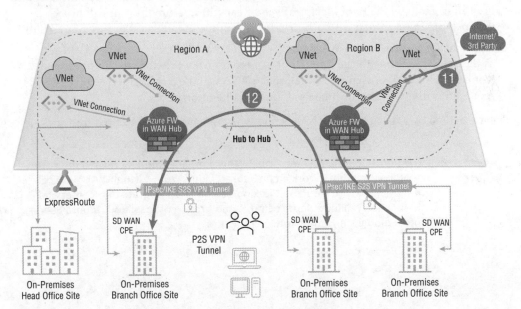

Branch-to-Internet or Third-Party Security Service (11)   This connection type allows branches to connect to the Internet via the Azure Firewall in the Virtual WAN hub. With the Azure Firewall, traffic from supported third-party security services does not pass through. With Azure Firewall Manager, you can configure the branch-to-Internet path using a supported third-party security service.

Cross-Region Secured Branch-to-Branch Transit (12)   Branches can be connected to an attached virtual hub with Azure Firewall by using ExpressRoute circuits and site-to-site VPN connections. Branches can be connected to the Virtual WAN hub in the region nearest the branch.

You can connect your branches to the Azure backbone using this option. But you should weigh the benefits of connecting branches over a private WAN versus Azure Virtual WAN.

There is no support for inter-hub traffic processing through a firewall as of this writing. Traffic will be routed to the appropriate branch; however, the Azure Firewall will not block traffic between hubs.

Branch-to-VNet Secured Transit (13)   Through a branch-to-VNet secured transit service, branches can communicate with virtual networks located in the same region as the Virtual WAN hub and another virtual network connected to another Virtual WAN hub situated in another region.

Inter-hub communication with the firewall is not supported as of this writing. The Azure firewall in each hub will not block traffic between hubs. Azure firewall will process traffic destined for virtual networks located within the same region in the secured hub.

When deployed in a Virtual WAN hub (Secure Virtual Hub), Azure firewall can act as the default gateway to the Internet or Trusted Security Provider for all branches (connected by VPN or ExpressRoute), spoke VNets, and users (connected by P2P VPN). Azure Firewall Manager must be used for this configuration.

Figure 5.17 shows the any-to-any connection type branch-to-VNet secured transit (13).

The introduction of Azure Virtual WAN simplified and increased the scale of global transit network architectures. With Azure Virtual WAN, you can streamline Azure cloud networking design and integrate datacenter and co-location facilities, large campus and branch offices, and remote users into a global transit network architecture.

FIGURE 5.17   Virtual WAN traffic path 13

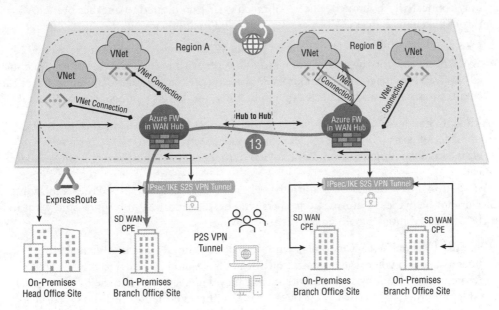

Choosing SKUs and Services for Virtual WANs

Virtual WANs are categorized into two types (SKUs): Basic and Standard. Table 5.2 shows the configuration options for each type, and the rest of this section provides more detail.

TABLE 5.2   Virtual WAN SKU comparison

Virtual WAN type	Hub type	Available configurations
Basic	Basic	Site-to-site VPN only
Standard	Standard	ExpressRoute Point-to-site Site-to-site Inter-hub and VNet-to-VNet transiting via the virtual hub Azure firewall NVA in a Virtual WAN

Basic Virtual WAN   This category of WAN consists of hub types that provide VPN-only connectivity to branch offices. A branch can be connected to another branch through a single hub or a VNet can be connected to another VNet.

Standard Virtual WAN   The *Standard Virtual WAN* category builds on the Virtual WAN Basic category by adding standard hub types with branch connection options such as user VPN (point-to-site), standard VPN (site-to-site), and ExpressRoute. Branches can connect to other branches, hubs can link to hubs, and VNets can connect to VNets.

Although Standard Virtual WAN is the service of most large global organizations, the primary offering is also available for less complex connectivity scenarios. Consumers of the Azure cloud can upgrade from Basic to Standard, but they cannot revert from Standard to Basic.

Association and propagation features have been added to route tables. Preexisting route tables do not have these features. Consumers who have preexisting hub routes and want to use the new capabilities should consider the following:

Standard Virtual WAN Customers with Already Existing Routes in a Virtual Hub   Consider a scenario where the organization already has routes assigned to the hub in the Azure portal's Routing section. In that case, they will need to delete the existing route tables and then try to create new ones (available through the Route Tables section for the hub in the Azure portal). Microsoft strongly recommends deleting all Virtual WAN hubs.

Basic Virtual WAN Customers with Already Existing Routes in a Virtual Hub   The organization already having routes in the Routing section for the hub in Azure will need to upgrade their Basic Virtual WAN to Standard Virtual WAN. Microsoft strongly recommends deleting all Virtual WAN hubs.

Concerning point-to-site, clients are supported with the following limitation. Each VPN P2S user gateway has two instances. There is a limit to how many connections each instance can support as the scaling units change. Scale units 1–3 support 500 connections, scale units 4–6 support 1,000 connections, scale units 7–12 support 5,000 connections, and scale units 13–18 support up to 10,000 connections.

Assume, for example, that the organization chooses one scale unit. There would be one active-active gateway per scale unit, and each of the cases (in this case, two) would support up to 500 connections. Organizations can only get 500 connections * 2 per gateway; this does not mean you plan to use 1,000 instead of 500 for this scale unit. If you exceed the Microsoft recommended connection count, instances may need to be serviced, resulting in connectivity interruptions for the extra 500.

Plan for downtime when organizations change the point-to-site configuration on the VPN gateway or scale up or down on the scale unit.

A scale unit is a unit assigned to pick a gateway's aggregate throughput in a virtual hub. In VPN, 500 Mbps is 1 scale unit. An ExpressRoute scale unit is 2 Gbps. In the previous example, 10 scale units of VPN would mean 500 Mbps × 10 = 5 Gbps.

Organizations can estimate the expense of an Azure Virtual WAN solution by determining:

- Amount of Virtual WAN Hubs required
- The entire amount of site-to-site and point-to-site VPN via required per region
- The complete number of VPN tunnels needed per region
- The total number of ExpressRoutes required per region
- Amount of data traversing between hubs in different regions
- Amount of data traversing between VNets inside or among regions
- Number of ExpressRoute circuits needed per region
- Amount of data egress from Azure to the organization branch or end user

Connect a VNet Gateway to an Azure Virtual WAN and Build a Hub in a Virtual WAN

To set up connectivity from an Azure VNet gateway to an Azure Virtual WAN, the following are the prerequisites:

- Azure Virtual WAN and virtual hub
- Azure virtual network
- Connect a VNet to the virtual hub (optional)

The first two need to be well established. In this section, you learn about setting up an Azure Virtual WAN and its hub.

It is not uncommon for the network topology to become very complex in many cases. Network connections, gateways, and peering processes can be challenging to keep track of. With Azure Virtual WAN, you can manage them all from one place.

The Azure Virtual WAN combines multiple network services into one. You can manage, control, and monitor connections such as site-to-site, point-to-site, ExpressRoute, and connections between virtual networks. Organizations may have multiple site-to-site connections or multiple virtual networks; keeping them all straight can be confusing. Fortunately, Virtual WANs simplify this process.

To create a Virtual WAN using the Azure portal, follow the steps in Exercise 5.2.

EXERCISE 5.2

Create a Virtual WAN Using the Azure Portal

1. Log into a personal or business account in the Azure portal at `portal.azure.com`.

2. Click Create A Resource and choose Virtual WAN under Networking.

3. In the new pane (see the following image), enter the following information:

Subscription	Choose the subscription.
Resource Group	Generate a new resource group or use an existing one.
Resource Group Location	Choose a resource location from the drop-down menu. A WAN is a global resource and does not live in a particular region. However, you must select a region to manage and locate the organization's WAN resource.
Name	Type a name for your Virtual WAN.
Type	Select Basic or Standard.

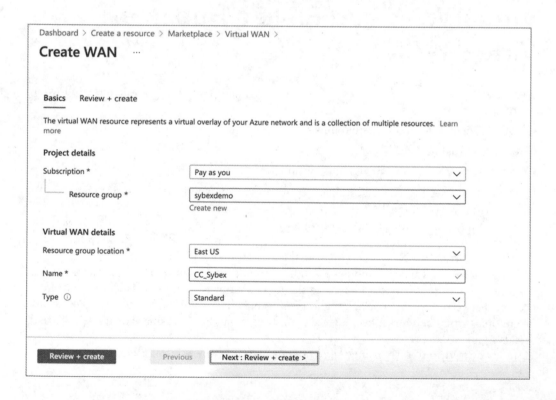

4. Once completed, choose Review + Create and after validation is completed (see the following image), click Create to create the Virtual WAN.

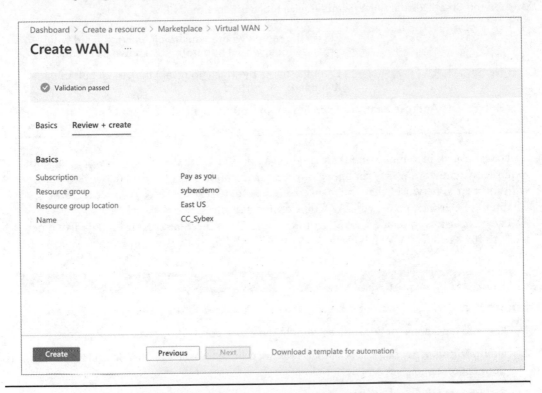

A virtual hub serves as a regional connection point. Multiple service endpoints connect different networks and services through them. Networking is built on these endpoints.

The hub is a virtual network that contains gateways for site-to-site, ExpressRoute, or point-to-site functionality. In the next exercise, you fill out the Basics tab for the virtual hub. You can build an empty hub without gateways and then later add gateways such as site-to-site, point-to-site, and ExpressRoute. Your organization will be charged for the hub even if no sites are attached to it or gateways are created within it.

To create a virtual hub in Virtual WAN using the Azure portal, follow the steps in Exercise 5.3.

EXERCISE 5.3

Create a Virtual HUB in a Virtual WAN Using the Azure Portal

1. Log into a personal or business account in the Azure portal at `portal.azure.com`.

2. Click Virtual Networks and choose the Virtual WAN you previously created. Choose Hubs under the Connectivity section. Select the option to attach a new hub.

3. On the Create Virtual Hub Wizard's Basics tab, complete the following fields:

Region	This is the region where you are planning to build your organizational virtual hub (formerly known as Location).
Name	Enter the name by which you want the virtual hub to be identified.
Hub Private Address Space	To create a hub, you need an address space of /24.

The next task is to make sure the virtual network is created; the virtual network does not require any gateways. Verify that none of your organization's on-premises networks overlap with the virtual networks that you want to connect to. (Creating a VNet was covered in Chapter 1, "Getting Started with AZ-700 Certification for Azure Networking.")

The next task is to connect the VNet to the hub. To connect an organizational virtual network to the Virtual WAN Hub using the Azure portal, follow the steps in Exercise 5.4.

Connect a Virtual Network to a Virtual WAN Hub Using the Azure Portal

1. Log into a personal or business account in the Azure portal at `portal.azure.com`.

2. On the Virtual WAN page, click Virtual Network Connection, and on the Virtual Network Connection page, click Add Connection.

3. Provide the following information to create the connection in Add Connection:

Connection Name	Provide a consumer connection to the cloud.
Hubs	Select the hub you wish to associate with this connection.
Subscription	Select your validated subscription for your organization.
Virtual Network	Specify the virtual network that organizations want to connect to this hub. No existing gateway (VPN or ExpressRoute) can be attached to the virtual network.

Now that the prerequisites are in place, take a look at the high-level process to connect a VNet gateway to Azure Virtual WAN, as shown in Figure 5.18.

In Exercise 5.5 you complete the steps shown in Figure 5.18.

FIGURE 5.18   Workflow for Azure Virtual WAN deployment

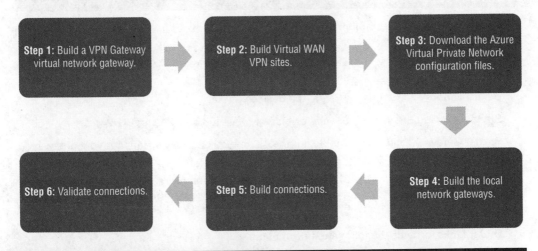

EXERCISE 5.5

Connect a VNet Gateway to Azure Virtual WAN

1. Build two instances of VPN Gateway virtual network gateway.

    Review Exercise 2.1 in Chapter 2, "Design, Deploy, and Manage a Site-to-Site VPN Connection and Point-to-Site VPN Connection," to create and configure a virtual network gateway.

    Configure the Azure Virtual WAN as follows.

    a. Microsoft recommends building a VPN Gateway virtual network gateway in the active-active mode for virtual networks. When you create the gateways, you can either use existing public IP addresses for the two instances of the gateway or create new public IPs. You can use these public IPs when setting up the Virtual WAN sites.

    b. On the virtual network gateway Configuration page, you can select Configure BGP ASN if you are familiar with BGP configuration. You can change the default ASN value via the Azure portal.

    c. Assign two public IP addresses, one for primary and another for secondary. When the gateways are created, you can configure them on the Virtual Network Properties page.

2. Build Virtual WAN VPN sites.

    Under Connectivity, select VPN sites, then navigate to Virtual WAN VPN sites and create them. Using the virtual network gateways you created in step 1, create and configure a virtual network gateway. This process creates two Virtual WAN VPN sites.

Click Create Site and complete the following fields:

Region	Select the Azure region where the Azure VPN Gateway virtual network gateway exists.
Device Vendor	Provide the device vendor.
Private Address Space	Specify a value or leave it blank if using BGP.
Border Gateway Protocol	Enable it if the Azure VPN Gateway virtual network gateway supports BGP.
Connect To Hubs	Choose the hub created in the prerequisites from the drop-down menu. If you do not see a hub, verify that the network engineer created a site-to-site VPN gateway for the hub.

Under Links, provide the following information:

Provider Name	Type the name of the link provider.
Speed	Provide the Speed value.
IP Address	Type the IP address of the virtual network gateway.
BGP Address And ASN	Enter the BGP address and ASN. It must be the same as the IP addresses and ASN of the BGP peers from the virtual network gateway configured in step 1.

Click Confirm to create the site.

Repeat this step to make the second site match the second instance of the VPN Gateway virtual network gateway. You keep the same settings, except that they use a second public IP address and a second peer IP address from the VPN Gateway configuration.

3. Download the Azure Virtual Private Network configuration files.

    On the Virtual WAN VPN Sites page, click the site, then click Download Site-to-Site VPN Configuration. The settings are written into a file created by Azure. You can view the file by downloading it and opening it.

4. Review Exercise 2.2 in Chapter 2 to build the local network gateways.

    A site-to-site connection requires configurations for both sides (Azure and on-premises) when it is created. Despite being created in Azure, a local network gateway is part of a local network (on-premises). Connections between virtual and local networks require the creation of VPN connections. The following information is needed to complete the setup:

IP Address	Set the gateway configuration to the IP address shown in the configuration file; for example, Instance0.
BGP	Select Configure BGP Settings and enter the ASN **65515** if the connection is over BGP. Enter the peer's IP address. For gateway configuration, use `Instance0 BgpPeeringAddresses` in the configuration file.
Address Space	Enter the organization address spaces needed by the gateway to advertise. You can enter a range of addresses. Ensure the ranges don't overlap if you want to connect to other networks. If the connection uses BGP, leave the Configure BGP Settings check box clear.
Subscription, Resource Group, And Location	These are identical to the Virtual WAN hub.

The configuration will look like the following figure.

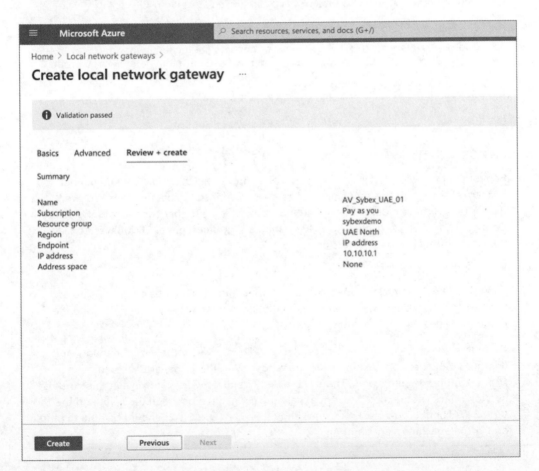

To create another local network gateway, repeat the steps, but in the configuration file, use the 'Instance1' values instead of the 'Instance0' values.

5. Build your connections.

In this step you create a connection between the VPN Gateway local network gateways and the virtual network gateway. The following instructions are the high-level configuration to build the connections.

a. Navigate to the virtual network gateway in the Azure portal and click Connections. At the top of the Connections page, click Add to open the Add Connection page.

b. On the Add Connection page, configure the following information for connection:

Name	Name your connection.
Connection Type	Choose Site-to-Site (IPsec).
Virtual Network Gateway	The value is fixed because you connect from this gateway.
Local Network Gateway	This connection connects the local network gateway to the virtual network gateway. Identify the gateway you created earlier.
Shared Key	Type a shared key.
IKE Protocol	Keep the IKE protocol.

Click OK to create a connection.

Repeat the preceding steps to build a second connection. Creating a second connection is preferable to using the local network gateway. Suppose the connections are over BGP. After you have created a cloud connection, navigate to that connection and select Configuration. Select Enabled for BGP on the Configuration page. Click Save. Repeat the steps for the second connection.

6. Validate the connections.

You can use Azure to test connectivity by creating virtual machines on either side of the virtual network gateway and one in a virtual network for the Virtual WAN, and then pinging the two virtual machines.

To do this, create a virtual machine for Azure VPN Gateway in the virtual network and another virtual network to connect to the Virtual WAN. Place the virtual machine in a subnet of this virtual network. There can be no virtual network gateways in this virtual network. Click OK to create the virtual network connection between the VNet and the Virtual WAN hub. The virtual machines should be connected. You should be able to ping one virtual machine from another.

Virtual WAN is a form of *software-defined WAN (SD-WAN)*. Virtual WAN connects SD-WAN devices, services, and technology via a seamless, scalable, and unbreakable backbone network. Aggregation of SD-WANs and backbone extensions can be considered as one system. A software-defined WAN ecosystem would benefit significantly from its inclusion.

Virtual WAN offers many services in the field provided by solution partners and Azure networking managed services partners.

Build a Virtual Network Appliance (NVA) in a Virtual Hub

Through collaboration with networking partners, Azure Virtual WAN has built automation that simplifies the process of connecting *customer premises equipment* (CPE) to Azure VPN gateways. Firewalls, routers, or SD-WAN edge devices connect a customer's on-premises network to the Internet or to their own private network.

CPE partners are working with Azure Virtual WAN. The following is a list of all the available partners the authors used when writing this book.

- Barracuda Networks
- Check Point
- Cisco Meraki
- Citrix
- CloudGenix
- Fortinet
- HPE Aruba
- NetFoundry
- Nuage/Nokia
- Open Systems
- Palo Alto Networks
- Riverbed Technology
- Silver-Peak
- VMware SD-WAN
- Versa

Using select networking partners, Azure enables organizations to deploy third-party *network virtual appliances* (NVAs) directly into the virtual hub. Customers can connect their branch CPE to the same brand of NVA within the virtual hub to take advantage of proprietary end-to-end SD-WAN capabilities.

Engineers can configure zero-touch deployments of CPEs with support from those partners. In other words, you can preconfigure an environment for a new CPE (out of the box). Directly connected to their vendor's management service, those devices obtain the connection details needed to connect to a customer's Virtual WAN.

In addition to managing connections to other branches and other connected services, Virtual WAN will also contain the connections with other Virtual WANs.

In 2020, Microsoft announced the first network appliance partnership and natively integrated appliances into Virtual WANs. With their CloudGen WAN appliance, Barracuda Networks was the first partner. Cisco, VMware, and Barracuda were the only partners available as of this writing, but there will be many more in the future.

The NVAs are deployed directly to the Virtual WAN hub by Barracuda Networks and Cisco Systems.

The NVA will be configured automatically during deployment by partners. To configure the NVA after it has been provisioned into the virtual hub, the NVA partner portal or management application must be used. No direct access is available to the NVA.

To connect branch sites to NVA in the Virtual WAN hub, you do not need to create site resources, site-to-site connection resources, or point-to-site connection resources, unlike with Azure VPN Gateway configurations. Through the NVA partner, it is all handled.

According to Microsoft, you should establish hub-to-VNet connections to connect Virtual WAN hubs to Azure virtual networks. Hubs are virtual networks that contain sites-to-site, ExpressRoute, point-to-site, and NVA gateways. Unlike site-to-site, ExpressRoute, or point-to-site, you must first create a hub VNet before you can deploy an NVA into it. Even if you do not attach any sites your organization will be charged. An organization can create a site-to-site VPN gateway in the virtual hub within 30 minutes.

Let's start creating the NVA in the hub. For this purpose, we'll use Barracuda CloudGen WAN Gateway.

Barracuda CloudGen WAN combines the benefits of next-generation firewalls and secure SD-WAN with cloud integration and automation to deliver a practical cloud-based secure access service edge (SASE) solution. Barracuda CloudGen WAN provides companies with a secure on-ramp to Azure Virtual WAN and the Microsoft global network via its web-based interface. CloudGen WAN can connect, secure, and manage all locations.

The following are various service benefits from Barracuda CloudGen WAN Gateway:

- Azure and the Microsoft global network can be accessed via SD-WAN.

- It offers a high-performance WAN backbone for Azure and the Microsoft global network.

- You can connect endpoints to consumer cloud applications (VPN) in a secure and reliable manner.

- SD-WAN SaaS on the cloud replaces inflexible multiprotocol label switching (MPLS) connections and long-term contracts.
- SD-WAN allows organizations to migrate legacy WANs in a fraction of the time it takes to migrate existing solutions.
- You can dynamically scale the SD-WAN network.
- You can optimize Microsoft 365 fulfillment and cloud access out of the box with smart defaults for cloud and SaaS apps.
- You can secure branches without existing security solutions with next-generation firewalls.
- A web filter is provided to protect online data.

Follow the steps in Exercise 5.6 to create an NVA via the Azure portal.

EXERCISE 5.6

Create an NVA via the Azure Portal

1. Log into a personal or business account in the Azure portal at `portal.azure.com`.

2. Locate the Virtual WAN hub you created and open it from the Azure portal.

3. Choose the Create link under the Network Virtual Appliances tile.

4. From the Network Virtual Appliance blade, choose Barracuda CloudGen WAN, then click the Create button.

   The Azure Marketplace offers Barracuda CloudGen WAN gateways. Be sure to review the terms and conditions.

   In the Basics wizard, you need to provide the following information:

Subscription	Select your subscription for the Virtual WAN and hub deployment.
Resource Group	Use the same as those used to deploy the Virtual WAN.
Region	Select the same region as the virtual hub resource.
Application Name	NextGen WAN, the Barracuda next-generation wireless network, is managed. The resource will appear when it appears in the subscription. Choose a name that is easy to remember.
Managing Resource Groups	These are groups in which Barracuda deploys resources that it manages. There should already be a title for this.

EXERCISE 5.6 *(continued)*

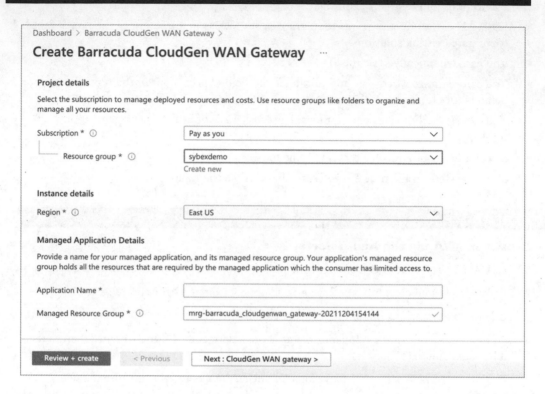

5. Click the Next: CloudGen WAN Gateway button.

In the CloudGen WAN Gateway Wizard, provide the following information:

Virtual WAN Hub	Name the Virtual WAN hub where you want to deploy this NVA.
NVA Infrastructure Units	Provide the number of NVA Infrastructure Units this NVA will require. You can select the aggregate bandwidth you would like across all branch sites connected to this hub through this NVA.

NVA infrastructure units represent the aggregate bandwidth capacity of an NVA in the Virtual WAN hub. NVA infrastructure units are similar to VPN scale units regarding capacity and sizing. The scale unit determines how many resources are deployed and how large they are. Scale units increase the amount of traffic that can be handled.

▪ At the cost of $0.25/hour, one NVA infrastructure unit represents 500 Mbps of aggregate bandwidth for all branch site connections coming into this NVA.

- For a given NVA virtual hub deployment, Azure supports up to 80 NVA infrastructure units.

- Various NVA infrastructure unit bundles may be offered by partners that are subsets of all supported NVA infrastructure unit configurations.

- Barracuda requires you to provide an *authentication token* to identify you as a registered user of this product. You need to obtain this from Barracuda.

As shown in the next image, you must supply a valid token to configure CloudGen WAN Gateway automatically.

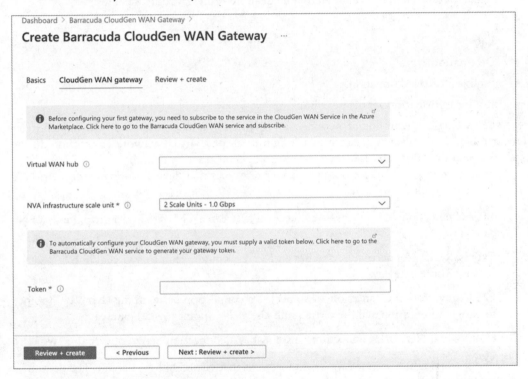

6. Finally, click the Review + Create button to continue. You must accept Co-Admin Access. Select the "I agree with the terms and conditions above" option and click Create.

Virtual WAN partners automate IPsec connectivity to Azure VPN endpoints. A Virtual WAN partner that provides SD-WAN is implied to manage automation and IPsec connectivity to Azure VPN endpoints via the SD-WAN controller. The device may require its endpoint instead of Azure VPN for any proprietary SD-WAN functionality. In that case, Azure Virtual WAN can coexist with SD-WAN endpoints deployed in a cloud VNet.

Set Up Virtual Hub Routing

In a virtual hub, routing is managed by a router using Border Gateway Protocol (BGP), which contains all routing between gateways. There can be more than one gateway in a virtual hub, such as a site-to-site VPN gateway, ExpressRoute gateway, point-to-site gateway, and Azure Firewall. As well as providing transit connectivity between virtual networks, this router also supports an aggregate throughput of 50 Gbps. Those who own Standard Virtual WAN can take advantage of these routing capabilities.

A virtual hub route table can contain one or more routes. A route includes:

- Name
- Label
- Destination types
- Prefixes for the destination
- Router information for the next hop

The routing configuration of a connection is typically associated with or propagated to a route table. You can set up the routing configuration for a virtual network connection during setup. A default route table is associated with all connections by default.

The following are Azure Resource Manager resources that have a routing configuration and Azure network connections:

VPN Connection   Establishes a connection between a VPN site and a virtual hub VPN gateway.

ExpressRoute Connection   Attaches an ExpressRoute circuit to a virtual hub ExpressRoute gateway.

P2S Configuration Connection   Establishes a connection between the User VPN (point-to-site) configuration and the virtual hub User VPN (point-to-site) gateway.

Hub Virtual Network Connection   Establishes a connection between virtual networks.

Default route tables are used for all connections in a virtual hub by default. The default route table of each virtual hub can be edited to add static routes. For the same prefix, routes that are added statically take precedence over routes learned dynamically.

From a propagation perspective, connections dynamically update a route table. By using BGP, routes are propagated from the virtual hub to the on-premises router over a VPN connection, ExpressRoute connection, or point-to-site configuration connection. Route tables can be established for either one or multiple routes.

Each virtual hub also includes a None route table. A route propagating to the None route table implies that no routes should be propagated from the connection. The routes propagated by VPN, ExpressRoute, and user VPN connections are stored in the same route tables.

Network traffic in Azure is routed in subnets by default. In some cases, however, Azure's network engineers want to define how and where traffic flows through custom routes. Microsoft encourages the use of route tables in such cases. Route tables determine where the network traffic needs to go next and describe the next hop for the traffic.

In Exercise 5.7 you create a route table via the Azure portal.

EXERCISE 5.7

Create a Route Table via the Azure Portal

1. Log into a personal or business account in the Azure portal at `portal.azure.com`.

2. Look for Connectivity, then choose Routing. In the Routing Wizard, check out the Default and None route tables.

3. Click Create Route Table to open the Create Route Table Wizard's Basics tab and complete the following fields:

Subscription	Choose the subscription.
Resource Group	Generate a new resource group or use an existing one.
Region	Choose your Azure region.
Name	Enter a name for the route table.
Propagate Gateway Routes	Select Yes.

4. Select the Review + Create tab, or click the blue Review + Create button in the wizard.

5. Choose Go To Resource or search for *yourroutetable* in the portal search box; on the resulting page, choose Routes from the Settings section, and on the Routes page, click the Add button. In the Add Route screen, provide the following information:

Route Name	Enter a name for the route.
Address Prefixes Destination	Choose your IP address.
Destination IP Address/CIDR Ranges	Provide the address range of the private subnet.
Next Type	Choose your virtual appliances.
Next Hop Address	Enter the address of the VM appliance you created.

6. To associate connections with the route table, click the Associations tab. Branches, virtual networks, and the current settings of the connections are available to you.

You can use route tables to create custom routing in Azure virtual networks despite network routing being automatic. Traffic flow is controlled by route tables and subnet associations in virtual networks. New route tables are empty when they're created. To use a route table for the traffic flow, you must define rules and subnets after the resource is created.

You can adjust the settings for a resource after it has been created. The only setting you can change before configuring routes and subnets is the Border Gateway Protocol (BGP) route propagation. After creation, you can change other settings.

You can enable or disable gateway route propagation in the route table settings at any time. Disabling this option prevents on-premises routes from being propagated via BGP to the network interfaces in a virtual network subnet. The settings allow you to add, delete, and change routes and subnets.

The Azure portal will display the route table for the virtual hub. For effective routes, click the ellipsis button (...) and choose Effective Routes. In the route table, the propagated routes are automatically populated in the Effective Routes section.

Nothing happens once a route table is created until it is configured properly. Let's look at how and which resources are affected. Resources involved in an Azure subnet and route table must be associated with a subnet.

Build a Connection Unit

Any on-premises/non-Microsoft endpoint can access Azure gateways through a connection unit:

▪ For (site-to-site) S2S VPN, this value indicates branches.

▪ For (point-to-site) P2S VPN, this value indicates remote users.

▪ For ExpressRoute, this value indicates ExpressRoute circuit connections.

Figure 5.19 is a very high-level process for establishing a Virtual WAN connection to organization resources in Azure through an S2S-based IPsec/IKE (IKEv1 and IKEv2) VPN connection.

For instance, say a branch connection to Azure VPN costs $0.05/hour in a virtual hub. Therefore, 100 branch connections connecting to an Azure virtual hub would cost $0.05 per hour.

The VPN site-to-site scale unit represents the aggregate speed of all branch sites connecting to the hub, and it is scalable up to 20 Gbps. Each Azure region supports a maximum of 1,000 VPN site-to-site connection units, representing the number of branch sites connected to a hub.

FIGURE 5.19   Workflow for establishing a Virtual WAN

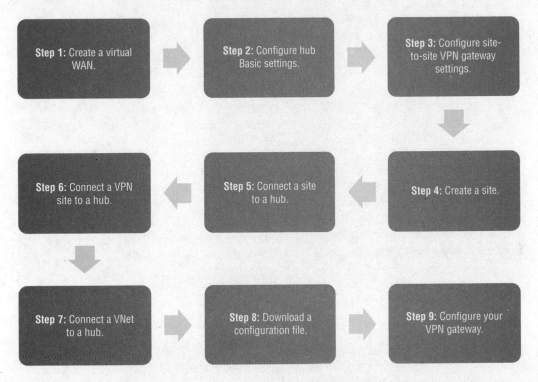

Figure 5.20 is a high-level process for establishing connectivity to Azure using the user's VPN (point-to-site) connection over OpenVPN or IPsec/IKE (IKEv2). Connecting to a VPN over a native client requires the VPN client to be installed on each computer.

For instance, it would cost $0.03 * 3/hour to connect three remote users to the Azure virtual hub point-to-site gateway.

FIGURE 5.20   Workflow for establishing a connection to Azure using a user VPN

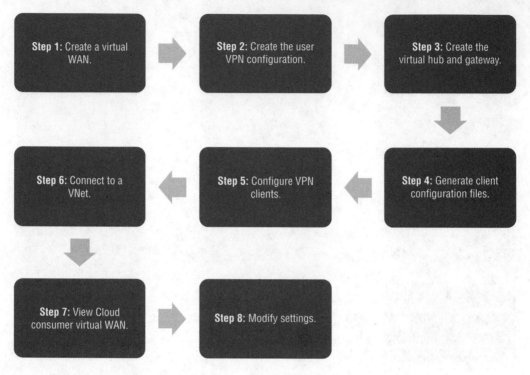

Figure 5.21 is a high-level process for establishing connectivity to Azure over an ExpressRoute circuit.

For instance, a virtual hub that connects two ExpressRoute circuits costs $0.05 * 2/hour.

FIGURE 5.21 Workflow for establishing an Azure connection over an ExpressRoute circuit

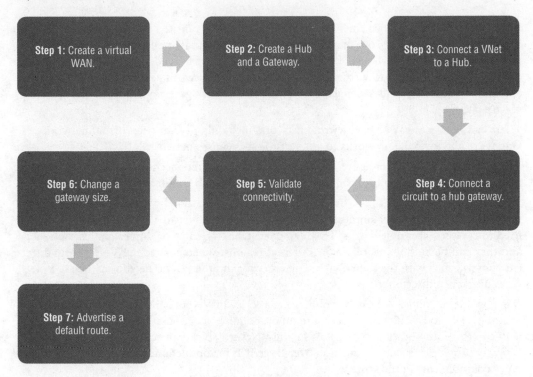

Summary

This chapter explored cross-VNet connectivity and provided a detailed look into Virtual WAN in the Azure cloud.

You learned in detail about designing service chaining, including Gateway Transit, creating VPN connectivity between VNets, and configuring VPN Gateway Transit for virtual network peering. You also learned about four models for deployment.

You also learned about Azure Virtual WAN architecture, how to choose Azure Virtual WAN SKUs and services, how to connect a VNet gateway to Azure Virtual WAN, how to build a hub in a Virtual WAN and an NVA in a virtual hub, and how to configure virtual hub routing.

You now have the detailed insight required to design and deploy Azure cross-VNet connectivity and design and deploy Azure Virtual WAN architecture.

Exam Essentials

Know how to design service chaining, including Gateway Transit.   By using service chaining, traffic can be routed from one virtual network to a virtual appliance or gateway in another virtual network via user-defined routes. As the next-hop address, configure user-defined routes that point to virtual machines in a virtual network peering to enable service chaining. In addition to user-defined routes, virtual network gateways can be used to enable service chaining.

There can be a gateway on each virtual network, including peer-to-peer virtual networks. Gateways allow virtual networks to connect to on-premises networks.

When both options are configured for virtual network interconnection, traffic flows through the peering configuration between the virtual networks, and traffic goes through the Azure backbone.

Know how to design VPN connectivity between VNets.   VNet-to-VNet connections can be used to connect virtual networks. They can come from the same or different subscriptions, and they can be in the same region or different regions. When connecting VNets from different subscriptions with the same Active Directory tenant, there is no need to associate VNets from different subscriptions.

It is possible to connect VNets by configuring a VNet-to-VNet connection. It is similar to creating a site-to-site IPsec connection to an on-premises location when connecting a virtual network to another virtual network using the VNet-to-VNet connection type. The VPN gateway provides a secure connection over IPsec/IKE for both connectivity types, and both types communicate in the same way.

Understand how to deploy VNet peering.   With virtual network peering, you can seamlessly connect two or more virtual networks in Azure. The virtual networks will appear to be connected as a single network. In peer-to-peer virtual networks, Microsoft's backbone infrastructure carries traffic between virtual machines, and Microsoft's private network is used to route traffic between virtual machines on the same network.

There are two types of peering available in Azure:

- Virtual network peering: establishing connections between virtual networks in the same Azure region
- Global virtual network peering: establishing an interconnection between Azure regions

Know how to design an Azure Virtual WAN architecture, including selecting types and services.   Azure Virtual WAN combines routing, security, and networking capabilities under a single operational interface. Having scale and performance built in for branches (VPN/SD-WAN), users (Azure VPN/OpenVPN/IKEv2), ExpressRoute circuits, and virtual networks are what the Virtual WAN architecture offers.

Virtual WANs from Azure come in two types, Basic and Standard.

Site-to-site VPN is an available configuration for the Basic SKU Virtual WAN type. For the Standard SKU type of Virtual WAN, ExpressRoute, User VPN (P2P), VPN (site-to-site), Inter-hub, and VNet-to-VNet transiting through the virtual hub, Azure Firewall and NVA are available.

Be able to connect a VNet gateway to Azure Virtual WAN. It is the same process as setting up a connection between a VPN gateway (virtual network gateway) and a Virtual WAN (VPN gateway) from a branch VPN site.

Set up an active-active VPN gateway virtual network gateway for your virtual network. You can either create new public IP addresses for the two gateway instances when creating the gateway or use existing public IP addresses. When setting up Virtual WAN sites, you'll use these public IPs.

Be able to create a network virtual appliance (NVA) in a virtual hub. An NVA in an Azure Virtual WAN hub connection requires a VPN device located on-premises with an externally facing public IP address assigned to it.

Know how to configure virtual hub routing. Multiple gateways can be located in a virtual hub, including site-to-site VPN gateways, ExpressRoute gateways, point-to-site gateways, and Azure Firewalls. The virtual hub uses Border Gateway Protocol (BGP) to manage all routing, including transit routing, between the gateways. It can support up to an aggregate throughput of 50 Gbps between virtual networks connected to a virtual hub. These routing capabilities apply to Standard Virtual WAN customers.

Know how to create a connection unit. Connections are Resource Manager resources that have a routing configuration. The four types of connections are VPN connection, ExpressRoute connection, P2S configuration connection, and hub virtual network connection.

During the setup process, routing configurations for virtual network connections can be set up. The Default route table is associated and propagated by default for all connections.

Review Questions

1. You must specify a VPN type when creating the virtual network gateway for a VPN gateway configuration. Which of the following are the two VPN types?

    A. Policy-based

    B. Dynamic-based

    C. Static-based

    D. Route-based

2. How do VPN gateways have high availability configured by default?

    A. Active-active

    B. Dual redundancy

    C. Multiple on-premises VPN devices

    D. VPN Gateway redundancy (active-standby)

3. What factors do you need to cover during the Azure VPN Gateway planning? (Choose all that apply.)

    A. Throughput

    B. Scalability

    C. Dynamic IP

    D. Backbone

4. When you create the gateway subnet, you specify which of the following?

    A. Gateway VMs

    B. Gateway services

    C. The number of IP addresses that the subnet contains

    D. Default Gateway

5. Consider that CompanyXYZ has the hybrid network shown in the following network diagram.

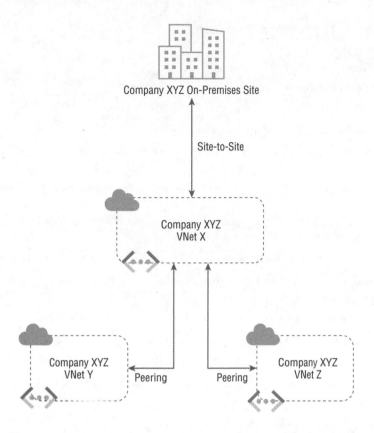

From a transitive peering standpoint, which of the following is valid?

A. Transitive peer VNet Y to peer VNet Z routing is not supported by default in Company XYZ.

B. Transitive peer VNet Y to peer VNet Z routing is supported by default in Company XYZ.

C. Transitive peer VNet X to peer VNet Y routing is not supported by default in Company XYZ.

D. None of the above.

6. Which connection lets you create a secure connection to a virtual network from an individual client computer?

A. A site-to-site (S2S) VPN gateway connection

B. A point-to-site (P2S) VPN gateway connection

C. Local network gateway

D. Gateway subnet

7. What can use one of the following protocols OpenVPN protocol?

   A. A site-to-site (S2S) VPN

   B. The Point-to-Site (P2S) VPN protocol

   C. Local network gateway

   D. Gateway subnet

8. Which of the following is valid for Azure connectivity?

   A. Organizations can connect virtual networks in different regions and from different subscriptions.

   B. Organizations can connect only from virtual networks within the same regions and same subscriptions.

   C. Organizations cannot connect from virtual networks within different regions and different subscriptions.

   D. None of the above.

9. Azure solutions can be deployed and managed using which of the following methods?

   A. Azure Resource Manager

   B. Cloud portal

   C. Azure Classic

   D. A and C

10. Who operates and supports the components of an Azure Virtual WAN?

   A. Microsoft

   B. Cisco

   C. Customer

   D. A and C

11. Which of the following services enables streamlining a hub-and-spoke virtual network WAN deployment?

   A. VMware SDN

   B. Barracuda

   C. Azure Virtual WAN

   D. Cisco

12. Which of the following component is used to secure a Virtual WAN hub?

   A. VMware NSX-T

   B. Azure Active Directory

   C. Microsoft Defender

   D. Azure Firewall and Firewall Manager

13. To set up connectivity from an Azure virtual network gateway to an Azure Virtual WAN, which of the following are the prerequisites?

   A. Azure Virtual WAN and virtual hub.

   B. Azure virtual network.

   C. Connect a VNet to the virtual hub (optional).

   D. All the above.

14. Which of the following statement is valid for NVAs in a Virtual WAN hub?

   A. Organizations cannot implement preferred NVAs directly into a Virtual WAN hub Azure Firewall and Firewall Manager.

   B. Organizations can only implement preferred NVAs directly into a Virtual WAN hub Azure Firewall and not in Firewall Manager.

   C. Organizations cannot implement preferred NVAs directly into a Virtual WAN hub Azure Firewall and can implement them in Firewall Manager.

   D. Organizations can implement preferred NVAs directly into a Virtual WAN hub Azure Active Directory.

15. Which of the following Resource Manager resources have a routing configuration and Azure network connections?

   A. VPN connection and ExpressRoute connection

   B. P2S configuration connection

   C. Hub virtual network connection

   D. All the above

16. Any on-premises/non-Microsoft endpoint can access Azure gateways via which of the following connection units?

   A. Site-to-site (S2S) VPN

   B. Point-to-site (P2S) VPN

   C. ExpressRoute

   D. All the above

17. Virtual WANs are categorized into which of the two types of SKUs?

   A. Basic and Standard

   B. Standard and Enterprise

   C. Enterprise and advanced

   D. Standard and Advanced

18. From an IPsec tunnel from a gateway instance to a consumer's on-premises VPN device, which of the following statements is valid?

    A. The IPsec tunnel from a gateway instance to the consumer's on-premises VPN device will be active during planned maintenance or an unplanned event.

    B. The IPsec tunnel from a gateway instance to the consumer's on-premises VPN device will be deactivated during planned maintenance or an unplanned event.

    C. The IPsec tunnel from a gateway instance to the consumer's on-premises VPN device will be intermittent during planned maintenance or an unplanned event.

    D. None of the above.

19. For Azure VPN gateways connecting the on-premises network of the cloud consumer to the Azure virtual network, which of the following statements is valid?

    A. An Azure VPN gateway does not support the encrypted link between the Azure virtual network and cloud consumer on-premises network.

    B. An Azure VPN gateway does support the encrypted link between the Azure virtual network and cloud consumer on-premises network.

    C. An Azure VPN gateway does not support the encrypted link between the Azure virtual network and co-location datacenter.

    D. None of the above.

20. Site-to-site VPN gateways allow Azure network engineers to connect securely to a cloud consumer virtual network from another network, whether virtual or physical. Which of the following statements are valid?

    A. Site-to-site VPN gateways allow you to connect securely to a cloud consumer virtual network from another network, whether virtual or physical.

    B. Site-to-site VPN gateways do not allow you to connect securely to a cloud consumer virtual network from another network, whether virtual or physical.

    C. Site-to-site VPN gateways do not allow you to connect securely to a cloud consumer virtual network from another network, when it is cloud-hosted.

    D. None of the above.

Chapter

6

Design and Deploy VNet Routing and Azure Load Balancer

THE MICROSOFT AZ-700 EXAM OBJECTIVES COVERED IN THIS CHAPTER INCLUDE:

✓ **Design, implement, and manage VNet routing**

- Design and implement user-defined routes (UDRs)
- Associate a route table with a subnet
- Configure forced tunneling
- Diagnose and resolve routing issues
- Design and implement Azure Route Server

✓ **Design and implement an Azure Load Balancer**

- Choose an Azure Load Balancer SKU (Basic versus Standard)
- Choose between public and internal
- Create and configure an Azure Load Balancer (including cross-region)
- Implement a load balancing rule
- Create and configure inbound NAT rules
- Create explicit outbound rules for a load balancer

You need to know how to design and implement a routing and load balancing solution that addresses an organization's cloud networking requirements.

The following are critical prerequisites for reading this chapter: you must have experience with networking concepts, including IP address, DNS, routing, and connecting to networks such as VPNs or WANs. You should also be familiar with the Azure portal and Azure PowerShell.

This chapter has two parts. In the first part, you learn how Azure routes traffic between Azure, on-premises, and Internet resources. In Azure virtual networks, Azure automatically creates a route table for each subnet and adds system default routes. Custom routes can be overridden on some of Azure's system routes, and more can be added to route tables. Routes in a subnet's route table determine how outbound traffic is routed from a subnet.

In the second part of this chapter, you learn about the design and deployment of an Azure Load Balancer. It is a Layer 4 (TCP, UDP) load balancer that distributes incoming traffic among healthy virtual machines. A load balancer health probe monitors a given port on each virtual machine and only routes traffic to an operational machine.

By the end of this chapter, you will know how to design, deploy, and manage virtual routing in Microsoft Azure, as well as how to design and deploy Azure Load Balancer.

Design and Deploy User-Defined Routes

This section introduces the basic concepts and terminology of routing before diving into a discussion of user-defined routes (UDRs) and how to create and implement them.

Basic Routing Concepts

In networking, routing is the process of moving data across networks in an efficient manner. In OSI Layer 3, logical addressing information is used for routing decisions.

Routers are the main devices for routing data. Routers are used to connect two or more networks so that packets can flow freely between them. They determine the best route for packets to travel from one network to another.

Routers are network hardware devices that forward packets to their destinations. In enterprise networking, it is vital to have a router in your network. Routers are mainly helpful for dividing a network into subnets, creating separate broadcast domains, and increasing security. Routers can also improve network performance.

Routers handle hierarchical addressing schemes, routing data packets between routers on the Internet according to the IP address class contained within them. More precise information can be provided at the destination network to send the data to the exact destination, such as the subnet or host address. Since routers can handle groups of addresses, they don't have to keep massive route tables containing every address in the world.

Any enterprise network is incomplete without a router, and almost every network requires a router to perform the following tasks:

Connecting to the Internet   Every network that needs access to the Internet requires a router. The device is called an Internet gateway because it serves as a gateway to the Internet.

Connecting Branch Offices   A router also commonly links geographically separated offices into one network that spans multiple locations. You can establish a secure virtual private network (VPN) between the two networks using gateway routers.

Classifying Large Networks   Large networks often need routers that are internal to the network itself. Consider a company that has more than a thousand employees across several dozen buildings on a single campus. When a network is divided into smaller, more manageable networks, routers are used to manage the network.

A router keeps a list of all the networks it can reach via its interfaces, and route tables contain this information. Upon receiving a packet on one of the router's interfaces, the router examines the destination IP address of the packet, consults the route table to determine which interface the packet should be forwarded to, and then forwards the packet to the correct interface. Figure 6.1 depicts the routing function between User A and User B.

FIGURE 6.1   Network routing overview

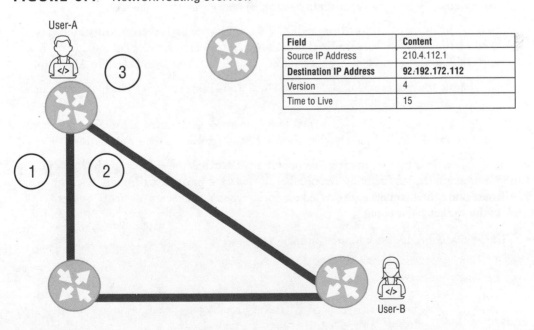

Field	Content
Source IP Address	210.4.112.1
Destination IP Address	**92.192.172.112**
Version	4
Time to Live	15

Internet Protocol (IP) packets travel from their origin (User A) to their destination (User B) along routes selected by routers in packet-switching networks like the Internet. Routers, specialized pieces of network hardware, determine Internet routing decisions.

The route table stored on the router is a list of all possible paths in the network. The router examines the packet's destination IP address when it receives IP packets from User A that need to be forwarded to User B in the network. Using the route table, it looks up the routing information.

User A sends the first packet to the nearest router. A router looks at the IP header of the packet. The destination IP address is the most crucial field in the header, as it points the packet in the right direction. The router has several possible routes for sending packets (as depicted in Figure 6.1, paths numbered 1, 2, and 3), and it aims to send them to the closest router to its destination.

Route tables can be either dynamic or static. Static route tables do not change, and a network administrator manually configures them. As a result, routes are set in stone unless the administrator manually updates the tables. Dynamic route tables are automatically updated. Dynamic routing protocols determine the shortest and fastest paths. In addition, they choose how long packets take to reach their destination.

A routing protocol is a standard way of formatting data so that any computer connected can understand it. Identifying or announcing network paths is the function of a routing protocol.

A routing algorithm determines the optimal path to the destination based on hop count, bandwidth, delay, and current load on the path.

The following protocols help data packets find their way across the Internet:

IP   A data packet's origin and destination are determined by its Internet Protocol (IP). To determine where packets should be sent, routers check the IP header.

BGP   The Border Gateway Protocol (BGP) is a distance path-vector protocol that is used on the Internet. Decentralized routing was intended to replace centralized routing with BGP, and data packets are transferred using BGP's Best Path Selection Algorithm.

A dynamic routing protocol, BGP is used by autonomous systems, which are large networks that announce BGP.

OSPF   Open Shortest Path First (OSPF) is a protocol that network routers employ for determining the fastest and shortest routes to send packets to their destinations.

RIP   The Routing Information Protocol (RIP) calculates the shortest path from one network to another by counting the number of routers it must pass through. Each traversal from one router to the next is called a hop, so when a packet travels from one network to another, it is "hopping."

The next section discusses Azure routing.

Azure Routes

Azure routes traffic between Azure and on-premises, and it also routes traffic between Azure and Internet resources. Azure automatically creates a route table for each subnet in an Azure virtual network (VNet) and adds system default routes. A subnet's route table determines how traffic from that subnet is routed outbound.

Azure automatically creates system routes and assigns them to each subnet in a virtual network. You cannot create or remove system routes, but you can override some system routes with custom routes.

For the AZ-700 exam, keep in mind that user-defined routes let organizations create network routes to connect their Azure virtual appliances to the Internet from their subnets. IP forwarding must be enabled for the network interfaces to receive and forward traffic. When multiple route types are present in a UDR route table, user-defined routes are preferred over the default system routes. More specific routes are used when numerous routes correspond to the destination.

Azure automatically assigns system routes to each subnet. A system route cannot be created or removed, but it can be overridden with a custom route. Azure creates default system routes for each subnet, and when you use specific Azure capabilities, it can also create additional default routes in specific subnets or across all subnets.

Each route specifies the next hop type and the address prefix. Azure uses the route that contains the prefix when traffic leaving a subnet goes to an IP address in the address prefix of a route. For every subnet within a virtual network, Azure automatically creates default routes. These are each described in Table 6.1.

TABLE 6.1   Default Routes

Source	Prefixes	Next Hop Type
Default	Specific to the virtual network	Default
Default	`0.0.0.0/0`	Internet
Default	`10.0.0.0/8`	None
Default	`192.168.0.0/16`	None
Default	`100.64.0.0/10`	None

Next-hop types represent how Azure routes traffic destined for the address prefix listed in the previous table.

Here's a list of next-hop types:

Virtual Network   A virtual network's address space allows traffic to be routed between address ranges. Azure creates a route with an address prefix corresponding to every address range defined in the address space of a virtual network. In the case of multiple address ranges defined in the virtual network address space, Azure creates individual routes for each address range. Azure uses routes created for each address range to route traffic between subnets. Azure routes traffic between subnets without the use of gateways. Address ranges within a virtual network define subnets, but Azure does not create default routes for subnet address ranges. Each subnet address range is within an address range of the virtual network's address space.

Internet   A prefix specifies how traffic is routed to the Internet. System default routes use the 0.0.0.0/0 address prefix. Azure routes traffic from any address not limited by a virtual network range to the Internet when you don't override its default routes. Azure routes traffic directly to one of its services over its backbone network rather than routing it over the Internet if the destination address belongs to one of Azure's services. Any traffic between Azure services does not transit the Internet, regardless of the Azure region where the virtual network is located or where an Azure service instance is deployed. You can override Azure's default system route with a custom route for the 0.0.0.0/0 address prefix.

None   Instead of sending traffic outside the subnet, the None type next-hop traffic is dropped. In Azure, the following address prefixes are automatically routed:

- In RFC 1918, 10.0.0.0/8, 172.16.0.0/12, and 192.168.0.0/16 were reserved for private use.
- RFC 6598 reserved 100.64.0.0/10.

Consider assigning any of the previous address ranges within the address space of a virtual network. As a result, Azure changes the next-hop type from None to VNET. If the address range you assign to the address space of a virtual network includes, but isn't the same as, one of the four reserved address prefixes, Azure removes the route for the prefix. It adds a route for the address prefix you added, with VNET as the next-hop type.

Azure adds more default system routes for different Azure capabilities, but only when the abilities are enabled. Azure will either add default routes to specific virtual networks or all virtual networks, depending on the ability. These are each described in Table 6.2.

TABLE 6.2 Optional default route

Source	Address prefixes	Next-hop type	Subnet within VNet
Default	Specific to the virtual network.	VNet peering	All
VNet gateway	Prefixes are advertised from on-premises via BGP or configured in the local network gateway.	VNet gateway	All
Default	Multiple	VNet Service Endpoint	Exclusively the subnet a service endpoint is enabled for.

Virtual Network Peering   When you build a VNet peering between two VNets, a route is created for each address range within the address space of each VNet peer.

Virtual Network (VNet) Gateway   When a virtual network gateway is connected to a virtual network, one or more routes with a virtual network gateway listed as the next hop-type are added to the virtual network. Because the gateway adds the routes to the subnet, the source is also a virtual network gateway. A virtual network gateway on Azure exchanges BGP routes with your on-premises network gateway. In that case, every route propagated from the on-premises network gateway is added to the route table. Microsoft recommends summarizing on-premises routes to the largest address ranges possible so that the fewest routes are propagated to the Azure virtual network gateway.

Virtual Network (VNet) Service Endpoint   You enable a service endpoint by allowing the public IP address for the service in the Azure's route table. As service endpoints are enabled for specific subnets within a virtual network, routes are added to the route table only for subnets for which they are enabled. The public IP addresses of Azure services change occasionally, and Azure automatically updates the addresses in the route table when they do.

When creating a user-defined route, you can specify next-hop types such as Virtual Appliance, Virtual Network Gateway, Virtual Network, Internet, and None. These are each described in the following list:

Virtual Appliance   Virtual appliances are typically virtual machines that run network applications, such as firewalls. As part of creating a route using the virtual appliance hop type, you can specify a next-hop IP address. It can be the private IP address of a virtual machine's NIC (Network Interface Card) or the private IP address of an Azure internal load balancer.

Private IP Address of a Virtual Machine's NIC   IP forwarding must be enabled for any network interface attached to a virtual machine that forwards network traffic to an address other than the virtual machine's own. This setting disables Azure's check of a network interface's source and destination.

For the appliance to forward traffic between private IP addresses assigned to Azure network interfaces, you may also need to enable IP forwarding within the virtual machine's operating system.

Consider an appliance that must route traffic to a public IP address. (NAT) network address translate the private IP address of the source's private IP address to its own private IP address, which Azure then NAT (network address translates) to a public IP address, before sending the traffic to the Internet.

Private IP Address of an Azure Internal Load Balancer You can define a route with the address prefix 0.0.0.0/0 and a next-hop type of Virtual Appliance, enabling the appliance to inspect the traffic and determine whether it should forward or drop it. An organization that intends to create a user-defined route containing the 0.0.0.0/0 address prefix should first read the 0.0.0.0/0 address prefix.

Virtual Network Gateway   When an organization would like traffic destined for specific address prefixes to be routed to a virtual network gateway, the virtual network gateway should be deployed with VPN capabilities.

You can't specify a virtual network gateway to be created as a type of ExpressRoute in a user-defined route because they must use BGP for custom routes with ExpressRoute. If an organization has VPN and ExpressRoute connections coexisting, you cannot specify virtual network gateways.

Using a route-based virtual network gateway, you can route traffic to the 0.0.0.0/0 address prefix. You might have a device that inspects the traffic and decides whether to forward it or drop it to the on-premises network. Creating a user-defined route for 0.0.0.0/0 requires first reading the 0.0.0.0/0 address prefix.

Instead of configuring a user-defined route for the 0.0.0.0/0 address prefix, you can advertise the organization's route via BGP if you enable BGP for a VPN virtual network gateway.

Virtual Network   This next-hop type indicates that you want to override the default routing.

Internet   This next-hop type is used when you want to explicitly route traffic destined to an address prefix to the Internet or if they wish to keep traffic destined for Azure services with public IP addresses within the Azure backbone network.

None   When you want to drop traffic to an address prefix instead of forwarding the traffic, you may list None for some optional system routes if they have not fully configured the capability.

It is now possible to preview the much-awaited service tag feature to be considered in design and deployment. You can now specify a service tag instead of an IP address range as the address prefix for a user-defined route. Multiple IP address prefixes are often associated with a single Azure service in a service tag. Microsoft manages the address prefixes encompassed by the service tag by automatically updating the service tag when addresses change, reducing the need for frequent updates of user-defined routes and reducing the number of routes you must define. As of this writing, you can create up to 25 routes with service tags in each route table.

A virtual network in Azure can be monitored, diagnosed, and viewed, and logs can be enabled or disabled using Azure Network Watcher. Azure Network Watcher monitors and repairs the network health of IaaS (infrastructure as a service) products, including virtual machines, virtual networks, application gateways, and load balancers.

Your subscription will automatically enable Network Watcher in the region of your virtual network when you create or update it. Automating Network Watcher will not affect your resources or incur any charges.

Follow the steps in Exercise 6.1 to configure user-defined routing using the Azure portal.

EXERCISE 6.1

Configure User-Defined Routing Using the Azure Portal

1. Log in to a personal or business account in the Azure portal at `https://portal.azure.com`.

2. Click Create Resource, search for **route table** in the search box, and click Create.

3. Once the Route Table Wizard opens, configure the following settings on the Route tab (see the next image):

   Name: Provide the route table name.

   Subscription: Choose your Azure subscription.

   Resource Group: Choose an existing resource group to use or provide a unique name for creating a new resource group.

   Region: Pick the Azure datacenter where you want to deploy the VM. Virtual networks and virtual machines must share the same route table.

   It is safe to choose No for Propagate Gateway Routes since this prevents on-premises routes from propagating to the network interfaces in the associated subnets.

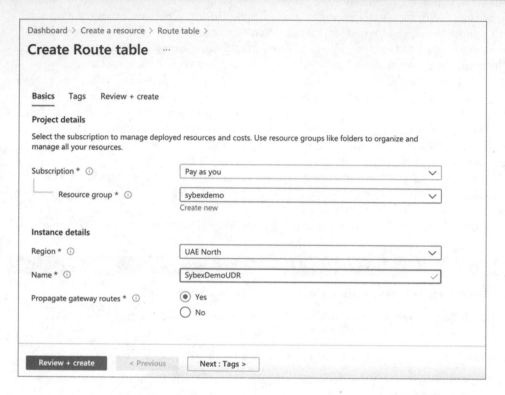

4. To create a route table, click Review + Create, then Create. Once the settings are validated, the route table will be deployed.

The following code demonstrates how to configure user-defined routing via Azure PowerShell:

```
$Route = New-AzRouteConfig -Name "SybexRoute" -AddressPrefix 10.1.0.0/16
-NextHopType "Sybexvnet"
New-AzRouteTable -Name "SybexRoute01" -ResourceGroupName "SybexRG"
-Location "UAECENTRAL" -Route $SybexRoute
Name               : Sybexroutetable01
ResourceGroupName  : SybexRG
Location           : UAECENTRAL
Id                 : /subscriptions/xxxx-xxxx-xxxx-xxxx/resourceGroups/
SybexRG1/
providers/Microsoft.Network
/routeTables/SybexRoute01
```

```
Etag                : W/"db5f4e12-3f34-465b-91dd-0ab4bf6fc286"
ProvisioningState : Succeeded
Tags                :
Routes              : [
                        {
                            "Name": "SybexRoute",
                            "Etag": "W/\"db5f4e12-3f34-465b-91dd-0ab4bf6fc286\"",
                            "Id": "/subscriptions/xxxx-xxxx-xxxx-
xxxx/resourceGroups
/ResourceGroup11/providers/Microsoft.Network/routeTables
/routetable01/routes/SybexRoute01",
                            "AddressPrefix": "10.2.0.0/16",
                            "NextHopType": "Sybexvnet",
                            "NextHopIpAddress": null,
                            "ProvisioningState": "Succeeded"
                        }
                    ]
Subnets             : []
```

You can change the settings as required. Follow the steps in Exercise 6.2 to change user-defined routing using the Azure portal.

You can modify only the BGP route propagation. You may change other settings after deployment as well.

EXERCISE 6.2

Change User-Defined Routing Settings Using the Azure Portal

1. Log into a personal or business account in the Azure portal at `https://portal. azure.com`.

2. Locate the route table you want to change. In the Azure portal search box, enter the route table's name.

3. When the route table appears, choose it. Under Settings, you can change the Propagate Gateway Routes settings in the Configuration pane at any time.

   The gateway route propagation setting can be disabled or enabled in the route table. If disabled, this option prevents BGP propagation of on-premises routes to the network interfaces in a virtual network subnet. You can customize the settings to create, delete, and change routes and subnets.

In the next section, you learn about associating a route table to and from a subnet.

Associate a Route Table with a Subnet

A route table can optionally be associated with a subnet in Azure, and one or more subnets can be linked to a route table. Even though route tables aren't virtual networks, you must associate a route table with each subnet that you want the route table associated with. Azure routes all traffic leaving the subnet based on the routes created by you in route tables, default routes, and routes propagated from an on-premises network if the virtual network is connected to an Azure virtual network gateway (ExpressRoute or VPN). Route tables in Azure can only be linked to subnets in virtual networks in the same Azure subscription and location.

Until a route table is configured correctly, it does nothing. Two items need to be considered: which resources are affected and how they are affected. You must associate a subnet and a route table by defining what resources are involved.

To associate a route table with a subnet using the Azure portal, follow the steps in Exercise 6.3.

EXERCISE 6.3

Associate a Route Table with a Subnet Using the Azure Portal

1. Log into a personal or business account in the Azure portal at `https://portal.azure.com`.

2. Click Virtual Networks and select the virtual network containing the subnet you want to associate with a route table.

3. Choose Subnets from the menu bar and, to associate a route table with a subnet, select the subnet.

4. Select the route table to associate with the subnet from the route table and save.

   The association is created once both options have been selected.

   A list of subnets will appear in the route table after a subnet has been associated.

   A route table that includes a route with a destination of `0.0.0.0/0` should not be associated with the gateway subnet of a virtual network connected to the Azure VPN gateway. The gateway will not function properly if this is done.

The following code demonstrates how to associate a route table with a subnet using Azure PowerShell:

```
az network vnet subnet update -g SybexRG -n SybexSubnet
--vnet-name SybexVNet --network-security-group SybexNsg
```

The next code demonstrates how to update a subnet with a NAT gateway using Azure PowerShell:

```
az network vnet subnet update -n SybexSubnet --vnet-name SybexVnet
-g SybexRG --nat-gateway SybexNatGateway
--address-prefixes "10.10.0.0/21"
```

> For the Microsoft AZ-700 exam, keep in mind that site-to-site VPNs between datacenters and Azure virtual networks will require the creation of a local network gateway and a user-defined route.
>
> It's important to note that even if a UDR points at the Azure firewall as the default gateway, traffic between directly peered VNets is routed directly. A UDR containing the target subnet network prefix on both subnets must explicitly contain the target subnet network prefix for traffic between subnets to be sent to the firewall in this scenario.

Set Up Forced Tunneling

Organizations can use forced tunneling to redirect or "force" all Internet traffic back to their on-premises location via a site-to-site VPN tunnel for inspection and auditing purposes. Most enterprise IT security and compliance policies consider this a critical security requirement. Without forced tunneling, Internet-bound traffic from VMs in Azure will always traverse directly from the Azure network out to the Internet without any option to allow you to inspect or audit the traffic. The disclosure of confidential information or other security breaches can result from unauthorized Internet access.

As of this writing, forced tunneling can be configured using Azure PowerShell, and it can't be configured using the Azure portal.

Figure 6.2 depicts forced tunneling.

The architecture shown in Figure 6.2 does not force a tunnel to the front-end subnet. Direct customer requests can continue to be accepted and processed in the front-end subnet, and subnets in the middle and back-end are tunneled. A site-to-site (S2S) VPN tunnel will be used to force or redirect all outbound connections from these two subnets to the Internet.

In this way, organizations can restrict and inspect Internet access while enabling multi-tier service architectures required for cloud consumption. The entire virtual network can also be accessed via forced tunneling if no workloads face the Internet.

Azure configures forced tunneling using virtual network custom user-defined routes. In Azure VPN, traffic is routed to an on-premises site using a default route.

FIGURE 6.2   Forced tunneling

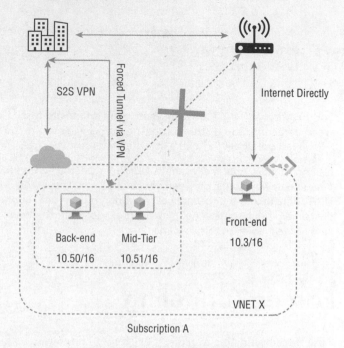

- Forced tunneling is associated with a VNet that has a route-based VPN gateway.
- Virtual network subnets all have a route table, which is divided into three groups:

Local VNet Routes   Direct access to VMs in the same virtual network.

Default Route   Directly connects to the Internet. All packets not covered by the previous two routes destined for private IP addresses are dropped.

On-Premises Routes   Access through Azure VPN.

As part of Exercise 6.4, you will use user-defined routes (UDRs) to create a route table that adds a default route and then associate the route table with the organization's VNet subnets to enable forced tunneling.

As shown in Figure 6.3, the configuration for this example is that the virtual network three-tier VNet has three subnets, front-end, mid-tier, and back-end, with four cross-premises connections inclusive of HQ and three branch offices.

FIGURE 6.3   Three-tier VNet demonstrates UDR

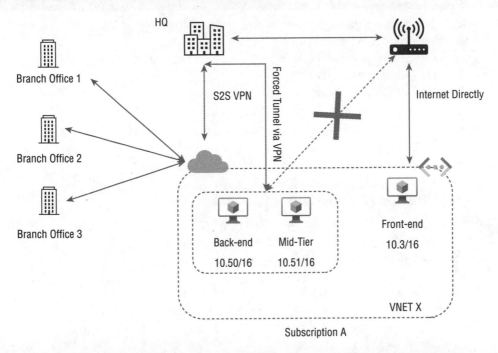

EXERCISE 6.4

Use User-Defined Routes to Create a Route Table That Adds a Default Route and Associates the Route Table with a Subnet to Enable Forced Tunneling

1. Use the `New-AzResourceGroup` command to create a resource group. The following example creates a resource group named `SybexFTRG` in the UAENorth location:

```
$rg = @{
    Name = 'SybexFTRG'
    Location = 'UAENorth'
}
New-AzResourceGroup @rg
```

2. Create a virtual network and provide the planned subnets. `New-AzVirtualNetwork` allows you to create a virtual network. The following code creates a default virtual network named `MultiTier-VNet` in the UAENorth location and provides the subnets for each group:

```
$FE1 = New-AzVirtualNetworkSubnetConfig -Name ""Frontend""
-AddressPrefix ""10.50.0.0/24""
```

```
$MT2 = New-AzVirtualNetworkSubnetConfig -Name ""Midtier""
-AddressPrefix "10.51.1.0/24"
$BE3 = New-AzVirtualNetworkSubnetConfig -Name "Backend"
-AddressPrefix "10.3.2.0/24"
$GS4 = New-AzVirtualNetworkSubnetConfig -Name "GatewaySubnet"
-AddressPrefix "10.5.100.0/28"
$vnet = New-AzVirtualNetwork -Name "MultiTier-VNet"
-Location "UAENorth" -ResourceGroupName "SybexFTRG"
-AddressPrefix "10.1.0.0/16" -Subnet $FE1,$MT2,$BE3,$GS4
```

3. Use the following code to create the local network gateways for each office inclusive of the head office and all branch offices:

```
$LNG1 = New-AzLocalNetworkGateway -Name "HQ"
-ResourceGroupName "SybexFTRG" -Location "UAENorth"
-GatewayIpAddress "110.110.110.111"
-AddressPrefix "172.168.1.0/24"
$LNG2 = New-AzLocalNetworkGateway -Name "Boffice1"
-ResourceGroupName "SybexFTRG " -Location "UAENorth"
-GatewayIpAddress "110.110.110.112"
-AddressPrefix "172.168.2.0/24"
$LNG3 = New-AzLocalNetworkGateway -Name "Boffice2"
-ResourceGroupName " SybexFTRG " -Location "UAENorth"
-GatewayIpAddress "110.110.110.113"
-AddressPrefix "172.168.3.0/24"
$LNG4 = New-AzLocalNetworkGateway -Name "Boffice3"
-ResourceGroupName "SybexFTRG" -Location "UAENorth"
-GatewayIpAddress "110.110.110.114"
-AddressPrefix "172.168.4.0/24"
```

4. Now create the route table and route rule:

```
New-AzRouteTable -Name "SyRouteTable" -ResourceGroupName "SybexFTRG"
-Location "UAENorth"
$rt = Get-AzRouteTable -Name "SyRouteTable"
-ResourceGroupName "SybexFTRG"
Add-AzRouteConfig -Name "SyDefaultRoute"
-AddressPrefix "0.0.0.0/0" -NextHopType VirtualNetworkGateway
-RouteTable $rt
Set-AzRouteTable -RouteTable $rt
```

5. Associate the route table to the middle tier and downstream subnets:

```
$vnet = Get-AzVirtualNetwork -Name "MultiTier-Vnet"
-ResourceGroupName "SybexFTRG"
Set-AzVirtualNetworkSubnetConfig -Name "MT" -VirtualNetwork $vnet
-AddressPrefix "10.50.1.0/24" -RouteTable $rt
Set-AzVirtualNetworkSubnetConfig -Name "BE" -VirtualNetwork $vnet
-AddressPrefix "10.51.2.0/24" -RouteTable $rt
Set-AzVirtualNetwork -VirtualNetwork $vnet
```

6. The virtual network gateway should now be created. Depending on the gateway SKU selected, it can take 45–60 minutes to create a gateway. Ensure that you have installed the latest version of PowerShell cmdlets if `ValidateSet` errors occur regarding the `GatewaySKU` value. PowerShell cmdlets have been updated with new valid values for the newest gateway SKUs. The following code provides an overview of creating a virtual network gateway:

```
$pip = New-AzPublicIpAddress -Name "GWIP" -ResourceGroupName "SybexFERG"
-Location "UAENorth" -AllocationMethod Dynamic
$gwsubnet = Get-AzVirtualNetworkSubnetConfig -Name "GWSubnet"
-VirtualNetwork $vnet
$ipconfig = New-AzVirtualNetworkGatewayIpConfig -Name "gwIpsetup"
-SubnetId $gwsubnet.Id -PublicIpAddressId $pip.Id
New-AzVirtualNetworkGateway -Name "GW1" -ResourceGroupName "SybexFERG"
-Location "UAENorth" -IpConfigurations $ipconfig
-GatewayType Vpn -VpnType RouteBased
-GatewaySku VpnGw1 -EnableBgp $false
```

7. A default site should be assigned to the virtual network gateway. You must correctly set the `-GatewayDefaultSite` cmdlet parameter to enable forced routing, as shown in this code:

```
$LocalGateway = Get-AzLocalNetworkGateway -Name "HQ"
-ResourceGroupName "SybexFERG"
$VirtualGateway = Get-AzVirtualNetworkGateway -Name "GW1"
-ResourceGroupName "SybexFERG"
Set-AzVirtualNetworkGatewayDefaultSite -GatewayDefaultSite $LocalGateway
-VirtualNetworkGateway $VirtualGateway
```

8. Finally, establish the site-to-site VPN connections:

```
$gateway = Get-AzVirtualNetworkGateway -Name "GW1"
-ResourceGroupName "SybexFERG"
$LNG1 = Get-AzLocalNetworkGateway -Name "HQ" -ResourceGroupName "SybexFERG"
$LNG2 = Get-AzLocalNetworkGateway -Name "Boffice1"
-ResourceGroupName "SybexFERG"
```

```
$LNG3 = Get-AzLocalNetworkGateway -Name "Boffice2"
-ResourceGroupName "SybexFERG"
$LNG4 = Get-AzLocalNetworkGateway -Name "Boffice3"
-ResourceGroupName "SybexFERG"
New-AzVirtualNetworkGatewayConnection -Name "Connection1"
-ResourceGroupName "SybexFERG" -Location "UAE North"
-VirtualNetworkGateway1 $gateway -LocalNetworkGateway2 $LNG1
-ConnectionType IPsec -SharedKey "preSharedKey"
New-AzVirtualNetworkGatewayConnection -Name "Connection2"
-ResourceGroupName "SybexFERG" -Location "UAE North"
-VirtualNetworkGateway1 $gateway -LocalNetworkGateway2 $LNG2
-ConnectionType IPsec -SharedKey "preSharedKey"
New-AzVirtualNetworkGatewayConnection -Name "Connection3"
-ResourceGroupName "SybexFERG" -Location "UAE North"
-VirtualNetworkGateway1 $gateway -LocalNetworkGateway2 $LNG3
-ConnectionType IPsec -SharedKey "preSharedKey"
New-AzVirtualNetworkGatewayConnection -Name "Connection4"
-ResourceGroupName "SybexFERG" -Location "UAE North"
-VirtualNetworkGateway1 $gateway -LocalNetworkGateway2 $LNG4
-ConnectionType IPsec -SharedKey "preSharedKey"
Get-AzVirtualNetworkGatewayConnection -Name "Connection1"
-ResourceGroupName "SybexFERG".
```

Diagnose and Resolve Routing Issues

This section describes how to troubleshoot a routing problem by viewing the effective routes for a network interface in a virtual machine (VM). As you read earlier, Azure creates several default routes for each virtual network subnet. However, you can override Azure's default routes by creating route tables and associating them with subnets. An organization's designed and deployed routes, Azure's default routes, and any routes propagated from the on-premises network through the Azure VPN gateway are the effective routes for all network interfaces in a subnet.

If a connection fails when you attempt to connect to a VM, you can view the effective routes for a network interface using the Azure portal, PowerShell, or the Azure CLI.

The following is the high-level information about VM configurations used in this example:

- **Name of VM:** SybexVM01
- **Name of VM network interface card:** SybexVMNic01

- **Name of the resource group:** SybexRG
- **Name of the location/region:** UAE North

The rest of this section describes the process for troubleshooting connection problems.

First, make sure troubleshooting tools are deployed in your local device. This example uses PowerShell. To confirm that Azure PowerShell cmdlets are deployed, execute the following cmdlet in PowerShell:

```
Get-Module -ListAvailable Az
```

Next, use Get-AzEffectiveRouteTable to get effective routes for a network interface. As an example, here are the effective routes for our network interface named SybexVMNic01, which belongs to a resource group named SybexRG:

```
Get-AzEffectiveRouteTable `
  -NetworkInterfaceName SybexVMNic01 `
  -ResourceGroupName SybexRG `
  | Format-Table
```

When the VM is in the running state, the output is returned. You can review the effective routes for each network interface attached to the VM if multiple network interfaces exist. Because each network interface can be in a different subnet, each interface can have a different effective route.

Here are additional items to help you diagnose the root cause of the connection issue:

- The problem may be due to the firewall software running within the VM's operating system if no routes are causing a VM's network communication to fail.

- Among routes defined, BGP, and system routes, the routing algorithm is based on the longest prefix match (LPM). Based on the available routes, you can only view effective routes that match the LPM.

- Ensure IP forwarding is enabled on the network virtual appliance (NVA) receiving the traffic if a route was created for an NVA.

- For virtual network peering traffic to work correctly, a system route must include a next-hop type of VNet Peering for the peered virtual network's prefix range.

- Although Azure assigns default routes to each Azure network interface, only the primary network interface within the VM's operating system is assigned a default route (0.0.0.0/0), or gateway.

- You can also use Network Watcher's connection troubleshoot capability to determine routing, filtering, and in-OS (Operating System) causes of outbound communication problems.

- If you tunnel traffic through a VPN gateway or NVA to an on-premises device, you may not access a VM from the Internet if the routing has not been configured for the devices. Confirm that you have configured the device to route traffic to either a private or a public IP address for the virtual machine.

- The next-hop capability of Network Watcher can determine the hop type for traffic destined for a location. A next hop specifies the next-hop type for traffic heading to a specific location.

- A VM's network communication problem might be caused by firewall software running on its operating system if no routes are pushing it to fail.

- If you want to determine the next-hop type for traffic destined for a particular location, use Network Watcher's next-hop feature.

- Due to how routing has been configured for the devices, you may not be able to connect to a VM from the Internet when forcing tunneling traffic to an on-premises device through a VPN gateway or NVA. Ensure that the routing configured for the device routes traffic either to a public or a private IP address for the VM.

Design and Deploy Azure Route Server

A fully managed Azure Route Server provides cloud customers with a more straightforward way to manage routing in Azure infrastructure, especially if they have an NVA. An organization's virtual networks and NVAs support BGP and software-defined (SD) networking, simplifying dynamic routing between them.

During provisioning, Route Server creates a virtual machine scale set, which provides high availability for the service. VMs are deployed into the availability zone if it is deployed in a region that supports zone redundancy to ensure service availability. If Route Server is deployed, the first two IP addresses from the subnet will be picked up.

Route Server can be deployed using the following architecture design patterns:

- Network topologies such as hub-and-spoke are supported. You can host Route Server and Azure Virtual Assistant within the hub network.

- Dual-homed networks can also host Route Server. Dual-homed networks pair a spoke network with two hubs.

Route Server provides route sharing with:

- Azure VPN gateway

- Azure ExpressRoute

- A network virtual appliance

You can enable or disable the route exchange. In addition, cloud users do not have to configure or maintain route tables manually.

You can exchange routing information directly with NVAs that support the BGP routing protocol.

Route Server simplifies dynamic routing between organizations' NVAs and virtual networks. This allows you to exchange routing information directly through the BGP routing protocol between any NVA that supports the BGP routing protocol and the Azure SD network in the Azure VNet without manually configuring and maintaining route tables. High availability is a fully managed service provided by Route Server.

Route Server allows network appliances to dynamically exchange route information with Azure virtual networks. This is done using Route Server, the organization's configured network appliances, ExpressRoute, and Azure VPN gateways without talking to each network manually.

Here are the key benefits of Route Server:

- Route Server can be deployed in any organization's new or existing virtual network.
- With Route Server, an organization's virtual networks can be configured, managed, and deployed more efficiently.
- There is no longer a need to manually update the route table on NVAs whenever a virtual network address changes.
- A single instance of an NVA can peer with multiple instances of Route Server. BGP attributes can be configured in NVA. You must let Route Server know whether NVA instances are active or passive based on the organization's design (e.g., active-active for performance or active-passive for resiliency).
- The NVA and Route Server interface is based on a standard protocol. An organization can peer with Route Server if their NVA supports BGP.
- User-defined routes no longer need to be manually updated whenever the organization's NVA announces new routes or withdraws old ones.

The following are the key prerequisites for Route Server:

- RouteServerSubnet allows Route Server to be deployed to an existing virtual network or a new virtual network within its empty dedicated subnet.
- The subnet must be at least /27.
- BGP should be able to benefit from the Route Server with NVA.

While designing Route Server, consider the following limitations:

- The maximum number of BGP peers supported is only eight.
- The maximum number of routes each BGP peer can advertise to Route Server is 1,000.
- The maximum number of routes that Route Server can advertise to ExpressRoute or a VPN gateway is 200.
- The maximum number of VMs in the virtual network (including peered virtual networks) that Route Server can support is 2,000.
- Route Server doesn't support network security group association to RouteServerSubnet.
- A UDR cannot be configured on RouteServerSubnet of Route Server.

- Route Server only supports autonomous system numbers (ASNs) with a maximum of 16 bits (2 bytes).
- Route Server propagates routes with BGP communities as is.
- Route Server exchanges only BGP routes with NVAs. NVA data traffic goes directly to the VM, and VM data traffic goes directly to the NVA.
- Virtual network peering is supported by Route Server.
- Route Server is designed with high availability by default. It will have zone-level redundancy if it is deployed in an Azure region with availability zones.

Route Server does not have an upper limit on how many VMs can be supported. Deploying Route Server infrastructure within an Azure region determines the number of VMs supported.

The next section discusses various design patterns in Route Server deployment.

Route Server Design Pattern 1

Route Server supports ExpressRoute and Azure VPN. With Route Server, third-party NVAs can run on Azure and integrate seamlessly with ExpressRoute and Azure VPN gateways. The gateway and Route Server don't require any configuration or management on devices. Azure Route Server and the gateway can exchange routes through a simple configuration change.

By default, Route Server does not propagate the routes it receives from NVAs and ExpressRoute gateways to each other when you deploy a Route Server along with ExpressRoute gateways and NVAs in a virtual network. ExpressRoute and the Cloud Virtual Assistant will learn each other's routes once you enable route exchange.

Example Reference Pattern 1

A software-defined wide area network (SD-WAN) appliance receives the route along with the virtual network route from Azure Route Server(ARS), on-premises 2, connected to ExpressRoute.

Figure 6.4 depicts Route Server Design Pattern 1.

Example Reference Pattern 2

The ExpressRoute gateway will receive route information from On-Premises 1 connected to an SD-WAN appliance, as well as virtual network information from Route Server.

Additionally, you can install an Azure VPN gateway using the SD-WAN appliance. Due to the fully managed nature of Azure VPN gateway and ExpressRoute, you can set up route exchange for the two on-premises networks to communicate.

The Azure VPN gateway should be configured in active-active mode and have an ASN of 65515.

FIGURE 6.4   Route Server Design Pattern 1

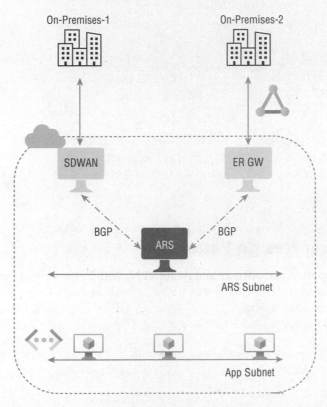

Figure 6.5 depicts Route Server Design Pattern 2.

Route Server Design Pattern 2

This design pattern is Route Server with a dual-homed network.

Organizations can use Azure Route Server to build hub-and-spoke network topologies. Route Servers and NVAs are part of the virtual hub network. A dual-homed network is another topology that can be configured for the Azure network using Route Server. You can configure this for a virtual spoke network peering with two or more hub virtual networks. Organizations on-premises or over the Internet may communicate with virtual machines in the spoke virtual network through either a virtual hub network or the Internet.

Figure 6.6 shows a high-level overview of the supported building blocks for Design Pattern 2.

A virtual machine in a spoke virtual network will see the security NVA or VPN NVA in the hub as its next hop in the data plane. Hybrid cross-premises or Internet-bound traffic will now be routed through the hub virtual network's NVAs.

FIGURE 6.5   Route Server Design Pattern 2

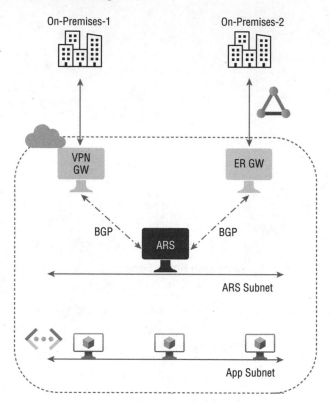

FIGURE 6.6   Route Server design with VNet peering pattern

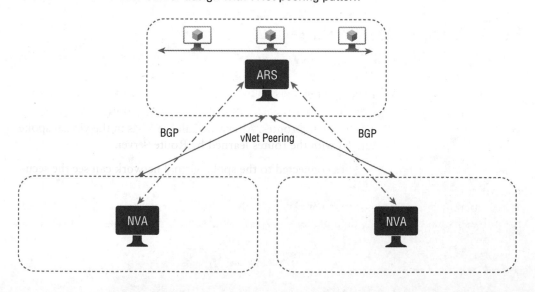

If they were deployed inside the same virtual network, the NVA and Route Server would exchange routes in the control plane. The NVA will be able to learn the virtual network addresses of spokes from Route Server, and routes will be learned from each NVA. All virtual machines in the spoke virtual network will then be programmed with the learned routes by Route Server.

Both hubs can be configured to be active-active or active-passive. A virtual machine's traffic to and from its active hub will fail over to another hub if it fails. NVA failures and service connectivity failures are examples of these failures. Organizations networks are configured in this way to ensure high availability.

Microsoft recommends the following three design and deployment essentials:

- In every virtual hub network, deploy an NVA and deploy a route server in every virtual spoke network.

- Make sure VNet peering is enabled between the virtual spoke and hub networks.

- Route Server and every NVA must be configured to peer with BGP.

Figure 6.7 explains how this works.

FIGURE 6.7   Dual-home network with Route Server

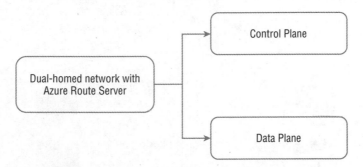

Azure Route server Dual home network is classified into two planes: control plane and data plane.

Control Plane   Route Server and the NVA share routes in the control plane as if they were in the same virtual network. From each NVA, Route Server will learn about the spoke virtual network addresses and routes. Afterward, all the VMs in the virtual spoke network will be programmed with the routes learned by Route Server.

Data Plane   Virtual machines connected to the spoke virtual network can see the security NVA or VPN NVA in the hub as the next hop. NVAs in the virtual hub network will then route Internet-bound traffic and hybrid cross-premises traffic.

Example Reference Pattern 1

This is an example of Route Server integration with ExpressRoute.

You can create dual-homed networks using two or more ExpressRoute connections. Follow these steps:

1. Each virtual hub network requires a Route Server with an ExpressRoute gateway.

2. Configure BGP peering between the NVA and Route Server in the virtual hub network.

3. The virtual hub network enables route exchange between the ExpressRoute gateway and Route Server.

4. In the spoke virtual network VNet peering configuration, make sure Use Remote Gateway Or Remote Route Server is disabled.

Figure 6.8 depicts dual-homed networks using ExpressRoute connections.

FIGURE 6.8 Dual-homed networks with ExpressRoute

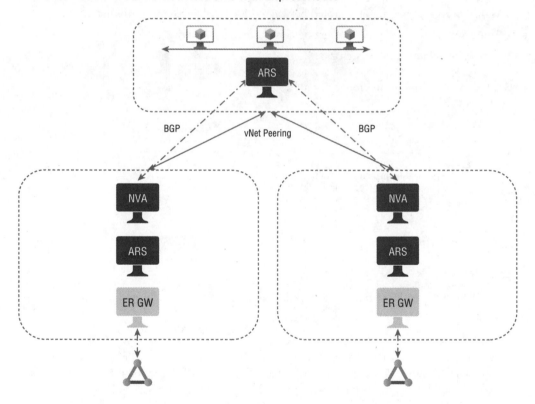

In the control plane, through route exchange with Route Server in the hub, the NVA in the virtual hub network learns about on-premises routes from the ExpressRoute gateway. Using the same Route Server, the NVA sends the addresses of the spoke virtual networks to the ExpressRoute gateway. In both the spoke and virtual hub networks, the Route

Server will assign the on-premises network addresses to the VMs in their respective virtual networks.

In the data plane, the VMs in the spoke virtual network will first send all traffic to the virtual hub network before sending it to the on-premises network. The NVA will forward the traffic through ExpressRoute to the on-premises network. The same data path will be used in the reverse direction for on-premises traffic.

By choosing a path with Route Server, an organization can route traffic through their SD-WAN NVA over the Internet to their on-premises networks.

The remainder of this section discusses how Route Server enables path selection, allowing you to configure your organization's SD-WAN NVAs to have a routing preference when communicating with on-premises networks.

Figure 6.9 depicts the path type with Route Server.

FIGURE 6.9   Route Server path type

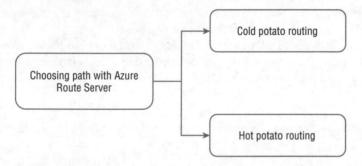

Cold Potato Routing   SD-WAN NVAs are configured with a Microsoft network IP address when deployed in the same virtual network as Route Server. On-premises traffic to the organization will use the Microsoft global network and exit the Microsoft network closest to its destination. Routing will enter the Microsoft network nearest the user on the return path from the on-premises network. Performance-optimized routing ensures the best possible experience while maintaining a reasonable cost.

Hot Potato Routing   To optimize costs, a second routing method assigns an Internet IP address to the organization's SD-WAN NVAs. When traffic is routed to the on-premises network, it will exit the Microsoft network in the same region where the service is hosted. Then it will use the ISP's network to connect to the Internet. Microsoft's network is the closest to the hosted service region, where routing occurs from on-premises. A routing method such as this will provide the best overall price when transferring a large amount of data.

Choosing an Azure Load Balancer SKU

Network load balancing is nothing more than evenly distributing incoming traffic across a group of back-end resources or servers. Optimum resource utilization, maximum throughput, and minimum response times are all realized by load balancing. Shared workloads across redundant computing resources can also improve availability. Load balancing services provided by Azure help distribute workloads between your networks. Load balancing maximizes throughput while minimizing response time by optimizing the use of your resources.

You can create internal and public load balancers to distribute network traffic within your networks and network traffic arriving from outside your organization's networks.

Azure Load Balancers help your organization improve application availability and scalability by distributing network traffic across multiple servers to prevent single points of failure. Azure Load Balancer operates at Layer 4 of the Open Systems Interconnection (OSI) model, and customers can only contact Azure Load Balancer from the end-user layer.

Figure 6.10 is an overview of the Azure Load Balancer.

Flows arriving at the load balancer's front-end are distributed to back-end pool instances by the load balancer. These flows are based on configured load balancing rules and health probes. Azure virtual machines or virtual machine scale sets can be used as back-end pool instances.

FIGURE 6.10   Azure Load Balancer overview

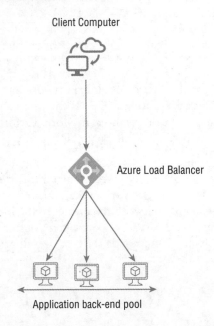

You can use Azure's load balancing services to distribute workloads across multiple compute resources. Figure 6.11 summarizes the Azure load balancing services by the categories described next:

FIGURE 6.11   Azure load balancing services

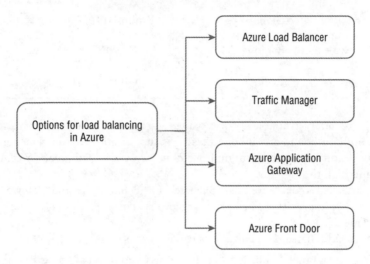

- Microsoft Azure Load Balancer is a high-performance, low-latency Layer 4 load balancing service (inbound and outbound) for all UDP and TCP protocols. Microsoft ensures your solution is highly available while handling millions of requests per second. Azure Load Balancer provides high availability across availability zones through zone redundancy.

- Using Traffic Manager, you can distribute traffic to services across global Azure regions optimally while ensuring high availability and responsiveness. Load balancing is only possible at the domain level because Traffic Manager is a DNS-based load balancing service. As a result, it cannot fail over as quickly as Front Door due to issues with DNS caching and systems that do not honor DNS TTLs.

- Application Gateway provides Layer 7 load balancing capabilities as part of its application delivery controller (ADC) service. The gateway can handle CPU-intensive SSL termination, which optimizes web farm productivity.

- Application delivery network Front Door provides web application acceleration and load balancing services. Layer 7 capabilities are available for your applications, such as SSL offload, path-based routing, fast failover, and caching, to improve performance and high availability.

Table 6.3 is a summary of these categories for each Azure load balancing service.

TABLE 6.3   Azure load balancing services

Service	Global/regional	Best protocol for traffic flow
Azure Front Door	Global	HTTP(S)
Traffic Manager	Global	non-HTTP(S)
Application Gateway	Regional	HTTP(S)
Azure Load Balancer	Regional	non-HTTP(S)

You can create highly available services using Azure Load Balancer, which scales business applications. Both outbound and inbound traffic is supported by load balancing. All TCP and UDP applications can scale up to millions of flows with a load balancer that provides low latency and high throughput.

There are three SKUs for Azure Load Balancer: Basic, Standard, and Gateway. (As of this writing, Gateway is in preview.) Each SKU targets a specific scenario and differs in features, scale, and pricing.

With Azure Load Balancer, organizations can achieve the following:

- Azure virtual machines can be load-balanced between internal and external traffic.

- Distribute resources across and within zones to increase availability.

- Azure virtual machines can be configured to have outbound connectivity.

- Health probes can be used to monitor load-balanced resources.

- Use port forwarding to access virtual machines with public IP addresses and ports on a virtual network.

- Enable IPv6 load balancing.

- Load balance services across multiple ports or IP addresses.

- Load-balance resources between internal and external Azure regions.

- Using high availability (HA) ports, balance UDP and TCP traffic across all ports.

- Through Azure Monitor, a standard load balancer provides multidimensional metrics. These metrics can be filtered, grouped, or broken out for each dimension. This gives your organization an overview of the service's performance and health over time. Insights for Azure Load Balancer visualize these metrics in a preconfigured dashboard. There is also support for resource health.

- Load balancers are designed to operate on the zero-trust network security model.

- The standard load balancer is secure by default as part of your organization's virtual network. Virtual networks are isolated and private.

- Load balancers and standard public IP addresses are closed to inbound connections unless opened by a network security group (NSG). An NSG allows specific traffic. Traffic cannot reach cloud virtual machine resources if organizations do not have NSGs on their subnets or NICs.

- In the basic load balancer, Internet access is enabled by default.

- The load balancer does not store any customer information.

> Microsoft recommends using standard load balancers. Only one SKU can be used to connect a stand-alone VM, an availability set, and a scale set. You must use load balancers and public IP SKUs that match when using public IP addresses, and load balancers and public IP SKUs can't be changed.
>
> Standard load balancers minimize administrative effort and provide high availability.

Organizations cannot alter existing resources' SKUs since SKUs are immutable. For production workloads, standard SKU load balancers are recommended by Microsoft.

Table 6.4 is a comparison of the Basic and Standard SKUs.

TABLE 6.4   Azure Load Balancer SKU comparison

Type	Standard load balancer	Basic load balancer
Use Case	Provides high performance and ultra-low latency for load balancing network layer traffic. Routes traffic within and across regions and availability zones to ensure high resilience.	The platform is designed for small-scale applications that don't require high availability or redundancy. Availability zones are not supported.
Supported Back-end type	NIC- and IP-based.	NIC
Supported Protocol	TCP, UDP	TCP, UDP
Front-end IP Configs	Supports up to 600 configurations	Supports up to 200 configurations
Back-end pool size	Supports up to 1,000 instances	Supports up to 300 instances
Back-end pool endpoints	Any VM or VM scale sets in a single virtual network	VM in a single availability set or VM scale set

TABLE 6.4 Azure Load Balancer SKU comparison *(continued)*

Type	Standard load balancer	Basic load balancer
Health probes	TCP, HTTP, HTTPS	TCP, HTTP
Health probe down behavior	Even when an instance probe goes down or when all probes go down, TCP connections remain active.	On a downed instance probe, TCP connections stay alive. Once all probes have been brought down, all TCP connections will close.
Availability Zones	Zone-redundant Zonal front-ends for inbound and outbound traffic	Not available (as of this writing)
Diagnostics	Azure Monitor multidimensional metrics	Azure Monitor logs
HA Ports	Available for internal load balancers	Not available (as of this writing)
Security	Inbound flows are prohibited unless a network security group allows it. Internal traffic between the virtual network and the internal load balancer is permitted.	Communication allowed by default.
Outbound Rules	Declarative outbound NAT configuration	Not available (as of this writing)
TCP Reset on Idle	Available on any rule	Not available (as of this writing)
Multiple front ends	Both inbound and outbound	Inbound but no outbound support.
Management Operations	Most operations < 30 seconds	60–90+ seconds typical
Service-level Agreement	99.99	Not available (as of this writing)
Global VNet Peering Support	Standard Internal Load Balancer (ILB) is supported via global VNet peering.	Not supported (as of this writing)
Supports NAT Gateway	Both standard ILB and Standard public LB are supported via NAT gateway.	Not supported (as of this writing)

Type	Standard load balancer	Basic load balancer
Supports Private Link	Standard ILB is supported via Private Link.	Not supported (as of this writing)
Cross-regional load balancing (Preview)	Standard public LB is supported via cross-region LB.	Not supported (as of this writing)

There are a few important factors to consider when choosing a load balancing option:

- Traffic type—is it for a web application?
- If it is a private application, who is the target audience?
- Does your application need to load-balance virtual machines and containers within a virtual network, load-balance across regions, or both?
- Does the service have a service level agreement (SLA)?
- As well as the actual cost, consider the operational costs associated with managing and maintaining a solution based on that service.
- Service provider features and limitations—what features and benefits does each service provider offer, and what are their limits?

Microsoft provides the decision chart shown in Figure 6.12 to guide you through a series of critical decision criteria to recommend the best load balancing solution. However, you should take this flowchart and recommendation only as a starting point and then perform a more detailed evaluation based on the criteria to select the best option for your environment.

Business applications may consist of multiple workloads, so evaluate each workload separately. Several load balancing solutions may be incorporated into a complete solution.

Choosing Between Public and Internal Load Balancers

The IP address of your organization's Azure Load Balancer is the point of contact for your end users' clients. These IP addresses can be either public or private.

A public load balancer can provide outbound connections for virtual machines inside an organization's virtual network. Private IP addresses are converted to public IP addresses to establish specific connections. Public load balancers are used to load-balance web traffic to VMs in the cloud. In other words, public load balancers map the public IP and port of the incoming traffic to the VM's private IP and port, and they map traffic the other way around when the VM responds.

FIGURE 6.12 Decision chart for Azure load balancing

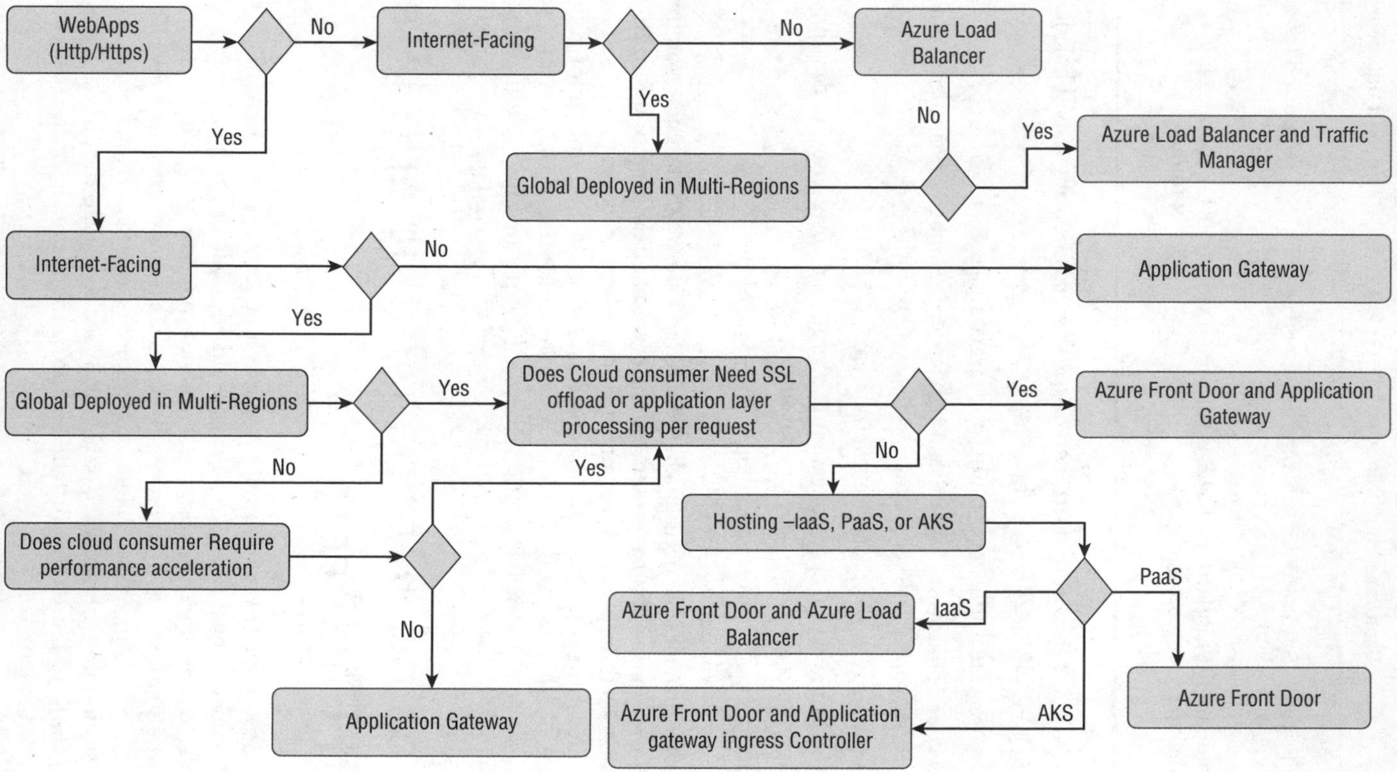

You can use load balancing rules to distribute traffic among multiple virtual machines or services. For instance, you can distribute a load of web requests across several web servers.

A private load balancer is used if only private IP addresses are required at the front-end. Load balancing is done internally within a virtual network using internal load balancers. Accessing an on-premises load balancer front-end from a hybrid network is possible. In other words, a virtual network's internal load balancer distributes traffic to virtual resources. An Azure load-balanced virtual network restricts access to its front-end IP addresses. IP addresses and virtual networks are never directly exposed to Internet endpoints on the front-end. Azure-based and on-premises resources are used to access internal line-of-business applications.

These Azure services support availability zones:

Zonal Services   Resources can be assigned to specific zones. It is possible to pin virtual machines, managed disks, or standard IP addresses to a particular zone to spread one or more instances of resources across several zones.

Consumers of cloud services can choose to have a front-end guaranteed to a single zone called a *zonal*. A single zone can handle an inbound or outbound flow in a region. Your organization's front-end shares the zone's health, and the data path is not affected by any failures in zones other than working zones. You can expose IP addresses per availability zone via zonal front-ends.

Further, load-balanced endpoints within each zone can be used directly via zonal front-ends. Consumers can use this configuration to expose per-zone load-balanced endpoints for monitoring each zone independently. Customers can integrate their cloud endpoints with a DNS load balancing product, such as Traffic Manager, and use a single DNS name.

Figure 6.13 shows a zone load balancer.

FIGURE 6.13   Zone load balancer

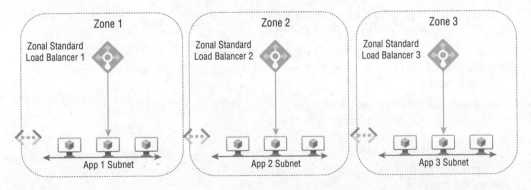

Zone-Redundant Services Zone-redundant services offer automatic replication or distribution across zones. Having data replicated across three zones ensures data availability in case of a zone failure.

> **Zone-Redundant** A standard load balancer can be zone-redundant in a region with availability zones. Only one IP address serves the traffic.

No matter the zone, only one front-end IP address will survive zone failure, and the front-end IP will be able to reach all (non-impacted) back-end pool members. The data path survives even if one zone in the region fails, as long as one zone in the region remains healthy.

Multiple infrastructure deployments in different availability zones serve the front-end's IP address. Retries or reestablishments will succeed in other zones unaffected by the zone failure.

Figure 6.14 shows a zone-redundant load balancer.

FIGURE 6.14 Zone-redundant load balancer

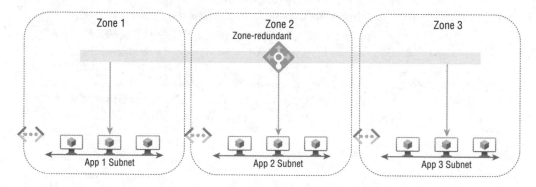

You can add a zone parameter to the public IP for a public load balancer front-end. This public IP address references front-end IP configurations.

Add a zones parameter to the internal load balancer front-end IP configuration for an internal load balancer front-end. Zone front-ends assign IP addresses to a specific zone in each subnet.

Nonregional Services Azure services are always available from any Azure region and can cope with zone-wide and regional outages.

Azure Load Balancer supports availability zones. By aligning resources and distribution across zones, you can increase availability across business applications through the standard load balancer.

Build and Configure an Azure Load Balancer (Including Cross-Region)

Before we create and configure Azure Load Balancer, we'll discuss its features.

In addition to load balancing, Azure Load Balancer is equipped with outbound connection, automatic reconfiguration, application-agnostic and transparent, health probes, and port forwarding features.

Load Balancing   With Azure load balancing, a five-tuple hash contains source IP, source port, destination IP, destination port, and protocol.

Outbound Connection   A front-end IP of the load balancer can be translated for all outgoing flows from a private IP address inside your virtual network to public IP addresses on the Internet.

Automatic Reconfiguration   Load balancers can adjust their configurations based on conditions when they increase or decrease instances. The load balancer will reconfigure itself automatically if additional virtual machines are added to the back-end pool.

Application Agnostic and Transparent   TCP and UDP are not directly impacted. URLs and multisite hosting can be used to route traffic.

Health Probe   The health probe stops routing traffic to any failed virtual machines it detects in the back-end pool's load balancer. Instances in the back-end pool can be monitored with a health probe.

Port Forwarding   The load balancer supports port forwarding so that you don't have to attach public IP addresses to each web server in the pool.

Figure 6.15 is a high-level building block view of the result of the procedure we described for building and configuring the public load balancer using a standard load balancer SKU.

Azure Load Balancer is built and configured via Azure PowerShell.

Begin by creating a virtual network, network security group, and bastion host, as shown in the following code:

What is Azure Bastion?

With Azure Bastion, you can connect to a virtual machine from your browser via Azure portals. You can provision within your virtual networks using a fully platform-managed PaaS service. Connect to virtual machines over TLS using the Remote Desktop Protocol (RDP)/ Secure Socket Shell (SSH). You can connect to Azure Bastion without a public IP address, agent, or special client software.

FIGURE 6.15 Load balancer building block

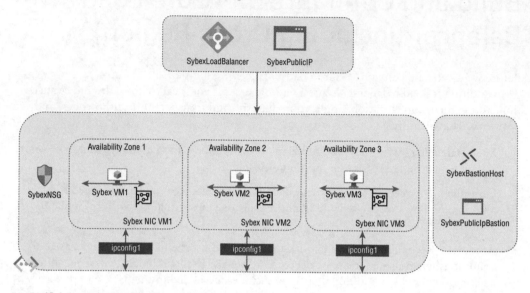

```
## Build backend subnet config ##
$subnet = @{
    Name = 'SybexBackendSubnet'
    AddressPrefix = '10.2.0.0/24'
}
$subnetConfig = New-AzVirtualNetworkSubnetConfig @subnet
## Build Azure Bastion subnet. ##
$bastsubnet = @{
    Name = 'AzureBastionSubnet'
    AddressPrefix = '10.2.1.0/24'
}
$bastsubnetConfig = New-AzVirtualNetworkSubnetConfig @bastsubnet
## Build the virtual network ##
$net = @{
    Name = 'sybexVNet'
    ResourceGroupName = 'CreatePubLBQS-rg'
    Location = 'UAENorth'
    AddressPrefix = '10.2.0.0/16'
    Subnet = $subnetConfig,$bastsubnetConfig
}
```

```
$vnet = New-AzVirtualNetwork @net
## Build public IP address for bastion host. ##
$ip = @{
    Name = 'sybexBastionIP'
    ResourceGroupName = 'PubLBQS-rg'
    Location = 'UAENorth'
    Sku = 'Standard'
    AllocationMethod = 'Static'
}
$publicip = New-AzPublicIpAddress @ip
## Build bastion host ##
$bastion = @{
    ResourceGroupName = 'PubLBQS-rg'
    Name = 'sybexBastion'
    PublicIpAddress = $publicip
    VirtualNetwork = $vnet
}
New-AzBastion @bastion -AsJob
## Build rule for network security group ##
$nsgrule = @{
    Name = 'sybexNSGRuleHTTP'
    Description = 'Allow HTTP'
    Protocol = '*'
    SourcePortRange = '*'
    DestinationPortRange = '80'
    SourceAddressPrefix = 'Internet'
    DestinationAddressPrefix = '*'
    Access = 'Allow'
    Priority = '2000'
    Direction = 'Inbound'
}
$rule1 = New-AzNetworkSecurityRuleConfig @nsgrule
## Build network security group ##
$nsg = @{
    Name = 'sybexNSG'
    ResourceGroupName = 'PubLBQS-rg'
    Location = 'UAENorth'
    SecurityRules = $rule1
}
New-AzNetworkSecurityGroup @nsg
```

Next, create the three virtual machines for the back-end pool of the load balancer, as shown in the following code. This code lets you:

- Initiate three network interfaces using the PowerShell cmdlet `New-AzNetworkInterface`.
- Set an administrator username and password for the VMs with the PowerShell cmdlet `Get-Credential`.
- Initiate the virtual machines with the following PowerShell cmdlets:
  - `New-AzVM`
  - `New-AzVMConfig`
  - `Set-AzVMOperatingSystem`
  - `Set-AzVMSourceImage`
  - `Add-AzVMNetworkInterface`

```powershell
# Create the administrator and password for the VMs. ##
$cred = Get-Credential
## Put the virtual network into a variable. ##
$vnet = Get-AzVirtualNetwork -Name 'SybexVNet' -ResourceGroupName 'PubLBQS-rg'
## Place the load balancer into a variable. ##
$lb = @{
    Name = 'sybexLoadBalancer'
    ResourceGroupName = 'PubLBQS-rg'
}
$bepool = Get-AzLoadBalancer @lb  | Get-AzLoadBalancerBackendAddressPoolConfig

## Place the network security group into a variable. ##
$nsg = Get-AzNetworkSecurityGroup -Name 'sybexNSG'
-ResourceGroupName 'PubLBQS-rg'

## For loop with variable to create VM for load balancer backend pool. ##
for ($i=1; $i -le 3; $i++)
{
## Command to create network interface for VMs ##
$nic = @{
    Name = "sybexNicVM$i"
    ResourceGroupName = 'PubLBQS-rg'
    Location = 'UAENorth'
    Subnet = $vnet.Subnets[0]
    NetworkSecurityGroup = $nsg
    LoadBalancerBackendAddressPool = $bepool
}
```

```
$nicVM = New-AzNetworkInterface @nic

## Create a virtual machine configuration for VMs ##
$vmsz = @{
    VMName = "sybexVM$i"
    VMSize = 'Standard_DS1_v2'
}
$vmos = @{
    ComputerName = "sybexVM$i"
    Credential = $cred
}
$vmimage = @{
    PublisherName = 'MicrosoftWindowsServer'
    Offer = 'WindowsServer'
    Skus = '2019-Datacenter'
    Version = 'latest'
}
$vmConfig = New-AzVMConfig @vmsz `
    | Set-AzVMOperatingSystem @vmos -Windows `
    | Set-AzVMSourceImage @vmimage `
    | Add-AzVMNetworkInterface -Id $nicVM.Id

## Create the virtual machine for VMs ##
$vm = @{
    ResourceGroupName = 'PubLBQS-rg'
    Location = 'UAENorth'
    VM = $vmConfig
    Zone = "$i"
}
New-AzVM @vm -AsJob
}
```

Create the outbound rule that configures source network address translation (SNAT) for VMs in the back-end pool.

In Azure, VMs that do not have a public IP address or that are part of an internal basic load balancer pool receive an outbound access IP address. An outbound IP address that cannot be customized is provided by default.

When a public IP address is assigned to the VM or when the VM is placed in the back-end pool of a standard load balancer with or without outbound rules, the default outbound access IP address is disabled. In case an Azure VNet NAT gateway resource is assigned to the subnet of the VM, the default outbound access IP address is disabled.

By default, outbound access is not enabled for VMs created by virtual machine scale sets in Flexible orchestration mode. (One of the main advantages of Flexible orchestration is that it provides orchestration features over standard Azure IaaS VMs, rather than scale set child virtual machines. With Flexible orchestration, you can use all the standard VM APIs, not just the ones you use with Uniform orchestration.)

You can connect to a VM's public IP address from the Internet. Use Get-AzPublicIpAddress to return the public IP address of a VM. Here is an example of how to retrieve the public IP address of the SybexVM1 VM:

```
Get-AzPublicIpAddress `
  -Name SybexVM1 `
  -ResourceGroupName SybexRG | Select IpAddress
```

Azure's outbound connectivity to the Internet can be configured as shown in Table 6.5.

TABLE 6.5   Azure outbound connectivity

Method	Type of port allocation	Production-grade?
Via the front-end IP address(s) of a load balancer for outbound via outbound rules	Static, explicit	Yes, but not at scale
Attaching a NAT gateway to the subnet	Static, explicit	Yes
Allocating a public IP address to the virtual machine	Static, explicit	Yes

Now create the public standard address using the following PowerShell cmdlet.

- New-AzPublicIpAddress to create a public IP address:

```
$publicip = @{
    Name = 'SybexPublicIP'
    ResourceGroupName = 'PubLBQS-rg'
    Location = 'UAENorth'
    Sku = 'Standard'
    AllocationMethod = 'static'
    Zone = 1,2,3
}
New-AzPublicIpAddress @publicip
```

- New-AzPublicIpAddress to assign a zonal public IP address in zone 1:

```
$publicip = @{
    Name = 'SybexPublicIP'
```

```
            ResourceGroupName = 'PubLBQS-rg'
            Location = 'UAENorth'
            Sku = 'Standard'
            AllocationMethod = 'static'
            Zone = 1
        }
        New-AzPublicIpAddress @publicip
```

Next, create the public standard load balancer. The load balancer should be built and configured with the following components:

- For the front-end IP pool, use `New-AzLoadBalancerFrontendIpConfig`. Through this IP address, the load balancer receives incoming traffic.

- Build a back-end address pool using `New-AzLoadBalancerBackendAddressPoolConfig` for traffic sent from the load balancer's front-end.

- Use `Add-AzLoadBalancerProbeConfig` to detect the health of back-end VM instances.

- Use `Add-AzLoadBalancerRuleConfig` to define how traffic will be distributed to the VMs with a load balancer rule.

- Using `New-AzLoadBalancer`, create a public load balancer.

The following code shows how this is done:

```
## put public IP deployed in previous steps into variable. ##
$publicIp = Get-AzPublicIpAddress -Name 'SybexPublicIP'
-ResourceGroupName 'PubLBQS-rg'
## Build load balancer frontend configuration and keep in variable. ##
$feip = New-AzLoadBalancerFrontendIpConfig -Name 'sybexFrontEnd'
-PublicIpAddress $publicIp
## Build backend address pool configuration and keep in variable. ##
$bepool = New-AzLoadBalancerBackendAddressPoolConfig -Name 'sybexBackEndPool'
## Build the health probe and keep in variable. ##
$probe = @{
    Name = 'sybexHealthProbe'
    Protocol = 'http'
    Port = '8080'
    IntervalInSeconds = '600'
    ProbeCount = '3'
    RequestPath = '/'
}
$healthprobe = New-AzLoadBalancerProbeConfig @probe
## Build the load balancer rule and keep in variable. ##
$lbrule = @{
    Name = 'sybexHTTPRule'
```

```
    Protocol = 'tcp'
    FrontendPort = '8080'
    BackendPort = '8080'
    IdleTimeoutInMinutes = '10'
    FrontendIpConfiguration = $feip
    BackendAddressPool = $bePool
}
$rule = New-AzLoadBalancerRuleConfig @lbrule -EnableTcpReset
-DisableOutboundSNAT
## Build the load balancer resource. ##
$loadbalancer = @{
    ResourceGroupName = 'PubLBQS-rg'
    Name = 'sybexLoadBalancer'
    Location = 'UAENorth'
    Sku = 'Standard'
    FrontendIpConfiguration = $feip
    BackendAddressPool = $bePool
    LoadBalancingRule = $rule
    Probe = $healthprobe
}
New-AzLoadBalancer @loadbalancer
```

Now you'll install the targeted roles. You can install a custom script extension by using `Set-AzVMExtension`. For example, it installs the IIS web server using the PowerShell command `Add-WindowsFeature Web-Server` and updates the `default.htm` page to show the hostname of the VM.

Now you just need to ensure that the previous steps of this VM deployment have been completed by using `Get-Job` to check the status of the VM deployment jobs.

Use the `Get-Job` cmdlet to retrieve objects representing the background jobs that have been started during the current session. The `Get-Job` cmdlet can retrieve jobs started using the `Start-Job` cmdlet or the `AsJob` parameter of any cmdlet.

```
## Install a script extension using a for loop with a variable. ##
for ($i=1; $i -le 3; $i++)
{
$ext = @{
    Publisher = 'Microsoft.Compute'
    ExtensionType = 'CustomScriptExtension'
    ExtensionName = 'IIS'
    ResourceGroupName = 'PubLBQS-rg'
    VMName = "SybexVM$i"
    Location = 'UAENorth'
```

```
    TypeHandlerVersion = '1.8'
    SettingString = '{"commandToExecute":"powershell Add-WindowsFeature
Web-Server; powershell Add-Content
-Path \"C:\\inetpub\\wwwroot\\Default.htm\"
-Value $($env:computername)"}'
}
Set-AzVMExtension @ext -AsJob
}
```

Finally, let's test and verify the load balancer. Find the load balancer's public IP address by using `Get-AzPublicIPAddress`:

```
$ip = @{
    ResourceGroupName = 'PubLBQS-rg'
    Name = 'SybexPublicIP'
}
Get-AzPublicIPAddress @ip | select IpAddress
```

To verify and validate the load balancer setup, copy the public IP address and paste it into the address bar. A default page will be displayed.

Customers can force-refresh the web browser on their client machine to view the load balancer distributing traffic across all three VMs.

Build and Configure Cross-Region Load Balancer Resources

The Azure Standard Load Balancer features cross-region load balancing, with these benefits:

- The ability to have multiple regions responsible for incoming traffic
- Immediate failover to the best regional deployment
- The ability to distribute loads across regions with the lowest possible latency to the nearest Azure region
- Scalability through multiple endpoints
- A static IP address for anycast
- The preservation of client IP addresses
- Reliance on an existing load balancing system with no learning curve

As of this writing, the cross-region load balancer is currently in preview and has the following limitations:

- Configurations of cross-regional front-end IP addresses are public only. Internal front-ends are not available at present.
- A private or internal load balancer cannot be added to the back-end pool of a cross-region load balancer.

- Configurations of cross-region IPv6 front-end IP addresses are not supported.

- On cross-region load balancers, UDP traffic is not supported.

- It is currently not possible to configure a health probe. Every 20 seconds, the default health probe automatically collects availability information about the regional load balancer.

- There is no integration with Azure Kubernetes Service (AKS). Connectivity will be lost if the AKS cluster is deployed in the back-end with a cross-region load balancer.

- The preview version is not recommended for production workloads because it does not have a service level agreement (SLA).

Service is available globally across multiple Azure regions with a cross-region load balancer. Traffic is routed to the next closest healthy load balancer if a load balancer fails.

Load Balancer's front-end IP address is static and advertised across regions in most Azure regions. Load balancing rules on cross-regional load balancers should match the inbound NAT rules on regional standard load balancers in terms of their back-end ports. Figure 6.16 shows a cross-regional load balancer.

FIGURE 6.16   Cross-regional load balancer

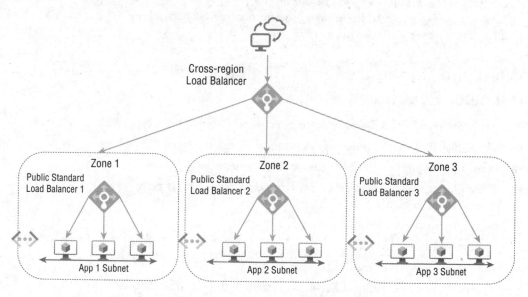

You can create regional redundancy by adding a global front-end public IP address to your organization's load balancers. When a regional load balancer fails, traffic is routed to the closest healthy region.

Health probes of cross-region load balancers collect availability information every 20 seconds. Cross-region load balancers will detect a failure if a regional load balancer becomes unavailable. At that point, the regional load balancer is removed from the rotation.

The Azure cross-region load balancer uses a geo-proximity load balancing algorithm to determine traffic routing. If multiple regional load balancers are used for geo-proximity, the final routing decision is made based on the load distribution mode of the regional load balancers.

You can add or remove regional deployments behind a global endpoint of a cross-region load balancer without interruption if they expose the global endpoint of the load balancer to customers. The public IP address of the cross-region load balancer remains the same.

The cross-regional load balancer is a Layer 4 pass-through network load balancer. The packet's original IP address is preserved during this pass-through, and the code running in the virtual machine has access to the original IP address. As a result, IP address-specific logic can be applied.

The rest of this section explains the process for configuring a public load balancer using a standard load balancer SKU. In this example, resources are built to support the cross-region load balancer and the Azure load balancer is built and configured via Azure PowerShell.

First, create a cross-region load balancer as detailed next. You will need a global standard SKU public IP address to manage cross-region load balancing:

- Generate the public IP address with `New-AzPublicIpAddress`.

- With `New-AzLoadBalancerFrontendIpConfig`, configure the front-end IP address.

- Use the `New-AzLoadBalancerBackendAddressPoolConfig` command to build an address pool for the back-end.

- With `Add-AzLoadBalancerRuleConfig`, you can create a load balancer rule.

- Implement a cross-region load balancer using `New-AzLoadBalancer`.

```
## Build global IP address for load balancer ##
$ip = @{
    Name = 'SybexPublicIP-CR'
    ResourceGroupName = 'SybexResourceGroupLB-CR'
    Location = 'UAENorth'
    Sku = 'Standard'
    Tier = 'Global'
    AllocationMethod = 'Static'
}
$publicIP = New-AzPublicIpAddress @ip
## Build frontend configuration ##
$fe = @{
    Name = 'SybexFrontEndCR'
    PublicIpAddress = $publicIP
}
```

```
$feip = New-AzLoadBalancerFrontendIpConfig @fe
## Build back-end address pool ##
$be = @{
    Name = 'sybexBackEndPool-CR'
}
$bepool = New-AzLoadBalancerBackendAddressPoolConfig @be
## Build the load balancer rule ##
$rul = @{
    Name = 'SybexHTTPRule-CR'
    Protocol = 'tcp'
    FrontendPort = '80'
    BackendPort = '80'
    FrontendIpConfiguration = $feip
    BackendAddressPool = $bepool
}
$rule = New-AzLoadBalancerRuleConfig @rul
## Build cross-region load balancer resource ##
$lbp = @{
    ResourceGroupName = 'sybexResourceGroupLBCR'
    Name = 'SybexLoadBalancerCR'
    Location = 'UAENorth'
    Sku = 'Standard'
    Tier = 'Global'
    FrontendIpConfiguration = $feip
    BackendAddressPool = $bepool
    LoadBalancingRule = $rule
}
$lb = New-AzLoadBalancer @lbp
```

Next, you'll configure a back-end pool, adding two regional standard load balancers to the cross-region load balancer's back-end pool:

- For regional load balancer information, use `Get-AzLoadBalancer` and `Get-AzLoadBalancerFrontendIpConfig`.

- `New-AzLoadBalancerBackendAddressConfig` is used to configure the load balancer's pool of back-end addresses.

- Add the regional load balancer front-end address pool to the cross-region back-end pool using `Set-AzLoadBalancerBackendAddressPool`.

```
## Keep the region 1 load balancer configuration in a variable ##
$region1 = @{
    Name = 'sybexLoadBalancer-R1'
    ResourceGroupName = 'PubLBQS-rg-r1'
}
```

```
$R1 = Get-AzLoadBalancer @region1
## Keep the region 2 load balancer configuration in a variable ##
$region2 = @{
    Name = 'sybexLoadBalancer-R2'
    ResourceGroupName = 'PubLBQS-rg-r2'
}
$R2 = Get-AzLoadBalancer @region2
## Keep the region 1 load balancer front-end configuration in a variable ##
$region1fe = @{
    Name = 'sybexFrontEnd-R1'
    LoadBalancer = $R1
}
$R1FE = Get-AzLoadBalancerFrontendIpConfig @region1fe
## Keep the region 2 load balancer front-end configuration in a variable ##
$region2fe = @{
    Name = 'sybexFrontEnd-R2'
    LoadBalancer = $R2
}
$R2FE = Get-AzLoadBalancerFrontendIpConfig @region2fe
## Build the cross-region backend address pool configuration for region 1 ##
$region1ap = @{
    Name = 'sybexBackendPoolConfig-R1'
    LoadBalancerFrontendIPConfigurationId = $R1FE.Id
}
$beaddressconfigR1 = New-AzLoadBalancerBackendAddressConfig @region1ap
## Build the cross-region backend address pool configuration for region 2 ##
$region2ap = @{
    Name = 'sybexBackendPoolConfig-R2'
    LoadBalancerFrontendIPConfigurationId = $R2FE.Id
}
$beaddressconfigR2 = New-AzLoadBalancerBackendAddressConfig @region2ap
## Attach the backend address pool config for the cross-region load
balancer ##
$bepoolcr = @{
    ResourceGroupName = 'sybexResourceGroupLB-CR'
    LoadBalancerName = 'sybexLoadBalancer-CR'
    Name = 'sybexBackEndPool-CR'
    LoadBalancerBackendAddress = $beaddressconfigR1,$beaddressconfigR2
}
Set-AzLoadBalancerBackendAddressPool @bepoolcr
```

Now, let's test and verify the cross-region load balancer at a very high level with the following approach. Connect to the public IP address in a web browser. Then, stop the virtual machines in one of the regional load balancer back-end pools and observe the failover.

Find the load balancer's public IP address using `Get-AzPublicIPAddress`:

```
$ip = @{
    ResourceGroupName = 'sybexResourceGroupLB-CR'
    LoadBalancerName = 'sybexLoadBalancer-CR'
}
Get-AzPublicIPAddress @ip | select IpAddress
```

Copy the public address and paste it into the address bar to verify and validate the load balancer setup. A default page will be displayed.

The next step is to stop the virtual machines in one of the load balancers' back-end pools. Refresh the web browser and observe how the connection to the other load balancer is failed over to.

Deploy a Load Balancing Rule

Azure Load Balancers distribute incoming traffic among healthy virtual machine instances as a Layer 4 service. The distribution algorithm used by load balancers is based on hashing. As a default, it maps traffic to available servers using a 5-tuple hash (source IP, source port, destination IP, destination port, protocol type). Load balancers can either be Internet-facing and accessible via public IP addresses or internally accessible via a virtual network only. In addition to network address translation (NAT), Azure Load Balancers support traffic routing between public and private IP addresses.

With Load Balancer, traffic can be configured according to rules. This section shows how to configure Azure load balancing rules.

The following are the type of rules for the Azure Load Balancer:

Load Balancing Rules   Load balancing rules are used to distribute incoming traffic to all instances in the back-end pool. In load balancing, an IP address and port on the front-end are mapped to several IP addresses and ports on the back-end. An example of a rule is defining how web traffic is load-balanced on port 80.

High Availability Ports   High availability ports are set to all protocols and port 0 in a load balancer rule. A single rule can be used to load-balance all TCP and UDP traffic arriving on all ports of a standard internal load balancer. Load balancing rules in the HA port help you create scalable and highly available network virtual appliances (NVAs) in virtual networks. This feature is useful when large numbers of ports must be load-balanced.

Inbound NAT Rule   As a result of using the inbound NAT rule, incoming traffic is forwarded to the front-end IP address and port combination. Traffic is directed to a specific virtual machine or instance in the back-end pool. This hash-based distribution also performs port forwarding and load balancing.

Outbound Rules   The outbound rules configure NAT for all VMs or instances in the back-end pool. Enabling this rule lets instances in the back-end communicate (outbound) with the Internet.

In Exercise 6.5 you build a load balancing rule that distributes incoming traffic sent to a specified IP address and port combination across instances in a back-end pool. The health probe only sends new traffic to instances deemed healthy by the probe.

The load balancing rules section of the health probes page of the load balancer can be found under Settings.

EXERCISE 6.5

Configure Azure Load Balancing Rules via the Azure Portal

1. Log into a personal or business account in the Azure portal at `https://portal.azure.com`.

2. Search for load balancers and select your load balancer.

3. Select Load Balancing Rules in Settings on the load balancing page.

4. Click Add In Load Balancing Rules to add a rule.

   Enter the following information on the Add Load Balancing Rule page (see the following table for the list).

Item	Description	Value
Name	The load balancing rule should have a unique name.	SybexLB01Rule
IP Version	Choose either IPv4 or Ipv6.	Ipv4 or Ipv6
Front-end IP Address	Enter the existing IP address of the load balancer that is visible to the public.	Choose the front-end IP address of the load balancer.
Back-end Pool	Choose a back-end pool already existing. Load-balanced traffic for this rule will be directed to the virtual machines in this back-end pool.	Choose the back-end pool of the load balancer.
Protocol	Choose either the TCP or UDP protocol.	Keep it default TCP.
Port	Load balancing rules require a port number. By default, port 80 is used.	Enter **80**.

Backend Port	By default, clients communicate with the load balancer using port 80. However, you can select a different port to route traffic to the VMs in the back-end pool.	Enter **80**.
Health Probe	A health probe can be selected or created. Using the health probe, the load balancing rule determines which VMs in the back-end pool are healthy and can therefore receive load-balanced traffic.	Choose Create new. In Name, enter **SybexHealthProbe**. Choose HTTP in Protocol. Leave the rest at the defaults or tailor to your requirements. Click OK.
Session Persistence	You can choose None, Client IP, or Client IP and protocol. Sessions persist when the same virtual machine handles client traffic from the back-end pool for the session duration. None: Allows any virtual machine to handle successive requests from the same client. Client IP address: Specifies that the same virtual machine will handle consecutive requests from the same IP address. Client IP address and protocol: The same virtual machine will be assigned to successive requests from the same client IP address and protocol combination.	Choose None or organization required persistence.
Idle Timeout (minutes)	Set the time for a TCP or HTTP connection to remain active without relying on clients to send keep-alive messages. Idle timeouts are set by default to 4 minutes, the minimum setting, and up to 30 minutes can be set.	By Default, 4 or move the slider to organization required idle timeout.
TCP Reset		Choose Enabled.

| Floating IP | Select either Disabled or Enabled. The VM instances' IP address is exposed for ease of use (with Floating IP disabled). Floating IP allows additional flexibility by mapping IP addresses to the Frontend IP of the load balancer when enabled. | Use the default, Disabled, or select Enabled if your deployment requires floating IP. |
| Outbound Source Network Address Translation (SNAT) | | Use the default, (Recommended) Use outbound rules to provide back-end pool members access to the Internet. |

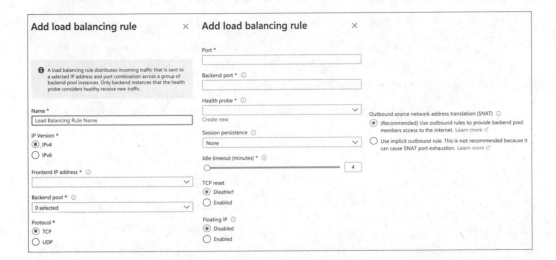

5. After providing the information, click Add Load Balancing Rule.

Load balancing rules in Azure can be reduced by enabling floating IP. When floating IP is enabled, Azure changes the IP address mapping to the front-end IP address of the load balancer front-end rather than the back-end IP address.

VM instances' IP addresses are exposed without floating IP. With floating IP enabled, the front-end IP of the load balancer changes to the IP address mapping of the load balancer.

Build and Configure Inbound NAT Rules

Connections to the back-end pool are routed via inbound NAT rules. Through an inbound NAT rule, incoming traffic directed to a specific IP address and port combination is forwarded to a virtual machine.

Follow the steps in Exercise 6.6 to configure Azure load balancing inbound NAT rules via the Azure portal.

EXERCISE 6.6

Configure Azure Load Balancing Inbound NAT Rules via the Azure Portal

1. Log into a personal or business account in the Azure portal at `https://portal.azure.com`.

2. Search for load balancers and select your load balancer.

3. Select Add In Load Balancing NAT Rule to add a rule.

   Enter the following information on the Add inbound NAT rule page (see the following table for the list):

Name	Provide a name for the NAT rule for VM.
Frontend IP Address	Choose LoadBalancerFrontend.
Service	Choose Custom.
Protocol	Use the default value: TCP.
Idle Timeout (Minutes)	Enter or choose **15**.
TCP Reset	Click Enabled.
Port	Enter **221**.
Target Virtual Machine	Choose, for example, SybexVM1.
Network IP Configuration	Choose ipconfig1 (10.1.0.4).
Port Mapping	Choose Custom.
Floating IP	By default, Disabled.
Target Port	Provide **22**.

Add inbound NAT rule

TEST

ℹ️ An inbound NAT rule forwards incoming traffic sent to a selected
IP address and port combination to a specific virtual machine.

Name *

[Inbound NAT Rule name]

Frontend IP address * ⓘ

[⌄]

IP Version ⓘ

IPv4

Service *

[Custom ⌄]

Protocol

◉ TCP ○ UDP

Idle timeout (minutes) ⓘ

[●━━━━━━━━━━━━━━━━━━━━━━━━━━━━] [4]

Max: 30

TCP Reset ⓘ

○ Enabled ◉ Disabled

Port *

[ ]

Target virtual machine

[None ⌄]

Port mapping ⓘ

◉ Default ○ Custom

[Add]

4. After providing the preceding information, click Add Inbound NAT Rule.

Build Explicit Outbound Rules for a Load Balancer

A public standard load balancer allows you to define SNAT explicitly. You can configure SNAT to provide outbound Internet connectivity for your organization's back-end instances to the load balancer's public IP addresses.

A public standard load balancer allows organizations to define source network address translation (SNAT) explicitly. You can configure this to provide outbound Internet connectivity for your organization's back-end instances to the load balancer's public IP addresses.

SNAT ports are allocated from front-end IP addresses to a back-end pool for outbound connections to the Internet by an outbound rule. The exact syntax applies outbound rules to load balancing and inbound NAT:

Front-end + parameters + back-end pool

By configuring an outbound rule, you ensure that all VMs identified by the back-end pool are translated to the front-end using outbound NAT. The outbound NAT algorithm can be fine-tuned even further with parameters.

A front-end that provides an additional IP address supplies 64,000 ephemeral ports the load balancer can use as SNAT ports.

A TCP connection can be kept open for a specified number of minutes. The idle timeout value must be the same when multiple outbound rules reference the same back-end pool or the same back-end IP configuration.

Outbound rules provide a configuration parameter that controls the idle timeout for outbound flows. The default value is 4 minutes.

- Outbound rules must last at least 4 minutes but no more than 100 minutes.

- Load balancer rules and inbound NAT rules have a minimum of 4 minutes to a maximum of 30 minutes.

The default behavior of a load balancer, when the outbound idle timeout is reached, is to drop the flow silently. Use the `enableTCPReset` parameter to enable predictable application behavior and control.

Let's get more insight into TCP Reset. With a standard load balancer, you can enable TCP Reset On Idle for a given rule to create more predictable application behavior. By default, the load balancer silently drops flows when the idle timeout of a flow is reached. The load balancer will send bidirectional TCP Resets (TCP RST packets) on idle timeout. If your application endpoints need to establish a new connection, this will let them know the connection has timed out.

Inbound NAT rules, load balancing rules, and outbound rules can all be configured to send TCP Resets on idle timeout. If enabled per rule, load balancer sends bidirectional TCP Reset packets to both client and server endpoints at idle timeout for all matching flows.

If the outbound idle timeout is reached, the parameter controls send bidirectional TCP Reset (TCP RST).

Outbound rules can be applied to the following scenarios:

- Create outbound connections to a specific set of public IPs or prefixes.

- Change SNAT port allocations.

- Only allow outbound connections.

- Only allow outbound NAT within VMs (no inbound).

- Internal load balancers can only use outbound NAT.

- A public standard load balancer should support both TCP and UDP protocols for outbound NAT.

Exercise 6.7 walks you through the steps to configure Azure load balancing outbound rules via the Azure portal.

EXERCISE 6.7

Configure Azure Load Balancing Outbound Rules via the Azure Portal

1. Log into a personal or business account in the Azure portal at `https://portal.azure.com`.

2. Search for load balancers and select your load balancer.

3. Select Add In Load Balancing Outbound Rule to add a rule. Enter the following information on the Add outbound NAT rule page:

Setting	Value for Example.
Name	Provide the name for the outbound rule for VMs.
IP Version	Choose either IPv4 or IPv6.
Frontend IP Address	Choose LoadBalancerFrontend.
Protocol	Select All for this example.
Idle Timeout (Minutes)	Keep the default of 4.
TCP Reset	Click Enabled.
Port Allocation	From the drop-down, choose Manually Choose Number Of Outbound Ports.

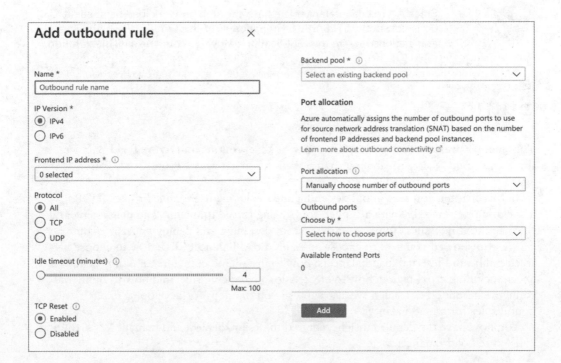

EXERCISE 6.7 *(continued)*

Here are a few limitations to consider:

- Each front-end IP address is allowed to have a maximum of 64,000 ephemeral ports.

- Outbound idle timeout is configurable between 4 and 120 minutes (240 and 7200 seconds).

- For outbound NAT, the load balancer does not support ICMP.

- A NIC's primary IP configuration is the only one that can be used for outbound rules. A VM or NVA cannot have an outbound rule for its secondary IP, and multiple NICs can be used.

- The back-end pool must contain all virtual machines in an availability set that requires outbound connectivity.

- Connectivity outbound must be provided by all virtual machines within a virtual machine scale set.

- Back-end pools should have the maximum number of instances, and you cannot increase these instances beyond this number. There are fewer ports per instance when instances increase unless you add more front-end IP addresses.

 Since Azure Load Balancer is a pass-through network load balancer, it does not support TLS/SSL termination as of this writing. If your business applications require this, application gateways could be a viable solution.

Summary

This chapter presented a high-level overview of VNet routing and Azure Load Balancer in the Azure cloud. You learned about Azure application gateways, Front Door, Traffic Manager Profile, and Azure Virtual NAT.

In this chapter, you read about designing and deploying user-defined routes (UDRs), associating a route table with a subnet, configuring forced tunneling, and diagnosing and resolving routing issues. You also learned about designing and deploying Azure Route Server.

We also showed you how to choose an Azure Load Balancer SKU; how to choose between public and internal load balancers; how to install and configure an Azure Load Balancer, including cross-region; how to create a load balancing rule; and how to build and configure inbound NAT rules. We also showed you the steps for developing explicit outbound rules for a load balancer.

You now have the detailed insight required to design, deploy, and manage VNet routing and Azure Load Balancer.

Exam Essentials

Know how to design and implement user-defined routes (UDRs).   To override Azure's default system routes or to add more routes to a subnet's route table, you can create custom or user-defined (static) routes in Azure. You create a route table in Azure, then associate it with zero or more virtual networks.

You can now specify a service tag as the address prefix for a user-defined route as an alternative to explicitly setting an IP range. A service tag represents a group of IP address prefixes from a given Azure service. Service tags are managed by Microsoft and updated as address prefixes change.

Know how to associate a route table with a subnet.   Azure automatically routes traffic between Azure subnets, virtual networks, and on-premises networks. The easiest way to change Azure's default routing is to create a route table.

A route table can also be associated with a subnet, and subnets can be associated with a route table. Since route tables are not associated with virtual networks, you must associate each route table with the subnet you want it associated with. A route table can only be associated with subnets in virtual networks in the same Azure subscription and location as the route table.

Understand how to configure forced tunneling.   You can use forced tunneling to send all Internet-bound traffic via a site-to-site VPN tunnel back to your on-premises location for inspection and auditing. This is a critical requirement for many enterprise IT policies. You will not be able to inspect or audit your Internet-bound traffic if you do not configure forced tunneling from Azure VMs to the Internet. Information disclosure and other security breaches may result from unauthorized Internet access.

Forced tunneling can be configured using Azure PowerShell, but not through the Azure portal.

Know how to design and implement Azure Route Server.   Your network virtual appliance (NVA) and virtual network can be dynamically routed using Azure Route Server. The Azure Software-Defined Network (SDN) in the Azure VNET allows you to exchange routing information directly through the Border Gateway Protocol (BGP) routing protocol without the need to configure or maintain route tables manually. Azure Route Server is a fully managed service configured with high availability.

Configuring, managing, and deploying your virtual network's NVA is easier with Azure Route Server.

Know how to select an Azure Load Balancer SKU (Basic versus Standard).   The Azure Load Balancer has three SKUs: Basic, Standard, and Gateway. The SKUs cater to specific scenarios and have varying scale, features, and pricing.

The Azure Load Balancer is equipped with load balancing capabilities for dealing with high latency and performance requirements at the Network layer. It enhances resilience by routing traffic between regions and availability zones.

The Azure Load Balancer is suitable for small-scale applications that do not require high availability or redundancy. Zones are not supported.

Understand how to build and configure an Azure Load Balancer (including cross-region).   Distributing load (incoming network traffic) among a set of back-end resources or servers is referred to as load balancing.

In the Open Systems Interconnection (OSI) model, Azure Load Balancer operates on Layer 4. For clients, this is the single interface.

Azure offers fully managed solutions for load balancing. The standard load balancer is open to the Internet by default based on the zero-trust network security model.

Load balancing with Azure Standard Load Balancer enables geo-redundant high availability.

Know how to deploy and configure inbound NAT rules.   An inbound NAT rule forwards load balancer front-end traffic to one or more instances in the back-end pool.

NAT rules can be of two types:

Single Virtual Machine   A NAT rule that targets a single machine in the load balancer's back-end pool

Multiple Virtual Machines   An inbound NAT rule that targets multiple virtual machines in the load balancer's back-end pool

Know how to deploy explicit outbound rules for a load balancer.   For a public standard load balancer, outbound rules can be used to configure SNAT (source network address translation). Using this configuration, you will be able to provide outbound Internet connectivity for your back-end instances using the public IP(s) assigned to your load balancer. It allows:

- IP masked traffic
- Simplified allow lists
- Fewer public IP resources for deployment

Review Questions

1. From a user-defined route perspective, which of the following statements is valid?

   A. The maximum number of user-defined routes per route table is 400, and the maximum number of user-defined routes per table is 200 for Azure subscriptions.

   B. The maximum number of user-defined routes per route table is 200, and the maximum number of user-defined routes per table is 400 for Azure subscriptions.

   C. The maximum number of user-defined routes per route table is 300, and the maximum number of user-defined routes per table is 600 for Azure subscriptions.

   D. The maximum number of user-defined routes per route table is 400, and the maximum number of user-defined routes per table is 300 for Azure subscriptions.

2. What must be enabled for network interfaces to receive and forward traffic?

   A. IP forwarding

   B. Virtual appliance

   C. User defined routes

   D. Virtual Gateway

3. What is preferred when multiple routes are present in a UDR route table?

   A. More specific routes

   B. Azure virtual appliances

   C. User-defined routes

   D. Azure Route Server

4. What happens if a route table is not associated with the gateway subnet of the organization's virtual network connected to the Azure VPN gateway?

   A. The gateway will function properly.

   B. The virtual appliance will not function properly.

   C. The gateway will not function properly.

   D. The virtual appliance will function properly.

5. Which of the following can you use so that forced tunneling will redirect or force all Internet traffic back to their on-premises location?

   A. Site-to-site VPN tunnel

   B. Point-to-point VPN Tunnel

   C. Client VPN

   D. Forced VPN tunnel

6.   From a Network Watcher perspective, which of the following statements is valid?

   A.   Using Network Watcher, you can determine the routing, filtering, and operating system causes of outbound communication problems.

   B.   Using Network Watcher, you cannot determine the routing, filtering, and operating system causes of outbound communication problems.

   C.   Using Network Monitor, you cannot determine the routing, filtering, and operating system causes of outbound communication problems.

   D.   None of the above.

7.   What does Azure Route Server support?

   A.   Redundancy within a region

   B.   Geo-replication across multiple regions

   C.   Zone redundancy

   D.   Regional and global

8.   A secure web application experiences a lot of traffic, and the engineer would like to distribute the workload using a load balancer. Is there a load balancer that can handle this traffic?

   A.   Azure Load Balancer

   B.   Azure Front Door

   C.   Both A and B

   D.   None of the above

9.   Which type of load balancing service distributes traffic between virtual machines within a virtual network?

   A.   Global

   B.   Regional

   C.   Both A and B

   D.   Zonal

10.   Which of the following services offers DNS-based load balancers that provide high availability and responsiveness for traffic distributed across many Azure regions?

   A.   Azure Load Balancer

   B.   Azure Traffic Manager

   C.   Azure Application Gateway

   D.   Azure Front Door

11.   Which of the following services offers an application delivery controller (ADC), providing various Layer 7 load balancing capabilities?

   A.   Azure Load Balancer

   B.   Azure Traffic Manager

   C.   Azure Application Gateway

   D.   Azure Front Door

12. Which of the following services offers a high-performance, ultra-low-latency Layer 4 load balancing service (inbound and outbound) for all UDP and TCP protocols?

   A. Azure Load Balancer

   B. Azure Traffic Manager

   C. Azure Application Gateway

   D. Azure Front Door

13. Company XYZ's objective is to reduce the cost. Provide three actions you should follow when setting up outbound connectivity for Company XYZ downstream systems.

   A. Deploy an internal load balancer in Standard SKU.

   B. Deploy a public load balancer in Standard SKU.

   C. Deploy a back-end pool that holds downstream.

   D. Define an outbound rule.

14. Concerning external load balancers, which of the following statements is true?

   A. External load balancers have public IP addresses.

   B. External load balancers do not have public IP addresses.

   C. External load balancers have private IP addresses.

   D. External load balancers do not have private IP addresses.

15. When users need to access the "closest" endpoint without a significant network delay, what traffic-routing method should be used?

   A. Performance

   B. Weighted

   C. Geographic

   D. Multi-Value

16. From the Azure region and Azure Traffic Manager perspective, which of the following is a valid statement?

   A. It is possible to fail any Azure region without affecting Azure Traffic Manager ultimately.

   B. It is not possible to fail any Azure region without affecting Azure Traffic Manager ultimately.

   C. It is only possible to fail specific Azure regions without affecting Azure Traffic Manager ultimately.

   D. It is only possible to fail specific Azure regions with affecting Azure Traffic Manager ultimately.

17. What is the maximum number of nesting layers that Azure Traffic Manager supports?

   A. 5

   B. 10

   C. 15

   D. 20

18. Outbound rules allow you to define SNAT explicitly for a public standard load balancer. Which of the following does this configuration enable? (Choose all that apply.)

    A. IP masked traffic.

    B. Simplified allow lists.

    C. Fewer public IP resources are needed for deployment.

    D. A and B only.

19. From the Azure inbound NAT perspective, which of the following is a valid statement?

    A. An inbound NAT rule is used to forward traffic from a load balancer front-end to one or more instances in the back-end pool, such as a single virtual machine or multiple virtual machines.

    B. An inbound NAT rule redirects traffic from a load balancer front-end to one or more instances in the back-end pool, such as a single virtual machine or two virtual machines at maximum.

    C. An inbound NAT rule redirects traffic from a load balancer front-end to one or more instances in the back-end pool, such as a single virtual machine or three virtual machines at maximum.

    D. An inbound NAT rule is used to forward traffic from a load balancer front-end to one or more instances in the back-end pool, such as a single virtual machine or two virtual machines at maximum.

20. From the Azure Load Balancer HA port perspective, which of the following is a valid statement?

    A. A single rule can be used to load-balance all TCP and UDP traffic arriving on all ports of a standard internal load balancer.

    B. The Azure Load Balancer does not support load balancing TCP and UDP flow on all HA ports simultaneously.

    C. The Azure Load Balancer does support load balancing only TCP flow on all HA ports simultaneously.

    D. The Azure Load Balancer does support load balancing only UDP flow on all HA ports simultaneously.

Chapter

7

Design and Deploy Azure application gateway, Azure front door, and Virtual NAT

THE MICROSOFT AZ-700 EXAM OBJECTIVES COVERED IN THIS CHAPTER INCLUDE:

✓ **Design and implement Azure Application Gateway**

- Recommend Azure Application Gateway deployment options
- Choose between manual and autoscale
- Create a back-end pool
- Configure health probes
- Configure listeners
- Configure routing rules
- Configure HTTP settings
- Configure Transport Layer Security (TLS)
- Configure rewrite sets

✓ **Implement Azure Front Door**

- Choose an Azure Front Door SKU
- Configure health probes, including customization of HTTP response codes
- Configure SSL termination and end-to-end SSL encryption
- Configure multisite listeners

- Configure back-end targets
- Configure routing rules, including redirection rules

✓ **Implement an Azure Traffic Manager profile**

- Configure a routing method (mode)
- Configure endpoints
- Create HTTP settings

✓ **Design and implement an Azure Virtual Network NAT**

- Choose when to use a Virtual Network NAT
- Allocate public IP or public IP prefixes for a NAT gateway
- Associate a Virtual Network NAT with a subnet

You must ensure that end users have consistent access to applications, services, and data as your organization migrates infrastructure, applications, and data to Azure. Azure provides load balancing services that facilitate consistency of access. Load balancing ensures that no single server bears too much load by distributing network traffic across multiple servers. It increases user availability and application responsiveness by evenly spreading the work. Some load balancers also provide application security.

Critical prerequisites for reading this chapter include experience with networking concepts, including application load balancing and DNS; you should also be familiar with the Azure portal and Azure PowerShell.

In this chapter, you first learn how Azure Application Gateway works. We then show you how to set it up, including configuring health probes and listeners. Next, you learn about request routing, redirection, and rewrite policies.

Then, you see how to deploy Azure Front Door and how to choose an Azure Front Door SKU. You'll also learn about health probe operation and securing Front Door with SSL. SSL termination and end-to-end SSL encryption are covered, as are back-end pools, host headers, and health probes. The chapter then moves on to routing and routing rules, as well as URL redirection and rewriting.

Deploying an Azure Traffic Manager profile and Traffic Manager routing methods are next, followed by using VNet address translation, allocating public IP addresses or public IP prefixes for a NAT gateway, and finally associating a VNet NAT with a subnet.

Azure Application Gateway Overview

During migration to Azure, you must ensure that end users have consistent access to applications, services, and data.

Azure's load balancing tools support consistency of access. Load balancing distributes network traffic among multiple servers to prevent any server from carrying too much load. As a result of distributing work evenly, load balancing improves application responsiveness and increases application and service availability. Furthermore, load balancers offer additional security features.

Azure Application Gateway manages traffic to web applications by serving web traffic load balancers. Load balancers traditionally operate at the Transport layer (OSI Layer 4, TCP and UDP) and route traffic based on IP address and port information. It helps create highly available, scalable, and secure web front-ends. By utilizing Azure's application-level load balancing and routing features, you can create a scalable and highly available web front-end, and you can automatically scale Application Gateway instances as web application traffic increases.

Avoid web vulnerabilities such as SQL injection and cross-site scripting by protecting your business applications. Use custom rules and rule groups to monitor your web applications and eliminate false positives.

Several Azure services can be integrated with Application Gateway:

- Azure Traffic Manager supports multiple-region redirections, automatic failovers, and zero-downtime maintenance.

- You can use Azure Virtual Machines, Azure Virtual Machine scale sets, or Azure App Service Web Apps for back-end pools.

- Monitoring and alerting are provided by Azure Monitor and Azure Security Center and an application health dashboard.

- In Key Vault, SSL certificates can be managed centrally and automatically renewed.

Organization data is protected with strong encryption from front to back. Application Gateway routes traffic to back-end server pools based on URL paths and multiple web applications using host headers. Reduce encryption and decryption overhead on your servers by offloading SSL to business applications and centralizing SSL certificate management.

Application Gateway offers the following capabilities:

- An application delivery controller that is platform-managed, scalable, and highly available

- Centralized SSL policy and offloading

- For multi-instance deployments, a service level agreement (SLA) of 99.95 percent uptime

- Support for cookie-based session affinity and public, private, or hybrid websites

- Layer 7 load balancing solutions that you can customize

- Integration with your web application firewall

Application Gateway has the following features:

- Protocols supported include HTTP, HTTPS, HTTP/2, and WebSocket.

- It offers protection against web application vulnerabilities using a web application firewall.

- End-to-end request encryption is provided.

- It offers autoscaling for dynamically adjusting capacity as needs change.

- You can redirect to another site or switch from HTTP to HTTPS.

- Clients and servers can exchange parameter information using HTTP headers.

- Rather than displaying default error pages, Application Gateway allows you to create custom error pages with your own branding and layout.

- HTTP request attributes can be used by Application Gateway to make routing decisions, including URI paths and host headers.

- Consumers of the Azure cloud can route traffic based on the incoming URL.

How Application Gateway Works

This section explains how an application gateway accepts incoming end-user requests and routes them to the back-end.

Applications can be loaded through Application Gateway both internally and externally. This gateway uses public IP addresses and DNS names for Internet-facing application gateways, which must resolve their private IP addresses to public IP addresses. As a result, Internet-facing application gateways can route client requests.

Internal application gateways use private IP addresses. You can use a custom or private DNS zone, and the domain name should be internally resolvable to the Application Gateway's private IP address. So, internal load balancers can only route requests from clients with access to an application gateway's virtual network. Figure 7.1 is an overview of Application Gateway.

FIGURE 7.1   Application Gateway overview

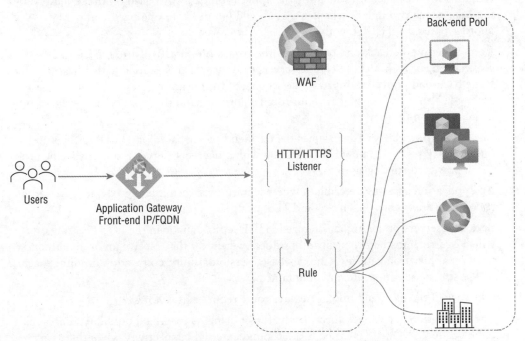

Gateways accept requests using the following methods:

- Using a Domain Name System (DNS) server, a client resolves the domain name of an application gateway before sending a request to the gateway. Because all application gateways are under the `azure.com` domain, Azure controls the DNS entry.

- In Azure DNS, the front-end IP address of the application gateway is returned to the client.

- One or more listeners accept traffic from the application gateway. Listeners are logical entities that receive connection requests and are configured with an IP address, protocol, and port number for client connections to the application gateway.

- Web application firewalls (WAFs) check request headers and bodies, if they are present, against WAF rules. They use this information to determine whether the request is legitimate or a security threat. If the request is valid, it is sent to the back-end. A WAF in Prevention mode blocks a request that isn't valid, considering it a security threat. It is evaluated and logged if it is in Detection mode but is still forwarded to the back-end server if it is not a security threat.

Gateways route requests using the following methods:

- The gateway evaluates the routing rule associated with the listener if a request is valid and not blocked by WAF. Based on this, the gateway routes requests to the appropriate back-end pool.

- Requests for a listener are routed by the application gateway based on the request routing rule, which determines whether they should be routed to one back-end pool or another based on the URL path.

- Upon selecting the back-end pool or another based on the URL Path, the gateway requests one of its healthy back-end servers (y.y.y.y). This is done with a health probe. If the back-end pool contains multiple servers, the application gateway routes requests among healthy servers using a round-robin algorithm, and this load-balances the recommendations on the servers.

- The application gateway determines the back-end server based on HTTP settings and opens a TCP session. A new HTTP session with a back-end server requires specific protocol, port, and routing settings.

- An application gateway determines whether traffic between it and a back-end server is encrypted (thus achieving end-to-end TLS) or not.

- Back-end servers honor any customized HTTP settings made in the HTTP settings, which override hostname, path, and protocol, whenever they receive an original request from an application gateway. Cookies-based session affinity, connection draining, back-end hostname selection, etc. are maintained.

In the case of the back-end pool, gateways route requests as follows:

- The application gateway connects to the server using its front-end public IP address as a public endpoint. One is assigned for outbound external connectivity when there isn't a front-end public IP address.

- Application gateway routes the request to the back-end server using its private IP address.

- The back-end server's front-end public IP address routes requests to a back-end server with an external endpoint or an externally resolvable FQDN. A private DNS zone or custom DNS server is used to resolve DNS, or Azure provides its own DNS. An IP address is assigned for outbound external connectivity if there isn't one.

The next three sections discuss what you need to consider when you deploy Azure Application Gateway.

> For the Microsoft AZ-700 exam, keep in mind that, to minimize administrative effort and provide high availability for network virtual appliances (NVAs), Microsoft recommends including Azure Application Gateway in the solution.

Approaches to Application Gateway Routing

Clients send requests to your organization's web apps to the gateway's IP address or DNS name. Requests are routed through the gateway to a selected web server in the back-end pool, according to rules configured for the gateway to determine where the appeal should be directed.

There are two primary approaches for routing traffic:

Path-Based Routing   Path-based routing routes requests to different pools of back-end servers using different URL paths.

For instance, if a user wants to play a video, the request is routed to the path /video/*, which is hosted in a pool of autoscale servers optimized for handling video streaming. If the user wants an image, then the request is routed to the path /images/*, which is hosted in a pool of servers optimized for image retrieval.

Multiple-Site Routing   Multiple-site routing is helpful when you need to configure several web applications' routing on the same application gateway instance. In a multisite configuration, you can register multiple DNS names (CNAMEs) for the Application Gateway IP address, specifying the name of each site. Different listeners handle requests for each site in Application Gateway. Every listener passes the request to a different rule, which routes the request to servers in different back-end pools.

Multisite configurations facilitate the use of multitenant applications in which each tenant has its own virtual machine or other resources for hosting a web application.

Choosing Application Gateway SKU

Standard_v2 SKU supports Application Gateway, and WAF_v2 SKU supports Web Application Firewall (WAF). The v2 SKUs offer essential features such as autoscaling, redundancy in zones, and static virtual IP (VIP) support for static IP addresses. The Standard and WAF v2 SKUs continue to support existing features.

Table 7.1 provides an overview of the Azure Application Gateway and WAF SKUs.

TABLE 7.1   Overview of the Azure Application Gateway and WAF SKUs

Type	Description
Autoscaling	With the autoscaling SKU, a WAF or Application Gateway can scale out in response to changing traffic loads. Additionally, autoscaling removes the requirement to choose a deployment size or instance count when provisioning. The SKU is highly elastic. With the Standard_v2 and WAF_v2 SKUs, Application Gateway can operate in autoscaling-disabled (fixed-capacity) and autoscaling-enabled modes. A restricted capacity mode is beneficial for scenarios with consistent and predictable workloads, whereas an autoscaling mode is beneficial for unpredictable application traffic.
Zone redundancy	A single Application Gateway deployment can cover multiple availability zones, thus eliminating the need to deploy separate instances of an application gateway in each zone with Traffic Manager. You can choose to deploy Application Gateway instances in a single zone or multiple zones, increasing zone resilience. Applications' back-end pools can also be distributed among availability zones. As of this writing, availability zones aren't supported by every Azure region.
Static VIP	The Application Gateway v2 SKU supports the static VIP type. Even after restarting the deployment, the VIP associated with the application gateway remains unchanged. You must use the application gateway URL instead of the IP address for domain name routing to App Services via the application gateway.
Header Rewrite	You can add, remove, or update HTTP requests and response headers with the v2 SKU of Application Gateway.
Key Vault Integration	With Application Gateway v2, certificates attached to HTTPS-enabled listeners can be stored in the Key Vault.
Azure Kubernetes Service Ingress Controller	An Azure Application Gateway can be used as an ingress for an Azure Kubernetes Service (AKS) cluster using the Application Gateway v2 Ingress Controller.
Performance enhancements	The TLS offload performance of the v2 SKU is up to 5 times better than the Standard/WAF SKU.
Faster deployment and update time	Compared to the Standard/WAF SKU, the V2 SKU offers a faster deployment, and the update process includes WAF configuration changes.

Azure Application Gateway v2 and Web Application Firewall v2 are available in separate SKUs.

You need to consider several factors when choosing whether to deploy Web Application Firewall or Application Gateway, such as your organization's scaling strategy and the cost of the service.

Scaling Options for Application Gateway and WAF

There are two ways to configure Application Gateway and WAF for scaling:

Autoscaling   With autoscaling allowed, the Application Gateway and WAF v2 SKUs scale in or out based on application traffic requirements. This model offers better elasticity to your application, eliminating the need to guess the gateway size and the number of instances.

The Application Gateway does not need to run at peak capacity for the anticipated maximum traffic load using this mode. You must specify a minimum instance count, and, optionally, a complete instance count. With minimum capacity, Application Gateway and WAF v2 ensure they don't fall below the minimum instance count specified, even in the absence of traffic. In terms of reserved capacity units, each model corresponds to 10 or more units, and 0 is an autoscaling model that has no reserved capacity.

You can also specify a maximum instance count to prevent Application Gateway from scaling beyond specified limits. The gateway will only be charged for the traffic it serves. A complete instance count of 20 is the default if no value is specified. The instance count can range from 0 to 125.

Azure Application Gateways are always deployed in a highly available environment. Instances of the service are created either as configured (if autoscaling is disabled) or as required by the application load (if autoscaling is enabled). It is important to note that users only have visibility into the Application Gateway service, not into individual instances. When an Application Gateway model is having a problem and is no longer functioning, a new instance will be created transparently.

Manual   You can also choose Manual mode, which disables autoscaling. If there is too much traffic, a traffic loss may result if Application Gateway or WAF cannot handle it. You must specify the number of instances for Manual mode, varying between 1 and 125.

Overview of Application Gateway Deployment

In Application Gateway, several components work together to send requests to a pool of web servers and check their health. Figure 7.2 depicts the building blocks involved in deploying Application Gateway.

FIGURE 7.2 Building blocks of Application Gateway

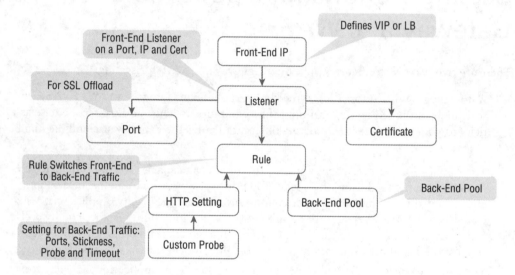

Front-End Setup

IP addresses associated with application gateways are called front-end IP addresses. You can configure the IP address in an application gateway to be public, private, or both. Application gateways support one public and one private IP address. You must have the same virtual network and public IP address to use your application gateway. Listeners are assigned a front-end IP address after they are created.

Back-End Setup

Back-end servers receive requests and route them to the back-end pool, which processes them. A back-end pool can be composed of NICs, virtual machine scale sets, public IP addresses, internal IP addresses, and multitenant back-ends like Azure App Service. You can create an empty back-end pool and add back-end targets to the pool following application gateway creation.

Health Probes Setup

By default, Azure Application Gateway automatically removes any resources from its back-end pool when they are deemed unhealthy. Once they become available and respond to health probes, Application Gateway adds the formerly unhealthy instances back to the healthy pool. The application gateway uses the same port as the HTTP back-end settings to send health probes by default. This can be changed by using a custom probe.

Source IP addresses used by Application Gateway for health probes depend on the back-end pool:

- An application gateway's public IP address is the back-end pool's server address's source address.
- The source IP address comes from the application gateway subnet's private IP address space if the server address in the back-end pool is a Private Endpoint.

Default Health Probe

An application gateway automatically configures a default health probe when you do not set up any custom probe configurations. Monitoring is performed by making an HTTP GET request to the configured IP addresses or FQDNs in the back-end pool. Default probes use HTTPS to test the health of the back-end servers if the back-end HTTP settings are configured for HTTPS.

For instance, let's say you configure an application gateway to receive HTTP network traffic on port 80 using back-end servers X, Y, and Z. With default health monitoring, the three servers are tested for a healthy HTTP response every 30 seconds with a 30-second timeout for each request. The HTTP status code for a healthy response is 200 to 399. For this health probe, the HTTP GET request will look like `http://127.0.0.1/`.

If server X fails the default probe check, the application gateway stops forwarding requests. Server X is checked every 30 seconds by the default probe. The application gateway starts forwarding requests to server X after server X responds successfully to a health probe request.

Table 7.2 provides definitions for the properties of default health probe settings.

TABLE 7.2   Default health probe configuration

Probe Property	Value	Description
Probe URL	`<protocol>://127.0.0.1:<port>/`	The protocol and port of the probe are inherited from the back-end HTTP settings.
Interval	30 Seconds	In seconds, the time between health probes.
Time-Out	30 Seconds	In seconds, the amount of time the application gateway waits for a probe response before marking the probe as unhealthy. After a probe returns as healthy, the corresponding back-end is also marked as healthy.

TABLE 7.2   Default health probe configuration *(continued)*

Probe Property	Value	Description
Unhealthy	3	If the standard health probe fails, it determines how many probes should be sent. In the v1 SKU, these additional health probes are sent immediately to determine the back-end's health instead of waiting for the probe interval. A health probe remains in place for the interval with the v2 SKU. In case of consecutive probe failures, the back-end server is marked as unhealthy.

Application Gateway instances probe the back-end independently, and the same probe configuration applies to each Application Gateway instance. For example, if the probe configuration sends health probes every 30 seconds, both instances of the application gateway will send the health probe every 30 seconds. There may be more than one listener, and each probes the back-end independently.

Custom Health Probe

With custom probes, you have more control over health monitoring. You can configure custom probes to work with a custom hostname, URL path, and probe interval, as well as specify how many failed responses to accept before marking the back-end pool instance as unhealthy.

Table 7.3 provides definitions for the properties of custom health probes.

TABLE 7.3   Custom health probe configuration

Probe Property	Description
Name	The probe's name. In the back-end HTTP settings, the probe is identified by this name.
Protocol	The protocol for sending the probe. In the back-end HTTP settings, it must match the protocol it is associated with.
Host	This value is the name of the virtual host running on the application server (different from the VM hostname). `*protocol>://*host name>:*port>/*urlPath>` is the probe address. The server's private IP address, the public IP address, or the DNS entry for the public IP address can also be used. If used with a file-based path entry, this will attempt to access the server and verify that a certain file exists on the server as a health check.
Ports	A custom port ranging from 1 to 65535.

Probe Property	Description
Path	The relative path is followed by the probe. A valid path begins with a slash (/).
Port	The destination port is used if it has been defined. If not, the HTTP settings are used. It is only available with the v2 SKU.
Interval	The time in seconds between two successive probes.
Time-Out	Calculate the time-out in seconds. During this time-out period, if no valid response is received, the probe is marked as failed.
Unhealthy	Count the retries of a probe. If the consecutive probe failure count reaches an unhealthy level, the back-end server is marked as down.

Probe Matching

HTTP(S) responses with a status code between 200 and 399 are considered healthy by default. Custom health probes also support two additional matching criteria, which can be used to modify the default interpretation of what constitutes a healthy response.

- There is a probe matching criterion for accepting user-specified HTTP response codes or ranges of HTTP response codes. There is support for individual comma-separated response status codes or a range of status codes.

  The probe matching criterion looks at the HTTP response body and matches it with a user-specified string. It doesn't perform a full regular expression match and only looks for the presence of a user-specified string in the response body.

- Using the `New-AzApplicationGatewayProbeHealthResponseMatch` cmdlet, you can specify match criteria.

Configuring Listeners

An incoming connection request is received by a listener that checks port, protocol, host, and IP address. You have to configure a listener; they enter values that match those in the incoming request on the gateway.

In addition to creating an application gateway using the Azure portal, you should generate a default listener by selecting the protocol and port. If HTTP2 support is enabled on the listener, it can be selected. After creating the application gateway, you can edit the settings of the default listener (`appGatewayHttpListener`) or create new listeners.

When you create a new listener, you must choose between basic and multisite:

- With a basic listener, every request will be accepted and forwarded to the back-end pools of the domain.

- With a multisite listener, requests are routed to different back-end pools according to the host header or hostname. Incoming requests must match the hostname specified. To host multiple websites on the same public IP address and port, Application Gateway uses HTTP 1.1 host headers.

The following items describe rules to configure for listeners:

Front-End IP   Select the address that will associate with this listener. Requests will be routed to this address.

Front-End Port   A new front-end port can be created, or an existing port should be selected. There are a variety of ports that can be chosen. You can use well-known ports, such as 80 and 443, and any custom port that's allowed. There are two types of ports: public and private.

Protocol: Choose HTTP or HTTPS

You must select the protocol to use:

HTTP   Nothing is encrypted between a client and an application gateway.

HTTPS   Enables the termination or encryption of TLS. At the application gateway, the TLS connection ends, and client and application traffic are encrypted. You must configure the back-end HTTP settings if you want end-to-end TLS encryption. It is reencrypted when traffic travels from the application gateway to the back-end.

Certificate   The certificate must be added to the listener so that the application gateway can derive a symmetric key to configure TLS termination and end-to-end encryption. The TLS protocol specifies this requirement. Traffic sent to the gateway is encrypted and decrypted using the symmetric key. A PFX format certificate must be used for creating the certificate. You can decrypt and encrypt traffic using this gateway by exporting the private key.

Order of Processing Listeners   The v1 SKU matches requests according to the order of the rules and the type of listener. The rules with a simple listener come first, are processed first, and accept requests for that port and IP combination. To avoid this, configure the rules with multisite listeners first, then push the basic listeners to the end.

Listeners for SKU v2 are processed before listeners for SKU v1.

Redirection Overview

Traffic can be redirected using an application gateway. This software allows traffic from one listener to be routed to another listener or a remote website using a generic redirection mechanism. The method simplifies application configuration, optimizes resource usage, and supports new redirection scenarios, such as global and path-based redirection.

Classless Inter-Domain Routing (CIDR) is the format in which you define the internal address space of a virtual network. Any network you connect to must have a unique address space within your subscription.

The virtual network address space can be partitioned into one or more subnets within each address range. If it's not partitioned, you can define custom routes to route traffic between subnets. Alternatively, all virtual networks' address ranges can be combined into one subnet.

6. Click OK to create a virtual network.

7. Click the Next: Frontends tab to open the page shown in the following image, confirm that Frontend IP Address Type is set to Public, click Add New for the public IP address, and enter your public IP address.

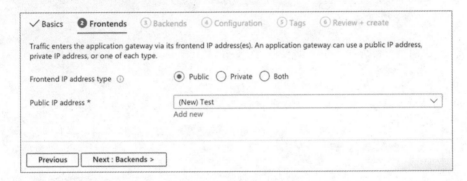

8. Click Next: Backends and, on the Backends tab, choose to add a back-end pool. In the Add A Backend Pool page that opens (see the next image), provide the following values to build an empty back-end pool:

Name	Enter your back-end pool for the name of the back-end pool.
Add Backend Pool Without Targets	Choose Yes or No, Yes to build a back-end pool with no targets. After creating an application gateway, you can add back-end targets.

9.   On the Add A Backend Pool page, click Add to save the back-end pool settings and to
     return to the Backends tab. Then, choose Next: Configuration to open the Configuration
     tab shown in the next image.

10. In this step, you'll connect the front-end and back-end pool you built using a routing rule on the Configuration tab; under the Routing Rules icon, choose Add A Routing Rule to open the page shown in the next image. In the Rule Name input field, provide your Routing Rule.

It is necessary to have a listener for routing rules. On the Add A Routing Rule page, on the Listener tab (shown in the next image), enter the following values:

Listener Name	Type a name for the listener.
Frontend IP	Choose Public to select the public IP you created for the front-end.
Port	Provide the port number for the listener. Ports 80 and 443 are well-known, as are ports 1 to 65199 (v1 SKU) or 1 to 65502 (v2 SKU).

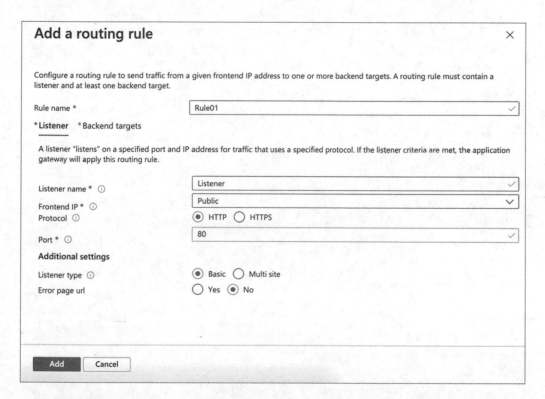

Leave the other settings at their defaults on the Listener tab, then choose the Backend Targets tab to set up the rest of the routing rule.

11. Under Backend Targets, provide or choose the following information:

Target Type	Choose your back-end pool.
Backend Target	Choose your back-end target.
Backend Settings	The HTTP configuration will specify how the routing rule works. In the Add An HTTP setting window that opens, provide your HTTP configuration for the HTTP setting name and choose 80 for the back-end port. Obtain the default values for the different settings in the Add An HTTP Setting window.

12. Click Add to return to the Add A Routing Rule window shown next.

13. Click Add to save the routing rule and to return to the Configuration tab.

14. In this step, on the Tags tab, you can organize the resource per your organization's standards.

Tags are used to organize Azure resources, resource groups, and subscriptions logically. As you apply the same tag to multiple resources and groups, you can categorize them and view consolidated billing.

15. On the Review + Create tab, wait for the validation pass status before you click Create.

Features and Capabilities of Azure Front Door SKUs

Azure Front Door is an entry point that utilizes Microsoft's global edge network to create quick, secure, and globally scalable web applications. You can use Front Door to convert worldwide consumer and enterprise apps into robust, high-performance applications with content that reaches a global audience through Azure.

Front Door allows you to develop, operate, and scale static and dynamic web applications. The service enables you to define, manage, and monitor end-user performance and reliability, allowing quick global failover for a top-of-the-line end-user experience.

Front Door uses the Anycast protocol, a split TCP, and Microsoft's global network to improve global connectivity at Layer 7 (HTTP/HTTPS).

Using split TCP, you can reduce latencies and TCP problems by breaking a long-running connection into smaller pieces.

A client's TCP connection can be split to terminate near the user's Front Door edge location.

You can ensure Front Door routes end-user client requests to the most efficient and available application back-end based on your organization's routing method. In Azure, an application back-end is any service that can be accessed through the Internet. Front Door provides a variety of traffic-routing methods and back-end health monitoring options to meet a wide range of application requirements and scenarios. As with Traffic Manager, Front Door is resilient to failures, including failures to an entire Azure region.

Application Gateway and Front Door are both Layer 7 load balancers, but Front Door is a global service whereas Application Gateway is a regional service. Front Door can balance loads across scale units, clusters, and stamp units in different regions. A scale unit's Application Gateway load-balances virtual machines and containers.

Front Door includes the following features and capabilities:

- A split TCP-based Anycast protocol improves application performance.

- Back-end resources are monitored with intelligent health probes.

- Requests are routed on a URL-path basis.

- Multiple websites can be hosted efficiently.
- An affinity cookie is used to identify sessions.
- You can manage SSL offloading and certificates.
- You can configure custom domains.
- Application security is provided with Web Application Firewall.
- You can use URL redirects or rewrites to forward HTTP traffic to HTTPS.

HTTP/2 and IPv6 connectivity are supported natively.

In addition to Azure Front Door, Azure Front Door Standard and Azure Front Door Premium (both in preview as of this writing) are available. Combined with Azure Content Delivery Network (CDN) Standard and Azure WAF, Azure Front Door Standard/Premium provides a robust, secure cloud CDN platform with intelligent threat protection.

Table 7.4 shows a high-level capabilities comparison.

TABLE 7.4   Front Door Standard vs. Front Door Premium

Azure Front Door Standard SKU	Azure Front Door Premium SKU
Optimized content delivery	All the capabilities of the Standard SKU
Static and dynamic content	A wide range of security capabilities across WAF, including protection against bots
Global load balancing	Private Link
SSL offloading	Security analytics and integration with Microsoft Threat Intelligence
Domain and certificate management	
Improved traffic analytics	
Basic security	

Table 7.5 is a high-level feature comparison.

TABLE 7.5   Front Door Standard and Front Door Premium Feature comparison

Feature	Standard	Premium
Custom domains	Yes	Yes
SSL offload	Yes	Yes
Caching	Yes	Yes
Compression	Yes	Yes
Global load balancing	Yes	Yes
Layer 7 routing	Yes	Yes
URL rewrite	Yes	Yes
Rules Engine	Yes	Yes
Private Origin (Private Link)	No	Yes
WAF	Custom Rules only	Yes
Bot protection	No	Yes
Enhanced metrics and diagnostics	Yes	Yes
Security report	No	Yes
Traffic report	Yes	Yes

Health Probe Characteristics and Operation

To determine each back-end's health and proximity to a Front Door environment, Front Door sends a synthetic HTTP/HTTPS request (a health probe) to each configured back-end. Front Door then determines which back-end resources will best route an end-user's client requests using the responses from the probe.

Each Azure Front Door edge POP emits health probes to your origins, resulting in a high volume of health probes for your origins. The number of probes depends on your customer's traffic location and the frequency at which health probes are sent. Azure Front Door edge POPs reduce the frequency of the health probe if they do not receive real traffic from your end-users. Based on the frequency of your health probes, the health probe volume can be high if there is customer traffic to all Azure Front Door edge POPs.

Using the default probe frequency of 30 seconds, estimate the volume of health probes to your origin per minute. A probe volume equals two requests per minute multiplied by the number of edge POPs on each origin. There will be fewer probing requests if all POPs are not contacted.

You can send probes to Front Door via HTTP or HTTPS. The probes are sent over the same TCP ports configured for routing client requests and cannot be overridden.

Supported HTTP Methods for Health Probes

Front Door supports the following HTTP methods for sending health probes:

GET   GET retrieves whatever the Request-URI identifies as information (as an entity).

HEAD   A HEAD request is identical to a GET request, except the server *must not* return a message-body. For new Front Door profiles, the probe method by default is HEAD since it has a lower load and cost for back-ends.

Health Probe Responses

Table 7.6 summarizes the health probe responses.

TABLE 7.6   Health Probe responses

Response	Description
Determining health	A 200 OK status code indicates a healthy back-end. If a valid HTTP response is not received (including network failures), the back-end has failed.
Measuring latency	A probe's latency is the wall-clock time elapsed between when the request is sent and when the last byte of the response is received. As each request uses a new TCP connection, this measurement is not biased toward back-ends with existing warm connections.

Secure Front Door with SSL

You can ensure that sensitive data is delivered securely via TLS/SSL encryption to your organization's custom domain (for example, `https://www.sybexdemo.com`). The web browser validates the URL with HTTPS and verifies that a legitimate certificate authority issued the security certificate. Your organization's websites are secured and protected by this process.

Custom HTTPS features should have the following critical attributes:

No Additional Charges   There are no charges for certification or HTTPS traffic.

Easy Provisioning   One-click provisioning is available in the Azure portal. In addition to the REST API, you can use other developer tools to enable this feature.

Complete Certificate Management   All certificate procurement and management are handled for your organization. Certificates are automatically provisioned and renewed before expiration, which removes the risks of service interruption due to a certificate expiring.

You can enable the HTTPS protocol for a custom domain associated with Front Door under the front-end host's section. HTTPS is enabled by default on a Front Door default hostname in Azure Front Door. The HTTPS protocol is automatically enabled for requests made to `https://sybexdemo.azurefd.net` when you create a Front Door (for example, `https://contoso.azurefd.net`). You must allow HTTPS for this front-end host once your organization has registered the custom domain `www.sybexdemo.com`.

Front Door for Web Applications with a High-Availability Design Pattern

In this section, you build a pool of two instances for a web application from different Azure regions by using Azure Front Door. With this configuration, Front Door monitors the web application continuously and directs traffic to the nearest site that runs the application. Also, you perform a failover to the next available site. The network configuration is shown in Figure 7.8.

FIGURE 7.8   Front Door design pattern

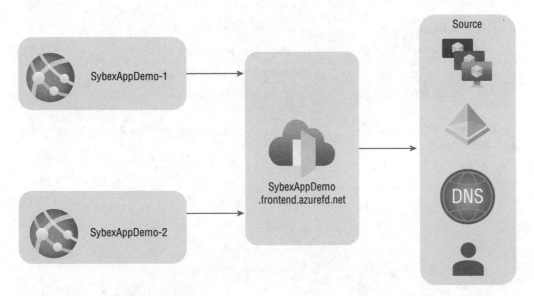

To complete Exercise 7.2, you perform the following two activities:

- **Activity 1:** Build two instances of a web application.
- **Activity 2:** Build a Front Door for the web applications.

EXERCISE 7.2

Deploy Front Door for Web Applications with a High-Availability Design Pattern

Start with Activity 1.

1. Log into a personal or business account in the Azure portal at `https://portal.azure.com`.

2. Select Create A Resource, then choose App Services.

3. In the Create Web App page that opens (see the next image), enter the following information:

Subscription	Choose your subscription.
Resource Group	Choose your resource group.
Name	For this example, use **Sybexapp1**.
Publish	Choose Code.
Runtime Stack	Choose .NET Core 6 (LTS).
Operating System	For this example, choose Windows.
Region	Choose your preferred region.
App Service Plan	Choose Create New and provide your preferred name or use the auto-created name in the text box.
SKU, Size, ACU, Memory	Choose Standard, Small, 100 total ACU, 1.75 GB memory.

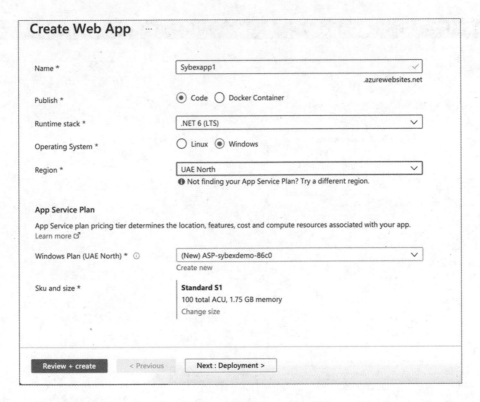

4. Click Review + Create, review the summary that opens (see the next image), then click Create. The deployment may take a while to complete.

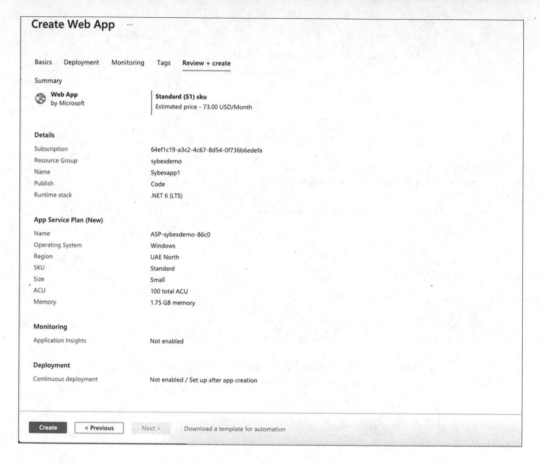

Repeat the preceding steps to build the second web application.

Next you proceed to Activity 2, building a Front Door for the web application.

1. Log into a personal or business account in the Azure portal at `https://portal.azure.com`.

2. Select Create A Resource, then choose Front Door.

3. On the Basics tab of the Create A Front Door Wizard that opens (see the next image), enter the following information:

Subscription	Choose your subscription.
Resource Group	Choose your resource group.
Resource Group Location	Choose your preferred region.

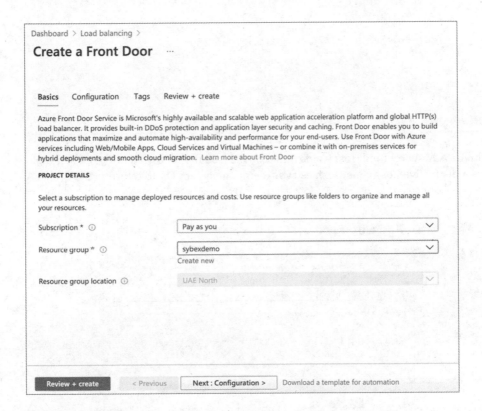

4. Click Next: Configuration. This is a three-stage process:

    a. On the Configuration tab, click + at the top of the Frontends/Domains box to add a front-end host, as shown in the following image:

EXERCISE 7.2 *(continued)*

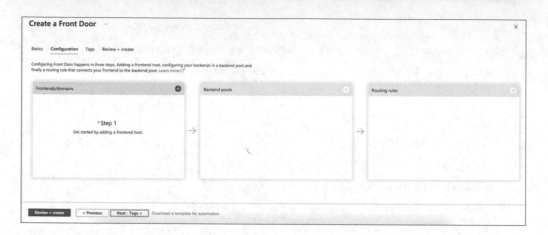

In the Add A Frontend Host window that opens (see the following image), enter a globally distinctive hostname, such as sybexdemo, then click OK to return to the Create A Front Door page.

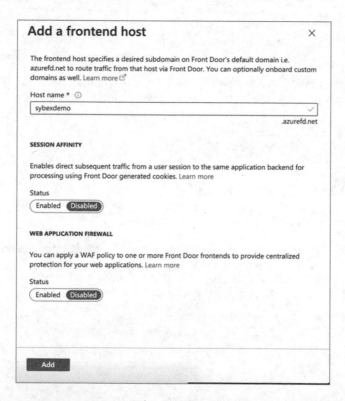

b. Click the plus symbol (+) in the Backend Pools box, and in the page that opens, enter a uniquely identifying hostname, such as BackendPool.

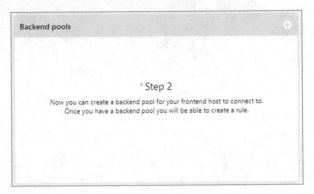

Components	Add a description.
Backend Host Type	Choose your service.
Subscription	Choose your subscription.
Backend Host Name	Choose the first web app you have created.

Select + Add a back-end, and then on the Add A Backend Pool blade, click Add to complete the configuration of the back-end pool.

c. Click the plus symbol (+) it exists at top the corner in the Routing Rules box in the image shown in the next figure to add routing rules to the back-end pool. Each routing rule routes requests to your back-end pool.

EXERCISE 7.2 *(continued)*

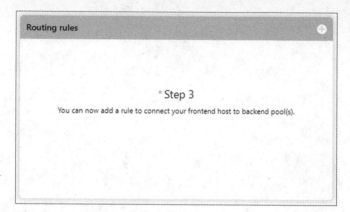

In the Create A Front Door Wizard, click + to configure a routing rule. Click Add A Rule to open the window shown next, and for Name, enter **LocationRule**. Accept all the default values, click Add The Routing Rule, click Review + Create, and then click Create.

Keep in mind that only when one or more HTTP settings are associated with the probe it will monitor the health of the back-end. The probe will monitor the back-end resources of those back-end pools associated with the HTTP setting(s) to which it was assigned. The syntax used for probing is $*protocol>://*hostName>:*port>/*urlPath>$.

SSL Termination and End-to-End SSL Encryption

Secure Sockets Layer (SSL) was the previous name for Transport Layer Security (TLS), a technology that establishes an encrypted link between a web server and a browser. All data passed between the web server and the web browser remains private and encrypted using this link.

Front Door supports end-to-end TLS encryption to meet security and compliance requirements. By terminating the TLS connection, Front Door TLS/SSL offloads the traffic at the Front Door, decrypts it, and re-encrypts it before forwarding it to the back-end. Because connections to the back-end are made over a public IP, you must configure HTTPS as the forwarding protocol on your Front Door to enforce end-to-end TLS encryption from the client to the back-end.

Secure data in transit to the back-end with end-to-end TLS while taking advantage of Front Door features like global load balancing and caching. URL-based routing, TCP split, caches close to clients, and the ability to customize HTTP requests at the edge are included.

Front Door decrypts client requests at the edge, offloading TLS sessions. Requests are then routed to the appropriate back-end pool by the configured routing rules. When Front Door transmits a request, it establishes a new TLS connection to the back-end and re-encrypts all data using the back-end's certificate. The back-end response to the end-user is encrypted through the same process. Your Front Door can be configured to use HTTPS as a forwarding protocol to enable end-to-end TLS.

The Front Door platform supports three versions of TLS: versions 1.0, 1.1, and 1.2. Since September 2019, all Front Door profiles use TLS 1.2 by default, but TLS 1.0 and TLS 1.1 are still available for backward compatibility.

Front Door currently does not support client/mutual authentication, despite TLS 1.2, which introduces client/mutual authentication through RFC 5246.

You can set the minimum TLS version in the custom domain HTTPS settings by using the Azure portal or the Azure REST API. Currently, you can select between 1.0 and 1.2 TLS to control the minimum TLS version Front Door will accept from a client. You can specify TLS 1.2 as the minimum. Front Door will attempt to negotiate the best TLS version the back-end can reliably and consistently accept when sending TLS traffic.

Your organization must create the certificate chain for your TLS/SSL certificate with an approved certificate authority (CA) on the Microsoft trusted CA list. Organizations whose CAs are not allowed will have their requests rejected. Self-signed certificates and certificates issued by internal CAs are not allowed.

Front Door is configured to Online Certificate Status Protocol (OCSP) by default, so no configuration is needed.

Front Door requires a valid CA certificate from the back-end that matches the back-end hostname for HTTPS connections. This certificate must contain the leaf and intermediate certificates, and Microsoft's trusted CA list must exist for the root CA. If a certificate without a complete chain is presented, requests involving that certificate may not work as expected. From a security perspective, Microsoft recommends that certificate subject name-checks be disabled. During testing, however, this is not necessary.

To enable the HTTPS protocol for secure delivery of contents on a Front Door custom domain, you can use a certificate that Front Door manages or use your organization's certificate. Managed certificates for Front Door are provided via DigiCert and are stored in Front Door's Key Vault. If you want to use certificates, you can use a certificate from a supported CA, such as a standard TLS, extended validation certificate, or a wildcard certificate. It is not possible to use self-signed certificates.

In the Front Door managed certificate option, the certificates are managed and auto-rotated by Front Door within 90 days of the expiry date. By default, Front Door orders and automatically rotates certificates every 45 days for Standard/Premium managed certificates.

Cipher suites that are supported for TLS 1.2 include:

- TLS_ECDHE_RSA_WITH_AES_256_GCM_SHA384
- TLS_DHE_RSA_WITH_AES_256_GCM_SHA384
- TLS_ECDHE_RSA_WITH_AES_128_GCM_SHA256
- TLS_DHE_RSA_WITH_AES_128_GCM_SHA256

The following cipher suites can be used with custom domains with TLS 1.0/1.1 enabled:

- TLS_ECDHE_ECDSA_WITH_AES_128_GCM_SHA256
- TLS_ECDHE_ECDSA_WITH_AES_256_GCM_SHA384
- TLS_ECDHE_RSA_WITH_AES_128_GCM_SHA256
- TLS_ECDHE_RSA_WITH_AES_256_GCM_SHA384
- TLS_ECDHE_ECDSA_WITH_AES_128_CBC_SHA256
- TLS_ECDHE_ECDSA_WITH_AES_256_CBC_SHA384
- TLS_ECDHE_RSA_WITH_AES_128_CBC_SHA256
- TLS_ECDHE_RSA_WITH_AES_256_CBC_SHA384
- TLS_ECDHE_ECDSA_WITH_AES_256_CBC_SHA
- TLS_ECDHE_ECDSA_WITH_AES_128_CBC_SHA
- TLS_ECDHE_RSA_WITH_AES_256_CBC_SHA
- TLS_ECDHE_RSA_WITH_AES_128_CBC_SHA
- TLS_RSA_WITH_AES_256_GCM_SHA384
- TLS_RSA_WITH_AES_128_GCM_SHA256
- TLS_RSA_WITH_AES_256_CBC_SHA256
- TLS_RSA_WITH_AES_128_CBC_SHA256
- TLS_RSA_WITH_AES_256_CBC_SHA
- TLS_RSA_WITH_AES_128_CBC_SHA

- TLS_DHE_RSA_WITH_AES_128_GCM_SHA256
- TLS_DHE_RSA_WITH_AES_256_GCM_SHA384

Multisite Listeners

Listeners are logical entities that listen for incoming connection requests using the port, protocol, host, and IP addresses. You need to enter values that match the values in the incoming request on the gateway when they configure the listener.

You can create an application gateway using the Azure portal, and it is also possible to choose a default listener by selecting the listener's port and protocol. You can choose whether HTTP2 support should be enabled on the listener. After you complete setting up the application gateway, it is also possible to edit the settings of that default listener (per Microsoft, it is appGatewayHttpListener) or build a new listener.

When you build a new listener, you can choose between basic and multisite.

- Choose basic if you want all requests (for any domain) to be accepted and forwarded to back-end pools.

- Choosing a multisite listener is necessary if you wish to redirect requests to different back-end pools based on the host header or hostname. Also, you must specify a hostname that matches incoming requests. Multiple websites can be hosted on the same public IP address and port using HTTP 1.1 host headers.

Requests are matched based on the order of the rules and the type of listener for the v1 SKU. In the ordering, rules with basic listeners appear first and will be handled first and accept requests for those ports and IP addresses. Set up rules with multisite listeners first and push the basic listener rule to the last list to avoid this. Listeners from multisites are processed before listening from basic sites when using the v2 SKU.

A listener must allow the application gateway to enable traffic to be routed appropriately to the back-end address pools. As an example, let's create listeners for two domains: sybexdemo1.com and sybexdemo2.com.

With the front-end configuration and the front-end port, create the first listener using New-AzApplicationGatewayHttpListener. If incoming traffic is to be handled by a pool, the listener needs a rule. Use the New-AzApplicationGatewayRequestRoutingRule command to create a basic rule named contosoRule.

```
$sybexdemo1listener = New-AzApplicationGatewayHttpListener `
    -Name sybexdemo1Listener `
    -Protocol Http `
    -FrontendIPConfiguration $fipconfig `
    -FrontendPort $frontendport `
    -HostName "www.sybexdemo1.com"
$sybexdemo2listener = New-AzApplicationGatewayHttpListener `
```

```
 -Name sybexdemo2Listener `
 -Protocol Http `
 -FrontendIPConfiguration $fipconfig `
 -FrontendPort $frontendport `
 -HostName "www.sybexdemo2.com"
$sybexdemo1Rule = New-AzApplicationGatewayRequestRoutingRule `
 -Name sybexdemo1Rule `
 -RuleType Basic `
 -HttpListener $sybexdemo1Listener `
 -BackendAddressPool $sybexdemo1Pool `
 -BackendHttpSettings $poolSettings
$sybexdemo2Rule = New-AzApplicationGatewayRequestRoutingRule `
 -Name sybexdemo2Rule `
 -RuleType Basic `
 -HttpListener $sybexdemo2Listener `
 -BackendAddressPool $sybexdemo2Pool `
 -BackendHttpSettings $poolSettings
```

Back-Ends, Back-End Pools, Back-End Host Headers, and Back-End Health Probes

In this section we consider back-ends and back-end pools for Azure Front Door.

A back-end is a web application deployment in a specific region, and Front Door supports Azure and non-Azure resources in the pool. The application can either be hosted in the on-premises datacenter or another cloud provider's datacenter.

Back-end Front Doors refer to your application's public IP address or hostname. Cloud back-ends are not the same as the database or storage tier. Your organization's application back-ends should be viewed as public endpoints. It would be best to consider adding the following when adding back-ends to a Front Door back-end pool:

Back-End Host Type   This is all about the type of resource you want to add. Front Door supports autodiscovery of application back-ends from App Service, Cloud Service, or Storage; if you wish to use a different resource in Azure or even a non-Azure back-end, select the custom host type.

Subscription and Back-End Hostname   You must select a custom host for the back-end host type if you haven't selected your organization's back end. Select the relevant subscription and the corresponding back end hostname in the UI.

Back-End Host Header   The host header is sent with each request to the back-end server.

Priority   When all traffic is routed through a primary service back-end, assign priorities to different back-ends. In addition, if the backup or the primary back-ends are unavailable, provide backups.

Weight   You can be assigned weights distributed between various back-ends, either evenly or based on weight coefficients.

Requests forwarded by Front Door to back-ends include a host header field used to locate the requested resource. This field usually contains the host header and port information from the back-end URI.

To add the back-end host header to the back-end, configure the back-end host header field in the back-end pool section of Front Door:

1. Open Front Door and select the back-end pool with the back-end to configure.

2. Create a back-end if you have not yet done so or edit one already there.

3. Leave the back-end header field blank or put a custom value in. A host header value will be set based on the incoming request hostname.

The Front Door back-end pool refers to back-ends that receive similar traffic. It's a group of app instances across the globe that receive the same traffic and respond as expected. Each back-end is based in a separate area or region. Active-active deployment or active-passive configuration is available for all back-ends.

Back-end pools specify how health probes should be applied to different back-ends and how load balancing should take place between them.

Each of the back-ends you configure receives periodic HTTP/HTTPS probe requests from Front Door. To load-balance end-user requests, probe requests pick the proximity and health of each back-end. Back-end pool health probe settings determine how you poll application back-ends for health status. You can configure the following settings:

Path   All back-ends in the back-end pool use this URL to conduct probe requests. Health probe paths are case-sensitive.

Protocol   Used for traffic exchange between Front Door and your back-ends via HTTP or HTTPS.

Message Method   Defines how health probe messages should be sent: GET (default) or HEAD (alternative).

Interval (Seconds)   Sets how frequently your back-ends will send health probes or how often each environment will send a health probe.

Health probes are evaluated based on the load balancing settings of the back-end pool. Based on these settings, the health of a back-end is determined. The health probe also checks how traffic is balanced between the different back-ends in the back-end pool. To achieve load balancing, the following configuration settings are available:

Sample Size   Determines how many health probe samples should be considered for back-end health evaluation.

Successful Sample Size   Establish the sample size, which is the number of successful samples needed to call the back-end healthy. Consider 30 seconds for a Front Door health probe, a sample size of 5, and a success rate of 3. Each time back-end health probes are considered, the last five samples over 150 seconds are evaluated (5 × 30). The back-end must pass three successful tests before it can be declared healthy.

Latency Sensitivity (Additional Latency)   Determines whether Front Door will send your request to back-ends within a specific latency measurement sensitivity range or whether it will forward the request to the closest back-end.

Routing and Routing Rules

Front Door can perform one of two actions when receiving client requests from your organization regarding routing. Respond to them if you enable caching or forward them to the appropriate application back-end as a reverse proxy.

The following are the five high-level routing architectures that exist as of this writing:

Routing Traffic Using the Front Door Environment (Anycast)   All DNS and HTTP traffic routed to the Front Door environments uses Anycast, which allows users to reach the closest Azure environment with the fewest network hops. With this architecture, Front Door provides better round-trip times by utilizing split TCP. It organizes its environments into primary and fallback "rings." The outer ring is closer to users, offering lower latencies.

The inner-ring environments can handle any issues with the outer-ring environment. All traffic should be directed to the outer ring, and the inner ring handles traffic overflow from the outer ring. All front-end hosts and domains served by Front Door are assigned a primary VIP (Virtual Internet Protocol) address. Inner-ring environments only support a fallback address.

As a result, the closest Front Door environment is always reached by requests from end users. All traffic automatically moves to the closest environment if the preferred Front Door environment is unhealthy.

Connecting to Front Door Using Split TCP   In split TCP, a connection is broken into smaller pieces to reduce latencies. Due to Front Door's closest location to end users, TCP connections terminate within Front Door environments. An application back-end TCP connection has a two-round-trip time (RTT). Due to the "short connection" between the Front Door environment and the end user, the connection is established over three short round-trips instead of three long ones, resulting in lower latency. There is the ability to make a preestablished "long connection" between the Front Door environment and the back-end environment, which can be reused across other end users' requests to save time connecting to the back-end environment. When SSL/TLS is used, the effect of split TCP is multiplied since there are more round-trips required for securing the connection.

Processing Requests According to Routing Rules   Once a connection is established in a Front Door environment and a TLS handshake has been completed, the next step is to match the request to the routing rule. Configuration determines which routing rule should be applied to each request on Front Door.

Finding Out Which Back-Ends Are Available in the Back-End Pool   If there is no caching, Front Door uses a health probe to determine the status of the back-end pool associated with the routing rule.

Forwarding Requests to Your Application's Back-End   The user request will be forwarded to the "best" back-end, assuming caching isn't configured according to your routing method configuration.

The Azure Front Door Standard/Premium Route outlines how incoming requests are handled when they arrive at the Front Door environment. It is possible to associate a domain with a back-end origin group via the Route settings. Turn on advanced features such as Pattern To Match and Ruleset for greater control over traffic.

"Left-hand side" and "right-hand side" are the two main components of a Front Door Standard/Premium routing configuration. The left-hand side of the route describes how Microsoft matches the incoming request, and the right-hand side describes how Microsoft processes the request.

Basically, Microsoft matches based on the most specific match first, looking only at the left-hand side. Microsoft matches based on HTTP protocol, then front-end host, then path.

URL Redirection and URL Rewriting in Front Door Standard and Premium

Preview versions of Front Door Standard and Premium were available as of this writing.

Traffic can be redirected by Front Door at the following levels: protocol, hostname, path, query string, and fragment. Since the redirection is based on paths, these functions can be configured for each micro-service. By using URL redirect, you can optimize resource usage and implement new redirection scenarios, including global redirection and path-based redirection.

End-user clients can understand the purpose of the redirect based on the response status code set by the redirect type. Redirect types supported include the following:

301 (Moved Permanently)   There is now a permanent URI for the target resource. The enclosed URIs will be used in any future references to this resource. The HTTPS redirection status code is 301.

302 (Found)   There is a temporary change of URI for this resource. Despite the redirections changing from time to time, the client should continue to use the effective request URI in the future.

307 (Temporary Redirect)   A temporary URI has been assigned to the target resource. When a user agent does an automatic redirection to a URI, the request method *may not* be changed. The client should use the original URI request for future requests since redirections can change over time.

308 (Permanent Redirect)   Accordingly, the target resource will now have a permanent URI. The enclosed URI should be used for any future references to this resource.

You can specify the redirection protocol. A redirect feature is most commonly used to set HTTP to HTTPS redirection.

Use HTTPS Only   Only set the protocol to HTTPS if you wish to redirect traffic from HTTP to HTTPS. Microsoft recommends always turning to HTTPS only when using Front Door.

Use HTTP Only   Directs the incoming request to HTTP. This value should only be used if you desire nonencrypted HTTP traffic.

Match Request   This option retains the protocol used by the incoming request. Thus, HTTP requests remain HTTP and HTTPS requests remain HTTPS after redirection.

When configuring redirect routing, you can also change the domain or hostname for redirect requests. In this field, you can change the URL hostname for the redirection or preserve the hostname from the incoming request. You can set this field to the new path value to replace the path segment during redirection. However, you can preserve the path value during redirection.

You can also replace the query string parameters in the redirected URL. Set this field to Replace and set the appropriate value to return any existing query string from the incoming request URL. If you keep the original query strings, the field can be set to Preserve.

When the browser lands on a web page, the destination fragment is the part of the URL that follows #. You can set this field to add fragments to redirect URLs.

It is possible to redirect the path of a request route to an origin using Front Door URL rewriting. You can use URL rewrite to specify conditions to ensure URLs or headers are only rewritten when certain conditions are met. Rewrite criteria are determined by request and response information. You can redirect users to different origins based on the scenario, device type, and requested file type with this feature.

Using a rule set, you can configure URL redirection. In source patterns, URL paths replace the original URL path. Prefix-based matching is currently used. Use the forward slash (/) in the source pattern value to match all URL paths. The URL rewrite source pattern is applied only to the path following the route configuration Patterns To Match.

The following is the incoming URL format: `*Front-end>/ *route-patterns-to-match-path>/*Rule-URL-Rewrite-Source-pattern>`. The rule engine will only consider `/*Rule-URL-Rewrite-Source-pattern>` as the source pattern to rewrite. In the case of URL rewrite rules with source pattern matching, the output URL format will be *<Front-end>/<route-patterns-to-match-path>/<Rule-URL-Rewrite-destination>*.

The Origin path of the Origin group in route configuration can be set to / in scenarios where the *route-patterns-to-match-path* segment of the URL path must be removed. Rewrites can be configured. Source paths are overwritten by destination paths. You can add the remaining path to the new path by selecting Preserve Unmatched Path.

For the AZ-700 exam, keep in mind that by using Application Gateway, you can disable TLS1.0, TLS1.1, and TLS1.2 by default. SSL 2.0 and 3.0 are disabled by default and are not configurable. Application Gateway can use a maximum of 100 TLS/SSL certificates.

You also need to enable the SSL profile for the listener to configure the listener for HTTPS by uploading an enterprise-signed certificate.

Design and Deploy Traffic Manager Profiles

Azure Traffic Manager is a load balancer based on DNS. Azure Traffic Manager enables you to distribute traffic to your public-facing applications across Azure regions. Traffic Manager also has highly available and responsive public endpoints. It has six options for routing traffic:

- Priority
- Weighted
- Performance
- Geographic
- Multivalue
- Subnet

Depending on the application, you can select the best one.

Traffic Manager directs clients' requests to the appropriate service endpoint using DNS based on a traffic-routing method. Traffic Manager also monitors every endpoint's health.

Any Azure-hosted or externally hosted Internet-facing service can be an endpoint. Traffic Manager provides a range of traffic routing methods and endpoint monitoring options for different application needs and automatic failover models. It is secure and resilient to failures, including losing an entire Azure region.

Traffic Manager monitors cloud services such as Azure as well as external sites and services, and it automatically redirects users to an alternate location if a failure occurs.

By directing users to the Azure or external location with the lowest network latency, Traffic Manager makes applications more responsive and improves content delivery times. User traffic can be routed across several places, such as numerous cloud services or multiple Azure web applications. Traffic Manager can distribute traffic equally or based on weights.

Traffic Manager can also be used in burst-to-cloud scenarios, cloud migrations, and failovers, as well as on-premises. Use it for datacenters on-site without inconveniencing customers.

The features of Traffic Manager include:

- Increased application availability and performance
- No interruption of service
- Integrated hybrid applications
- Delivery of complex deployments without disruption of service

How Traffic Manager Works

A public endpoint is assigned to Traffic Manager, and it must be an FQDN. Using the routing method you specified, all traffic arriving at the endpoint will be distributed to endpoints in the back-end. By default, performance routing is used, which distributes traffic based on its performance characteristics. The traffic will be evenly distributed when multiple back-end endpoints are in the same region. Depending on the geographical location and minimum network latency of the endpoints, Traffic Manager will delegate traffic to one or more endpoints closest to the incoming traffic.

The architecture shown in Figure 7.9 provides a high-level overview of Traffic Manager's working method.

The following provides an in-depth description of the flow:

1. `demo.sybex.com` is resolved by sending a DNS query to the client's configured recursive DNS service. Recursive DNS services, sometimes called local DNS servers, do not host any DNS domains directly. To resolve a DNS name, the client is freed from the burden of contacting all the authoritative DNS servers across the Internet.

2. The recursive DNS service resolves the DNS name by finding the name servers for the `Sybex.com` domain. These name servers are then contacted to obtain the DNS record for `demo.sybex.com`. The DNS servers return CNAME records pointing to `sybexdemo.trafficmanager.net` for `sybex.com`.

3. The recursive DNS service finds the name servers of the `trafficmanager.net` domain, provided by the Azure Traffic Manager service. The application then sends a request for the `sybex.trafficmanager.net` DNS record to those DNS servers.

4. A request is sent to Traffic Manager's name servers. The name servers choose an endpoint based on:

   - The configuration state of each endpoint (disabled endpoints won't be returned)
   - The Traffic Manager's health checks, which determine the current health of each endpoint
   - Choice of routing method

5. A CNAME record for the chosen endpoint is returned. Let's assume `sybex-eu.cloudapp.net` is returned.

6. A recursive DNS service is used to determine the name servers for the domain `cloudapp.net`. A DNS record for `sybex-eu.cloudapp.net` is requested from those name servers. In this case, a DNS A record containing the IP address of the service endpoint in the EU is returned.

7. Recursive DNS offers a single DNS response to the client by consolidating the results.

8. DNS results are sent to the client, connecting to the given IP address. Clients connect to application service endpoints directly, not through Traffic Manager. Since it is an HTTPS endpoint, the client performs the SSL/TLS handshake and then requests `/login.aspx` through HTTP GET.

FIGURE 7.9   Azure Traffic Manager Overview

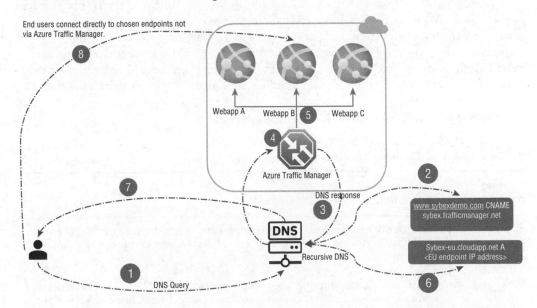

The recursive DNS service caches the DNS responses it receives, and the client device's DNS resolver also caches their results. As a result of caching, subsequent DNS requests are answered faster by utilizing the cached data rather than querying other name servers. A DNS record's time-to-live (TTL) property determines the duration of its cache. With shorter values, the cache expires faster, resulting in a higher number of round-trips to the Traffic Manager name servers. Traffic can take longer to divert from a failed endpoint with longer values. You can configure the TTL used in Traffic Manager DNS responses to be as low as 0 seconds and as high as 2,147,483,647 seconds (the maximum range compliant with RFC-1035), allowing them to pick the value that best suits their needs.

For the AZ-700 exam, keep in mind that Traffic Manager does not provide endpoints or IP addresses clients can connect to. You must configure static IP addresses at the service level rather than in Traffic Manager when assigning static addresses to services.

Traffic Manager Routing Methods

Traffic Manager supports six traffic-routing methods to determine how network traffic should be routed to the various service endpoints. Whenever Traffic Manager receives a DNS query, it applies the traffic-routing method associated with that profile. Which DNS endpoint is returned in the response depends on the traffic-routing method.

A health monitor and an automatic failover feature are available in every Traffic Manager profile. Traffic Manager profiles allow you to configure only one traffic-routing method at a time. You can choose a different traffic-routing method at any time for their profile.

Settings you change will be applied without downtime within one minute. You can use nested Traffic Manager profiles to combine different routing methods. In order to meet the needs of more extensive and complex applications, nesting profiles are a flexible way of configuring traffic routing.

Table 7.7 summarizes the six different routing methods.

TABLE 7.7   Routing methods

Routing methods	Description
Priority	Use Priority routing if you want a single service point for all traffic. When a primary or one backup endpoint is unavailable, you can provide multiple backups.
Weighted	Consider weighted routing when you want traffic distributed across a set of endpoints based on their importance. This method distributes equal weight across all endpoints.

Routing methods	Description
Performance	You can choose performance routing if your endpoints are located in different geographic regions and you want end users to use the closest endpoint to minimize latency.
Geographic	When you select Geographic routing, users can be directed to specific endpoints (Azure, External, or Nested) depending on the geographic origin of their DNS queries. It is possible to comply with scenarios such as data sovereignty mandates, localizing content and ensuring a good user experience, and measuring traffic from different regions with this routing technique.
Multivalue	Choose Multivalue when the only endpoints of a Traffic Manager profile are IPv4 or IPv6 addresses. All healthy endpoints are returned when a query for this profile is received.
Subnet	Use Subnet traffic routing to transform a set of end-user IP address ranges into specific endpoints. When a request is received, an endpoint is mapped to an IP address based on the request's source address.

Priority-Based Traffic Routing

To ensure the reliability of their services, enterprises usually deploy one or more backup services in case their primary service fails. Azure customers can quickly implement this failover pattern by implementing the Priority traffic-routing method.

Various service endpoints are prioritized in Traffic Manager profiles. By default, Traffic Manager forwards all traffic to the primary (highest priority) endpoint. The traffic is routed to the second endpoint if the primary endpoint cannot be reached. A scenario in which both primary and secondary endpoints are unavailable results in traffic going to the third. Endpoint availability depends on its configured status (enabled or disabled) and its ongoing monitoring. Figure 7.10 shows the architecture of Priority-based traffic routing.

Using the Priority property in Resource Manager, you can set the endpoint priority explicitly. A lower value represents a higher priority, and a value between 1 and 1000 denotes a lower priority. Priority values cannot be shared across endpoints, and it is not mandatory to set this property. If omitted, the endpoint order will be used as the priority.

Weighted-Based Traffic Routing

Users of the Weighted traffic-routing method can choose whether traffic should be distributed equally or according to predetermined weightings. You can assign weights to each endpoint in a profile configuration. The weight can be an integer between 1 and 1000. By default, Traffic Manager uses 1 as the weight, which means a higher priority.

FIGURE 7.10   Priority-based traffic routing

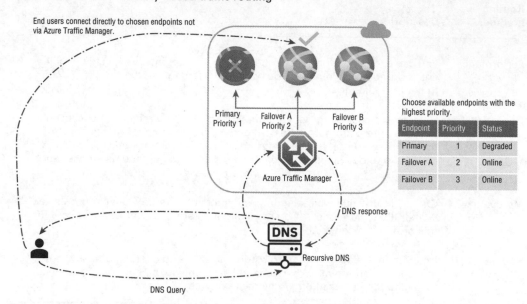

Traffic Manager randomly selects an endpoint for each DNS query it receives. All endpoints are assigned weights based on their selection probabilities, and using the same weight on all endpoints ensures even traffic distribution. In the DNS response, endpoints with a higher or lower weight are more or less likely to be returned. Figure 7.11 shows the architecture of Weighted-based traffic routing.

FIGURE 7.11   Weighted-based traffic routing

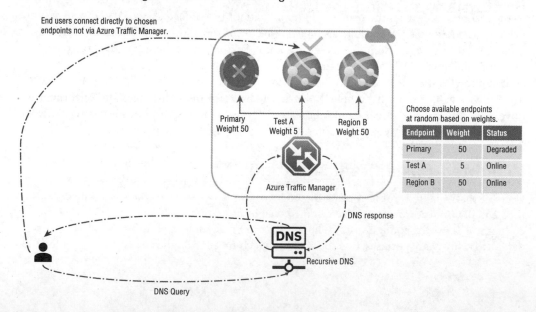

Several scenarios are enabled by the weighted method:

- An incremental application upgrade involves gradually increasing the amount of traffic to a new endpoint from a small percentage.

- To migrate an application to Azure, create a profile that includes Azure and external endpoints. The weight of the new endpoints should be adjusted to prefer the endpoints.

- Expand an on-premises deployment into Azure by placing it after a Traffic Manager profile. When you require extra capacity in Azure, you can add or enable more additional endpoints and specify what allotment of traffic moves to each endpoint.

The Azure portal, Azure PowerShell, CLI, and REST APIs can be used to set weights.

It is important to remember that clients cache DNS responses, that the recursive DNS servers cache them, and that clients use them to resolve DNS names. If clients cache DNS responses, weighted traffic distributions may change. The traffic distribution works as expected when the number of clients and recursive DNS servers is large. Caching, however, can significantly skew traffic distribution when there are few clients or recursive DNS servers.

The following are some everyday use cases:

- Testing and development environments

- Communication between applications

- Users of an application who share a common recursive DNS infrastructure (such as employees of a company connecting through a proxy)

All DNS-based traffic-routing systems, not just Traffic Manager, exhibit these DNS caching effects. It's possible to bypass DNS caching by explicitly clearing the cache, and if that doesn't work, an alternative traffic-routing method may be more appropriate.

Performance-Based Traffic Routing

Your applications can be made more responsive by deploying endpoints at two or more locations across the globe. With Azure's Performance method of traffic routing, you can route traffic to the nearest user location. Figure 7.12 shows the architecture of Performance-based traffic routing.

The "closest" endpoint isn't always the closest by geographic distance. The Performance traffic-routing method determines the closest endpoint by measuring network latency. Traffic Manager tracks the round-trip times between the Azure datacenters' IP addresses using an Internet latency table.

The Internet latency table is used to determine the source IP address of incoming DNS requests in Traffic Manager. Once that IP address range is identified, Traffic Manager chooses an available endpoint in the Azure datacenter that has the lowest latency. The DNS response includes Traffic Manager's selection.

Clients do not directly submit DNS queries to Traffic Manager. On the other hand, recursive DNS queries come from clients configured to use recursive DNS. This means that the recursive DNS server's IP address is used to find the "closest" endpoint, not the clients. The client can use this address as a proxy.

FIGURE 7.12 Performance-based traffic routing

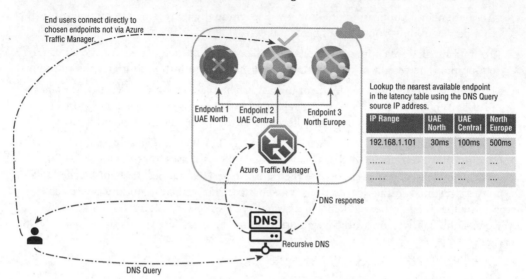

As changes in the global Internet and Azure regions occur, Traffic Manager regularly updates the Internet latency table. However, application performance varies due to real-time variations in traffic across the Internet. A given service endpoint is not monitored for load by Performance traffic routing. If an endpoint becomes unreachable, it won't be included in the DNS query results.

Geographic-Based Traffic Routing

Geographic routing can be configured in Traffic Manager profiles to send users to specific endpoints (Azure, External, or Nested) depending on where they originate from. You can use this routing method to comply with data sovereignty mandates, localize content and user experiences, and measure traffic across multiple regions. Every endpoint associated with a profile configured for Geographic routing must have a set of geographic regions.

Each geographic region can have the following granularity levels:

- World – any region
- Regional Grouping
- Country/Region
- State/Province

If an endpoint is assigned a region or series of regions, any requests from those regions will only be routed to that endpoint. Traffic Manager uses the source IP address of the DNS query to identify the region from which a user is querying—commonly identified as the local DNS resolver's IP address. Figure 7.13 shows the architecture of Geographic-based traffic routing.

FIGURE 7.13   Geographic-based traffic routing

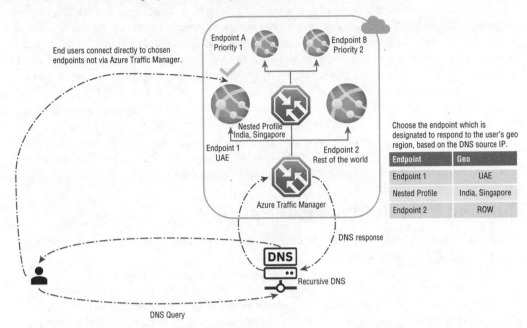

Upon reading the source IP address of a DNS query, Traffic Manager determines which geographic region it originates from. Then it checks to see if an endpoint is mapped to this geographic region. Lookups start at the lowest level of granularity (State/Province or Country/Region, where supported) and go all the way up to the highest level, which is World. The first match is chosen to return in the query response using this traversal. A child profile is returned when matching with a nested type endpoint based on its routing method.

Multivalue-Based Traffic Routing

Multiple healthy endpoints can be obtained by using the Multivalue traffic-routing method. In an unresponsive endpoint, this configuration allows the caller to perform client-side retries with other endpoints. In this way, you can increase the availability of services and reduce the latency of a DNS query to obtain a healthy endpoint. The Multivalue routing method only works if all the endpoints of type External are IPv4 or IPv6 addresses. This profile returns all healthy endpoints and a configurable maximum number of results when a query is received.

Subnet-Based Traffic Routing

Organizations can use the Subnet traffic-routing method to map a set of end-user IP address ranges to their specific endpoints. Traffic Manager inspects the source IP address of a DNS query for that profile, determines the endpoint it is mapped to, and returns it in the query response. The source IP address is the DNS resolver that the caller uses most of the time.

The IP address to be mapped to an endpoint can be specified as CIDR ranges (for example, 1.2.3.0/24) or as an address range (1.2.3.4-5.6.7.8). You must define an endpoint with no address range and take traffic from any remaining subnets if the IP address range within a profile is not the same as the IP address range of another endpoint within that profile. Any undefined ranges will result in a NODATA response from Traffic Manager if no fallback endpoint has been specified. Microsoft recommends defining a fallback endpoint to ensure all possible IP ranges are specified.

Users connecting from a specific IP space may experience different results depending on the subnet routing. You can, for example, have all requests from their corporate office routed to another endpoint. You can use this routing method to test an internal version of an app. In another scenario, users connecting from a specific ISP are provided with a different experience (for example, users connecting from a given ISP are blocked).

Building a Traffic Manager Profile

This section covers creating a Traffic Manager profile to provide high availability for Company XYZ's web application.

In Exercise 7.2 you created and deployed two web application instances in two regions, and you reuse them in Exercise 7.3. Traffic Manager will act as the primary endpoint in the first region and a failover endpoint in the second region. Exercise 7.3 involves creating a Traffic Manager profile based on endpoint priority. Users will be redirected to the primary web application site through this profile. Traffic Manager will always monitor the web application. If the primary site goes down, the backup site will automatically fail.

You will deploy an environment as shown in Figure 7.14.

FIGURE 7.14   Architecture overview of Azure Traffic Manager (ATM)

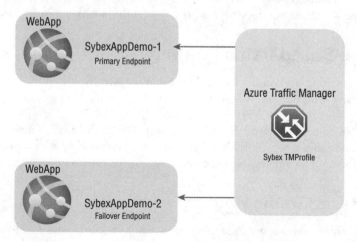

To complete the exercise, you need to perform the following three activities.

- **Activity 1:** Build two instances of a web app.
- **Activity 2:** Build a Traffic Manager profile.
- **Activity 3:** Add Traffic Manager endpoints.

Traffic Manager profiles control traffic distribution to cloud services or website endpoints through traffic-routing methods. Creating Traffic Manager profiles is possible through the Azure portal, and the Azure portal allows you to configure endpoints, monitoring, and other settings after creating your profile. There can be up to 200 profiles in Traffic Manager. Many scenarios only require a few endpoints.

Exercise 7.3 starts with Activity 2, since you performed Activity 1 in Exercise 7.2.

EXERCISE 7.3

Build a Traffic Manager Profile

1. Log into a personal or business account in the Azure portal at `https://portal.azure.com`.

2. Click Create A Resource and choose Traffic Manager Profile. Enter the following information in the Create Traffic Manager Profile Wizard (see the next image):

Name	Choose your preferred name.
Routing Method	Choose your preferred routing method; for this exercise, use Priority.
Subscription	Choose your subscription.
Resource Group	Choose a resource group or create a new resource group.
Resource Group Location	For this exercise, use UAE North.

There is no location restriction on Azure Traffic Manager. You must, however, designate where the metadata associated with Traffic Manager profiles should reside in the resource group. Due to this location, there will be no impact on the profile's runtime availability.

Dashboard > Load balancing >

Create Traffic Manager profile ⋯

Name *

SybexdemoTM

.trafficmanager.net

Routing method

Priority

Subscription *

Pay as you

Resource group *

sybexdemo

Create new

Resource group location ⓘ

UAE North

[Create]   Automation options

3. Review and click Create.

Traffic Manager lets you control how network traffic is distributed to applications deployed in different datacenters. Each deployment of an application is configured as an endpoint in Traffic Manager. The DNS response from Traffic Manager is selected based on the endpoints that are available to return. It chooses the route based on the status of the endpoints and the traffic-routing method.

Now let's move forward with Activity 3, Add Traffic Manager Endpoints.

1. Log into a personal or business account in the Azure portal at `https://portal.azure.com`.

2. Click SybexdemoTM in the resource list, browse to Setting, choose Endpoints, and click Add. In the page that opens, enter the following information (see the next image):

Type	Microsoft supports three types of endpoints— Azure endpoints, external endpoints, and nested endpoints—to load-balance traffic to a cloud service, web application, or public IP address within the same subscription.
Name	Enter your preferred name.
Target resource type	For Azure endpoints:

You can choose from the following resource types when you want to use the Azure endpoint type: Cloud service App Service slot Public IP address.

Priority	Give this endpoint a priority. If you enter **1**, all traffic will go to this endpoint when it is healthy.
Custom Header Settings	The custom headers need to be configured as host. An unlimited number of pairs can be used. Compatible with HTTPS and HTTP. The profile setting overrides custom header settings.

3. Click Add.

When you add endpoints to a Traffic Manager profile, their status will be checked, and once they have been checked, their Monitor status changes to Online.

Repeat steps 1–2 to add the secondary failover endpoint.

By setting Priority to 2, you ensure that traffic will route to the configured failover endpoint if the primary endpoint becomes unavailable.

You can test if the Traffic Manager profile successfully sends traffic to the failover endpoint post-deployment by bringing down the primary endpoint.

For the Microsoft AZ-700 exam, keep in mind that when configuring Traffic Manager, you should use Priority to direct users to the instance with the lowest latency.

Virtual Network NAT

Network address translation (NAT) provides outbound Internet connectivity for virtual networks while serving as a network address translation service.

Virtual Network Address Translation (VNet NAT) is a fully managed, highly resilient service. With VNet NAT, virtual networks can connect outbound to the Internet. All outbound connectivity on a subnet is established using the VNet NAT's static public IP addresses.

You can have your private IP address virtual machine connected to the Internet via a known and predetermined IP address. You can assign VMs a public IP address, and the VMs will use that to communicate with the Azure cloud.

You can place the VMs behind a load balancer, which has a public IP, and that would be used for communication.

Consider an organization that doesn't have public IP addresses for their virtual machines. An organization can't grant virtual machine private access through a firewall to another network without authorizing several Azure outbound addresses. The organization will access a remote virtual machine from a predetermined static address.

NAT can be deployed in a specific availability zone and has built-in redundancy. When creating availability zone scenarios, NAT can be isolated within a particular zone by default. These deployments are known as *zonal deployments*.

From the beginning, NAT has been scaled out fully. Scaling or ramping up is not required, and Azure will handle the NAT process for you. Multiple fault domains allow NAT to handle numerous failures without service interruption.

VNet NAT's key benefits are illustrated in Figure 7.15.

FIGURE 7.15   Virtual network NAT benefits

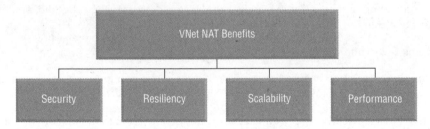

A NAT gateway resource can use a public IP and public IP prefix.

It is possible to create flows between the virtual network and services outside the virtual network. Services outside your organization's VNet cannot establish connections to instances due to return traffic from the Internet.

NAT can be used with public IP addresses, public IP prefixes, or both. Public IP prefixes can be assigned directly to organizations or distributed across multiple NAT gateway resources. The network address translation will shape up all traffic to the prefix's range of IP addresses. Load balancers and public IP addresses are not compatible with NAT, and basic resources must reside on a subnet associated with a gateway. The NAT gateway allows basic load balancers and public IP to be upgraded to standard.

For the AZ-700 exam, keep in mind that the following are limitations of VNet NAT:

- The NAT feature is compatible with the public IP, public IP prefix, and load-balancer resources in standard SKU. Essential resources (for example, basic load balancers) and products derived from them aren't compatible with NAT. Subnets without NAT configuration must be used for the resources needed.

- There is support for IPv4 addresses. NAT does not impact the IPv6 address family. IPv6 prefixes cannot be used for NAT.

- NAT cannot span multiple virtual networks.

- There is no support for IP fragmentation.

- NAT supports TCP and UDP protocols only. ICMP is not supported.

Using a Virtual Network NAT

There is a shortage of IPv4 address ranges globally, and accessing Internet resources can be expensive. To gain access to external resources on a public network, internal resources on a private network needed routable IPv4 addresses. This is where network address translation (NAT) comes in. As an alternative to purchasing an IPv4 address for each resource that needs Internet access, you can use a NAT service to translate outgoing requests from internal resources to an external IP address, enabling communication.

Microsoft offers NAT services for mapping a single IP address, IP prefixes for a range of IP addresses, and ports associated with an IP address. Public IP address resources or public IP prefix resources, or a combination of both, can be used with NAT. You can directly use a public IP prefix or distribute the public IP addresses of the prefix across NAT gateways. Any traffic between the prefix and its IP address range will be routed through NAT. NAT creates flows between the virtual network and the Internet. Internet traffic can only return if there is an active flow.

You can configure NAT for each VNet subnet to enable outbound connectivity by specifying a NAT gateway resource. Any virtual machine instance that connects to the Internet via UDP or TCP will use NAT after NAT is configured. You don't need to create user-defined routes, and no further configuration is required. NAT replaces the default Internet destination over all other outbound scenarios.

As NAT scales to support dynamic workloads, you can avoid extensive pre-planning or pre-allocating addresses. NAT supports up to 64,000 concurrent UDP and TCP, respectively, using port network address translation (PNAT or PAT). NAT can support up to 16 public IP addresses.

Figure 7.16 shows the high-level workflow to deploy a NAT.

FIGURE 7.16 High-level workflow to deploy NAT

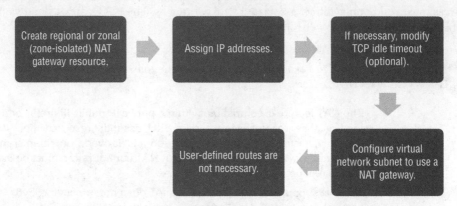

NAT is recommended for connecting to a public endpoint in all outbound scenarios for production workloads. In the following examples, NAT gateways are used for inbound and outbound traffic.

Example 1: Public IP Addresses for NAT and VM Instances Outbound traffic will be routed through NAT gateways. No outbound traffic will be affected.

Figure 7.17 shows a NAT gateway with a public load balancer.

FIGURE 7.17 NAT gateway with a public load balancer

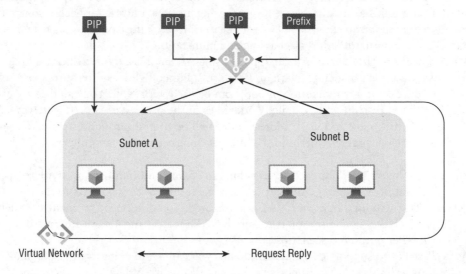

Example 2: Public IP Address at Instance Level and Standard Public Load Balancer with NAT and VM   The NAT gateway supersedes a load balancing or outbound rule that specifies outbound connectivity, and inbound connections are unaffected.

Figure 7.18 depicts a NAT gateway with a public load balancer at instance level.

FIGURE 7.18   NAT gateway with a public load balancer at instance level

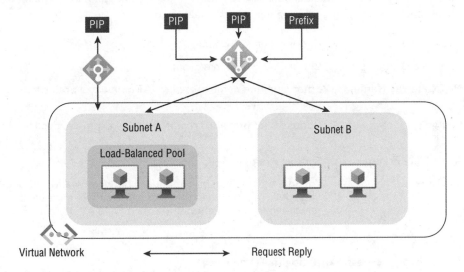

In Azure network security groups (NSGs), a VM's inbound and outbound traffic can be filtered. NAT outbound traffic can be monitored with NSG flow logs enabled in Azure.

NAT gateways can provide up to 50 Gbps of bandwidth. You can split deployments into multiple subnets and assign a NAT gateway to scale out. Each assigned outbound IP address can receive up to 64,000 TCP and UDP flows.

From the perspective of design and deployment, consider the following while using NAT:

- Public IP addresses and basic load balancers are not compatible with NAT. Instead, use public IP addresses and load balancers with standard SKUs.
- The NAT gateway does not support IP fragmentation.

Allocate Public IP or Public IP Prefixes for a NAT Gateway

In Exercise 7.4 you create a NAT gateway resource. You can use one or more public IP address resources, public IP prefixes, or both.

In this exercise, the provisioning of public IP addresses is already done.

EXERCISE 7.4

Create a NAT Gateway

1. Log into a personal or business account in the Azure portal at `https://portal .azure.com`.

2. Click Create A Resource, then choose NAT Gateway and click Create. In the page that opens, enter the following information (see the next image):

Subscription	Choose your subscription.
Resource Group	Choose your resource group.
NAT Gateway Name	Enter a unique name for your NAT gateway. For this example, use AppDemo.
Region	Choose your preferred region. For this example, use UAE North.
Availability Zone	For this example, keep the Default Zone.
Idle Timeout	The idle timeout can be configured between 4 and 120 minutes, determining when the NAT gateway will remove idle flows. Whenever an endpoint uses a flow, a TCP Reset is sent.

Dashboard > NAT gateways >

Create network address translation (NAT) gateway   ...

Basics   Outbound IP   Subnet   Tags   Review + create

Azure NAT gateway can be used to translate outbound flows from a virtual network to the public internet.
Learn more about NAT gateways.

Project details

Select a subscription to manage deployed resources and costs. Use resource groups like folders to organize and manage all your resources.

Subscription * | Pay as you   ∨ |

└── Resource group * | sybexdemo   ∨ |
                                          Create new

Instance details

NAT gateway name * | AppDemo   ✓ |

Region * | UAE North   ∨ |

Availability zone | ∨ |

ℹ No availability zones are available for the location you have selected. To view locations that support availability zones, go to aka.ms/zonedregions.

Idle timeout (minutes) * ⓘ | 4 |
                                                                                      4-120

| Review + create | | < Previous | | Next : Outbound IP > | | Download a template for automation |

3.   Select the Outbound IP tab, click Next: Outbound IP to open the page shown here:

4.   Choose SybexappPublicIP-1 for Public IP address on the Outbound IP tab, then select the Review + Create tab or click the Review + Create button.

As of this writing, public IPv6 addresses and public IPv6 prefixes are not supported by NAT gateways.

Associate a Virtual Network NAT with a Subnet

All computing resources in a subnet can use NAT if it's associated with the subnet. In addition, all subnets in a VNet can share resources. When associated with a Public IP prefix, NAT will automatically scale to the number of IP addresses required for outbound connections.

With NAT, each subnet can define its outbound connectivity. Within a single virtual network, multiple subnets can have different NATs. It is also possible to use the same NAT for numerous subnets within the same virtual network. Configuration of a subnet involves specifying which NAT gateway resource should be used. The outbound traffic for the subnet is handled by NAT automatically without custom configuration. Users do not need to define routes. The NAT protocol takes precedence over other outbound scenarios and replaces the default Internet destination.

There can be only one NAT per subnet, and NAT cannot be deployed within a gateway subnet.

There can be no association between NAT and IPv6 Public IP addresses or IPv6 Public IP prefixes. The subnet can be associated with a dual-stack network, however.

In Exercise 7.4, you created a virtual network NAT; now in Exercise 7.5 you associate a virtual network NAT with a subnet.

EXERCISE 7.5

Associate a VNet NAT with a Subnet

1. Log into a personal or business account in the Azure portal at `https://portal.azure.com`.

2. Click Create A Resource, then choose NAT Gateway and click Create to open the page in the next image. Enter the following information:

Subscription	Choose your subscription.
Resource Group	Choose your resource group.
NAT Gateway Name	Enter a unique name for your NAT gateway. For this example, use AppDemo.
Region	Choose your preferred region. For this example, use UAE North.
Availability Zone	For this example, keep Default Zone.
Idle Timeout	The idle timeout can be configured between 4 and 120 minutes, determining when the NAT gateway will remove idle flows. Whenever an endpoint uses a flow, a TCP Reset is sent.

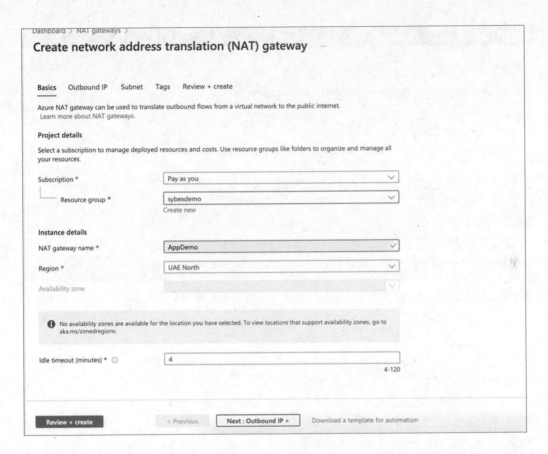

3. Select the Outbound IP tab, or click Next: Outbound IP to open the page shown here:

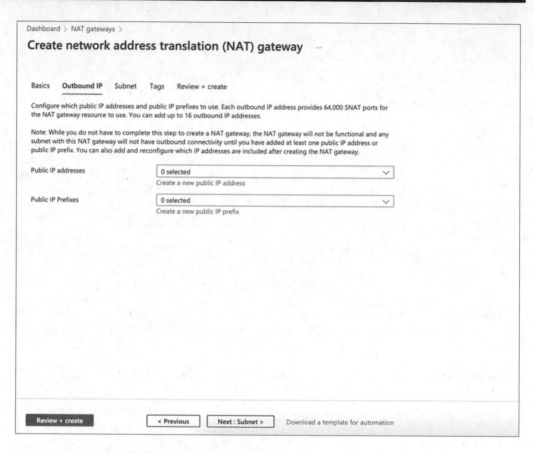

Dashboard > NAT gateways >

Create network address translation (NAT) gateway   ...

Basics   **Outbound IP**   Subnet   Tags   Review + create

Configure which public IP addresses and public IP prefixes to use. Each outbound IP address provides 64,000 SNAT ports for the NAT gateway resource to use. You can add up to 16 outbound IP addresses.

Note: While you do not have to complete this step to create a NAT gateway, the NAT gateway will not be functional and any subnet with this NAT gateway will not have outbound connectivity until you have added at least one public IP address or public IP prefix. You can also add and reconfigure which IP addresses are included after creating the NAT gateway.

Public IP addresses   0 selected   ⌄
                           Create a new public IP address

Public IP Prefixes   0 selected   ⌄
                           Create a new public IP prefix

Review + create   < Previous   Next : Subnet >   Download a template for automation

4. Choose SybexappPublicIP-1 for Public IP Address.

5. Click Add Subnet and enter the following information in the page that opens:

Subnet Name	Enter your subnet. For this example use SybexSubnet.
Subnet address range	Enter your preferred IP range.

6. Select the Review + Create tab or click the Review + Create button.

From the perspective of management, consider the following:

- You cannot directly modify an existing virtual network's NAT IP address. You must create a new public IP address and attach it to a VNet NAT. Make sure the new IP address is associated with the NAT gateway resource. Remove the old address from the NAT gateway resource.

- There will be no traffic disruption if one of the IP addresses is removed while multiple public IP addresses are assigned to a NAT gateway resource.

- NAT gateways cannot connect directly to private IP addresses with public IP addresses over the Internet.

Summary

This chapter provided a high-level overview of the many load balancing options available to Azure networking engineers in the Azure cloud. You learned about four of those: Azure application gateways, Azure Front Door, Azure Traffic Manager, and Azure Virtual NAT.

You also learned how to load-balance network traffic effectively to ensure high availability of services.

We also discussed designing and implementing Application Gateway, including Application Gateway deployment options and how to choose between manual and autoscaling. You also learned how to create a back-end pool and configure health probes, listeners, routing rules, HTTP settings, Transport Layer Security (TLS), and rewrite sets.

Next, you learned how to deploy Azure Front Door, choose an Front Door SKU, and configure health probes, including customization of HTTP response codes, SSL termination, end-to-end SSL encryption, multisite listeners, back-end targets, routing rules, and redirection rules.

Then you learned how to deploy an Azure Traffic Manager profile, configure a routing method (mode), and configure HTTP settings.

Finally, we showed you how to design and implement an Azure VNet NAT and choose when to use it, how to allocate public IP or public IP prefixes for a NAT gateway, and how to associate a VNet NAT with a subnet.

Exam Essentials

Understand Azure Application Gateway deployment options.   You can manage traffic to your web applications using Azure Application Gateway, a load balancer for web traffic. Application Gateway offers features such as load-balancing HTTP traffic, web application firewalls, and TLS/SSL encryption support between users and application servers and between application gateways and servers.

In addition to the URI path, Application Gateway can use host headers to decide how to route requests. By using the incoming URL, for instance, you can choose how to route traffic. The incoming URL containing/images can be routed to a specific set of servers (known as a pool) configured for images. In URLs that contain videos, the traffic is routed to a pool dedicated to videos.

Understand the differences between manual and autoscaling configurations.   WAF and Application Gateway can be configured to scale in two different ways: automatically and manually. With autoscaling enabled, the Application Gateway and WAF v2 SKUs scale out or in according to application traffic. Using this model makes your application more elastic, and it doesn't need to guess gateway size or instance count. The gateway will not need to run at maximum capacity for maximum traffic loads when you use this mode, so you will save money. Microsoft recommends that you specify a minimum and optional complete instance count.

A manual mode is also available, which disables autoscaling. When the Application Gateway or WAF can't handle all the traffic, it could result in traffic loss. In manual mode, instance counts must be specified, and there are 125 possible instances.

Know how to create a back-end pool.   Web traffic is directed to specific back-end resources through the application gateway. You can create listeners, rules, and back-end resources and assign them to ports. Here is a simple setup: a public IP address for the front-end, a listener to host the single site on the application gateway, two virtual machines in the back-end pool, and a basic request routing rule.

Be able to configure health probes.   All Azure Application Gateway back-end resources are monitored by default, and any resource deemed unhealthy is automatically removed. When unhealthy instances become available and respond to health probes, Application Gateway adds them back to the healthy back-end pool. Health probes are sent using the same port as the back-end HTTP settings by default. Using a custom health probe, you can change this.

Understand how to configure listeners.   A listener is a logical entity that monitors incoming connection requests' port, protocol, host, and IP address. Configuring the listener requires entering values that match the values in the incoming request on the gateway. A default listener is created when you create an application gateway through the Azure portal by selecting the protocol and port. An HTTP2   listener can be enabled if needed. The settings of that default listener (`appGatewayHttpListener`) can be edited after creating the application gateway, or new listeners can be created.

Be able to configure routing rules.   A default rule is created when you create an application gateway using the Azure portal (rule1). The `appGatewayHttpListener` rule binds the default listener to the default back-end pool (`appGatewayBackendPool`) and the default back-end HTTP settings (`appGatewayBackendHttpSettings`). Once the gateway has been created, you can edit the settings of the default rule or create new ones.

Know how to configure HTTP settings. This configuration directs traffic to the back-end servers using the application gateway. An HTTP setting must be associated with one or more request-routing rules after it is created.

Know how to configure Transport Layer Security (TLS). A secure connection between a web server and a browser is established using Transport Layer Security (TLS), formerly known as Secure Sockets Layer (SSL). Using this link, all data passed between a web server and browser remains private and encrypted. Application gateways support both TLS termination at the gateway and end-to-end TLS encryption.

Gateways support TLS termination at the gateway, and traffic is typically unencrypted to the back-end servers.

Know how to select an Azure Front Door SKU. With Front Door, you can deliver content and files, build global apps and APIs, and provide a more reliable, secure, and scalable experience for your users. Front Door is a cutting-edge cloud content delivery network (CDN) that provides fast, reliable, and secure access to your applications' static and dynamic content worldwide. Front Door uses Microsoft's global edge network with hundreds of international and local POPs (An Internet service provider [ISP] local access point is a POP [Point Of Presence].) Users can connect to the Internet through their Internet service provider through a point of presence (POP) close to your enterprise and consumer end users.

Be able to configure health probes, including customization of HTTP response codes. For each Front Door environment, a synthetic HTTP/HTTPS request is sent periodically to each of your configured origins to determine the health and proximity of each back-end. Front Door uses the probe results to determine the best source to route your client requests. This can be done either using HTTP or HTTPS. Probes are sent over the same TCP port used to route client requests and cannot be overridden.

Know how to configure SSL termination and end-to-end SSL encryption. TLS is the standard security technology for establishing an encrypted link between a web server and a browser. All data exchanged between the web server and the browser remains private and encrypted through this link. Front Door (AFD) supports end-to-end TLS encryption to meet your security or compliance requirements. With Front Door TLS/SSL offload, the TLS connection is terminated, the traffic is decrypted at the Front Door, and then re-encrypted before being sent back to the back-end. To enforce TLS encryption from the client to the back-end, configure HTTPS as the forwarding protocol on your Front Door so that connections to the back-end occur over the public IP address.

Know how to configure routing rules, including redirection rules. It is possible to change the path of a request routed to your origin using Front Door. In addition to adding conditions, URL rewrite can also ensure that URLs or specified headers get rewritten only when certain conditions are met. Based on the request and response information, these conditions can be specified.

Traffic is routed over multiple stages for Front Door. First, clients route traffic from Front Door to the client. Then Front Door determines the origin of traffic based on your configuration. Front Door's firewall, routing rules, rules engine, and caching configuration affect the routing process.

Be able to configure a routing method (mode).   Traffic Manager offers six methods of traffic routing to determine how to route network traffic to the various service endpoints. Each DNS query Traffic Manager receives gets routed according to the traffic-routing method associated with that profile, and traffic-routing methods determine which endpoints are returned in DNS responses.

There are six routes for routing traffic: Priority routes, Weighted routes, Performance routes, Geographic routes, Multivalue routes, and Subnet routes.

Be able to configure endpoints.   You can specify the endpoint priority for each endpoint explicitly using the Priority property in Resource Manager. Values for this property range from 1 to 1000, with a lower value representing a higher priority. A priority value cannot be shared between endpoints, and it is optional to set this property. When omitted, a default priority is calculated based on the order of the endpoints.

Know how to create HTTP settings.   The Traffic Manager probing agent initiates a GET request to the endpoint using the given port, protocol, and relative path when the monitoring protocol is set as HTTP or HTTPS. Endpoints are considered healthy if the probing agent receives a 200-OK response or expected status codes. The response might be different, or there may not be a response within the timeout period. If the Tolerated Number Of Failures setting is set to 0, Traffic Manager is probing agent re-attempts. The result is that no re-attempts are made. If the Tolerated Number Of Failures setting is exceeded, the endpoint is marked unhealthy.

Understand when to use a VNet NAT.   NAT (network address translation) with virtual networks is a managed, highly resilient service. With VNet NAT, virtual networks can easily access the Internet. VNet NAT uses static public IP addresses on a subnet when configured on a subnet.

Understand how to allocate public IP or public IP prefixes for a NAT gateway.   There are two types of public IP for NAT gateways: public IP and public IP prefix. The VNet NAT feature is compatible with standard SKU public IP addresses and public IP prefix resources. Public IP addresses of a prefix can be used directly or distributed across multiple NAT gateway resources. All traffic is shaped up to the range of IP addresses for the prefix by the NAT gateway. A basic load balancer or a basic public IP address cannot be used with a VNet NAT gateway. Basic resources must be located on a separate subnet from the NAT gateway. You can upgrade the basic load balancer and basic public IP to work with a NAT gateway.

Understand how to associate a VNet NAT with a subnet.   All compute resources in a subnet can use the NAT gateway resource associated with that subnet. Virtual networks can share this resource across all subnets. In the case of NAT gateways related to public IP addresses, scaling is automatic based on the number of outbound IP addresses.

Review Questions

1. Azure Application Gateway should be configured so that users will not experience performance degradation during peak hours. How should this be done?

    A. Using autoscaling

    B. Using manual scaling

    C. Via health probes

    D. Tuning methods

2. A company's app service has 20 instances. The components reside in a different Azure region and are accessible through a public endpoint.

    HRMSApp is an application being developed by the HR department at the company. HRMSApp uses endpoints every 15 minutes and connects to the first available one.

    Cloud consumers will use Traffic Manager to hold the list of endpoints.

    DNS caching can be minimized by configuring Traffic Manager profiles.

    Which algorithm fits this requirement?

    A. Performance

    B. Multivalue

    C. Weight

    D. Geographic

3. There are two primary methods of routing traffic in Application Gateway. Which of the following are applicable? (Choose all that apply.)

    A. Path-based routing

    B. Event-based routing

    C. Multisite routing

    D. All the above

4. Which of the following is true of Front Door and Application Gateway?

    A. Front Door is a global service, whereas Application Gateway is a regional service.

    B. Front Door is not a global service, and Application Gateway is a not a regional service.

    C. Front Door is a global service, and Application Gateway is a not a regional service.

    D. Front Door is not a global service, and Application Gateway is a regional service.

5. From the Front Door perspective, which of the following incoming traffic patterns determines whether the incoming request matches the routing rule?

    A. Host

    B. Path matches

    C. Host and path matches

    D. None of the above

6. Which of the following is true of Front Door's back-end health probes?

    A. Health probes are used to monitor Front Door's back-end.

    B. Health probes are not used to monitor Front Door's back-end.

    C. Health probes are used to log events about Front Door's back-end.

    D. Health probes are not used to log events about Front Door's back-end.

7. How many edge environment requests can Front Door handle?

    A. 99 to 1,000 requests per minute

    B. 32 to 500 requests per minute

    C. 25 to 1,200 requests per minute

    D. 75 to 1,000 requests per minute

8. The Traffic Manager listener checks an incoming connection request based on which of the following?

    A. Port and protocol

    B. Host and IP address

    C. A and B

    D. None of the above

9. What is Traffic Manager based on?

    A. DNS

    B. DHCP

    C. NAT

    D. Subnet

10. What enables an organization to distribute traffic to their public-facing applications across Azure regions?

    A. Azure Traffic Distribution

    B. Azure Traffic Consolidation

    C. Azure Traffic Segmentation

    D. Azure Traffic Controller

11. What is the name of the virtual machine instance's network protocol that connects to the Internet? (Choose all that apply.)

    A. TCP

    B. UDP

    C. HTTPS

    D. SFTP

12. What do you specify for each VNet subnet to enable outbound connectivity?

   A. NAT gateway resource

   B. Azure Traffic Manager

   C. Azure Application Gateway

   D. Azure Virtual appliance

13. How many options for routing traffic does Azure Traffic Manager give you?

   A. 3

   B. 6

   C. 10

   D. 9

14. What does Front Door use the Anycast protocol and a split TCP and Microsoft's global network for to improve global connectivity?

   A. Layer 7 HTTP HTTPS

   B. Layer 6 Presentation layer SSL

   C. Layer 7 SSH DNS

   D. Layer 2 Switching Security

15. How many endpoints does Traffic Manager support per profile?

   A. 821

   B. 401

   C. 200

   D. 221

16. Which of the following are features of Azure Traffic Manager?

   A. Increased application availability and performance

   B. No interruption of service

   C. Integrated hybrid applications

   D. All the above

17. Which of the following protocols allows a custom domain associated with a Front Door?

   A. HTTPS

   B. HTTP

   C. SFTP

   D. SSL

18. Which of the following does Front Door support?

   A. End-to-end TLS encryption

   B. Up-to-downstream systems

   C. Up to load balancers

   D. Up to VM level

19. What is the routing rule used to associate the rewrite configuration with the source listener?

    A. Global header rewrite

    B. Reevaluate path map

    C. Path-based routing

    D. Host header

20. Which three options can an organization choose for load balancers with Availability Zone?

    A. No-zone (the default option)

    B. A specific zone, or zone redundant

    C. Region specific

    D. A and B

Chapter

8

Design, Deploy, and Manage Azure Firewall and Network Security Groups

THE MICROSOFT AZ-700 EXAM OBJECTIVES COVERED IN THIS CHAPTER INCLUDE:

✓ **Design, implement and manage an Azure Firewall deployment**

- Design an Azure Firewall deployment
- Create and implement an Azure Firewall deployment
- Configure Azure Firewall rules
- Create and implement Azure Firewall Manager policies
- Create a secure hub by deploying Azure Firewall inside an Azure Virtual WAN hub
- Integrate an Azure Virtual WAN hub with a third-party NVA

✓ **Implement and manage network security groups (NSGs)**

- Create an NSG
- Associate an NSG to a resource
- Create an application security group (ASG)
- Associate an ASG to a NIC
- Create and configure NSG rules
- Interpret NSG flow logs
- Validate NSG flow rules
- Verify IP flow

Azure Firewall is a cloud-native network firewall that works with Azure Services Fabric to provide security and threat protection. It's a stateful firewall as a service with built-in high availability and unrestricted scalability in the cloud and zero maintenance.

In this chapter, you will first learn about Azure Firewall design and deployment and how to configure its rules and policies. You will also learn how to deploy and configure a secure hub within an Azure Virtual WAN hub to integrate it with third-party network virtual appliances (NVAs).

Next, you will learn the steps to build an Azure network security group (NSG) and attach it to a resource, and how to make an application security group (ASG) and connect it to a NIC. You will also learn how to create and configure NSG rules and read NSG flow logs, how to validate NSG flow rules, and how to verify IP flow.

Network security groups filter network traffic between Azure resources and Azure virtual networks. They contain security rules that allow or deny inbound or outbound network traffic to and from several types of Azure resources. You can specify each rule's source and destination, port, and protocol.

Azure Firewall and Firewall Manager Features

Firewalls typically block all network traffic by default, analyze that traffic and check whether predefined conditions (rules) are met before allowing the traffic to pass. These conditions could include a specified IP address, FQDN, network port, or network protocol.

Firewall rules are defined by these conditions together. There may be only one rule on a firewall, but most firewalls have multiple rules. Traffic passing through the firewall must meet the conditions of all its rules.

In some cases, firewalls are hardware-based, meaning they reside inside devices specifically designed to act as firewalls. Other firewalls run as software programs on computers of any kind.

Firewalls are security features that separate trusted networks from untrusted networks. The firewall will analyze all incoming and outgoing network traffic, determining whether the firewall permits or denies the traffic. In a firewall, legitimate traffic is allowed while malicious traffic, such as malware and intrusion attempts, is prohibited.

With Azure Firewall, organizations can control and monitor access to Azure resources to protect their Azure virtual networks (VNets). They can manage multiple Azure Firewall instances from a central location with Azure Firewall Manager.

Using Azure Firewall, you can protect your Azure network resources from inbound and outbound threats.

Using Azure Firewall, you can build a firewall in the cloud. In most instances, Azure Firewall is provisioned within a hub virtual network. On-premises traffic to and from the spoke virtual networks crosses the firewall with traffic to the hub network.

Azure Firewall includes the following features:

Built-In High Availability   High availability is built-in, so no load balancing is required, and no configuration is required.

Unrestricted Cloud Scalability   You don't need to budget for your peak traffic with Azure Firewall because it scales out as much as is necessary to accommodate changing traffic flows.

Application FQDN Filters   You can restrict outbound HTTP/S traffic or Azure SQL traffic to a specified list of fully qualified domain names (FQDNs), including wildcards. These filters do not require TLS termination.

Network Traffic Filtering Rules   You can create filters based on source IP address, port, and protocol. Azure Firewall is fully stateful, which enables it to distinguish legitimate connections from invalid ones. The firewall enforces and records rules across multiple virtual networks and subscriptions.

FQDN Tags   FQDN tags can enable well-known Azure services to pass through firewalls if you want to allow Windows Update network traffic through the firewall. It would be best to create an application rule and include the Windows Update tag. Now, Windows Update network traffic can pass through the firewall and be accessed by cloud users.

Service Tags   Tags serve to group IP address prefixes and minimize security rule creation complexity. Consumers of cloud services cannot create tags or specify which IP addresses should be included in a tag, because Microsoft manages the service tags and updates them as address prefixes change.

Threat Intelligence   Threat intelligence-based filtering can enable an organization's firewalls to block traffic from or to know malicious IP addresses and domains. The IP addresses and domains are gathered by Microsoft Threat Intelligence.

SNAT   Source Network Address Translation (SNAT) is used to translate all outbound virtual network traffic IP addresses to the Azure Firewall public IP address. You can identify and allow traffic originating from an organization's virtual networks to remote Internet destinations.

Inbound DNAT Support   The traffic coming from the Internet to an organization's firewall public IP addresses is translated by Destination Network Address Translation (DNAT) and filtered into the private IP addresses on the Organizations' virtual networks.

Multiple Public IP Addresses   You can assign additional public IP addresses (up to 250) to an organization's firewall to enable specific DNAT and SNAT scenarios.

Azure Monitor Logging   Events are automatically integrated with Azure Monitor, enabling organizations to archive logs to their storage accounts, stream events to their Event Hubs, or send them to Azure Monitor logs.

Forced Tunneling   An Azure Firewall can be configured to route all Internet-bound traffic to the next hop instead of directly to the Internet. Consumers of cloud services may use edge firewalls or network virtual appliances (NVAs) to process network traffic before it enters the Internet.

Web Categories   Administrators can control access to website categories such as social media websites, gambling websites, and others with web categories. In Azure Firewall Standard, web categories are included, but they are more refined in Azure Firewall Premium Preview. Standard SKU's Web categories are based on an FQDN, while Premium SKUs are based on the entire URL.

Certifications   The Azure Firewall is compliant with the Payment Card Industry (PCI), Service Organization Control (SOC), International Organization for Standardization (ISO), and ICSA Labs.

Azure Firewall provides East-West traffic inspection as well as north-south traffic inspection, so it can be used both for traffic to and from the Internet and internal traffic. Inter-cloud traffic filtering includes spoke-to-spoke traffic and hybrid cloud traffic between Azure virtual and on-premises cloud networks.

There are two types of Azure Firewall: Standard and Premium.

Azure Firewall Standard provides OSI Layer 3-Layer7 filtering and threat intelligence. Filtration based on intelligence can detect and block traffic from/to known malicious IP addresses and domains, updated in real-time to protect against new threats.

Figure 8.1 is an overview of Azure Firewall Standard.

Table 8.1 illustrates the key features of Azure Firewall Standard.

TABLE 8.1   Key features of Azure Firewall Standard

Features	Detailed Description
Source network address translation (SNAT)	The Azure Firewall instance sends all outbound traffic to a private IP address. During the translation process, the IP address of each source virtual machine becomes a static public IP address of the Azure Firewall instance. There is a single public IP address from which organizations send all network traffic to external destinations.

Features	Detailed Description
Destination network address translation (DNAT)	The Azure Firewall instance acts as a gateway for traffic coming in from external sources. Organizations' virtual networks translate allowed traffic to the private IP address of the destination resource.
Application rules	Outbound traffic restrictions are based on a list of FQDNs. Organizations can access the FQDN of a specified SQL database instance via outbound traffic.
Network rules	Network parameters determine incoming and outgoing traffic rules. Among these parameters are the source or destination IP address, the network port, and the protocol.
Threat intelligence	Protects against malicious traffic by filtering incoming and outgoing traffic according to Microsoft threat intelligence rules, defining known malicious IP addresses and domain names. Azure Firewall users can set one of two threat intelligence modes: notify when traffic fails a threat intelligence rule or notify when traffic is denied.
Stateful	The packets are examined in context rather than individually. Packets arriving unexpectedly are denied as malicious if the current traffic indicates that the packets are malicious.
Forced tunnelling	Azure Firewall routes all outgoing traffic to a specified network resource instead of directly to the Internet. Network resources may include hardware firewalls installed on-premises or virtual network appliances that filter traffic before it is allowed to pass through an Internet connection.
Tag support	Service tags and FQDN tags are supported to make rule configuration easier. Service tags represent services. For example, AzureCosmosDB is the service tag for Azure Cosmos DB. FQDN tags are text entities that represent a group of domain names connected to popular Microsoft services. For example, the FQDN WindowsVirtualDesktop identifies Microsoft Azure Virtual Desktop traffic.
Monitoring	Using Azure Monitor, Power BI, Excel, and other tools, organizations can analyze the logs of the Azure Firewall.

FIGURE 8.1   Azure Firewall Standard overview

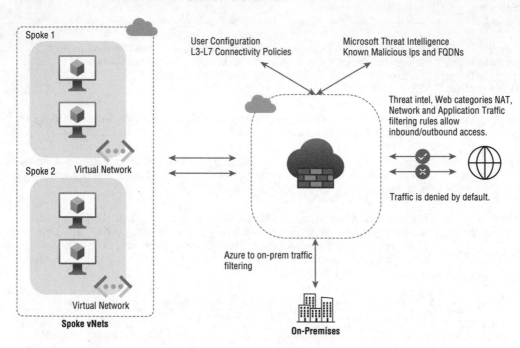

Azure Firewall Premium includes advanced features such as a signature-based intrusion detection and prevention system (IDPS) that quickly detects attacks based on specific patterns. Bitstream pattern analysis can be applied to network traffic or known malware instruction sequences. Microsoft protects against new and emerging exploits by updating our signatures in real-time against 58,000 categories. There are four types of exploits: malware, phishing, coin mining, and Trojan attacks.

Figure 8.2 is an overview of Azure Firewall Premium.

Table 8.2 illustrates the key features of the Azure Firewall Premium.

TABLE 8.2   Key features of Azure Firewall Premium

Features	Detailed Description
TLS Inspection	Outgoing traffic is decrypted, processed, encrypted, and sent to the destination.
IDPS	A network intrusion detection and prevention system (IDPs) allows you to monitor network activities for malicious activity, log information about it, report it, and attempt to block it.
URL filtering	Adds full URL filtering to Azure Firewall's FQDN functionality. For instance, www.sybexdemo.com/a/c rather than www.sybexdemo.com.
Web categories	Administrators can allow or deny user access to various categories of websites, such as social networking sites and gambling websites.

FIGURE 8.2   Azure Firewall Premium overview

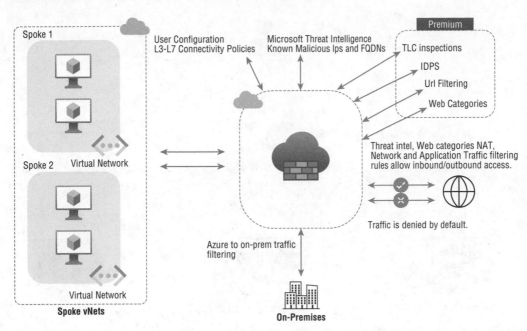

Azure Firewall Premium includes all the features of the Standard SKU, plus the additional features in Table 8.2.

> Azure Firewall is an Azure virtual network resource security service that's managed, and cloud based. With built-in high availability and unrestricted cloud scalability, it is a fully stateful firewall-as-a-service.
>
> There was an Azure network security group (NSG) before Azure Firewall. A new compute resource is deployed with NSGs automatically generated.

You can use Azure Firewall Manager to centrally manage Azure Firewalls across multiple subscriptions. Firewall Manager leverages firewall policy to apply a standard set of network/ application rules and configuration to an organization's tenant firewalls.

Access to Azure resources is a priority for organizations with Azure resources. Security perimeters are usually created by implementing security technologies such as firewalls. The perimeter can control how traffic flows to and from hosted apps and other resources. However, as security requirements grow, it might become difficult to manage these security technologies. To simplify the management of cloud-based security, use Azure Firewall Manager to centralize firewall-security policies and route management for cloud-based security perimeters.

Figure 8.3 is an overview of Azure Firewall Manager.

FIGURE 8.3   Azure Firewall Manager overview

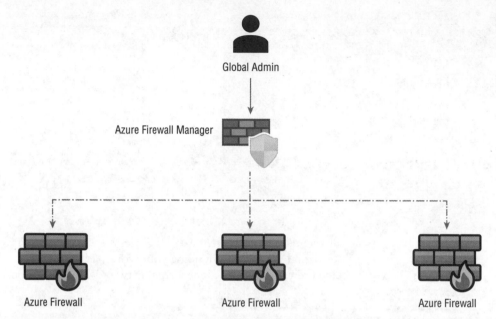

As shown in Figure 8.3, managing multiple firewalls simultaneously without centralized firewall management can be challenging since it is hard to maintain different firewalls individually. Organizations might need to reconfigure their firewalls to ensure that all of an organization's security settings match as their security needs change. You may be required to update all the organization's firewalls if security requirements grow. Firewall Manager simplifies the management of firewalls.

Azure Firewall Manager gives you the following capabilities:

- Centralized firewall management.
- Span multiple Azure subscriptions and regions.
- Deploy hub-and-spoke architectures that support traffic governance and protection.

Creating firewall policies is the foundation of Firewall Manager. The following are the items a firewall policy should include:

- NAT settings
- Network rule collections
- Application rule collections
- Threat intelligence settings

You can apply firewall policies to firewalls. After creating policies, you can associate them with one or more virtual networks or virtual hubs.

Among Firewall Manager's features and capabilities are:

- Configuration and deployment are centralized. It is possible to set up multiple instances of Azure Firewall simultaneously. Each instance can potentially span multiple subscriptions and regions.

- The centralized software routing bypasses the need for users to create routes on manually spoked virtual networks.

- Across multiple secured virtual hubs, policies can be managed centrally. Organizations' IT security teams can create global firewall policies and apply them across their organizations. This is done through hierarchical approaches.

- A third-party security provider can be integrated.

- There is cross-regional capability available. Azure Firewall policies created in one region can be applied to other regions.

You can implement Firewall Manager in one of two architectures:

Hub Virtual Network   Hub virtual networks are security policies associated with hubs. In addition to peering spoke virtual networks containing your workload servers and services, you can also manage firewalls in stand-alone virtual networks that do not peer with any other spokes.

After a policy is created, it can be associated with a firewall in a Virtual WAN hub (aka secured virtual hub) or a firewall in a virtual network (aka hub virtual network).

Secured Virtual Hub   Hub-and-spoke architectures can be easily created using a Microsoft-managed Azure Virtual WAN hub. The secured virtual hub refers to a hub that has routing and security policies associated with it.

How Azure Firewall Manager Works

As discussed previously, a policy is the basic building block of a Firewall Manager. You can create policies and associate them with Azure Firewall instances in secured virtual hubs or hubs VNet.

Azure Firewall policies control traffic in protected resources based on rules and settings.

The firewall policy in Azure Firewall Manager consists of one or more sets of the following policy rule collections and settings.

Threat Intelligence Settings   Configures Azure Firewall to use threat intelligence for policy filtering. Detects potentially malicious traffic. Moreover, you can block traffic from and to malicious IP addresses and domains.

NAT Rule Collection   Advises Azure Firewall engineers on how to configure DNS translation (DNAT).

Network Rule Collection   Controls non-HTTP/S traffic flowing through the firewall.

Application Rule Collection   Controls HTTP/S traffic flowing through the firewall.

Firewall policies are a resource offered by Azure. You can create firewall policies as an instance of this resource. Using Azure Firewall Manager as a separate resource, you can quickly apply policies to multiple firewalls. Azure engineers can create one policy that will be the base policy and then inherit the rules from more specialized policies.

Table 8.3 illustrates the key features of the Azure Firewall Manager.

TABLE 8.3   Features of the Azure Firewall Manager

Features	Detailed Description
Centralized management	Configure firewalls throughout the cloud customers' entire networks.
Manage multiple firewalls	Configure, monitor, and manage multiple firewalls from one interface.
Supports multiple network architectures	Azure Virtual WAN hubs, as well as standard virtual networks, are protected.
Automated traffic routing	Network traffic is automatically routed to the firewall when connected to the Azure Virtual WAN hub.
Hierarchical policies	Creating so-called parent and child firewall policies is possible. Children inherit all the settings and rules of their parents; a parent policy contains all the rules and settings that users want to apply globally.
Support for third-party security providers	Provides third-party Security as a Service (SECaaS) solutions for organizations to protect their network's Internet connection.

Now that Azure Firewall and Azure Firewall Manager's basic features are familiar to you, the next section will examine how these technologies provide Azure resources' security.

How Azure Firewall and Firewall Manager Protect VNets

Understanding Azure Firewall and how it protects a virtual network requires understanding two critical characteristics:

- All inbound traffic is directed to the public IP address of the firewall instance.
- All outbound traffic is routed through the firewall instance's private IP address.

The firewall handles all traffic inbound and outbound. Default settings prevent all access to the firewall. A network engineer's task is to configure the firewall so that traffic can pass through the firewall under specific conditions. The conditions are called "rules," and each rule applies a set of checks to the data. Every firewall rule must be passed before traffic is allowed to pass through.

Azure Firewall manages network traffic differently depending on the origin:

- For inbound traffic allowed by Azure Firewall, DNAT converts the firewall's public IP address to the private address of the corresponding destination resource in the virtual network.

- With Azure Firewall, the source IP address is translated to the firewall's public IP address for outbound traffic.

To work effectively, Azure Firewall must be set up as a barrier between the trusted network you want to protect and an untrusted network that may pose a threat.

A hub and spoke network topology is the best way to deploy Azure Firewall:

- A virtual network that serves as a central point of connection. The hub network is such a network.

- The hub network is peer to one or more virtual networks. Workload servers are accessed through these peer virtual networks.

You can install the firewall instance in a subnet of the hub virtual network, and all traffic in and out of the network is configured to go through the firewall.

A firewall created with Azure allows you to create the three types of rules shown in Table 8.4.

TABLE 8.4   Three Types of Rules

Features	Detailed Description
Application	Filter traffic based on an FQDN. For example, organizations might use an application rule to allow outbound traffic to access an Azure SQL Database instance using the FQDN `xyz.sybexdemo.net`.
NAT	Translate and filter inbound Internet traffic using the public IP address and port number of a firewall. You can create a NAT rule that turns the firewall's public IP address and port 3389 into the virtual machine's private IP address to enable a remote desktop connection.
Network	Filter traffic based on the IP address, port, or network interface protocol. Using a network rule, you might allow outbound traffic to access a specific DNS server at a specified IP address using port 53, for instance.

Azure Firewall prioritizes rules. The priority is always given to rules based on threat intelligence. Following that, rules are applied based on their type: NAT rules, network rules, and application rules. According to the priority values organizations assign when creating rules, rules are processed within each type in ascending order.

Azure Firewall contains several features that make creating and managing rules easier. These features include FQDN, FQDN tag, Service tag, IP groups, and custom DNS.

> For the Microsoft AZ 700 exam, keep in mind that by creating rules by source and destination IP address, port, and protocol, you can centrally define if a network should be allowed or denied. Using Azure Firewall, legitimate packets can be distinguished for different types of connections.
>
> Firewalls can be configured to alert and deny traffic from/to known malicious IP addresses and domains using threat intelligence-based filtering. Microsoft Threat Intelligence feeds provide IP addresses and domains that are known to be malicious.

Now that you know why Azure Firewall and Azure Firewall Manager are suitable for cloud-based organizations, use the following capabilities to evaluate their suitability. You should use them when any of the following use cases apply.

Use Case 1 You want to protect an organization's networks against infiltration.

Several malicious actors target an organization's network with the intent of infiltrating it. The intruders may want to use network resources or examine, steal, or destroy sensitive or proprietary information.

> **Design Consideration** Azure Firewall prevents such intrusions. Malicious hackers might gain access to a network resource, for example, to infiltrate the network. The Azure Firewall examines the context of network packets using stateful inspection. The firewall will likely allow a request if it responds to earlier legitimate activity. However, if a request comes seemingly out of nowhere, as would the bid sent by a would-be infiltrator, the firewall will deny it.

Use Case 2 You want to protect an organization's networks against user error.

Infiltrating networks or installing malware on network computers is often accomplished by tricking a user into clicking a link in an email message. Users are directed to a hacker-controlled website that either installs malware or tricks them into entering their credentials.

> **Design Consideration** Azure Firewall uses threat intelligence to block access to known malicious domains and IP addresses.

Use Case 3   You want to protect a business that includes e-commerce or credit card payments.

A company might need to comply with the Payment Card Industry Data Security Standard (PCI DSS). Developed and maintained by the PCI Security Standards Council, the PCI DSS is a set of security standards. Key requirements must be met to achieve PCI compliance and protect cardholder data by installing and maintaining a firewall.

> **Design Consideration**   According to PCI DSS, you must set up a firewall that restricts all traffic from untrusted networks and hosts. The firewall must block all traffic except that required for processing payment cards.

Use Case 4   You want to configure spoke-to-spoke connectivity.

Hub and spoke topologies typically have the following characteristics:

- An interconnection points between several virtual networks—the hub.
- A spoke is a virtual network that is peer to the hub. The on-premises network connected to ExpressRoute circuits or VPN gateways can also be considered a spoke.

> **Design Consideration**   Data can be exchanged between spoke and hub networks, but spokes cannot directly communicate. Organizations might require this capability. An application programming interface (API) might need information from a SQL database on another spoke.
>
> One solution is to peer the spoke networks with each other. As the number of connections increases, that solution becomes unwieldy for a few of these connections.
>
> Direct connectivity between spokes can be established using Azure Firewall, a more accessible and more secure solution. Having an Azure Firewall instance installed in the hub can enable you to achieve this connectivity. As a result, you can configure the virtual spoke networks with user-defined routes (UDRs) that route traffic through a firewall and to the other spoke.

Use Case 5   You want to monitor incoming and outgoing traffic.

Companies might want to analyze detailed reports on inbound and outbound network traffic. There are many reasons for requiring such reports, including regulatory compliance, enforcing company policies on Internet usage, and troubleshooting problems.

> **Design Consideration**   Organizations can configure Azure Firewall to maintain diagnostic logs of four types of firewall activity:
>
> - Application rules
> - Network rules
> - Threat intelligence
> - DNS proxy

A firewall's application rule log might contain the following entries for an outbound request:

HTTPS request from 10.1.0.50:24352 to some website.com:443.

- Action: Allow.
- Rule Collection: collection100.
- Rule: rule102.

The logs for firewalls might include entries such as those below for an inbound request:

TCP request from 54.101.126.14:12354 to 10.0.0.80:3389. Action: Allow.

Once you enable diagnostic logging, they can monitor and analyze the logs in the following ways:

- examine the logs directly in their native JSON format.
- examine the logs in Azure Monitor.
- examine and analyze the logs in Azure Firewall Workbook.

Use Case 6   The network requires multiple firewalls.

A company's Azure footprint spans multiple Azure regions. When a company has multiple Internet connections, you need to deploy firewall instances for each of these connections.

Design Consideration   You can configure and manage those firewalls separately, but this creates several issues:

- A great deal of work goes into managing multiple firewalls.
- Each firewall must be updated with global settings and rules.
- Maintaining consistency across all firewalls is difficult.

This problem can be solved by Azure Firewall Manager, which provides a centralized management interface for all Azure Firewall instances across all Azure regions and subscriptions. Microsoft Azure engineers can create firewall policies, which can be applied to each firewall instance, and changes to a policy are propagated automatically.

Use Case 7   You want to deploy hierarchical firewall policies.

One-size-fits-all firewall policies are suitable for many smaller companies. For small businesses, it is often possible to create a single firewall policy that covers all users and resources on the network.

For larger companies, however, an in-depth and nuanced approach is required. Consider the following examples:

- DevOps marts may have virtual networks for developing apps, staging apps, and production versions.

- Large companies might have separate teams for database users, engineering, and sales. These teams run their applications through different virtual networks.

  Design Consideration   Although all virtual networks will undoubtedly have firewall rules in common, each will also have its own firewall rules. As a result, large companies almost always need hierarchical firewall policies. A hierarchical firewall policy consists of two components:

  - A single base firewall policy that implements the rules must be implemented company-wide.

  - A local firewall policy implements rules specific to a particular application, team, or service. The firewall policy is inherited from the base policy in local policies, and rules related to the underlying application, group, or service are added.

  Azure Firewall Manager lets you configure a base firewall policy, create local policies that inherit that policy, and implement specific rules for each resource.

The critical consideration for the upcoming use case 8, 9, 10, and 11 demands Azure premium SKU.

Associations can prevent malware and viruses from spreading horizontally across networks using Azure Firewall Premium. Azure Firewall Premium uses more powerful virtual machines to meet the performance demands of IDPs and TLS inspection. As with the Standard SKU, the Premium SKU supports seamless scaling up to 30 Gbps and integrates with availability zones to ensure a 99.99 percent service level agreement (SLA). The Premium SKU is compliant with PCI DSS environment requirements.

Use Case 8   You want to inspect outbound TLS encrypted network traffic through multiple firewalls.

  Design Consideration   Azure Firewall Premium TLS Inspection decrypts outbound traffic, processes it, encrypts it, and then sends it to its intended location.

  Azure Firewall Premium terminates inbound and outbound TLS connections. With Azure Application Gateway, TLS inspection is supported for inbound data, allowing end-to-end encryption. Using Azure Firewall, traffic is re-encrypted, and value-added security functions are performed.

Use Case 9   You need to protect your network using signature-based malicious traffic detection.

  Design Consideration   You can monitor an organization's network for malicious activity using an intrusion detection and prevention system (IDP), log information about the activity, report it, and attempt to block the move.

  In Azure Firewall Premium, IDPs is based on signatures to detect attacks based on patterns, such as bytes in network traffic or known malicious instructions used by malware. IDPS signatures cover applications and network-level traffic (Layers 4-7). This signature is updated continuously. IDPs can handle inbound, spoke-to-spoke (East-West), and outbound traffic.

Characteristics, features, and considerations of the Azure Firewall signatures/rulesets are:

- Traditional prevention methods miss malicious activity in the wild, Command and Control, exploit kits, and actual malware that has been fingerprinted.

- Fifty thousand rules in more than 50 categories.

- There are many categories of malware, such as malware command and control, DoS attacks, botnets, informational events, exploits, vulnerabilities, SCADA network protocols, exploit kit activity, etc.

- The number of new rules released each day varies from 20 to 40.

- The system uses a global sensor network feedback loop and a state-of-the-art malware sandbox to reduce false positives.

The IDPs in Azure allow engineers to detect attacks on non-encrypted traffic on all ports and protocols. When HTTPS traffic needs to be inspected, Azure Firewall can decrypt it and detect malicious activity better by using its TLS inspection capabilities.

You can use the IDPs bypass list to block traffic from IP addresses, ranges, and subnets specified in the bypass list.

You can also use signature rules if the IDPs mode is set to Alert. However, they want to block one or more specific signatures and their associated traffic. By setting the TLS inspection mode to deny, they can add new signature rules.

Use Case 10   You need to extend Azure Firewall's FQDN filtering capability to an entire URL.

Design Consideration   Azure Firewall Premium can filter an entire URL. For example, `www.sybex.com/a/c` instead of `www.sybex.com`.

HTTPS and HTTP traffic can be filtered with URL filtering. Azure Firewall Premium's TLS inspection capability can decrypt HTTPS traffic and extract the target URL to verify whether access is allowed. You must enable TLS inspection at the application rule level. Once enabled, you can filter using URLs with HTTPS.

Use Case 11   You want to control access based on categories.

Design Consideration   Administrators use web categories to control access to websites such as gambling sites, social media sites, etc. Azure Firewall Standard will also support web categories, but it will be more fine-tuned in Azure Firewall Premium. The Premium SKU fits the type according to the entire URL for HTTP and HTTPS traffic, unlike the Standard SKU's Web categories that use an FQDN.

As an example, if Azure Firewall intercepts an HTTPS request for
www.google.com/news, it should categorize the request as follows:

- **Firewall Standard** — just the FQDN part will be identified so that
  www.google.com will be classed as a Search Engine.

- **Firewall Premium** — the entire URL will be examined so that
  www.google.com/news will be categorized as News.

There are six categories based on severity: Liability, High-Bandwidth, Business
Use, Productivity Loss, General Surfing, and Uncategorized.

Critical considerations for Azure Firewall design:

- Azure Firewall can be used to filter East-West traffic, non-HTTP/S access
  to the Internet (VMs and services that connect to the internet), and Internet outbound traffic (VMs and services that access the Internet).

- For managing multiple Azure Firewalls across hub-and-spoke deployments and Azure Virtual WAN hubs, consider Firewall Manager.

- To manage the security posture of the global network environment,
  assign a global Azure Firewall policy to all Azure Firewall instances.

- The Firewall in Azure uses autoscaling. There is a 30Gbps maximum.

- Microsoft recommends starting using an Azure Firewall with two
  instances. After an auto-scale, Azure Firewall releases one or more
  instances based on CPU and network throughput.

- Upon reaching 60% throughput or CPU consumption, Azure Firewall
  gradually scales. By default, deployments have a maximum throughput
  of 2.5 - 3 Gbps; when 60% of that number is reached, they start scaling
  out. It usually takes between 5 and 7 minutes to scale out.

- Whether Azure Firewall is deployed in a single Availability Zone or multiple Availability Zones it has different SLAs.

- Recognize that Azure Firewalls and Virtual Networks are regional
  resources when designing workloads designed to be fault-tolerant and
  resistant to failures.

- Keep close tabs on SNAT port utilization, firewall health state, and
  throughput metrics.

- A next-generation firewall, Azure Firewall Premium, provides the capabilities needed for regulated and compassionate environments.

- Azure Firewall, Performance Logs, and Azure Access Logs are available as
  diagnostic logs. Organizations can use these logs in Azure to manage and
  troubleshoot their Azure Firewall instances.

Build and Configure an Azure Firewall Deployment

Microsoft recommends a hub-and-spoke configuration when deploying an Azure Firewall, and Azure's reference architecture details this topology. The hub virtual network is a central point of connection between many spoke virtual networks, and the hub can also facilitate connectivity to an organization's on-premises networks. With spoke virtual networks, work-loads can be isolated from the hub and peer with it. An ExpressRoute or VPN gateway connection connects the on-premises datacenter and the hub.

Figure 8.4 shows an overview of Azure Firewall deployment architecture.

 For the Microsoft AZ 700 exam, keep in mind that using Azure Portal, Azure PowerShell, and Azure Resource Manager template, you can deploy Azure Firewall using Availability Zones on an organizations' networks.

FIGURE 8.4   Azure Firewall deployment architecture overview

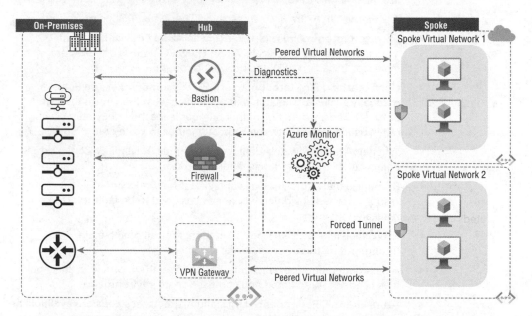

Using a hub and spoke configuration includes cost savings, overcoming subscription limits, and workload isolation.

The benefits of this topology include:

- You can reduce costs by centralizing services such as network virtual appliances (NVAs) and DNS servers, which multiple workloads can share.
- To overcome subscription limits, connect virtual networks from different subscriptions to the central hub.
- It is essential to separate IT operations (SecOps, InfraOps) from workloads (DevOps).

The Azure Firewall allows you to configure three different types of rules.

NAT Rules   Inbound traffic to subnets can be translated and filtered by Azure Firewall Destination Network Address Translation (DNAT). This rule collection translates public IP addresses and ports on an organization's firewalls to private addresses and ports. SSH, RDP, and other applications that are not HTTP/S are examples of scenarios where NAT rules might be helpful. To allow traffic, NAT rules must be accompanied by matching network rules.

Table 8.5 illustrates the key configuration settings for NAT Rules.

TABLE 8.5   Key configuration for NAT rules

Features	Detailed Description
Name	A Name that is the label for the rule.
Protocol	TCP or UDP.
Source Address	The Internet address or CIDR block of the source.
Destination Addresses	The firewall address to be examined by the rule.
Destination Ports	On the firewall's external IP address, the rule will listen on the TCP or UDP ports.
Translated Address	Privately hosted or presented services (virtual machines, internal load balancers, etc.) may have a private IP address.
Translated Ports	The port that the Azure Firewall will route to the inbound traffic.

Network Rules   A network rule is required for all non-HTTP/S traffic going through the firewall. If, for example, resources in one subnet must communicate with those in another subnet, organizations would configure a network rule from the source to the destination.

Table 8.6 illustrates the key configuration settings for network rules.

TABLE 8.6 Key configuration for network rules

Features	Detailed Description
Name	A friendly label for the rule.
Protocol	TCP, UDP, ICMP (ping and traceroute) or Any.
Source Address	The address or CIDR block of the source.
Destination Addresses	The addresses or CIDR blocks of the destination(s).
Destination Ports	The destination port of the traffic.

Application Rules A subnet can be accessed through application rules that define fully qualified domain names (FQDN). A firewall rule can be used to allow Windows Update network traffic.

Table 8.7 illustrates the key configuration settings for application rules.

TABLE 8.7 Key configuration for application rules

Features	Detailed Description
Name	A friendly label for the rule.
Source Address	The IP address of the source.
Protocol	HTTP/HTTPs and the port of the app server it is listening on.
Target FQDN	Domain name for the service, for example, www.sybex.com. Wildcards are permitted. A group of FQDNs represents known Microsoft services called an FQDN tag. FQDN tags include Windows Update, App Service Environment, and Azure Backup.

If you configure both network rules and application rules, network rules will be applied in priority order before application rules. Furthermore, all rules are terminating; no other rules are run when a match is found in a network rule.

A packet is evaluated by the application rules if there is no network rule match and if the protocol is HTTP, HTTPS, or MSSQL. Azure Firewall looks for a matching application rule in response to the HOST HEADER. Azure Firewall only examines server name indications (SNI) for HTTPS applications.

Configuring DNAT enables inbound Internet connectivity. Specifically, DNAT rules will be applied before network rules. When a match is found, the translated traffic is implicitly added to the network rule. DNAT should only be allowed access to the network through a specific Internet source and not via wildcards for security reasons.

Inbound connections are not subject to applicable rules. You can use Web Application Firewalls (WAF) to filter inbound HTTP/S traffic.

Web Application Firewalls (WAF) protect web applications from exploits and vulnerabilities by centralizing their protection. Malicious attacks exploiting commonly known vulnerabilities increasingly target web applications, and SQL injection and cross-site scripting are among the most common threats. It can take a great deal of maintenance, patching, and monitoring at multiple layers of the application topology to prevent such attacks in application code. Using a Web application firewall simplifies security management, and a WAF gives application administrators better assurance that their applications are protected from threats and intrusions.

When you create a Web Application Firewall (WAF) policy, the WAF policy is in Detection mode, and you can change it to Prevention mode.

You can modify rules so that previously allowed traffic is denied access to ensure enhanced security. Existing sessions will be dropped when this occurs.

With all this basic understanding, let's explore the high-level deployment considerations for Azure Firewall.

- The application and network connectivity policies can be centrally created, enforced, and logged.

- Virtual network resources have a static, public IP address. Outside firewalls can identify virtual networks in this way.

- Monitoring and analytics are fully integrated into Azure Monitor.

- The FQDN tag should always be used when creating firewall rules.

- Azure Firewall does not require a subnet bigger than /26.

Availability Zones are one of the critical features of the Azure Firewall.

You can configure Azure Firewall to span multiple Availability Zones when deploying it for increased availability. Azure Firewall configuration increases the VNet's availability to 99.99%. With two or more Availability Zones selected, a 99.99% uptime guarantee is offered.

- Azure Firewall can also be assigned to a specific zone based on the 99.95% SLA.

- An Availability Zone firewall does not incur any additional costs. However, there are other costs associated with inbound and outbound data transfers.

- Availability Zones have only been supported by regions where Azure Firewall is available.

- Firewall deployment is the only time to configure Availability Zones. It is not possible to add Availability Zones to an existing firewall.

Now let's consider deploying and configuring Azure Firewall using the Azure portal.

Controlling outbound network access is an integral part of an overall network security plan. For example, you may want to limit access to websites. Or you may wish to restrict the outbound IP addresses and ports they can access.

You can control outbound network access from an Azure subnet with Azure Firewall. You can configure:

- An application rule that defines fully qualified domain names (FQDNs) accessible through a subnet.
- Network rules consisting of an address, a protocol, a destination port, and a destination address.

You can route organizations' network traffic to the firewall according to the configured firewall rules as the default gateway for each subnet.

Let us create a simplified single VNet with two subnets for easy deployment for this section—one for Azure Firewall and one for server workload (website).

Figure 8.5 depicts the Azure Firewall for one VNet.

FIGURE 8.5   Azure Firewall for one VNet

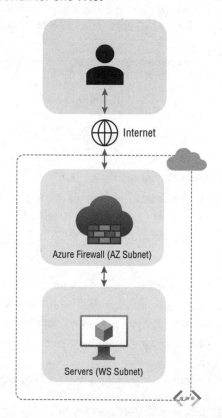

To create the environment shown in Figure 8.5, you will follow this six-stage deployment process:

Stage 1: Deploy network pre-requisites.

Stage 2: Deploy an Azure Firewall.

Stage 3: Deploy a default route.

Stage 4: Configure an application rule to permit access to `www.google.com`.

Stage 5: Configure a network rule to permit access to outward DNS servers.

Stage 6: Configure a NAT rule to permit a remote desktop connection to the VM.

Follow the steps in Exercise 8.1 to create a resource group.

EXERCISE 8.1

Deploy Network Prerequisites: Develop a Resource Group

1. Log in to a personal or business account in the Azure portal at `https://portal` `.azure.com`.

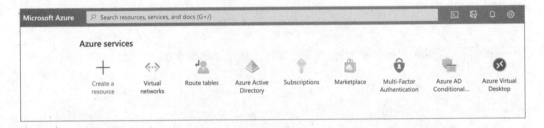

2. Choose Resource Groups from the landing page or search for and select Resource Groups from any page on the Azure portal menu. Then click Add.

3. For the Resource Group Name, enter **Sybex-FW-RG**.

   For Subscription, choose sybexdemo.

4. For Resource Group Location, choose a location. All other resources that you create must be in the same location.

5. Click Create.

To create a new virtual network using the Azure portal, follow the steps in Exercise 8.2.

EXERCISE 8.2

Deploy Network Prerequisites: Deploy a Virtual Network via the Azure Portal

1. Log in to a personal or business account in the Azure portal at `https://portal .azure.com`.

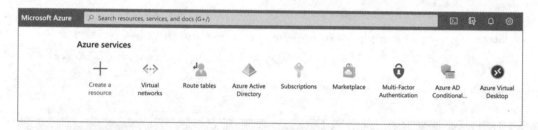

2. Type **virtual network** in the search box press Enter to open the window shown in the next image.

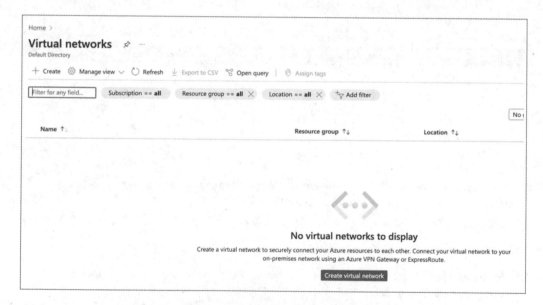

3. Click Create Virtual Network and, on the Basics tab in the wizard that opens (see the next image), provide the following input.

Subscription	Choose your subscription.
Resource Group	Choose a resource group or create a new resource group.

Name	Provide your new VNet's name per your defined naming standards. Here we use sy-vNET1-TEST-Demo.
Region	Choose the region you want to deploy to or one that's close to your resource needs.

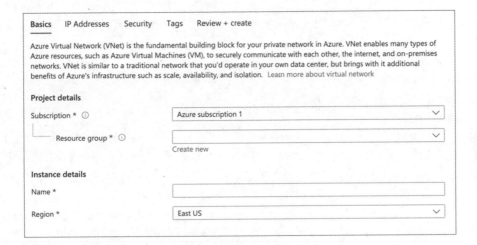

Once inputs are provided, go to the IP Addresses tab.

4. On the IP Addresses tab provide the following inputs.

IP Addresses space	In CIDR notation, one or more address prefixes define a virtual network's address space.

After creating the virtual network, you can add address spaces.

Classless Inter-Domain Routing (CIDR) is the format in which you define the internal address space of a virtual network. Any network you connect to must have a unique address space within your subscription.

For this exercise, choose an address space of `10.0.1.0/24` for Azure Firewall virtual network.

Subnet	Address range in CIDR notation for a subnet. Virtual networks must contain it within their address space.

No special characters are allowed in subnet names, only letters, numbers, underscores, periods, or hyphens.

EXERCISE 8.2 (continued)

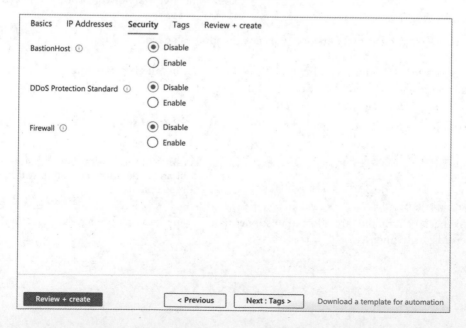

Basics | **IP Addresses** | Security | Tags | Review + create

The virtual network's address space, specified as one or more address prefixes in CIDR notation (e.g. 192.168.1.0/24).

IPv4 address space

10.0.0.0/16   10.0.0.0 - 10.0.255.255 (65536 addresses)

☐ Add IPv6 address space ⓘ

The subnet's address range in CIDR notation (e.g. 192.168.1.0/24). It must be contained by the address space of the virtual network.

+ Add subnet   🗑 Remove subnet

	Subnet name	Subnet address range	NAT gateway
☐	default	10.0.0.0/24	-

ⓘ Use of a NAT gateway is recommended for outbound internet access from a subnet. You can deploy a NAT gateway and assign it to a subnet after you create the virtual network. Learn more ⧉

Review + create   < Previous   Next : Security >   Download a template for automation

5. On the Security tab (see the next figure), choose whether to enable or disable Bastion Host, DDoS protection, and Firewall. If any of these options are allowed, you need to provide additional information for that service.

    For this exercise, we keep all three choices disabled.

Basics | IP Addresses | **Security** | Tags | Review + create

BastionHost ⓘ   ⦿ Disable
                       ○ Enable

DDoS Protection Standard ⓘ   ⦿ Disable
                       ○ Enable

Firewall ⓘ   ⦿ Disable
                       ○ Enable

Review + create   < Previous   Next : Tags >   Download a template for automation

6. For this exercise you will skip the Tags tab.

   Tags are used to organize Azure resources, resource groups, and subscriptions logically. As you apply the same tag to multiple resources and groups, you can categorize them and view consolidated billing.

7. On the Review + Create tab, wait for validation pass status, then click Create to finish creating your virtual network.

Next, follow the steps in Exercise 8.3 to create a virtual machine.

EXERCISE 8.3

Deploy Network Prerequisites: Create a Virtual Machine

1. Log in to a personal or business account in the Azure portal at `https://portal.azure.com`.

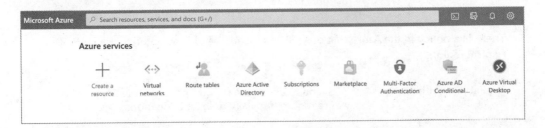

2. Type **virtual machine** in the search box and press Enter to display the page shown in the next image.

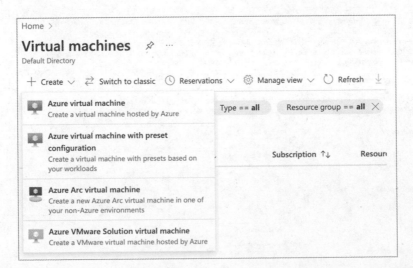

3. Select the Azure Virtual Machine option and click + Create.

4. Enter the following information on the Basics tab of the page shown in the next image.

Subscription	Choose your subscription.
Resource Group	Choose a resource group or create a new resource group or use the existing group.
Virtual Machine Name	Virtual machines in Azure have two distinct names: the virtual machine name used as the Azure resource identifier and the guest hostname. When creating a VM in the portal, the same name is used for the virtual machine and hostnames. The virtual machine name cannot be changed after the VM is created, and the Guest VM administrator can change the hostname when they log into the virtual machine.
Region	Choose the region you want to deploy to or close to your resource needs.

There is a policy in the Azure that only allows resources to be created in the UAE Central region.

Availability options	Availability Zones are unique physical locations within an Azure region (typically at least 3 locations).

Home > Virtual machines >

Create a virtual machine   ⋯

Basics   Disks   Networking   Management   Advanced   Tags   Review + create

Create a virtual machine that runs Linux or Windows. Select an image from Azure marketplace or use your own customized image. Complete the Basics tab then Review + create to provision a virtual machine with default parameters or review each tab for full customization. Learn more ⬀

Project details

Select the subscription to manage deployed resources and costs. Use resource groups like folders to organize and manage all your resources.

Subscription * ⓘ   [Azure Pass - Sponsorship   ∨]

    Resource group * ⓘ   [(New) Resource group   ∨]
                     Create new

Instance details

Virtual machine name * ⓘ   [   ]

Region * ⓘ   [(US) Central US   ∨]

Availability options ⓘ   [No infrastructure redundancy required   ∨]

[Review + create]   [< Previous]   [Next : Disks >]

Continue by entering the following information (see the next image).

Security Type	Different types of security can be applied to a virtual machine. Azure generation 2 virtual machines are more secure with features like Trusted launch and Confidential virtual machines. Additional security features do not support backup, managed disks, or ephemeral OS disks, among other limitations.
Image	Select the specific image version.
Gen1 vs. Gen2	Gen 2 (new feature Q1 2021), uses newer hardware, supports UEFI boot instead of BIOS and newer images, sizes, and capabilities.
Azure Spot Instance	Set maximum bid for unused Azure compute capacity. At any point in time when Azure needs the capacity back, the Azure infrastructure will evict Azure Spot Virtual Machines. Therefore, Azure Spot Virtual Machines are great for workloads that can handle interruptions like batch processing jobs, dev/test environments, large compute workloads, and more.
Size	Select VM size based on workload type and requirements. For a lab environment select smallest VM size to save costs and shutdown when not used, delete when not required.
Administrator Type	Select administrator SSH public key or password.
Username	Provide administrator username.
Password	Provide administrator password.
Confirm Password	Provide previously provided administrator password.

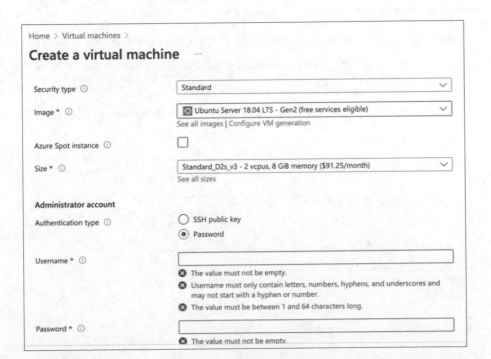

EXERCISE 8.3 *(continued)*

Continue by entering the following information (see the next image).

Inbound Port Ports that need to be opened from the public Internet (for Windows RDP-3389, for Linux SSH -22) For remote access, could also implement a Bastion host.

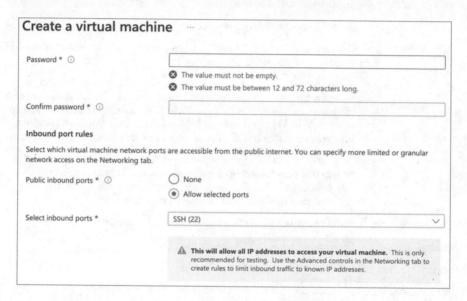

5. Go to the Disks tab (see the next image) and enter the following information.

OS disk Type	Select disk type, Standard HDD, Standard SSD, Premium SSD.
Delete with VM	The disk persists independently of the virtual machine. When a virtual machine is deleted, you can choose to automatically delete the associated disk.
Encryption at host	VMs can be encrypted at the host by encrypting their cache, temp disk, and ephemeral disks.

Then enter information for the data disk(s) as shown in the next image.

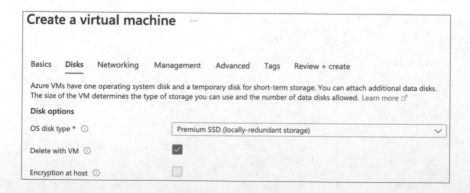

Data Disks   Create and attach a new disk or attach an existing disk.

Data disks

You can add and configure additional data disks for your virtual machine or attach existing disks. This VM also comes with a temporary disk.

LUN	Name	Size (GiB)	Disk type	Host caching	Delete with VM ⓘ

Create and attach a new disk   Attach an existing disk

6. On the Networking tab, enter the following information.

Virtual Network   Choose the name selected for the virtual network created in Exercise 8. 2.

Subnet   Choose the subnet selected in Exercise 8.2.

Public IP   (Assigned by default) For this setup, do not use a Public IP address since there will be additional costs.

NIC NSG   Security rules in a NSG (network security group) control whether inbound network traffic can reach or leave the virtual machine. It would be best if you associated network security groups with individual subnets rather than specific network interfaces within a subnet, whenever possible, to simplify the management of security rules.

Public inbound Ports   Default settings restrict access to the virtual machine to sources within the same virtual network, and traffic from Azure load balancing solutions. You can select None to confirm or one of these standard ports to allow traffic from the public internet.

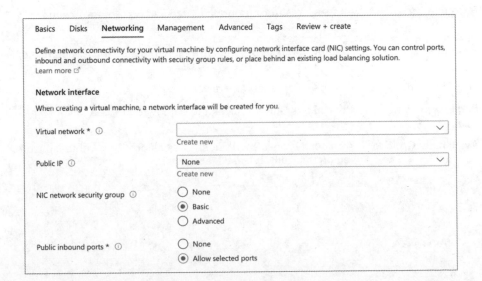

EXERCISE 8.3 *(continued)*

Keep all remaining configuration defaults.

7. On the Review + Create tab, wait for validation pass status before clicking Create.

To create a new Azure Firewall using the Azure portal, follow the steps in Exercise 8.4.

EXERCISE 8.4

Deploy an Azure Firewall

1. Log into a personal or business account in the Azure portal at `https://portal
    .azure.com`.

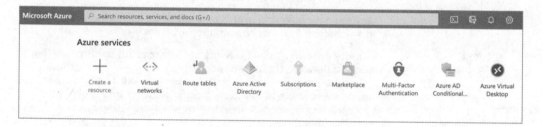

2. Type **Azure firewall** in the search box and press Enter.

    To configure the firewall, enter the following information (see the next image):

    Subscription   Choose your subscription.
    Resource Group   Choose a resource group or create a new resource group.

    Resources will be organized by, for example, department name and application name.

    Firewall Name   Provide a name for the firewall.
    Region   Choose the region you want to deploy to or close to your
                          resource needs.
    Availability Options Availability zones are unique physical locations within an Azure
                          region (typically at least 3 locations).

Create a firewall ...

Basics   Tags   Review + create

Azure Firewall is a managed cloud-based network security service that protects your Azure Virtual Network resources. It is a fully stateful firewall as a service with built-in high availability and unrestricted cloud scalability. You can centrally create, enforce, and log application and network connectivity policies across subscriptions and virtual networks. Azure Firewall uses a static public IP address for your virtual network resources allowing outside firewalls to identify traffic originating from your virtual network. The service is fully integrated with Azure Monitor for logging and analytics. Learn more.

Project details

Subscription * | Azure subscription 1 ⌄ |

    Resource group * | (New) SybexDemo ⌄ |
                                 Create new

Instance details

Name * | |

Region * | East US ⌄ |

Availability zone ⓘ | None ⌄ |

Continue by entering the following information (see the next image):

Firewall Tier	Choose Standard or Premium.
Firewall Management	For this example, click Use A Firewall Policy To Manage This Firewall. The other option is Use Firewall Rules (Classic) To Manage This Firewall.

You can create an Azure Firewall policy aligning to the SKU you selected.

Choose A Virtual Network	Options are Create New or Use Existing; for this exercise you can select the previously created or Create New.
Subnet	Choose your AzureFirewallSubnet.
Subnet Address Space	Choose the Subnet address space.

EXERCISE 8.4 *(continued)*

Firewall tier	⦿ Standard
	○ Premium
Firewall management	⦿ Use a Firewall Policy to manage this firewall
	○ Use Firewall rules (classic) to manage this firewall
Firewall policy *	(New) Sybex_Dev ⌄
	Add new
Choose a virtual network	⦿ Create new
	○ Use existing
Virtual network name *	SybexVNET01 ✓
Address space *	172.1.0.0/24 ✓
	172.1.0.0 - 172.1.0.255 (256 addresses)
Subnet	AzureFirewallSubnet
Subnet address space *	172.1.2.0/24 ✓
	172.1.2.0 - 172.1.2.255 (256 addresses)

Finish by entering the following information (see the next image):

Public IP address   None in this case. Assigning a Public IP here is not needed because you will not enable forced tunneling.

Forced Tunneling   For firewall management traffic, enable forced tunneling. A subnet with direct Internet access will be created (it's disabled for this exercise).

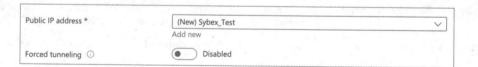

3. On the Review + Create tab, wait for the validation pass status before you click Create.

Next, in Exercise 8.5, you create a default route. The default route of 0.0.0.0/0 is sufficient for both outbound and inbound connectivity through the firewall. During a TCP handshake, the firewall responds to incoming requests by sending a response to the IP address that sent the traffic. This is by design. Due to this, the AzureFirewallSubnet IP range does not require an additional user-defined route (UDR).

EXERCISE 8.5

Configure the Outbound Default Route Through the Azure Firewall

1. Log into a personal or business account in the Azure portal at `https://portal`
   `.azure.com`.

2. On the Azure portal menu (see the next image), choose All Services or use the search
   bar to search for All services.

3. Under Networking, choose Route Tables, as shown in this image:

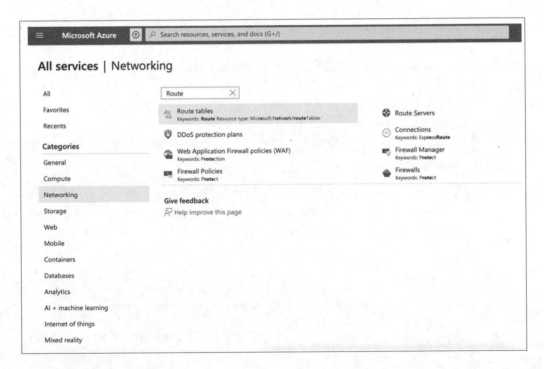

4. Click Create Route Table.

5. On the Basics tab, provide the following inputs (see the next image):

Subscription	Choose your subscription.
Resource Group	Choose a resource group or create a new one.
Region	Choose the region you want to deploy to or one that's close to your resource needs.
Name	Assign your new route table a name per your defined naming standards. Here we use AZ-FW-ROUTE.
Propagate Gateway Routes	Choose No to control the propagation of on-premises routes to the network interfaces in attached subnets.

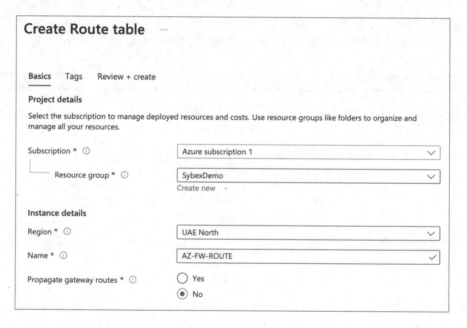

6. On the Review + Create tab, wait for the validation pass status before you click Create. After the deployment has completed, click Go To Resource as shown here:

7. On the AZ-FW-Route page, choose Subnets and select Associate (see the next image). For this exercise, use AZRouteFW.

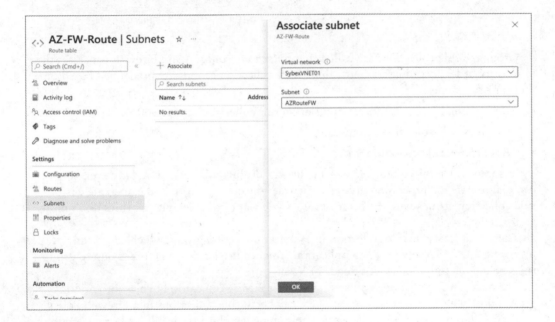

8. Click OK.

Azure Firewall Policy

Azure Firewall Policy consists of security and operational settings for the firewall. You can manage Azure Firewall rule sets by using Firewall Policy. Rule sets are organized, prioritized, and processed based on a hierarchy with three components: rule collection groups, rule collections, and rules, as shown in Figure 8.6.

FIGURE 8.6   Azure Firewall Policy management

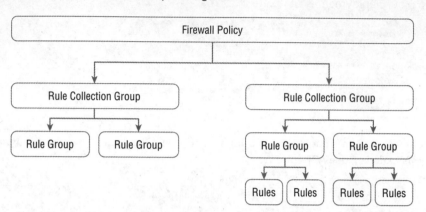

Groups of rule collections are called *rule collection groups*. Azure Firewall processes them in priority order according to their values. Rule collection groups are predefined based on their priority values:

- **Destination Network Address Translation rule collection group:** 100

- **Network rule collection group:** 200

- **Application rule collection group:** 300

It is impossible for you to delete or modify the default rule collection. However, you can manipulate the processing order for the rule collection groups. You can create custom rule collection groups with the priority values you want if the default priorities don't meet your needs.

There is at least one rule collection in each rule collection group, which can be any of the following—DNAT, Network, or Application. You can use a rule collection group to group rules belonging to the same workloads or VNet.

The maximum size of rule collection groups is 2 MB. You can split rules into multiple groups if they need more than 2 MB. There can be 50 rule collections in a Firewall Policy.

Each rule is part of a rule collection, determining which traffic is allowed or denied in the organization's network. The firewall processes them as the third unit, and they don't follow a priority order. Rules are processed from the top down. According to the rules, the firewall evaluates each packet passed through it for an allow or deny match. By default, no rules allow the traffic.

There are three types of rules: Application, DNAT, and Network. Let's get started with the Application rule.

Depending on how the Application layer (Layer 7) is configured, application rules can allow or deny inbound, outbound, and East-West traffic. Application rules are used when you want to filter traffic based on fully qualified domain names (FQDNs) and HTTP/HTTPS protocols. Depending on how the Network layer (Layer 3) and the Transport layer (Layer 4) are configured, network rules can allow or deny traffic inbound, outbound, and East-West. A network rule can be used to filter traffic according to IP addresses, protocols, and ports.

In the application rule you create in Exercise 8.6, www.sybex.com is allowed outbound access.

EXERCISE 8.6

Configure an Application Rule

1. Log into a personal or business account in the Azure portal at `https://portal.azure.com`.

2. On the Azure portal menu (see the next image), choose All Services or search for All services.

3. Under Networking, choose Azure Firewall.

4. On the Sybex_FW_Demo page, underneath Settings, Select Firewall Manager, as shown here:

EXERCISE 8.6 *(continued)*

5. Choose Azure Firewall Policies, Your Firewall Policy.

6. Choose the Application rule under Settings.

7. Choose Add Application Rule Collection to open the page shown in the next image and add the following information:

Name	Provide the name. For this example, use **Sybex-App-Coll01**.
Priority	Provide the priority. For this example enter **200**.
Action	The options are Allow and Deny. For this example, select Allow.

Under Rules (Target FQDNs):

Name	Type **Ap001**.
Source Type	You can choose IP Address or IP Group. For this example, choose IP Address.
Source	Enter the IP range. For this example, enter **10.0.0.0/24**.
Protocol	For Port, enter the desired HTTP or HTTPS port number. For this example, use http :80.
Target FQDNS or FQDN Tag	Enter ***.sybex.com**.

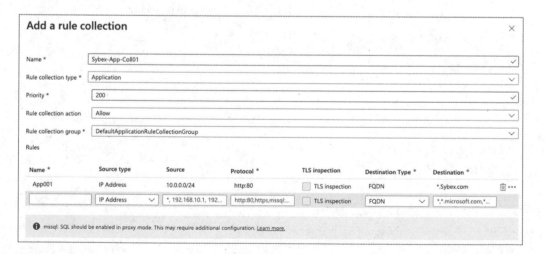

8. Click Add.

Traffic originating from the firewall's public IP address(es) can be allowed or denied via DNAT rules. Whenever you would like to translate a public IP address into a private IP address, you can use a DNAT rule. Azure Firewall public IP addresses can listen for Internet traffic, filter it, and translate the traffic to Azure resources.

You can connect remotely to your virtual machines with the rule you create in Exercise 8.7.

EXERCISE 8.7

Create DNAT Rule

1. Log into a personal or business account in the Azure portal at `https://portal.azure.com`.

2. On the Azure portal menu (see the next image), choose All Services or search for All services.

3. Under Networking, choose Azure Firewall.

4. On the Sybex_FW_Demo page, underneath Settings, choose Firewall Manager (see the next image).

EXERCISE 8.7 *(continued)*

5. Choose Azure Firewall Policies, Your Firewall Policy.

6. Choose the Application rule under Settings.

7. Click Add NAT Rule Collection to open the page shown in the next image and add the following information:

Name	Enter **MS_RDP**.
Priority	Type **200**.
Under Rules:	
Name	Type **rdp-nat**.
Protocol	Select TCP.
Source Type	Select IP Address.
Source	Enter *****.
Destination Address	Enter the firewall public IP address.
Destination Ports	Enter **3389**.
Translated Address	Enter the Server-SN private IP address.
Translated Port	Type **3389**.

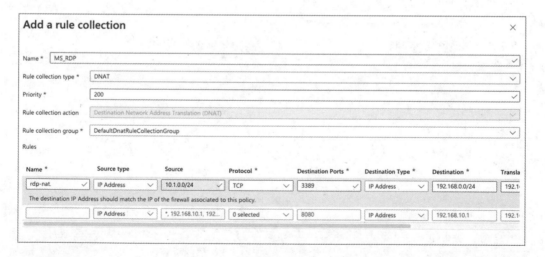

Add a rule collection

Name *	MS_RDP
Rule collection type *	DNAT
Priority *	200
Rule collection action	Destination Network Address Translation (DNAT)
Rule collection group *	DefaultDnatRuleCollectionGroup

Rules

Name *	Source type	Source	Protocol *	Destination Ports *	Destination Type *	Destination *	Transla
rdp-nat.	IP Address	10.1.0.0/24	TCP	3389	IP Address	192.168.0.0/24	192.1

The destination IP Address should match the IP of the firewall associated to this policy.

| | IP Address | *, 192.168.10.1, 192... | 0 selected | 8080 | IP Address | 192.168.10.1 | 192.1 |

8. Click Add.

Azure Firewall can protect any virtual network. Consumers typically deploy it as a hub-and-spoke model whereby it peers with other virtual networks on a central virtual network. Engineers can then change the default route from the peer virtual networks to point to this central virtual network. Microsoft does not recommend global VNet peering, which may negatively impact performance and latency in different regions. Deploy a firewall for each region to achieve the best performance.

One advantage of this model is the ability to control multiple spoke VNETs across multiple subscriptions centrally. In addition to saving money, you don't need to deploy a firewall in every VNet separately. You can determine the cost savings by comparing customer traffic patterns to the associate peering cost.

Build and Configure a Secure Hub within an Azure Virtual WAN Hub

Virtual hubs are managed by Microsoft and allow connectivity from external resources. In the Azure portal, the components of a virtual hub are a virtual hub VNet and gateways (optional).

The Azure Virtual WAN hub configuration includes securing a virtual hub using Firewall Manager. You can integrate native security and traffic governance features into transitive and hub-and-spoke architectures via secure virtual hubs.

You can filter traffic by using a secured virtual hub in Azure to filter traffic between virtual networks (virtual network to virtual network), between virtual networks and branch offices (branch to virtual network), and between virtual networks and the Internet (branch to Internet/virtual network to Internet). Secured virtual hubs enable traffic to be automatically routed, so you won't need to configure UDRs to make traffic flow through your firewalls.

You can choose the required security providers to protect and govern your network traffic, including Azure Firewall and third-party security (SECaaS) providers. Branch-to-branch (B2B) filtering and filtering across multiple hubs are currently not supported by a secured hub.

You can create a new secure virtual hub via Firewall Manager in the Azure portal. Alternatively, you can convert an existing secured virtual hub created via Azure Virtual WAN.

Firewall Manager allows cloud users to create secure virtual hubs to secure the network traffic flowing to private IP addresses, Azure PaaS, and the Internet. User-defined routes aren't required as traffic is routed to the firewall automatically.

Security management is provided by Azure Firewall Manager, which manages security policies and routes for cloud-based security perimeters. A single Firewall Manager instance can define network- and application-level rules for traffic filtering across multiple instances of Azure Firewall. You can set up hub-and-spoke architectures for governing and protecting traffic across different Azure regions and subscriptions.

Firewall Manager also supports hub virtual network architecture:

Hub Virtual Network   Whenever a security policy is associated with a virtual network, it is referred to as a hub virtual network. An Azure virtual network is something you create and manage yourselves. You can peer spoke virtual networks that contain your organization's workload servers and services. You can also manage firewalls in stand-alone virtual networks that have not peered to any spoke.

Secured Virtual Hub   Whenever security and routing policies have been associated with Azure Virtual WAN hubs, they are labeled secured virtual hubs. You can create hub-and-spoke architectures using an Azure Virtual WAN hub, which Microsoft manages.

Table 8.8 compares the two types of virtual hubs.

TABLE 8.8   Types of virtual hubs

Key performance indicators to consider	Hub virtual network	Secured virtual hub
Underlying resource	Virtual network (VNet)	Virtual WAN hub (VWAN Hub)
Hub and spoke	Uses virtual network peering	Automated using hub virtual network connection
On-premises connectivity	10 Gbps VPN Gateway, 30 S2S connections, ExpressRoute	Up to 20 Gbps VPN Gateway; 1000 S2S connections; ExpressRoute
Automated branch connectivity using SD-WAN	Not supported	Fully approved by Microsoft for usage
Hubs per AZ region	Multiple virtual networks per AZ region	Multiple virtual hubs per AZ region
Azure Firewall – multiple public IP addresses	Organization provided	Fully autogenerated
Azure Firewall Availability Zones	Fully supported	Fully approved by Microsoft for usage

Key performance indicators to consider	Hub virtual network	Secured virtual hub
Security as a service with third-party providers of advanced Internet security	VPN connectivity to partner service of choice established and managed by organizations	Automated through the use of security partner provider flows and partner management experiences
Centralized route management to route traffic to the hub	Organization managed UDR	Fully supported using BGP by Microsoft for usage
Multiple security provider support	Tunneling to third-party firewalls supported with manually configured forced tunneling	Azure Firewall's private traffic filtering and a third party's Internet filtering supported automatically by Azure Firewall
Web Application Firewall on Application Gateway	Supported in virtual network	Presently supported in a spoke network
Network Virtual Appliance	Supported in virtual network	Presently supported in a spoke network
Azure DDoS Protection Standard support	Supported in hub virtual network	Not supported

Build and Configure a Secure Hub within an Azure Virtual WAN Hub Using Azure PowerShell

This section shows the process of building a secure hub within Azure Virtual WAN using Azure PowerShell.

The first step is to define variables, creating the resource groups, virtual WAN instances, and virtual hubs:

```
# Define Variables
$RG = "Sybex-vwan-rg"
$Location = "UAECentral"
$VwanName = "Sybexvwan"
$HubName =  "Sybexhub1"
# Deploy Resource Group, Virtual WAN and Virtual Hub
New-AzResourceGroup -Name $RG -Location $Location
$Vwan = New-AzVirtualWan -Name $VwanName -ResourceGroupName $RG
-Location $Location -AllowVnetToVnetTraffic -AllowBranchToBranchTraffic
-VirtualWANType "Standard"
```

```
$Hub = New-AzVirtualHub -Name $HubName -ResourceGroupName $RG
-VirtualWan $Vwan
-Location $Location -AddressPrefix "172.168.1.0/24" -Sku "Standard"
```

Create two virtual networks and connect them to the hub as spokes:

```
# Deploy Virtual Network
$SybexSpoke1 = New-AzVirtualNetwork -Name "Sybexspoke1" -ResourceGroupName $RG
-Location $Location -AddressPrefix "10.50.51.0/24"
$SybexSpoke2 = New-AzVirtualNetwork -Name "Sybexspoke2" -ResourceGroupName $RG
-Location $Location -AddressPrefix "10.50.52.0/24"
# Establish Connection between Virtual Network to Virtual WAN
$SybexSpoke1Connection = New-AzVirtualHubVnetConnection -ResourceGroupName $RG
-ParentResourceName  $HubName -Name "Sybexspoke1"
-RemoteVirtualNetwork $SybexSpoke1
-EnableInternetSecurityFlag $True
$SybexSpoke2Connection = New-AzVirtualHubVnetConnection -ResourceGroupName $RG
-ParentResourceName  $HubName -Name "Sybexspoke2"
-RemoteVirtualNetwork $SybexSpoke2
-EnableInternetSecurityFlag $True
```

Once the virtual WAN is created successfully, it will provide any-to-any connectivity.

The next step is to install an Azure Firewall to secure a virtual hub. A Virtual WAN Azure Firewall instance can be managed efficiently using firewall policies. The following example also creates a firewall policy:

```
# Deploy Firewall Policy
$FWPolicy = New-AzFirewallPolicy -Name "SybexVwanFwPolicy"
-ResourceGroupName $RG -Location $Location
# Deploy Firewall Public IP
$AzFWPIPs = New-AzFirewallHubPublicIpAddress -Count 1
$AzFWHubIPs = New-AzFirewallHubIpAddress -PublicIP $AzFWPIPs
# Deploy Firewall
$AzFW = New-AzFirewall -Name "sybexazfw1" -ResourceGroupName $RG
-Location $Location `
          -VirtualHubId $Hub.Id -FirewallPolicyId $FWPolicy.Id `
          -Sku AZFW_Hub -HubIPAddress $AzFWHubIPs
```

Azure Monitor can be configured to log data from the Azure Firewall. You can still use the firewall logs to verify that traffic is passing through the firewall in this example:

```
# Additionally, enable logging to Azure Firewall
$LogWSName = "Sybexvwan-" + (Get-Random -Maximum 99999) + "-" + $RG
```

```
$LogWS = New-AzOperationalInsightsWorkspace -Location $Location
-Name $LogWSName
-Sku Standard -ResourceGroupName $RG
Set-AzDiagnosticSetting -ResourceId $AzFW.Id -Enabled $True -Category
AzureFirewallApplicationRule, AzureFirewallNetworkRule
-WorkspaceId $LogWS.ResourceId
```

Now configure the virtual network connections for organizations to propagate to the non-route table:

```
# Set virtual network connections to propagate to None
$VnetRoutingConfig = $SybexSpoke1Connection.RoutingConfiguration    #
$SybexSpoke1Connection is the baseline for the future vnet configuration.
All vnets will have the same configuration
$NoneRT = Get-AzVhubRouteTable -ResourceGroupName $RG -HubName $HubName
-Name "SybexnoneRouteTable"
$NewPropRT = @{}
$NewPropRT.Add('Id', $NoneRT.id)
$PropRTList = @()
$PropRTList += $NewPropRT
$VnetRoutingConfig.PropagatedRouteTables.Ids = $PropRTList
$VnetRoutingConfig.PropagatedRouteTables.Labels = @()
$Spoke1Connection = Update-AzVirtualHubVnetConnection -ResourceGroupName $RG
-ParentResourceName  $HubName -Name "Sybexspoke1" -RoutingConfiguration
$VnetRoutingConfig
$Spoke2Connection = Update-AzVirtualHubVnetConnection -ResourceGroupName $RG
-ParentResourceName  $HubName -Name "Sybexspoke2" -RoutingConfiguration
$VnetRoutingConfig
```

Static routes should be added to the default route table. To secure connectivity in a virtual WAN, Firewall Manager generates a default configuration, but you can customize the prefix list of the static route to fit specific requirements.

```
# Add static routes to the default Route table
$AzFWId = $(Get-AzVirtualHub -ResourceGroupName $RG
-name  $HubName).AzureFirewall.Id
$AzFWRoute = New-AzVHubRoute -Name "all_traffic" -Destination @("0.0.0.0/0",
"10.50.51.0/8", "172.16.0.0/12", "172.168.0.0/16") -DestinationType "CIDR"
-NextHop $AzFWId -NextHopType "ResourceId"
$DefaultRT = Update-AzVHubRouteTable -Name "sybexdefaultRouteTable"
-ResourceGroupName $RG -VirtualHubName  $HubName -Route @($AzFWRoute).
```

For hub virtual network deployment, follow these steps:

1. **Build a firewall policy.**   You can create or derive a new policy or customize an existing policy. Make sure NAT rules aren't applied to policies that apply to multiple firewalls.

2. **Build a hub-and-spoke architecture.**   Using Firewall Manager, create a hub virtual network and peer spoke virtual networks to it, or create a virtual network and add virtual network connections and peer spoke virtual networks to it.

3. **Choose security providers and associate firewall policy.**   There is currently only one supported firewall provider, Azure Firewall. When creating a hub virtual network or converting an existing virtual network to a hub virtual network, it is also possible to convert multiple virtual networks.

    Route traffic to your organization's virtual network firewall using UDRs.   You can create custom or user-defined (static) routes in Azure to override default system routes or add more routes to a subnet's route table. In Azure, you make a route table, then attach the route table to zero or more virtual network subnets.

For Firewall Manager to be deployed for secured virtual hubs, follow these steps:

1. **Create a hub-and-spoke architecture.**   You can create a secured virtual hub by using Firewall Manager and then add virtual network connections, or you can create a virtual WAN hub and add virtual network connections.

2. **Select security providers.**   Selecting an appropriate security provider can be performed while creating a secured virtual hub or restoring a current virtual WAN hub to a safe virtual hub.

3. **Create a firewall policy and associate it with your organization's hub.**   This only applies to Azure Firewall users. Security-as-a-service policies are configured through the partner's management interface.

    Configure route settings to route traffic to your organization's secured virtual hub.   You can easily route traffic to your secure hub for filtering and logging without using UDRs on the spoke's virtual networks' Secured Virtual Hub Route Setting page. Each virtual WAN consumer can have only one hub per region. Multiple virtual WANs can be added to the region. Across a virtual WAN, you cannot have overlapping IP spaces for hubs. You must connect hub VNets within the same region.

Connectivity to other resources is enabled through a virtual hub, which Microsoft manages. In the Azure portal, a virtual hub is created from a virtual WAN, and its components include a virtual hub VNet and gateways (optional).

Integrate an Azure Virtual WAN Hub with a Third-Party Network Virtual Appliance

You can deploy select network virtual appliances (NVAs) directly into the virtual WAN hub in a jointly managed solution by Azure and third-party NVA vendors. Virtual WAN hubs cannot be deployed with all NVAs in Azure Marketplace.

An NVA can be deployed as a third-party gateway with various functionalities in the virtual WAN hub. It can act as both an SD-WAN gateway and a firewall. NVAs deployed through the virtual WAN hub offer customers the benefits shown in Table 8.9.

TABLE 8.9 Features offered by NVAs deployed through the virtual WAN hub

Features	Description
Infrastructure choices that have been predefined and tested.	Microsoft and its partners work together to identify throughput and bandwidth limits before releasing the solution to customers.
Provides built-in availability and resilience.	Deployments of virtual WAN NVAs are aware of availability zones and are configured to be highly available automatically.
Bootstrapping and provisioning without hassle.	Prequalified managed applications can be provisioned and boot-strapped on the virtual WAN platform. They are available on the Azure Marketplace.
Streamlining routing.	Intelligent routing systems are available with Virtual WAN. As with Microsoft gateways, NVA solutions peer with the virtual WAN hub router and participate in virtual WAN routing decisions.
Providing integrated support.	Azure virtual WAN partners enjoy special support agreements that enable them to diagnose and solve problems quickly.
Life cycle management provided by the platform.	Azure virtual WAN includes updates and patches. In this way, if you deploy virtual appliance solutions, you can avoid the complexity of life cycle management.
Features integrated into the platform include:	Virtual hub route tables interoperate seamlessly with Microsoft gateways and virtual networks, and with Encrypted ExpressRoute (SD-WAN overlay over an ExpressRoute circuit).

TABLE 8.9   Features offered by NVAs deployed through the virtual WAN hub *(continued)*

Features	Description
Within the virtual WAN hub you can deploy the listed NVAs for SD-WAN connectivity.	Barracuda Cisco Cloud Services Router VWAN VMware SD WAN Versa Networks
Specified SD-WAN NVAs can be deployed in the virtual WAN hub to provide connectivity and security.	Fortinet Next-Generation Firewall (NGFW) All North-South, East-West, and Internet-bound traffic can be inspected using NGFW virtual appliances.

Azure virtual WAN hub NVAs explicitly designed for use in this hub are available for direct deployment. Azure Marketplace publishes NVA as a Managed Application that customers can deploy directly from Marketplace.

High-Level Use Case for Network Virtual Appliances

In the virtual WAN hub, there are three high-level use case for NVAs:

Any-to-Any Connectivity   Each Azure region with a footprint supports the deployment of NVAs. SD-WAN tunnels connect branch sites to Azure via virtual WAN hubs.

Microsoft's global backbone provides branch sites with access to workloads in Azure in virtual networks in the same region or other regions. Other branches connected to Azure via ExpressRoute, site-to-site VPN, or remote user connectivity can also communicate with SD-WAN-connected sites.

Security Provided by Azure Firewall along with NVA Connectivity   In addition to Azure Firewall, users can deploy NVAs based on connectivity. Azure Firewall can be configured to inspect all traffic sent over virtual WANs. Alternatively, you can configure virtual WANs to forward all Internet traffic to Azure Firewall for inspection.

Security Provided by NVA Firewalls   NVAs can also be deployed in the virtual WAN hub to provide SD-WAN connectivity and NGFW functionality. On-premises devices can be connected to the NVA in the hub to inspect North-South, East-West, and Internet-bound traffic.

Table 8.10 lists the regions that offer NVA in the virtual hub as of this writing.

TABLE 8.10   Azure regions currently offering NVA in virtual hubs

Geo Region	Azure regions
North America	Canada Central, Canada East, Central US, East US, East US 2, South Central US, North Central US, West Central US, West US, West US 2
South America	Brazil South, Brazil Southeast
Europe	France Central, France South, Germany North, Germany West Central, North Europe, Norway East, Norway West, Switzerland North, Switzerland West, UK South, UK West, West Europe
Middle East	UAE North
Asia	East Asia, Japan East, Japan West, Korea Central, Korea South, Southeast Asia
Australia	Australia South East, Australia East, Australia Central, Australia Central 2
Africa	South Africa North
India	South India, West India, Central India

The following are deployment considerations when integrating an Azure virtual WAN hub with a third-party NVA:

- Virtual WAN supports all routing scenarios through NVAs in the hub.
- Azure Firewall enables the deployment of partner NVAs into hubs.
- Users must deploy NVAs into a Standard hub.
- As of this writing, the virtual WAN hub can be deployed with Barracuda CloudGen WAN, Cisco Cloud virtual WAN application, and VMware SD-WAN.

Create and Attach a Network Security Group to a Resource

Network security groups (NSGs) are built-in tools in Azure that allow you to control incoming and outgoing traffic on individual network interfaces and a subnet level. Azure rules control which traffic is permitted or denied for specific resources or subnets. Security rules can either be applied to a subnet (by using them for all resources in that subnet) or to a NIC, which is accomplished by applying security rules to the VM associated with the NIC.

Azure NSGs can filter network traffic to and from Azure resources in an Azure virtual network. Several Azure resources are protected by NSGs that regulate inbound and outbound network traffic. You can specify each rule's source, destination, port, and protocol.

The security rules in network security groups are evaluated based on the five-tuple information (source, source port, destination, destination port, and protocol) to allow or deny traffic. Security rules created by Azure engineers cannot have the same priority and direction.

A flow record is created for existing connections, and based on the connection state, communication is allowed or denied. NSGs can be stateful if they have flow records. The response to any outbound traffic over port 80 does not require an inbound security rule if an outbound security rule is specified. When communication is initiated externally, only an inbound security rule is necessary, and vice versa. When inbound traffic is allowed over a port, it is unnecessary to specify an outbound security rule.

Existing connections may not be interrupted if you remove the security rule that enabled the flow. If connections are interrupted, no traffic will flow in either direction for a few minutes.

Within Azure subscription limits, a security group may contain zero rules or as many as desired. Table 8.11 shows the properties of a rule.

TABLE 8.11   Property and description for NSG

Property	Description
Name	An organization's unique name.
Priority	There are between 100 and 4,096 digits in this number. Because lower numbers have a higher priority than higher numbers, rules with lower numbers are processed first. Traffic matching a rule stops the processing of additional rules. Due to this, rules with lower priorities (higher numbers) with the same attributes as rules with higher priorities are not processed.
Source or destination	Can be set to Any, or an individual IP address, or Classless Inter-Domain Routing (CIDR) block (10.0.0.0/24, for example), service tag, or application security group.
	Select the private IP address assigned to an Azure resource if you specify the address. Azure processes NSGs for inbound traffic after converting public IP addresses to private IP addresses, and Azure translates private IP addresses into public IP addresses for outbound traffic.
	You can create fewer security rules by specifying a range, a service tag, or an application security group. With augmented security rules, you can specify multiple IP addresses and ranges in a rule. You cannot specify many service tags or application groups. Resource Manager deployment models can only create enhanced security rules within NSGs. NSGs created through the classic deployment model cannot have multiple IP addresses and IP ranges.

Property	Description
Protocol	TCP, UDP, ICMP, ESP, AH, or Any.
Direction	Inbound or outbound traffic is affected by this rule.
Port range	You can specify an individual port or range of ports, such as 80 or 10000–10005. When you select ranges, you create fewer security rules. The Resource Manager deployment model allows for enhanced security rules only within NSGs. You cannot specify multiple ports or port ranges in one security rule in a NSG created through the classic deployment model.
Action	Allow or Deny

Whenever you create an NSG, the default rules shown in Table 8.12 are automatically created.

VNet, Azure Load Balancer, and Internet are service tags in the Source and Destination columns of Table 8.12 instead of IP addresses. There are three protocol options in the Any column: TCP, UDP, and ICMP. When creating rules, the TCP, UDP, ICMP, and Any options are available. All addresses are represented by 0.0.0.0/0 in the Source and Destination columns. For this expression, you can use * or any in the Azure portal, Azure CLI, or PowerShell.

You can override the default rules by creating rules with a higher priority, but they cannot remove the default rules.

Enhancing the security rules simplifies virtual network security definitions, allowing you to define more complex and extensive network security policies with fewer rules. You can combine multiple ports, multiple explicit IP addresses, and multiple ranges of IP addresses into a single, easy-to-understand security rule. A rule's source, destination, and port fields may be enhanced with augmented rules. Security rules with service tags or application security groups can simplify the maintenance of created security rule definitions. An Azure service tag represents a group of IP address prefixes for a given service. Using service tags minimizes frequent updates on network security rules.

With application security groups, you can define security policies based on grouped virtual machines, which allows them to configure network security as a natural extension of the application structure. You can reuse your organization's security policies at scale without manually maintaining explicit IP addresses.

The following are design and deployment principles you should take into consideration:

Virtual IP of the Host Node   Virtualized host IP addresses 168.63.129.16 and 169.254.169.254 provide essential infrastructure services such as DHCP, DNS, Azure Instance Metadata Service, and health monitoring. The only virtualized IP addresses used across all regions belong to Microsoft. These platform rules will not be included in effective security rules. You can override this essential infrastructure communication by

TABLE 8.12 NSG default rules

Services	Traffic type	Priority	Source	Source ports	Destination	Destination ports	Protocol
AllowVNetInBound	Inbound	65,000	VNet	0–65535	VNet	0–65535	Any
AllowAzureLoadBalancer-InBound	Inbound	65,001	Azure Load Balancer	0–65535	0.0.0.0/0	0–65535	Any
DenyAllInbound	Inbound	65,500	0.0.0.0/0	0–65535	0.0.0.0/0	0–65535	Any
AllowVnetOutBound	Outbound	65000	VNet	0–65535	VNet	0–65535	Any
AllowInternetOutBound	Outbound	65001	0.0.0.0/0	0–65535	Internet	0–65535	Any
DenyAllOutBound	Outbound	65500	0.0.0.0/0	0–65535	0.0.0.0/0	0–65535	Any

defining security rules based on these service tags in your NSG rules: AzurePlatformDNS, AzurePlatformIMDS, and AzurePlatformLKM.

Licensing (Key Management Service)   Windows images running on virtual machines must be licensed. License requests are sent outbound through TCP port 1688 to the Key Management Service (KMS) host servers. Default routes `0.0.0.0/0` will disable this platform rule for deployments using this configuration.

Virtual Machines in Load-Balanced Pools   The originating computer's port and IP address range are applied, not the load balancers. Ports and addresses are for the destination computer, not the load balancer.

Azure Service Instances   Virtual network subnets are used to deploy Azure services such as HDInsight, application service environments, and VM scale sets. Before applying an NSG to a subnet that hosts a resource, review the port requirements. The service doesn't function correctly if you block ports required by the service.

Sending Outbound Email   Microsoft recommends that network engineers use authenticated SMTP relay services (typically connected via TCP port 587, but often others). SMTP relay services specialize in sending to reduce rejections by third-party email providers. SendGrid and Exchange Online Protection is an SMTP relay service. Azure provides SMTP relay services to all customers regardless of their subscription type.

You could send an email directly over TCP port 25 if you created a cloud subscriber's Azure subscription before November 15, 2017, using SMTP relay services. When designing organization subscriptions after November 15, 2017, you might not be able to send emails directly over TCP port 25. The outbound behavior depends on the type of subscription, as follows:

Enterprise Agreement   Outbound TCP port 25 communication is allowed under the Enterprise agreement. The Azure platform does not impose restrictions when sending emails to external email providers directly from VMs.

Pay-as-You-Go   The communication of all resources on TCP port 25 has been blocked. Suppose an Azure engineer needs to send an email directly from a VM to an external email provider (without using an SMTP relay). Requests of this nature may be granted. After conducting anti-fraud checks, Microsoft reviews and approves requests at its discretion. To submit a support request, the issue type Technical, Virtual Network Connectivity must be selected. In your support case, explain why your subscriptions cannot use authenticated SMTP relays but instead must send your emails directly to the mail provider. If your subscription is exempt, you can communicate outbound over TCP port 25 only after that date.

MSDN, Azure Pass, Azure in Open, Education, BizSpark, and Free Trial   All resources block outbound communication on TCP port 25, and requests to remove the restriction will not be granted. You need SMTP relay services if you wish to send emails from your virtual machines.

Cloud Service Provider   A cloud service provider can make an unblock request on behalf of Azure resource consumers if their cloud service providers cannot use a secure SMTP relay.

If Azure allows you to send an email over TCP port 25, Microsoft cannot guarantee inbound email will be accepted by email providers. Working directly with a provider to resolve message delivery or spam filtering issues, or using an authenticated SMTP relay service, is the best solution if a specific provider rejects mail from your virtual machines.

> Azure VNets are connected to NSGs, containing a list of security rules. An NSG can be attached to a subnet, an individual virtual machine (classic), or an individual NIC (Resource Manager).
>
> Within Azure VNets, you can utilize TCP, UDP, and ICMP TCP/IP protocols. Within VNets, Unicast is supported except for Dynamic Host Configuration Protocol (DHCP) via Unicast (source port UDP/68 destination port UDP/67) and UDP source port 65330, which is reserved for the host. VNets block multicast, broadcast, IP-in-IP, and generic routing encapsulation (GRE) packets.
>
> In the Layer 3 world, VNets are overlays, and Azure does not have support for Layer 2 semantics.
>
> You can create or configure a VNet using the Azure portal, Azure PowerShell, Azure CLI, or a network configuration file (netcfg—for traditional VNets only).

Using the Azure portal, you can create a new NSG by following the steps in Exercise 8.8.

EXERCISE 8.8

Create a Network Security Group

1.   Log into a personal or business account in the Azure portal at `https://portal .azure.com`.

2.   On the Azure portal menu, choose All Services or search for All services.

3. Under Networking, Network Security Groups is selected (see the following image):

All services | Networking

All

Favorites

Recents

Categories

General

Compute

Networking

Storage

Web

Mobile

Containers

Databases

Analytics

AI + machine learning

Internet of things

Mixed reality

Filter services

↔ Virtual networks

◆ Load balancers

🔍 Network Watcher

🖥 Network interfaces

🗒 Public IP Prefixes

🛡 Application security groups

📄 Service endpoint policies

🌐 Web Application Firewall policies (WAF)

🌐 Virtual WANs

🌐 DNS zones

🛡 Application gateways

🗒 IP Groups

⬡ Azure Synapse Analytics (private link hubs)

🚪 Front Door and CDN profiles

🛡 Network security groups

🖥 Public IP addresses

🗒 Route tables

🛡 DDoS protection plans

⬤ Private DNS zones

🔗 Private Link

✕ Bastions

🌐 Traffic Manager profiles

◇ NAT gateways

🛡 Firewall Manager

4. Select the Basics tab, shown in the next image, and configure the NSG as follows:

Subscription — Choose your subscription.

Resource Group — Choose a resource group or create a new resource group.

Name — Provide a name for the NSG. We're using SybexDemo.

Region — Choose the region you want to deploy to or one close to your resource needs.

EXERCISE 8.8 *(continued)*

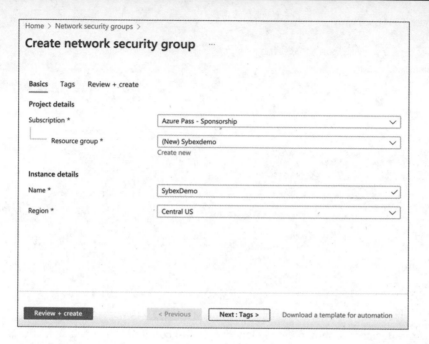

5. On the Review + Create tab, wait for confirmation that your NSG has been validated, then click Create, as shown here:

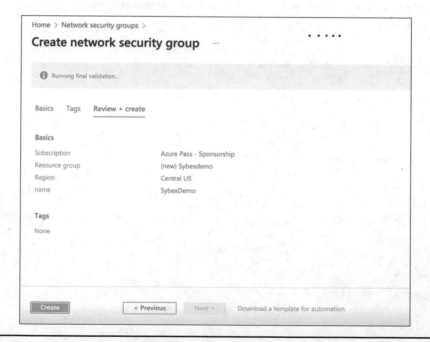

The NSG is ready for use once the deployment has been validated and started (which takes a few seconds).

It is possible to deploy the NSG during VM deployment, which will connect the NSG to the deployed NIC. Considering that the NSG is already associated with the resource, any rules defined in it will only apply to the associated VM.

Here is an example on Exercise 8.9 where the NSG deployed separately. It is not attached until an association is made with the NIC or the subnet, and its rules cannot be applied. As a result, the NSG rules will be applied to all subnet resources when attached with a subnet. In Exercise 8.9, you use the Azure portal to attach an NSG to a resource.

EXERCISE 8.9

Attach a Network Security Group to a Resource

1. Log into a personal or business account in the Azure portal at `https://portal.azure.com`.

2. In the Search box, type **Network security group** and press Enter.

3. Choose Sybex_Demo from the Network Security Group list, and then choose Subnets underneath Settings, as shown here:

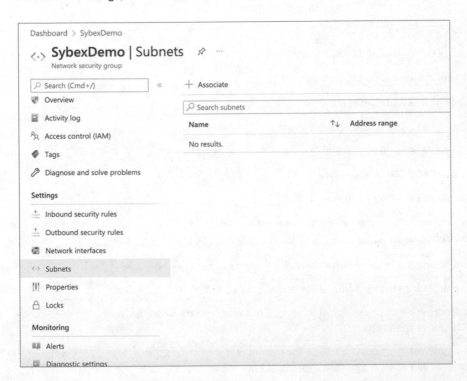

4. Click Associate, select the virtual network that includes the subnet you want to associate the NSG with, and then choose the subnet.

5. After submitting the change, the associated subnet will appear.

When an NSG is associated with a subnet, all resources within the subnet will be subject to its rules. It is important to note that a subnet can be associated with more than one NSG, in which case all the NSGs' rules will apply. Considering a single NSG, priority is a critical factor, but if the rules of more NSGs are observed, the Deny rule will prevail. Therefore, if you have two NSGs on the same subnet, one with the Allow rule on TCP port 443 and another with the Deny rule, traffic on this port will be denied.

Key Considerations for IP Subnet Planning for NSGs

The IETF has designated a number of address ranges in RFC 1918 for private, nonroutable address spaces. Microsoft encourages you to use these ranges:

- `10.0.0.0–10.255.255.255` (10/8 prefix)
- `172.16.0.0–172.31.255.255` (172.16/12 prefix)
- `192.168.0.0–192.168.255.255` (192.168/16 prefix)

You cannot add the following address ranges:

- `224.0.0.0/4` (Multicast)
- `255.255.255.255/32` (Broadcast)
- `127.0.0.0/8` (Loopback)
- `169.254.0.0/16` (Link-local)
- `168.63.129.16/32` (Internal DNS)

Within each subnet, Azure reserves five IP addresses. `X.X.X.0–X.X.X.3` are the addresses for the subnet.

- The address `x.x.x.0` is reserved for the Virtual network address.
- The default gateway address for Azure is `x.x.x.1`.
- The addresses `x.x.x.2` and `x.x.x.3` are reserved by Azure for mapping the Azure DNS IPs to the VNets.
- The network broadcast address for subnets larger than /25 is `x.x.x.255`. Smaller subnets will have a different broadcast address.

Create an Application Security Group and Attach It to a NIC

Application security groups (ASGs) enable you to configure network security as a natural extension of an application's structure, grouping virtual machines and defining network security policies based on those groups. You can reuse your security policy at scale without maintaining explicit IP addresses manually. The platform handles the complexity of exact IP addresses and multiple rule sets, allowing you to focus on your organization's business logic. Figure 8.7 shows an overview of the NIC ASG attachment.

FIGURE 8.7   Overview of the NIC ASG attachment

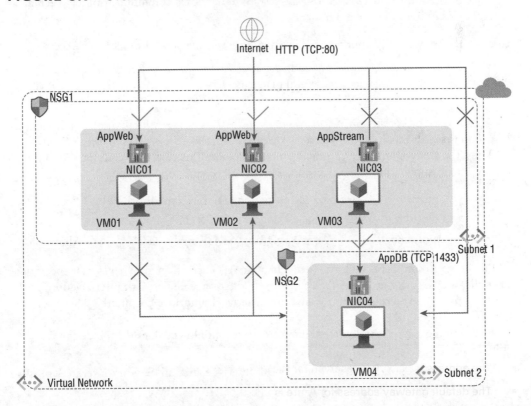

There are two members of the AppWeb ASG in Figure 8.7: NIC01, NIC02. In addition to NICO3, NIC04 is a member of the AppStream application security group. In this example, each network interface belongs to only one NSG, but network interfaces can belong to more than one ASG. Each network interface has no associated NSG.

Both subnets have NSG1, which contains the following rules:

Allow-HTTP-Inbound-Internet   This is the only rule that needs to be enabled. Because of the DenyAllInbound default security rule, no additional rule is necessary for the App-Stream and AppDB ASGs.

Priority	Source	Source ports	Destination	Destination ports	Protocol	Access
100	Internet	*	AppWeb	80	TCP	Allow

Deny-AppDB-All   This rule is required to deny traffic generated by all resources since the default security rule, AllowVNetInBound, allows communication between all resources in the same virtual network.

Priority	Source	Source ports	Destination	Destination ports	Protocol	Access
120	*	*	AppDB	1433	Any	Deny

Allow-AppDB-AppStream   AppStream traffic can enter the AppDB application security group through this rule. Unlike Deny-Database-All, this rule is given higher priority. Thus, the Deny-Database-All rule is processed before this rule, allowing traffic from the ASGLogic application security group, whereas all other traffic is blocked.

Priority	Source	Source ports	Destination	Destination ports	Protocol	Access
110	AppLogic	*	AppDB	1433	TCP	Allow

Only network interfaces that are members of an ASG are affected by rules that specify the application security group as the source or destination. The network interface does not belong to an ASG. The rule is not applied to the network interface despite the NSG being associated with the subnet.

The following are the fundamental limitations you should consider during design and deployment:

- The ASG must contain at least one network interface, and all network interfaces must be part of the same virtual network.

- You can specify an ASG as a source or destination of a security rule, but both ASGs must be part of the same virtual network.

- The maximum number of ASGs is 3,000, the maximum number of IP configurations per ASG is 20, the maximum number of IP configurations per ASG is 4,000, and the maximum number of ASGs per network security group is 100.

Follow the steps in Exercise 8.10 to use the Azure portal to create a new ASG.

EXERCISE 8.10

Create a New Application Security Group

1. Log into a personal or business account in the Azure portal at `https://portal`
    `.azure.com`.

2. In the Search box, type **Application security group** and press Enter.

3. Choose Application Security Group to open the Create An Application Security Group
    Wizard (see the next image). Provide the following information to configure the ASG.

Subscription	Choose your subscription.
Resource Group	Choose a resource group or create a new resource group.
Name	Provide a name for your ASG.
Region	Choose the region you want to deploy to or one that's close to your resource needs.

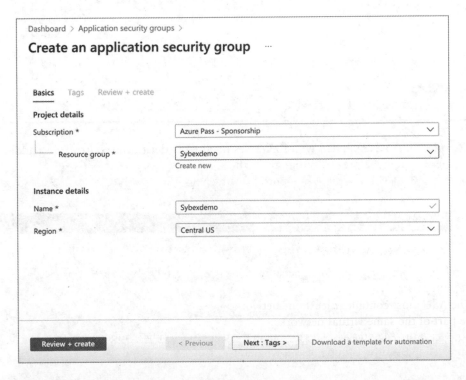

4. On the Review + Create tab, wait until the ASG is validated, as shown in the following
    image, then click Create.

EXERCISE 8.10 *(continued)*

NSG rules must be combined with ASG rules to allow better traffic control, with additional checks applied before permitting traffic flow.

In Exercise 8.11 you use the Azure portal to attach an ASG to a NIC.

EXERCISE 8.11

Create a New Application Group

1. Log into a personal or business account in the Azure portal at `https://portal`
   `.azure.com`.

2. In the Search box, type **Virtual machine** and press Enter.

3. Choose your VM and click Networking. In the page that opens, choose Configure The
   Application Security Groups, as shown here:

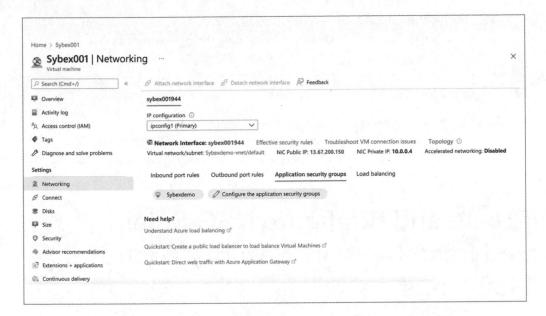

4. In the new pane that opens (see the following image), choose the ASG that needs to be associated with this VM from the list of available ASGs.

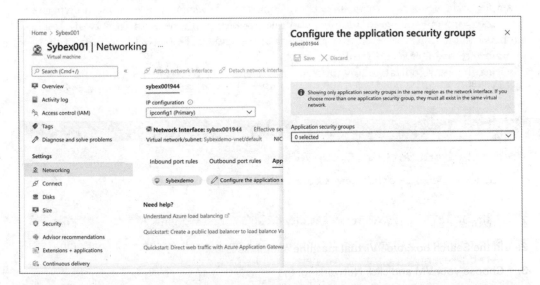

5. As soon as you click Save, the changes will be applied and the VM will be associated with the ASG.

Associating the VM with the ASG is essential, and you can associate more than one VM with each ASG. NSG rules are then created by combining the ASG with the NSG.

Key Consideration for ASGs

Plan the security rules on-demand and create rules instead of individual or ranges of IP addresses to minimize the number of security rules and the need to change them.

Create and Configure NSG Rules and Read Network Security Group Flow Logs

You can create rules based on only NSGs to allow or deny traffic based on a range of IP addresses, and ASGs will enable you to broaden or narrow this range of IP addresses. For example, you can specify which subnets can connect to a specific ASG without allowing VMs from the front-end subnet. In addition, multiple VMs from different virtual networks and subnets can only be accessed if they all belong to the same ASG. Network security groups contain zero or more security rules.

Using the Azure portal, follow the steps in Exercise 8.12 to create and configure NSG rules.

EXERCISE 8.12

Create Network Security Group Rules

1. Log into a personal or business account in the Azure portal at https://portal
    .azure.com.

2. In the Search box, type **Network security group** and press Enter.

3. Select Inbound Security Rules or Outbound Security Rules from the menu bar of the
    network security group, as shown here:

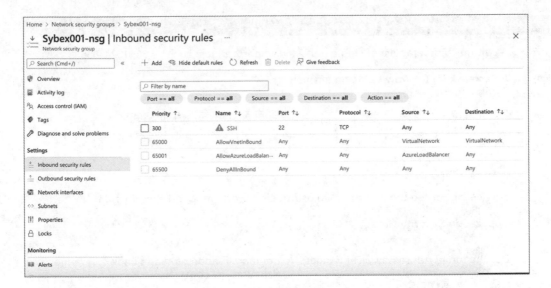

4. From the Inbound [or Outbound] Security Rule page that opens, enter the following values (see the next image):

Source	Choose one of the following:
	Any
	IP Addresses
	Service Tag (inbound security rule) or VirtualNetwork (outbound security rule)
	Application Security Group
Source IP Addresses/CIDR Ranges	Enter CIDR ranges and IP addresses separated by commas.
Source Service Tag	Choose a service tag from the drop-down menu.
Source Application Security Group	Select a security group that already exists.
Source Port Ranges	Choose one of the following:
	A single port, such as 80
	A range of ports, such as 1024–65535

A comma-separated list of single ports and/or port ranges, such as 80, 1024–65535

An asterisk (*) to allow traffic on any port.

Destination	Choose one of the following:
Any	
IP Addresses	
Service Tag (outbound security rule) or VirtualNetwork (inbound security rule)	
Application Security Group	
Destination IP Addresses/CIDR Ranges	Enter an IP address range and CIDR range delimited by commas.
Destination Service Tag	Choose a service tag from the drop-down menu.
Destination Application Security Group	Choose a security group that already exists.
Destination Port Ranges	Choose one of the following:
A single port, such as 80	
A range of ports, such as 1024–65535	
A comma-separated list of single ports and/or port ranges, such as 80, 1024–65535	
An asterisk (*) to allow traffic on any port	
Protocol	Select TCP, UDP, or ICMP.
Action	Select Allow or Deny.
Priority	This value is unique for all security rules in the NSG and ranges between 100 and 4096.
Name	Enter the name of the rule within the group of network security rules. Up to 80 characters can be used for the name.
Description	Enter a text description. The maximum length for the description is 140 characters.

Add inbound security rule
Sybex001-nsg

Source ⓘ

Any ⌄

Source port ranges * ⓘ

*

Destination ⓘ

Any ⌄

Service ⓘ

Custom ⌄

Destination port ranges * ⓘ

8080

Protocol

⦿ Any
◯ TCP
◯ UDP
◯ ICMP

Action

[Add] [Cancel]

5. Click Add.

You must have Network Security Group Flow Logging enabled on one or many NSGs in your organization's accounts.

The Azure Network Watcher flow logs feature lets you log information about IP traffic flowing through NSGs. Data is sent to Azure Storage accounts, from which it can be accessed and exported to visualization tools, security information and event management (SIEM), or the intrusion detection system of your choice.

Your network must be monitored, managed, and known to ensure that security, compliance, and performance are not compromised. The environment of your organization must be known in order to protect and optimize it. You often need to know the current state of your networks, which of them is connecting, where they are connecting from, what ports are open to the Internet, expected network behavior, irregular network behavior, and when a sudden increase in traffic occurs.

Cloud environments rely on flow logs to determine the truth about all network activity. It doesn't matter if your organization is an up-and-coming startup looking to optimize resources or a large enterprise looking to detect an intrusion; flow logs are the best tool. The cloud allows consumers to maximize network flows, monitor throughput, verify compliance, and detect intrusions, among other things.

To read logs, blobs of blocks are used to store NSG flow logs. Each log is a separate block blob generated every hour, and block blobs are made up of smaller blocks. New entries are added to the logs with the latest information every hour.

Here's an example PowerShell script that sets up all the variables necessary to query the NSG flow log blob and list the blocks in the `CloudBlockBlob` block blob. You should update the script to include valid values for your organization's environments.

```
function Get-NSGFlowLogCloudBlockBlob {
    [CmdletBinding()]
    param (
        [string] [Parameter(Mandatory=$true)] $subscriptionId,
        [string] [Parameter(Mandatory=$true)] $NSGResourceGroupName,
        [string] [Parameter(Mandatory=$true)] $NSGName,
        [string] [Parameter(Mandatory=$true)] $storageAccountName,
        [string] [Parameter(Mandatory=$true)] $storageAccountResourceGroup,
        [string] [Parameter(Mandatory=$true)] $macAddress,
        [datetime] [Parameter(Mandatory=$true)] $logTime
    )
    process {
        # Retrieve the primary storage account key to access the NSG logs
        $StorageAccountKey = (Get-AzStorageAccountKey -ResourceGroupName
$storageAccountResourceGroup -Name $storageAccountName).Value[0]
        # Create a new storage context to be used to query the logs
        $ctx = New-AzStorageContext -StorageAccountName $StorageAccountName
-StorageAccountKey $StorageAccountKey
        # Container name used by NSG flow logs
        $ContainerName = "insights-logs-networksecuritygroupflowevent"
        # Name of the blob that holds the NSG flow log
        $BlobName = "resourceId=/SUBSCRIPTIONS/${subscriptionId}/
RESOURCEGROUPS
/${NSGResourceGroupName}/PROVIDERS/MICROSOFT.NETWORK/NETWORKSECURITYGROUPS
/${NSGName}/y=$($logTime.Year)/m=$(($logTime).ToString("MM"))
/d=$(($logTime).ToString("dd"))/h=$(($logTime).ToString("HH"))
/m=00/macAddress=$($macAddress)/PT1H.json"
        # Obtain the storage blog
        $Blob = Get-AzStorageBlob -Context $ctx -Container $ContainerName
-Blob $BlobName
        # Obtain the block blog of type 'Microsoft.Azure.Storage.Blob.
CloudBlob'
from the storage blob
        $CloudBlockBlob = [Microsoft.Azure.Storage.Blob.CloudBlockBlob]
$Blob.ICloudBlob
```

```
        #Return the Cloud Block Blob
        $CloudBlockBlob
    }
}
function Get-NSGFlowLogBlockList  {
    [CmdletBinding()]
    param (
        [Microsoft.Azure.Storage.Blob.CloudBlockBlob]
[Parameter(Mandatory=$true)] $CloudBlockBlob
    )
    process {
        # Stores the block list in a variable from the block blob.
        $blockList = $CloudBlockBlob.DownloadBlockListAsync()
        # Return the Block List
        $blockList
    }
}
$CloudBlockBlob = Get-NSGFlowLogCloudBlockBlob -subscriptionId
"CCSubscriptionId"
-NSGResourceGroupName "FLOWLOGSVALIDATIONWESTCENTRALUS" -NSGName
"V2VALIDATIONVM-NSG"
-storageAccountName "CCStorageAccountName" -storageAccountResourceGroup
"ml-rg"
-macAddress "000D3AF87856" -logTime "11/11/2018 03:00"
$blockList = Get-NSGFlowLogBlockList -CloudBlockBlob $CloudBlockBlob.
```

A list of the blocks in a blob can be obtained from the `$blockList` variable. Blobs generally contain two blocks. In the first block, there are 12 bytes; this block includes the opening brackets of the JSON log. Two bytes make up the closing brackets.

The data can be retrieved by reading the `$blockList` variable. This example reads the bytes from each block and stores them in an array. The `DownloadRangeToByteArray` method is used to retrieve the data.

```
function Get-NSGFlowLogReadBlock  {
    [CmdletBinding()]
    param (
        [System.Array] [Parameter(Mandatory=$true)] $blockList,
        [Microsoft.Azure.Storage.Blob.CloudBlockBlob]
[Parameter(Mandatory=$true)] $CloudBlockBlob
    )
    # Define the size of the byte array to the largest block
    $maxvalue = ($blocklist | measure Length -Maximum).Maximum
```

```
    # Create an array to store values in
    $valuearray = @()
    # Create the starting index to track the current block being read
    $index = 0
    # Loop through each block in the block list
    for($i=0; $i -lt $blocklist.count; $i++)
    {
        # Build a byte array object to story the bytes from the block
        $downloadArray = New-Object -TypeName byte[] -ArgumentList $maxvalue
        # Bytes from the current block are downloaded into the ByteArray,
starting with the current index. Reading increases index by 3 to remove
preceding comma.
$CloudBlockBlob.DownloadRangeToByteArray($downloadArray,0,$index,
 $($blockList[$i].Length)) | Out-Null
        # Increment the index by adding the current block length to
the previous index
        $index = $index + $blockList[$i].Length
        # Retrieve the string from the byte array
        $value = [System.Text.Encoding]::ASCII.GetString($downloadArray)
        # Add the log entry to the value array
        $valuearray += $value
    }
    #Return the Array
    $valuearray
}
$valuearray = Get-NSGFlowLogReadBlock -blockList $blockList
-CloudBlockBlob $CloudBlockBlob
```

Each string value in the array $valuearray now represents a block. Using $valuearray[$valuearray.Length-2], find the second to last value in the array. Since it is the closing bracket, you do not need the last value.

The preceding example shows how NSG flow log entries can be read without parsing the entire log.

NOTE   A block blob contains all NSG flow logs. Microsoft's system generates a block blob for every log entry every hour, and each block blob is composed of smaller blocks. The logs are updated with the latest data every few minutes, and new entries are generated every hour.

Validate NSG Flow Rules

Network Watcher is a feature of the Azure platform that allows network traffic logs to be collected from NSGs and stored in an Azure blob container. In Network Watcher, this is done through NSG flow logs. Flow logs are managed outside of the path of the network traffic, so there is no latency impact.

Inbound and outbound flows are logged per NSG rule in JSON format. Each record includes the network interface the flow applies to, 5-tuple information, and the traffic decision.

NSG log files can be stored in Azure blob containers, and retention periods can be configured. Additionally, you can collect log data in a Log Analytics workspace (if Traffic Analytics is enabled). This data is retained for the duration of the workspace.

Enabling NSG flow logs can be achieved via the following management solutions: Azure portal, PowerShell, CLI, REST, and Azure Resource Manager. Let's use PowerShell for the following examples.

To ensure flow logging works correctly, the Microsoft Insights provider must be registered. Use the following command to deploy the provider:

```
Register-AzResourceProvider -ProviderNamespace Microsoft.Insights
```

Flow logs can enable NSG flow logs and traffic analytics using the following code:

```
#Define Variables
$NW = Get-AzNetworkWatcher -ResourceGroupName NetworkWatcherRg
-Name NetworkWatcher_uaenorth
$nsg = Get-AzNetworkSecurityGroup -ResourceGroupName nsgRG -Name nsgName
$storageAccount = Get-AzStorageAccount -ResourceGroupName StorageRG
-Name sybexstorage123
Get-AzNetworkWatcherFlowLogStatus -NetworkWatcher $NW -TargetResourceId
$nsg.Id
#KPIs for Traffic Analytics.
$workspaceResourceId = "/subscriptions/bbbbbbbb-bbbb-bbbb-bbbb-bbbbbbbbbbbb
/resourcegroups/trafficanalyticsrg/providers/microsoft.operationalinsights
/workspaces/taworkspace"
$workspaceGUID = "cccccccc-cccc-cccc-cccc-cccccccccccc"
$workspaceLocation = "UAENorth"
#Define Version 1 Flow Logs
Set-AzNetworkWatcherConfigFlowLog -NetworkWatcher $NW -TargetResourceId
$nsg.Id
```

```
-StorageAccountId $storageAccount.Id -EnableFlowLog $true
-FormatType Json -FormatVersion 1
#Define Version 2 Flow Logs, and Define Traffic Analytics
Set-AzNetworkWatcherConfigFlowLog -NetworkWatcher $NW -TargetResourceId
$nsg.Id
-StorageAccountId $storageAccount.Id -EnableFlowLog $true -FormatType Json
-FormatVersion 2
#Define Version 2 Flow Logs with Traffic Analytics Configured
Set-AzNetworkWatcherConfigFlowLog -NetworkWatcher $NW -TargetResourceId
$nsg.Id
-StorageAccountId $storageAccount.Id -EnableFlowLog $true -FormatType Json
-FormatVersion 2 -EnableTrafficAnalytics
-WorkspaceResourceId $workspaceResourceId
-WorkspaceGUID $workspaceGUID -WorkspaceLocation $workspaceLocation
#Validate Flow Log Status
Get-AzNetworkWatcherFlowLogStatus -NetworkWatcher $NW -TargetResourceId
$nsg.Id
```

Flow logs can disable traffic analytics and NSG flow logs using the following code:

```
#Method to Disable Traffic Analytics by removing -EnableTrafficAnalytics
property
Set-AzNetworkWatcherConfigFlowLog -NetworkWatcher $NW -TargetResourceId
$nsg.Id
-StorageAccountId $storageAccount.Id -EnableFlowLog $true -FormatType Json
-FormatVersion 2 -WorkspaceResourceId $workspaceResourceId
-WorkspaceGUID $workspaceGUID -WorkspaceLocation $workspaceLocation
#Method to Disable Flow Logging
Set-AzNetworkWatcherConfigFlowLog -NetworkWatcher $NW -TargetResourceId
$nsg.Id
-StorageAccountId $storageAccount.Id -EnableFlowLog $false
```

Network flows will be logged only for NSG resources with flow logs enabled, and flow logs will not be logged for NSG resources without flow logs enabled. You can verify NSG flow log status by typing the following commands:

```
# You can list NSGs with flow logs is disabled
az network nsg list --query "[?flowLogs!='null']" -o table
# You can list NSGs with flow logs is disabled
az network nsg list --query "[?flowLogs=='null']" -o table
```

Common use cases for NSG flow logs are network monitoring, usage monitoring, proactive threat detection, compliance insights, network forensics, and security analysis.

The following are key concepts of NGS flow logs you should consider:

- In a flow log, each IP flow that enters and leaves an NSG is recorded at Layer 4.

- The Azure platform collects logs at 1-minute intervals without affecting customer resources or network performance.

- JSON logs show inbound and outbound flows according to NSG rules.

- The log record includes the NIC to which the flow applies, 5-tuple information, traffic decision, and throughput information (version 2 only).

- Flow logs are automatically deleted after one year if they are not accessed.

The following are core concepts of NGS flow logs and rules you should consider:

- Virtual networks (VNets) and subnetworks are the building blocks of software-defined networks. NSGs can be used to manage the security of VNets and subnets.

- NSGs contain rules that define how network traffic is allowed or denied in resources they connect to. Virtual machines can be configured with NSGs for each virtual network interface and virtual network subnet.

- The rules in the applicable NSG are applied to all traffic flows in your organization's network.

- NSG flow logs are the result of these evaluations. In Azure, flow logs are collected without requiring customers to modify their resources.

- Storage accounts are used for NSG flow logs, where they can be accessed.

NSG flow logs can be viewed via the NSG Flow Logs portal and by using PowerShell functions (as described in previous sections). Logs can also be exported to Splunk via export NSG flow logs.

Although flow logs target NSGs, they are not displayed like other logs. Flow logs are stored in an account. The following is an example of a storage location:

```
https://{yourstorageaccountname}.blob.core.windows.net
/insights-logs-networksecuritygroupflowevent/resourceId=/SUBSCRIPTIONS
/{yoursubscriptionID}/RESOURCEGROUPS/{yourresourceGroupName}/PROVIDERS
/MICROSOFT.NETWORK/NSG/{yournsgName}/y={year}/m={month}/d={day}/h={hour}
/m=00/macAddress={yourmacAddress}/PT1H.json
```

Traffic Analytics can be used to visualize NSG flow logs; it is an Azure native service that processes flow logs, extracts insights, and visualizes them. Use Power BI to visualize NSG flow logs, Elastic Stack to display NSG flow logs, and Grafana Labs' Grafana, Cisco Secure Network Analytics Stealthwatch, and Graylog Inc.'s Graylog to manage and analyze NSG flow logs.

NSGs associated with the flow log are stopped when the flow log is disabled. Flow logs as resources continue to exist with all their settings and associations. Flow logging on a configured NSG can be enabled at any time.

By deleting a flow log, the associated flow logging is shut off, and its associated settings and associations are deleted. Flow logging must be restarted for that NSG by creating a new flow log resource. The Azure portal will support deleting flow logs in the future. Flow logs can be deleted via PowerShell, CLI, or the REST API.

Here are the essential best practices you should apply while designing and deploying NSG logs:

- Separate subscriptions should be used for storing logs.

- Each subnet in production should have an NSG, and each Azure region with virtual network resources should have a Network Watcher instance.

- Every Azure region with virtual network resources should have one Standard tier storage account.

- Activate an Activity Log alert to be notified when keys for storage accounts are rotated or if key-based access is disabled.

- Using Azure Policy, enforce the collection of NSG flow logs.

NSGs are a way to group and manage Azure network resources. Logging with NSG flow logs enables you to sync all traffic going through NSGs in a 5-tuple format. Raw flow logs are written to an Azure Storage account accessed later for further processing, analysis, and querying.

The flow logs' data is collected outside your organization's network paths, so they do not impact your networks' throughput or latency. There is no risk to network performance when you create or delete flow logs.

Service endpoints are compatible with NSG flow logs without any extra configuration needed.

Verify IP Flow

The IP flow verify checks whether packets are allowed or denied to or from a virtual machine. There is direction, protocol, local IP address, remote IP address, local port, and a remote port. The name of the rule that denied the packet is returned if a security group denies the packet. Any source or destination IP can be used, but IP flow verification enables administrators to quickly diagnose connectivity issues, whether on or off the Internet.

An NSG is applied to the network interface, such as for a subnet or NIC in a virtual machine. IP Flow Verify in Network Watcher checks the rules for all NSGs applied to the network interface. A network interface's traffic flow is then determined by its configured settings. IP Flow Verify can be used to confirm whether an NSG rule blocks traffic from or to a virtual machine. The Azure Virtual Network Manager rules will also be evaluated along with the NSG rules.

Azure Virtual Network Manager (AVNM) lets users manage virtual networks globally across subscriptions, including grouping, configuring, and deploying them. AVNM security configuration allows users to define a group of rules that are applicable to one or more NSGs. NSG rules are given less priority than these security rules. The major difference is that AVNM manages admin rules in a central location controlled by governance and security teams, which then flow down to each VNet. An NSG is a resource controlled by the VNet owner, which applies at a subnet or NIC level.

A Network Watcher instance needs to be created in every region where IP flow verification will be performed. Network Watcher can only monitor resources within a single region as a regional service. It does not affect the results of IP Flow Verify, since any routes associated with the NIC or subnet will still be returned.

Azure permits and denies traffic to and from virtual machines by default. Azure administrators may later override Azure's defaults to allow or deny additional traffic types.

Follow the steps in Exercise 8.13 to use the Azure portal to configure IP Flow Verify.

EXERCISE 8.13

IP Flow Verify Using the Azure Portal

1. Log into a personal or business account in the Azure portal at `https://portal` `.azure.com`.

2. In the search box, type **Network Watcher** and press Enter.

3. Look for IP Flow Verify under Network Diagnostics Tools.

4. When the IP Flow Verify Wizard opens, enter the following configuration information:

Resource Group	Choose a resource group or create a new resource group.
VM	Assign the VM name.
Network Interface	Enter **myvm**. (The name of the network interface of the portal created when you created the VM is different.)
Protocol	Select TCP or UDP.
Direction	Select Outbound or Inbound.
Local IP Address	Enter **10.0.0.4** or your preferred IP.
Local Port	Enter **60000** or your preferred local port.
Remote IP Address	Enter **13.107.21.200** (one of the addresses for www.bing.com or your preferred remote IP).
Remote Port	Enter **443** or your preferred port.

5. Click Check.

After a few seconds, the result returned informs you that access is allowed or blocked per the configured network security rules.

The concept of flow state is introduced in flow logs version 2, along with information about transmitted bytes and packets.

The following are the typical use cases to turn on flow logging:

- Network Monitoring
- Usage monitoring and optimization
- Compliance
- Network forensics and security analysis

Summary

In this chapter, you read about the design and deployment of Azure Firewall, how to configure Azure Firewall rules and policies, and how to deploy and configure a secure hub within an Azure virtual WAN hub to integrate an Azure virtual WAN hub with a third-party NVA.

You also read about the steps to build an NSG and attach it to a resource, efforts to make an application security group (ASG) and connect it to a NIC, how to create and configure NSG rules and read NSG flow logs, and the process to validate NSG flow rules and verify IP flow.

As your organization moves to Azure, you should design your networks to protect your resources from unauthorized access or attack by applying network traffic controls to permit only legitimate traffic. This chapter provides you with an overview of a range of network security solutions you can implement to meet your network security needs.

You now know how to design and implement secure network environments in Azure.

Exam Essentials

Understand how to design an Azure Firewall deployment.   In Azure Firewall, you get the best-of-breed threat protection for your cloud workloads that is cloud-native and intelligent. This fully functional firewall is a service with built-in high availability and unrestricted cloud scalability. East-west traffic inspection is available, as well as north-south traffic inspection.

There are two versions of the Azure Firewall: Standard and Premium.

Microsoft Cyber Security provides Azure Firewall Standard with L3-L7 filtering and threat intelligence feeds. By monitoring and blocking traffic from/to known malicious IP addresses and domains, threat intelligence-based filtering can protect against new and emerging threats.

Azure Firewall Premium includes a signature-based IDPS that detects attacks based on specific patterns, allowing rapid detection of attacks. A pattern can be a sequence of bytes in network traffic or a known malicious instruction sequence used by malware. A total of over 58,000 signatures in more than 50 categories are updated in real time to protect against new and emerging exploits. Trojan attacks, malware, phishing, and coin mining are the exploit types.

Know how to create and implement an Azure Firewall deployment.   You want to ensure the security of your network's outbound connections. This may include limiting access to websites, and you might also want to restrict access to specific outbound IP addresses and ports.

Azure Firewall and Firewall Policy allow you to control outbound network access from an Azure subnet. These features include:

- An application rule that defines a fully qualified domain name (FQDN) can be accessed from a subnet.
- A network rule specifies the source address, the protocol, the destination port, and the destination address.

Network traffic is subject to the firewall rules whenever the firewall is configured as the default gateway for a subnet.

Understand how to configure Azure Firewall rules.   Using classic rules or Firewall Policy, you can configure NAT, network, and application rules on Azure Firewall. Azure Firewall denies all traffic by default until rules are manually configured to allow traffic.

With Firewall Policy, rules are organized inside rule collections and rule collection groups. Rule collection groups contain zero or more rule collections, and rule collections are type NAT, Network, or Applications. You can define multiple rule collection types within a single rule group and specify zero or more rules in a rule collection, and rules in a rule collection must be of the same kind (NAT, Network, or Application).

Know how to create and implement Azure Firewall Manager policies.   Firewall policies are the recommended method for configuring your Azure Firewall. Firewall policies are a global resource that can be shared across multiple Azure Firewall instances in hub virtual networks and secured virtual hubs. These policies work across subscriptions and regions.

You can create and manage a policy using the Azure portal, the REST API, templates, Azure PowerShell, and the Azure CLI.

Know to integrate an Azure virtual WAN hub with a third-party NVA.   With a solution jointly managed by Azure and third-party network virtual appliance (NVA) vendors, customers can deploy NVAs directly into a virtual WAN hub. There are some NVAs in Azure Marketplace that cannot be deployed into a virtual WAN hub.

Understand how to create an NSG.   Azure network security groups can be used to filter traffic to and from Azure resources in an Azure virtual network. Several Azure resources are protected by an NSG that contains security rules to allow or deny inbound and outbound traffic between them. Each rule specifies port and protocol information and allows inbound or outbound traffic between them.

Be able to associate an NSG with a resource. When using the classic deployment model, NSGs are associated with subnets or virtual machines, and when using the Resource Manager deployment model, they are associated with network interfaces.

Know how to create an application security group (ASG). In application security groups, you can define network security policies based on groups of virtual machines, allowing you to configure network security as a natural extension of each application's structure. Without maintaining IP addresses manually, you can reuse your security policies at scale. By handling IP addresses and rule sets explicitly, the platform allows you to concentrate on your business logic.

Understand how to create and configure NSG rules. An NSG consists of zero or more security rules that are applied to a network. Security rules can be added, viewed, edited, and deleted.

Understand how to validate NSG flow rules. You can log IP traffic flowing through an NSG using the flow logs provided by Azure Network Watcher. Azure Storage accounts are used to store flow data, which can then be exported to any visualization tool, SIEM, or IDS of your choice.

Know how to verify IP flow. A virtual machine's IP flow determines whether a packet from or to it can be allowed. Direction, protocol, local IP, remote IP, local port, and remote port are all included in the information. A security group can deny a packet, in which case the rule that denied it is returned. Although any source or destination IP can be used, IP flow verification helps administrators quickly diagnose connectivity issues from or to the Internet and the on-premises environment.

Review Questions

1. Which of the following provides advanced threat protection that meets the needs of highly sensitive and regulated environments, such as the payment and healthcare industries?

    A. Azure Firewall Standard

    B. Azure Firewall Premium

    C. Azure Firewall Standard and Premium

    D. None of the above

2. What is the name of the security service that protects Azure virtual networks?

    A. Azure Firewall

    B. Azure Kubernetes Services

    C. Azure Container Services

    D. Azure Security Benchmark

3. What standard rule does Azure Firewall use to configure NAT rules, network rules, and application rules?

    A. Azure Firewall Policies

    B. Azure Firewall Rules

    C. Azure Sentinel

    D. Azure Firewall Manager

4. Firewall Policy rules are organized into rule collections; which of the following is valid?

    A. Firewall Policy rules are organized into rule collections, Compute, Storage, NAT, DNAT, Network, and Application groups.

    B. Firewall Policy rules are organized into rule collections, Storage, NAT, DNAT, Network, and Application groups.

    C. Firewall Policy rules are organized into rule collections, Compute, NAT, DNAT, Network, and Application groups.

    D. Firewall Policy rules are organized into rule collections, DNAT, Network, and Application groups.

5. What is used to centrally manage Azure Firewalls across multiple subscriptions?

    A. Azure Kubernetes Services

    B. Azure Monitor

    C. Azure Sentinel

    D. Azure Firewall Manager

6. What SLA is offered by Microsoft Azure when more than two availability zones are selected?

   A. 99.9999

   B. 99.9

   C. 99.999

   D. 99.99

7. From Azure Firewall Manager's perspective, which of the following is valid?

   A. Two types of network architecture can be managed by Firewall Manager: secured virtual hubs and hub virtual networks.

   B. Only one type of network architecture can be managed by Firewall Manager: secured virtual hubs.

   C. Only one type of network architecture can be managed by Firewall Manager: hub virtual networks.

   D. None of the above.

8. Azure Firewall can be used to filter which of the following traffic type?

   A. East-West traffic

   B. Non-HTTP/S access to the Internet

   C. Internet outbound traffic

   D. All of the above

9. What is the maximum number of characters supported for an Azure Firewall?

   A. 100

   B. 80

   C. 60

   D. 90

10. From the Azure DDoS protection perspective, which of the following is valid?

   A. Azure DDoS protection provides the service tiers Basic, Standard, Advanced, and Enterprise.

   B. Azure DDoS protection provides the service tiers Standard, Advanced, and Enterprise.

   C. Azure DDoS protection provides the service tiers Basic and Standard only.

   D. Azure DDoS protection provides the service tiers Standard and Advanced.

11. What are the security rules that allow inbound network traffic to Azure resources? (Choose all that apply.)

   A. Source

   B. Destination

   C. Port

   D. Protocol

12. Which of the following is true about network security group rules?

    A. Network security group rules allow all outbound traffic to the Internet (destination by default).

    B. Network security group rules do not allow all outbound traffic to the Internet (destination by default).

    C. Network security group rules allow all outbound traffic to the Internet (source by default).

    D. Network security group rules do not allow all outbound traffic to the Internet (source by default).

13. You can configure Azure Firewall and Azure Firewall Policy to provide which of the following?

    A. Application rules and network rules

    B. System rules and DNAT rules

    C. DNAT and network rules

    D. System and network rules

14. From the perspective of the firewall, VNet, and the public IP address, which of the following is valid?

    A. The firewall, VNet, and the public IP address all must be in the same resource group.

    B. The firewall, VNet, and the public IP address can all be in different resource groups.

    C. The firewall and the public IP address can be in different resource groups.

    D. The VNet and the public IP address can be in different resource groups.

15. Which of the following is valid about Azure application security groups?

    A. The application security group must contain at least one network interface, and all interfaces must be part of the same virtual network.

    B. The application security group must contain at least one network interface, and all interfaces can be part of different virtual networks.

    C. The application security group must contain at least two network interfaces, and all interfaces can be part of different virtual networks.

    D. The application security group must contain at least two network interfaces, and all interfaces must be part of the same virtual network.

16. From the Azure Firewalls subnet support perspective, which of the following is valid?

    A. Azure Firewalls need a subnet bigger than /26.

    B. Azure Firewalls need a subnet bigger than /32.

    C. Azure Firewalls do not need a subnet bigger than /32.

    D. Azure Firewalls do not need a subnet bigger than /26.

17. From the Azure Firewall deployment perspective, which of the following is valid?

   A. You can deploy Azure Firewall without a public IP address.

   B. You cannot deploy Azure Firewall with a public IP address.

   C. You can deploy Azure Firewall with a public IP address.

   D. None of the above.

18. What is the maximum number of application security groups supported?

   A. 1,000

   B. 2,700

   C. 3,000

   D. 5,000

19. Using which one of the following can you use to log IP traffic flow?

   A. Azure Traffic Manager

   B. Traffic Analytics

   C. Azure Monitor

   D. Azure Network Watcher

20. NSG flow logs can be visualized using which of the following?

   A. Azure Traffic Manager

   B. Traffic Analytics

   C. Azure Monitor

   D. Azure Sentinel

Chapter

9

Design and Deploy Azure Web Application Firewall and Monitor Networks

---

THE MICROSOFT AZ-700 EXAM OBJECTIVES COVERED IN THIS CHAPTER INCLUDE:

✓ **Implement a Web Application Firewall (WAF) deployment**

- ▪ Configure detection or prevention mode

- ▪ Configure rule sets for Azure Front Door, including Microsoft managed and user-defined

- ▪ Configure rule sets for Application Gateway, including Microsoft managed and user defined

- ▪ Implement a WAF policy

- ▪ Associate a WAF policy

✓ **Monitor networks**

- ▪ Configure network health alerts and logging by using Azure Monitor

- ▪ Create and configure a Connection Monitor instance

- ▪ Configure and use Traffic Analytics

- ▪ Configure NSG flow logs

- ▪ Enable and configure diagnostic logging

- ▪ Configure Azure Network Watcher

Microsoft Azure is everywhere. Organizations are rapidly migrating workloads from their on-premises datacenters to Azure, using new technologies such as containers, serverless, and machine learning to reap the advantages the cloud provides, such as flexible capacity and scalability, improved availability, and expanded agility. With continuous access to applications, data, and infrastructure seamlessly connected, Azure is an inextricable part of our everyday lives.

Despite the many advantages that come with the adoption of Azure, organizations are faced with new challenges and concerns. Among them, security remains a crucial challenge. You should design organization networks in a protected manner to secure them from unauthorized access or attack by applying network traffic controls to permit only legitimate traffic.

This chapter provides an overview of a range of network security solutions for Azure that you can implement to meet your network security requirements.

In the first part of this chapter, you will learn about the Azure Web Application Firewall, Azure Front Door, and Application Gateway.

The Azure Web Application Firewall is a cloud-native service protecting web apps from standard exploits such as SQL injections and cross-site scripting attacks. You get complete visibility into organization environments and block malicious attacks in minutes with the service.

In the second part of this chapter, you will learn about the Azure Monitor, the Connection Monitor instance, Traffic Analytics, NSG flow logs, diagnostic logging, and Azure Network Watcher.

Network Insights from Azure Monitor provides a comprehensive overview of all deployed network resources without requiring configuration. Aside from network monitoring features, it also offers flow logging for network security groups (NSGs) and traffic analytics. Additionally, it provides network diagnostic tools.

By the end of this chapter, you will know how to design and implement secure network environments in Azure.

Azure Web Application Firewall Functions and Features

Azure WAF is a Web Application Firewall that safeguards your web applications or APIs against common web exploits and bots that may impact availability and security, or consume more underlying resources.

Azure WAF offers you control over how traffic calls your applications by allowing you to make security rules that prevent bot traffic and block common attack patterns, such as SQL injection or cross-site scripting. You can also customize rules that filter out specific traffic patterns.

You can create rules quickly by using Managed Rules for Azure WAF, a preconfigured set of rules managed by Azure to handle problems like the OWASP Top 10 security risks and automated bots that consume more underlying resources and skew KPIs or that can force downtime. These rules are frequently updated as new issues arise. Azure WAF includes a full-featured API that you can use to automate the build, deployment, and management of security rules.

There are most often one or more common vulnerabilities in web apps that are tested. Threat actors could use the following exploits if these vulnerabilities are found:

- SQL injection
- Cross-site scripting
- HTTP/HTTPS request smuggling
- Local and remote file inclusion

The application code must be maintained, patched, and monitored to prevent such attacks. Writing code to close the most common security holes is a common task in the web app development cycle. It takes time, expertise, and testing to write the security code.

That said, you can deploy Azure Web Application Firewall in just a few minutes. Your organization's web apps are protected immediately from known threats without you writing a single line of code.

In this section, you'll learn what Azure Web Application Firewall is, how it works, and when you should use it. Web Application Firewalls (WAFs) are Azure services that provide centralized protection for web apps hosted in Azure. WAFs protect web applications from common attacks such as SQL injections and cross-site scripting.

Centralized WAFs simplify security management, improve response times for security threats, and make patching known vulnerabilities easier than securing individual web applications. Application administrators can also rest assured that their applications are protected from threats and intrusions when using a WAF. Figure 9.1 shows an overview of Azure WAF.

Cloud services from Microsoft, including Azure Application Gateway (AAG), Azure Front Door (AFD), and Azure Content Delivery Network (CDN), can be used with WAF. There are customized features for each service.

The following features are included in the Azure Web Application Firewall:

Managed Rules   Azure Web Application Firewall uses rules created, maintained, and updated by Microsoft's security team to detect and prevent common exploits. The Azure Web Application Firewall automatically updates itself when modified by a rule or core rule set.

Custom Rules   Rules can be customized. You can create a custom rule if Azure Web Application Firewall's managed rules don't cover the threat to their web application.

FIGURE 9.1 Azure WAF overview

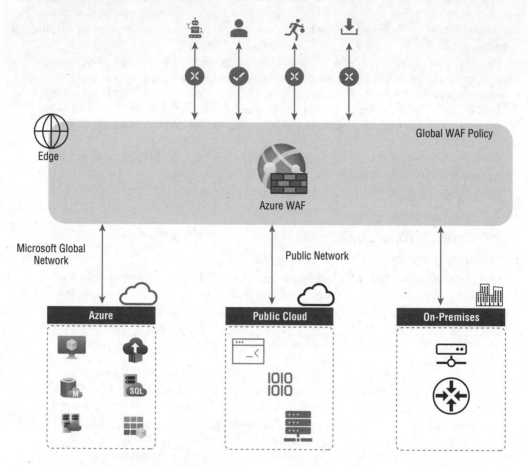

Modes   There are two modes of operation for the Azure WAF. Input HTTP/HTTPS requests that match one of the rules should be processed in one of two ways:

   Detection Mode   The request is logged, but it is allowed to pass.

   Preventive Mode   This logs the request, but it does not allow it to pass.

When you create a WAF policy, the policy is in Detection mode by default. Requests matching WAF rules are not blocked when WAF is in Detection mode; instead, they are logged in the WAF logs. You can change the mode setting from Detection to Prevention. WAF blocks and logs requests that match rules defined in the Default Rule Set (DRS).

Testing an app often involves running Azure WAF in Detection mode. In Detection mode, you can look for two kinds of problems:

> **False Positives**   Legitimate requests that are flagged as malicious by the firewall

> **False Negatives**   Malicious requests allowed by the firewall

You can switch to prevention mode when the app is ready to be deployed.

Exclusion Lists   Customers can configure Azure WAF to ignore specific attributes when analyzing requests.

Policies   An Azure WAF policy combines managed rules, custom rules, exclusions, and other Azure WAF settings into a single element. Users can then apply that policy to multiple web apps and manage and maintain them easily.

Request Size Limits   Azure WAF can be configured to flag too large or too small requests.

Alerts   Azure WAF and Azure Monitor are fully integrated. With this integration, you will receive near-real-time alerts when the firewall detects a threat.

Azure WAF can be deployed via Azure Application Gateway, Azure Front Door Service, and Azure CDN.

WAF on Application Gateway

The *WAF on Application Gateway* protects web applications based on the Core Rule Set (CRS) 3.1, 3.0, or 2.2.9 from the Open Web Application Security Project (OWASP).

WAF policies contain all the features listed in this section. Consumers of the cloud can create multiple policies, each of which can be associated with an application gateway, individual listeners, or path-based routing rules for an application gateway. Depending on the need, you can have separate policies for each website behind their application gateway.

Gateways serve as application delivery controllers (ADCs). A variety of features are available, including Transport Layer Security (TLS), formerly Secure Sockets Layer (SSL); termination; cookie-based session affinity; round-robin load distribution; content-based routing; the capability to host multiple websites; and security enhancements.

A new enhancement to the application gateway includes TLS policy management and end-to-end TLS support. Application security is further enhanced by the integration of WAF with the application gateway. By combining the two, you can protect your web applications against common vulnerabilities. Furthermore, it provides you with an easy-to-manage central location to manage your web applications.

The *WAF SKU* is available in two versions in Application Gateway: WAF_v1 and WAF_v2. Application Gateway WAF_v2 SKUs can only be associated with WAF policy associations.

Protection, monitoring, customization, and a long list of features are the main benefits of WAF on Application Gateway:

The following are the protection benefits:

- Without modifying back-end code, protect the web applications against web vulnerabilities and attacks.

- Secure multi-application environments simultaneously. A WAF protects up to 40 websites on a single instance of Application Gateway.

- WAF policies can be tailored for different sites behind a WAF.

- The IP reputation rule set protects the web applications from malicious bots.

The following are the monitoring benefits:

- Using a real-time WAF log, you can monitor attacks on web applications. Monitoring trends is easy with the log integrated with Azure Monitor.

- Microsoft Defender for Cloud is integrated with Application Gateway WAF. Defender for Cloud provides a comprehensive view of the security state of all Azure, hybrid, and multicloud resources.

The following are the customization benefits:

- WAF rules and rule groups can be customized to meet application requirements and eliminate false positives.

- Each site should have its own WAF policy to allow site-specific configuration behind WAF.

- You can create custom rules that meet the needs of applications.

The following are the features:

- Protection against SQL injection.

- Prevention of cross-site scripting attacks.

- Among the protections against common web attacks are command injection, HTTP request smuggling, HTTP response splitting, and remote file inclusion.

- HTTP protocol violations are also prevented.

- Affected host user-agents and accept headers are protected against HTTP protocol anomalies.

- Some countries/regions can gain access to applications via geo-filtered traffic, while others can't.

- Apply bot mitigation rules to applications to prevent bot attacks.

- Inspect request bodies for JSON and XML.

- You can exclude specific request attributes from WAF evaluations using exclusion lists. Tokens inserted into Active Directory can be used for authentication or password fields.

- Define custom rules for applications.

- Scanners and crawlers are protected.

- Misconfigurations of common applications are prevented (for example, Apache and IIS).

- Configurable request size limits.

WAF on Front Door

The *WAF on Front Door* solution is global and centralized, and locations worldwide support its deployment. A WAF-enabled web application inspects each incoming request delivered by Front Door at the network edge.

WAF prevents malicious attacks from entering your virtual network before they can enter the attack sources. The protection is global at scale without compromising performance. Each Front Door subscription can be associated with a WAF policy. The ability to deploy new rules within minutes enables you to quickly react to change threat patterns.

There are two new SKUs for Azure Front Door in preview: Front Door Standard and Front Door Premium SKU. WAF is natively integrated with Front Door Premium SKU with full functionality. Custom rules only support Standard SKU.

With Front Door, web applications are protected from common vulnerabilities and exploits. Azure-managed rule sets make deploying protection against a standard set of threats convenient. Azure manages these rule sets, so the rules are updated as needed to protect against new attack signatures. Figure 9.2 depicts the types of Azure WAF rules.

FIGURE 9.2   Types of Azure WAF rules

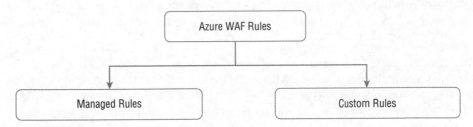

The Azure-managed DRS includes rules against the following threat categories:

Cross-Site Scripting   A threat actor sends malicious code to another user's web browser using a web application. The script runs on the browser, allowing access to the user's session data, cookies, and other information.

PHP Injection Attacks   During an attack, the attacker inserts text that is specially configured to trick the server into running PHP commands. PHP commands allow the attacker to run local or remote scripts. The attacker would then be able to access sensitive data and run commands on the server.

Session Fixation   An attacker exploits a web app vulnerability to obtain a valid session ID. An attacker deceives a user into authenticating with that ID for a new session and then hijacks that session.

SQL Injection Protection   The attacker injects specially crafted text into a web form field to trick the server into running SQL commands. The attacker can access sensitive data, insert, update, or delete data, and run SQL operations by using these commands.

Remote Command Execution   A server is tricked into running commands associated with its operating system by the attacker. The attacker might, for instance, run `ls` on a Unix system to get a directory listing.

Java Attacks   A Java-based application called Log4j was found to contain a flaw (or lousy code). Attackers are actively hunting for systems they can hijack through this Log4j.

Local File Inclusion   In most cases, an attacker exploits vulnerabilities in PHP scripts that handle `include` statements incorrectly. An attacker can include files that are locally present on the server by passing specially configured text to a script's `include` statement. In this case, the attacker might be able to access sensitive information and execute commands on the server.

Remote File Inclusion   An attacker uses this method to pass a remote file—just like a local file inclusion—into a script's `include` statement, except they send a particular configuration to the server that allows the attacker to control the remote server.

Protocol Attackers   An attacker inserts specially configured text into HTTP/HTTPS request headers. A server could be tricked into displaying sensitive data or running code by using specific text injected into the header.

An Azure-managed DRS is enabled by default, and DefaultRuleSet_1.0 is selected. You can find the recently released rule set Microsoft_DefaultRuleSet_1.1 in the drop-down list under WAF-Managed Rules ➢ Assign.

Azure WAF with Front Door lets you set up conditions for controlling access to the web applications. There are four parts to a custom WAF rule: priority number, type, match condition, and action.

Custom rules are divided into two kinds: match rules and rate-limit rules. Matching rules control access based on a set of matching conditions, whereas rate limit rules limit access based on matching requirements and the rates of incoming requests. You can disable a custom rule without changing the configuration to prevent it from being evaluated.

WAF on Azure CDN from Microsoft

Azure Content Delivery Network (CDN) for WAF offers a centralized and global solution. Azure CDN for WAF is deployed at network edge locations around the world. A WAF stops malicious attacks close to its source before reaching end users. They are protected globally without sacrificing performance.

WAF policies are easily linked to any CDN endpoint you have subscribed to. So that you can respond rapidly to changing threats, new rules can be deployed within minutes.

Set Up Detection or Prevention Mode

A WAF setting is an addition to the application gateway. Besides providing centralized protection, it helps increase the security of applications behind the application gateway.

Web application owners are at risk from malicious attacks such as SQL injection, cross-site scripting (XSS), and other OWASP top 10 threats.

 You can read more about OWASP top 10 threats at `https://owasp.org/www-project-top-ten`.

By protecting web applications from common web attacks, WAFs keep your services available and help them meet compliance requirements.

You can use WAFs to support the following use cases:

- Web apps that contain highly sensitive or proprietary data.
- Web apps that require users to log in.
- Web app developers who lack security expertise have other priorities, budget constraints, and time constraints.
- The web app must be developed and deployed quickly.
- The web app launch will be a high-security profile.

Follow the steps in Exercise 9.1 to set up detection or prevention mode using the Azure portal.

EXERCISE 9.1

Set Up Detection or Prevention Mode Using the Azure Portal

1. Log into a personal or business account in the Azure portal at `https://portal.azure.com`.

2. Click Create A Resource, enter **Web Application Firewall** in the search box, and click Create WAF Policy to display the screen in the next image. Enter the following information:

Policy For	Select Regional WAF (Application Gateway), Global WAF (Front Door), or Azure CDN (as of this writing, it was in preview).
Subscription	Choose your subscription.

EXERCISE 9.1 *(continued)*

Resource Group	Choose a resource group or create a new one.
Policy Name	Enter a unique name for the policy.
Policy State	WAF policies can be enabled or disabled. Deactivating a WAF policy will prevent it from being applied to any websites.
Policy Mode	Choose Detection Mode or Prevention Mode.

A log file is kept for each threat alert that is registered in Detection mode. A WAF policy action of Log should be set for Front Door diagnostics. A WAF action is taken if a rule matches a request in Prevention mode.

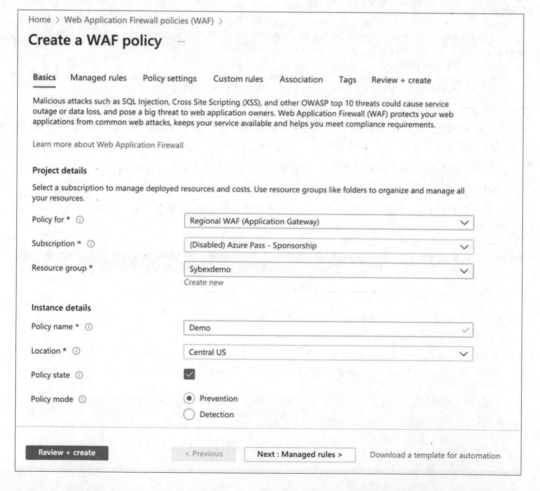

3. On the Review + Create tab, wait for the validation pass status before you click Create.

You pay only for what you use with Azure Web Application Firewall; there are no up-front costs.

Azure Front Door WAF Policy Rule Sets

A cloud customer can configure a WAF policy and assign it to one or more Front Door front-ends for protection. There are two categories of security rules in a WAF policy:

Microsoft-Managed Azure-managed preconfigured rule sets

Custom Rules User-defined/custom rules that are managed by organizations

A managed rule set is processed before custom rules when both are present. An action comprises a priority, a match condition, and a rule. Supported action types include ALLOW, BLOCK, LOG, and REDIRECT. You can create custom rules combining managed and managed rules to meet their specific application protection requirements.

The rules in a policy are processed in order of priority. A priority number identifies how the process's rules will be applied. Rules with a smaller integer value are considered more important, so they are evaluated before rules with a higher integer value. The request is then handled based on the corresponding action specified in the rule. Those rules with lower priorities are not processed after such a match is processed.

The *WAF policy* associated with a web application delivered by Front Door can only be processed one at a time. You can have a Front Door configuration without any WAF policies. A WAF policy is replicated to all Microsoft edge locations to ensure that security policies are consistent worldwide.

There are two ways to configure Azure WAF policy:

Detection Mode In Detection mode, WAF does nothing except monitor and log the requests, and it matches the WAF rule to the WAF logs. Customers can enable Front Door logging diagnostics. Click Diagnostics in the portal.

Prevention Mode A WAF responds to a request if it matches a rule if it is in Prevention mode. Once a match is found, lower priority rules are not evaluated. Logging of matched requests is also performed for every matched request.

You can choose to run from one of the following actions when a request matches a rule's conditions:

Allow Requests are forwarded to the back-end via the WAF, and the WAF does not block requests with lower priorities.

Block In this case, WAF blocks the request and sends a response to the client without forwarding the request to the back-end.

Log   In the WAF logs, the request is logged, and lower-priority rules continue to be evaluated.

Redirect   WAF redirects it to the specified URI upon receiving a request. That URI is set at the policy level. Whenever the Redirect action is configured, all requests matching that action are redirected to that URI.

Azure WAF policies can include two types of *security rules*: custom rules authored by the customer-managed rule sets and preconfigured rule sets managed by Azure.

You can configure custom rules WAF as follows:

IP Allow List and Block List   You can control access to web applications hosted by assigning IP addresses or ranges of IP addresses to clients. The list supports IPv4 and IPv6 addresses and can be configured to block or allow requests from IP addresses to match those on the list.

Geographic-Based Access Control   You can control access to clients' web applications according to the country code associated with their IP address.

HTTP Parameters-Based Access Control   You can use string matches in HTTP/HTTPS request parameters to create rules. Request URI, Request Header, and Request Body are examples of query strings, POST args, request body, and request headers.

Request Method-Based Access Control   Based on cloud consumption rules on HTTP request methods. Examples include GET, PUT, or HEAD.

Size Constraint   You can create rules based on the length of a query string, URI, or request body.

Rate Limiting Rules   Typically, a rate control rule limits high traffic from a client IP address. You may configure the maximum number of web requests a client IP can send for one minute. This rule differs from IP list-based let/block custom rules, which either allow or block all requests from the client IP address. In addition to rate limits, additional conditions can be used to control rates, such as matching HTTP(S) parameters.

With Azure-managed rule sets, you can deploy protection against a standard set of threats quickly and easily. Due to Azure's management of these rule sets, new attack signatures are protected against when necessary. The Azure-managed DRS includes rules for the following threat categories:

- Cross-site scripting
- Java attacks
- Local file inclusion
- PHP injection attacks
- Remote command execution
- Remote file inclusion
- Session fixation

- SQL injection protection
- Protocol attackers

Custom rules are consistently applied before the DRS rules are evaluated. The corresponding rule action is used if a request matches a custom rule, and the demand is blocked or passed through to the back-end. No other custom rules or the rules in the DRS are processed. You can also remove the DRS from WAF policies.

A managed bot protection rule set allows you to take custom actions when known bots are requested. Bots are divided into three categories: Bad, Good, and Unknown. The WAF platform manages the signature of bots, which updates them dynamically.

A bad bot comes from a malicious IP address or one that has falsified its identity. Microsoft Threat Intelligence feeds malicious IP addresses every hour, and Microsoft Threat Intelligence and Microsoft Defender for Cloud use the Intelligent Security Graph.

Search engines that are validated are considered good bots. Different bot groups identify themselves as bots, such as market analysts, feed fetchers, and data collectors.

User agents published without additional validation are used to classify unknown bots. For different types of bots, you can set custom actions to block, allow, log, or redirect.

The `FrontdoorWebApplicationFirewallLog` logs incoming requests matching bot rules if bot protection is enabled. You may access WAF logs through their storage accounts, event hubs, or log analytics.

With the Azure portal, REST APIs, Azure Resource Manager templates, and Azure Power-Shell, you can deploy and configure all WAF rule types.

Azure Monitor is integrated with WAF at Front Door to monitor alerts and identify traffic trends.

Managed Rule Sets

When you use an Azure-managed preconfigured rule set, your web applications will be protected from common threats outlined in OWASP's categories:

- Cross-site scripting
- Java attacks
- Local file inclusion
- PHP injection attacks
- Remote command execution
- Remote file inclusion
- Session fixation
- SQL injection protection
- Protocol attackers

Table 9.1 shows the 16 rule groups included in DRS 2.0. There are multiple rules in each group, which can be disabled. DRS 2.0 is only available in Azure Front Door Premium accounts.

TABLE 9.1   Default Rule Set 2.0 rule groups

Security rule group	Description
METHOD-ENFORCEMENT	Lock-down methods (PUT, PATCH)
PROTOCOL-ENFORCEMENT	Secure against protocol and encoding issue
PROTOCOL-ATTACK	Secure against from header injection, request smuggling, and response splitting
APPLICATION-ATTACK-LFI	Secure against from file and path attacks
APPLICATION-ATTACK-RFI	Secure against from remote file inclusion (RFI) attacks
APPLICATION-ATTACK-RCE	Secure against from remote code execution attacks
APPLICATION-ATTACK-PHP	Secure against from PHP-injection attacks
APPLICATION-ATTACK-NodeJS	Secure against from Node JS attacks
APPLICATION-ATTACK-XSS	Secure against from cross-site scripting attacks
APPLICATION-ATTACK-SQLI	Secure against from SQL-injection attacks
APPLICATION-ATTACK-SESSION-FIXATION	Secure against from session-fixation attacks
APPLICATION-ATTACK-SESSION-JAVA	Secure against from JAVA attacks
MS-ThreatIntel-WebShells	Secure against from web shell attacks
MS-ThreatIntel-AppSec	Secure against from AppSec attacks
MS-ThreatIntel-SQLI	Secure against from SQLI attacks
MS-ThreatIntel-CVEs	Secure against from CVE attacks

Table 9.2 shows the 13 rule groups included in DRS 1.1. There are multiple rules in each group, which can be disabled.

TABLE 9.2   Default Rule Set 1.1

Security rule group	Description
PROTOCOL-ATTACK	Secure against header injection, request smuggling, and response splitting
APPLICATION-ATTACK-LFI	Secure against file and path attacks
APPLICATION-ATTACK-RFI	Secure against remote file inclusion attacks
APPLICATION-ATTACK-RCE	Secure aside from remote command execution
APPLICATION-ATTACK-PHP	Secure against PHP-injection attacks
APPLICATION-ATTACK-XSS	Secure against cross-site scripting attacks
APPLICATION-ATTACK-SQLI	Secure against SQL-injection attacks
APPLICATION-ATTACK-SESSION-FIXATION	Secure against session-fixation attacks
APPLICATION-ATTACK-SESSION-JAVA	Secure against JAVA attacks
MS-ThreatIntel-WebShells	Secure against m web shell attacks
MS-ThreatIntel-AppSec	Secure against AppSec attacks
MS-ThreatIntel-SQLI	Secure against SQLI attacks
MS-ThreatIntel-CVEs	Secure against CVE attacks

Table 9.3 shows the eight rule groups included in DRS 1.0. There are multiple rules in each group, which can be disabled.

TABLE 9.3   Default Rule Set 1.0

Security rule group	Description
PROTOCOL-ATTACK	Secure against header injection, request smuggling, and response splitting
APPLICATION-ATTACK-LFI	Secure against file and path attacks

Security rule group	Description
APPLICATION-ATTACK-RFI	Secure against remote file inclusion attacks
APPLICATION-ATTACK-RCE	Secure against remote command execution
APPLICATION-ATTACK-PHP	Secure against PHP-injection attacks
APPLICATION-ATTACK-SQLI	Secure against SQL-injection attacks
APPLICATION-ATTACK-SESSION-FIXATION	Secure against session-fixation attacks
APPLICATION-ATTACK-SESSION-JAVA	Secure against JAVA attacks

Table 9.4 shows the three rule groups included in Bot Rules. There are multiple rules in each group.

TABLE 9.4 Bot Rules

Security rule group	Description
BadBots	Secure aside from bad bots
GoodBots	Detects good bots
UnknownBots	Detects unknown bots

Custom Rule Sets

Match rules and rate limit rules are two types of custom rules that control access based on either matching requirements or incoming request rates.

You can disable custom rules so they will not be analyzed but keep the configuration.

An action and a condition make up a custom rule, and match rules are all custom rules for a WAF policy. Table 9.5 shows the custom rule fields and their descriptions.

TABLE 9.5 Custom rule fields and descriptions

Field	Description
Custom rule name	Unique name for WAF custom rule.
Status	Enable or Disable: The enabled/disabled status of a rule. A disabled rule will not be processed by WAF.
Rule Type	Match or Rate Limit: Access can be controlled based on match conditions or rate limits. Match conditions control access and rate limits control access based on the rates of incoming requests.
Priority	The priority of a WAF rule is expressed as a unique integer. Lower priority rules are evaluated first, and each custom rule must have a unique priority number. Evaluation of lower-valued rules takes place before higher-valued rules are assessed. For ease of reprioritizing rules, assign numbers in increments of 100.
Match Condition	A match condition defines an operator, a variable, and a value. Rules can contain multiple match conditions. The match condition may be based on geolocation, client IP addresses (CIDR), size, or string matching.
Match Type: Geo-Location	Match variable supported is RemoteAddr and it is a fixed variable. Two types of operations are supported: "is" and "is not." Choose from a list of worldwide countries/regions.
Match Type: IP Addresses	Match variables supported are RemoteAddr and Socket address. Two types of operations are supported: "Does Contain" and "Does Not Contain." IP addresses need to be populated.
Match Type: Size	Match variables such as QueryString, RequestUri, RequestHeader, PostArgs, RequestBody, and Cookies. Two types of operations are supported: "is" and "is not." Supported operators include LessThan: *size constraint*, GreaterThan: *size constraint*, LessThanOrEqual: *size constraint*, and GreaterThanOrEqual: *size constraint*. Before comparison, the value is transformed. Transforms are applied in the order in which they appear in the list, each being used once. A list of strings with names of transformations to do before the match is attempted. These can be Uppercase, Lowercase, Trim, RemoveNulls, UrlDecode, and UrlEncode. Match values can be positive numbers only.

TABLE 9.5   Custom rule fields and descriptions *(continued)*

Field	Description
Match Type: String	Match variables such as `RequestHeader`, `QueryString`, `RequestUri`, `RequestHeader`, `PostArgs`, `RequestBody`, and `Cookies`.
	Header Name indicates whether the request header field is standard or nonstandard.
	Two types of operations are supported: "is" and "is not."
	Supported operators include Any, Equal, Contains, Begins with, End with, and Regex.
	Note that Regex does not support backreferences and capturing subexpressions, arbitrary zero-width assertions, subroutine references and recursive patterns, conditional patterns, backtracking control verbs, the \C single-byte directive, the \R newline match directive, the \K start of match reset directive, callouts and embedded code, atomic grouping, and possessive quantifiers.
	Before comparison, the value is transformed. Transforms are applied in the order in which they appear in the list, each being used once.
	A list of strings with names of transformations to do before the match is attempted. These can be Uppercase, Lowercase, Trim, RemoveNulls, UrlDecode, and UrlEncode.
	Match values: Several HTTP request method values are supported, including GET, POST, PUT, HEAD, DELETE, LOCK, UNLOCK, PROFILE, OPTIONS, PROPFIND PROPPATCH, MKCOL, COPY, and MOVE.

WAF Policies

There are two possible WAF policies for Azure Front Door:

- When a policy is enabled, WAF inspects incoming requests and takes appropriate actions by rules defined in the policy.

- When a policy is disabled, WAF inspections are paused. Bypassing WAF, requests will be routed to the back-end based on Front Door routing.

Following is the list of WAF Policies's setting:

Enable request body inspection.   WAF does not evaluate the HTTP message body if the request body inspection is disabled. A WAF enforces its rules on headers, cookies, and URIs in such cases. As long as the request body inspection is turned off, the maximum request body size field will not be available.

Redirect URL.   When the REDIRECT action is selected for any of the rules in a WAF policy, you are required to specify a URI to redirect requests to. The redirect URI must be a valid HTTP(S) site, and after configuration, all requests matching rules with a REDIRECT action will be redirected to the specified website.

A WAF policy can be set to redirect requests to a redirect URL if the redirect action is selected for any of the rules.

Block response status code.　The WAF status code was sent in response to a blocked request.

The WAF returns a 403-status code with the text "The request has been blocked" when a matched rule blocks a request. Logging is also enabled for this status code.

When WAF blocks a request, you can define a custom response code and message. Currently, the custom status codes shown in Table 9.6 are supported.

TABLE 9.6　Supported custom status codes

Code	Description
200	Ok
403	Forbidden
405	Method not allowed
406	Not acceptable
429	Too many requests

The response message and custom response status code are set at the policy level. A customized response status and response message are assigned to all blocked requests once they are configured.

Block response body.　You can add a custom response message when a WAF rule blocks a request.

For example, you can keep the response code 403 and add a short Forbidden message, as shown in the figure for step 4 of Exercise 9.2.

Adding the `[[azure-ref]]` property to the request body inserts the unique reference string. The `TrackingReference` field in `FrontdoorAccessLog` and `FrontdoorWebApplicationFirewallLog` contains the same value.

Exercise 9.2 walks you through the steps to set up rule sets for Azure Front Door using the Azure portal.

EXERCISE 9.2

Set Up Rule Sets for Front Door Using the Azure Portal

1.　Log into a personal or business account in the Azure portal at `https://portal.azure.com`.

2. Click Create A Resource, enter **Web Application Firewall** in the search box, and click Create WAF Policy to display the screen shown in the next image. Enter the following information:

Policy For   Select Regional WAF (Application Gateway), Global WAF(Front Door), or Azure CDN (as of this writing, it was in preview). For this exercise, choose Global WAF(Front Door).

Front Door SKU   Choices include Basic, Standard, and Premium SKU.

Subscription   Choose your subscription.

Resource Group   Choose a resource group or create a new one.

Policy Name   Provide a unique name for the policy.

Policy State   WAF policies can be enabled or disabled. Deactivating a WAF policy will prevent it from being applied to any websites.

Policy Mode   Select Detection Mode or Prevention Mode.

A log file is kept for each threat alert that is registered in Detection mode. A WAF policy action of Log should be set for Front Door diagnostics. A WAF action is taken if a rule matches a request in Prevention mode.

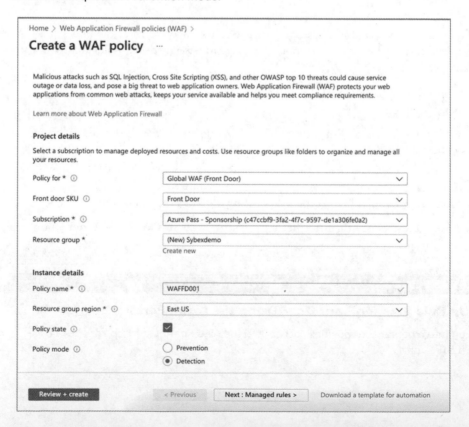

3. Click Next: Managed Rules to configure managed rules on the screen shown in the following image.

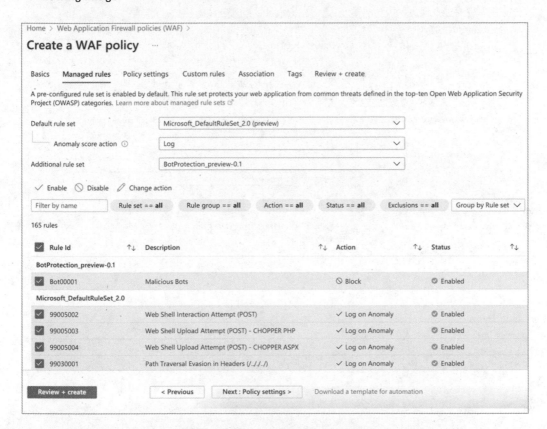

For this exercise, you can configure WAF policies in Detection mode and use the Default Rule Set. Individual rules within the DRS can be disabled or enabled according to your organization's needs. You can also set specific actions in the cloud (ALLOW/ BLOCK/REDIRECT/LOG).

The default action is BLOCK. Default rules in the DRS can be bypassed by configuring custom rules in the same WAF policy.

4. Click Next: Policy Settings to configure policy settings.

A Web Application Firewall (WAF) policy setting lets you manage access to web applications. It includes multiple settings per rule.

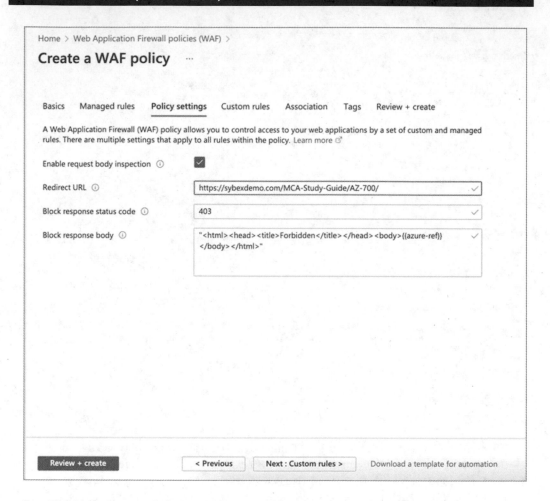

5. Click Next: Custom Rules to configure custom rules.

    You will now be able to add a custom rule to the system. Fill out the Custom Rule
    Name field and set Priority to 1.

    You can create conditions using match types and variables that must match to trigger a
    rule. You can set a response (allow, deny, or log) as shown in the following image.

You will be able to proceed to the Association section once the custom rule has been created and appears in the list.

6. On the Review + Create tab, wait for the validation pass status before you click Create.

Use the Azure Web Application Firewall as part of your front-end solution for web applications. Begin by creating an Azure Web Application Firewall policy, which includes the following settings:

- Which managed rule set you wish to use
- Which rules within that rule set you want to disable
- Any custom rules you want to add
- Which mode you want to use

You can create Azure Web Application Firewall policies and associate them with existing Azure Front Door profiles.

Application Gateway WAF Policy Rule Sets

Your organization's business applications are protected using OWASP rules using the WAF. SQL injection, cross-site scripting attacks, and session hijacking are among the rules included here. You can assign listeners to ports, create rules, and add resources to back-end pools to direct the application web traffic to specific resources to use Azure Application Gateway.

An *Application Gateway web application firewall* can be enabled by creating a WAF policy. It contains managed rules, custom rules, exclusions, and other customizations, such as file upload limits.

You may configure a WAF policy and associate the policy with single or multiple application gateways. There are two types of security rules in WAF policies:

Custom Rules   User-defined/custom rules managed by the organization

Microsoft-Managed   Azure-managed preconfigured rule sets that Microsoft manages

A custom rule set is processed before managed rules when both are present. The three actions that can be taken in a rule are ALLOW, BLOCK, and LOG. Combining managed and custom rules allow you to create fully customized application protection policies.

Priority is given to rules within a policy. Priority specifies the order in which the rules of a process will be applied. Integer values with a lower value indicate a higher priority, and those rules are evaluated before rules with a higher integer value. In response to matching a rule, the requested action is executed. The rules with lower priorities are no longer processed after processing such a match.

WAF policies can be associated with web applications delivered by Application Gateway on a global level, per-site level, per-URI level, or both.

The Application Gateway supports three rule sets:

- CRS 3.1
- CRS 3.0
- CRS 2.2.9

These rule sets protect your web applications from malicious activity.

Custom rules are also supported by Application Gateway. Custom rules enable you to create your own rules, which are then evaluated for each request that passes through WAF. These rules are given a higher ranking than the rest of the managed rule sets. An action is taken if certain conditions are met. A custom rule can now be created for the geomatch operator.

 The geomatch operator allows you to fit the exact requirements of your business applications and security requirements by limiting entry to your web applications by country/region. As with all custom rules, this can be combined with additional rules to fit the requirements of your application.

WAF can enable managed rule sets for bot protection to block or log requests from malicious IP addresses alongside the managed rule sets. Microsoft Threat Intelligence feeds the IP addresses, and intelligent Security Graph powers Microsoft Threat Intelligence. It is used by multiple services, including Microsoft Defender for Cloud.

You can access WAF logs from the storage account, event hub, or log analytics if you enable bot protection. The firewall log contains incoming requests that match the malicious bot's client IP addresses.

There are two modes of operation for the Application Gateway WAF. Input HTTP/HTTPS requests that match one of the rules should be processed in one of two ways:

Detection Mode   The request is logged, but it is allowed to pass the incoming traffic.

Preventive Mode   This logs the request, but it does not allow it to pass. As a result, the attacker receives an exception for 403 Unauthorized Access, and the connection is closed. These attacks are logged in the WAF records.

All WAF settings and configurations are contained in WAF policies. Exclusions, custom rules, managed rules, and so forth fall under this category. For these policies to take effect, they must be associated with an application gateway (global), a listener (per-site), or a path-based rule (per-URI).

You can create policies. Policies must be related to an application gateway, a listener, or a path-based rule to take effect.

The WAF SKU has two versions: Application Gateway WAF_v1 and Application Gateway WAF_v2. Associations with WAF policies are only supported for the Application Gateway WAF_v2 SKU.

As soon as you associate a WAF policy globally, every website protected by the Application Gateway WAF is protected with the same managed rules, custom rules, exclusions, and any other settings that have been configured.

Per-Site WAF Policy

Consumers of cloud services can use *per-site WAF policies* to secure multiple sites with different security needs behind a single WAF. If a WAF protects five sites, for example, you can set up five different WAF policies (one for every listener) to customize exclusions, custom rules, managed rule sets, and other WAF settings.

Let's say that a global policy is applied to your application gateway. You can use a different policy than an application gateway listener, and listener policies now only apply to the listener. If an application gateway does not have a specific policy, the global policy still applies to all other listeners and path-based rules.

Per-URI Policy

You can associate a WAF policy with a path-based rule for even more customization down to the *per-URI level*. Certain pages within a single site may require different policies, so you can set WAF policies that only apply to a particular URI. For example, a payment page or a sign-in page may require a more specific WAF policy than other websites protected by WAFs.

The more specific the WAF policy, the more likely it is to override a less specific one. Per-URI policies on URL path maps override any WAF policies that are above them.

A healthy application gateway should be monitored regularly. Integration of Microsoft Defender for Cloud, Azure Monitor, and Microsoft Azure Monitor logs allows WAF to monitor health.

Each threat detected by the Application Gateway WAF is reported in detail. Azure Diagnostics logs automate this process. Alerts are recorded using the JSON file format, and logs from Azure Monitor can be integrated with these alerts.

Managed Rules

Managed rules are enabled by default to use a preconfigured rule set. The OWASP top-ten categories, which are included in a managed rule set, protect your web application against common threats. The Azure WAF service manages the default rules. As new attack signatures emerge, rules are updated.

WAFs like Application Gateway protect web applications from common vulnerabilities. OWASP core rule sets (CRS) 3.2, 3.1, 3.0, and 2.2.9 are applied. Disabling these rules on a rule-by-rule basis is possible.

CRS 3.1 comes preconfigured with the Application Gateway WAF by default. CRS 3.2, 3.0, and 2.2.9 can be used instead by cloud customers.

A new engine, rule sets that defend against Java infections, file upload checks, and a fix for false positives are among the features of CRS 3.2 (which was in preview as of this writing).

Compared to CRS 3.0 and 2.2.9, CRS 3.1 has fewer false positives.

Microsoft Azure-managed rules defend against web vulnerabilities, including SQL-injection attacks, cross-site scripting attacks, command injection attacks, HTTP request smuggling attacks, HTTP response splitting attacks, remote file inclusion attacks, HTTP protocol violations, HTTP protocol anomalies like missing host user-agents, bots, crawlers, and scanners, and application misconfigurations (for example, Apache and IIS).

There are 13 rule groups in CRS 3.2, as shown in Table 9.7. Rules can be disabled within each group. Only the WAF_v2 SKU supports CRS 3.2 (in preview as of this writing).

TABLE 9.7   Core rule set 3.2

Security rule group	Description
KNOWN-CVES	Help detect new and known CVEs
REQUEST-911-METHOD-ENFORCEMENT	Lock-down methods (PUT, PATCH)
REQUEST-913-SCANNER-DETECTION	Secure against port and environment scanners
REQUEST-920-PROTOCOL-ENFORCEMENT	Secure against protocol and encoding issues
REQUEST-921-PROTOCOL-ATTACK	Secure against header injection, request smuggling, and response splitting
REQUEST-930-APPLICATION-ATTACK-LFI	Secure against file and path attacks
REQUEST-931-APPLICATION-ATTACK-RFI	Secure against remote file inclusion (RFI) attacks
REQUEST-932-APPLICATION-ATTACK-RCE	Secure against remote code execution attacks
REQUEST-933-APPLICATION-ATTACK-PHP	Secure against PHP-injection attacks
REQUEST-941-APPLICATION-ATTACK-XSS	Secure against cross-site scripting attacks
REQUEST-942-APPLICATION-ATTACK-SQLI	Secure against SQL-injection attacks
REQUEST-943-APPLICATION-ATTACK-SESSION-FIXATION	Secure against session-fixation attacks
REQUEST-944-APPLICATION-ATTACK-SESSION-JAVA	Secure against JAVA attacks

There are 13 rule groups in CRS 3.1, as shown in Table 9.8. Rules can be disabled within each group. Only the WAF_v2 SKU supports CRS 3.1.

TABLE 9.8 Core rule set 3.1

Security rule group	Description
KNOWN-CVES	Help detect new and known CVEs
REQUEST-911-METHOD-ENFORCEMENT	Lock-down methods (PUT, PATCH)
REQUEST-913-SCANNER-DETECTION	Secure against port and environment scanners
REQUEST-920-PROTOCOL-ENFORCEMENT	Secure against protocol and encoding issues
REQUEST-921-PROTOCOL-ATTACK	Secure against header injection, request smuggling, and response splitting
REQUEST-930-APPLICATION-ATTACK-LFI	Secure against file and path attacks
REQUEST-931-APPLICATION-ATTACK-RFI	Secure against remote file inclusion (RFI) attacks
REQUEST-932-APPLICATION-ATTACK-RCE	Secure against remote code execution attacks
REQUEST-933-APPLICATION-ATTACK-PHP	Secure against PHP-injection attacks
REQUEST-941-APPLICATION-ATTACK-XSS	Secure against cross-site scripting attacks
REQUEST-942-APPLICATION-ATTACK-SQLI	Secure against SQL-injection attacks
REQUEST-943-APPLICATION-ATTACK-SESSION-FIXATION	Secure against session-fixation attacks
REQUEST-944-APPLICATION-ATTACK-SESSION-JAVA	Secure against JAVA attacks

There are 12 rule groups in CRS 3.0, as shown in Table 9.9. Rules can be disabled within each group. Only the WAF_v2 SKU supports CRS 3.0.

TABLE 9.9   Core rule set 3.0

Security rule group	Description
KNOWN-CVES	Help detect new and known CVEs
REQUEST-911-METHOD-ENFORCEMENT	Lock-down methods (PUT, PATCH)
REQUEST-913-SCANNER-DETECTION	Secure against port and environment scanners
REQUEST-920-PROTOCOL-ENFORCEMENT	Secure against protocol and encoding issues
REQUEST-921-PROTOCOL-ATTACK	Secure against header injection, request smuggling, and response splitting
REQUEST-930-APPLICATION-ATTACK-LFI	Secure against file and path attacks
REQUEST-931-APPLICATION-ATTACK-RFI	Secure against remote file inclusion (RFI) attacks
REQUEST-932-APPLICATION-ATTACK-RCE	Secure against remote code execution attacks
REQUEST-933-APPLICATION-ATTACK-PHP	Secure against PHP-injection attacks
REQUEST-941-APPLICATION-ATTACK-XSS	Secure against cross-site scripting attacks
REQUEST-942-APPLICATION-ATTACK-SQLI	Secure against SQL-injection attacks
REQUEST-943-APPLICATION-ATTACK-SESSION-FIXATION	Secure against session-fixation attacks

Table 9.10 summarizes the 10 rule groups in CRS 2.2.9. The rules in each group can be disabled.

TABLE 9.10   Core rule set 2.2.9

Security rule group	Description
crs_20_protocol_violations	Secure against protocol violations (such as invalid characters or a GET with a request body)
crs_21_protocol_anomalies	Secure against incorrect header information
crs_23_request_limits	Secure against arguments or files that exceed limitations
crs_30_http_policy	Secure against restricted methods, headers, and file types

TABLE 9.10   Core rule set 2.2.9 *(continued)*

Security rule group	Description
crs_35_bad_robots	Secure against web crawlers and scanners
crs_40_generic_attacks	Secure against generic attacks (such as session fixation, remote file inclusion, and PHP injection)
crs_41_sql_injection_attacks	Secure against SQL-injection attacks
crs_41_xss_attacks	Secure against cross-site scripting attacks
crs_42_tight_security	Secure against path-traversal attacks
crs_45_trojans	Secure against backdoor trojans

WAF Policies

A WAF policy lets you control access to web applications using a set of custom and managed rules. Multiple settings apply to all rules within the policy.

A WAF may sometimes prevent you from allowing requests for their application. You can use WAF exclusion lists to exclude specific request attributes from a WAF evaluation, and the rest of the request remains untouched. Lists of exclusions are global in scope. Exclusion lists can include the following attributes by name. The chosen field's values are not evaluated against WAF rules, and the exclusion lists do not allow inspection of the field's value.

- Request headers.
- Request cookies.
- Request attribute; as an exclusion element, the request attribute name arguments can be added, such as Form field name, JSON entity, and URL query string arguments.

Clients of the cloud can match exact request headers, body attributes, cookies, or query string attributes. Partial matches can also be specified. Rules for exclusions are global in scope and apply to every page and every rule.

You can specify a request header, body, cookie, or query string attribute match. Partial matches can also be specified. Rule exclusions are global in scope and apply to all pages and rules.

The following operators are supported for matching criteria:

Equals   An exact match is performed with this operator. For example, use the equals operator with the selector set to `bearerToken` to select a header named `bearerToken`.

Starts With   All fields starting with the specified selector value will be matched by this operator.

Ends With   All request fields that end with the specified selector value are matched using this operator.

Contains   Specify a selector value, and this operator will match all request fields.

Equals Any   This operator matches all fields in the request. * will be the selector value.

Selectors   There is no case sensitivity when matching, and regular expressions are not allowed as selectors.

The HTTP message body is not evaluated when the request body inspection is disabled in WAF. In such cases, WAFs enforce their rules on headers, cookies, and URIs. If the request body inspection is off, the maximum request body size field will not be visible.

The maximum request body size, including any file uploads, determines the request size limit.

Custom Rules

Match rules and rate limit rules are two types of custom rules. Access is controlled by each, based on matching requirements or incoming request rates. You can disable custom rules so they will not be analyzed but keep the configuration.

An action and a condition make up a custom rule, and match rules are all custom rules for a WAF policy.

Table 9.11 shows the custom rule fields and their descriptions.

TABLE 9.11   Custom rule fields and descriptions

Field	Description
Custom rule name	Unique name for WAF custom rule
Priority	The priority of a WAF rule is expressed as a unique integer. Lower priority rules are evaluated first, and each custom rule must have a unique priority number.
	Evaluation of lower-valued rules takes place before higher-valued rules' assessment. For ease of reprioritizing rules, assign numbers in increments of 100.
Match Condition	A match condition defines an operator, a variable, and a value. Rules can contain multiple match conditions. The match condition may be based on geolocation, client IP addresses (CIDR), size, or string matching.
Match Type: Geo-Location	Match variable supported is RemoteAddr and it is a fixed variable.
	Two types of operations are supported: "is" and "is not."
	Worldwide list of country/region to choose from.

TABLE 9.11 Custom rule fields and descriptions *(continued)*

Field	Description
Match Type: IP Addresses	Match variables supported are `RemoteAddr` and `Socket address`. Two types of operations are supported: "Does Contain" and "Does not Contain." IP addresses need to be populated.
Match Type: Size	Match variables such as `QueryString`, `RequestUri`, `RequestHeader`, `PostArgs`, `RequestBody`, and `Cookies`. Two types of operations are supported: "is" and "is not." Supported operators include LessThan: *size constraint*, GreaterThan: *size constraint*, LessThanOrEqual: *size constraint*, and GreaterThanOrEqual: *size constraint*. Before comparison, the value is transformed. Transforms are applied in the order in which they appear in the list, each being used once. A list of strings with names of transformations to do before the match is attempted. These can be Uppercase, Lowercase, Trim, RemoveNulls, UrlDecode, and UrlEncode. Match values can be positive numbers only.
Match Type: String	Match variables such as `RequestHeader`, `QueryString`, `RequestUri`, `RequestHeader`, `PostArgs`, `RequestBody`, and `Cookies`. Header Name indicates whether the request header field is standard or nonstandard. Two types of operations are supported: "is" and "is not." Supported operators include Any, Equal, Contains, Begins With, End With, Regex. Note that Regex does not support backreferences and capturing subexpressions, arbitrary zero-width assertions, subroutine references and recursive patterns, conditional patterns, backtracking control verbs, the \C single-byte directive, the \R newline match directive, the \K start of match reset directive, callouts and embedded code, atomic grouping, and possessive quantifiers. Before comparison, the value is transformed. Transforms are applied in the order in which they appear in the list, each being used once. A list of strings with names of transformations to do before the match is attempted. These can be Uppercase, Lowercase, Trim, RemoveNulls, UrlDecode, and UrlEncode. Match values: Several HTTP request method values are supported, including GET, POST, PUT, HEAD, DELETE, LOCK, UNLOCK, PROFILE, OPTIONS, PROPFIND PROPPATCH, MKCOL, COPY, and MOVE.

To set up rule sets for Azure Application Gateway using the Azure portal, take the steps detailed in Exercise 9.3.

EXERCISE 9.3

Set Up Rule Sets for Azure Application Gateway Using the Azure Portal

1. Log into a personal or business account in the Azure portal at `https://portal.azure.com`.

2. Click Create A Resource, enter **Web Application Firewall** in the search box, and click Create WAF Policy to launch the screen shown in the next image. Enter the following information:

Policy For	Select Regional WAF (Application Gateway), Global WAF(Front Door), or Azure CDN (as of this writing, it was in preview). For this exercise, choose Regional WAF(Application Gateway).
Subscription	Choose your subscription.
Resource Group	Choose a resource group or create a new one.
Policy Name	Provide a unique name for the policy.
Location	Select your Azure location.
Policy State	WAF policies can be enabled or disabled. Deactivating a WAF policy will prevent it from being applied to any websites.
Policy Mode	Select Detection Mode or Prevention Mode.

A log file is kept for each threat alert that is registered in detection mode. A WAF policy action of Log should be set for Front Door diagnostics. A WAF action is taken if a rule matches a request in Prevention mode.

Home > Web Application Firewall policies (WAF) >

Create a WAF policy   ···

Basics   Managed rules   Policy settings   Custom rules   Association   Tags   Review + create

Malicious attacks such as SQL Injection, Cross Site Scripting (XSS), and other OWASP top 10 threats could cause service outage or data loss, and pose a big threat to web application owners. Web Application Firewall (WAF) protects your web applications from common web attacks, keeps your service available and helps you meet compliance requirements.

Learn more about Web Application Firewall

Project details

Select a subscription to manage deployed resources and costs. Use resource groups like folders to organize and manage all your resources.

Policy for * ⓘ	Regional WAF (Application Gateway) ⌄
Subscription * ⓘ	(Disabled) Azure Pass - Sponsorship (275288f2-45e6-4d43-87a8-8be493a... ⌄
Resource group *	Sybexdemo ⌄
	Create new

Instance details

Policy name * ⓘ	WDF001 ✓
Location * ⓘ	UAE North ⌄
Policy state ⓘ	☑
Policy mode ⓘ	⦿ Prevention
	◯ Detection

[Review + create]   < Previous   Next : Managed rules >   Download a template for automation

3.   Click Next: Managed Rules to configure managed rules (see the following image).

4.   Click Next: Policy Settings to configure policy settings.

EXERCISE 9.3 *(continued)*

Home > Web Application Firewall policies (WAF) >

Create a WAF policy ...

Basics   Managed rules   **Policy settings**   Custom rules   Association   Tags   Review + create

A Web Application Firewall (WAF) policy allows you to control access to your web applications by a set of custom and managed rules. There are multiple settings that apply to all rules within the policy. Learn more ☐

Exclusions

Select specific parts of incoming requests to exclude. All other items in the request will be evaluated.

> ℹ The maximum number of exclusions is 40.

Match variable	Operator	Selector
Select what to exclude ⌄	Select an operator ⌄	Enter a selector

Global parameters

Inspect request body ⓘ   ● On ○ Off

Max request body size (KB) * ⓘ   128   ✓

Max file upload size (MB)   100   ✓

| Review + create | | < Previous | Next : Custom rules > | Download a template for automation |

---

5. Click Next: Custom Rules to configure custom rules.

You will now be able to add a custom rule to the system. Fill out the Custom Rule Name field and set Priority to 1. You can create conditions using match types and variables that must match to trigger a rule. You can set a response (ALLOW, DENY, or LOG).

You will be able to proceed to the Association section once the custom rule has been created and appears in the list.

6.   On the Review + Create tab, wait for the validation pass status before you click Create.

NOTE

A WAF tier can be selected when creating your application gateway. You can upgrade your existing application gateways to use Web Application Firewalls as an alternative. Afterward, you associate the WAF policy with your application gateway.

Deploy and Attach WAF Policies

Using *WAF policies*, you can handle WAF settings and configurations separately. The same policy can be applied to multiple resources rather than individual application gateways. There are three types of WAF policies: Application Gateway, Front Door, and CDN.

Follow the steps in Exercise 9.4 to set up rule sets for a WAF Policy using the Azure portal.

EXERCISE 9.4

Set Up Rule Sets for a WAF Policy Using the Azure Portal

1. Log into a personal or business account in the Azure portal at `https://portal .azure.com`.

2. Click Create A Resource, enter **Web Application Firewall** in the search box, and click Create WAF Policy to open the page shown in the next image. Enter the following information:

Policy For	Select Regional WAF (Application Gateway), Global WAF(Front Door), or Azure CDN (as of this writing, it was in preview).
Subscription	Choose your subscription.
Resource Group	Choose a resource group or create a new one.
Policy Name	Provide a unique name for the policy.
Location	Select your Azure location.
Policy State	WAF policies can be enabled or disabled. Deactivating a WAF policy will prevent it from being applied to any websites.
Policy Mode	Select Detection Mode or Prevention Mode.

A log file is kept for each threat alert that is registered in detection mode. A WAF policy action of Log should be set for Front Door diagnostics. A WAF action is taken if a rule matches a request in Prevention mode.

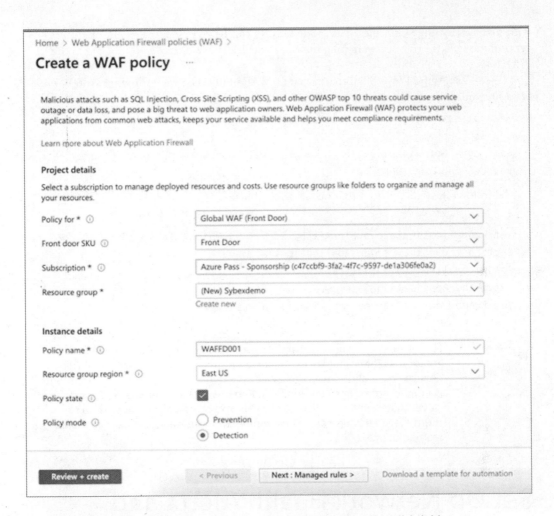

3. Choose from the following options on the Association tab, then click Add:

| Associate Application Gateway | Choose your application gateway profile name. |
| Associate Listeners | Choose the name of your application gateway listener. |

4. On the Review + Create tab, wait for the validation pass status before you click Create.

When you create a WAF policy, it is automatically set to Detection mode. The WAF doesn't block any requests when it's in Detection mode. As a result, the WAF logs are filled with matches for the WAF rules. The mode settings can be changed to Prevention. In Prevention mode, CRS rule sets matching the rules you select are blocked and logged in the WAF logs.

You can use Azure PowerShell to associate a WAF policy. Use the following syntax to create a firewall policy:

```
New-AzApplicationGatewayFirewallPolicy -Name <policy name>
-ResourceGroupName <"RG name">
   $policy = Get-AzApplicationGatewayFirewallPolicy -Name <policy name>
-ResourceGroupName <RG name>`
```

The following syntax is used to attach a WAF policy:

```
#Save the policy itself
Set-AzApplicationGatewayFirewallPolicy -InputObject $policy`
#Attach the policy to an Application Gateway
$gw.FirewallPolicy = $policy`
#Save the Application Gateway
Set-AzApplicationGateway -ApplicationGateway $gw`
```

By combining Azure WAF and Azure Policy, you can monitor WAF resources for compliance at scale to enforce organizational standards. Azure Policy allows users to assess the overall state of their environment using an aggregate view while drilling down to a per-resource, per-policy level. Additionally, Azure Policy helps you bring your resources up to compliance through automatic remediation for new resources and bulk remediation.

Set Up Network Health Alerts and Logging Using Azure Monitor

Monitoring Network Insights from *Azure Monitor* provides a holistic view of health and metrics across all deployed network resources without any configuration required. Besides providing network monitoring capabilities, it provides flow logging for network security groups (NSGs) and traffic analytics. In addition, it offers other network diagnostics.

Azure Monitor improves the performance and availability of applications and services. Cloud telemetry can be collected, analyzed, and acted upon by Azure tenants and on-premises environments. Let's discuss how applications perform and proactively identify any issues affecting them or their resources.

Monitoring telemetry from both on-premises and cloud environments is possible with Azure Monitor. Based on that analysis, appropriate actions can be taken.

Azure Monitor includes the following capabilities and features:

- Applications and dependencies can be detected and diagnosed with Application Insights.
- VM Insights provide insights into infrastructure issues.
- Monitoring container workloads deployed to Azure Container Instances, Azure Kubernetes Services, and other containers in Azure and on-premises is supported by Azure Monitor for Containers.
- Using Log Analytics, you can troubleshoot and perform deep diagnostics on monitoring data.
- Using alerts and automated actions, you can support operations at scale.
- Build visualizations with Azure dashboards and workbooks.
- Use Azure Monitor Metrics to collect data from monitored resources.

As part of Azure Monitor Network Insights, users can access network health and metrics, connections, traffic, and Diagnostic Toolkit. Figure 9.3 shows Azure Monitor's network insights capabilities.

FIGURE 9.3 Azure Monitor overview

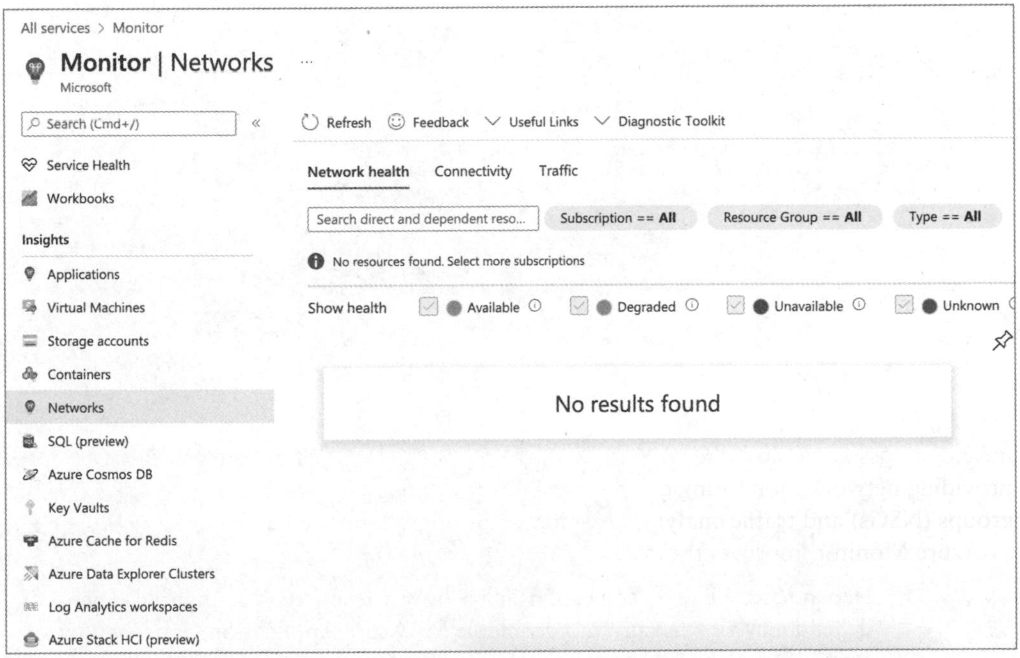

Azure Monitor Network Insights is developed around the following listed vital components:

Network Health and Metrics   On the Azure Monitor Network Insights Overview page, you can easily see the inventory and health of networking resources. It consists of four primary functional areas: search and filtering, resource health and metrics, alerts, and dependency view.

Search and Filtering   You can customize the resource health and alerts view using filters such as Subscription, Resource Group, and Type.

You can find resources and their associated resources using the search box. An application gateway, for example, is associated with a public IP address. Searching for the DNS name of the public IP address will return both the public IP address and the related application gateway.

Alerts   You can view all alerts generated for selected resources across all subscriptions in the Alert box on the right side of the page, shown in Figure 9.4. Click the alert count to go to a detailed alerts page if there is a value for the alerts on an item.

FIGURE 9.4   Azure Monitor alerts

Dependency Views   You can visualize how a resource is configured. The dependency view is currently available for Azure Application Gateway, Azure Virtual WAN, and Azure Load Balancer. For example, if you select the Application Gateway resource name in the metrics grid view, you can see the dependency view of the Application Gateway resource. Load balancers and Virtual WAN can be configured the same way in Azure.

Connectivity   You can view all tests configured in *Connection Monitor* and *Connection Monitor* (classic) for the selected subscriptions using the Connectivity tab.

The reachability status of each test is displayed for each of the Sources and Destinations tiles. You can configure their reachability criteria based on the percentage of failed checks and the round-trip time (RTT) (milliseconds) they experienced. Depending on the selection criteria, you can update the status for each test based on those values.

The grid view allows you to select any item. By clicking the icon in the Reachability column, you can access the Connection Monitor page and see hop-by-hop topology and connectivity affecting issues. From the Alert column, select the appropriate value to access the alerts. Go to the metrics page of the Connection Monitor chosen by clicking the graphs in the Checks Failed Percent and Round-Trip Time (ms) columns.

All connectivity tests configured across all subscriptions are displayed in the Alert box on the right side of the page. Click an alert count to see a detailed alerts list.

Traffic   The Traffic tab shows a list of all NSGs configured for *NSG flow logs and Traffic Analytics* for the selected subscriptions. On this tab, you can identify the NSGs configured for the searched IP address using the search functionality. You can search for any IP address within your environment. A tiled regional view will show the NSG flow logs and Traffic Analytics configuration status for all NSGs. When you choose any region tile, a grid view appears. The grid provides NSG flow logs and Traffic Analytics in an easy-to-read and configured statement.

You can select any item in the grid view. The Flowlog Configuration Status column icon allows you to edit NSG flow log and Traffic Analytics configurations. Go to the traffic alerts for the selected NSG by selecting the value in the Alert column. The Traffic Analytics workspace can also be accessed by selecting the Traffic Analytics view.

All workspace-based alerts across all subscriptions are displayed in the Alert box on the right side of the page. You will be taken to a detailed alerts page if you select an alert count.

Diagnostic Toolkits   *Diagnostic Toolkits* provide access to all diagnostic features available for troubleshooting the network. This drop-down list (see Figure 9.5) allows you to access features such as packet capture, VPN troubleshooting, connection troubleshooting, next hop, and IP Flow Verify.

Azure Monitor Network Insights' Diagnostic Toolkit provides access to all diagnostic tools available to troubleshoot networks and their components.

This Diagnostic Toolkit provides access to the following network monitoring features:

> **Capture Packets on Virtual Machines**   Using the Network Watcher packet capture network diagnostic tool, you can create capture sessions to track traffic to and from virtual machines. The capture session includes filters to ensure that only the traffic is captured. Packet capture is useful for detecting network anomalies both reactively and proactively. Packet capture can be started remotely via a virtual machine extension using Network Watcher.

Troubleshoot VPN   Diagnose a virtual network gateway or connection using the Network Watcher VPN troubleshoot tool.

Connectivity Troubleshooting   Provides access to the Network Watcher connection troubleshoot tool to verify that a VM is directly connected to another VM, the fully qualified domain name (FQDN), URI, or IPv4 address.

Identify Next Hops   Use the Network Watcher next-hop network diagnostic tool to find out a packet's next-hop type and IP address originating from a specific VM and NIC. Identifying the next hop allows you to determine if traffic is being sent to the correct destination or if it is being lost.

Identify Traffic Filtering Issues   Open the Network Watcher IP Flow Verify network diagnostic tool to determine if a packet is permitted or denied, from or to a virtual machine, based on 5-tuple information. Azure returns the security group decision and the rule name that denied the packet.

FIGURE 9.5   Azure Monitor: Networks

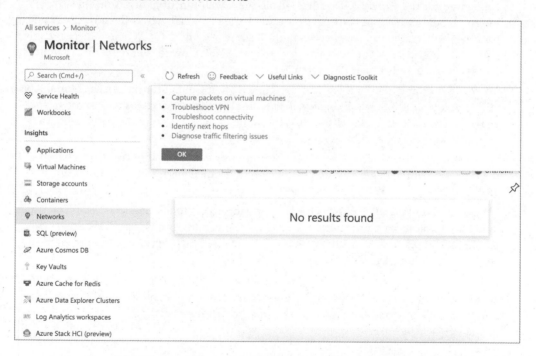

Azure Monitoring Network Insights, by default, displays all networking resources. View the health and metrics of the resource type, subscription details, location, and so forth by clicking on the resource type. Microsoft has onboarded an initial set of networking resources. Onboarded resources can access a resource-specific topology view and an integrated metrics workbook. Exploring resource metrics and troubleshooting issues is easier using these out-of-the-box experiences.

Resources onboarded include Virtual WAN, Application Gateway, Load Balancer, ExpressRoute, Private Link, NAT Gateway, Public IP, and NIC.

To set up network health alerts using the Azure portal, follow the steps in Exercise 9.5.

EXERCISE 9.5

Set Up Network Health Alerts Using the Azure Portal

1. Log into a personal or business account in the Azure portal at `https://portal.azure.com`.

2. Click Monitor. Monitoring settings and data are consolidated in the Monitor blade.

3. Click Alerts, then open the Create menu and choose Alert Rule (see the following figure).

EXERCISE 9.5 *(continued)*

4. Select the Scope tab and click Select Scope.

5. Select your target resource (or resources) in the context pane that appears.

   To find resources in monitoring, use the Filter By Subscription, Filter By Resource Type, and Filter By Location drop-down menus. You can also search for resources using the search bar.

You can create alert rules on metrics when the selected resource has them; available signal types on the bottom right will include metrics.

Click Done after selecting a target resource.

6. Select the Condition tab. In the context pane that loads, you see a list of signals that are supported for the resource. A new alert will be created on the metric you selected.

Let's use the All Administrative Operations as an example.

Select a signal   ✕

Choose a signal below and configure the logic on the next screen to define the alert condition.

Signal type ⓘ   Monitor service ⓘ

| All | ⌄ | | All | ⌄ |

Displaying 1 - 8 signals out of total 8 signals

🔎 Search by signal name

Signal name	↑↓	Signal type	↑↓	Monitor service	↑↓
Custom log search		Log		Log analytics	
All Administrative operations		Activity Log		Administrative	
Create or Update Network Interface (Microsoft.Network/networkInterfaces)		Activity Log		Administrative	
Join Virtual Machine to a network interface. (Microsoft.Network/networkInterfaces)		Activity Log		Administrative	
Delete Network Interface (Microsoft.Network/networkInterfaces)		Activity Log		Administrative	
Get Network Interface Effective Route Table (Microsoft.Network/networkInterfaces)		Activity Log		Administrative	
Get Network Interface Effective Security Groups (Microsoft.Network/networkInterf...		Activity Log		Administrative	
Update parent NIC on the elastic NIC (Microsoft.Network/networkInterfaces)		Activity Log		Administrative	

Done

You can view a chart that shows the metric's behavior over the last six hours. To specify an extended metric history, open the Chart Period drop-down menu.

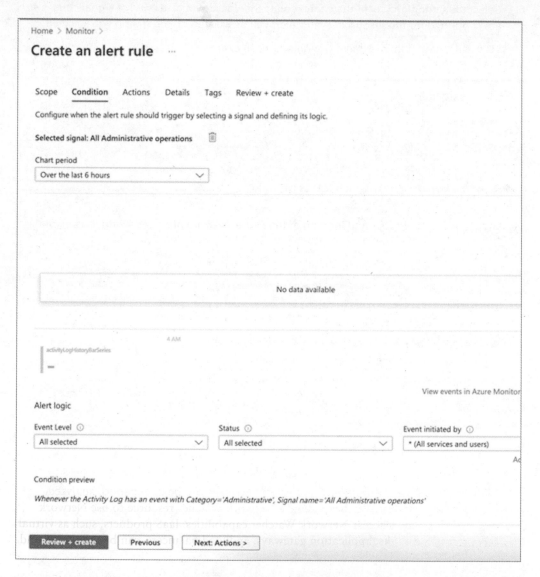

Under Alert Logic, you can optionally define more filtering criteria:

Event Level	Select the severity level of the event; choices include Verbose, Informational, Warning, Error, and Critical.
Status	Specify the event status: Started, Failed, or Successful.
Event Initiated By	Known as the caller, this is a unique identifier for the user who performed the action, such as an email address or an Azure Active Directory ID.

7. Navigate to the Actions tab, where you can define what actions and notifications are triggered when a rule generates an alert. You can select an existing action group or create a new action group when creating an alert rule.

8. Click the Details tab and select the resource group where the alert rule resource will be stored under Project details. Click the alert rule name to view details. You can also describe the alert rule.

9. Click Review + Create and wait for validation to complete.

 Monitoring and logging of the Azure WAF are provided using logging and by integrating with Azure Monitor and Azure Monitor logs.

Build and Configure Azure Network Watcher

Azure Network Watcher provides tools for monitoring, diagnosing, displaying metrics, and enabling or disabling logs for resources in Azure virtual networks. A network health monitoring program, Network Watcher monitors and repairs the health of virtual machines, virtual networks, application gateways, load balancers, and other IaaS products. Note however, that it is not intended for monitoring or tracking web analytics or PaaS.

Using Azure Network Watcher, you can monitor and diagnose conditions based on network scenarios as well, from Azure. You can diagnose problems at an end-to-end network level with scenario-level monitoring. Your Azure networks can be understood, analyzed, and viewed using Network Watcher. Create a Network Watcher resource to use Network Watcher, allowing you to access Network Watcher capabilities. IaaS products, such as virtual machines, virtual networks, application gateways, and load balancers, can be monitored and repaired with Network Watcher.

The following is the list of Key capabilities of the Azure Network watcher.

Automate remote network monitoring with packet capture.   Monitoring and diagnosing networking issues without logging into your VMs is made possible with Network Watcher. Get real-time performance information at the packet level by setting alerts and capturing packets. You can investigate an issue in detail for better diagnoses when you observe a problem.

Analyze the network traffic.   Network security group flow logs can help you better understand your network traffic patterns. Flow logs provide you with data for compliance, auditing, and monitoring network security profiles.

Troubleshoot VPN connectivity problems.   You can diagnose most common VPN gateway and connection issues with Network Watcher. In addition to identifying the problem, you can use detailed logs to help further investigate.

Monitoring connection status and performance in Network Watcher is unified and end-to-end with Connection Monitor. As part of the Connection Monitor feature, hybrid cloud deployments are supported, and Network Watcher provides tools for monitoring, diagnosing, and viewing connectivity-related metrics.

Monitoring a platform as a service resource is limited in Network Watcher. The tools available in Network Watcher are classified into four categories, as shown in Figure 9.6.

FIGURE 9.6   Network Watcher overview

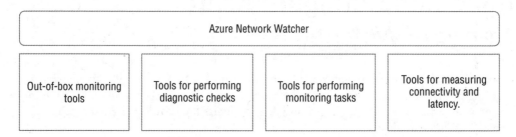

Network Insight and Network Topology   The out-of-box monitoring feature offers two important components: Network Insights and the network topology capability.

You can use the topology capability to generate a visual diagram of the resources and relationships in a virtual network.

The topology tool provides a graphical representation of your Azure virtual networks, their resources, interconnections, and relationships with each other. You can utilize this tool to visualize all components involved in the problem you are troubleshooting at the beginning of the troubleshooting process, which might not be apparent by looking at the contents of resource groups in the Azure portal.

Diagnostic Tools   Network Watcher offers five important components: IP Flow Verify, next hop, packet capture, VPN troubleshoot, and effective security rules.

IP Flow Verify   Diagnose connectivity issues from or to the Internet and from and to the on-premises environment. Check if a security rule is blocking traffic to or from a virtual machine. IP Flow Verify helps ensure security rules are correctly applied. Whenever IP Flow Verify is used for troubleshooting, you will need to examine other areas such as firewall restrictions if it does not reveal an issue.

Next Hop   Showing the next hop helps you determine if traffic is directed to the intended destination and if routing is correctly configured. You can also get the next-hop routing table. The user-defined route is returned if the route has been defined, and otherwise, the system route is returned. You can choose between the Internet, Virtual Appliances, Virtual Network Gateways, VNet Locals, VNet Peers, or None as your next hop. There is no next hop for routing traffic when the value None is specified, even if there is a valid system route. Azure creates several default outbound routes when you create virtual networks. A virtual network's outbound traffic is routed according to Azure's default routes. You may override Azure's default routes or create additional routes.

Packet Capture   Network Watcher's variable packet capture gives you the ability to track traffic to and from a virtual machine. It captures packets that assist in diagnosing network anomalies both reactively and proactively. It can also be used to gather network statistics, identify intrusions on networks, and debug client-server communications.

VPN Diagnostics   You troubleshoot gateways and connections using VPN Diagnostics. It provides an abundance of information. Portal information is summarized, and log files contain more detailed information. Storage account log files contain connection statistics, CPU and memory information, packet drops, packet security errors, and buffers and events.

Effective Security Rules   Network security groups must be associated with a subnet or NIC. In the case of a subnet, it applies to all instances of the VMs on the subnet. The Effective Security Rules view returns all the configured NSGs and rules for a virtual machine at a NIC level and a subnet level, providing insight into how it is configured. In addition, the effective security rules for each NIC are returned. You can examine a VM's network vulnerability using the Effective Security Rules view.

Monitoring Tools   The monitoring feature offers two important components: Connectivity Monitoring and Network Performance Monitor.

Network Connections Monitoring   Azure Network Watcher Connection Troubleshoot is the most recent addition to the Network Watcher suite of tools and capabilities. You can use Connection Troubleshoot to troubleshoot network performance issues and connectivity problems. Connectivity troubleshooting checks TCP connectivity between two virtual machines.

Network Performance Monitor   With the Network Performance Monitor tool, you can track latency and packet loss. You can configure alerts to be triggered when latency and packet loss exceed thresholds.

Traffic Monitoring Tools   The Traffic Monitoring feature offers two important components: NSG Flow Logs and Traffic Analytics.

NSG Flow Logs   NSG flow logs are used to map IP traffic through network security groups. Auditing and compliance can be accomplished using them. You can define a prescriptive set of security rules in an organization. A periodic compliance audit can be implemented programmatically by comparing prescriptive rules with applicable rules for each VM within the network.

Traffic Analytics   With this, you can monitor your cloud environment and see what users and applications are doing across Azure.

Exercise 9.6 provides the steps for building and configuring an Azure Network Watcher using the Azure portal.

EXERCISE 9.6

Build and Configure an Azure Network Watcher

1. Log into a personal or business account in the Azure portal at `https://portal.azure.com`.

2. Select All Services, then Networking, then Network Watcher to open the window shown in the next image.

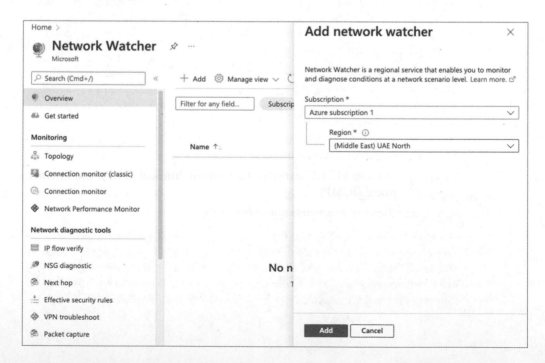

You can select all the subscriptions you want to enable Network Watcher. A Network Watcher is created for every region that is available.

The name of the Network Watcher instance is automatically set to NetworkWatcher_*region_name* when you enable the instance from the Azure portal, where *region_name* corresponds to the Azure region where the instance is enabled.

3. Click Add to complete the Azure Network Watcher deployment.

In addition to detecting threats, WAF with Front Door provides detailed reports. The JSON file format is used for logging and alerts in Azure Diagnostics. Azure Monitor logs can also be integrated with these logs.

Build and Configure a Connection Monitor Instance

Azure Network Watcher provides end-to-end monitoring of connections with Connection Monitor. The Connection Monitor feature provides tools for monitoring, diagnosing, and viewing connectivity-related metrics for hybrid and Azure cloud environments.

To measure latency between resources, use the Connection Monitor tool. Connection Monitor can detect changes to network configuration or NSG rules. You can configure Connection Monitor to probe VMs periodically for errors or alterations in the cloud. With Connection Monitor, you can diagnose problems and determine why they occurred and how to fix them.

Figure 9.7 shows an overview of the Connection Monitor.

Here are a few of the benefits of Connection Monitor:

- A unified, intuitive monitoring experience for Azure and hybrid environments
- Monitoring of connectivity across regions and workspaces
- Enhanced visibility into performance and higher probing frequencies
- Provides faster alerts for hybrid deployments
- Checks of connectivity using HTTP, Transmission Control Protocol (TCP), and Internet Control Message Protocol (ICMP)
- Analyze metrics and logs for Azure and non-Azure tests

You need to install monitoring agents on the hosts you wish to monitor to use Connection Monitor. Connection Monitor uses lightweight executable files when running connectivity checks, regardless of whether a host is in an Azure virtual network or on-premises. You can install the Network Watcher Agent VM, also known as the Network Watcher extension, on Azure VMs. You can install the Log Analytics agent for on-premises computers.

FIGURE 9.7   Connection Monitor overview

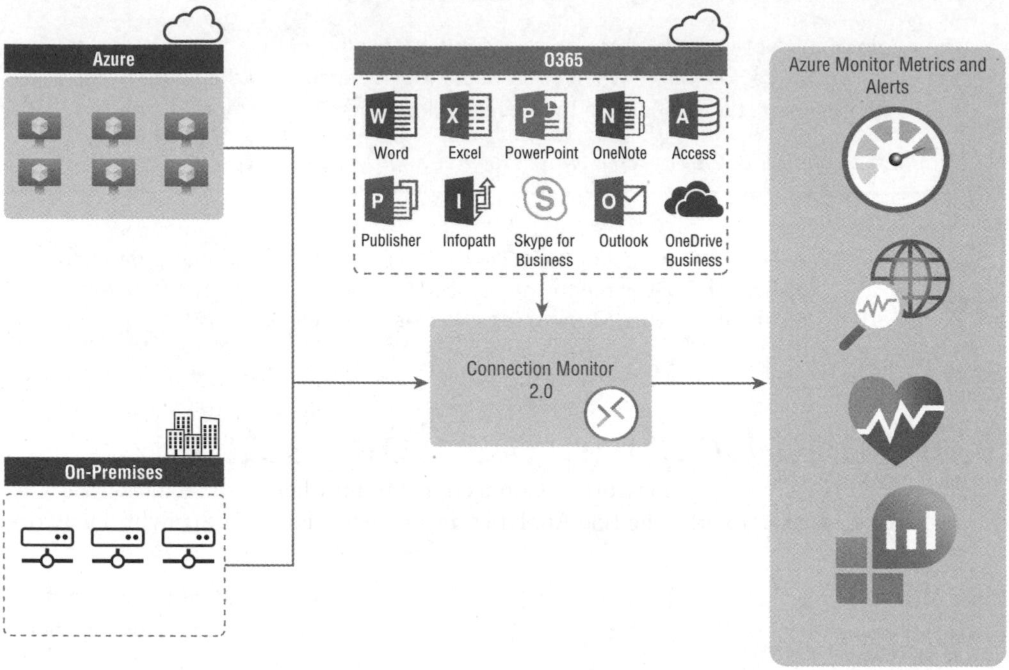

Activate the Connection Monitor to combine the Network Watcher Connection Monitor (Classic) feature and the NPM Service Connectivity Monitor, ExpressRoute Monitoring, and Performance Monitoring features.

Connection Monitor can be used in the following situations:

- Your organization's front-end VM interacts with a database server VM through a multi-tier application. You need to check the two virtual machines' network connectivity.

- Your organization wants, for instance, East US region VMs to ping Central US region VMs, and you want to compare network latencies across regions.

- An Azure storage account endpoint is required to connect a hybrid application. On-premises sites and Azure applications share the same endpoint. On-premises users want to compare the latencies of Azure applications with the latencies of the on-premises sites.

- Consumers of cloud services want to ensure that their on-premises setups and Azure VMs that host cloud applications are connected.

Building and configuring a Connection Monitor for monitoring is a five-stage process:

Stage 1: Deploy monitoring agents.   Connection Monitor relies on lightweight executable files to run connectivity checks, and it supports connectivity checks from both Azure environments and on-premises environments.

Stage 2: Enable Network Watcher.   Network Watcher is enabled for all subscriptions with virtual networks. Network Watcher is automatically enabled in the virtual network's region and subscription when you create a virtual network in your subscription. You are not charged or affected by this automatic enabling.

Stage 3: Build a Connection Monitor.   Communication is monitored regularly by Connection Monitor. You are notified if reachability or latency changes. You can also view the historical and current network topology between source agents and destination endpoints. Azure VMs and on-premises machines with monitoring agents can serve as sources. The destination endpoints can be Microsoft 365 URLs, Dynamics 365 URLs, custom URLs, Azure VM resource IDs, IPv4, IPv6, FQDN, or any domain name.

Stage 4: Configure data analysis and alerts.   Log Analytics stores data collected by Connection Monitor. You can set up this workspace when you create Connection Monitors, and monitoring data is also available in Azure Monitor Metrics. Log Analytics can be used to store monitoring data indefinitely, while Azure Monitor stores metrics for 30 days by default.

Stage 5: Diagnose issues in network.   Connection Monitor helps you diagnose the problems in your network. The Log Analytics agents detect issues in the hybrid network that was installed earlier. The Network Watcher extension detects problems in Azure, and you can view problems in the Azure network in the network topology.

You can create Connection Monitors that include both on-premises machines and Azure VMs as sources. Endpoint connectivity can also be monitored with these Connection Monitors. Regardless of the location or IP address of the endpoint, it can be monitored.

Connection Monitor consists of the following:

Connection Monitor Resource   An Azure resource specific to a particular region. Its properties are as follows:

> **Endpoint**   Connectivity checks are performed as a destination or a source. The endpoints include Azure virtual machines, on-premises agents, URLs, and IP addresses.
>
> **Test Configuration**   Configuration is specific to a protocol for a test. You can define the port, thresholds, and test frequency based on the chosen protocol.
>
> **Test Group**   There are source endpoints, destination endpoints, and test configurations in the group. Test groups can be included in a Connection Monitor.
>
> **Test**   A test is the combination of a source endpoint, destination endpoint, and test configuration. Monitoring data is available at the most granular level, the test. Monitoring data include failed checks and round-trip time (RTT).

To build and configure a Connection Monitor using the Azure portal, take the steps in Exercise 9.7.

EXERCISE 9.7

Build and Configure a Connection Monitor Instance

1. Log into a personal or business account in the Azure portal at `https://portal`
   `.azure.com`.

2. Click the Network Watcher icon. Under Monitoring, choose Connection Monitor in the
   left pane, and then click Create to open the window shown in the next image. Enter the
   following information:

Connection Monitor Name	Provide a unique name for your Connection Monitor.
Subscription	Choose your subscription.
Region	Choose your region.
Workspace Configuration	Choose a custom workspace or the default workspace. Make the workspace holds your monitoring data.

   If you choose to use the default workspace, click the check box.

   To choose a custom workspace, deselect the check box. Then choose the subscription
   and region for your custom workspace.

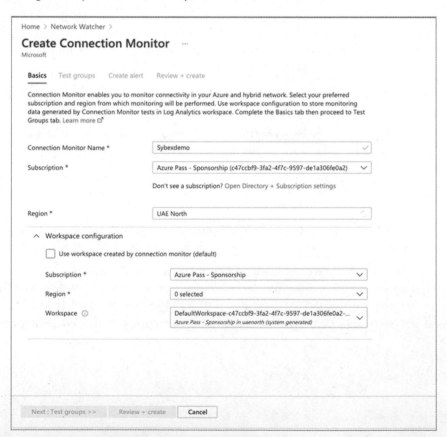

3. Click Next: Test Groups.

   On the next page, you can add sources, configurations, and destinations in test groups. Connection Monitors test sources and destinations based on network parameters for each test group. Test configurations are measured for a percentage of failed checks and round-trip time (RTT).

4. Click Add Test Group, then Next: Create Alerts.

   You can set alerts on the Create Alert tab to notify them when tests fail based on thresholds set in test configurations. Here are the configuration options:

Create Alert	Select this check box to create metric alerts. The other fields will be editable when you select Create Alert. Note that there will be an added charge for the alert.
Scope (Resource/Hierarchy)	Values are filled in automatically based on the values you specify on the Basics tab.
Condition	A new alert is generated for the Test Result (preview) metric. A Connection Monitor test result that is failing will trigger the alert rule.
Action Group	Emails can be entered directly or alerts can be created via an action group. The NPM Email ActionGroup is created if you enter your email directly, populated with the email ID. You can use action groups if they have already created one.
Alert Rule Name	You have already filled in this field for the Connection Monitor.
Enable Rule Upon Creation	The condition-based alert rule is enabled (default setting). You can deselect this option if you want to create the rule without enabling it—perhaps for evaluation and testing purposes or just because you are not ready to deploy it.

5. On the Review + Create tab, review the configuration and confirm for deployment.

Network Watcher includes Connection Monitor, which provides unified end-to-end connections monitoring. Network Watcher's Connection Monitor is compatible with hybrid cloud deployments. You can monitor, diagnose, and view connectivity-related metrics with Network Watcher.

Build, Configure, and Use Traffic Analytics

Cloud-based Traffic Analytics gives you visibility into user and application activity in cloud networks. With Traffic Analytics, Network Watcher NSG flow logs are analyzed for insights into traffic flows in Azure clouds and rich visualization of data written to NSG flow logs.

For ensuring uncompromised security, compliance, and performance, it is crucial to monitor, manage, and know your networks. Protecting and optimizing the cloud environment is essential. You often need to know which hosts are connecting, from where they are connecting, which ports are open to the Internet, expected network behavior, irregular network behavior, and sudden spikes in traffic.

An enterprise network on-premises is different from a cloud network. On-premises networks are equipped with routers and switches that support the NetFlow protocol, which provides the capability to collect IP network traffic as it enters or exits a network interface. You can analyze network traffic flow and volume by analyzing traffic flow data.

The Azure virtual networks have NSG flow logs, which provide information about IP traffic egressing and incoming through network interfaces, virtual machines, or subnets associated with NSGs. By analyzing raw NSG flow logs and integrating security, topology, and geography intelligence, Traffic Analytics can provide valuable insights into traffic flow in cloud environments. In addition to traffic distribution by Azure datacenter, virtual network, subnets, or rogue networks, Traffic Analytics provides information on hosts, application protocols, host pairs, inbound/outbound traffic, open Internet ports, and blocking rules.

As a result of Traffic Analytics, you can:

- Visualize network activity across Azure subscribers and identify hotspots.

- Identify security threats and secure networks with information such as open ports, applications trying to access the Internet, and VMs connecting to rogue networks.

- Understand traffic patterns across Azure regions and the Internet to optimize network deployment for performance and capacity.

- Never misconfigure pinpoint networks. Doing so would result in failed connections in your organization's networks.

The raw NSG logs are examined in Traffic Analytics, and reduced logs are captured by aggregating similar flows among the same source and destination IP addresses, destination ports, and protocols.

An Azure virtual machine (for example, `10.10.20.10`) communicates 1,000 times over 10 hours with Azure VM 2 (for example, `10.10.10.20`) through port 80 and protocol HTTP. As opposed to 1,000 entries, the reduced log only has one entry stating that Azure VM 1 and Azure VM 2 communicated 1,000 times over 10 hours using port 80 and the HTTP protocol. A Log Analytics workspace enriches reduced logs with geospatial, security, and topology data.

An example of how data flows is shown in Figure 9.8.

FIGURE 9.8   Log Analytics workspace's data flow

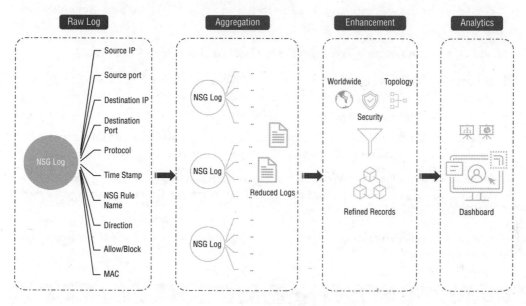

You will analyze traffic for cloud users whose NSGs you want to analyze by using a Network Watcher or by enabling a Network Watcher in every region in which those cloud users have NSGs. Any supported Azure region can enable traffic analytics for NSGs.

The following is a list of the critical components of Traffic Analytics:

Network Security Group (NSG)   The security rules within this file allow or deny network traffic to resources connected to an Azure VNet. An NSG can be associated with a subnet, a VM (classic), or a network interface attached to a VM (Resource Manager).

NSG Flow Logs   An NSG provides access to ingress and egress IP traffic information. JSON-based NSG flow logs provide outbound flow information. On a per-rule basis, NSG flow logs provide information about inbound flows, NICs the flows apply to, and five-tuple details on the flow (source/destination IP address, source/destination port, and protocol) and whether the traffic was allowed or denied.

Log Analytics   Monitoring data is collected by an Azure service and stored in a central repository. The Azure API can be used to manage events, performance data, or custom data. Once the information is collected, it can be analyzed and exported. Several monitoring applications rely on Azure Monitor logs as a foundation, such as Network Performance Monitor and Traffic Analytics.

Log Analytics Workspace   This workspace is an Azure Monitor log, which contains account-related data.

Network Watcher Azure provides a regional service for monitoring and diagnosing conditions at the scenario level. You can turn on and off NSG flow logs using Network Watcher.

Building and configuring a Traffic Analytics Dashboard is a three-stage process:

Stage 1: Enable Network Watcher. You must have an existing Network Watcher or enable a Network Watcher in each region where they have NSGs that they wish to analyze. Analyzing traffic is available for all regions that host NSGs.

Stage 2: Enable flow logging. You must first create an NSG before enabling flow logging. They can create one using the Azure portal, the Azure CLI, or PowerShell.

Stage 3: View via Network Watcher. View Traffic Analytics by searching for Network Watcher in the portal search bar. From the left menu, select Traffic Analytics to explore traffic analytics and its capabilities.

Exercise 9.8 walks you through the steps to build and configure an NSG flow log using the Azure PowerShell.

EXERCISE 9.8

Build and Configure an NSG Flow Log Using the Azure PowerShell

1. Register Insight Provider via AZ PowerShell.

   Microsoft is required to enable flow logging. When you are unsure whether Microsoft uses Microsoft.insights, the provider must be registered. To do so, use the following syntax:

   ```
   Register-AzResourceProvider –ProviderNamespace Microsoft.Insights
   ```

2. Set up flow logs and Traffic Analytics for NSGs using the following code:

   ```
   #Defining Variables
   $SybexNW = Get-AzNetworkWatcher –ResourceGroupName NetworkWatcherRg
   –Name NetworkWatcher_westcentralus
   $Sybexnsg = Get-AzNetworkSecurityGroup –ResourceGroupName nsgRG –Name nsgName
   $SybexstorageAccount = Get-AzStorageAccount –ResourceGroupName StorageRG
   –Name contosostorage123
   Get-AzNetworkWatcherFlowLogStatus –NetworkWatcher $SybexNW
   –TargetResourceId $Sybexnsg.Id
   ```

```
#Activate Traffic Analytics Parameters
$SybexworkspaceResourceId = "/subscriptions/aaaa---aaaa--aaaaaaa--aaaaa/
resourcegroups/trafficanalyticsrg/providers/microsoft.operationalinsights/
workspaces/taworkspace"
$SybexworkspaceGUID = "aaaaaaa-aaa-aaaa-aaaaa-aaaaaaaaaa"
$SybexworkspaceLocation = "easteurope"
#Setup Version 1 Network Flow Logs
Set-AzNetworkWatcherConfigFlowLog -NetworkWatcher $SybexNW
-TargetResourceId $Sybexnsg.Id -StorageAccountId $storageAccount.Id
-EnableFlowLog $true -FormatType Json -FormatVersion 1
#Setup Version 2 Network Flow Logs, and Enable Traffic Analytics
Set-AzNetworkWatcherConfigFlowLog -NetworkWatcher $SybexNW
-TargetResourceId $Sybexnsg.Id -StorageAccountId $storageAccount.Id
-EnableFlowLog $true -FormatType Json -FormatVersion 2
#Setup Version 2 Flow Logs with Traffic Analytics enabled
Set-AzNetworkWatcherConfigFlowLog -NetworkWatcher $SybexNW
-TargetResourceId $Sybexnsg.Id -StorageAccountId $SybexstorageAccount.Id
-EnableFlowLog $true -FormatType Json -FormatVersion 2 -EnableTrafficAnalytics
-WorkspaceResourceId $SybexworkspaceResourceId
-WorkspaceGUID $SybexworkspaceGUID
-WorkspaceLocation $SybexworkspaceLocation
#Query Flow Log Standing
Get-AzNetworkWatcherFlowLogStatus -NetworkWatcher $SybexNW
-TargetResourceId $Sybexnsg.Id
```

Storage accounts specified cannot have network rules limiting access to only Microsoft services or specific virtual networks. The storage account can be part of the same Azure subscription or in a different subscription, and then you can enable the flow log for the NSG. You must use additional subscriptions that are associated with the same Azure Active Directory tenant. Every subscription must be associated with a valid account that has the necessary permissions.

3. View Traffic Analytics by searching for Network Watcher in the portal search bar. From the left menu, select Traffic Analytics to explore traffic analytics and its capabilities after you have completed the first two steps in this exercise.

   The following figure is an overview of Traffic Analytics.

EXERCISE 9.8 *(continued)*

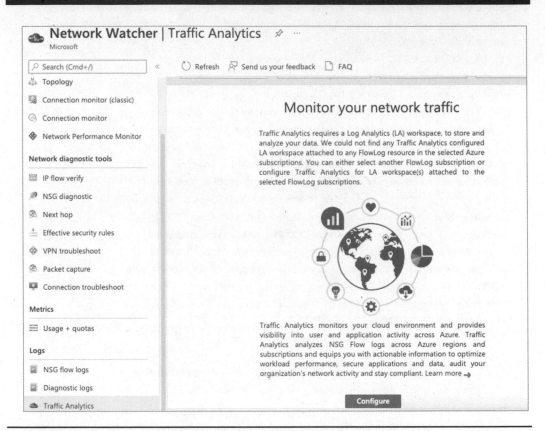

In cloud networks, Traffic Analytics provides visibility into user and application activity. In the Azure cloud, Traffic Analytics analyzes Network Watcher NSG logs to provide insights about traffic flow. Traffic Analytics collects the NSG flow logs at a frequency of 10 minutes and examines the raw NSG flow logs by aggregating common flows between the same source address, a destination address, destination port, and protocol.

Build and Configure NSG Flow Logs

An NSG allows or denies traffic to a virtual machine's network interface. NSGs are a way of combining and managing Azure network resources. You can log 5-tuple flow information about all traffic passing through NSGs. From an Azure Storage account, raw flow logs can be processed, analyzed, queried, or exported.

Network Watcher's NSG flow logs provide access to information about IP traffic flowing through an NSG. You can use NSG flow logs to log source and destination IP addresses, ports, protocols, and whether traffic was allowed or denied by an NSG. You can analyze logs with various tools, including Power BI and the Traffic Analytics feature in Network Watcher.

Network traffic data is collected outside the flow logs, so it does not affect network latency or throughput. You can create and delete flow logs without impacting network performance.

The following are everyday use cases for NSG flow logs:

Monitor a Network   NSG flow logs can help you identify undesired traffic. Filter flow logs by IP and port to capture application behavior. You can export flow logs to analytics and visualization tools of your preference to set up monitoring dashboards.

Monitor and Optimize Usage   Using NSG flow logs, you can identify top talkers in the network, identify cross-regional traffic using GeoIP data, analyze traffic growth for capacity forecasting, and eliminate traffic rules that overtly restrict traffic.

Monitor Compliance   Examine flow data to verify network isolation and compliance with enterprise access policies.

Network Forensics and Security Analysis   Network forensics and security analysis of network flow from compromised IP addresses and network interfaces. The flow logs can be exported to any security information and event management (SIEM) or intrusion detection system (IDS) tool of your choice.

You can enable NSG flow logs using Azure PowerShell, Azure portal, Azure CLI, REST, and Azure Resource Manager.

In Exercise 9.9, you use the Azure portal to create and configure NSG flow logs.

Build and Configure NSG Flow Logs Using the Azure Portal

1. Log into a personal or business account in the Azure portal at `https://portal.azure.com`.

2. In Network Watcher, Under NSG Flow Logs, you can open the Flow Log settings pane by clicking the name of the NSG, as shown here:

EXERCISE 9.9 *(continued)*

3. Click Create NSG Flow Log and enter the following information:

    Subscription   Choose your subscription.

    Network Security Group   Choose your network security group.

    Flow Log Name   Assign a unique name to the flow log.

    Location   Choose your Azure location.

    Subscription   Select your storage subscription.

    Storage Account   Choose your storage account.

    Retention (days)   Specify how long logs should be kept.

    If you want to retain data forever and do not want to apply any retention policy, set Retention (Days) to 0.

4. Click Configuration.

    You can select version 1 or version 2.

Version 1 records IP traffic flows, both allowed and denied, for both ingress and egress. Version 2 includes additional throughput data (bytes and packets) per flow.

The second version of Flow Logs introduces the concept of Flow State and stores data about transmitted bytes and packets.

5. Review your selections in the Review + Create tab and confirm to proceed.

Organizational standards can be enforced, and Azure Policy can assess compliance. Azure Policy can be used to implement governance for resource consistency, regulatory compliance, security, cost, and management.

Enable and Set Up Diagnostic Logging

You can use Network Configuration Diagnostics to determine which traffic will be allowed or denied in your Azure VNets and reported in your debugging information. You can also use this tool to determine whether NSG rules have been set up correctly. Your organization's subscriptions must include Network Watcher if you wish to use Network Configuration Diagnostics.

Azure Monitor Metrics automatically sends platform metrics by default and without configuration. Logs from Azure resources and Azure platforms, such as the activity logs and resource logs, provide detailed diagnostic and auditing information. Resource logs are collected after they are routed to a destination, but activity logs exist independently.

Each Azure resource has a diagnostic setting that defines the following criteria:

Source   Metrics and logs to be sent to destinations specified in the setting. Types of metrics and logs vary.

Destinations   A list of destinations.

There can only be one diagnostic setting per destination. If you want to send data to more than one destination type (for example, two different Log Analytics workspaces), you must create multiple settings. There are five diagnostic settings for each resource.

Diagnostic logging can be used in the following ways:

- Troubleshoot network traffic filtering in or out of a VM.
- Troubleshoot a VM's network routing.
- Analyze outbound connections from a VM.
- Capture packets going to and coming from a virtual machine.

- Troubleshoot Azure VNet gateways and connections.
- Compare the latencies of Azure regions with those of Internet service providers.
- View security rules for network interfaces.

Enabling Diagnostic Logging

Diagnostic logs form the basis for enabling and disabling Azure network resource logs in Network Watcher. Resources such as NSGs, public IP addresses, load balancers, and app gateways may be required. When you enable the logs, you can use the tools to query and view the log's entries.

You can analyze diagnostic logs using PowerBI and other tools. You can enable diagnostics logging using Azure PowerShell, the Azure portal, Azure CLI, REST, and Azure Resource Manager. For this example, we'll use PowerShell.

An example CLI command for creating a diagnostic setting with all three destinations follows. Based on your requirements, there might be slight differences in the syntax.

With `Set-AzDiagnosticSetting`, you can enable or disable each time querying and log category for a specific resource. Data is stored in the specified storage account. By implementing the ShouldProcess pattern, this cmdlet may seek confirmation from the user before actually creating, modifying, or removing the resource.

```
az monitor diagnostic-settings create `
--name KeyVault-Diagnostics `
--resource /subscriptions/aaaa-aaaa-aaaa-aaaa-aaa/resourceGroups/
myresourcegroup/providers/Microsoft.KeyVault/vaults/mykeyvault `
--logs    '[{""category"": ""AuditEvent"","""enabled"": true}]' `
--metrics '[{""category"": ""AllMetrics"","""enabled"": true}]' `
--storage-account /subscriptions/aaaa-aaaa-aaaa-aaaa-aaa/resourceGroups/
myresourcegroup/providers/Microsoft.Storage/
storageAccounts/mystorageaccount `
--workspace /subscriptions/aaaa-aaaa-aaaa-aaaa-aaa/resourcegroups/
myresourcegroup/providers/microsoft.operationalinsights/
workspaces/myworkspace `
--event-hub-rule /subscriptions/aaaa-aaaa-aaaa-aaaa-aaa/resourceGroups/
myresourcegroup/providers/Microsoft.EventHub/
namespaces/myeventhub/authorizationrules/RootManageSharedAccessKey
```

Azure diagnostic logging provides advanced filtering options and fine-tuned controls, such as time and size limits. The capture can be stored in Azure Storage, on the virtual machine's disk, or both. Several standard network analysis tools can be used to analyze the capture file.

Summary

In this chapter, you read about the design and deployment of Azure WAF, how to configure Azure WAF rules and policies, and how to monitor networks.

In the first part of this chapter, you learned to design and deploy Azure WAF, how to set up Detection or Prevention mode, and how to set up rule sets for Azure Front Door, including Microsoft-managed and user-defined. You also learned how to set up rule sets for Application Gateway, including Microsoft-managed and user-defined, and how to deploy and attach WAF policy.

In the second part of this chapter, you read about the steps to set up network health alerts and logging by using Azure Monitor; how to build and configure a Connection Monitor instance; how to build, configure, and use Traffic Analytics; how to build and configure NSG flow logs; and how to enable diagnostic logging and Azure Network Watcher.

You now know how to implement Azure WAF and monitor your networks.

Exam Essentials

Be able to configure Detection or Prevention mode.   The Azure WAF protects your web applications from common threats such as SQL injection, cross-site scripting, and other web exploits. Access to your web applications can be controlled by WAF policies consisting of both custom and managed rules. A WAF policy can protect applications hosted on Azure Front Door or Application Gateway.

Know how to configure rule sets for Front Door, including Microsoft-managed and user-defined.   In addition to OWASP Core Rule Sets (CRS), the Microsoft-managed Default Rule Set also includes Microsoft Threat Intelligence Collection rules. There is a common expectation that WAF rules must be tailored to suit the specific needs of the application or organization using the WAF. A common approach is to define rule exclusions, create custom rules, and disable rules that are causing issues. If requests that should be handled by your WAF are being blocked, you can take a few steps.

Be able to configure rule sets for Application Gateway, including Microsoft-managed and user-defined.   WAFs protect web applications against common vulnerabilities and exploits using Application Gateway. The OWASP core rule sets 3.2, 3.1, 3.0, and 2.2.9 are used to accomplish this. You can disable these rules individually.

Know how to implement a WAF policy.   The WAF policy contains all the WAF settings and configurations. Exclusions, custom rules, managed rules, and so forth fall into this category. For these policies to take effect, they must be assigned to an application gateway (global), a listener (per-site), or a path-based rule (per-URI).

It is possible to create as many policies as you wish. An application gateway must be associated with a policy before it takes effect, and the application gateway may be associated with any combination of listeners, path-based rules, and gateways.

Know how to configure network health alerts and logging by using Azure Monitor. Using Azure and on-premises telemetry data, collect, analyze, and act on it. You can proactively identify problems with Azure Monitor and optimize the performance and availability of your applications.

Be able to create and configure a Connection Monitor instance. Network Watcher's Connection Monitor provides end-to-end monitoring of all connections. It supports hybrid cloud deployments as well as Azure deployments. Monitoring, diagnosing, and viewing connectivity-related metrics for Azure deployments are all possible with Network Watcher.

Know how to configure and use Traffic Analytics. Cloud-based Traffic Analytics is a solution that tracks the activity of users and applications in cloud networks. Network Watcher analyzes flow logs from NSGs in your Azure cloud to provide traffic analytics.

Understand how to enable and configure diagnostic logging. You can view Azure diagnostic logs and save them to one or more destinations, including Azure Storage, Log Analytics workspace, and Azure Event Hubs.

Know how to configure Network Watcher. An Azure virtual network can be monitored, diagnosed, and viewed, and metrics and logs can be enabled or disabled using Network Watcher. Using Network Watcher, you can monitor and repair infrastructure-as-a-service (IaaS) elements, such as virtual machines, virtual networks, application gateways, and load balancers. This is not intended for and will not work for monitoring or analytics of platform-as-a-service (PaaS) elements.

Review Questions

1. An organization wants to prevent malicious requests from being submitted to a web application. Which mode does the company need to apply?

   A. Detection

   B. Prevention

   C. Reconnaissance

   D. Exclusion

2. An attacker injects specially crafted text into a web form field to trick the server into running SQL commands. Which of the following can the attacker access? (Choose all that apply.)

   A. Insert, update, or delete sensitive data

   B. Insert data

   C. Update or delete data

   D. Run SQL operations

3. A WAF policy can use one of two modes. What are they?

   A. Default mode or Custom mode

   B. Default Rule Set mode or Detection mode

   C. Prevention mode or Detection mode

   D. Managed mode or Custom mode

4. Assume your company wants to deploy a web application and is wondering if it should use its developers to code against common exploits. What scenario does not support the use of the Azure WAF?

   A. User accounts and proprietary data are stored on your web application.

   B. Employees, customers, and vendors can access your web applications through a private network connection.

   C. Security expertise is lacking in the development team.

   D. There is a lack of time and money for development teams.

5. Azure WAF with Front Door enables you to control access to web applications based on conditions you specify. Which of the following can be specified in a custom WAF rule? (Choose all that apply.)

   A. Priority number

   B. Rule type

   C. Match conditions

   D. Action

6. A WAF policy contains which of the following two types of custom rules?

   A. String rules and match rules

   B. Match rules and rate limit rules

   C. Priority rules and rate limit rules

   D. String rules and priority rules

7. Microsoft-Managed Azure Rules include rules against which of the following threat categories? (Choose all that apply.)

   A. Cross-site scripting

   B. Java attacks

   C. Local file inclusion

   D. PHP injection attacks

8. What are the two types of data that Azure Monitor uses?

   A. Policies and locks

   B. Database and storage

   C. Metrics and logs

   D. Compute and memory

9. Which of the following statements is correct?

   A. Azure Monitor logs can be accessed without a workspace.

   B. All Azure resources are automatically logged in the Azure Monitor logs.

   C. Logs and performance data are collected and organized by Azure Monitor logs.

   D. Azure Monitor logs can be accessed with a workspace.

10. Traffic Analytics consists of which of the following components?

    A. The back-end pools

    B. Flow logs for network security groups (NSGs)

    C. Availabilities zones

    D. Resource group in Azure

11. What is the most accurate statement regarding Network Watcher?

    A. It is necessary to enable Network Watcher for each virtual network manually.

    B. By default, Network Watcher is enabled for all regions.

    C. As soon as you create a virtual network, Network Watcher is enabled automatically.

    D. It is necessary to enable Azure monitor before allowing Network Watcher.

12. Network Insights is organized around which of the following key components? (Choose all that apply.)

    A. Network health and metrics

    B. Network connectivity

    C. Network traffic

    D. Diagnostic Toolkit

13. To get an overview of the health status of various network resources, which of the following components is used?

    A. Health and metrics

    B. Alerts

    C. Dependency view

    D. Search and filtering

14. Which of the following features of Azure Monitor Network Insights provides access to all diagnostic features available to troubleshoot networks and components?

    A. Network health and metrics

    B. Network connectivity

    C. Network traffic

    D. Diagnostic Toolkit

15. On which tab of Azure Monitor Network Insights can you view flow logs and traffic analytics for all NSGs configured for the selected subscriptions grouped by location?

    A. Network health and metrics

    B. Connectivity

    C. Traffic

    D. Diagnostic Toolkit

16. On which tab of Azure Monitor Network Insights can you see a visual representation of all tests configured via Connection Monitor and Connection Monitor (classic) for the selected subscriptions?

    A. Network health and metrics

    B. Connectivity

    C. Traffic

    D. Diagnostic Toolkit

17. On which tab of Azure Monitor Network Insights can you see information about the network services used, along with health alerts?

    A. Network Health and Metrics

    B. Connectivity

    C. Traffic

    D. Diagnostic Toolkit

18. Which tool is designed to monitor and repair the network health of IaaS products, including virtual machines, virtual networks, application gateways, and load balancers?

    A. Azure Network Watcher

    B. Azure WAF

    C. Azure Monitor

    D. Azure Sentinel

19. NSG flow logs are used to map IP traffic through network security groups. Which of the following can be accomplished using NSG flow logs?

   A. Auditing

   B. Compliance

   C. A and B

   D. None of the above

20. By combining which of the following can WAF resources be monitored for compliance at scale to enforce organizational standards?

   A. Azure WAF

   B. Azure Policy

   C. A and B

   D. None of the above

Chapter 10

Design and Deploy Private Access to Azure Services

THE MICROSOFT AZ-700 EXAM OBJECTIVES COVERED IN THIS CHAPTER INCLUDE:

✓ **Design and implement Azure Private Link Service and Azure Private Endpoint**

- Create a Private Link service
- Plan private endpoints
- Create private endpoints
- Configure access to private endpoints
- Integrate Private Link with DNS
- Integrate a Private Link service with on-premises clients

✓ **Design and implement service endpoints**

- Create service endpoints
- Configure service endpoint policies
- Configure service tags
- Configure access to service endpoints

✓ **Configure VNet Integration for dedicated platform as a service (PaaS) services**

- Configure App Service for regional VNet integration
- Configure Azure Kubernetes Service (AKS) for regional VNet integration
- Configure clients to access App Service Environment

In this chapter, you learn the fundamentals of Azure Private Link service, Azure Private Endpoint, service endpoints, and VNet integration for dedicated platform as a service (PaaS). We'll show you what VNet integration for dedicated platform as a service (PaaS) is, how it works, and when to use it.

Imagine that your company has several Azure PaaS services connected to your Azure virtual network. You also use Azure ExpressRoute and several peer virtual networks to access Azure PaaS services. Connections require the public Internet, and due to security concerns, you would prefer that these connections not use a public IP address.

As a network engineer, you are responsible for finding a solution to enable end users to access services on the Azure platform privately. Azure Private Link can bypass the Internet and provide private connections.

After reading this chapter, you will understand how to create solutions that enable private access to Azure services. Using this knowledge, you can connect a virtual network to Azure PaaS services, customer-owned services, or Microsoft Partner services. You will be able to create and manage private connections to Azure resources, integrate on-premises and peering networks, protect Azure resources from data exfiltration, and deliver services directly to organizations.

Overview of Private Link Services and Private Endpoints

In this section you learn what Azure Private Link services and Private Endpoints are, how they work, and when you should use them.

You can access Azure PaaS services and your own organization's or partner's services hosted by Azure over a Private Endpoint in your virtual network. The *Azure Private Link* service can be used to accomplish this. It provides Private Link connections to your custom Azure services so you can access those services privately from your Azure virtual networks without using the public Internet.

You use the Microsoft backbone network to connect your virtual network to the service, so it is no longer necessary to expose your service to the public Internet. It is possible to create your own Private Link service in your virtual network and deliver it to your customers. Azure Private Link can be set up and consumed across Azure PaaS, customer-owned services, and shared partner services.

Behind Private Link is a technology called *Private Endpoint*. Private Endpoint provides a private and secure connection between a virtual network and an Azure service, and it replaces the resource's public endpoint.

Private Link access can be enabled for end-user services running behind Azure Standard Load Balancer so that users can access them privately from their own VNets. Your VNet can be mapped to services by creating a Private Endpoint.

Azure Private Endpoints are network interfaces that use the virtual network address. Through Azure Private Link, you can access a service powered by Azure privately and securely. You can integrate the service into their virtual networks using a Private Endpoint. Figure 10.1 shows the Azure Private Link and Azure service endpoint connectivity.

FIGURE 10.1   Overview of Azure Private Link and Azure service endpoint

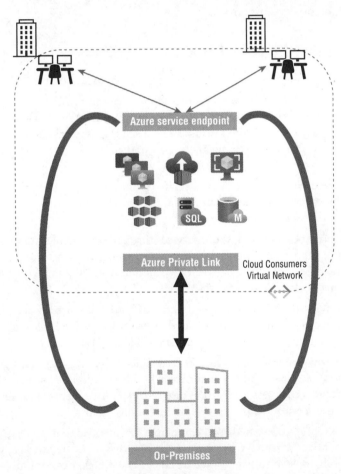

The critical difference between Private Link and service endpoints is that you inject the multi-tenant PaaS resource into your virtual network with Private Link. The traffic still leaves your VNet and hits the public endpoint of the PaaS resource with service endpoint; with Private Link, the PaaS resource gets a private IP on your VNet. The virtual network is not left open when traffic is sent to the PaaS resource.

Azure Private Link is included with different Azure PaaS services. Secure access to Azure services is provided by Private Link. A Private Link replaces the public endpoint with a private network interface to provide that security. Here are three key considerations:

- Your virtual network becomes a part of the Azure resource.

- As an alternative to the public Internet, the connection to the resource now uses the Azure backbone network.

- You can securely configure Azure resources to no longer expose public IP addresses, eliminating potential security risks.

Key Benefits of Private Link

The following are the benefits of using Private Link in conjunction with Private Endpoints:

- On Azure, you can have private access to PaaS services and Microsoft Partner services. Using Private Endpoints, Azure services are mapped to the Azure virtual network. It makes no difference if the Azure resource is in a separate virtual network and Active Directory tenant. The resource appears to be a part of the Azure virtual network to users.

- Private Link gives you access to Azure services from anywhere. Even if the Azure service's virtual network is in a different region than your own virtual network, the private connection to that service works.

- Private Link provides access to Azure services through non-public routes. An Azure service's traffic route changes once it's mapped to your virtual network. The Azure backbone network carries all traffic between a virtual network and the Azure service. Traffic from public networks is never sent to Azure.

- There is no longer a need for public endpoints. A mapped Azure service no longer requires a public endpoint since all traffic flows over the Azure backbone. By disabling the public endpoint, you can eliminate potential security risks.

- Private Link–powered resources are also accessible to peering at Azure virtual networks. In the case with multiple Azure virtual networks, no additional configuration is needed for those networks to access a private Azure resource. Any client on a peer network can access the Azure service mapped to Private Endpoint clouds.

- Exfiltration of data is prevented. You can map a Private Endpoint to a specific instance of an Azure service. When you set up the private access to Azure Storage, you map the access to a blob, table, or other storage instance. The attacker cannot move or copy data from a compromised virtual machine of one to another instance.

- Azure services can be accessed privately. The Private Link service allows you to offer your customers private access to custom Azure services.

You should now have a basic understanding of the features and benefits of Private Link. Next we'll look at how Private Link works. We'll explore how it integrates with Private Endpoint and the Private Link service to provide secure access to Azure services. This section will assist you in determining whether Private Link is the best option for cloud users.

How Private Link Integrates into an Azure Virtual Network

Private Link allows you to access Azure services securely. The term "private" here refers to using the Azure backbone network rather than the Internet for the connection. To do this, Private Link transforms the Azure resource's connectivity method from public endpoint to Private Endpoint.

Although you don't use the public endpoint, it still exists. It is still a security risk to have a public endpoint, even if it's unused. Azure resources' public endpoint can be disabled to avoid this potential security vulnerability.

This means that Azure resources are now part of the virtual networks. Clients on your network have access to this Private Link resource just like any other network resource. An Azure backbone network is now used to connect to the resource for even greater security. No traffic is routed through the public Internet to or from the resource.

Despite this, the public endpoint of the resource still exists, even though you do not use it. Public endpoints, even unused ones, pose a security risk. Fortunately, this issue can be avoided by disabling the Azure resource's public endpoint.

How Azure Private Endpoint Works

You might ask, what is involved in shifting a public resource interface to a private one? The answer is you configure an Azure Private Endpoint in consumers' network configurations. Private Endpoints create a private connection between virtual networks and Azure resources.

Your virtual networks are provided with an unused private IP address from the address space of a specified subnet by the Private Endpoint. For example, you might have a subnet that uses the address space `10.2.0.0/24`, and virtual machines on that subnet might have IP addresses such as `10.2.0.20` or `10.2.0.155`.

IP addresses from the same address space are used by Private Endpoint. A specific Azure service is then mapped to the IP address. A private IP address effectively integrates the service into a virtual network.

Here are a few key considerations when designing and deploying Azure Private Endpoints:

- Virtual machines and other clients on the Azure virtual network and Private Link–powered Azure services can communicate privately through Private Endpoint.

- In Private Link–powered Azure services, Private Endpoint provides private connectivity between regional peer-to-peer virtual networks.

- Private Link–powered Azure services and globally peering virtual networks can be connected privately via Private Endpoint.

- With Private Endpoint, you gain private connectivity between your on-premises networks—connected via ExpressRoute Private Peering or a VPN—and Azure services powered by Private Link.

- You can deploy up to 1,000 Private Endpoint interfaces per virtual network.

- Azure subscriptions can support up to 64,000 Private Endpoint interfaces.

- You can map a maximum of 1,000 Private Endpoint interfaces to the same Private Link resource.

- A Private Endpoint interface can only be accessed by clients, meaning that only those clients can access it. If an Azure service is mapped to a Private Endpoint interface, that service provider will be unable to interact with (or even perceive) the Private Endpoint interface.

- Private Endpoint interfaces are read-only, which means they cannot be modified. For example, there is no way to map the interface to another resource or change its IP address.

- Although you must deploy the Private Endpoint in the same region as your virtual network, the Private Link resource can be deployed in a different region.

NOTE A Private Endpoint in a virtual network lets you access Azure PaaS services (for example, Azure Storage and SQL Database) and Azure-hosted customer-owned/partner services.

An Azure Private Endpoint is a network interface that connects privately and securely to a service using Azure Private Link. Connect privately to an Azure PaaS service that supports Private Link or your organization's own Private Link service using Private Endpoints.

A service provider creates the Azure Private Link service. As of now, a Private Link service can be added to a Standard Load Balancer's front-end IP configuration.

Traffic is sent privately over the Microsoft backbone, and it doesn't cross the Internet. Microsoft does not store customer data.

Organizations' custom Azure services can now benefit from Azure Private Link service. You only need to run their custom services behind an Azure Standard Load Balancer, and then they can attach a Private Link service resource to that load balancer.

Azure creates an alias for the Private Link service resource with the syntax *prefix*.*guid* .*suffix*: once you generate the resource.

- *prefix*—A name that you provide.

- *guid*—A globally unique ID that Azure generates automatically.

- *suffix*—region.azure.privatelinkservice region indicates the region where the Private Link service is deployed.

Users of custom services share the Private Link service alias. Afterward, each consumer creates their own Azure virtual network with a Private Endpoint, and consumers then map the endpoint to the Private Link service alias.

When designing and deploying a Private Link service, it is essential to consider the following points:

- Customers can access a Private Link service via Private Endpoints in any public region.

- The Private Link service must be deployed in the same region as the load balancer and the virtual network hosting your custom Azure service.

- Cloud customers may deploy a maximum of 800 Private Link services per Azure subscription.

- A maximum of 1,000 Private Link service resources can map to a single Private Endpoint interface.

- You can deploy multiple Private Link service resources on a single standard load balancer without having to change the front-end IP configuration.

Consider a scenario where there is a way to access Azure resources without using the public Internet or that there is a way that the network cloud providers are interested in using Azure to provide private resources. When either or both scenarios are met, Private Link, Private Endpoint, and Private Link service provide the following solution:

- You can create a Private Endpoint in your Azure virtual network subnet to access an Azure PaaS or Azure service from a Microsoft Partner. Through Private Link, the endpoint accesses the Azure service using a private IP address over the Azure backbone. On-premises networks and peer-to-peer virtual networks using ExpressRoute private peering or a VPN tunnel can also access Azure services via the Private Endpoint.

- To provide private access to customized Azure service, put the service behind a standard load balancer, create a Private Link service resource, and connect it to the load balancer's front-end IP.

The following scenarios can be used with Azure Private Links:

Integrating Azure PaaS Services into Your Virtual Network   Depending on the resource and its configuration, Azure PaaS services can be complicated to connect to. Azure services through Private Link become just another virtual node in your Azure virtual network. With a Private Link resource now integrated into an Azure virtual network, clients can leverage a straightforward FQDN to connect.

Securing Traffic between Your Network and the Azure Cloud   Cloud computing presents a paradox: a cloud-based virtual machine must connect and communicate outside the cloud to access a service within the same provider. Cloud-based endpoints require Internet-based traffic, even though they are in the cloud.

Those packets become "public" once they leave the cloud. Nefarious actors can use a long list of exploits to steal, monitor, or corrupt traffic.

In Private Link, traffic is rerouted not to traverse the Internet, thus eliminating that risk. Microsoft's Azure backbone serves as the connection to ensure that all traffic between your organization and a Private Link resource is secure and private.

Eliminating Internet Exposure for PaaS Services   Most Azure PaaS resources are accessible via the Internet. Clients can connect to these resources via the Internet by using their public endpoint, which provides clients with an IP address.

It is by design exposed to the Internet through the public endpoint. However, black-hat hackers can use that endpoint to infiltrate or disrupt that service as well.

Once you create a Private Endpoint and map it to an Azure resource, you no longer need the public endpoint. You can disable the resource's public endpoint so that it no longer presents an attack surface to the Internet.

Accessing Azure PaaS Resources across Networks   A virtual network is rare, and most network setups include at least one of the following components:

- One or more peering networks connected by Azure virtual networks
- One or more on-premises networks connected through private peering with ExpressRoute or a VPN tunnel

Those networks cannot connect to Azure resources without Private Link, which typically requires the public Internet. In virtual networks, that changes once Private Endpoint maps the Azure resource to a private IP address. Peer networks within all networks are able to access the Private Link resource directly, without configuration.

Lowering the Risk of Data Exfiltration   It's often possible to access multiple Azure resources on a virtual machine. Azure Storage, for example, allows users to access various blobs, tables, files, and so forth.

Assume a virtual machine connected to an Azure service is part of your network. If a hacker has gained control over the virtual machine, the user is now a malicious infiltrator. In such a scenario, the attacker could control a resource that the user moves data to.

Data exfiltration is demonstrated in this scenario. Through Private Link, a Private Endpoint is mapped to a single instance of an Azure resource, reducing the risk of data exfiltration. Despite viewing the data, an attacker has no means of copying or moving it.

Offering Customers Private Access to Company-Created Azure Services   Imagine a company that uses Azure to create custom services. Who will use those services? Here are some examples:

- Consumers who purchase cloud products
- Vendors or suppliers of the company
- Users of a company's cloud services

Each of these consumers is a customer of your services.

Your company's data is likely as important as the data accessed and created by those customers. Data of companies should be protected.

Private Link is deemed to be the best choice for securing your company data. You should take that security model and extend it to your customized Azure services. Azure

Standard Load Balancer can be used to deploy custom services. You can then access the services through Private Endpoints.

Consumers will be able to offer their customers private and secure access to their custom Azure services.

Azure Private Link integrates with Azure Monitor. With this combination, logs can be archived to a storage account, events can be streamed to cloud event consumers, and Azure Monitor logs can be seen.

Azure Monitor provides the following information to consumers: Private Endpoints (data processed by Private Endpoints [Inbound and Outbound]) and Private Links (data processed by Private Links [Inbound and Outbound]).

In Exercise 10.1, you use a Private Endpoint to connect securely to a web application in Azure using Azure Private Link. You can create endpoints using a variety of methods, including the Azure portal, CLI, and PowerShell.

Access to Private Endpoints provides granular segmentation of the network behind a given service. You can access the service resource from on-premises without using public endpoints.

Public endpoints are publicly routable addresses, and Private Endpoints are private IP addresses in the address space of the virtual network where the Private Endpoint is configured.

Several types of Private Links can be accessed via Private Endpoints. You can use Azure PaaS services and your own Private Link service, and it's a one-to-many relationship.

Multiple Private Endpoints connect to one Private Link service, and a Private Endpoint connects to multiple Private Link services.

EXERCISE 10.1

Set Up a Private Link service and Private Endpoints

1. Build a resource group using the following syntax.

```
New-AzResourceGroup -Name 'SybexPLS-rg' -Location 'UAENorth'
```

2. Build a virtual network with the following code:

```
## Build backend subnet config ##
$subnet = @{
    Name = 'mySubnet'
    AddressPrefix = '10.2.0.0/24'
    PrivateLinkServiceNetworkPolicies = 'Disabled'
}
```

```
$subnetConfig = New-AzVirtualNetworkSubnetConfig @subnet

## Build the virtual network ##
$net = @{
    Name = 'myVNet'
    ResourceGroupName = 'CreatePrivLinkService-rg'
    Location = 'UAENorth'
    AddressPrefix = '10.2.0.0/16'
    Subnet = $subnetConfig
}
$vnet = New-AzVirtualNetwork @net
```

3. Build an internal Azure Load Balancer.

    The following are the various cmdlets used to build an internal Azure Load Balancer:

    ▪ Build the front-end IP pool with New-AzLoadBalancerFrontendIpConfig.
      Traffic from this IP is forwarded to the load balancer.

    ▪ For traffic originating from the front-end of load balancing, create a back-end
      address pool with New-AzLoadBalancerBackendAddressPoolConfig. You
      can deploy your virtual machines into this pool.

    ▪ Create a health probe using Add-AzLoadBalancerProbeConfig to determine
      the health of the back-end VM instance.

    ▪ Create a load balancer rule that defines how traffic is distributed to the VMs using
      Add-AzLoadBalancerRuleConfig.

    ▪ Use New-AzLoadBalancer to create a public load balancer.

Use the following syntax to build an Azure Load Balancer:

```
## Keep virtual network created in task into a variable. ##

$vnet = Get-AzVirtualNetwork -Name 'SybexVNet' -ResourceGroupName 'SybexPLS-rg'

## Build a load balancer frontend configuration and place in variable. ##
$lbip = @{
    Name = 'SybexFE'
    PrivateIpAddress = '10.2.0.5'
    SubnetId = $vnet.subnets[0].Id
}
```

```
$feip = New-AzLoadBalancerFrontendIpConfig @lbip

## Build a backend address pool configuration and place in variable. ##
$bepool = New-AzLoadBalancerBackendAddressPoolConfig -Name 'SybexBE'

## Create the health probe and place in variable. ##
$probe = @{
    Name = 'SybexHP'
    Protocol = 'http'
    Port = '80'
    IntervalInSeconds = '360'
    ProbeCount = '5'
    RequestPath = '/'
}
$healthprobe = New-AzLoadBalancerProbeConfig @probe

## Build a load balancer rule and place in variable. ##
$lbrule = @{
    Name = 'SybexHTTPRule'
    Protocol = 'tcp'
    FrontendPort = '80'
    BackendPort = '80'
    IdleTimeoutInMinutes = '15'
    FrontendIpConfiguration = $feip
    BackendAddressPool = $bePool
}
$rule = New-AzLoadBalancerRuleConfig @lbrule -EnableTcpReset

## Build the load balancer resource. ##
$loadbalancer = @{
    ResourceGroupName = 'CreatePrivLinkService-rg'
    Name = 'myLoadBalancer'
    Location = 'UAENorth'
    Sku = 'Standard'
    FrontendIpConfiguration = $feip
    BackendAddressPool = $bePool
    LoadBalancingRule = $rule
    Probe = $healthprobe
}
New-AzLoadBalancer @loadbalancer
```

4. Build a Private Link service.

    ▪   Configure the Private Link service IP with
        New-AzPrivateLinkServiceIpConfig.

    ▪   Build the Private Link service with New-AzPrivateLinkService.

    Use the following syntax to build a Private Link service.

```
## Keep the virtual network into a variable. ##
$vnet = Get-AzVirtualNetwork -Name 'SybexVNet' -ResourceGroupName 'SybexPSL-rg'

## Config the IP for the private link service. ##
$ipsettings = @{
    Name = 'SybexIPconfig'
    PrivateIpAddress = '10.2.0.5'
    Subnet = $vnet.subnets[0]
}
$ipconfig = New-AzPrivateLinkServiceIpConfig @ipsettings

## Keep the load balancer frontend configuration into a variable. ##
$par = @{
    Name = 'SybexLoadBalancer'
    ResourceGroupName = 'SybexPSL-rg'
}
$fe = Get-AzLoadBalancer @par | Get-AzLoadBalancerFrontendIpConfig

## Build the private link service for the load balancer. ##
$privlinksettings = @{
    Name = 'SybexPrivateLinkService'
    ResourceGroupName = 'SybexPSL-rg'
    Location = 'UAENorth'
    LoadBalancerFrontendIpConfiguration = $fe
    IpConfiguration = $ipconfig
}
New-AzPrivateLinkService @privlinksettings
```

5. Build a Private Endpoint virtual network using the following syntax:

```
## Deploy backend subnet config ##
$subnet = @{
    Name = 'SybexSubnetPE'
    AddressPrefix = '12.2.0.0/24'
    PrivateEndpointNetworkPolicies = 'Disabled'
```

```
    }
    $subnetConfig = New-AzVirtualNetworkSubnetConfig @subnet

    ## Deploy the virtual network ##
    $net = @{
        Name = 'SybexVNetPE'
        ResourceGroupName = 'SybexPSL-rg'
        Location = 'eastus2'
        AddressPrefix = '12.2.0.0/16'
        Subnet = $subnetConfig
    }
    $vnetpe = New-AzVirtualNetwork @net
```

6. Build a Private Endpoint using the following syntax:

```
    ## Keep the private link service configuration into variable. ##
    $par1 = @{
        Name = 'SybexPLS'
        ResourceGroupName = 'SybexPSL-rg'
    }
    $pls = Get-AzPrivateLinkService @par1

    ## Build the private link configuration and place in variable. ##
    $par2 = @{
        Name = 'SybexPLC'
        PrivateLinkServiceId = $pls.Id
    }
    $plsConnection = New-AzPrivateLinkServiceConnection @par2

    ## Keep the virtual network into a variable. ##
    $par3 = @{
        Name = 'SybexVNetPE'
        ResourceGroupName = 'SybexPSL-rg'
    }
    $vnetpe = Get-AzVirtualNetwork @par3

    ## Build private endpoint ##
    $par4 = @{
        Name = ' SybexPE'
        ResourceGroupName = 'SybexPSL-rg'
        Location = 'UAENorth'
        Subnet = $vnetpe.subnets[0]
```

```
        PrivateLinkServiceConnection = $plsConnection
    }
    New-AzPrivateEndpoint @par4 -ByManualRequest
```

7. Approve the Private Endpoint connection with the following code:

```
    ## Keep the private link service configuration into variable. ##
    $par1 = @{
        Name = 'SybexPLS'
        ResourceGroupName = 'SybexPLS-rg'
    }
    $pls = Get-AzPrivateLinkService @par1

    $par2 = @{
        Name = $pls.PrivateEndpointConnections[0].Name
        ServiceName = 'SybexPLS'
        ResourceGroupName = 'CreatePrivLinkService-rg'
        Description = 'Approved'
    }
    Approve-AzPrivateEndpointConnection @par2
```

Plan Private Endpoints

You can use *Private Endpoints* to connect to your virtual networks. The Azure Private Link network interface allows you to connect privately and securely to Azure Private Link–powered services. You enable Private Endpoints to bring the service into your virtual network.

Services provided by Azure include Azure Storage, Azure Cosmos DB, Azure SQL Database, and your own services using Private Link services.

Figure 10.2 provides an overview of Private Endpoints.

FIGURE 10.2   Overview of Private Endpoints

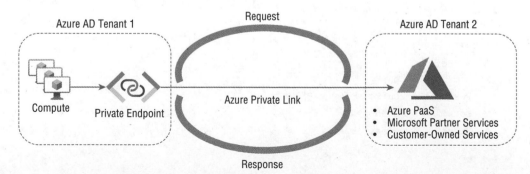

The properties of a Private Endpoint are as follows:

Name   The name given to the resource group.

Subnet   The network subnet on which the private IP address will be assigned.

Private Link Resource   Use one of the available types of Private Link to connect to the resource by using its ID or alias. The traffic sent to this resource is uniquely identified by its network identifier.

Target Subresource   This property identifies the resource to be connected to. There are various options to choose from when creating a Private Link resource.

Connection Approval Method   Connection approval can be either manual or automatic. Private Endpoints can be approved automatically based on Azure's role-based access control (RBAC) permissions. If you connect to Private Link resources without Azure RBAC permissions, you should use the manual method to allow the resource owner to approve the connection.

Request Message   Connectivity requests can be approved manually by sending a message to the resource owner. This message identifies the specific request.

Connection Status   The active property specifies whether the Private Endpoint is active. For traffic to be sent, only approved Private Endpoints are allowed. Connection state options include:

>   **Approved**   The connection was approved automatically or manually.
>
>   **Pending**   Currently, the Private Link resource owner needs to approve the connection created manually.
>
>   **Rejected**   This connection was rejected by the Private Link resource owner.
>
>   **Disconnected**   The Private Link resource owner disconnected the connection. It should be deleted for cleanup since the Private Endpoint has become inactive.

Considerations for designing and deploying Azure Private Endpoints follow:

- Through Private Endpoints, customers can connect from the same location:
  - Virtual network
  - Regionally peered virtual networks
  - Globally peered virtual networks
  - On-premises environments that use VPNs or ExpressRoutes
  - Services provided by Private Link
- Connections to a Private Endpoint can only be initiated by clients that are connected to the endpoint. Router configurations are not available for service providers to connect with customers, and only one direction of the connection is possible.

- For the life cycle of the Private Endpoint, a network interface with read-only capabilities is automatically created. The interface receives a dynamic private IP address in the subnet that maps to the Private Link resource. Private IP addresses remain unchanged for the entire life cycle of Private Endpoints.

- The Private Endpoint must reside in the same region and subscription as the virtual network.

- The Private Link resource can be deployed in a separate region from the virtual network and the Private Endpoint.

- Multiple Private Links can be created with a single Private Link resource. As a rule, a single Private Endpoint should be used for all Private Link resources on a single network with a standard DNS server configuration. In this way, duplicate DNS entries can be avoided.

- Creating more than one Private Endpoint on the same subnet or different subnets within the same virtual network is possible. Cloud subscribers are limited in the number of Private Endpoints they can create.

- The Private Link subscription must also be registered with the Microsoft network resource provider.

Consumers of cloud services can have multiple Private Endpoints in the same VNet or subnet, connected to different services. Users have access to Azure PaaS resources across different Azure regions.

Consumers of the cloud do not need dedicated subnets for Private Endpoints. In a VNet where services are deployed, you can choose a Private Endpoint IP from any subnet.

Azure Active Directory tenants can connect to Private Link services or Azure PaaS services using Private Endpoints. Connecting Private Endpoints across tenants needs to be approved manually.

In Exercise 10.2 you create a Private Endpoint using the Azure portal.

EXERCISE 10.2

Create a Private Endpoint Using the Azure Portal

1. Log into a personal or business account in the Azure portal at https://portal.azure.com and select Create A Resource.

2. Select Networking. In the left pane, search for Private Link and select it in the search results.

3. On the Private Link page that opens, click Create.

4. In the Private Link Center, in the left pane, choose Private Endpoints.

5. In the Private Endpoints pane, choose Create.

6. In the Create A Private Endpoint pane, choose the Basics tab, and then provide the following values:

Subscription	Choose your subscription.
Resource Group	Choose a resource group or create a new one.
Name	Enter a unique name for the endpoint.
Region	Choose your region.

7. Select the Resource tab and, in the Resource pane, provide the following values:

Connection Method	Choose Connect To An Azure Resource In My Directory.
Subscription	Select your subscription.
Resource type	Choose Microsoft.Web/sites.
Resource	Select your web app. Choose the name of the web app that you created earlier.
Target Sub-Resource	Choose Sites.

8. Select the Configuration tab and, in the Configuration pane, provide the following values:

Virtual Network	Choose your virtual network.
Subnet	Choose your virtual network subnet.
Integrate with Private DNS Zone	Keep the default of Yes.
Subscription	Select your subscription.
Private DNS Zones	Keep the default of (New) privatelink.azurewebsites .net.

9. On the Review + Create tab, wait for the validation pass status before you click Create.

Configure Access to Private Endpoints

Service providers can manage a Private Endpoint connection through Azure Private Link. In the *approval workflow* for accessing Private Link resources, an Azure Private Link service consumer can request a connection to the service provider to use the service. If the service provider allows the connection, the consumer can connect.

Connecting to a Private Link resource can be approved by one of the following methods:

Automatic Approval   Use this method if you own the resource or have permission to access it. Based on the type of Private Link resource, the following permissions are required:

```
Microsoft.<Provider>/<resource_type>/privateEndpointConnectionsApproval/
action
```

Manual Approval   This method should be used if you do not have the necessary permissions. This initiates an approval process. Pending connections will be created for the Private Endpoint and any subsequent Private Endpoint connections, and Private Link resource owners must approve connections.

As shown in Figure 10.3, the Private Endpoint is enabled to send traffic normally once it has been approved.

FIGURE 10.3   Private Endpoint enablement process

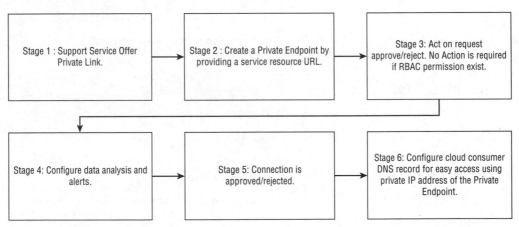

Private Link resource owners have the following capabilities over a Private Endpoint connection:

Approve   Connect the Private Endpoints. The responding Private Endpoint will be able to send traffic to the Private Link.

Reject   Reject a connection to a Private Endpoint. This will be reflected on the Private Endpoint.

Delete   Any Private Endpoint connection can be deleted. A disconnected state will be added to the Private Endpoint in response to the action. Only the resource may be deleted from the Private Endpoint during this time.

Table 10.1 shows the various service provider actions for Private Endpoints and their resulting connection states. The service provider can change the connection state without the consumer's involvement, and consumers will then be notified of the change.

TABLE 10.1   Service provider action for Private Endpoints

Service provider action	Service consumer Private Endpoint state	Description
None	Pending	The Private Link resource owner must approve the connection before it can be published.
Approve	Approved	The connection has been automatically or manually approved and is ready to use.
Reject	Rejected	This connection was rejected by the owner of the Private Link resource.
Remove	Disconnected	As a result of the Private Link resource owner removing the connection, and it should be deleted.

Azure PowerShell can be used to manage access:

- To get Private Link connection states:

```
Get-AzPrivateEndpointConnection -Name myPrivateLinkService
-ResourceGroupName myResourceGroup
```

- To approve a Private Endpoint connection:

```
Approve-AzPrivateEndpointConnection -Name myPrivateEndpointConnection
-ResourceGroupName myResourceGroup -ServiceName myPrivateLinkService
```

- To deny a Private Endpoint connection:

```
Deny-AzPrivateEndpointConnection -Name myPrivateEndpointConnection
-ResourceGroupName myResourceGroup -ServiceName myPrivateLinkService
```

- To remove a Private Endpoint connection:

```
Remove-AzPrivateEndpointConnection -Name myPrivateEndpointConnection
-ResourceGroupName myResourceGroup -ServiceName myPrivateLinkService.
```

Azure Private Link RBAC Permissions

Cloud resource access management is a vital function for role-based access control. Azure RBAC manages the access and operation of Azure resources.

User roles such as Owner, Contributor, and Network Contributor are required to deploy a Private Endpoint or Private Link service. By creating a custom role with the permissions, you can also provide more granular access.

Integrate Private Link with DNS and Private Link Services with On-Premises Clients

Your organization's DNS settings must be configured correctly to resolve the Private Endpoint IP address to the connection string's fully qualified domain name (FQDN). Existing Azure services might already have a DNS configuration for a public endpoint, and this configuration must be overridden to connect using a Private Endpoint.

A Private Endpoint's network interface contains the information needed to configure their DNS. Network interface information includes the Private Link resource's FQDN and private IP address.

To configure DNS settings for Private Endpoints, you can use the following options:

- Microsoft recommends using the host file only for testing. Consumers can override the DNS on a virtual machine by using the host file.

- You can use a private DNS zone to override the DNS resolution for a Private Endpoint. A private DNS zone can be linked to the virtual network to resolve specific domains.

- You can use *DNS forwarders*. If you want to override DNS resolution for private links, use a DNS forwarder. A DNS forwarder establishes a DNS forwarding rule to use a private DNS zone on a virtual network's DNS server.

- Azure creates a CNAME record for the canonical name on the public DNS. Through the CNAME record, the resolution is redirected to the private domain name. The organization's private IP address can be used to override the DNS resolution.

- Applications using the cloud do not have to change their connection URLs. Your organization's Private Endpoints will be resolved when resolving a public DNS service. This process doesn't impact existing cloud applications.

- FQDNs of services are automatically assigned public IP addresses. Change the DNS settings to resolve the endpoint's private IP address.

- An application's success relies on DNS successfully resolving the Private Endpoint IP address.

You can choose from the following use cases with DNS resolution integrated:

- Workloads on virtual networks without a custom DNS server
- Workloads that use a DNS forwarder on-premises
- Using a DNS forwarder for virtual network workloads and on-premises workloads

Use Case 1: Workloads on Virtual Networks without a Custom DNS Server

Workloads on virtual networks without a custom DNS server are suitable for this use case. A client queries `178.73.123.12` as an Azure-provided DNS service to determine the Private Endpoint IP address. The client will use Azure DNS to resolve private DNS zones.

If the client uses a private DNS zone, they require the following resources for SQL Database:

- A private DNS zone (`privatelink.database.windows.net` with type A record)
- Private Endpoint information (FQDN record name and private IP address)
- A client virtual network

Figure 10.4 shows the DNS resolution sequence from virtual network workloads using a private DNS zone.

FIGURE 10.4 Workloads on virtual networks without a custom DNS server

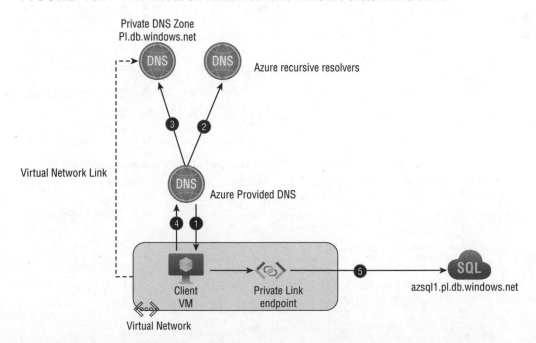

The following is the high-level DNS resolution flow depicted in Figure 10.4. (The numbering refers to the numbers in the figure.)

1. DNS query for `azsq1.db.windows.net`
2. Authoritative DNS query for `azsql1.db.windows.net` response CNAME `azsq1.pl.db.windows.net`
3. DNS query for `azsql1.pl.db.windows.net` response private IP address 10.10.1.5
4. Response CNAME `azsql1.pl.db.windows.net` A `azsql.ps.db.windows.net` 10.10.1.5
5. Private connection to IP address

Peer virtual networks associated with the same Private Endpoint can be extended. You can add new virtual network links to the private DNS zone to all peer virtual networks.

This configuration requires a single private DNS zone, and manual operations would be necessary to merge DNS records from multiple zones with the same name for different virtual networks.

Customers using a Private Endpoint in a hub-and-spoke model from a different subscription or even within the same subscription should link the same private DNS zones to all spokes and hubs with clients that require DNS resolution from these zones.

In this scenario, the network topology is hub and spoke. The spoke networks share one Private Endpoint and a private DNS zone, as shown in Figure 10.5.

FIGURE 10.5   Hub-and-spoke networking topology

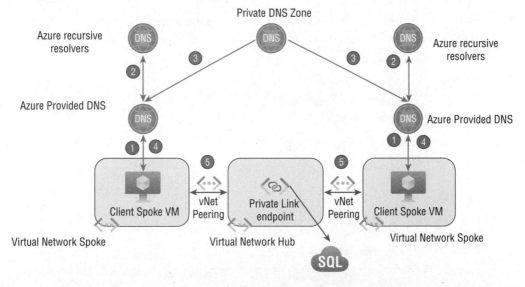

The following is the high-level DNS resolution flow as depicted in Figure 10.5. (The numbering refers to the numbers in the figure.)

1. DNS query for `azsq1.db.windows.net`
2. Authoritative DNS query for `azsql1.db.windows.net` response CNAME `azsq1.pl.db.windows.net`
3. DNS query for `azsql1.pl.db.windows.net` response private IP address
4. Response CNAME `azsql1.pl.db.windows.net` A `azsql.ps.db.windows.net` IP address
5. Private connection to IP

Use Case 2: Workloads That Use a DNS Forwarder On-Premises

This use case is for Azure SQL Database using a private DNS zone.

To resolve the FQDN of an on-premises Private Endpoint, use a DNS forwarder to resolve the Azure service public DNS zone in Azure. DNS forwarders are virtual machines running on the virtual network linked to the Private DNS Zone and able to proxy DNS queries from other virtual networks or on-premises. In order to get an Azure DNS response from a virtual network, the query must originate from the virtual network. There are several DNS proxy options, including running Windows DNS services, running Linux DNS services, and using Azure Firewall.

This scenario shows an on-premises network using a DNS forwarder in Azure. With this forwarder, DNS queries are forwarded to the Azure-provided DNS server `168.63.129.16` via a server-level forwarder.

The following resources are prerequisites that must be configured:

- On-premises network
- A virtual network connected to an on-premises network
- Implemented DNS forwarder in Azure
- A record of type A for `privatelink.database.windows.net`
- Endpoint information (FQDN name and IP address)

Using an on-premises network, Figure 10.6 illustrates DNS resolution. DNS forwarders are deployed in Azure.

A private DNS zone linked to a virtual network is used to resolve the name.

The following is the high-level DNS resolution flow as depicted in Figure 10.6. (The numbering refers to the numbers in the figure.)

1. DNS query for `azsq1.db.windows.net`
2. Server-level forwarder public IP address
3. Authoritative DNS query for `azsql1.db.windows.net` response CNAME `azsq1.pl.db.windows.net`
4. DNS query for `azsql1.pl.db.windows.net` response private IPC address `10.10.1.5`

5A and 5B. Response CNAME `azsql1.pl.db.windows.net A azsql.ps.db` `.windows.net` IP address

6. Private connection to IP address

FIGURE 10.6 Workloads that use a DNS forwarder on-premises

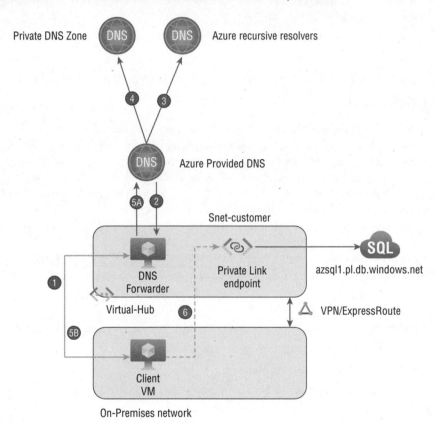

Using this configuration, an on-premises network with a DNS solution can be extended. Using a conditional forwarder, on-premises DNS traffic is forwarded to Azure DNS, and the conditional forwarder connects to the Azure DNS forwarder.

To configure correctly for this use case, you need the following resources:

- Custom DNS solution for on-premises networks
- A virtual network connected to an on-premises network
- Implemented DNS forwarder in Azure
- Private DNS zones with type A records for `pl.db.windows.net`
- Information about Private Endpoints (FQDN record name and private IP address)

Figure 10.7 shows DNS resolution from an on-premises network. DNS resolution is conditionally forwarded to Azure.

FIGURE 10.7   On-premises workloads using a DNS forwarder

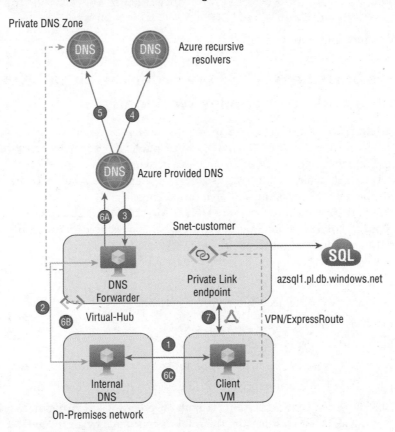

A private DNS zone is linked to a virtual network to resolve the name.

The recommended public DNS zone forwarder should be used if conditional forwarding is required. Instead of `privatelink.database.windows.net`, use `database.windows.net`.

The following is the high-level DNS resolution flow as depicted in Figure 10.7. (Numbering refers to the numbers in the figure.)

1. DNS query for `azsql.db.windows.net`

2. Conditional forward for `db.windows.net` to `10.10.1.254`

3. Server level forwarder to `192.62.128.14`

4. Authoritative DNS query for `azsql1.db.windows.net` response CNAME `azsq1.pl.db.windows.net`

5. DNS query for `azsql1.pl.db.windows.net` response private IP address `10.10.1.5`

6A, 6B and 6C. Response CNAME `azsql1.pl.db.windows.net A azsql.ps.db.windows.net IP address`

7. Private connection to IP address

Use Case 3: Using a DNS Forwarder for Virtual Network Workloads and On-Premises Workloads

Azure SQL Database uses a private DNS zone in this scenario.

Use a DNS forwarder to resolve the Azure service public DNS zone for workloads accessing a Private Endpoint from virtual or on-premises networks.

In the following example, both networks access an endpoint in a hub network located at a shared location, and the endpoint is located on-premises.

DNS queries are forwarded to the Azure DNS service `168.63.129.16` using a server-level forwarder. For this configuration, a single private DNS zone is needed. All on-premises and peering connections must use the same private DNS zone.

The following resources are prerequisites that must be configured:

- On-premises network

- On-premises network connected to a virtual network

- Peered virtual network

- A DNS forwarder is deployed in Azure

- The private DNS zone `privatelink.database.windows.net` has an A record

- Private Endpoint information (private IP address and FQDN record name)

Figure 10.8 shows the DNS resolution for both on-premises and virtual networks. The resolution is using a DNS forwarder, and the resolution is made by a private DNS zone linked to a virtual network.

The following is the high-level DNS resolution flow as depicted in Figure 10.8. (The numbering refers to the numbers in the figure.)

1. DNS query for `azsq1.db.windows.net`

2. Authoritative DNS query for `azsql1.db.windows.net` response CNAME `azsq1.pl.db.windows.net`

3. DNS query for `azsql1.pl.db.windows.net` response private IP address `10.10.1.5`

4. Response CNAME `azsql1.pl.db.windows.net A azsql.ps.db.windows.net` IP address

5. Private connection IP address

FIGURE 10.8   DNS forwarder for virtual network workloads and on-premises workloads

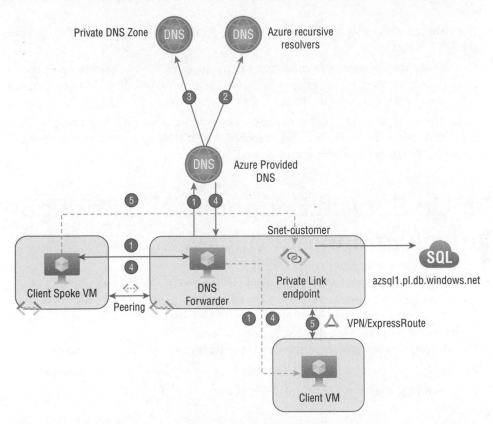

Organizations can also create a private DNS zone group by integrating their Private End-point with a private DNS zone. An association between a DNS zone group and a Private Endpoint enables auto-updating the private DNS zone when an update is made to the Private Endpoint. A private DNS zone is automatically updated when adding or removing regions.

A Private Endpoint's DNS records were previously created using scripting (by retrieving certain information about the endpoint and adding it to the zone). When using the DNS zone group, no additional PowerShell/CLI lines are required for every DNS zone. An orga-nization will also delete all DNS records when the Private Endpoint is deleted within a DNS zone group.

Frequently, a DNS zone group is used in a hub-and-spoke topology, in which the private DNS zones are created in the hub and registered to the spokes, rather than creating separate zones in each spoke.

A DNS zone group can support up to five DNS zones, and more than one DNS zone group can't be added to one Private Endpoint.

To summarize this section, here are the options for configuring Private Endpoint DNS settings:

- For testing, use the host file. The host file on a virtual machine can be used to override the DNS in Azure.

- Create your own private DNS zone. You can use private DNS zones to override the DNS resolution for a Private Endpoint. Domains can be resolved by linking a private DNS zone to the virtual network.

- DNS forwarding is optional. You can use your organization's DNS forwarder to override DNS resolution for Private Link resources. Use a DNS server in a virtual network to create a DNS forwarding rule for a private DNS zone.

Set Up Service Endpoints and Configure Service Endpoint Policies

Virtual Network (VNet) service endpoints provide direct and secure access to Azure services over the Azure backbone network. Organizations can limit access to Azure resources to only their virtual networks by using endpoints. Private IP addresses in a VNet can reach *Azure service endpoints* without using a public IP address in the VNet.

The following Azure regions and services are available with service endpoints:

- Microsoft Azure Storage (Microsoft Storage) is now available in all Azure regions.

- Microsoft SQL Database (Microsoft.SQL): Generally available (GA) in all Azure regions.

- Dedicated SQL pools (formerly SQL DW) for Azure Synapse Analytics (Microsoft.Sql) are GA across all Azure regions.

- Azure regions with database service, Azure Database for PostgreSQL (Microsoft.SQL) is GA.

- MySQL Database for Azure (Microsoft.Sql): GA in Azure regions where database service is available.

- Microsoft.SQL Azure Database for MariaDB (Microsoft.Sql): GA in Azure regions that support database services.

- All Azure regions can use Azure Cosmos DB (Microsoft.AzureCosmosDB).

- Microsoft.KeyVault (Azure Key Vault) is GA across all Azure regions.

- Microsoft.ServiceBus is now available in all Azure regions.

- Microsoft.EventHub: All Azure regions are now GA for Azure Event Hubs (Microsoft.EventHub).

- Azure Data Lake Store Gen 1 (Microsoft.AzureActiveDirectory) is GA in all Azure regions that support ADLS Gen1.

- Microsoft Azure App Service (Web): GA in all Azure regions where the service is available.

- All Azure regions where Cognitive services are available to support Azure Cognitive Services (Microsoft.CognitiveServices).

The following benefits are provided by service endpoints:

- Improved security for Azure service resources: VNet private address spaces can overlap, and you can't use overlapping areas to uniquely identify traffic originating from their VNet. Service endpoints can secure Azure service resources to virtual networks by extending VNet identity to the service. Once you enable service endpoints in their virtual network, they can add a virtual network rule to secure the Azure service resources to their virtual network. The rule also improves security by removing public Internet access to resources and allowing traffic only from virtual networks.

- Virtual networks should optimally route Azure service traffic. Currently, any routes from virtual networks that force Internet traffic to their on-premises and virtual appliances also force Azure service traffic to take the same route as the Internet traffic. Service endpoints facilitate Azure traffic routing optimally.

- Virtual networks always route traffic directly to Microsoft Azure backbone network services via their endpoints. By forcing tunneling on the Azure backbone network, you can continue auditing and monitoring outbound Internet traffic from your virtual networks without impacting service traffic.

- A cloud firewall does not require reserved public IP addresses in virtual networks to secure Azure resources. No network address translation (NAT) device or gateway is needed to set up the service endpoints. Consumers can configure cloud service endpoints by clicking on a subnet, and there's no additional overhead to maintaining the endpoints.

Consider the following limitations while designing and deploying service endpoints:

- Virtual networks deployed through the Azure Resource Manager deployment model can benefit from this feature.

- On Azure virtual networks, endpoints can be configured on subnets. Azure services cannot be accessed via endpoints from on-premises.

- A service endpoint for Azure SQL applies only to Azure service traffic within a virtual network's region. The preview version of Azure Storage allows you to access virtual networks in other regions.

- Currently, Azure Data Lake Storage (ADLS) Gen1 only supports VNet integration for virtual networks within the same region. Also, it is important to note that virtual network integration for ADLS Gen1 generates additional security claims in the access token based on what occurs between virtual networks and Azure Active Directory (Azure AD). Virtual networks are authenticated against their Data Lake Storage Gen1 accounts using these claims. In the service endpoints section, the `Microsoft .AzureActiveDirectory` tag is used only to support ADLS Gen1 service endpoints. Authentication through Azure AD is not supported.

- The virtual network service endpoint provides the Azure service with information about virtual networks. You can add virtual network rules to secure Azure service resources within their virtual networks once they enable service endpoints in their virtual networks.

- Public IP addresses are currently used as source IP addresses for Azure service traffic. When accessing the Azure service from a virtual network, service traffic switches use virtual network private addresses as their source IP addresses. Switches like this enable access to the services without using reserved IP addresses for IP firewalls.

- Azure service resources aren't accessible from on-premises networks by default. You need to allow on-premises traffic from public IP addresses (typically NAT) from their on-premises or via ExpressRoute, to be able to allow traffic from on-premises. You can add these IP addresses by configuring the IP firewall for Azure service resources.

- You need to identify the NAT IP addresses used by using ExpressRoute for public peering or Microsoft peering from their premises. Every ExpressRoute circuit employs two NAT IP addresses by default to apply to Azure service traffic once it enters the Azure network backbone. Microsoft peering relies on either the service provider's or the customer's NAT IP addresses. To access Azure resources, these public IP addresses must be allowed in the resource IP firewall settings. Open a support ticket with ExpressRoute via the Azure portal to find IP addresses for public peering ExpressRoute circuits.

To enable a service endpoint, you must do the following two things:

- Turn off the service's public access.
- Create a virtual network for the service endpoint.

Traffic flow into Azure VMs to access the service directly from their private address is not accessible from public networks. If you examine effective routes for a deployed VM vNIC, you'll notice that the service endpoint is the Next Hop type.

Service endpoints are enabled per service and per subnet. Consumers of cloud services have a VM in a private subnet and a storage account in the same region. You want to avoid having traffic go through the Internet between the former and the latter.

Follow the steps in Exercise 10.3 to create a subnet and enable a service endpoint.

EXERCISE 10.3

Create a Subnet

1. Log into a personal or business account in the Azure portal at `https://portal .azure.com`.

2. Choose Subnets under Settings, and then choose Subnet.

3. Select Microsoft.Service under the Service endpoints header.

4. Click Save.

Follow the steps in Exercise 10.4 to modify the default network access rule on a Microsoft service (Storage in this example).

EXERCISE 10.4

Enable a Service Endpoint

1. Navigate to the storage account and select Firewalls And Virtual Networks in the sidebar. Under Allow Access From, choose Selected Networks.

2. Choose Add An Existing Virtual Network, then select the virtual network and subnet you just edited.

3. Click Add and then click Save.

Service endpoints are free. VNet resources and service resources are always charged, but service endpoints do not incur an extra charge.

You can enable a service endpoint; all VMs in the associated subnet are assigned private IP addresses instead of public ones. Remember this since firewall rules set to public IP addresses can fail. You may temporarily interrupt traffic from the subnet to the service resource during the switch, so be sure that specific critical tasks aren't running when you enable or disable a service endpoint.

Your organization's virtual network identities are provided to Azure via a virtual network service endpoint. As soon as you enable service endpoints in their virtual networks, you can add a virtual network rule to secure Azure service resources within your virtual networks.

When a virtual machine is assigned a service endpoint, its IP address changes from a public IPv4 address to a private IPv4 address. As a result of this change, existing Azure service firewall rules based on Azure public IP addresses will not work. Before setting up service endpoints, please check that Azure's service firewall rules allow this switch. While configuring service endpoints from this subnet, you may experience temporary interruptions in service traffic.

Any BGP or UDR route for the address prefix match of an Azure service is overridden by the service endpoint route.

Overview of Service Tags and Access to Service Endpoints

A *service tag* is a collection of prefixes from an Azure service. Microsoft manages the prefixes covered by the service tag and updates the service tag automatically as address changes occur, reducing the complexity of updating network security rules frequently.

Azure Firewall, network security groups, and user-defined routes can all be controlled via service tags. Create security rules and routes using service tags instead of specific IP addresses. An API management service tag can be specified in a security rule's appropriate source or destination field.

Traffic for each cloud service can be allowed or denied. If the service tag name is specified in the address prefix of a route, you can route traffic intended for any of the prefixes encapsulated by the service tag to the next-hop type you prefer.

You can use service tags to protect Azure resources from Internet access and prevent users from accessing Azure services when connecting to Azure from public endpoints. Set inbound/outbound rules for network security groups to block traffic to/from the Internet and allow traffic to/from Azure Cloud.

The classic deployment model (before Azure Resource Manager) supports a subset of the tags listed in Table 10.2. Each tag has its own spelling.

TABLE 10.2   Subset of supported tags

Classic spelling	Equivalent Resource Manager tag
Azure_LOADBALANCER	AzureLoadBalancer
INTERNET	Internet
VIRTUAL_NETWORK	VirtualNetwork

Service tags of Azure services refer to the address prefixes from the specific cloud being used. The underlying IP ranges corresponding to the SQL tag value on the Azure China cloud, for example, will be different from those corresponding to the SQL tag value on the Azure public cloud.

Consider the case of organizations implementing a virtual network service endpoint for a service like Azure Storage or Azure SQL Database. Azure adds a route to the service's virtual network subnet when that happens. The route has the same address prefixes, or CIDR ranges, like those corresponding to the service tag.

Table 10.3 contains all the service tags available in network security group rules. Columns show whether the tag can be used in rules that cover inbound or outbound traffic, that support regional scope, and that can be used in Azure Firewall rules.

The service tags reflect the ranges of the entire cloud by default. Some service tags can also restrict the corresponding IP ranges to a specific region. For example, Azure Storage's service tag represents the entire cloud, but Storage and WestUS limit the range to only the IP address ranges from the WestUS region. Table 10.3 indicates whether each service tag supports this scope.

TABLE 10.3   Service tag supports

Tag	Can use inbound or outbound?	Can be regional?	Can use with Azure Firewall?
ActionGroup	Inbound	No	No
ApiManagement	Inbound	Yes	Yes
ApplicationInsightsAvailability	Inbound	No	No
AppConfiguration	Outbound	No	No
AppService	Outbound	Yes	Yes
AppServiceManagement	Both	No	Yes
AzureActiveDirectory	Outbound	No	Yes
AzureActiveDirectoryDomainServices	Both	No	Yes
AzureAdvancedThreatProtection	Outbound	No	No
AzureArcInfrastructure	Outbound	No	Yes
AzureAttestation	Outbound	No	Yes
AzureBackup	Outbound	No	Yes
AzureBotService	Outbound	No	No
AzureCloud	Outbound	Yes	Yes
AzureCognitiveSearch	Inbound	No	No
AzureConnectors	Inbound / Outbound	Yes	Yes
AzureContainerRegistry	Outbound	Yes	Yes

TABLE 10.3   Service tag supports *(continued)*

Tag	Can use inbound or outbound?	Can be regional?	Can use with Azure Firewall?
AzureCosmosDB	Outbound	Yes	Yes
AzureDatabricks	Both	No	No
AzureDataExplorerManagement	Inbound	No	No
AzureDataLake	Outbound	No	Yes
AzureDeviceUpdate	Both	No	Yes
AzureDevSpaces	Outbound	No	No
AzureDevOps	Inbound	No	Yes
AzureDigitalTwins	Inbound	No	Yes
AzureEventGrid	Both	No	No
AzureFrontDoor.Frontend AzureFrontDoor.Backend AzureFrontDoor.FirstParty	Both	No	No
AzureHealthcareAPIs	Both	No	Yes
AzureInformationProtection	Outbound	No	No
AzureIoTHub	Outbound	Yes	No
AzureKeyVault	Outbound	Yes	Yes
AzureLoadBalancer	Both	No	No
AzureMachineLearning	Both	No	Yes
AzureMonitor	Outbound	No	Yes
AzureOpenDatasets	Outbound	No	No
AzurePlatformDNS	Outbound	No	No
AzurePlatformIMDS	Outbound	No	No

Tag	Can use inbound or outbound?	Can be regional?	Can use with Azure Firewall?
AzurePlatformLKM	Outbound	No	No
AzureResourceManager	Outbound	No	No
AzureSignalR	Outbound	No	No
AzureSiteRecovery	Outbound	No	No
AzureSphere	Both	No	Yes
AzureStack	Outbound	No	Yes
AzureTrafficManager	Inbound	No	Yes
AzureUpdateDelivery	Outbound	No	No
BatchNodeManagement	Both	No	Yes
CognitiveServicesManagement	Both	No	No
DataFactory	Both	No	No
DataFactoryManagement	Outbound	No	No
Dynamics365ForMarketingEmail	Outbound	Yes	No
EOPExternalPublishedIPs	Both	No	Yes
EventHub	Outbound	Yes	Yes
GatewayManager	Inbound	No	No
GenevaActions	Inbound	No	Yes
GuestAndHybridManagement	Outbound	No	Yes
HDInsight	Inbound	Yes	No
Internet	Both	No	No
LogicApps	Both	No	No
LogicAppsManagement	Inbound	No	No

TABLE 10.3   Service tag supports *(continued)*

Tag	Can use inbound or outbound?	Can be regional?	Can use with Azure Firewall?
M365ManagementActivityApi	Outbound	Yes	No
M365ManagementActivityApiWebhook	Inbound	Yes	No
MicrosoftAzureFluidRelay	Outbound	No	No
MicrosoftCloudAppSecurity	Outbound	No	No
MicrosoftContainerRegistry	Outbound	Yes	Yes
PowerBI	Both	No	No
PowerPlatformInfra	Outbound	Yes	Yes
PowerQueryOnline	Both	No	No
ServiceBus	Outbound	Yes	Yes
ServiceFabric	Both	No	No
Sql	Outbound	Yes	Yes
SqlManagement	Both	No	Yes
Storage	Outbound	Yes	Yes
StorageSyncService	Both	No	No
WindowsAdminCenter	Outbound	No	Yes
WindowsVirtualDesktop	Both	No	Yes
VirtualNetwork	Both	No	No

REST, Azure PowerShell, and Azure CLI are available for retrieving the current list of service tags and IP address range information.

New service tag data can propagate in the API results across all Azure regions as of this writing, taking up to four weeks. You must be authenticated and access Azure's current subscription. A subset of the tags currently in the downloadable JSON file is represented in the API data, which provides access to tags that can be used with NSG rules.

Configure Access to Service Endpoints

Public IP addresses are currently used as source IP addresses for Azure service traffic from a virtual network. When accessing the service from a virtual network with service endpoints, Azure service traffic switches use the virtual network private addresses as source IP addresses. With this switch, you can access cloud services without reserving public IP addresses for IP firewalls.

You can limit some Azure service resources to a virtual network subnet by using virtual network service endpoints. You can also turn off the resources' Internet access. Virtual networks are directly connected to Azure services, allowing you to access Azure services using their private network's address space. Traffic destined for Azure resources is always routed over the Azure backbone network through Microsoft Azure service endpoints.

The VNet service endpoints extend the private address scope of the virtual network. Additionally, the endpoints extend the VNet's connection to Azure and enable the protection of Azure resources.

Service tags represent groups of IP addresses associated with an Azure service. By managing the address prefixes covered by the service tag, Microsoft minimizes the complexity of updating security rules frequently.

You can use service tags to define network access controls on Azure firewalls and network security groups. Instead of specifying a specific IP address, use a service tag. In the source or destination field of a rule, specify the name of the service tag, such as API management.

In Exercise 10.5 you bind network access to Azure PaaS resources using Azure PowerShell.

EXERCISE 10.5

Bind Network Access to Azure PaaS Resources

Task 1: Create one subnet for the virtual network.

It is necessary to create a resource group for the virtual network and all other resources created in this section before creating the virtual network. We do this by using the New-AzResourceGroup command.

1. Create SybexRG using the following code:

```
New-AzResourceGroup -ResourceGroupName SybexRG -Location WestUS
```

2. Use New-AzVirtualNetwork to build a virtual network. The following code creates a virtual network named SybexvNet with the address prefix 10.10.1.0/16.

```
$virtualNetwork = New-AzVirtualNetwork `
  -ResourceGroupName SybexRG `
```

```
-Location WestUS `
-Name SybexvNet `
-AddressPrefix 10.10.1.0/16.
```

3. Using New-AzVirtualNetworkSubnetConfig, create a subnet named Internet:

```
$subnetConfigInternet = Add-AzVirtualNetworkSubnetConfig `
  -Name Internet `
  -AddressPrefix 10.1.1.0/24 `
  -VirtualNetwork $virtualNetwork
```

4. Use Set-AzVirtualNetwork to create the subnet in the virtual network:

```
$virtualNetwork | Set-AzVirtualNetwork
```

Task 2: Configure the subnet and enable the service endpoint.

You can only enable service endpoints for services that support service endpoints. Get-AzVirtualNetworkAvailableEndpointService returns a list of endpoint-enabled services available in an Azure location. The following example returns a list of the services that service endpoints in the WestUS region can access. Service endpoints will enable more and more Azure services over time, increasing the list of services returned.

```
Get-AzVirtualNetworkAvailableEndpointService -Location westus | Select Name
```

5. In the virtual network, create an additional subnet.

The following code is an example of a private subnet configured with a Microsoft. Storage service endpoint:

```
$subnetConfigPrivate = Add-AzVirtualNetworkSubnetConfig `
  -Name Private `
  -AddressPrefix 10.1.1.0/24 `
  -VirtualNetwork $virtualNetwork `
  -ServiceEndpoint Microsoft.Storage
$virtualNetwork | Set-AzVirtualNetwork
```

Task 3: Create an Azure resource that is accessible from only a subnet and allow network access to it.

You can create an Azure-accessed resource only from a specific subnet and allow network access to the resource. New-AzNetworkSecurityRuleConfig can be used to do this.

6. Using `New-AzNetworkSecurityRuleConfig`, create network security group security rules. A public IP address assigned to the Azure Storage service may be accessed via the following rule:

```
$rule1 = New-AzNetworkSecurityRuleConfig `
  -Name Allow-Storage-All `
  -Access Allow `
  -DestinationAddressPrefix Storage `
  -DestinationPortRange * `
  -Direction Outbound `
  -Priority 100 `
  -Protocol * `
  -SourceAddressPrefix VirtualNetwork `
  -SourcePortRange *
```

Public IP addresses are denied access with the following rule. The previous rule overrides this rule because it has a higher priority, allowing access to the public IP addresses in Azure Storage.

```
$rule2 = New-AzNetworkSecurityRuleConfig `
  -Name Deny-Internet-All `
  -Access Deny `
  -DestinationAddressPrefix Internet `
  -DestinationPortRange * `
  -Direction Outbound `
  -Priority 110 `
  -Protocol * `
  -SourceAddressPrefix VirtualNetwork `
  -SourcePortRange *
```

Remote Desktop Protocol (RDP) traffic can enter the subnet from anywhere with the following rule. You can connect a remote desktop to the subnet in a later step to confirm network access to the resource.

```
$rule3 = New-AzNetworkSecurityRuleConfig `
  -Name Allow-RDP-All `
  -Access Allow `
  -DestinationAddressPrefix VirtualNetwork `
  -DestinationPortRange 3389 `
  -Direction Inbound `
  -Priority 120 `
  -Protocol * `
  -SourceAddressPrefix * `
  -SourcePortRange *
```

EXERCISE 10.5 *(continued)*

7. Use New-AzNetworkSecurityGroup to create a network security group. MySybexPrivate is a network security group formed in the following example.

```
$nsg = New-AzNetworkSecurityGroup `
  -ResourceGroupName myResourceGroup `
  -Location WestUS `
  -Name mySybexPrivate `
  -SecurityRules $rule1,$rule2,$rule3
```

8. With Set-AzVirtualNetworkSubnetConfig, associate the network security group with the private subnet and then write the subnet configuration to the virtual network. The following example assigns the SybexPrivate network security group to the private subnet:

```
Set-AzVirtualNetworkSubnetConfig `
  -VirtualNetwork $VirtualNetwork `
  -Name Private `
  -AddressPrefix 10.1.1.0/24 `
  -ServiceEndpoint Microsoft.Storage `
  -NetworkSecurityGroup $nsg
$virtualNetwork | Set-AzVirtualNetwork
```

Task 4: Restrict network access to a resource.

The steps essential to limit network access to resources developed via Azure services enabled for service endpoints vary across services.

9. Create a storage account.

As shown in the following code, use New-AzStorageAccount to create an Azure storage account. The name for the storage account must be unique across all Azure locations, with between 3 and 24 characters and using all lowercase letters and numbers.

```
$storageAcctName = '<replace-with-cloudconsumer-unique-storage-account-name>'
New-AzStorageAccount `
  -Location WestUS `
  -Name $storageAcctName `
  -ResourceGroupName myResourceGroup `
  -SkuName Standard_LRS `
  -Kind StorageV2
```

10. With `Get-AzStorageAccountKey`, retrieve the key for the storage account after it is created:

```
$storageAcctKey = (Get-AzStorageAccountKey `
  -ResourceGroupName myResourceGroup `
  -AccountName $storageAcctName).Value[0]
```

Use `$storageAcctKey` to create a file share. (In a later step you use it again to map the file share to a drive in a VM.)

11. Set up a file share in the storage account

First, using `New-AzStorageContext`, create a context for storage accounts and keys. It encapsulates the name and key for storage accounts:

```
$storageContext = New-AzStorageContext $storageAcctName $storageAcctKey
```

Next, use `New-AzStorageShare` to create a file share:

```
$share = New-AzStorageShare my-file-share -Context $storageContext
```

12. Deny all network access to an account.

Clients in any network can connect to storage accounts by default. With `Update-AzStorageAccountNetworkRuleSet`, set the default action to Deny to limit access to selected networks. When network access is denied, the storage account becomes inaccessible.

```
Update-AzStorageAccountNetworkRuleSet `
  -ResourceGroupName "SybexRG" `
  -Name $storageAcctName `
  -DefaultAction Deny
```

`Get-AzVirtualNetwork` returns the created virtual network, and `Get-AzVirtualNetworkSubnetConfig` returns the private subnet object into a variable:

```
$privateSubnet = Get-AzVirtualNetwork `
  -ResourceGroupName "SybexRG" `
  -Name "myVirtualNetwork" `
  | Get-AzVirtualNetworkSubnetConfig `
  -Name "Private"
```

13. Now allow network access to the storage account from the private subnet.

`Add-AzStorageAccountNetworkRule` allows network access from the private subnet to the storage account.

```
Add-AzStorageAccountNetworkRule `
  -ResourceGroupName "SybexRG" `
  -Name $storageAcctName `
  -VirtualNetworkResourceId $privateSubnet.Id.
```

Task 5: Deploy a virtual machine (VM) to each subnet.

New-AzVM can be used to create a virtual machine on the public subnet. The following command requires credentials. Those values are used to configure the username and password for the virtual machine. You can move on to Task 6 by using the -AsJob option to create the VM in the background.

14. In the private subnet, create a virtual machine:

```
New-AzVm `
    -ResourceGroupName "SybexRG" `
    -Location "WestUS" `
    -VirtualNetworkName "SybexVirtualNetwork" `
    -SubnetName "Private" `
    -Name "SybexVmPrivate"
```

Repeat this step to create a second VM.

Azure creates the virtual machine within a few minutes. Continue until Azure has finished creating the VM and has returned results to PowerShell.

Task 6: Confirm access to a resource from a subnet.

As a final task, you must validate the access for the provisioned resource.

15. Return a VM's public IP address using Get-AzPublicIpAddress. The following shows how to retrieve the public IP address of SybexVMPrivate VM:

```
Get-AzPublicIpAddress `
  -Name SybexVMPrivate `
  -ResourceGroupName SybexRG `
  | Select IpAddress
```

16. Replace <publicIpAddress> in the following command with the public IP address returned from the previous command, and then execute the following command:

```
mstsc /v:<publicIpAddress>
```

RDP files are created and downloaded to your computer. You can then open the RDP files.

17. Select Connect if prompted and enter your username and password when prompted to do so.

To determine what credentials you entered when creating the VM, you may need to select More Choices and use another account. During the sign-in process, you may receive a certificate warning. Click OK and Connect.

18. Using PowerShell, map the Azure file share to drive Y on SybexVmPrivate. Replace `<*storage-account-key>` and `<*storage-account-name>` with the values you supplied or retrieved when you completed step 9 before running the following commands.

```
$sybexacctKey = ConvertTo-SecureString -String "<storage-account-key>"
-AsPlainText -Force
$ID = New-Object System.Management.Automation.PSCredential -ArgumentList
"Azure\
<storage-account-name>", $acctKey
New-PSDrive -Name Y -PSProvider FileSystem -Root "\\
    <storage-account-name>.file.core.windows.net\my-file-share" -Credential
$ID.
```

19. Confirm that the VM has no outbound connectivity to any public IP addresses other than the Azure file share mapped to the Y drive.

    Customers receive no replies because the network security group associated with the private subnet does not allow outbound access to public IP addresses other than the addresses assigned to Azure Storage.

    SybexVmPrivate VM's remote desktop session will be closed.

Integrating App Services into Regional VNets

Azure services can be integrated into an Azure virtual network, allowing virtual machines and compute resources within the virtual network to access the service privately. Here are some options for integrating Azure services into a virtual network:

- Dedicated instances of the service can be hosted on a virtual network. These services can be accessed privately by using virtual networks and on-premises networks.

- Your organization's virtual and on-premises networks can be used to access a specific service instance privately through Private Link.

- In addition, your organization can extend a virtual network to the service through service endpoints, which allows you to access the service using public endpoints.

    By using service endpoints, virtual network resources can be secured.

    Azure consumers are limited in how many resources they can deploy from Azure. Most Azure networking limitations are set to maximum values.

    Azure VNets allow you to place Azure resources in a non-Internet-routable network. Using VNet integration, your business applications can access resources within or through a VNet. However, VNet integration does not allow applications to be accessed privately.

In Azure App Service, VNet integration is available in two variations:

- All multi-tenant plans except Isolated are supported.
- Support for isolated pricing plan apps deployed into your VNets.

In multi-tenant apps, VNet integration is used. The applications is already in a VNet and doesn't require VNet integration in an App Service environment.

Applications can access resources from their VNet through VNet integration, but inbound private access to their apps cannot be granted. Private site access refers to making an app accessible only from within a private network, such as an Azure virtual network. You can use VNet integration only to make outbound calls into your VNet from your apps. When used with a VNet in the same region, the VNet integration feature performs differently than when used with a VNet in another region. It comes in two variations:

Regional VNet Integration   A dedicated subnet must exist in the VNet that you are integrating when you connect to Azure Resource Manager virtual networks in the same region.

Gateway-Required VNet Integration   You need an Azure VNet gateway provisioned in the target VNet to connect to VNets in other regions or to classic virtual networks in the same region.

Integration requires a Standard, Premium, PremiumV2, PremiumV3, or Elastic Premium pricing plan, supports TCP and UDP, and works with Azure App Service apps and function apps.

The gateway-required VNet integration provides access to resources only in the target VNet or networks connected to the target VNet with peering or VPNs. Accessing resources over Azure ExpressRoute connections or using service endpoints is impossible with gateway-required VNet integration.

Business applications can access resources in VNet regardless of the integration version used, but it does not grant applications private access from the VNet. Private site access enables applications to be accessed only within a private network, such as within an Azure VNet. The VNet integration feature only works for outbound calls from the business applications into the VNet.

Azure Regional VNet Integration

Virtual networks in the same region can be connected without a gateway using regional virtual network integration. This allows you to access:

- Virtual network resources
- Resources in virtual networks that are peering with your virtual network, including global peering connections
- Service endpoint-secured services
- Resources on Azure ExpressRoute connections
- Private endpoint-enabled services

You can use the following Azure networking features when you use regional virtual network integration:

Network Security Groups (NSGs)   You can block outbound traffic by placing an NSG on the integration subnet. You cannot use virtual network integration to provide inbound access to applications, so inbound rules do not apply.

Route Tables (UDRs)   Route tables can be placed on the integration subnet to send outbound traffic.

How Azure Regional VNet Integration Works

Worker roles are used to host apps in App Service. In regional virtual network integration, worker roles are mounted with virtual interfaces corresponding to addresses in the delegated subnet. Since the address is in the virtual network, it has access to most things in or through the virtual network, like a VM in the virtual network. As a result, some networking features aren't available yet for this feature that are available when running a VM within a virtual network.

Figure 10.9 is an overview of Azure regional VNet integration.

FIGURE 10.9   Overview of Azure regional VNet integration

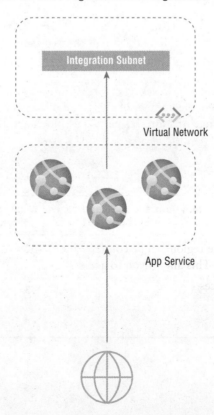

When regional virtual network integration is enabled, the business applications make outbound calls through their virtual network. The outbound addresses listed in the app properties portal are the addresses still used by the applications. However, suppose the outbound call is to a virtual machine or Private Endpoint in the integration virtual network or peered virtual network. In that case, the outbound address will be an address from the integration subnet. The private IP address assigned to an instance is exposed via the WEBSITE_PRIVATE_IP environment variable.

All outbound traffic is routed through the virtual network when all traffic routing is enabled. Only private traffic (RFC1918) and service endpoints configured on the integration subnet will be sent to the virtual network if all traffic routing is not allowed. Outgoing traffic toward the Internet will be routed normally.

Only one worker can use each virtual interface. One virtual network integration per App Service plan corresponds to one virtual interface per worker. There is only one virtual network integration per App Service plan for a specific subnet. You will need to create another App Service plan if an app needs to connect to another virtual network or another subnet in the same virtual network. Customers do not have direct access to the virtual interface used.

The traffic generated by virtual network integration does not appear in Azure Network Watcher or NSG due to how this technology works.

Subnet Requirements

A dedicated subnet is required for virtual network integration. Azure subnets lose five IP addresses if you create a subnet. An IP address will be used from the integration subnet for each plan instance. For example, four addresses will be used if you scale applications to four instances.

The required IP address space doubles when organizations grow or shrink for a short time. A change like this affects the number of real, available instances for a given subnet size. Table 10.4 shows the full range of addresses per CIDR block and the effect on a horizontal scale.

TABLE 10.4 Full range of addresses per CIDR block

CIDR block size	Maximum available addresses	Maximum horizontal scale (instances)
/28	11	5
/27	27	13
/26	59	29

Because a subnet's size can't be changed once it has been assigned, choose a large subnet to accommodate the scale an application may reach. You can use a /26 with 64 addresses to avoid any issues with subnet capacity. You must create subnets with a minimum of /27 sizes before integrating with virtual networks.

To reach an existing virtual network that is already connected by apps in another plan, you should choose a different subnet than the one used by the current virtual network integration.

Access Management

If you are configuring regional virtual network integration via the Azure portal, using the CLI, or when setting the `virtualNetworkSubnetId` property directly, you need at least the role-based access control permissions shown in Table 10.5.

TABLE 10.5   Role-based access control permission

Action	Description
Microsoft.Network/virtualNetworks/read	Read the virtual network definition
Microsoft.Network/virtualNetworks/subnets/read	Read a virtual network subnet definition
Microsoft.Network/virtualNetworks/subnets/join/action	Joins a virtual network

Suppose the virtual network is in a different subscription than the app. In that case, you must ensure that the subscription with the virtual network is registered with a Microsoft .Web resource provider.

When creating the first web app in a subscription, consumers can explicitly register the provider, but it will also be automatically registered.

Route Management

Virtual network integration allows you to control what traffic goes through virtual network integration. There are three routing types you should consider when configuring regional virtual network integration:

- Application routing determines what traffic is routed from your application and into your virtual network.

- Configuration routing involves operations before or during your application's startup—for instance, container image pull and application settings with Azure Key Vault reference.

- Network routing manages how application and configuration traffic is routed from your virtual network.

Virtual network integration routes only private traffic (RFC1918 traffic) sent from the applications. Otherwise, all traffic will not be routed through the virtual network integration unless you configure application routing or routing options. Only traffic that passes through the virtual network integration is subject to network routing.

Application Route Management

Once the applications are running, application routing applies to the traffic it sends. You can route all traffic or only private traffic into the virtual network when you configure application routing. You can configure this behavior through the Route All setting. When Route All is disabled, applications only route private traffic into their virtual network. Ensure that Route All is enabled on your virtual network if all outbound app traffic is routed.

To enable the routing of all traffic, Microsoft recommends you use the Route All configuration setting. With this setting, you can audit the behavior. You can still use the existing WEBSITE_VNET_ROUTE_ALL app setting to enable all traffic routing.

Configuration Route Management   You can configure how parts of configuration traffic are managed using virtual network integration. Configuration traffic, by default, goes directly over the public route. Nevertheless, in VNet integration, it can be configured to be routed through the virtual network.

Content Storage   Content storage traffic can be routed through VNet integration by adding the app setting WEBSITE_CONTENTOVERVNET with the value 1. You must also make sure that firewalls or network security groups configured on traffic from the subnet permit traffic to ports 443 and 445 and add the app setting.

Container Image Pull   You can pull the container over the virtual network integration when using custom containers for Linux. You must add the app setting WEBSITE_PULL_IMAGE_OVER_VNET with the value true to route traffic through the virtual network integration.

Application Settings Using Azure Key Vault   When Key Vault references are used in app settings, the public route will be taken to get secrets. An attempt will be made to get the secrets through VNet integration if the Key Vault blocks public traffic.

Routing   Route tables can route outbound traffic from applications to any desired destination. A route table affects destination traffic, and it only applies to traffic routed through VNet integration. For example, firewall devices or gateways can serve as destinations. Your integration subnet routes will not affect inbound app requests.

You can use a route table to send outbound traffic to the Azure ExpressRoute gateway to route outbound traffic on-premises. Configure routes in the external network to send replies if they route traffic to a gateway.

Border Gateway Protocol (BGP) routes can also affect application traffic. Application outbound traffic is affected if they have BGP routes from something like an ExpressRoute gateway. Your routing scope settings such as user-defined routes influence BGP routes.

Network Security Group   A VNet integration app can block outbound traffic to resources in virtual networks or the Internet by using a network security group. The only option is to enable Route All. RFC1918 traffic from the application is only subject to NSGs when Route All is not enabled.

Your integration subnets are covered by NSGs regardless of route tables.

Since virtual network integration only affects outbound traffic from the application, inbound rules in an NSG don't apply. Use the Access Restrictions feature of applications to control inbound traffic.

Service Endpoints   Integrating regional virtual networks allows you to access Azure services secured with service endpoints. You can access an endpoint-secured service by following these steps:

- Integrate regional virtual networks with web apps so that you can connect to a specific subnet for integration.
- Configure the service endpoints for the destination service against the integration subnet.

Private Endpoints   Make sure that DNS lookups resolve to Private Endpoints if you wish to call these endpoints. There are several ways to enforce this behavior:

- Integrate private zones with Azure DNS. The integration is automatically performed when zones are linked to a virtual network without a custom DNS server.
- Control the Private Endpoint in the DNS server used by the application. Customers must know the IP address of the Private Endpoint to configure the application. Use an A record to direct consumers to the endpoint cloud address.
- You can configure your own DNS servers to forward to Azure DNS private zones.

Azure DNS Private Zones   When an app is integrated with a VNet, it uses the same DNS server as the VNet. Apps won't work with Azure DNS private zones by default. Azure DNS private zones can only be used with the following app settings:

- 168.63.129.16 is the value for `WEBSITE_DNS_SERVER`
- 1 is the value of `WEBSITE_VNET_ROUTE_ALL`

These settings send all outbound calls from the app into their VNet and enable the app to access an Azure DNS private zone. Applications can use Azure DNS by querying the DNS private zone at the worker level with these settings.

Figure 10.10 depicts Azure Kubernetes Service (AKS) for regional VNet integration.

FIGURE 10.10 Azure Kubernetes Service (AKS) for regional VNet integration

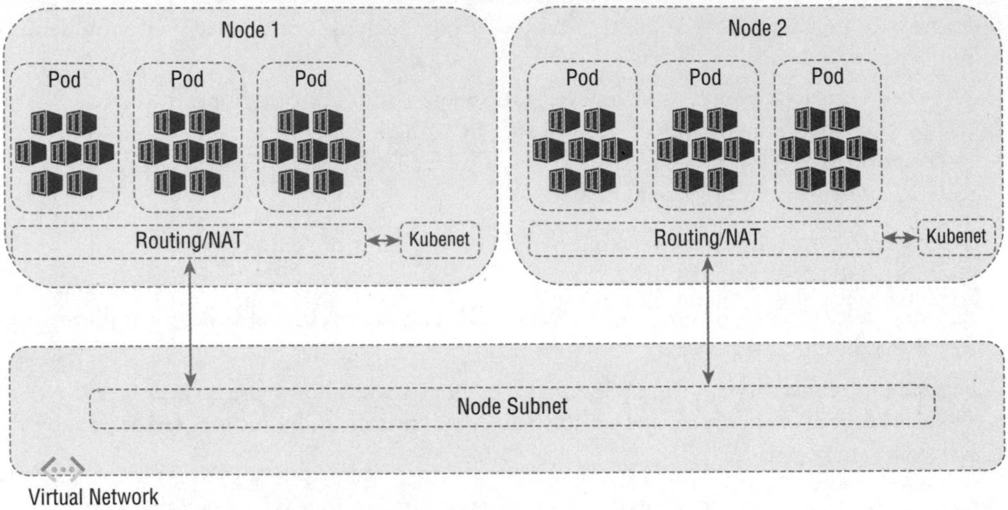

The use of regional virtual networks has some limitations:

- All App Service deployments, including Premium v2 and Premium v3, can benefit from this feature. It is also available in Standard, but only in newer app service deployments. Consumers on an older deployment cannot use the feature unless they are on a Premium v2 App Service plan. Cloud consumers who want to make sure that they can use the feature with a Standard App Service plan should create the app in a Premium v3 App Service plan, and only the newest deployments support that plan. You can scale down a plan after it has been created.

- In an App Service environment, isolated plans cannot use the feature.

- With classic virtual networks, you can't access resources through peering connections.

- Azure Resource Manager virtual networks must have an unused IPv4 /28 block or larger subnet to use this feature.

- There must be a shared virtual network between the app and the virtual network.

- Integration virtual networks cannot be configured with IPv6 address spaces.

- Integration subnets cannot be configured with service endpoint policies.

- Each App Service plan can use only one integration subnet.

- Integrated apps cannot delete virtual networks in the cloud. Ensure the integration is removed before you delete the virtual network.

- Each App Service plan can only have one integration for a regional virtual network, and multiple apps can share the same virtual network.

- While an app uses regional virtual network integration, cloud subscribers cannot change their subscription.

Azure VNet regional integration is available in two different variations in Azure App Service:

- All pricing plans, except Isolated, are supported on the multi-tenant systems.
- Isolated pricing plans are supported by the App Service Environment (ASE), which deploys into the VNet.

The Azure App Service Environment (ASE) is one of the Premium features of the Azure App Service. It provides network isolation and improved scaling capabilities by delivering a single-tenant Azure App Service instance within your own VNet.

Configure Azure Kubernetes Service (AKS) for Regional VNet Integration

Kubernetes is an open source platform for managing, automating deployment, scaling, and running containerized applications. It consists of a master, a group of worker nodes, and namespaces. A namespace is a mechanism for partitioning resources into logically named groups. Figure 10.11 is an overview of Kubernetes.

FIGURE 10.11   Kubernetes overview

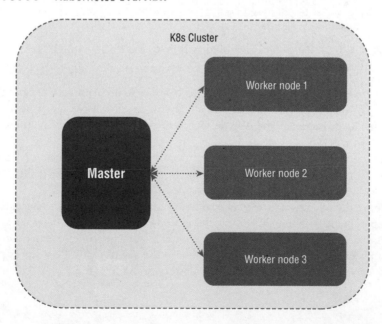

The following are key terms used in Kubernetes.

Container   An executable image containing software and its dependencies that is lightweight and portable.

Container Runtime   Container runtimes are software that run containers.

Docker   The Docker Engine (also known as Docker) is a software technology that provides operating system-level virtualization.

Pod   The simplest and smallest Kubernetes object. Pods represent containers running on your cluster.

Cluster   Containerized applications run on worker machines called nodes. Worker nodes are present in every cluster.

Namespace   Within a Kubernetes cluster, an abstraction supports the isolation of groups of resources.

Service   An abstract way of exposing a set of Pods running an application as a network service.

Node   Kubernetes nodes are machines that perform work.

kube-controller-manager   Runs controller processes from the control plane.

kube-proxy   Each node in your cluster runs Kube-proxy, which is part of the Kubernetes Service concept.

Kubectl   An API-based command-line tool for communicating with Kubernetes clusters.

Kubelet   Cluster node agents run on each node. Pods are used to run containers.

Kubernetes API   Kubernetes functionality is provided through a RESTful API, and a cluster state is stored.

As you learned in the previous section of this chapter, Azure App Services have a feature called regional VNet integration, which will allow you to join a VNet. As long as your VNet is located in the same region as the App Service, Azure Kubernetes Service (AKS) for regional VNet integration will work.

Kubernetes clusters can be directly accessed from your App Service using AKS. Customers no longer must make Kubernetes services available to the public Internet if they don't want to.

By offloading the operational overhead to Azure, the *Azure Kubernetes Service (AKS)* simplifies the deployment of managed Kubernetes clusters. Azure hosts Kubernetes and handles critical tasks, such as health monitoring and maintenance. Due to Azure's management of Kubernetes masters, you only manage and maintain the agent nodes. Customers pay only for the agent nodes within their clusters, not the masters, so AKS is free.

AKS cluster deployment involves deploying and configuring the Kubernetes master and all nodes. Advanced networking, Azure Active Directory integration, monitoring, and other features can be configured during the deployment process.

Cloud users define virtual networks and subnets in many environments and assign IP address ranges. Users can deploy multiple applications and services on these virtual networks. Kubenet (basic networking) or Azure Container Networking Interface (CNI) advanced networking can be used for network connectivity by AKS clusters.

Kubenet assigns an IP address to its nodes only. Pods cannot directly communicate. Instead, connectivity between pods between nodes is handled by UDR and IP forwarding.

Typically, UDRs and IP forwarding configurations are created and maintained by the AKS service. However, you can use your own route table for custom route management. Pods could also be deployed behind a service that receives a specific IP address and balances traffic for the application.

Azure *Container Networking Interface (CNI)* provides each pod with an IP address from the subnet and allows direct access. IP addresses must be unique across network space. The number of pods that a node supports is configured in its configuration parameter, and the equivalent number of IP addresses for each node is reserved up front. When application demands grow, this approach requires more planning and often results in IP address exhaustion or the need to re-create clusters in a larger subnet.

The following are design and deployment limitations and considerations for Kubenet:

- In the design of Kubenet, there is an additional hop, which adds minor latency to pod communication.

- Using Kubenet requires route tables and UDRs, adding complexity to operations.

- Due to the design of Kubenet, direct pod addressing is not supported.

- Additionally, Kubenet clusters cannot share a subnet as Azure CNI clusters.

- Kubenet supports Calico network policies, but Azure network policies, pools of Windows nodes, and the virtual nodes add-on are not supported.

AKS clusters typically use a network plug-in balancing flexibility and advanced configuration requirements. Considerations that help identify when each network model may be the best choice are outlined here. Kubenet should be used when:

- You have limited IP address space.

- Pods communicate mostly within clusters.

- Consumers of cloud services do not require advanced AKS features like virtual nodes or Azure network policies.

Azure CNI can be used when:

- IP addresses are available.

- Pods communicate mostly with resources outside the cluster.

- You don't want to manage routes defined by users.

- AKS advanced features, such as virtual nodes or Azure network policies, are needed.

The following AKS VNet integration limitations should be taken into consideration:

- The Azure Kubernetes service is an entirely different service than Azure App Services. Microsoft manages a portion of the platform, even though it is considered a platform as a service (PaaS). With infrastructure as a service (IaaS), you have greater control over the environment than with Azure App Service. In addition, it gives you more networking integration capabilities.

- You should begin by defining the resources you will use when you deploy an Azure Kubernetes cluster.

- Depending on the networking model, the virtual network can either be manually configured or automatically created.

- A load balancer is necessary to support scalability in the AKS solution. Azure Kubernetes recommends clusters of three VMs at a minimum, so the load balancer must be present at that level for Kubernetes to function, let alone support applications in the cloud.

- A network security group must be applied to the subnets in which the cluster is placed to prevent traffic that should not be flowing.

In Azure Kubernetes, VMs serve as nodes for the Azure Kubernetes cluster. You may use VM scale sets for scaling your Kubernetes cluster if you know your user base will grow and shrink over time and you want to take advantage of that fact, if you provide any scale for your Kubernetes cluster.

Azure supports two networking models. Kubenet, the default Kubernetes deployment model, is used by most customers. A cloud consumer who deploys Kubernetes on-premises or in another cloud service provider achieves the following:

- Preserves IP address space.

- For reaching pods, Kubernetes uses an internal and external load balancer.

- UDRs can be manually maintained by the user.

- Provides for a maximum of 400 nodes per cluster.

The Azure CNI adds IP addresses to the pods and nodes of the second deployment networking model supported by Microsoft. Thus, you must provide exceptionally well-defined network IP addresses before implementing a cluster, depending on how many nodes you believe will be deployed within your cluster and how many pods will reside in each node.

In this model, the pods are connected to a virtual network and are directly reachable over their private IP addresses from other networks. This requires a much larger number of IP addresses, which requires a lot more planning.

You can automatically configure VNet resources in both networking models as per your preferences. They both support manual creation and the attachment of VNet resources.

You can create a VNet automatically via the Azure portal if you select Kubenet as your networking deployment model. The Azure portal does not allow you to attach Kubernetes to an existing VNet. You have greater control if you need to perform operations via the CLI or PowerShell. The Azure CNI, by default, will allow manual creation and attachment.

Azure Kubernetes service's network policies can be defined, and they can be changed in either model. In manual VNet resource creation, routes and service endpoint configurations can be defined, whereas automatic VNet resource creation does not allow such configurations. Go through the wizard for Kubenet; when the VNet is created, UDRs will be automatically configured to enable Kubernetes.

Azure CNI users only know the requirements for a UDR when their IP addresses are attached to their pods.

Table 10.6 illustrates the differences in behavior between Kubenet and Azure CNI.

TABLE 10.6   Kubenet versus Azure CNI

Capabilities	Kubenet	CNI
Deploy cluster in new or choose existing VNet	Yes, works; UDRs manually applied	Yes, works
Pod-pod network connectivity	Yes, works	Yes, works
Pod-VM connectivity; VM in the VNet	Yes, works when initiated by pod	Yes, works in both ways
Pod-VM connectivity; VM in peered VNet	Yes, works when initiated by pod	Yes, works in both ways
On-premises access using VPN or ExpressRoute	Yes, works when initiated by pod	Yes, works in both ways
Access to Azure resources; protected by service endpoints	Yes, works	Yes, works
External Kubernetes services using a load-balancer service, App Gateway, or ingress controller	Yes	Yes
Default Private Zones and Azure DNS	Yes	Yes
Windows node pools	No	Yes

Kubernetes provides a virtual networking abstraction layer to access applications or between application components. The Kubernetes nodes are connected to a virtual network that provides connectivity for pods inbound and outbound. To deliver these features, the Kube-proxy component runs on each node.

AKS clusters can also be virtualized on the Azure platform. You can create and configure Azure Load Balancer resources when you create a Kubernetes. The corresponding Azure NSG rules are configured as you open network ports to pods. As new ingress routes are configured, Azure can also configure external DNS for HTTP application routing.

Kubernetes Services, offered by Azure, allow you to deploy a cluster that uses both Kubenet and Azure Container Networking Interface (CNI) networking.

- The AKS cluster's network resources are created during deployment using Kubenet.
- AKS Clusters are connected to existing virtual network resources and configurations using Azure CNI.

Configure Clients to Access the App Service Environment

Azure *App Service* hosts web applications, REST APIs, and mobile apps over HTTP. Customers can choose from .NET, .NET Core, Java, Ruby, Node.js, PHP, or Python to develop in the cloud. They can run applications on Windows or Linux.

Azure App Service provides developers with a fully managed PaaS. Among App Service's key features are:

- Multiple languages and frameworks
- Managed production environment
- Containerization
- Docker
- Security and compliance
- Connections to SaaS platforms and on-premises data
- Global scale with high availability
- Visual Studio and Visual Studio Code integration
- Serverless programming

The App Service Environment (ASE) feature of the Azure App Service provides a secure, highly scalable, isolated, and dedicated environment to run App Service apps. An ASE can host apps such as Windows web apps, Linux web apps, Docker containers (Windows and Linux), Functions, and Logic apps (Standard). ASEs are suitable for applications requiring large-scale isolation, secure network access, high memory utilization, and high requests per second (RPS). A single Azure region or multiple Azure regions can be used to create various ASEs. As a result, an ASE is ideal for horizontally scaling stateless applications with high RPS requirements.

ASEs can host one customer's applications on one of their virtual networks. The customer can fine-tune inbound and outbound application traffic. Through VPN connections, applications can access on-premises corporate resources with high speed and security.

ASEs have numerous use cases, including internal line-of-business applications, applications requiring more than 30 instances, single-tenant applications for compliance or security reasons, network-isolated applications, and multi-tier applications. In a multi-tenant App Service, many networking features allow apps to reach network-isolated resources or become network-isolated themselves. App-level networking can be enabled using these features. ASEs do not require any additional configuration for apps to be on a virtual network. Apps are deployed into an isolated network environment on a virtual network. ASEs are single-tenant Azure App Service deployments that run on virtual networks.

App service plans are created in ASEs, where they serve as provisioning profiles for hosting applications. Scaling App Service plans results in more application hosts running all the apps on each host. Combined, all App Service plans result in 200 App Service plan instances per v3 App Service Environment. No limit applies to the number of App Service Isolated v2 (Iv2) plans.

When you deploy to dedicated hardware (hosts), they are limited in scaling across all App Service plans to the number of cores in this environment. ASEs deployed on dedicated hosts have 132 virtual cores. Each instance of I1v2 has two vCores, I2v2 has four vCores, and I3v2 has eight vCores.

ASE deploys Azure App Service into a single subnet on a virtual network. You deploy apps into an ASE, where they are exposed to the inbound address assigned to the environment. The inbound address for all apps deployed in an ASE will be the address of the ASE subnet if it is deployed with an internal virtual IP address (VIP). An external VIP address is assigned to the ASE. The app will use a public Domain Name System (DNS) in that case, and the inbound address will be Internet addressable.

The number of instances and traffic in an ASE will vary based on the number of addresses it uses in its subnet. Some infrastructure roles are automatically scaled based on the number of App Service plans and the load. CIDR blocks with 256 addresses are recommended for App Service Environment v3. An ASE v3 can be scaled to its maximum with that size.

No features need to be enabled for apps in an ASE to access resources within the same virtual network. The apps in the ASE can access resources in the extended networks if the ASE virtual network is connected to another network. The users can control the traffic in the network.

App Service multi-tenant allows apps to connect to various networks with numerous features. Apps can act as though they are running on a virtual network if they have these networking features. The virtual network doesn't require any additional configuration for an ASE v3.

An advantage of using an ASE instead of a multi-tenant service is that any network access controls for apps hosted in the ASE are external to the application configuration. Users of the multi-tenant service must enable each app's features individually and use role-based access control or a policy to prevent any configuration changes.

ASEs can either be Internet-facing using a public IP address or internally facing by only using an Azure internal load balancer (ILB) address.

The NSG restricts inbound network communications to ASEs on that subnet. NSGs enable you to run apps behind upstream devices and services such as WAFs and network SaaS providers.

Furthermore, corporate resources such as internal databases and web services are often accessed by apps. You can access on-premises resources through the ASE if the ASE is deployed in a virtual network with a VPN connection to the on-premises network. Any site-to-site or Azure ExpressRoute VPN can provide this capability.

Microsoft will manage App Service, a PaaS service with all of the same features and capabilities that a standard App Service has. Isolated Tier App Plans, however, are deployed. Because of this, Microsoft will ask for a virtual network that it can be placed into, and it exists only within that virtual network.

The App Service still offers all of its other features and capabilities. It will exist within the virtual network rather than having an IP address and a name. Microsoft will assign it a CNAME, but it will be accessible only from within the virtual network until you decide otherwise.

Besides internal endpoints, the virtual network can have external endpoints. Use an appliance such as a virtual network appliance, use Azure Application Gateway, or set up a public endpoint allowing inbound and outbound traffic.

ASEs allow traffic to be initiated in both directions. Internal services, as well as ASEs, can communicate with one another.

From a client access perspective, end users will access the ASE in the same way they used to do with any IaaS-based solution. For example, you can allow for port forwarding from a jump box or Azure Bastion.

You can direct traffic through an internal or external load balancer. Default App Services are equipped with a load balancer to facilitate scalability. Microsoft can provide different CNAMEs for different solutions, and you can decide whether the load balancer should have a Private Endpoint or a public endpoint.

You can route traffic going into and out of the App Service using UDRs. As a result, you can force traffic to go through an intrusion detection/prevention device or a web application firewall.

Many cloud customers have created App Services over the years to reduce administration overhead and allow their internal users on their internal networks on-premises to access the

App Services through ExpressRoute. Therefore, you have several different options for accessing the App Service, but the most important thing is still in App Service. The network has just been isolated, and it is secured like an IaaS model.

 As a Premium service option of Azure App Service, App Service Environments (ASEs) provide enhanced configuration capabilities that are not available with the multi-tenant stamps. The ASE feature deploys the Azure App Service into the virtual network of a customer.

Compute resources in an ASE are distributed between the front-end and the worker pool. Front-ends serve as HTTP/HTTPS endpoints and transmit data to workers, which host applications.

No features need to be enabled for apps in an App Service Environment to access resources within the same virtual network. The apps in the ASE can access resources in the extended networks if the ASE virtual network is connected to another network. A user can block network traffic.

Summary

This chapter covered designing and deploying private access to Azure Services. Now you understand how to create solutions that enable private access to Azure services. You can plan, build, configure, and create access to Private Endpoints.

You also learned how to integrate a Private Link with DNS and on-premises clients. We showed you how to create, configure, and provide access to service endpoints, and we described the method for configuring VNet integration for App Services.

Exam Essentials

Know how to create a Private Link service.   You can build your own service using Azure Private Link. Private Link access can be enabled for your service running behind Azure Standard Load Balancer so that you can access it privately from within your own VNets.

Understand how to plan Private Endpoints.   A Private Endpoint is a network interface on your virtual network using a private IP address. An Azure Private Link–powered service is brought into your virtual network by enabling a Private Endpoint through this network interface.

Through Private Endpoints, customers can connect from the same virtual network, regionally peer-to-peer virtual networks, globally peer-to-peer virtual networks, on-premises VPNs, and Private Link–based services.

Understand how to integrate Private Link with DNS.   The public DNS creates a CNAME record for the canonical name. Resolving the private domain name is done with the help of the CNAME record. Private endpoints can be overridden with their private IP addresses.

The connection URL does not need to be changed in your applications. If you resolve to a public DNS service, your Private Endpoints will be resolved. Thanks to this process, you won't need to make any changes to your existing applications.

Understand how to create service endpoints.   Over an optimized route over the Azure backbone network, VNet service endpoints provide secure and direct connectivity to Azure services. Using endpoints, your Azure service resources can be secured to only your virtual networks. By using service endpoints, private IP addresses in the VNet can access Azure services without needing a public IP address.

Know how to configure service endpoint policies.   Endpoint policies for VNets enable you to filter outbound virtual network traffic to Azure Storage accounts and allow data exfiltration only to specific Azure Storage accounts. When connected over a service endpoint to Azure Storage, virtual network traffic can be controlled through endpoint policies.

Know how to configure service tags.   In Azure, service tags represent groups of IP address prefixes. By managing the prefixes covered by the service tag, Microsoft minimizes the complexity of updating network security rules frequently as addresses change.

Know how to configure App Service for regional VNet integration.   Azure virtual networks let you place many Azure resources in a network that isn't Internet-routable. With the App Service, you can integrate your apps with virtual networks and access resources through them. Virtual network integration does not allow private access to your apps.

In addition to Basic, Standard, and Premium tiers, there are Premium v2 and Premium v3. Isolated and Isolated v2 pricing tiers are available for App Service Environments deployed directly into your virtual network.

Know how to configure Azure Kubernetes Service (AKS) for regional VNet integration. Compared to Azure App Services, Azure Kubernetes is a very different beast. Microsoft manages only a portion of platform as a service, despite it being termed a platform as a service. Unlike Azure App Services, it is deployed as infrastructure as a service, giving you greater control over the environment. In addition, it gives you a greater level of networking integration.

Know how to configure clients to access App Service Environment.   Using Azure App Service Environment v2, you can run an App Service application securely on a large scale in an isolated and dedicated environment. A Windows web application, a Linux web application, a Docker container, a mobile app, or a function can be hosted by this capability.

There is no limit to the number of ASEs customers can create within or across Azure regions. As a result of this flexibility, ASEs are ideal for horizontally scaling stateless application tiers that support high requests per second (RPS).

Review Questions

1. Microsoft Partner services and PaaS services in Azure can be accessed privately from Azure virtual networks using which of the following?

    A. ER

    B. Private Link

    C. S2S

    D. P2S

2. Which key network interface technology is behind Azure Private Link that allows virtual networks and an Azure service to establish a private and secure connection?

    A. Azure Private Endpoint

    B. Azure Private Link service

    C. Microsoft Backbone

    D. ExpressRoute

3. You want to offer a custom Azure resource privately. The Azure network requirement is to provide access to an Azure resource without using the public Internet. Which of the following helps achieve the need?

    A. Azure Private Link

    B. Azure Private Endpoint

    C. Private Link service

    D. All the above

4. A company might want to ensure that its Azure virtual network clients have secure access to a particular Azure resource. In this scenario, which of the following technologies should be added to the virtual network?

    A. Azure Private Link

    B. Azure Private Endpoint

    C. Private Link service

    D. All the above

5. An Azure virtual network enables a company to provide private access to Azure resources. How does Azure Private Endpoint offer private access to Azure resources?

    A. By using an IP address from a subnet of an Azure virtual network.

    B. Azure provides a private IP address.

    C. Private peering with Azure ExpressRoute is possible.

    D. All the above.

6. Assume a company wants to provide Azure Private Link service with access to custom Azure services. Which of the following technologies is a requirement for implementing Private Link service?

   A. Azure Basic Load Balancer

   B. Azure Standard Load Balancer

   C. Azure Application Gateway

   D. Azure Front Door

7. How do service endpoints and Private Endpoints differ?

   A. An endpoint is a system or service that connects to another system or service.

   B. External systems and services are connected to a Private Endpoint.

   C. Virtual network can be connected to Azure privately and securely by using a service endpoint.

   D. All of the above.

8. Which of the following is true?

   A. Subscriptions from Private Link resources must be registered with Microsoft.

   B. Subscriptions from Private Link resources should not be registered with Microsoft.

   C. Subscriptions from Private Link resources should be registered with the on-premises network.

   D. Subscriptions from Private Link resources should not be registered with the cloud carrier.

9. Which resource associated with a Private Endpoint contains information about configuring a Private Endpoint DNS?

   A. Azure virtual network

   B. The network interface

   C. The private DNS Zone

   D. Azure Active Directory

10. What is the importance of IP address 168.63.129.16?

    A. The IP address 168.63.129.16 is a nonvirtual (Classic) public IP address that facilitates communication with Azure platform resources.

    B. Azure platform resources can be accessed through 168.63.129.16, a public IP address.

    C. The static address 168.63.129.16 belongs to a DNS forwarder.

    D. Azure platform resources can be accessed via 168.63.129.16, a public virtual IP address.

11. What kind of access to Azure services is enabled when you integrate Azure services into an Azure virtual network?

    A. Private access

    B. Remote access

    C. Public access

    D. None of the above

12. From a regional VNet integration perspective, which of the following methods let you enable access to the application?

   A. A VNet in the same region as the application

   B. VNet resources that are peering with the VNet application

   C. Secured services at endpoints

   D. All of the above

13. What can you use to send all outbound traffic to an ExpressRoute gateway?

   A. Route table

   B. ExpressRoute

   C. Azure Firewall

   D. All of the above

14. What can you use to block inbound and outbound traffic to resources in a VNet?

   A. Route table

   B. ExpressRoute

   C. Network security group

   D. All the above

15. Which of the following is true?

   A. Regional VNet integration enables you to reach Azure services that are insecure with service endpoints.

   B. Regional VNet integration enables you to reach secure Azure services with service endpoints.

   C. Regional VNet integration does not allow you to reach secure Azure services with service endpoints.

   D. Regional VNet Integration allows you to reach open Internet Azure services with service endpoints.

16. Business apps won't work with Azure DNS private zones by default. To make them work with Azure DNS private zones, which of the following need to be added to the app settings?

   A. `WEBSITE_DNS_SERVER` with value `168.63.126.16` and `WEBSITE_VNET_ROUTE_ALL` with value 1

   B. `WEBSITE_DNS_SERVER` with value `168.63.127.16` and `WEBSITE_VNET_ROUTE_ALL` with value 1

   C. `WEBSITE_DNS_SERVER` with value `168.63.128.16` and `WEBSITE_VNET_ROUTE_ALL` with value 1

   D. `WEBSITE_DNS_SERVER` with value `168.63.129.16` and `WEBSITE_VNET_ROUTE_ALL` with value 1

17. Which of the following is true?

    A. User-defined routing (UDR) and IP forwarding are used for connectivity between pods across nodes in AKS services.

    B. Azure Route Server and IP filtering are used for connectivity between pods across nodes in AKS services.

    C. Route tables and IP filtering are used for connectivity between pods across nodes in AKS services.

    D. Route tables and IP forwarding are used for connectivity between pods across nodes in AKS services.

18. Which of the following can use Kubenet basic networking or Azure CNI advanced networking?

    A. Azure virtual machine

    B. Azure Virtual Desktop

    C. Azure Function

    D. Azure Kubernetes Services

19. Which of the following statements about networking deployment models is true?

    A. Azure AKS networking deployment of Kubenet does offer advanced AKS features such as virtual nodes or Azure network policy.

    B. Azure AKS networking deployment of Kubenet does not offer advanced AKS features such as virtual nodes or Azure network policy.

    C. Azure AKS networking deployment of Azure CNI does offer basic AKS features such as pod communication outside the cluster.

    D. Azure AKS networking deployment of Azure CNI does offer basic AKS features such as unlimited IP.

20. Which of the following is true?

    A. Azure App Service is a fully managed IaaS.

    B. Azure App Service is a fully managed PaaS.

    C. Azure App Service is a fully managed SaaS.

    D. Azure App Service is a fully managed DaaS.

Appendix

Answers to Review Questions

Chapter 1: Getting Started with AZ-700 Certification for Azure Networking

1.   A, B, C. Report as a service is not provided.

2.   A. The private cloud infrastructure is provisioned for exclusive use by a single organization comprising multiple consumers (e.g., business units). It may be owned, managed, and operated by the organization, a third party, or some combination of them, and it may exist on- or off-premises.

3.   C. The community cloud infrastructure is provisioned for exclusive use by a specific community of consumers from organizations that have shared concerns (e.g., mission, security requirements, policy, and compliance considerations). It may be owned, managed, and operated by one or more of the organizations in the community, a third party, or some combination of them, and it may exist on- or off-premises.

4.   B. The public cloud infrastructure is provisioned for open use by the general public. It may be owned, managed, and operated by a business, academic organization, a government organization, or some combination. It exists on the premises of the cloud provider.

5.   A. Azure Firewall protects your Azure virtual network resources by providing managed, cloud-based network security. You can create, enforce, and log policies across subscriptions and virtual networks by using Azure Firewall.

6.   B. IoT modules within the Azure network provide capabilities to connect to Internet devices.

7.   B. By using Azure Peering, customers can connect to Microsoft cloud services such as Microsoft 365, Dynamics 365, SaaS services, Azure, and any other Microsoft service accessible on the Internet.

8.   A. Azure Zonal Services provide several features, including provisioning VMs and disk management capabilities.

9.   B. Subscriptions to Azure doesn't require any approval from Microsoft; they are self-service capabilities that are to be enabled through the Internet and don't require complex contracting procedures as well.

10. C. Azure management groups can support up to 6 levels.

11. C. A subnet is a logical subdivision of an IP network that can be either public or private based on enterprise needs.

12. A. A web application firewall can protect application resources from SQL injection.

13. A, B, D, E. Azure Networking Services are broadly classified as connectivity services, application protection services, application delivery services, and network monitoring services, including:

Connectivity Services   Virtual Network, ExpressRoute, VPN Gateway, Virtual WAN, Azure DNS, Azure Bastion, Virtual Network NAT Gateway, Azure Peering Service

Application Protection Services   DDoS Protection, Azure Private Link, Azure Firewall, Web Application Firewall, Network security groups, service endpoints

Application Delivery Services   Content Delivery Network, Azure Front Door Service, Traffic Manager, Load Balancer, Application Gateway

Network Monitoring Services   Network Watcher, Azure Monitor Network Insights, ExpressRoute Monitor, Azure Monitor

14. B. VNet Peering is one of the methods by which Azure communicates securely with its resources.

15. A, C. ExpressRoute only allows traffic between on-premises and the Azure Cloud; no other public traffic is allowed between them.

WAN optimization cannot be achieved through routing tables; this requires various other techniques to be followed such as deduplication, compression data packets, latency optimization, caching/proxy, forward error correction, spoofing, and traffic shaping.

16. A. Azure subscriptions and regions can span across multiple virtual networks.

17. A,B. Azure follows standards for network address and default gateways to follow the patterns shown in A and B.

18. A. Azure resources can be added only to one resource group but they are optional when creating subnets. Tags can be added to an Azure subnet to identify them easily and report on them. Firewall is allowed to be chosen by the user; it is neither disabled or enabled when creating an Azure VNet.

19. A. A NAT system can provide up to 64,000 concurrent flows for UDP and TCP, respectively, for each attached public IP address, by using port network address translation (PNAT or PAT).

20. B. NAT can support 16 public IP addresses.

Chapter 2: Design, Deploy, and Manage a Site-to-Site VPN Connection and Point-to-Site VPN Connection

1. A. IP addresses assigned to Basic SKUs can be assigned statically or dynamically.

2. A, C. The Azure virtual private network can be route-based or policy-based.

3. E. Key design elements are network throughput (either Mbps or Gbps), network backbone (either Internet or private), the Azure VPN gateway SKU, VPN device compatibility, VPN gateway type, method of routing (either route-based or BGP) and network connection resiliency pattern (either active/passive or active/active).

4. A, D. Site-to-site supports both active/active and active/passive, whereas point-to-site and ExpressRoute supports only the active/passive disaster recovery pattern.

5. A. Dynamic routing is route-based and is supported only in Site-to-site VPN configuration.

6. B. Point-to-site and ExpressRoute support various network protocols for tunneling such as SSTP, IPSec/IKEv2, OpenVPN, MPLS, and VPLS; however, site-to-site supports only IPsec.

7. D. ExpressRoute supports various peering services and configurations, including private peering, Azure peering (but not CDN, Azure Front Door, Azure Virtual Desktop, MFA, Logical Apps, or Traffic Manager), public peering, point-to-site, and site-to-site.

8. D. Static routing is supported only by site-to-site VPN configuration. Only ExpressRoute supports BGP for routing, and it also supports active/passive DR configuration like point-to-site VPN configuration.

9. B. VPN gateways can support both static routing and dynamic routing. Static routing is policy-based and dynamic routing is route-based.

10. C. Only one site-to-site connection can be supported by policy-based VPN gateways, unlike route-based VPN gateways, which can support multiple connections, up to 30.

11. D. Policy-based VPN devices support only the IKE v1 protocol.

12. A. 1 GB per tunnel is the maximum limit set for site-to-site VPN connections.

13. A, D. The number of applications that transact through the tunnel or data transfer speeds are not accounted for when calculating the VPN gateway cost. Organizations consuming Azure VPN gateways pay for two items: one is the hourly compute costs for the virtual network gateway, and another one is the egress data transfer from the virtual network gateway. Data transfer prices are determined based on egress traffic from the origin virtual network gateway with varying scenarios.

14. A, B, D. Route-based VPN gateways are not classified by high performance.

15. D. Building a VPN gateway should be the first step before creating your VNet, which should be followed by VPN client setup to complete the point-to-site configuration.

16. A. Two active/standby instances are used for every Azure VPN gateway.

17. D. Azure users can connect with their organization's domain credentials using AD Domain authentication. The RADIUS server must be integrated with AD.

18. E. A point-to-site VPN connection allows all the types of authentication mechanisms listed.

19. F. To resolve a point-to-site VPN client-side issue, you must check certificates and configuration files; verify that the client OS is compatible; verify that proper NIC drivers exist in the client OS; verify that local firewall policies and the execution of apps are not blocked; check that specific client hibernate or sleep time is configured after a specified or sufficient time; ensure that you have Internet access, valid client credentials, and a resolvable DNS server, and that you can reach the VPN server and that it is responding. With macOS, make sure it is using Mac OS X using the native VPN client and IKEv2.

20. A, B, C, D. OpenVPN (SSL) and SSTP (SSL) tunneling cannot be combined, and they are exclusive tunneling types. IKEv2 can be an independent tunnel option.

Chapter 3: Design, Deploy, and Manage Azure ExpressRoute

1. A. ExpressRoute is the most preferred method to connect between on-premises and Azure networks. It allows you to create private connections between Azure datacenters, Azure services, and infrastructure on your premises securely and reliably.

2. C. ExpressRoute Premium allows you to extend connectivity across geographic boundaries for global connectivity over the Microsoft core network. An ExpressRoute circuit can be connected to a VNet in a different geopolitical region.

3. E. All of these bandwidth options are available when choosing to connect via ExpressRoute.

4. D. Microsoft 365 services are available through the Internet, and you can also connect to Azure PaaS services from Microsoft 365 services through peering. Azure PaaS services and Microsoft 365 services are connected by Microsoft peering. The Microsoft peering routing domain allows bidirectional connectivity between an organization's WANs and Microsoft cloud services. Organizations must use public IP addresses owned or controlled by their connectivity providers to access Microsoft cloud services. They should also adhere to all cloud service regulations.

5. A, B, C. Direct Connect offers customers a direct connection to the Microsoft global network through peering locations around the world. Dual 100 Gbps connectivity is provided by ExpressRoute Direct, which supports active/active connections. Organizations can also take advantage of the ExpressRoute direct service through a service provider. It is established for data ingestion for a large volume of data transfer during migration, for regulated industries that need more bandwidth, or for any customer requiring more bandwidth than usual.

6. B. A maximum of 10,000 prefixes are allowed in Azure private peering.

7. B. Microsoft 365 and PaaS services are distinct services that are applicable for varied contexts. Through Microsoft peering, Microsoft public services such as Microsoft 365, Dynamics 365, and PaaS services are accessed.

8. D. ExpressRoute supports both BGP and active-passive DR; only point-to-site VPN supports static routing.

9. D. All of these billing models are supported by Azure ExpressRoute.

10. C. You can connect your Microsoft resources using ExpressRoute through a carrier-grade, private network. As a result, the ExpressRoute path within Microsoft's network has no single point of failure and provides high availabitiy and disaster recovery.

11. C. A route filter provides access to a subset of supported Microsoft peering services.

12. D. IPv4 is supported by all peering types, but IPv6 is not supported by Azure private peering.

13. A. Azure private peering supports a maximum of 4,000 prefixes by default. It supports 10,000 with ExpressRoute Premium.

14. A. Azure private peering can support any valid IP address within an organization's WAN. Azure public peering and Microsoft peering require public IP addresses owned by the organization or their own connectivity providers.

15. E. The maximum number of circuit connections supported by the UltraPerformance gateway SKU (ErGw3Az/UltraPerformance SKU) is 16.

16. B. Circuits established by third-party network service providers can provide a maximum speed of 50 Mbps to 10 Gbps.

17. C. For organizations to use FastPath, the virtual network gateway must be either UltraPerformance or ErGw3AZ.

18. A. Through FastPath, network traffic is sent directly to virtual machines within the virtual network, bypassing the gateway.

19. A, C. When designing ExpressRoute connectivity for disaster recovery, the following critical Microsoft recommended best practices need to be applied:

- Apply geo-redundant ExpressRoute circuits.
- Apply diverse service provider network(s) for different ExpressRoute circuits.
- Develop each of the ExpressRoute circuits with high availability.
- Terminate the different ExpressRoute circuits in different locations on your organization's network.

20. A. An ExpressRoute circuit, once set up, allows you to access services within a virtual network and other Azure services simultaneously. It is essential to have an existing Azure account to access Azure ExpressRoute.

Chapter 4: Design and Deploy Core Networking Infrastructure: Private IP and DNS

1. D. The default limit per virtual network is 3,000 subnets, but that can be scaled up to 10,000 with Microsoft support.

2. A. Per Microsoft, you will not be able to ping default routers within a VNet.

3. C. Azure VNet does not support multicast or broadcast.

4. D. VMs, the App Service Environment, the Azure Kubernetes Service, and virtual machine scale sets can all be connected via Azure VNets. Additionally, service endpoints can be used to connect to other Azure resource types, such as Azure SQL databases and storage accounts.

5. A. Internet resources can communicate inbound to Azure resources using public IP addresses. An IP address is assigned based on the location of the resource.

6. A. Azure public IP addresses for Basic SKUs can be allocated statically or dynamically.

7. C. You can connect different VNets seamlessly through virtual network peering, regardless of where they are located (VNet peering) or what region they are located in (Global VNet peering).

8. A. Azure Firewall is a cloud-native security service that protects cloud consumer workloads from threats using a well-designed intelligent firewall. With Azure Application Gateway, cloud consumers can manage cloud consumer web applications using a web traffic load balancer. In a virtual network, a Private Endpoint is an interface using a private IP address. Azure Private Link provides you with a secure and private connection to the service.

9. A, B, C. A virtual network uses private IP addresses for communication. There are three types of resources that can have IP addresses assigned to them in Azure virtual networks: virtual machine network interfaces, load balancers, and application gateways.

10. A. One thousand private DNS zones are the maximum configuration per subscription.

11. A. Private DNS zones in Azure or Azure-provided name resolution are best for this scenario. The DNS suffix should be the hostname or the fully qualified domain name.

12. B. Private DNS zones in Azure or a cloud consumer managed DNS server are best for this scenario. The DNS suffix should be a fully qualified domain name.

13. A, B, C. Azure DNS private zones provide name resolution within and between virtual networks. They support resolution across virtual networks, resolution scoped to a single virtual network, and split-horizon functionality.

14. B. One thousand per second is the maximum number of requests that can be sent to an Azure DNS resolver from a virtual machine.

15. A. A maximum of 1,000 private DNS zones can be linked to a virtual network.

16. A. Private DNS from Azure provides a secure and reliable DNS service for your virtual network. Use Azure Private DNS to manage and resolve domain names in the virtual network without configuring a custom DNS server.

17. B. 168.63.129.16 is the Azure DNS IP address. This is a fixed IP address that will not change.

18. A. Azure creates a DNS canonical name record (CNAME) on the public DNS. The resolution is then redirected to the private domain. Your private IP address can override the resolution.

19. B. It is not possible to modify the DNS suffix created by Azure-provided name resolution because it is fully managed by Microsoft.

20. D. Private DNS zones in Azure, Azure-provided name resolution, and the organization's managed DNS server are the methods that can be used by resources deployed in virtual networks to resolve domain names to internal IP addresses.

Chapter 5: Design and Deploy Core Networking Infrastructure and Virtual WANs

1. A, D. VPNs fall into two categories: policy-based and route-based.

Policy-based VPNs encrypt packets and route them through IPsec tunnels based on the IPsec policies configured between an on-premises network and the Azure VNet.

In a route-based VPN, packets are routed into tunnel interfaces using "routes" in the IP forwarding table.

2. D. Every Azure VPN gateway consists of two instances in an VPN Gateway redundancy (active-standby) configuration. This results in improved connection availability.

3. A, D. You must consider several factors during the planning process. These include throughput in Mbps or Gbps, the backbone being Internet or private, the availability of a public IP address (static), VPN device compatibility, multiple client connections, or a site-to-site link, VPN gateway type, and Azure VPN Gateway SKU.

4. C. The number of IP addresses that the gateway subnet contains should be specified when you create the subnet. A gateway subnet has IP addresses assigned to gateway virtual machines and gateway services, and different configurations require different numbers of IP addresses.

5. A. Peer-to-peer transitive routing is currently unavailable in Azure virtual networking but can be enabled with a virtual network appliance and custom routing rules.

6. B. An individual client can connect to your virtual network using a point-to-site (P2S) VPN gateway. The computer connecting to the VPN must start the P2S connection first. Telecommuters can use this method.

7. B. The VPN protocol is based on SSL/TLS and OpenVPN. Because most firewalls open TCP port 443 outbound, TLS uses a TLS VPN solution can penetrate firewalls. Mobile devices (Android, iOS, and Windows) and Mac computers (macOS 10.13 and later) can connect to OpenVPN using OpenVPN.

8. A. Organizations can connect virtual networks and can be in different regions and from different subscriptions. Organizations can connect VNets from different subscriptions, and the subscriptions don't need to be associated with the same Active Directory tenant.

9. D. Azure solutions can be deployed and managed using Resource Manager and classic deployment models.

10. A. Azure Virtual WAN is a fully managed service and supported by Microsoft.

11. C. Microsoft Azure Virtual WAN with Virtual WAN hubs simplifies a complex virtual network WAN.

12. D. A secured virtual hub is an Azure Virtual WAN Hub with associated security and routing policies configured by Azure Firewall Manager.

13. D. To set up connectivity from an Azure virtual network gateway to an Azure Virtual WAN, the prerequisites are Azure Virtual WAN and Virtual Hub, and Azure virtual network, and you must connect a VNet to the virtual hub.

14. D. Organizations can implement preferred NVAs directly into a Virtual WAN hub in a jointly managed solution by Microsoft Azure and third-party NVA vendors.

15. D. Azure Resource Manager resources that have a routing configuration and Azure network connections are VPN connection, ExpressRoute connection, P2S configuration connection, and hub virtual network connection.

16. D. Any on-premises/non-Microsoft endpoint can access Azure gateways through a connection unit such as site-to-site (S2S) VPN, point-to-site (P2S) VPN, and ExpressRoute.

17. A. Virtual WANs are categorized into two types (SKUs): Basic and Standard.

18. D. The IPsec tunnel from the cloud consumer on-premises VPN device to the gateway instance is disconnected when a planned or unplanned event happens to the gateway instance. Cloud consumer VPN devices should automatically remove or withdraw the corresponding routes so that traffic will be routed to the other active IPsec tunnel.

19. A. Azure VPN gateways connects the on-premises network of the cloud consumer to the Azure virtual network. Azure VPN gateways include four components: virtual network gateways, local network gateways, connections, and gateway subnets.

20. A. A site-to-site VPN gateway connection securely connects two networks.

Chapter 6: Design and Deploy VNet Routing and Azure Load Balancer

1. A. A route table created by administrators and associated with a subnet will combine with, or override, the default routes Azure adds to the subnet. User-defined route tables have a maximum limit of 200, and user-defined routes per route table have a maximum limit of 400 per Azure subscription.

2. A. IP forwarding must be enabled for the network interfaces to receive and forward traffic.

3. C. When multiple route types are present in a user-defined route (UDR) table, user-defined routes are preferred over the default system routes.

4. C. A route table that includes a route with a destination of 0.0.0.0/0 should not be associated with the gateway subnet of the virtual network connected to the Azure VPN gateway. The gateway will not function properly if this is done.

5. A. Organizations can use forced tunneling to redirect or "force" all Internet traffic back to their on-premises location via a site-to-site VPN tunnel for inspection and auditing purposes.

6. A. You can use Network Watcher's connection troubleshooting capability to determine routing, filtering, and operating system causes of outbound communication problems.

7. C. During provisioning, Azure Route Server creates a VMSS, which provides high availability for the service. VMs are deployed into the availability zone if it is deployed in a region that supports zone redundancy to ensure service availability.

8. C. HTTPS is used for secure web applications. HTTPS traffic can be facilitated by Azure Application Gateway and Azure Front Door.

9. B. Traffic is distributed within virtual networks across virtual machines (VMs) or zones and zone-redundant service endpoints within a region through regional load balancing services.

10. B. DNS-based traffic load balancers allow organizations to optimally distribute traffic across global Azure regions without sacrificing high availability and responsiveness. Traffic Manager load-balances only at the domain level because it is a DNS-based service. Therefore, it can't fail over as quickly as Front Door due to DNS caching and systems that ignore DNS time-to-live values (TTLs).

11. C. An ADC offers Layer 7 load balancing capabilities with Azure Application Gateway, which provides application delivery controllers as a service. Offload CPU-intensive SSL termination to the gateway to optimize web farm productivity.

12. A. Using Azure Load Balancer, you can achieve high performance, low-latency interconnection for any UDP or TCP protocol (inbound and outbound). The solution is designed to handle millions of requests per second while ensuring high availability. Load balancers in Azure are redundant across availability zones, ensuring high availability.

13. **B, C, D.** For incoming traffic, public load balancers map the public IP and port to the private IP and port of the VM, and load balancers map traffic the other way around for response traffic from the VM. Applying load balancing rules allows you to distribute specific types of traffic across multiple VMs or services. You can distribute traffic between different web servers to spread a load of web requests.

    High availability (HA) port rules are load-balancer rules configured with `protocol-all` and `port-0`. With this rule, a single rule can load-balance all TCP and UDP flows that arrive on the different ports of an internal standard load balancer.

    An outbound rule configures outbound network address translation (NAT) for all virtual machines or instances identified by the back-end pool. An outbound rule configures outbound network address translation (NAT).

14. **A.** A public load balancer can provide outbound connections for virtual machines (VMs) in the virtual network. The load balancer translates private IP addresses into public addresses. Public load balancers are used to load-balance Internet traffic to cloud organizations' VMs.

    Traffic is distributed according to several traffic-routing methods and continuous monitoring of endpoint health and automatic failover when endpoints fail.

15. **A.** You should choose this method when there are multiple geographic endpoints and you want their end users to access the nearest endpoint with the lowest network delay.

16. **A.** As per Microsoft, in the unlikely event of an outage affecting an entire Azure region, Traffic Manager should continue to operate normally. Application traffic can be directed to an instance of the application that is available in several Azure regions with Traffic Manager.

17. **B.** Profiles in Azure Traffic Manager can be nested up to 10 levels deep. Loops aren't allowed.

18. **A, B, C.** For a public standard load balancer, outbound rules can be used to configure SNAT (source network address translation). Using this configuration, you will be able to provide outbound Internet connectivity for your back-end instances using the public IP(s) assigned to your load balancer. It allows IP masked traffic, simplified allow lists, and fewer public IP resources for deployment.

19. **A.** An inbound NAT rule forwards load balancer front-end traffic to one or more instances in the back-end pool.

    NAT rules can be of two types:

    - Single virtual machine: A NAT rule targeting a single machine in the load balancer's back-end pool
    - Multiple virtual machines: An inbound NAT rule that targets multiple virtual machines in the load balancer's back-end pool

20.   A. High availability ports are set to all protocols and port 0 in a load-balancer rule. A single rule can be used to load-balance all TCP and UDP traffic arriving on all ports of a standard internal load balancer. Load balancing rules in the HA port help you create scalable and highly available network virtual appliances (NVAs) inside virtual networks. This feature is useful when large numbers of ports must be load-balanced.

Chapter 7: Design and Deploy Azure application gateway, Azure front door, and Virtual NAT

1.   A. Application Gateway scales up or down based on application traffic requirements with autoscaling enabled.

2.   B. Choose Multivalue when creating a Traffic Manager profile with IPv4 or IPv6 addresses as endpoints. This profile returns all healthy endpoints when a query is received.

3.   A, C. There are two primary methods of routing traffic in Application Gateway: path-based routing and multisite routing.

4.   A. Organizations are offered various Layer 7 load balancing capabilities by Front Door and Application Delivery Network (ADN) or Application Gateway. Front Door and Application Gateway are Layer 7 load balancers (HTTP/HTTPS) that support global and regional services.

5.   C. Incoming traffic pattern matching determines whether the incoming request matches the routing rule.

- Hosts (for example, `www.sybex.com`, `*.sybex.com`)

- Paths (for example, `/*`, `/sybexusers/*`, `/book.png`)

- HTTP Protocols (HTTP/HTTPS)

Internally, these properties are expanded so that there is a possibility to match every combination of Protocol/Host/Path.

6.   A. Application Gateway Health probes are used to monitor Front Door's back-end.

7.   C. The health probe volume for back-ends for Front Door can be high as Front Door has edge environments globally—ranging from 25 to 1200 requests per minute, depending on the health probe frequency configured. The probe volume should be about 200 requests per minute using the default probe frequency of 30 seconds on the organization's back-end.

8.   C. Traffic Manager listeners check for incoming connection requests based on ports, protocols, host, and IP address.

9. A. Load balancing is based on DNS with Traffic Manager. Your public-facing applications can be distributed across multiple Azure regions using this service.

10. A. Azure Traffic Distribution enables organization to distribute traffic to their public-facing applications across Azure regions.

11. A, B. Any virtual machine instance's network protocol that connects to the Internet via UDP or TCP will use NAT after NAT is configured.

12. A. You configure the NAT configuration for each VNet subnet to enable outbound connectivity by specifying a NAT gateway resource.

13. B. Azure Traffic Manager gives you six options for routing traffic: Priority, Weighted, Performance, Geographic, Multivalue, and Subnet.

14. A. Front Door uses the Anycast protocol and a split TCP and Microsoft's global network to improve global connectivity at Layer 7 (HTTP/HTTPS).

15. C. Traffic Manager supports up to 200 endpoints per profile.

16. D. The features of Traffic Manager include increased application availability and performance, no interruption of service, integrated hybrid applications, and delivery of complex deployments without disruption of service.

17. A. Organizations can enable the HTTPS protocol for a custom domain associated with Front Door under the front-end host's section.

18. A. Front Door supports end-to-end TLS encryption to meet an organization's security and compliance requirements.

19. A. Router rules are used to associate the rewrite configuration with the source listener. The basic routing rule involves a source listener and global header rewrite for rewrite configurations. The URL path map defines the rewrite configuration using a path-based routing rule.

20. D. Azure load balancers can either be zone redundant, zone-based, or non-zone-based.

Chapter 8: Design, Deploy, and Manage Azure Firewall and Network Security Groups

1. B. Azure Firewall Premium delivers advanced threat protection that fulfills the requirements of highly sensitive and regulated environments.

2. A. With Azure Firewall, you can control and monitor access to Azure resources to protect your Azure VNets from incoming and outgoing threats.

3. A. Azure Firewall allows you to configure NAT rules, network rules, and application rules either by using classic rules or Firewall Policies.

4. D. As part of the Firewall Policy, rules are organized into rule collections, DNAT, Network, and Application groups (only three).

5. D. You can use Azure Firewall Manager to centrally manage Azure Firewalls across multiple subscriptions. Firewall Manager leverages firewall policy to apply a standard set of network/application rules and configuration to your organization's tenant firewalls.

6. D. A 99.99% uptime SLA is guaranteed for Azure Firewall deployment when more than two availability zones are selected.

7. A. Firewall Manager can manage two network architecture types: secured virtual hub and hub virtual network.

8. D. Azure Firewall can be used to filter East-West traffic, non-HTTP/S access to the Internet (VMs and services that connect to the Internet), and Internet outbound traffic (VMs and services that access the Internet).

9. B. The maximum length of the name is 80 characters.

10. C. In DDoS Protection Standard, three types of attacks are mitigated such as volumetric attacks, protocol attacks, and resource (application) layer attacks. Azure DDoS protection provides the service tiers Basic and Standard only.

11. A, B, C, D. Several Azure resources can have security rules that allow or deny inbound network traffic to or outbound network traffic from a network security group. You can specify each rule's source, destination, port, and protocol.

12. A. Network security group rules allow all outbound traffic to the Internet (destination).

13. A. An Azure Firewall and Firewall Policy allows network engineers to define application rules that define FQDNs accessed from a subnet and network rules that specify a source address, protocol, destination port, and destination address.

14. A. All three components—the firewall, the VNet, and the public IP address—must be in the same Azure resource group.

15. A. The application security group must contain at least one network interface, and all interfaces must be part of the same virtual network.

16. D. Azure Firewall do not need a subnet bigger than /26.

17. C. Azure Firewall needs to be deployed with a public IP address.

18. C. The maximum number of application security groups is 3,000, the maximum number of IP configurations per application security group is 20, the maximum number of IP configurations per application security group is 4,000, and the maximum number of application security groups per network security group is 100.

19. D. The Azure Network Watcher flow logs feature lets you log information about IP traffic flowing through NSGs.

20. B. NSG flow logs can be visualized using Traffic Analytics, an Azure native service that processes flow logs, then extracts and visualizes them.

Chapter 9: Design and Deploy Azure Web Application Firewall and Monitor Networks

1. B. The Azure Web Application Firewall Prevention mode not only logs a rule violation, but the request will also not be sent to the web application.

2. A, B, C, D. An attacker injects specially crafted text into a web form field to trick the server into running SQL commands. The attacker can access sensitive data; insert, update, or delete data; and run SQL operations by using these commands.

3. C. A WAF policy created by you is by default in Detection mode but can be changed to Prevention mode.

4. B. Web app traffic is never sent over the public Internet because the virtual network where it resides has private access. Therefore, the app is not at risk from common web exploits.

5. A, B, C, D. Front Door in Azure WAF lets you control access to your web applications based on conditions you specify. There is a priority number, a rule type, a match condition, and an action in a custom WAF rule.

6. B. There are two types of custom rules in Azure WAF: match rules and rate limit rules.

7. A, B, C, D. The following categories of threats are included in default settings of Microsoft-managed Azure Rules: cross-site scripting, Java attacks, local file inclusion attacks, PHP injection attacks, remote command execution, remote file inclusion, session fixation, SQL injection protection, and protocol attackers.

8. C. Microsoft Azure Monitor uses logs and metrics as its two primary data types.

9. C. The Azure Monitor logs feature collects and organizes logs and performance information from monitored resources.

10. B. You can use a network security group to view the ingress and egress of IP traffic.

11. C. Network Watcher will be enabled automatically when you create or update virtual networks in your region.

12. A, B, C, D. The Azure Monitor Network Insights feature is organized around the following key components: network health and metrics, connectivity, traffic, and Diagnostic Toolkit.

13. A. The health and metrics information can be used to run health checks on the various network resources.

14. D. Diagnose networks and components in the cloud with Azure Monitor Network Insights' Diagnostic Toolkit.

15. C. Traffic Analytics can be accessed using the Traffic tab of Azure Monitor Network Insights for all NSGs configured for NSG flow logs for the subscriptions selected by location. You can use this tab to identify NSGs configured for an IP address using the search functionality.

16. B. The Connectivity tab of Azure Monitor Network Insights lets you see all tests configured for the selected subscriptions via Connection Monitor and Connection Monitor (classic).

17. A. The Network Health tab of Azure Monitor Network Insights offers a simple method for visualizing an inventory of networking resources and resource health and alerts.

18. A. Network Watcher is designed to monitor and repair the network health of IaaS products, including virtual machines, virtual networks, application gateways, and load balancers.

19. C. NSG flow logs are used to map IP traffic through network security groups. Auditing and compliance can be accomplished using them.

20. C. By combining Azure Web Application Firewall (WAF) and Azure Policy, WAF resources can be monitored for compliance at scale to enforce organizational standards.

Chapter 10: Design and Deploy Private Access to Azure Services

1. B. Microsoft Partner services and PaaS services in Azure can be accessed privately from Azure virtual networks using Azure Private Link.

2. A. The key technology behind Private Link is the Private Endpoint. Private Endpoints are network interfaces that allow virtual networks and an Azure service to establish a private and secure connection.

3. D. Private Link, Private Endpoint, and Private Link Service can fulfill an organization's needs.

4. B. Clients can access an Azure resource privately by adding a Private Endpoint to their virtual network.

5. A. An unused IP address is mapped by Private Endpoint to the address space of the subnet in which it resides.

6. B. Azure's Private Link service must use the Standard Load Balancer. The Azure Basic Load Balancer does not support Private Link service.

7. C. External resources are connected to a Service Endpoint. Azure's virtual network can connect securely to Private Endpoints. Azure's virtual network can connect to virtual networks through a Private Endpoint. A Service Endpoint accesses external resources.

8. A. Subscriptions from Private Link resources need to be registered with Microsoft.

9. B. The network interface information includes the Private Link resource's FQDN and private IP addresses.

10. D. Virtual public IP addresses are used to facilitate communication with Azure platform resources. Azure customers can also define any virtual network address space for their private virtual networks.

11. A. Azure virtual networks enable private access to Azure services from virtual machines and compute resources located within the virtual network. Azure services can be integrated into cloud consumers' virtual networks.

12. D. Using regional VNet integration enables applications to access:

- Resources in a VNet in the same region as applications
- Resources in VNets that are peering with the VNet application
- Service Endpoint secured services
- Resources across Azure ExpressRoute connections
- Resources across peered connections, which include Azure ExpressRoute connections

13. A. You can use a route table to send all outbound traffic to an ExpressRoute gateway.

14. C. In an Azure virtual network, you can filter network traffic to and from Azure resources using Azure NSGs. Several types of Azure resources are protected by NSGs, which contain security rules that regulate inbound and outbound traffic.

15. B. Azure services secured by Service Endpoints can be accessed via Regional VNet integration. You must configure regional VNet integration with a web application to access a Service Endpoint–secured service. Configure the integration subnet's Service Endpoints in the destination service.

16. D. You need to add the settings `WEBSITE_DNS_SERVER` and `WEBSITE_VNET_ROUTE_ALL` to the application to work with Azure DNS private zones.

All outbound calls from business applications are forwarded to the VNet, and business applications can access an Azure DNS private zone. Business applications can query the DNS private zone at the worker level and use Azure DNS with these settings.

17. A. In a Kubenet subnet, IP addresses are only assigned to the nodes, and a pod cannot directly communicate with another pod. Pods are connected by UDR and IP forwarding instead.

18. D. Azure Kubernetes Services clusters can use Azure CNI (advanced networking) or Kubenet (basic networking).

19. B. Azure AKS networking deployment of Kubenet doesn't offer advanced AKS features like virtual nodes and Azure network policy.

20. B. Azure App Service provides consumers and developers with a fully managed platform (PaaS). A few of App Service's key features include multiple languages and frameworks, managed production environment, containerization, Docker, security and compliance, connectivity to SaaS platforms and on-premises data, global scale with high availability, Visual Studio, API, mobile features, Visual Studio Code integration, and serverless programming.

Index

A

access. *See also* private access
    Azure DNS and, 232–233
    to Azure service endpoints, 646–650
    configuring to Private Endpoints,
        632–634
    management of, required for Azure
        regional VNet integration, 661
access control list (ACL), 210
ACL (access control list), 210
active/active connections, 160–161
AD (Azure Active Directory)
    about, 630
    configuration workflow for, 124–127
    configuring authentication, 116–133
    tenant, 125
Address Resolution Protocol (ARP), 195
address space
    about, 28–29
    VNets and, 208
agility, of Microsoft Azure, 13
AH (Authentication Header), 101
AKS (Azure Kubernetes Service)
    about, 26
    Azure Application Gateway and Ingress
        Controller for, 388
    configuring for regional VNet
        integration, 665–670
allocating public IP (prefixes) for NAT
    gateways, 445–447
American National Standards Institute
    (ANSI), 7
answers to review questions

Azure Application Gateway, 690–691
Azure DNS, 685–686
Azure ExpressRoute, 683–684
Azure Firewall/Azure Firewall
    Manager, 691–693
Azure Front Door, 690–691
Azure Load Balancer, 688–690
Azure Monitor, 693–694
Azure networking, 680–681
Azure Traffic Manager, 690–691
Azure Virtual Network NAT, 690–691
Azure Web Application Firewall
    (WAF), 693–694
cross-VNet connectivity, 686–687
network security groups
    (NSGs), 691–693
private access, 694–696
private IP, 685–686
virtual WANs, 686–687
VNet routing, 688–690
VPN Connections, 681–683
any-to-any (IPVPN) connectivity
    about, 152–153
    for Network Virtual Appliances
        (NVAs), 508
App Service Environment (ASE)
    about, 665
    configuring clients to access, 670–673
application delivery services, 25
application protection services, 25
application route management,
    required for Azure regional VNet
    integration, 662–665
application rules

about, 469
in Azure Firewall, 463, 468, 478
key configuration for, 478
application security groups (ASGs)
attaching to NICs, 519–524
creating, 519–524
application services, integrating into
regional VNets, 657–665
application settings, VNet integration apps
and, 662
ARCNet, 9
ARP (Address Resolution Protocol), 195
ASE (App Service Environment)
about, 665
configuring clients to access, 670–673
ASGs (application security groups)
attaching to NICs, 519–524
creating, 519–524
associating
route tables with subnets, 328–329
virtual network NATs with
subnets, 447–451
attaching
application security groups (ASGs) to
NICs, 519–524
network security groups (NSGs) to
resources, 509–518
Authentication Header (AH), 101
automated branch connectivity, using SD-
WAN, virtual hubs for, 502
autoscaling
Azure Application Gateway
and, 388, 389
WAF and, 389
availability sets (Microsoft Azure), 18–19
availability zones (AZs)
in Azure Firewall, 479, 502
Microsoft Azure, 18, 77, 94
AZ-700 certification, for Azure
networking, 2–73

AZs (availability zones)
in Azure Firewall, 479, 502
Microsoft Azure, 18, 77, 94
Azure Active Directory (AD)
about, 630
configuration workflow for, 124–127
configuring authentication, 116–133
tenant, 125
Azure Application Gateway
about, 20, 214, 345, 383–384
answers to review questions, 690–691
approaches to routing, 387
choosing SKUs, 387–389
deployment, 390–394
exam essentials, 451–454
exercises, 401–409
how it works, 385–387
redirection, 390–409
request routing rules, 395–396
review questions, 455–458
rewrite policies, 397–409
scaling options for, 389
Azure Az PowerShell module, 35–36
Azure Bastion, 353
Azure Content Delivery Network
(CDN), 20
Azure Cosmos DB, 642
Azure Data Lake Store, 643
Azure Databricks, 226
Azure Domain Name System (DNS)
about, 20, 204
answers to review questions, 685–686
configuring
about, 40–43
private DNS zones, 233–240
public DNS zones, 231–233
creating zones, 231–235
designing
name resolution inside
VNets, 240–245

private DNS zones, 233–240
public DNS zones, 231–233
exam essentials, 249–250
exercises, 234–235, 239–240, 247–248
linking private DNS zones to
   VNets, 245–248
recording PowerShell, 231–233
review questions, 251–254
VNet integration apps and Private
   Zones, 663
zones, 42–43, 231–235
Azure ExpressRoute
about, 27, 146
answers to review questions, 683–684
choosing
   circuit SKUs, 156
   circuits, 157–158
   between network service
      provider and ExpressRoute
      Direct, 153–155
   price based on SKUs, 156–157
   SKUs and tiers, 169–171
circuits, 157–158, 195
configuring
   encryption over, 191–192
   gateways, 182–186
connecting virtual networks to
   ExpressRoute circuits, 186–190
creating gateways, 182–186
deploying
   Azure cross-region connectivity
      between multiple
      locations, 156–169
   bidirectional forwarding
      detection, 192–193
   ExpressRoute FastPath, 175–176
   ExpressRoute Global
      Reach, 171–174
designing

Azure cross-region connectivity
   between multiple
   locations, 156–169
ExpressRoute FastPath, 175–176
ExpressRoute Global
   Reach, 171–173
diagnosing connection issues, 193–195
exam essentials, 196–198
exercises, 183–186, 194–195
getting started with, 146–153
Microsoft peering only, 176–178
as peering locations, 157
private peering only, 176–178
recommending route advertisement
   configurations, 190–191
resolving connection issues, 193–195
review questions, 199–202
setting up
   Microsoft peering, 181–182
   private peering, 178–180
Azure ExpressRoute Direct
about, 150
choosing between network service
   providers and, 153–155
Azure ExpressRoute FastPath, designing
   and deploying, 175–176
Azure ExpressRoute Global Reach
deploying, 171–174
designing, 171–173
Azure ExpressRoute Premium
   Add-On, 159
Azure Firewall Policy, 495–501
Azure Firewall/Azure Firewall Manager
about, 20, 213–214, 460
answers to review questions, 691–693
building
   deployments, 475–495
   secure hubs within Azure virtual
      WAN hubs, 501–506

configuring
    deployments, 475–495
    secure hubs within Azure virtual
        WAN hubs, 501–506
critical design considerations for, 475
exam essentials, 536–538
exercises, 481–495, 497–500
features of, 460–467
how it works, 467–468
integrating Azure virtual WAN hubs
    with third-party network virtual
    appliances, 507–509
policy, 495–501
protection of VNets by, 468–475
review questions, 539–542
Azure Front Door
    about, 345, 383
    answers to review questions, 690–691
    back-end health probes, 424–426
    back-end host headers, 424–426
    back-end pools, 424–426
    back-ends, 424–426
    end-to-end SSL encryption, 421–423
    exam essentials, 451–454
    exercises, 414–420
    features and capabilities of
        SKUs, 409–420
    health probe characteristics and
        operation, 411–412
    multisite listeners, 423–424
    review questions, 455–458
    routing and routing rules, 426–427
    secure, with SSL, 412–413
    SSL termination, 421–423
    URL redirection, 427–429
    URL rewriting, 427–429
    for web applications with high
        availability patterns, 413–420
Azure in Open subscription, 513
Azure Kubernetes Service (AKS)

about, 26
Azure Application Gateway and Ingress
    Controller for, 388
configuring for regional VNet
    integration, 665–670
Azure Load Balancer
    about, 20, 318
    answers to review questions, 688–690
    building
        about, 353–366
        explicit outbound rules, 371–374
        inbound NAT rules, 370–371
    choosing between public and internal
        load balancers, 349–352
    choosing SKUs, 344–349
    configuring
        about, 353–366
        inbound NAT rules, 370–371
    deploying load balancing rules, 366–369
    exam essentials, 375–376
    exercises, 367–369, 370–371, 373–374
    review questions, 377–380
Azure Monitor
    about, 544
    answers to review questions, 693–694
    building
        Azure Network Watcher, 591–595
        instances, 595–599
    configuring
        Azure Network Watcher, 591–595
        instances, 595–599
    enabling diagnostic logging, 607–608
    exam essentials, 609–610
    exercises, 587–591, 594–595, 598–599,
        602–604, 605–607
    logging in Azure Firewall, 462
    for Networks, 20
    NSG flow logs, 604–607
    review questions, 611–614
    setting up

diagnostic logging, 607–608
network health alerts
    and logging, 582–591
Traffic Analytics, 600–604
Azure NetApp Files, 226
Azure Network Watcher
  about, 20, 534–536
  building, 591–595
  configuring, 591–595
  Traffic Analytics and, 602
Azure Pass subscription, 513
Azure Policy, 607
Azure PowerShell
  building secure hubs within Azure
    Virtual WAN hubs using, 503–506
  configuring secure hubs within Azure
    Virtual WAN hubs using, 503–506
  deploying
    Azure Virtual Networks (VNETs)
      with, 35–37
    NAT gateways using, 54–56
  recording
    Azure DNS zones using, 42–43
    using, 233–235
Azure Private Endpoints
  about, 213, 616–618
  configuring access to, 632–634
  how it works, 619–623
  planning, 628–630
  VNet integration apps and, 663
Azure Private Link
  about, 616–618
  benefits of, 618–619
  integrating into Azure virtual
    networks, 619
  RBAC permissions, 634
Azure regional VNet integration, 658–665
Azure regions, 16–17, 30, 149, 157, 509,
  642, 643
Azure Resource Manager, 267–277

Azure Route Server
  configuring subnetting for, 226–231
  deploying, 336–343
  designing, 336–343
  planning subnetting for, 226–231
Azure service endpoints
  access to, 646–650
  configuring policies, 642–645
  setting up, 642–645
  VNet integration apps and, 663
Azure Subnet, 21, 23
Azure Traffic Manager
  about, 21, 345, 383
  answers to review questions, 690–691
  deploying profiles, 429–432
  designing profiles, 429–432
  exam essentials, 451–454
  exercises, 439–441
  how it works, 430–432
  review questions, 455–458
  routing methods, 432–441
Azure Virtual Network (VNet)
  about, 21, 26–28
  address space, 28–29
  Azure Firewall/Azure Firewall Manager
    and, 468–475
  concepts and best practices, 28–35
  configuring Azure Kubernetes
    Service (AKS) for regional
    integration, 665–670
  deploying
    about, 210–212
    with Azure PowerShell, 35–37
  designing
    name resolutions inside, 240–245
    private IP addressing for, 204–210
    VPN connectivity between, 263–266
  exercises, 31–35, 36–37
  integrating app services into
    regional, 657–665

linking private DNS zones to, 245–248
peering, 265–266
regions, 30
subnets, 29–30
subscriptions, 30
Azure Virtual Network Address
    Translation (NAT)
about, 383, 442–443
allocating public IP/public IP prefixes
    for gateways, 445–447
answers to review questions, 690–691
associating with subnets, 447–451
configuring Internet access with, 53–56
exam essentials, 451–454
exercises, 446–447, 448–450
review questions, 455–458
using, 443–445
Azure Virtual Network (VNet) gateways
about, 213, 323, 324
building, 94–97
choosing SKUs for point-to-site
    VPNs, 112–116
configuring, 94–97
connecting to Azure virtual
    WANs, 291–299
virtual network traffic routing
    and, 47–48
Azure Virtual Network (VNet) Peering
about, 21, 323
communicating via, 27
configuring cross-virtual network
    connectivity with, 43–46
deploying, 266–277
virtual network traffic routing and, 47
Azure Virtual Network (VNet) routing
about, 21, 318
answers to review questions, 688–690
associating route tables with
    subnets, 328–329
deploying

Azure Route Server, 336–343
    user-defined routes, 318–327
designing
    Azure Route Server, 336–343
    user-defined routes, 318–327
diagnosing routing issues, 334–336
exam essentials, 375–376
exercises, 325–326, 327, 328, 331–334
forced tunneling and, 52–53
resolving routing issues, 334–336
review questions, 377–380
setting up forced tunneling, 329–334
Azure Virtual Network (VNet) Service
    Endpoint
about, 21, 323
communicating via, 27
virtual network traffic routing and,
    48
Azure Virtual Network Terminal Access
    Point, 21
Azure Web Application Firewall (WAF)
about, 21, 544
answers to review questions, 693–694
attaching WAF policies, 580–582
on Azure Application Gateway, 547–549
Azure Application Gateway WAF policy
    rule sets, 566–579
on Azure CDN from
    Microsoft, 550–551
on Azure Front Door, 549–550
Azure Front Door WAF policy rule
    sets, 552–566
deploying WAF policies, 580–582
exam essentials, 609–610
exercises, 551–552, 561–565,
    575–579, 580–581
functions and features, 544–551
policies for, 479
review questions, 611–614
scaling options for, 389

setting up detection or prevention
mode, 551–553
virtual hubs for, 503

B

back-end health probes, 424–426
back-end host headers, 424–426
back-end pools, 424–426
back-ends, 390, 424–426
bandwidth, in Azure ExpressRoute, 150
Barracuda CloudGen WAN, 300–301
BFD (Bidirectional Forwarding Detection)
about, 162
deploying, 192–193
BGP (Border Gateway Protocol)
about, 94, 148, 320
Azure Route Server and, 226
configuring, 193
routes, 28
virtual hubs and, 304
Bidirectional Forwarding Detection (BFD)
about, 162
deploying, 192–193
billing models, selecting, 159
BizSpark subscription, 513
block blob, 530
Border Gateway Protocol (BGP)
about, 94, 148, 320
Azure Route Server and, 226
configuring, 193
routes, 28
virtual hubs and, 304
branch, 10–11
bridges, 9
building
application security groups
(ASGs), 519–524
Azure DNS zones, 233–235
Azure Firewall deployments, 476–495

Azure Load Balancer, 353–366
Azure Monitor instances, 595–599
Azure Network Watcher, 591–595
connection units, 306–308
cross-region load balancer
resources, 361–366
explicit outbound rules for load
balancers, 371–374
ExpressRoute gateways, 182–186
hubs in virtual WANs, 291–299
inbound NAT rules, 370–371
IPsec/IKE policy, 101–104
local network gateways, 97–101
network security group (NSG)
rules, 524–530
network security groups
(NSGs), 509–518
network virtual appliance (NVA) in
virtual hubs, 299–303
NSG flow logs, 604–607
secure hubs within Azure virtual WAN
hubs, 501–506
Traffic Analytics, 600–604
virtual network gateways, 94–97
business continuity and disaster recovery
(BC/DR), 162–169

C

campus, 10–11
CDN (Azure Content Delivery
Network), 20
centralized management
in Azure Firewall, 468
virtual hubs for, 503
certificate management, Azure Front Door
and, 413
certificate-based authentication
configuration workflow for, 117–124
configuring, 116–133

certifications, in Azure Firewall, 462
choosing
    Application Gateway SKUs, 387–389
    Azure Load Balancer SKUs, 344–349
    billing models, 159
    business continuity and
        disaster recovery (BC/DR)
        patterns, 162–169
    ExpressRoute circuit SKUs, 156
    ExpressRoute circuits, 157–158
    ExpressRoute SKUs and tiers, 169–171
    high availability design, 159–162
    between network service providers and
        ExpressRoute Direct, 153–155
    peering locations, 157
    between public and internal load
        balancers, 349–352
    services for virtual WANs, 289–291
    SKUs for virtual WANs, 289–291
    virtual network gateway SKUs for site-
        to-site VPN, 89–91
    VNet gateway SKUs for point-to-site
        VPNs, 112–116
CI/CD (continuous integration/continuous
    delivery), 35
circuits (Azure ExpressRoute), 195
Classless Inter-Domain Routing (CIDR)
    blocks, 26, 29–30, 205
clients, configuring to access App Service
    Environment, 670–673
client-side and authentication
    issues, 131–136
cloud computing
    basics of, 2–11
    deployment models, 4
    need for cloud, 3–5
cloud exchange co-location, 151–152
cloud networking, 5
cloud providers, 4
Cloud Scalability, in Azure Firewall, 461

Cloud Service Provider subscription, 514
cloud-based networks, 5
cloud-based Traffic Analytics, 600–604
cloud-defined networks, 4
cloud-enabled networks, 5
cloud-native network functions (CNFs), 5
cloud-native networks, 5
clusters, in Kubernetes, 666, 670
CNI (Container Networking
    Interface), 667–669
cold potato routing, 22, 343
community cloud, 4
configuration route management, VNet
    integration apps and, 662
configuring
    access
        to Private Endpoints, 632–634
        to Service Endpoints, 651
    Azure AD authentication, 116–133
    Azure DNS zones, 42–43
    Azure Firewall deployments, 476–495
    Azure Kubernetes Service (AKS) for
        regional VNet integration, 665–670
    Azure Load Balancer, 353–366
    Azure Monitor instances, 595–599
    Azure Network Watcher, 591–595
    basic SKU public IPs, 40
    Border Gateway Protocol (BGP), 193
    certificate-based
        authentication, 116–133
    clients to access App Service
        Environment, 670–673
    cross-region load balancer
        resources, 361–366
    cross-virtual network connectivity with
        peering, 43–46
    Domain Name System (DNS), 40–43
    encryption over ExpressRoute, 191–192
    ExpressRoute gateways, 182–186
    inbound NAT rules, 370–371

Internet access with Azure Virtual
NAT, 53–56
IPsec/IKE policy, 101–104
listeners, 393–394
local network gateways, 97–101
network security group (NSG)
rules, 524–530
NSG flow logs, 604–607
peering between two virtual
networks, 45–46
private DNS zones, 235–240
public DNS zones, 231–233
public IP addresses, 37–40
RADIUS authentication, 116–133
rewrites, 399
secure hubs within Azure virtual WAN
hubs, 501–506
service endpoint policies, 642–645
standard SKU public IPs, 40
subnet delegations, 223–226
subnetting
for Azure Route Server, 226–231
for services, 220–223
Traffic Analytics, 600–604
virtual network gateways, 94–97
virtual network traffic routing, 46–53
VPN gateway transit for virtual network
peering, 258–263
workflow for, 104–108
Connection Monitor, 599. *See also* Azure
Network Watcher
connections
active/active, 160–161
building units, 306–308
for cloud networking, 11
diagnosing issues with
ExpressRoute, 193–195
hub-to-hub, 280
passive, 161
point-to-point Ethernet, 152

resolving issues with
ExpressRoute, 193–195
virtual networks to ExpressRoute
circuits, 186–190
VNet gateways to Azure virtual
WANs, 291–299
Container Networking Interface
(CNI), 667–669
containers
in Kubernetes, 666
runtime of, in Kubernetes, 666
VNet integration apps and container
images, 662
content storage, VNet integration apps
and, 662
continuous integration/continuous delivery
(CI/CD), 35
control plane, in Route Server, 341
CPE (customer premises equipment),
299
creating
application security groups
(ASGs), 519–524
Azure DNS zones, 233–235
Azure Firewall deployments, 476–495
Azure Load Balancer, 353–366
Azure Monitor instances, 595–599
Azure Network Watcher, 591–595
connection units, 306–308
cross-region load balancer
resources, 361–366
explicit outbound rules for load
balancers, 371–374
ExpressRoute gateways, 182–186
hubs in virtual WANs, 291–299
inbound NAT rules, 370–371
IPsec/IKE policy, 101–104
local network gateways, 97–101
network security group (NSG)
rules, 524–530

network security groups
(NSGs), 509–518
network virtual appliance (NVA) in
virtual hubs, 299–303
NSG flow logs, 604–607
secure hubs within Azure virtual WAN
hubs, 501–506
Traffic Analytics, 600–604
virtual network gateways, 94–97
cross-region connectivity, designing
and deploying between multiple
locations, 156–169
cross-region load balancer
resources, 361–366
cross-virtual connectivity, configuring with
peering, 43–46
cross-VNet connectivity
about, 256
answers to review questions, 686–687
deploying VNet peering, 266–277
designing VPN connectivity between
VNets, 263–266
exam essentials, 310–311
exercises, 261–263
gateway transit, 256–263
review questions, 312–316
service chaining, 256–263
virtual network peering, 256–263
custom health probe, of Azure Application
Gateway, 392–393
customer premises equipment (CPE), 299

D

data exfiltration, 622
data plane, in Route Server, 341
DDNS (dynamic domain name
services), 243
dedicated SQL pools, 642

default health probe, of Azure Application
Gateway, 391–392
defense, of cloud networking, 11
deploying
Azure Application Gateway, 390–394
Azure cross-region connectivity between
multiple locations, 156–169
Azure ExpressRoute, 151–153
Azure Router Server, 336–343
Azure Traffic Manager
profiles, 429–432
Azure Virtual Networks (VNETs) with
Azure PowerShell, 35–37
Bidirectional Forwarding Detection
(BFD), 192–193
building Azure Firewall
deployments, 476–495
configuring Azure Firewall
deployments, 476–495
ExpressRoute FastPath, 175–176
ExpressRoute Global Reach, 171–174
load balancing rules, 366–369
models for, 4
NAT gateways using Azure
PowerShell, 54–56
user-defined routes, 318–327
VNet peering, 266–277
VNets, 210–212
deployment time, Azure Application
Gateway and, 388
designing
Azure cross-region connectivity between
multiple locations, 156–169
Azure Router Server, 336–343
Azure Traffic Manager
profiles, 429–432
Azure virtual WAN
architecture, 277–289
Azure VPN connections, 79–89

ExpressRoute FastPath, 175–176
ExpressRoute Global Reach, 171–173
name resolutions inside VNets, 240–245
private DNS zones, 235–240
private IP addressing for
    VNets, 204–210
public DNS zones, 231–233
user-defined routes, 318–327
VPN connections, 79–89
VPN connectivity between
    VNets, 263–266
Destination Network Address Translation
    (DNAT), Azure Firewall and, 462,
    463, 477
development, security, and operations
    (DevSecOps), 3
development and operations (DevOps), 3
DevOps (development and operations),
    3
DevSecOps (development, security, and
    operations), 3
DHCP (Dynamic Host Configuration
    Protocol), 243
diagnosing
    client-side and authentication
        issues, 131–136
    ExpressRoute connection
        issues, 193–195
    routing issues, 334–336
    VPN gateway connectivity
        issues, 109–112
diagnostic logging, 607–608
Diagnostic Toolkits, 585–586
diagnostic tools, in Network
    Watcher, 592–593
DNAT (Destination Network Address
    Translation), Azure Firewall and, 462,
    463, 477
Docker, in Kubernetes, 666

dynamic domain name services
    (DDNS), 243
Dynamic Host Configuration Protocol
    (DHCP), 243
dynamic IP address, 22
dynamic private IP addresses, 206
dynamic scaling, in Azure
    ExpressRoute, 150

E

Edge, of Microsoft Azure, 13
Edge Zones, 23
Education subscription, 513
elasticity, of Microsoft Azure, 13
enabling diagnostic logging, 607–608
Encapsulating Security Payload (ESP), 101
encryption
    configuring over
        ExpressRoute, 191–192
    end-to-end SSL, 421–423
end-to-end SSL encryption, 421–423
Enterprise Agreement subscription, 513
enterprise cloud networking, 4, 10–11
environment, setting, 130
ESP (Encapsulating Security Payload),
    101
estimating price based on ExpressRoute
    SKUs, 156–157
Ethernet, 9
exam essentials
    Azure Application Gateway, 451–454
    Azure ExpressRoute, 196–198
    Azure Firewall/Azure Firewall
        Manager, 536–538
    Azure Front Door, 451–454
    Azure Load Balancer, 375–376
    Azure Monitor, 609–610
    Azure networking, 56–57

Azure Traffic Manager, 451–454

Azure Virtual Network NAT, 451–454

Azure Web Application Firewall (WAF), 609–610

cross-VNet connectivity, 308–311

DNS, 249–250

network security groups (NSGs), 536–538

private access, 673–674

private IP, 249–250

virtual WANs, 309–311

VNet routing, 375–376

VPN connections, 136–139

exercises

Azure Application Gateway, 401–409

Azure DNS, 234–235, 239–240, 247–248

Azure ExpressRoute, 183–186, 194–195

Azure Firewall/Azure Firewall Manager, 481–495, 497–500

Azure Front Door, 414–420

Azure Load Balancer, 367–369, 370–371, 373–374

Azure Monitor, 587–591, 594–595, 598–599, 602–604, 605–607

Azure Traffic Manager, 439–441

Azure Virtual Network (VNET), 31–35, 36–37

Azure Virtual Network NAT, 446–447, 448–450

Azure Web Application Firewall (WAF), 551–552, 561–565, 575–579, 580–581

cross-VNet connectivity, 261–263

network security groups (NSGs), 514–516, 517–518, 521–523, 524–527, 535

private access, 623–628, 630–631, 644–645, 651–657

private IP, 211–212, 220–223, 225–226

virtual network traffic routing, 49–52

virtual WANs, 292–299, 301–303, 305

VNet routing, 325–326, 327, 328, 331–334

VPN connections, 94–97, 98–101, 105–108, 109–112, 125–127, 130–133

F

filtering network traffic, 27–28

firewalls, 9. *See also* Azure Firewall/Azure Firewall Manager

flexibility, of cloud networking, 11

Flexible Orchestration mode, 270

flow logs, network security group (NSG), 524–530

forced tunneling
about, 52–53
in Azure Firewall, 462, 463
setting up, 329–334

Free Trail subscription, 513

front-end setup, of Azure Application Gateway, 390

fully qualified domain name (FQDN)
about, 496
filters in Azure Firewall, 461
tags in Azure Firewall, 461

G

gateway transit
about, 256–263
configuring for virtual network peering, 258–263

gateways, types of, 170. *See also specific types*

geo-distribution, of Microsoft Azure, 13

Geographic-based routing method, 433, 436–437
geography (Microsoft Azure), 14–15
geo-presence, 264
geo-redundancy, 264
GET request, 412
global connectivity, in Azure ExpressRoute, 150
global infrastructure, of Microsoft Azure, 14–20

H

HA (high availability)
  in Azure Firewall, 461
  Azure Front Door for web applications with, 413–420
  Azure Load Balancer and ports, 366
  of Microsoft Azure, 13, 18
  selecting design, 159–162
hands-on labs, Azure networking, 57–69
HEAD request, 412
header rewrite, Azure Application Gateway and, 388
health probes
  back-end, 424–426
  characteristics and operation, 411–412
  load balancers and, 353
  responses, 412
  setting up in Azure Application Gateway, 391
  supported HTTP methods for, 412
hierarchical policies, in Azure Firewall, 468
high availability (HA)
  in Azure Firewall, 461
  Azure Front Door for web applications with, 413–420
  Azure Load Balancer and ports, 366
  of Microsoft Azure, 13, 18
  selecting design, 159–162

hop types, 47–48
hot potato routing, 22, 343
HTTP methods, supported for health probes, 412
hub route table, 280
hub virtual network, 280, 467
hub-and-spoke networks, 44, 259–260, 502
hubs
  building
    within Azure virtual WAN hubs, 501–506
    network virtual appliances (NVAs) in virtual, 299–303
    in virtual WANs, 291–299
  configuring within Azure virtual WAN hubs, 501–506
hub-to-hub connection, 280
hybrid cloud, 4, 10

I

IDPS (intrusion detection and prevention system), in Azure Firewall, 464
IEEE (Institute of Electrical and Electronics Engineers), 7
IETF (Internet Engineering Task Force), 192
IKE (Internet Key Exchange), 101
inbound NAT rules
  Azure Load Balancer and, 367
  building, 370–371
  configuring, 370–371
information technology (IT), 2
instances (Azure Monitor), 595–599
Institute of Electrical and Electronics Engineers (IEEE), 7
integrating
  app services into regional VNets, 657–665

Azure services, 28
Azure Virtual WAN hubs with
    third-party network virtual
    appliances, 507–509
Private Link with DNS and Private
    Link services with on-premises
    clients, 634–642
internal load balancer, compared with
    public load balancers, 349–352
International Telecommunications Union
    (ITU), 7
Internet
    about, 322–323, 324
    Azure network communication
        with the, 26
    configuring access to, with Azure Virtual
        NAT, 53–56
Internet Engineering Task Force
    (IETF), 192
Internet Key Exchange (IKE), 101
Internet of Things (IoT), 10–11
Internet Protocol (IP). *See also* private
    Internet Protocol (IP)
    about, 320
    address, 8, 22
    packets, 320
    subnet planning for NSGs, 518
    types of allocation, 22
    verifying flow, 534–536
intrusion detection and prevention system
    (IDPS), in Azure Firewall, 464
IoT (Internet of Things), 10–11
IP (Internet Protocol). *See also* private
    Internet Protocol (IP)
    about, 320
    address, 8, 22
    packets, 320
    subnet planning for NSGs, 518
    types of allocation, 22
    verifying flow, 534–536

IP Flow Verify, 534–536, 593
IPsec/IKE policy
    about, 92–93
    building, 101–104
    configuring, 101–104
IPv4, basic SKUs for, 38–39
IPv6, basic SKUs for, 38–39
IPVPN (any-to-any) connectivity
    about, 152–153
    for Network Virtual Appliances
        (NVAs), 508
IT (information technology), 2
ITU (International Telecommunications
    Union), 7

K

key use case, in Azure ExpressRoute,
    151
key vault integration, Azure Application
    Gateway and, 388
kube-controller-manager, in
    Kubernetes, 666
Kubectl, in Kubernetes, 666
Kubelet, in Kubernetes, 666
kube-proxy, in Kubernetes, 666
Kubernetes API, in Kubernetes, 666

L

LAN (Local Area Network), 6–7
layer 3 connectivity, in Azure
    ExpressRoute, 149
linking private DNS zones to
    VNets, 245–248
listeners
    configuring, 393–394
    multisite, 423–424
Local Area Network (LAN), 6–7

local connectivity, in Azure
    ExpressRoute, 150
local network gateways, 97–101
log analytics, Traffic Analytics and, 601
logging, setting up, 582–591

M

MAC (Media Access Control), 9, 191–192
Mac OS X, Wireshark for, 136
MACsec protocol, 191–192
MAN (Metropolitan Area Network), 6–7
management groups (Microsoft Azure), 20
Media Access Control (MAC), 9, 191–192
metered data, 159
Metropolitan Area Network (MAN), 6–7
Microsoft Azure
    about, 11–12
    availability sets, 18–19
    availability zones (AZs), 18, 77, 94
    Azure communication between
        resources, 26
    cloud foundation, 12–13
    geography, 14–15
    global infrastructure, 14–20
    integrating services, 28
    management groups, 20
    networking overview, 21–23
    networking services, 23–25
    networking terminology, 20–21
    regions, 16–17, 30
    resources groups, 18–19
    routes, 321–327
    subscriptions, 19, 30
Microsoft Azure App Service, 643
Microsoft Azure Online Resources
    (website), 38
Microsoft Azure Storage (Microsoft
    Storage), 642
Microsoft backbone infrastructure, 256

Microsoft Cloud services, connectivity to,
    in Azure ExpressRoute, 149
Microsoft Enterprise Edge (MSEE)
    router, 147–148
Microsoft peering
    setting up, 181–182
    using, 176–178
Microsoft SQL Azure Database for
    MariaDB, 642
Microsoft SQL Database (Microsoft
    SQL), 642
Microsoft.EventHub, 642
Microsoft.KeyVault, 642
Microsoft.ServiceBus, 642
monitoring
    in Azure Firewall, 463
    in Network Watcher, 593–594
MSDN subscription, 513
MSEE (Microsoft Enterprise Edge)
    router, 147–148
multiple-site routing, 387
multisite listeners, 423–424
Multivalue-based routing method,
    433, 437
MySQL Database for Azure, 642

N

name resolutions, designing inside
    VNets, 240–245
namespace, in Kubernetes, 666
national clouds, connectivity to, in Azure
    ExpressRoute, 150
National Institute of Standards and
    Technology (NIST)
    on cloud computing, 2
    on networking, 3
Network Address Translation (NAT)
    about, 10
    gateways, 20

pools, 161–162
Network Address Translation (NAT) rules
    about, 469
    Azure Firewall and, 477
    collection of, in Azure Firewall, 467
    key configuration for, 477
Network Functions Virtualization
    (NFV), 10
network insight, in Network Watcher, 592
network rules
    about, 469
    in Azure Firewall, 463
    Azure Firewall and, 477–478
    key configuration for, 478
network security groups (NSGs)
    about, 21, 347, 460
    answers to review questions, 691–693
    attaching
        application security groups to
            NICs, 519–524
        to resources, 509–518
    configuring rules, 523–530
    creating
        about, 509–518
        application security groups, 519–524
        rules, 523–530
    exam essentials, 536–538
    exercises, 514–516, 517–518, 521–523,
        524–527, 535
    key considerations for IP subnet
        planning for, 518
    reading flow logs for, 523–530
    review questions, 539–542
    Traffic Analytics and, 601
    validating flow rules, 531–534
    verifying IP flow, 534–536
    VNet integration apps and, 663
network service providers, choosing
    between ExpressRoute Direct
    and, 153–155

network topology, in Network
    Watcher, 592
Network Virtual Appliance (NVA)
    about, 28
    building in virtual hubs, 299–303
    virtual hubs for, 503
networking
    about, 3
    answers to review questions, 680–681
    AZ-700 certification for, 2–73
    basics of, 2–11
    exam essentials, 56–57
    hands-on lab, 57–69
    Microsoft Azure, 21–23
    review questions, 70–73
    services in Microsoft Azure, 23–25
    terminology for, 7–10, 20–21
networks
    architectures in Azure Firewall, 468
    cable types, 9
    connectivity services, 24–25
    filtering traffic, 27–28
    hub virtual, 280, 467
    hub-and-spoke, 44, 259–260, 502
    monitoring, 25
    peer-to-peer, 44–45
    registration, 236
    registration virtual, 245
    resolution, 236
    resolution virtual, 245–246
    rule collection, in Azure Firewall, 468
    security sets, 28
    segmentation of, 206
    setting up health alerts, 582–591
    traffic filtering rules, in Azure
        Firewall, 461
    types of, 6–7
next-hop types, 322–323
NFV (Network Functions
    Virtualization), 10

NICs, attaching application security groups (ASGs) to, 519–524

NIST (National Institute of Standards and Technology)
on cloud computing, 2
on networking, 3

node, in Kubernetes, 666

nonregional services (Microsoft Azure), 18, 352

NSG flow logs
building and configuring, 604–607
Traffic Analytics and, 601

O

on-premises
about, 190
connectivity in Azure ExpressRoute, 150
integrating Private Link with DNS and Private Link services with on-premises clients, 634–642
virtual hubs for connectivity, 502

Open Shortest Path First (OSPF), 320

Open Systems Interconnection (OSI), 7–8

optimization, of cloud networking, 11

organizational standards, 607

OSI (Open Systems Interconnection), 7–8

OSPF (Open Shortest Path First), 320

outbound rules
Azure Load Balancer and, 367
building explicit, for load balancers, 371–374

P

PaaS services, 621–622

packets
about, 10
capture of, 593

PAN (Personal Area Network), 6–7

partners, 160

passive connections, 161

path-based routing, 387

Pay-as-You-Go subscription, 513

peering locations, selecting, 157

peer-to-peer networks, 44–45

performance
Azure Application Gateway and, 388
Azure DNS and, 232

Performance-based routing method, 433, 435–436

Personal Area Network (PAN), 6–7

planning
Azure Private Endpoints, 628–630
subnetting for Azure Route Server, 226–231

pod, in Kubernetes, 666

point-to-point Ethernet connection, 152

point-to-site (P2S) VPNs
about, 27, 84–86
choosing VNet gateway SKUs for, 112–116
considerations for, 130

policies
Azure Firewall/Azure Firewall Manager, 495–501
for Web Application Firewall (WAF), 479

policy-based VPNs, route-based VPNs vs., 92–94

port forwarding, load balancers and, 353

ports, 9

preparing
subnet delegations, 223–226
subnetting for services, 213–220

price, selecting based on ExpressRoute SKUs, 156–157

Priority-based routing method, 432, 433

private access

about, 616
access to service endpoints, 646–657
answers to review questions, 694–696
Azure Private Endpoints, 616–618,
    619–623, 628–631, 632–634
Azure Private Link services,
    616–619, 634–642
configuring
    Azure Kubernetes Service
        (AKS) for regional VNet
        integration, 665–670
    clients to access app service
        environment, 670–673
    to Private Endpoints, 632–634
    service endpoint policies, 642–645
exam essentials, 673–674
exercises, 623–628, 630–631,
    644–645, 651–657
integrating
    app services into regional
        VNets, 657–665
    Private Link with DNS and Private
        Link services with on-premises
        clients, 634–642
planning Private Endpoints, 628–631
review questions, 675–678
service tags, 646–657
setting up service endpoints, 642–645
private cloud
    about, 4, 10
    Azure network communication
        with the, 27
private Internet Protocol (IP)
    about, 204
    answers to review questions, 685–686
    configuring
        subnet delegations, 223–226
        subnetting for Azure Route
            Server, 226–231
        subnetting for services, 220–223

deploying VNets, 210–212
designing addressing for
    VNets, 204–210
exam essentials, 249–250
exercises, 211–212, 220–223, 225–226
planning subnetting for Azure Route
    Server, 226–231
preparing
    subnet delegations, 223–226
    subnetting for services, 213–220
review questions, 251–254
private IP addresses
    of Azure Internal Load Balancer, 324
    of virtual machine's NIC, 324
private peering
    setting up, 178–180
    using, 176–178
probe matching, of Azure Application
    Gateway, 393
profiles (Azure Traffic Manager), 429–432
public cloud, 4
public IP addresses
    in Azure Firewall, 462
    configuring, 37–40
public IP prefixes, allocating for NAT
    gateways, 445–447
public load balancers, compared with
    public load balancers, 349–352

Q

query string headers, 398–401

R

RADIUS authentication,
    configuring, 116–133
RBAC permissions, Azure Private
    Link, 634

RDP (Remote Desktop Protocol), 270
reading network security group flow
    logs, 524–530
recommending route advertisement
    configuration, 190–191
recording, using PowerShell, 233–235
redirection, 394–395
redundancy, in Azure ExpressRoute, 149
regions (Azure), 16–17, 30, 149, 157, 509,
    642, 643
registration network, 236
registration virtual network, 245
reliability
    of Azure DNS, 232
    of Microsoft Azure, 13
Remote Desktop Protocol (RDP), 270
repeaters, 9
request headers, 397–398
resiliency
    of Azure DNS, 233
    of Microsoft Azure, 13
resolution network, 236
resolution virtual network, 245–246
resolving
    client-side and authentication
        issues, 131–136
    ExpressRoute connection
        issues, 193–195
    routing issues, 334–336
    VPN gateway connectivity
        issues, 109–112
resources, attaching network security
    groups (NSGs) to, 509–518
resources groups (Microsoft Azure),
    18–19
response headers, 397–398
review question answers
    Azure Application Gateway, 690–691
    Azure DNS, 685–686
    Azure ExpressRoute, 683–684

Azure Firewall/Azure Firewall
    Manager, 691–693
Azure Front Door, 690–691
Azure Load Balancer, 688–690
Azure Monitor, 693–694
Azure networking, 680–681
Azure Traffic Manager, 690–691
Azure Virtual Network NAT, 690–691
Azure Web Application Firewall
    (WAF), 693–694
cross-VNet connectivity, 686–687
network security groups
    (NSGs), 691–693
private access, 694–696
private IP, 685–686
virtual WANs, 686–687
VNet routing, 688–690
VPN Connections, 681–683
review questions
    Azure Application Gateway, 455–458
    Azure ExpressRoute, 199–202
    Azure Firewall/Azure Firewall
        Manager, 539–542
    Azure Front Door, 455–458
    Azure Load Balancer, 377–380
    Azure Monitor, 611–614
    Azure networking, 70–73
    Azure Traffic Manager, 455–458
    Azure Virtual Network NAT, 455–458
    Azure Web Application Firewall
        (WAF), 611–614
    cross-VNet connectivity, 312–316
    DNS, 251–254
    network security groups
        (NSGs), 539–542
    private access, 675–678
    private IP, 251–254
    virtual WANs, 312–316
    VNet routing, 377–380
    VPN connections, 140–143

rewrite policies, Azure Application
Gateway, 397–401
rich connectivity, in Azure
ExpressRoute, 150
RIP (Routing Information Protocol), 320
role instances, virtual machines (VMs)
and, 243
route management, required for Azure
regional VNet integration, 661–662
route network traffic, 28
route tables
about, 28
associating with subnets, 328–329
route-based VPNs, policy-based VPNs
vs., 92–94
routers, 9
routing
about, 321–327
Azure Front Door and, 426–427
Azure Traffic Manager
methods, 432–441
basic concepts, 318–320
cold potato, 22
diagnosing issues, 334–336
hot potato, 22
resolving issues, 334–336
VNet integration apps and, 662
Routing Information Protocol (RIP), 320
routing rules
Azure Application Gateway
and, 395–396
Azure Front Door and, 426–427
rules
network security group (NSG),
524–530, 531–534
prioritizing, 470
types of, 469

S

scalability
of Azure Application Gateway, 389
of cloud networking, 11
of Microsoft Azure, 13
of WAF, 389
SDN (Software-Defined Networking), 10
Secure Socket Tunneling Protocol
(SSTP), 116
Secure Sockets Layer (SSL)
Azure Front Door and, 412–413
end-to-end SSL encryption, 421–423
termination, 421–423
secured virtual hub, 467
security
of Azure DNS, 232
of cloud networking, 11
of Microsoft Azure, 13
of Network Virtual Appliances
(NVAs), 508
security-as-a-service, virtual hubs for, 503
selecting
Application Gateway SKUs, 387–389
Azure Load Balancer SKUs, 344–349
billing models, 159
business continuity and
disaster recovery (BC/DR)
patterns, 162–169
ExpressRoute circuit SKUs, 156
ExpressRoute circuits, 157–158
ExpressRoute SKUs and tiers, 169–171
high availability design, 159–162
between network service providers and
ExpressRoute Direct, 153–155
peering locations, 157
between public and internal load
balancers, 349–352
services for virtual WANs, 289–291
SKUs for virtual WANs, 289–291
virtual network gateway SKUs for site-
to-site VPN, 89–91
VNet gateway SKUs for point-to-site
VPNs, 112–116
service chaining, 256–263
service providers, 147

service tags
    about, 646–650
    in Azure Firewall, 461
services
    choosing for virtual WANs, 289–291
    configuring subnetting for, 220–223
    in Kubernetes, 666
    preparing subnetting for, 213–220
setting
    environment, 130
    redirection, 397
setup
    diagnostic logging, 607–608
    forced tunneling, 329–334
    logging, 582–591
    Microsoft peering, 181–182
    network health alerts, 582–591
    private peering, 178–180
    service endpoints, 642–645
    virtual hub routing, 304–306
Site-to-Site VPN, 27, 79–83,
        89–91, 306–308
SKUs
    Azure Front Door, 409–420
    Azure Load Balancer, 344–349
    basic, 38–39
    choosing
        ExpressRoute, 169–171
        for virtual WANs, 289–291
    gateway, 170
    standard, 39–40
SNAT (source network address
        translation), 357, 371, 461, 462
Software-Defined Networking (SDN), 10
source network address translation
        (SNAT), 357, 371, 461, 462
split TCP, 426–427
SSL (Secure Sockets Layer)
    Azure Front Door and, 412–413
    end-to-end SSL encryption, 421–423
    termination, 421–423

SSTP (Secure Socket Tunneling
        Protocol), 116
stateful, in Azure Firewall, 463
static IP address, 22
static routing, 93
static VIP, Azure Application Gateway
        and, 388
Subnet-based routing method,
        433, 437–438
subnets/subnetting
    about, 29–30
    associating
        route tables with, 328–329
        virtual network NATs with, 447–451
    configuring
        for Azure Route Server, 226–231
        for services, 220–223
    design considerations for, 214–218
    gateway, 171
    preparing
        for Azure Route Server, 226–231
        delegations for, 223–226
        for services, 213–220
    required for Azure regional VNet
            integration, 660–661
    subnet configuration, 223–226
    VNets and, 209
subscriptions, Microsoft Azure, 19, 30
switches, 9
switching, 9

T

tag support, in Azure Firewall, 463
TCP Reset, 372
TCP/IP (Transmission Control Protocol/
        Internet Protocol), 7–8
termination, Secure Sockets Layer
        (SSL), 421–423
terminology, for networking, 7–10, 20–21

third-party network virtual appliances, integrating Azure Virtual WAN hubs with, 507–509

third-party security provider support, in Azure Firewall, 468

threat intelligence, in Azure Firewall, 461, 463, 467

tiers, choosing ExpressRoute, 169–171

time-to-live (TTL) property, 432

TLS inspection, in Azure Firewall, 464

Token Ring, 9

traffic routing, in Azure Firewall, 468

Transmission Control Protocol/Internet Protocol (TCP/IP), 7–8

TTL (time-to-live) property, 432

tunnels, 120

U

unlimited data, 159

update time, Azure Application Gateway and, 388

URL filtering, in Azure Firewall, 464

URL path headers, 398–401

URL redirection, in Azure Front Door, 427–429

URL rewriting, in Azure Front Door, 427–429

user-defined routes, designing and deploying, 318–327

V

validating network security group flow rules, 531–534

verifying IP flow, 534–536

virtual appliances, 323

virtual hub routing, 304–306

virtual hubs, 280, 502–503

virtual machines (VMs)
diagnosing and resolving routing issues, 334–336
private IP addresses of, 324
role instances and, 243

virtual network gateway SKUs (VpnGw SKUs), choosing for site-to-site VPNs, 89–91

virtual networks (VNs)
about, 322, 324
association Network Address Translation (NAT) with subnets, 447–451
communicating via, 27
configuring
peering between two, 45–46
traffic routing, 46–53
VPN gateway transit for peering, 258–263
connecting to ExpressRoute circuits, 186–190
integrating Azure Private Link into, 619
peering, 44–45, 256–263
traffic routing, 49–52

Virtual Private Network (VPN), 7, 10, 76

Virtual Private Network (VPN) connections
about, 76
answers to review questions, 681–683
Azure VPN Gateway, 76–79
building
IPsec/IKE policy, 101–104
local network gateways, 97–101
virtual network gateways, 94–97
choosing
virtual network gateways SKUs for site-to-site VPNs, 89–91
VNet gateway SKUs for point-to-site VPNs, 112–116
configuration workflow, 104–108

configuring
    Azure AD authentication, 116–133
    certificate-based
        authentication, 116–133
    IPsec/IKE policy, 101–104
    local network gateways, 97–101
    RADIUS authentication, 116–133
    virtual network gateways, 94–97
designing
    about, 79–89
    between VNets, 263–266
diagnosing
    client-side and authentication
        issues, 133–136
    VPN gateway connectivity
        issues, 109–112
exam essentials, 136–139
exercises, 94–97, 98–101, 105–108,
    109–112, 125–127, 130–133
resolving
    client-side and authentication
        issues, 133–136
    VPN gateway connectivity
        issues, 109–112
review questions, 140–143
using policy-based VPNs *vs.* route-based
    VPNs, 92–94
Virtual Private Network (VPN) gateways
    about, 21, 45–46
    diagnosing connectivity issues, 109–112
    resolving connectivity issues, 109–112
virtual wide area networks (WANs)
    about, 6–7, 11, 23, 256
    answers to review questions, 686–687
    building
        connection units, 306–308
        hubs in, 291–299
        secure hubs within, 501–506
        virtual network appliances (NVAs) in
            virtual hubs, 299–303

    choosing SKUs and services
        for, 289–291
    configuring secure hubs
        within, 501–506
    connecting VNet gateways to, 291–299
    designing architecture, 277–289
    exam essentials, 310–311
    exercises, 292–299, 301–303, 305
    integrating with third-party network
        virtual appliances, 507–509
    review questions, 312–316
    setting up virtual hub routing, 304–306
virtualization, 10
virtualWAN, 279–280
VNet-Integrated Platform Services, 214
VNet-to-VNet connections, 264
VPN Diagnostics, 593

W

web applications, 243–245, 413–420
web categories, in Azure Firewall, 462, 464
websites
    Azure AD tenant, 125
    cryptographic algorithm support, 103
    Microsoft Azure Online Resources, 38
Weighted-based routing method,
    432, 433–435
Windows
    configuration workflow for Active
        Directory (AD), 127–133
    VPN certificate location in, 135
    VPN client configuration
        location in, 135
    VPN client log location in, 135
Wireless Local Area Network
    (WLAN), 6–7
Wireshark, for Mac OS X, 136
workflow, for configuration, 104–108

Z

zero-trust standards, of cloud
 networking, 11
zonal deployments, 442

zonal services (Microsoft Azure), 18, 351
zone redundancy, Azure Application
 Gateway and, 388
zone-redundant services (ZRS), 18,
 352

Online Test Bank

Register to gain one year of FREE access after activation to the online interactive test bank to help you study for your MCA Azure Network Engineer certification exam—included with your purchase of this book! All of the chapter review questions and the practice tests in this book are included in the online test bank so you can practice in a timed and graded setting.

Register and Access the Online Test Bank

To register your book and get access to the online test bank, follow these steps:

1. Go to www.wiley.com/go/sybextestprep. You'll see the "How to Register Your Book for Online Access" instructions.
2. Click "here to register" and then select your book from the list.
3. Complete the required registration information, including answering the security verification to prove book ownership. You will be emailed a pin code.
4. Follow the directions in the email or go to www.wiley.com/go/sybextestprep.
5. Find your book on that page and click the "Register or Login" link with it. Then enter the pin code you received and click the "Activate PIN" button.
6. On the Create an Account or Login page, enter your username and password, and click Login or, if you don't have an account already, create a new account.
7. At this point, you should be in the test bank site with your new test bank listed at the top of the page. If you do not see it there, please refresh the page or log out and log back in.